ESSENTIAL SOLITUDE

August W. Derleth

ESSENTIAL SOLITUDE

THE LETTERS OF H. P. LOVECRAFT AND AUGUST DERLETH: 1926–1931

Edited by David E. Schultz and S. T. Joshi

Hippocampus Press

New York

Essential Solitude: The Letters of H. P. Lovecraft and August Derleth
Published by Hippocampus Press
P.O. Box 641, New York, NY 10156
www.hippocampuspress.com

Cover Design by Barbara Briggs Silbert.
Hippocampus Press logo designed by Anastasia Damianakos.
Introduction and editorial matter © 2013 by
David E. Schultz and S. T. Joshi
Cover art depicting Sauk City's Eagle House Hotel & Saloon (c. 1888)
© 2013 by David C. Verba.

First Paperback Edition
978-1-61498-060-5 (Volume 1)
978-1-61498-062-9 (2 Volume Set)

Contents

Introduction

Paradox and tension, friction and contrast, can break open the hard kernels in which the potential for creativity and life itself lie dormant. The life of H. P. Lovecraft (1890–1937) is itself a study in contrasts, but perhaps no aspect of it was more incongruous, yet fruitful, than his relationship with August Derleth (1909–1971) of Sauk City, Wisconsin.

Could two writers be more different? Lovecraft was conservative by nature; by inclination a lifelong amateur writer. He published three dozen stories professionally (nearly all in *Weird Tales* magazine), but those tales represent a very small percentage of his total writings, little of which was fiction and most of which appeared in numerous amateur journals. For a "professional writer," three dozen published stories over a period of a dozen years is a paltry amount—not enough by which to earn a living. Lovecraft's trade, if such it could be called, was freelance editing, which he seems to have pursued irregularly and for which his fees were very meager. Derleth, on the other hand, was the consummate professional. True, he had much work published in little magazines without pay, but his purpose was to get his name in front of people. He tirelessly championed and promoted his own writing, and why not? If a writer does not believe in his own work, why should anyone else?

Derleth, like Lovecraft, lived with his family, but self-reliance came soon to Derleth, who shortly after writing Lovecraft was off to college in Madison. For Lovecraft, who lived with his mother and aunts for most of his life, maturity came late. When his mother died in 1921, and he was thirty years of age, he first began to shed the callowness of youth—about ten years later than most young men might. But it was several years before he really learned how to manage his personal affairs. In 1924, he eloped and moved to New York City to seek his fortune. Even though it was two years before he acknowledged the venture as a failure on both counts by returning home, his marriage basically had ended well before that time, and the career he sought never materialized. The reason for the New York debacle might best be found in Lovecraft's own words: "A man belongs where he has roots—where the landscape & milieu have some relation to his thoughts & feelings, by virtue of having formed them." Transplanted to New York, Lovecraft was a man ill-grounded in alien soil.

Once resettled in the familiar surroundings of Providence, he was imbued with a vitality not felt since the days before the death of his beloved grandfather Whipple V. Phillips in 1904. Lovecraft had no real career in the sense that most adults now have one, but the general progression of his working or professional life was toward the (occasional) writing of spectral stories and, more important, toward nurturing the same instinct in others. He acknowledged, "My reason for writing stories is to give myself the satisfaction of wonder, beauty, adventurous expectancy." (One can imagine Lovecraft saying much the same about reading—at least with respect to the outré fiction he favored.) And so his impulse to write was not for monetary gain or fame, but something associated with emotions that can be experienced only rarely, and cherished when they unexpectedly occurred. A true amateur, Lovecraft avoided the yoke imposed by the dollar, but freedom from the yoke came at a heavy cost. Because he had no real job, he lived less than modestly—in his later years, one might even say he lived on the brink of poverty. He ate poorly, though vigorously defended his diet against the protestations of others that his sustenance was inadequate.

At the time Derleth first wrote Lovecraft, Lovecraft was entering his most fruitful period as a fiction writer, but that was not to last. Let us reflect on Lovecraft's final year. He saw two stories published, one written several years before but not submitted to any publisher because of disgust not only with the work itself but also with the insensitive treatment of his work at the hands of Farnsworth Wright of *Weird Tales,* the other a story written fairly recently in a burst of enthusiasm following the acceptance of two stories (submitted on Lovecraft's behalf by others) by *Astounding Stories.* The elation and confidence-boosting by *Astounding*'s acceptances were shattered by the actual publication of the stories, for they had been clumsily edited to the extent that Lovecraft considered at least one of the stories "unpublished." Other appearances of his work in that last year fared much the same: the short story "The Nameless City," a pet favorite of his, oft-rejected over the last dozen years, was marred by more than fifty misprints in a humble semi-professional publication. Following numerous rejections over the years of his work for a collection of his tales (always solicited by others), his novelette "The Shadow over Innsmouth" was published as a slim booklet. Unlike the brochure of *The Shunned House,* which, though well-printed and completely free of error, did not see actual distribution until the 1960s, *The Shadow over Innsmouth* was so riddled with errors and printed and bound so poorly as to be an acute embarrassment to its author; even the book's lengthy errata sheet had errors.

As if these circumstances were not bad enough, Lovecraft suffered other personal setbacks. His surviving aunt's illness imposed a serious threat on their already shaky finances. The year 1936 was marked by the deaths of kindred spirits M. R. James (one of Lovecraft's favorite authors), George Allen England, and, most devastating, his close correspondent Robert E. Howard. A revision job that Lovecraft slaved over saw print with most of his work rejected. All this occurred as Lovecraft suffered, unknowingly, from the intestinal cancer that killed him early the following year.

As Lovecraft's star flickered and waned, the nova that was August Derleth grew steadily and blazed forth. Of all Lovecraft's friends and correspondents, Derleth surely was the least like any of the others. For one, he earned a living as a working writer. Few of Lovecraft's colleagues could say the same. Early on, and for his entire life, he exuded great self-confidence. His ear was deaf to the word "no." Where Lovecraft had let the rejection of a single tale sour him forever on writing for the professional magazines, Derleth relentlessly submitted and resubmitted work—sometimes a dozen times, even to the same magazine—until ultimately it was accepted. Lovecraft, who wrote to give himself "the satisfaction of wonder, beauty, adventurous expectancy," had a view of the writing game quite different from that of his protégé. Derleth kept detailed records of writings and earnings, and seemed more interested in how many more pieces he could write each year than the previous, how many more words, how much more he could earn. In later years, he turned the slur that he was a "one-man fiction factory" into a boast. Derleth was writing professionally while still in high school, but it was following his graduation from college that he underwent (though more than a decade younger than Lovecraft) a kind of liberating epiphany not unlike Lovecraft's of 1924. Derleth had gone to Minneapolis to edit a magazine, but like Lovecraft (who had once declined editorship of *Weird Tales* because it would have necessitated a move to Chicago) he found that, separated from the land where he had sunk his roots, he was displaced and ineffectual. Before long, he was back in Sauk City, and was thoroughly revitalized upon being re-acclimated with his native soil.

Derleth wrote weird fiction his entire life, but it was when he had resettled in Sauk City that he branched out and committed himself to the writing he wanted to do—regional writing about Wisconsin, about the land and people that he knew best (as declared by the title of one of his later books, *Wisconsin in Their Bones*). In fact, he envisioned a body of work so vast that it would encompass fifty books to tell it. He still wrote much commercial work—mere froth—but that was to pay the bills so that he could devote himself to his serious writing. Writing potboilers for *Weird Tales* and the detective magazines, and slight but fairly popular detective novels, allowed him eventually to build himself a house to his specifications, and to continue to keep his personal library well-stocked. But whereas Lovecraft was free of the yoke of debt, Derleth was virtually always under it, and so had to write with great speed, regularity, and prolificacy. For a writer living in rural Wisconsin, he did well. By 1937, when Lovecraft died, August Derleth, at age twenty-eight and nearly a decade younger than Lovecraft at the age when the two began corresponding, was at the beginning of a long career.

As Lovecraft lay dying, he received a copy of Derleth's sixth published book, while still others were in various stages of preparation. He himself had only one book to his name, a shoddily printed affair by an aspiring fan publisher. But that dire circumstance was to result in profound and long-lasting effects.

The two writers crossed paths in the summer of 1926. Lovecraft, then in his mid-thirties, had only recently resettled in Providence. Over the past three years, he had become something of a mainstay in the pages of *Weird Tales* magazine. Derleth had begun to see his own work published there, and before long would rival and soon exceed Lovecraft in the number of stories accepted for publication, and likely in total remuneration, despite his more modest rate of pay. Even as Lovecraft was deliberating his future in December 1925, following the failure of his marriage and the unsuccessful attempt to develop a writing career in America's publishing mecca, young Derleth was writing to Farnsworth Wright of *Weird Tales* asking for Lovecraft's address. In later years, countless young writers would get in touch with Lovecraft, expressing admiration for his writing, but Derleth was a notable exception to that bunch. Despite his youth—he was still in high school—he approached Lovecraft not as a fan or admirer but as a peer, both as a writer and as a fellow connoisseur of weird fiction. He did not contact Lovecraft immediately upon receiving Lovecraft's address—an odd circumstance for the impulsive and methodical young writer—and so his first letter to Lovecraft went circuitously to Brooklyn before arriving in Providence, whence Lovecraft had returned in April. When Lovecraft replied he pointed out that he had recently moved back to Providence, noting in a somewhat defiant postscript, "That Brooklyn address was temporary & is obsolete. I am 100% Rhode-Islander by birth & upbringing."

Derleth's object was simple: he wanted to know where he might find M. P. Shiel's story "The House of Sounds," which Lovecraft had praised in a letter published years before in *Weird Tales*. Lovecraft, never one to refuse a correspondent, cordially replied, informing Derleth that the book he sought was difficult to come by. If it could not be obtained from a used book dealer, he might try to borrow it, as Lovecraft himself had once done, from W. Paul Cook, Lovecraft's friend and another enthusiast of weird fiction. It is almost unimaginable these days that anyone would recommend to a complete stranger that he contact a third party to borrow a rare and precious item. But Lovecraft, always generous with his time (and with the libraries of others), took especial pains to nurture and cultivate any burgeoning interest in weird fiction. It was perfectly natural that Lovecraft would welcome into his circle an acolyte such as Derleth.

Lovecraft's recommendation about how Derleth might obtain the rare Shiel story was the inauspicious beginning of a lengthy and lively correspondence. Before long, Lovecraft was lending manuscripts of his unpublished stories to Derleth—again, almost unthinkable in an age without computers, when a duplicate could not be run off in seconds if a manuscript were lost or destroyed. They enthusiastically suggested and lent books to each other— Lovecraft recommending the classics of weird fiction, and Derleth ever on the prowl for new books as they were published. In time Derleth was even exchanging letters with many of Lovecraft's associates. Lovecraft's letter-writing is now near legendary, in number of correspondents, in sheer volume, even in bulk of individual letters, but especially in its often weighty but nevertheless stimulating content and manner of expression. His letters to Derleth are not distinguished by length or profundity but by sheer quantity—more than 380 by Lovecraft alone, written over an eleven-year period, the most not only to survive, but in all likelihood that he was ever to write to a single correspondent. (Only the lengthy near-daily letters to his aunt Lillian Clark during his stay in New York City can surpass this correspondence in wordage.) The correspondence also is characterized by the great frequency and regularity of exchange, for the two wrote nearly weekly for much of its duration.

It is likely that Lovecraft and Derleth would have encountered each other eventually, but the time Derleth chose may have been most fortuitous. Derleth had had a handful of mediocre stories published in *Weird Tales,* alone and in collaboration with his school chum Mark Schorer. His stories showed promise, but they were strictly conventional—mere ghost and vampire stuff. In 1926, Lovecraft was beginning to develop the fiction that we today recognize as uniquely "Lovecraftian": "The Call of Cthulhu," "The Silver Key," "Pickman's Model," "The Colour out of Space," and others—his cosmic fiction. Until that time, he had been writing basically macabre fiction. The macabre tales—including "The Outsider" and "The Rats in the Walls"—long remained Derleth's favorite among Lovecraft's works.

Because the two wrote very frequently, their letters rarely come to more than a sheet or two of paper and thus are quite short—by Lovecraftian standards. Both compulsively replied immediately, Derleth in deference to his self-imposed "ten-day rule," Lovecraft because of his innate courtesy and his tacit acknowledgment of Derleth's stringent requirement for prompt replies. Their letters tend to be prosaic at times, but they are noteworthy because of their focus on the craft and business of writing—a little-understood aspect of Lovecraft's career. Derleth's letters constitute in large part catalogues of his own current writing projects and attempts, successful or otherwise, at placements of his work. He sent many manuscripts to Lovecraft for criticism, some—like the ever-evolving novel *Evening in Spring*—many times. Derleth himself often did not understand Lovecraft's detailed comments about how he might improve his work—he seemed merely to want praise, although on occasion he did incorporate a suggestion from Lovecraft. Lovecraft himself at first sent manuscripts of unpublished stories to Derleth. In time, the younger writer felt compelled to offer suggestions as to how Lovecraft could make his stories more salable, ignoring the fact that Lovecraft professed not to be much interested in that. Lovecraft, at Derleth's promptings, seems not only to have tried to break into new markets for his work, but also to have shaped his work for acceptance by certain magazines. That Lovecraft did so is not evident in his letters to others, but it is in his letters to Derleth.

One will not find a discussion such as that which follows in any of Lovecraft's letters to Derleth. Compare this *extract* from a letter to any entire letter written to Derleth from the same period, bearing in mind that by early 1931, Lovecraft and Derleth had comfortably exchanged hundreds of letters:

Fantastic literature cannot be treated as a single unit, because it is a composite resting on widely divergent bases. I really agree that "Yog-Sothoth" is a basically immature conception, and unfitted for really serious literature. The fact is, I have never approached serious literature as yet. But I consider the use of actual folk-myths as even more childish than the use of new artificial myths, since in employing the former one is forced to retain many blatant puerilities and contradictions of experience which could be subtilised or smoothed over if the supernaturalism were modelled to order for the given case. The only permanently artistic use of Yog-Sothothery, I think, is in symbolic or associative phantasy of the frankly poetic type; in which fixed dream-patterns of the natural organism are given an embodiment and crystallisation. The reasonable permanence of this phase of poetic phantasy as a *possible* art form (whether or not favoured by current fashion) seems to me a highly strong probability. It will, however, demand ineffable adroitness—the vision of a Blackwood joined to the touch of a De la Mare—and is probably beyond my utmost powers of achievement. I hope to see material of this sort in time, though I hardly expect to produce anything even remotely approaching it myself. I am too saturated in the empty gestures and pseudo-moods of an archaic and vanished world to have any successful traffick with symbols of an expanded dream-reality. But there is another phase of cosmic phantasy (which may or may not include frank Yog-Sothothery) whose foundations appear to me as better grounded than these of ordinary oneiroscopy; personal limitation regarding the *sense of outsideness*. I refer to the aesthetic crystallisation of that burning and inextinguishable feeling of mixed wonder and oppression which the sensitive imagination experiences upon scaling itself and its restrictions against the vast and provocative abyss of the unknown. This has always been the chief emotion in my psychology; and whilst it obviously figures less in the psychology of the majority, it is clearly a well-defined and permanent factor from which very few sensitive persons are wholly free. Here we have a natural biological phenomenon so untouched and untouchable by intellectual disillusion that it is difficult to envisage its total death as a factor in the most serious art. Reason as we may, we cannot destroy a normal perception of the highly limited and fragmentary nature of our visible world of perception and experience as scaled against the outside abyss of unthinkable galaxies and unplumbed dimensions—an abyss wherein our solar system is the merest dot (by the same *local* principle that makes a sand-grain a dot as compared with the whole planet earth) *no matter what relativistic system we may use in conceiving the cosmos as a whole*—and this perception cannot fail to act potently upon the natural physical instinct of *pure curiosity;* an instinct just as basic and primitive, and as impossible of destruction by any philosophy whatsoever, as the parallel instincts of hunger, sex, ego-expansion, and fear.

. . . At any rate, the lure of the unknown abyss remains as potent as ever under any conceivable intellectual, aesthetic, or social order; and will crop out as a forbidden thing even in societies where the external ideal of altruistic collectivism reigns. In types where this urge cannot be gratified by actual research in pure science, or by the actual physical exploration of unknown parts of the earth, it is inevitable that a symbolic aesthetic outlet will be demanded. You can't dodge it—the condition must exist, under all phases cosmic interpretation, as long as a sense-chained race of inquirers on a microscopic earth-dot are faced by the black, unfathomable gulph of the Outside, with its forever-unexplorable orbs and its virtually certain sprinkling of utterly unknown life-forms. A great part of religion is merely a childish and diluted pseudo-gratification of this perpetual gnawing toward the ultimate illimitable void. Superadded to this simple curiosity is the galling sense of *intolerable restraint* which all sensitive people (except self-blinded earth-gazers like little Augie Derleth) feel as they survey their natural limitations in time and space as scaled against the freedoms and expansions and comprehensions and adventurous expectancies which the mind can formulate as abstract conceptions. Only a perfect clod can fail to discern these irritant feelings in the greater part of mankind—feelings so potent and imperious that, if denied symbolic outlets in aesthetics or religious fakery, they produce actual hallucinations of the supernatural, and drive half-responsible minds to the concoction of the most absurd hoaxes and the perpetuation of the most absurd specific myth-types. Don't let little Augie sidetrack you. The general revolt of the sensitive mind against the tyranny of corporeal enclosure, restricted sense-equipment, and the laws of force, space, and causation, is a far keener and bitterer and better-founded one than any of the silly revolts of long-haired poseurs against isolated and specific instances of cosmic inevitability. But of course it does not take the form of personal petulance, because there is no convenient scapegoat to saddle the impersonal ill upon. Rather does it crop out as a pervasive sadness and unplaceable impatience, manifested in a love of strange dreams and an amusing eagerness to be gulled by the quack cosmic pretensions of the various religious circuses. Well—in our day the quack circuses are wearing pretty thin despite the premature senilities of fat Chesterbellocs and affected Waste Land Shantih-dwellers, and the nostalgic and unmotivated "overbeliefs" of elderly and childhood-crippled physicists. The time has come when the normal revolt against time, space, and matter must assume a form not overtly incompatible with what is known of reality—when it must be gratified by images forming *supplements* rather than *contradictions* of the visible and mensurable universe. And what, if not a form of *non-supernatural cosmic art*, is to pacify this sense of revolt—as well as gratify the cognate sense of curiosity? "Dunt esk", as they say in your decadent cosmopolis! No, young Belloc, you can't rule out a phase of human feeling and expression which springs from instincts wholly basic and physical. Cosmic phantasy *of some sort* is as assured of possible permanence (its status subject to caprices of fashion) as is the literature of struggle and eroticism. But of course, as I have said before, its later and less irresponsible forms will doubtless differ vastly from most of the weird literature we have had so far. Like the lighter forms of dream-phantasy and Yog-Sothothery, it will require a delicate and precise technique; so that a crude old-timer like myself would never be likely to excel in it. Nevertheless, if I live much longer, I may try my hand at something of the sort—for it is really closer to my serious psychology than anything else on or off the earth. In "The Colour Out of Space" I began to get near it—though "Dunwich" and the "Whisperer" represent a relapse. In using up the ideas in my commonplace-book, I shall doubtless perpetrate a great deal more childish hokum, (gratifying to me only through personal association with the past) yet the time may come when I shall at least try something approximately serious. There is, of course, no need of becoming serious so long as thinly-veiled childishness retains power to gratify me; but I am assuming that my real senility has not so far advanced as to check, just yet, that gradual mental maturing perceptible in me since 1919 or 1920 (the period of Galpinian activation) and apparently somewhat accelerated (perhaps through Providence re-orientation) since 1927. I am still a primitive and retarded type as measured by good intellectual standards; but not quite so pathetic a case of belated infantility as I was in 1920 or 21 or 22, when I spewed forth such insufferable maundering as "The Tree", "Hypnos", "The Moon-Bog", "The Hound", etc. etc., though a fat middle-aged clod who ought to have known better a decade before; or even in 1925, when (during the Clinton Street period) I allowed myself to sign such mawkish drivel as "The Horror at Red Hook" and (worse yet) "He". The only decent things I wrote in those days were sheer luck-shots—"Arthur Jermyn", "Erich Zann", and a few others. And yet I had a better time, in some ways, than I have now; for my very infantility (repulsive as it was in a middle-aged man) allowed me to retain as a subjective reality something of that sense of adventurous expectancy which is now only a wistful aesthetic memory. I shall never find another Dunsanian city of wonder as utterly unreal and linked with incredible cloud-mysteries as the exotic and unexplored labyrinth of sea-born towers that was the dim, half-fabulous Manhattan of 1922. Least of all could I find such a Dunsanian place in any Manhattan of any later date. I grant, then, the virtues of infantility *so long as they are valid*—even though such phaenomena must of necessity appear absurd to the mental adult. What is hollow and insincere is the parade of infantility in art, and its feigning by the adult artist after its real essence has passed away. Dead childhood rattling its own bones in a mocking and hellish danse macabre.[1]

Lovecraft and Derleth could not sustain a correspondence at this level. (Derleth, aside from not being Lovecraft's intellectual peer, could not afford the time to write such lengthy screeds himself.) It is significant that Lovecraft's longest letter to Derleth is an exhaustive attempt to demolish Derleth's belief in the occult and spiritualism—a topic to which the two writers returned repeat-

---

1. HPL to Frank Belknap Long, 27 February 1931, *SL* 3.293–97.

edly, with little apparent headway on either side. It seemed the one subject in which they could engage in argumentative debate, but time constraints militated against the kind of long, leisurely, almost stream-of-consciousness letters that Lovecraft habitually wrote to such correspondents as Frank Belknap Long, James F. Morton, Robert E. Howard, J. Vernon Shea, and Woodburn Harris.

Despite differences in upbringing, beliefs, tastes, and age, Lovecraft and Derleth were in some senses astonishingly similar. Both were avowed students of weird fiction. Both inclined more to the more literary kinds of imaginative fiction, although both made no apologies for reading popular stuff as well (mostly with scant satisfaction). Lovecraft himself had written "Supernatural Horror in Literature" as his pronouncement of what constituted weird fiction that was worth the trouble to read, and Derleth, for his college thesis, wrote "The Weird Tale in English Since 1890" (clearly meant to serve as an expansion of Lovecraft's essay).

Both writers had profoundly deep roots in the regions of their birth and upbringing. Both had ventured from those roots seeking success—Lovecraft to New York City, Derleth to Minneapolis—but both ultimately realized that satisfaction would be found only in their natal regions. The failed rebellion against the past was necessary, though, for only through separation could they come to recognize how they were meant to live and, in consequence, what they were meant to write. Lovecraft's "exile" in New York ended with the research for and the writing of "Supernatural Horror in Literature," which he completed in Providence. It was soon followed by a burst of creativity that forged the trail he followed for the rest of his life and along which he attempted to lead others, for Lovecraft basically abandoned the macabre fiction he had been writing thus far. Derleth had gone to Minneapolis to edit a magazine, but his stay there was much less short-lived than Lovecraft's temporary exile (which might not have been so long had Lovecraft not been too proud to admit defeat). Upon returning to Sauk City, where he spent the rest of his life, Derleth devoted his energies primarily to his regional writing. To be sure, he never abandoned weird fiction or any purely commercial writing. He managed, to Lovecraft's amazement, to wear simultaneously the hats of many different writers for his entire career.

The two writers were headstrong and staunchly defended their principles. It is only natural that of the two, Lovecraft would have been exerted the greater influence on the other, because of his age, but Derleth was not incapable of influencing Lovecraft. Derleth managed, with not much resistance from Lovecraft, to get *Weird Tales* to accept two Lovecraft stories (though he failed with two others). Lovecraft seems to have written a few stories in response to Derleth's suggestions, but Derleth's harping on Lovecraft to write his "coral reef" story seems to have gotten Lovecraft not only to write "The Shadow over Innsmouth" but also to do so with a market other than *Weird*

Tales in mind, and employing a motif that Lovecraft ordinarily would not attempt to use in any work of fiction—an "action" scene. Lovecraft ultimately did not submit the story to the magazine in question—nor to any magazine, for that matter—and he resisted Derleth's suggestion to revise the story so as to make it more salable. Lovecraft also briefly attempted to write commercial fiction, even to the extent of acquiring a "plot robot" to help him develop purely commercial fiction. His experiments were conducted only on work done for clients and published, if at all, under their names.

For all their similarities, the two were, oddly enough, at polar opposites when it came to Lovecraft's writing. Derleth long favored Lovecraft's macabre early work, preferring it to the later "cosmic" tales. Lovecraft's subtle use of his "pseudomythological" conceptions as "background," not as the "message," was lost on him. Derleth wanted the background to be pulled well-lit into the foreground, and also to be more rigorously systematized. Lovecraft was not terribly interested in such systematization, finding slight discrepancies between story elements to be more suited to his notion of "background." Most puzzling of all, even though Derleth could publish, on several occasions, Lovecraft's manifesto about his aims in weird fiction, he could also publish the spurious and antithetical "black magic" quotation,[2] making it the foundation of his view that Lovecraft's work was basically a retelling of the Christian story of good versus evil.

It is no secret that Derleth exerted more energy than Lovecraft did into shaping the latter's celebrated "pseudomythology." Derleth recognized that there was considerable marketing potential in doing so, and pointed this out to Lovecraft as early as 1931. After all, the Conan stories of Robert E. Howard and the Jules de Grandin tales of Seabury Quinn were perennial reader favorites in *Weird Tales*. Derleth himself worked several literary veins. Recognizing the popularity of A. Conan Doyle's Sherlock Holmes tales, he embarked on his own series of detective stories featuring his sleuth, Solar Pons. In imitation of Edgar Lee Masters's *Spoon River Anthology*, Derleth developed a similar body of poems, published under the heading "Sac Prairie People" in his various poetry collections. He developed a series of yarns featuring the recurring characters Gus Elker, great-aunt Lou Stoll, and great-uncle Joe Stoll. Once he recognized that Lovecraft had a few recurring thematic elements in a handful of stories, it would be only natural for Derleth to develop those themes in greater detail to give readers more of the same. Derleth did not understand (or care) that Lovecraft wrote only to satisfy himself, not readers. To be sure, Lovecraft was not immune to the pleasures nearly any writer would derive from having his work published—money, recognition, and so on. Lovecraft's letters to Derleth show that he is not an elitist above such satisfaction, though he wanted to be one. He makes it clear that he writes when moved to express himself, and not by any

---

2. David E. Schultz, "The Origin of Lovecraft's 'Black Magic' Quote," *Crypt of Cthulhu* No. 48 (1987): 9–13.

other motive. On the rare occasions when he relaxed his principles, the results were substandard in various ways.

This might be most readily apparent in the way both writers employed Lovecraft's commonplace book—the notebook in which Lovecraft jotted ideas for stories. Lovecraft's purpose for his notebook, as he himself clearly stated at the head of it, was this: "This book consists of ideas, images, & quotations hastily jotted down for possible future use in weird fiction. Very few are actually developed plots—for the most part they are merely suggestions or random impressions designed to set the memory or imagination working" (*CE* 5.219). Derleth, on the other hand, typically knew what he wanted to do before he began the actual writing, and often had ideas well worked out in his head long before he sat down to work on them. Lovecraft's writing was more capricious. Kernels of story ideas might sit dormant for years in his commonplace book, until in an inspired moment he could develop the proper vehicle for expression. The seven-year hiatus in developing what ultimately became a minor scene in "The Call of Cthulhu" is but one example. When Lovecraft wrote a story, he wrote until he had no more to say. A story that seemed as though it would not need many pages to tell often spun out to greater length because of the need to develop the atmosphere properly. Derleth, on the other hand, could declare "Next week I shall write a 75,000-word novel" and inevitably turn in the work as described in the allotted amount of time. And so Lovecraft's notes for stories represented not plots but suggestions of a mood to be developed. Derleth obtained Lovecraft's commonplace book following his death and published it (twice). In an inspired moment, he determined that he could use the ideas in Lovecraft's notebook for writing stories that he would publish under the joint byline of Lovecraft (always first) and Derleth, even though most of the stories had no Lovecraft prose in them. Unlike the Derleth-Schorer collaborations, the Lovecraft-Derleth "posthumous collaborations" were written entirely by one author only. It is telling that many of the Lovecraft-Derleth stories are built, rather flimsily, on Lovecraft's "pseudomythological" concepts, even though no entry in Lovecraft's commonplace book mentions those concepts. And most of those stories do not ring true as Lovecraft's work because they simply aren't.

Misguided as all that was, Derleth without a doubt saw Lovecraft as his mentor. Many other aspiring writers surely did as well but not so keenly. Derleth published numerous pieces about Lovecraft that speak directly and indirectly to Lovecraft's influence in his life. "Lovecraft as Mentor" is a weak essay, mostly stitched together from excerpts of Lovecraft's letters to him, and thus containing more wordage by Lovecraft than Derleth. Yet the sentiment, though clumsily expressed, is strong. Derleth's admiration and respect for Lovecraft were boundless, as is evident from his numerous writings on Lovecraft following the latter's death, but perhaps most poignantly in a letter to E. Hoffmann Price: "You can readily understand how a youngster virtually isolated from every other intellectual contact would respond to HPL's invariable patience and kindness—and surely no one was ever more kind or ever more patient with the vagaries of youth! Lovecraft was perhaps my most important contact outside of Sauk City for twelve years, and it is only natural that his death would affect me with a profound sense of loss, from which I should say that, psychically, at least, I did not recover."[3] But when Lovecraft was alive, at times he might have found Derleth's admiration difficult to conceive. After all, Derleth was not content merely to sit submissively at the feet of the master. The two disagreed on many points, though never with acrimony. Derleth seemed rarely to take Lovecraft's advice, mostly regarding petty details, because after all, Derleth had far greater success than Lovecraft in having his work published, even with errors. And yet Lovecraft knew well that detail can contribute significantly to realism and verisimilitude. Lovecraft never successfully convinced Derleth that Derleth's work depended too heavily on convenient coincidences to move a plot forward; that details often did not seem to ring true; that "The Rats in the Walls," an early macabre piece and Derleth's favorite Lovecraft story, is not a terribly significant work (or that *At the Mountains of Madness* is).

Derleth's few surviving letters to Lovecraft, and Lovecraft's abundant responses to nearly all Derleth's letters, seem to cast Derleth in the role of anything but protégé. As noted, Derleth ignored many of Lovecraft's suggestions. He rarely conceded that Lovecraft was right in certain matters, though Lovecraft almost invariably was. Lovecraft's suggestion that Derleth put aside his eccentric modes of dress went unheeded far longer than Lovecraft predicted. Derleth's brash suggestions to Lovecraft, though made good-naturedly, strike us as impolite and impertinent (as when Derleth addresses Lovecraft as "poor deluded grandpa!"). Derleth's blasting (in Lovecraft's eyes) of "The Dreams in the Witch House" and "Through the Gates of the Silver Key" seems harsh, especially since Lovecraft himself exercised great restraint in commenting on Derleth's work, finding positives in even the weakest pieces. Lovecraft's polite yet sometimes vague comments often were perceived as strong praise by an author who seemed always looking to have his ego stroked.

Lovecraft was not without his own respect and admiration for Derleth, his comment about the "self-blinded earth-gazer" notwithstanding. He sincerely championed most of his youthful adherents, but his praise for Derleth was unmatched:

> As for Derleth—I don't wonder you find his W.T. stuff mediocre! He holds all records for leading a literary double life—for his serious work is no more like this commercial junk than Marcel Proust is like Nictzin Dyalhis! He despises his pot-boilers utterly & eloquently—but continues to write them because they bring in highly welcome cheques. His

---

3. Letter by AWD to E. Hoffmann Price, 18 March 1948, in "A 'Special' Halloween Letter to Knock the Socks Off H. P. Lovecraft Fans!" *August Derleth Society Newsletter* 15, No. 3 (Autumn 1994): 1.

real work is of a minor-keyed, delicate quality—brooding memories & impressions woven together as they impinge on a single life-stream, & brief tragic vignettes of hidden lives & strange, lonely people. Some day he will probably go farther in literature than anyone else in the whole W.T. crowd. . . . He is a small-towner, living at his birthplace, Sauk City, Wis., & having his literary roots deep in the soil. Vast promise there—mark an old man's words![4]

The reason Derleth doesn't contribute serious work to W.T. is that his serious work isn't at all in the weird vein. He places some of it in such select "intelligentsia" sheets as "This Quarter"—published by American expatriates in Paris. When I say that Derleth will soon lead all the rest of the "gang" I speak seriously & advisedly. He has a profundity, seriousness, simplicity, & human insight that none of the rest of us can even begin to duplicate. In comparison with his promise-laden sketches my own tales are the superficial tinsel of a played-out never-was. My stuff represents the last thin output of a small-timer who has nothing fresh in reserve—but Derleth is a mine of ideas & crystallised experiences just beginning to yield abundantly. His only peril is that his incessant pot-boiling may subtly & unperceivedly pollute his genuine aesthetic work—just as Wright's goddam insistence on obvious plots has insidiously given some of my work a naive & rather cheap twist without my knowing it. But so far he has kept the work of his right & left hands astonishingly separate & dissimilar.[5]

Although Lovecraft felt many of his protégés would have promising futures as writers of fiction, few made good on his predictions. Some, like R. H. Barlow and Carl F. Strauch, became noteworthy scholars in their fields. Fritz Leiber, Henry Kuttner, C. L. Moore, and Robert Bloch became well-known and respected authors of science fiction and related writing. August Derleth fulfilled Lovecraft's vision in some respects, but he did not become a Proust of the Midwest as Lovecraft felt he might. Nor did he become nationally recognized as a writer. Derleth gained some celebrity in the 1940s for his regional writing, but most of that work has long been out of print, and it was Derleth himself—ever the self-promoter—who saw that it remained in print as long as it did by buying the printers' plates for his books and reprinting them at his own expense. Derleth's work that is in print these days is primarily his writings in the "Cthulhu mythos," and thus is carried more by interest in Lovecraft's fictional themes than the actual merit of the fiction on its own. The title of a late collection of this work—*In Lovecraft's Shadow*—has an unfortunate irony to it, but August Derleth would not have minded one bit.

4. HPL to J. Vernon Shea, 14 August 1931, *SL* 3.396–97.
5. HPL to J. Vernon Shea, 21 August 1931, *SL* 3.398.

Lovecraft makes his prediction "advisedly," noting that Derleth showed great promise, but also that certain tendencies could well prevent him from fulfilling that promise.

Derleth had, as early as 1926, urged Lovecraft to seek a publisher for a book of his stories, but Lovecraft continually demurred. Derleth had even persuaded his own publisher, Loring & Mussey, to consider such a book, but upon receiving an assortment of Lovecraft's stories, they declined. Like most publishers, they were not interested in collections of short stories but in novels, such as the kind they published by Derleth. Lovecraft's death in 1937 affected Derleth profoundly, when he learned of it for the first time: "I opened Howard [Wandrei]'s letter on the bridge across the Wisconsin and from the moment I read of H.P.L.'s death, I have no distinct knowledge of making my way down the near-mile to the place where I sat to read, and I remember only Thoreau, the sun, the brook that afternoon, and the looming meaning like a mountain on the horizon, of Lovecraft's death. For something like 48 hours, my mind simply rejected the fact, by refusing to admit it. That night, I read his letters to me over—part of them—and I knew that in one sense, as long as any of us who had corresponded with him or known him, were left alive, H.P.L would never die."[6] After the immediate shock of Lovecraft's death had passed, Derleth acted swiftly to see his dream of a collection of Lovecraft's work fulfilled. Derleth attempted to find a publisher for the bulky manuscript he had assembled, starting with Scribner's, his own publisher. He soon realized that he would fare no better than Lovecraft himself had in seeing a book of Lovecraft's work into print if he tried only to persuade major publishing companies to take the work. Lovecraft himself had failed with *Weird Tales,* Vanguard, Putnam's, and Knopf. He simply was not well enough known to make a publisher willing to take a chance on his shorter work, especially the immense, half-million-word collection that Derleth was marketing.

Derleth and Wandrei decided that the only way to get Lovecraft's work into print would be to do the job themselves, and so they published *The Outsider and Others,* under the imprint of Arkham House, a name selected from Lovecraft's fiction. (It is telling that Lovecraft, in 1932, doubtless in response to a comment by Derleth, notes that if Derleth wants to see of a book of Lovecraft's work he may well have to publish it himself. Even more tellingly, Lovecraft ultimately designated R. H. Barlow, a boy of eighteen, his literary executor, perhaps because Lovecraft felt Barlow was more sympathetic and sensitive to his work as a whole.) The book was envisioned as the first of three large volumes, and the effort expended was Herculean. Derleth was a busy man in 1937, with many publishing obligations. Nevertheless, he and

---

6. Letter by AWD to E. Hoffmann Price, 18 March 1948, in "A 'Special' Halloween Letter . . .," p. 2.

Donald Wandrei wrote to as many of Lovecraft's correspondents as they could find, borrowing letters, manuscripts, and amateur publications, and transcribing as much of it as they deemed valuable. Most of that effort was to stock material for future use, before it was lost forever. Derleth also submitted many of the stories he obtained to *Weird Tales* for publication, and many of the pieces—either unpublished or published previously only in amateur journals of very limited circulation—that Lovecraft himself had been unable to sell to *Weird Tales* were now eagerly accepted, for there would be no more tales from Lovecraft's pen. In this sense Lovecraft grimly confirms the adage that "Death is a good career move." The years 1931–36 saw few appearances of Lovecraft—mostly reprints—but now that Lovecraft was dead, there was a veritable flood of his work in *Weird Tales,* thanks to Derleth's tireless efforts. Payment for all these items was sent directly to Lovecraft's surviving aunt. The cost of publishing *The Outsider* was borne in part by subscribers to the book, the balance by Derleth and Wandrei.

Even as Derleth undertook to sell Lovecraft's work to *Weird Tales* and to find a publisher for *The Outsider,* he dusted off a story he had started six years previously and put aside uncompleted. He now finished "The Return of Hastur" and eagerly sent it to Clark Ashton Smith, expecting nothing but enthusiastic approval; but Smith's response was not as favorable as he had hoped.[7] No matter. Derleth eventually submitted the story to *Weird Tales,* which accepted it, and thus opened the floodgates for many more Derleth stories in a Lovecraftian vein in years to come. Derleth sincerely believed that Lovecraft had entrusted him personally with not only the task of getting a book of Lovecraft's writings published, which he ultimately did in 1939, but also of carrying on Lovecraft's work—as though Lovecraft's unique conception needed to be carried on!

Derleth's inquiry to Lovecraft about Shiel's "The House of Sounds" had at least one further repercussion. It was Lovecraft who had praised the story, and it was Derleth who, eighteen years later in 1944, was first to reprint the story in the U.S. in his anthology of horror fiction, *Sleep No More.* Close scrutiny of this book (Derleth's thirty-second) shows that virtually its entire contents are infused with Lovecraft's presence—especially so in his own "The Rats in the Walls."

One could almost say that the whole of Arkham House's catalogue over the first thirty years reflects the influence of H. P. Lovecraft. That is not to say that Derleth relied on Lovecraft's recommendation in his decision about what to publish. Nevertheless, the contents of many of the books Derleth edited and published find their roots in the letters they exchanged, many items being his own discoveries. It is impossible to tell what may have happened had they not

---

7. Smith's several letters on the subject were printed in his *Letters to H. P. Lovecraft* (West Warwick, RI: Necronomicon Press, 1987), pp. 54–67.

exchanged some 800 letters between them. Would Derleth have become a book publisher? His desire to see Lovecraft's work gathered in a permanent format, and his impatience with the publishing industry's disinclination to take on the job, resulted in his founding of Arkham House with Donald Wandrei as a means of achieving his goal—and achieving it *his* way—but initially they meant to publish only one book, later considering that three volumes (stories, miscellany, and letters) would be needed to accomplish what they wished to accomplish regarding Lovecraft's work. But then, plans changed, and Arkham House began to publish other titles as well. It was only natural that Arkham House develop a personality, and what other personality than that of its larger partner? And so Derleth published works that appealed to him, and naturally many of those also would have appealed to H. P. Lovecraft.

Lovecraft's legacy is well known and need not be inventoried here. Derleth's may not be as expansive, or even well understood by those who know him only as a writer of "Cthulhu mythos" stories or detective fiction, or as the proprietor of a small publishing company, but it is nevertheless profound. He was the author or editor of more than 160 books. Besides writing weird fiction, he also wrote historical fiction and nonfiction, science and mystery fiction, and reams of poetry. He kept an enormous journal for decades. He edited several competent anthologies of science fiction. With Donald Wandrei, he founded Arkham House, initially to publish only a scant few Lovecraft collections. But Arkham House remains in business today, and during Derleth's day published many books of importance. He published the first books of Ray Bradbury, Fritz Leiber, Robert Bloch, A. E. van Vogt, Donald Sidney-Fryer, Brian Lumley, and Ramsey Campbell. In fact, Derleth became something of a mentor to many neophyte writers. To be sure, some Arkham House books were published as favors to their authors, but even so, they required Derleth's investment of capital and patience. H. P. Lovecraft without a doubt had a large hand in the shaping of modern horror fiction. His disciple August Derleth had a hand in shaping the field of horror fiction commercially, as one of the earliest and most important small-press publishers, and as advocate and inspiration of subsequent generations of authors and publishers.

Many have opined that in the long run August Derleth was more harmful than helpful to the legacy of H. P. Lovecraft. That possibility was first broached by W. Paul Cook—the man to whom Lovecraft sent Derleth in quest of "The House of Sounds"—who in the early 1940s expressed concern about what he felt was the indiscriminate publication of Lovecraft's work.[8] But what's done is done. No one can say that H. P. Lovecraft would have been better off if Scribner's, say, had published *The Outsider and Others*—or a more carefully selected book of his stories—or that Lovecraft would have been doomed to obscurity had not Derleth sacrificed to publish Lovecraft's

---

8. W. Paul Cook, "A Plea for Lovecraft," *Ghost* No. 3 (May 1945): 55–56.

work himself. In what was probably the last piece Derleth wrote about Lovecraft, he reflected: "By the kind of slow but persistent growth that creates a reputation in letters far longer lasting than the occasional meteoric literary reputation that bursts into prominence virtually overnight and fades as quickly, H. P. Lovecraft's literary status may be said to be firm; his place as a major writer in the minor division of the macabre is secure."[9] Derleth's backhanded compliment, dubbing Lovecraft "a major writer in the minor division of the macabre," was realistic but inevitably short-sighted. Nearly thirty years after Derleth's piece was published, Lovecraft now is recognized as a canonical American writer, rather than merely an extraordinary pulp writer, in large part because of the untiring efforts of August Derleth.

—DAVID E. SCHULTZ AND S. T. JOSHI

A Note on This Edition

We have sought to present the letters of H. P. Lovecraft and August Derleth with minimal editorial alteration. In a few instances, however, we have silently corrected obvious typographical or stenographic errors on both sides. We have supplied postmarks on envelopes or postcards only in cases where this information is necessary to the correct dating of the letter or postcard. Text printed on the fronts of postcards is supplied in brackets following the written text of the postcard.

In order to reduce the number of notes in the text, we have relegated much explanatory information to the Bibliography. Full bibliographical information on all works by Lovecraft or Derleth mentioned or alluded to in the text (including reprints in anthologies) is provided, as is information on all works of fiction mentioned or alluded to in the text. Stories published in pulp magazines are identified in notes, but because of the extensive discussion of stories in *Weird Tales* and their relative merits, stories that appeared in *Weird Tales* are for the most part listed in the bibliography (Section C). Further explanatory notes appear at the end of each letter.

The State Historical Society of Wisconsin owns virtually all existing letters and postcards by H. P. Lovecraft to August Derleth. Thus, our descriptions of Lovecraft's correspondence to Derleth identify only the type of document, not the owning repository. An exception to this is the six postcards owned by the John Hay Library of Brown University. As for the correspondence of August Derleth, many of the few surviving pieces are owned by the John Hay Library (most items are on the reverse sides of story drafts written by Lovecraft). However, a few of Derleth's letters are owned by the State Historical Society of Wisconsin. For clarity's sake, we note the owning repositories of all the surviving forty-six items by Derleth.

---

9. AWD, "H. P. Lovecraft: The Making of a Literary Reputation, 1937–1971," *Books at Brown* 25 (1977): 25.

Acknowledgments

Harry Miller and the staff of the State Historical Society of Wisconsin have, over the last twenty-odd years, been most helpful in providing materials from the Derleth papers for consultation. John H. Stanley and Rosemary Cullen of the John Hay Library have performed the same service with the Lovecraft papers in their care. Colleagues who lent valuable assistance in various ways to the preparation of this volume include Mike Ashley, Eric Carlson, Sean Donnelly, Alistair Durie, Stefan Dziemianowicz, Kenneth W. Faig, John D. Haefele, Dwayne H. Olson, Peter Ruber, Brian Showers, and John R. Squires.

We are grateful to the John Hay Library and the State Historical Society of Wisconsin for permission to publish the letters in this book. We also are grateful to Lovecraft Properties LLC for permission to publish the letters of H. P. Lovecraft and to April Derleth for permission to publish the letters of August Derleth.

Abbreviations

AHT	Arkham House transcripts of Lovecraft's letters
ALS	autograph letter, signed
ANS	autograph note (e.g., postcard), signed
AWD	August W. Derleth
CAS	Clark Ashton Smith
CB	Lovecraft, *Commonplace Book* (numbers refer to entries)
CE	Lovecraft, *Collected Essays,* five volumes
CG	Derleth, *Country Growth*
ColM	Derleth, *Colonel Markesan and Less Pleasant People*
CP	Derleth, *Collected Poems*
CSP	Derleth, *The Casebook of Solar Pons*
D	Lovecraft, *Dagon and Other Macabre Tales*
DAW	Donald A. Wandrei
DD	Derleth, *Dwellers in Darkness*
DH	Lovecraft, *The Dunwich Horror and Others*
FBL	Frank Belknap Long
FF	*Fantasy Fan*
FW	Farnsworth Wright
HDP	Derleth, *Here on a Darkling Plain*
HW	Derleth, *Hawk on the Wind*
JHL	John Hay Library, Brown University
LL	S. T. Joshi, comp., *Lovecraft's Library: A Catalogue* (numbers refer to entries)
LR	Peter Cannon, *Lovecraft Remembered*
MC	Derleth, *The Mask of Cthulhu*

MM	Lovecraft, *At the Mountains of Madness and Other Novels*
MSP	Derleth, *The Memoirs of Solar Pons*
MTH	Derleth, *Man Track Here*
MTS	Lovecraft-Wandrei, *Mysteries of Time and Spirit*
MW	Lovecraft, *Miscellaneous Writings*
NAPA	National Amateur Press Association
NLW	Derleth, *Not Long for This World*
NS	Derleth, *The Night Side*
NYP	Derleth, *Night's Yawning Peal*
OSM	Derleth, *The Other Side of the Moon*
PH	Place of Hawks (the Derleth residence in Sauk City, WI)
PH	Derleth, *Place of Hawks*
QG	Derleth, *In a Quiet Graveyard*
REH	Robert E. Howard
RHB	R. H. Barlow
S&D	Derleth, *The Sleeping and the Dead*
SD	Derleth, *Someone in the Dark*
SH	Derleth, *In RE: Sherlock Holmes*
SHL	Lovecraft, "Supernatural Horror in Literature"
SHSW	State Historical Society of Wisconsin, Madison
SL	Lovecraft, *Selected Letters*, five volumes
SN	Derleth, *Something Near*
SNM	Derleth, *Sleep No More*
SP	Derleth, *Selected Poems*
SPC	Derleth, *Strange Ports of Call*
SPP	Derleth, *Sac Prairie People*
WB	Derleth, *Wisconsin in Their Bones*
WE	Derleth, *Wind in the Elms*
WK	Derleth, *Who Knocks?*
WoT	Derleth, *Worlds of Tomorrow*
WT	*Weird Tales*

1926

[1]   [TLS, JHL]

[AUGUST W. DERLETH
SAUK CITY, WISCONSIN][1]

Sauk City, Wisconsin
30 July, 1926.

Mr. Howard P. Lovecraft
169 Clinton Street
Brooklyn, New York

My dear Mr. Lovecraft:—

Please pardon the impropriety of my writing you an informal letter such as this. Mr. Wright of WEIRD TALES was kind enough to give me your address when I requested it some time ago, and I am about to make use of it.

A short time ago, as I was perusing back copies of WEIRD TALES, I came across a letter from you to the *Eyrie* in the January 1924 issue. In this letter you mention two tales, THE HOUSE OF SOUNDS by M. P. Shiel, and THE PALE APE. Your note on these tales caught my fancy at once and I would like to know if these stories are procurable in the United States, and where, and at what price. Can you give me this information? I am enclosing a stamped and addressed envelope for your convenience in this matter.

Very sincerely yours,
August W. Derleth

Notes

1. AWD's earliest letters to HPL were on stationery with only this information. In later years, he adopted stationery with printed woodcuts that changed from season to season (about which HPL continually ribbed him).

[2]   [ALS]

10 Barnes St.,
Providence, R.I.,
August 3, 1926

Dear Mr. Derleth:—

You will find "The House of Sounds" in the volume entitled "The Pale Ape & Other Stories", of which I know of no American edition.[1] The copy I read was lent me by a friend, & the only ready way that occurs to me for you to see the book is to ask this same genial & accomodating gentleman for the loan of it—explaining your anxiety to read so notable a specimen of weird literature & mentioning my name in connexion with the matter. The person in question is

W. Paul Cook,
Box 215,
Athol, Mass.

As a steady follower of Weird Tales—& incidentally as the one who induced H. Warner Munn (also of Athol) to contribute to it[2]—Cook will recognise your name at once, and, I am sure, be glad to accomodate you in the matter of the book.

Let me add that I have noted many of your tales in the magazine,[3] & admired the thread of genuine weirdness & terror which runs through them. I hope that you, like Mr. Munn, will remain devoted to the spectral ideal, & bring to it the fruits of your increased practice & expanding technique. The weird has always fascinated me prodigiously, & I have only just now—at the suggestion of the same Mr. Cook whom I am recommending to you as the source of the book loan—finished a short historical account of spectral fiction as a literary form—to the typing of which I am looking forward with something like real horror![4]

Hoping that Mr. Cook will be able to accomodate you, I am
Very cordially yours,
H P Lovecraft

P.S. That Brooklyn address was temporary & is obsolete.[5] I am 100% Rhode-Islander by birth & upbringing.

Notes

1. HPL had mentioned Shiel's story at length in a letter published in *WT* (January 1924). AWD was the first to reprint the story in the U.S. The actual title of Shiel's book is *The Pale Ape and Other Pulses*.

2. Munn's first contribution to *WT* was "The Werewolf of Ponkert" (July 1925).

3. By this time AWD had had four stories published in *WT*: "Bat's Belfry"; "The Elixir of Life" (with Mark Schorer); "The Devil's Pay"; and "The Marmoset" (with Schorer).

4. I.e., SHL.

5. AWD had obtained HPL's former address of 169 Clinton Street, Brooklyn (where HPL lived from 31 December 1924 until 17 April 1926) from *WT*. FW, who typically forwarded letters to contributors rather than giving out their addesses, had given AWD HPL's in early December 1925, but AWD uncharacteristically delayed writing to HPL until 30 July 1926.

[3]   [ALS]

10 Barnes St.,
Providence, R.I.,
August 9, 1926

Dear Mr. Derleth:—

I was interested to hear of your recent literary acquisitions, & am reminded that I have never read "Brood of the Witch Queen",[1] which I saw advertised a year or two ago. I'll have to look it up! "The Hill of Dreams" is magnificent, but not so frankly horrible as others of Machen[']s. The tales in "The House of Souls" & "The Three Impostors" are the strongest in that especial line. Blackwood's "Listener" is magnificent—in fact, I'm not sure but that "The Willows" therein is the best weird tale ever written. Have you read B's "John Silence"?

I am glad you find my products readable, & hope you'll continue to do so. Wright favours those with a more prosaic tone, although I have a leaning toward phantasy of the Dunsany sort. The only things I ever did with commercial ends in view were not for Weird Tales, & were always miserably unsatisfactory to me. I shall look with interest for your "Night Rider". October & November will have nothing by me, December will contain a small bit of my verse, & in January will occur the longish "Horror At Red Hook", in which I vent some more of that disgust at New York & everything connected with it which appears in "He". Wright has rejected my latest story "Cool Air", though I really think it is not nearly so bad as many he has taken.

That historical outline of the weird tale was written for private publication in a non-professional magazine to be issued by that same W. Paul Cook to whom I've just referred you. Whether he still plans to issue it, I'm not quite sure, but I found the writing a pleasant exercise & good discipline. Just now I'm dreading the job of typing the thing.

No—I've had nothing published lately except in *Weird Tales,* though I've been thinking of trying some stories on others if I ever get the time. I had two serials in another magazine—a wretched rag called *Home Brew*—some five years ago,[2] but don't think much of them as I consider them in retrospect.

With best wishes, & appreciation of the interest you express in my lucubrations,

I remain
Most cordially & sincerely yrs
H P Lovecraft

Notes

1. By Sax Rohmer.
2. "Herbert West—Reanimator" and "The Lurking Fear."

[4]   [ALS]

> 10 Barnes St.,
> Providence, R.I.,
> Aug. 13, 1926

Dear Mr. Derleth:—

Well—I have secured from the library & read with interest "Brood of the Witch Queen", & am now ¾ way through the same author's "Green Eyes of Bast". These tales are very clever, & contain authentic suspense; though it cannot be said that they show the genuine art & sincerity of work like Machen's & Blackwood's. Their horror is mechanical rather than of the soul.[1] I shall certainly try to get "Grey Face", & trust it will prove as good as the other two. Year's [*sic*] ago I read Rohmer's "Bat Wing" & his "Romance of Sorcery".

You are right in according "The Hill of Dreams" first place among Machen's works—for I think that it is without doubt the fullest & truest expression of his ethereal genius. It is the least touched with conscious artifice of all his longer productions, & forms an almost characteristic record of the life of the dreamer's soul. Lucian's dream-life as a Roman in old Isca Silurum is something really quite unapproached in literature. "The Three Impostors", though, is very much worth reading. Stark horror never went beyond the limits reached in such chapters as "The White Powder" or "The Black Seal". Dunsany does not go in so much for sheer horror, as for fantastic beauty & the unreal world in general. You can get the cream of him in the Modern Library—90¢ each—in the volumes called "The Book of Wonder" & "A Dreamer's Tales". This is really a very good bargain, for these two small-type volumes comprise *four* of the regular edition.

As to editorial rejections of tales dear to their authors—apparently that is a very frequent type of phenomenon. Commercial standards have twists & phases incomprehensible to the artist, & the eyes of an editor are fixed on points of which an author would never think. Acceptance or rejection, indeed, forms no criterion whatsoever of absolute merit. My coming "Red Hook" is really one of the poorest things—shapeless, & with touches of almost tawdry melodrama—that I have ever perpetrated; but Wright snapped it up as quickly as he fired back "The Nameless City"—an archaeological phantasy[2] of which I am really rather fond.

I don't know when Cook will publish that *Recluse*, but I'll be glad to lend you a carbon of my weird tale article when I get it typed. It is not of much intrinsic merit, but will at least give you the names of stacks of weird books worth reading—some of which you may not have come across. Do you know the tales, for instance, of Montague Rhodes James? If not, lose no time in getting hold of the following:

> Ghost Stories of an Antiquary
> More Ghost Stories of an Antiquary

A Thin Ghost & Others
A Warning to the Curious.

James, who is Provost of Eton College, is a very profound scholar, antiquarian, & expert in palaeography & cathedral history. These weird stories form his pastime & avocation.

With every good wish, & abundant gratitude for putting me in touch with the Rohmer books, I remain
Most cordially & sincerely yrs—
H P Lovecraft

Notes

1. HPL to CAS, 9 August 1926 (*Book Sail* Catalog): "I'm reading Sax Rohmer's 'Brood of the Witch Queen' on somebody's recommendation. It's naive, crude, boresome—but I deserve the punishment for having fancied that anything by that egregious hack could be any good!"
2. Written 1921. Other "archaeological phantasies" of HPL include "The Rats in the Walls" (1923), "Under the Pyramids" (1924), and later *At the Mountains of Madness* (1931), and "The Shadow out of Time" (1934–35).

[5]   [ALS]

10 Barnes St.,
Providence, R.I.,
Aug. 18, 1926

Dear Mr. Derleth:—

I am glad to hear that you are on the trail of "The Pale Ape", & hope you will soon have M. R. James & Dunsany as well. If I had the cash, I would like to possess nearly all the leading specimens of weird fiction; but as it is, I have to content myself with library facilities except in a few modest instances. For example—I don't own so much as a single work of Algernon Blackwood's.

I have now read "Grey Face", but do not think it equals "Brood of the Witch Queen"—which is the only Rohmer book, I fancy, that requires inclusion in a brief outline of weird writing. I've also just read Blackwood's "Tongues of Fire", which was a distinct disappointment to me. Blackwood can be discouragingly insipid when he chooses!

Enclosed is a carbon of my "Nameless City", which you may peruse at leisure. It is nothing very marvellous—but I wondered a bit at Wright's rejection of it because he has accepted so many still worse things of mine. I don't mind rejections, though, for I attach no importance to judgments based on commercial expediency.

I trust your play may prove a success[1]—& sympathise regarding the incidental typing. When I get my article typed, you shall certainly see a carbon; & I only hope you'll find enough new names of weird writers to warrant your wading through it.

With every good wish,

Most cordially & sincerely yrs—

H P Lovecraft

Notes

1. Unidentified (but not the play *This Business Called Life*, which was written with Mark Schorer c. 1928).

[6]   [ALS]

10 Barnes St.,

Providence, R.I.,

Aug. 26, 1926

Dear Mr. Derleth:—

I am glad you found "The Nameless City" readable, & hope that some day some magazine may find it worth printing.[1] With me it is always an open question which type of weird tale is to be preferred—this wholly unreal sort, or that with a closer linkage to the external aspect of reality. Perhaps both have equal validity—each suiting some particular mood of the sensitive imagination.

I hope you will succeed in getting "The Pale Ape". When you do, I know you will find "The House of Sounds" one of the most powerful weird tales you have ever read. Some complain that it follows too closely the spirit of Poe's "House of Usher", but it seems to me that there is enough of distinct originality to give it a place among the few weird masterpieces on its own account. It is obviously the result of great care & frequent re-writing on its author's part—for an earlier version is extant,[2] in which the style is more or less cluttered up with the flashiness & showiness of the spectacular 'nineties. Apparently Shiel recognised this defect, & later decided to practice some artistic pruning—which he did, with eminently successful results. Yes—the price of weird classics is indeed a sad deterrent in the matter of accumulating a library of them. This same Janvier you are partonising had Maturin's "Melmoth, the Wanderer["][3] catalogued last winter, but the expense proved excessive for me. Have you read "Melmoth"? I consider it the best (as it is the last) of the early "Gothic" novels of terror. It is seldom found in public libraries.

Glad your play-typing is accomplished. I keep postponing the dreaded job on my article, but will certainly let you see it when it's done.

With all good wishes,

Cordially & sincerely yrs—

H P Lovecraft

P.S. Have you tried any fiction on *Ghost Stories,* 1926 Broadway, N.Y. City? I've just sent them three tales—though I expect them back.[4]

Notes

1. The story remained unpublished until 1936, when it appeared in severely misprinted form.
2. "Vaila," in *Shapes in the Fire* (1896).
3. See letter 299.
4. *Ghost Stories* was published by Constructive Publishing Co. (Bernarr MacFadden) from July 1926 to March 1930; Good Story Magazine Co. from April 1930 to December 1931/January 1932. It was a companion magazine to *True Story* and *True Detective Stories,* and its stories followed a confessional format. HPL submitted "In the Vault," "Cool Air," and probably "The Nameless City." "Pickman's Model," written c. September 1926, has a "somewhat colloquial" tone (as HPL notes in letter 10) not previously found in HPL's fiction, and may have been written with *Ghost Stories* in mind, although it does not appear that HPL ever submitted the story there.

[7]   [TLS, JHL]

Sauk City, Wisconsin
31 August, 1926

My dear Mr. Lovecraft,

Yes, I certainly enjoyed your THE NAMELESS CITY, and I am looking forward to the time when I shall peruse your article. As to the question you state regarding which type of weird tale is the preferred—personally, I prefer the wholly unreal type, though I do enjoy any other type.

I have not read WELWORTH [*sic*] THE WANDERER, nor have I ever heard of it before. I am listing it, and I will attempt to procure it some time later.

No, I have not tried any fiction on GHOST STORIES. I purchased a copy of the magazine, but the stories in it were of such inferior quality that I did not even read them. However, the magazine might have improved. Personally I despise the other Macfadden publications, TRUE STORY especially. Do let me know whether or not you have any of your stories accepted by it. You probably will receive your tales back, for I got the impression that it was not artistic ghost stories that they desired, but rather unpolished things.

May I ask, do you receive any writer's magazines? Such as THE WRITER, THE PLOTWEAVER, WRITER'S DIGEST? If so which do you consider the best?

Hoping to be able to peruse your article soon, I am

Very cordially yours,

August W. Derleth

[8]   [ALS]

10 Barnes St.,

Providence, R.I.,

Sept. 2, 1926

My dear Mr. Derleth:—

Confound my wretched script—& my disinclination to use the machine! Before you give a bookseller a false lead, let me say that the ponderous old book I cited is MELMOTH—*not* Welworth! You will find it long-winded and rambling, but it's the earliest work (1820) I can find which contains the true touch of cosmic horror except in thin spots. Incidentally—have you read other early horror work? If not, let me advise the following as worthy ingredients (if only for historical reasons) for any fantaisiste's library:

> Mysteries of Udolpho (1793) by Anne Radcliffe
> The Monk (1795) by Matthew Gregory Lewis.[1]

Oh, yes—& the earliest of all, though very clumsy & unconvincing, is Horace Walpole's "Castle of Otranto", from which the whole tradition of weird or "Gothic" fiction derived its vogue. There's quite a history of this early "Gothic" work published—"The Tale of Terror", by Prof. Edith Birkhead.[2] You ought to find that at any library.

My article may not be typed for some time yet, because somebody[3] has put me on the track of a list of weird fiction at the public library which (if I can get access to it) may cause me to expand the text considerably. If I get hold of the list & discover a stack of stuff I don't know, I shall have to indulge in a long course of reading first, & then almost rewrite the article!

Yes—I suppose I'll get my stuff back from *Ghost Stories*. It hasn't improved—& is about as poor as a magazine can be. I know the Macfadden junk is altogether impossible—in fact, I've never so much as opened one of these publications with the exception of that named! A man I know, however, picks up quite a little cash by deliberately catering to their needs. He's lucky to be able to catch their nauseously vulgar style—I'm sure I couldn't!

No—I don't take any writers' magazines, although those who do tell me that *The Writer's Digest* is the best. *The Writer's Monthly* is also good—I know a chap—Arthur Leeds—who used to conduct a column in it.[4] *The Writer* has changed so much since I last saw it that I don't know what it's like. It wasn't much in my day, but I think it's grown to be a very desirable & important publication.

With every good wish,

Most cordially & sincerely yrs—

H P Lovecraft

Notes

1. See George Saintsbury, ed., *Tales of Mystery*, containing extracts of Ann Radcliffe's

The Mysteries of Udolpho (1794), Matthew Gregory Lewis's *The Monk* (1796), and Charles Robert Maturin's *Melmoth, the Wanderer* (1820).

2. HPL obtained much of the information on Gothic fiction contained in SHL from Birkhead's book.

3. The tipster may have been C. M. Eddy, Jr.

4. Arthur Leeds and J. Berg Esenwein had a long-running series of articles, "Photoplay Construction," in the *Writer's Monthly* (then titled *Photoplay Author*) 1, No. 12 (May 1913)–5, No. 3 (March 1915). Leeds alone had a column, "Answers to Inquiries," 2, No. 1 (June–July 1913)–5, No. 2 (February 1915), followed by "Thinks and Things," 5, No. 3 (March 1915)–10, No. 6 (December 1917).

[9]   [TLS, JHL]

Sauk City, Wisconsin
6 September, 1926

My dear Mr. Lovecraft:—

I am infinitely sorry that I failed to carefully scrutinize your script in regard to MELMOTH THE WANDERER. I have made the change on my want list. I am acquainted with all of the books you mention except the book by Edith Birkhead. I will look them all up in the University of Wisconsin library in three weeks. I am beginning my University career there on the twenty-first.

I don't know whether I told you or not, but Mr. Wright finally took THE RIVER after its first revision. I am now writing a ghost story about THE SLEEPERS in a haunted Pullman car, in spite of the fact that Wright tells me that WEIRD TALES has quite a few ghost stories on file.

The longer your article is, the better I will like it.

Following your suggestion I sent some ghost tales to GHOST STORIES myself. Of course, I expect them back much faster than you'll get yours, if you do get them back.

Due to financial reverses I've had to cut two books from my order to Meredith Janvier, and I am now only getting THE THREE IMPOSTORS and THE PALE APE. Mr. Janvier is now searching for the latter book in the Brentano edition. I do hope that he finds it.

Very cordially yours,
August W. Derleth

[10]   [ALS]

10 Barnes St.,
Providence, R.I.,
Septr. 8, 1926

My dear Mr. Derleth:—

I am glad to hear that "The River" is to appear, & shall be on the watch for it. Your tale of a haunted Pullman sounds promising, & I trust it may find editorial favour. It makes no difference what other ghost tales Wright has—originality & uniquity lie in the treatment rather than in the basic theme. There are ghosts—& ghosts! I hope you can land something with *Ghost Stories,* for the rate there is 2¢ a word. My three yarns yet remain to be heard from, but I am not optimistic. I have a new one about nameless horrors beneath the hills of Old Boston which I may try on G. S.—not that it's of their moronic type, but that the style happens to be somewhat colloquial.[1]

Your choice of new books under a programme of retrenchment seems to me very wise, & I hope there will be no great difficulty in finding "The Pale Ape". I haven't yet looked up the list of weird fiction at the library.

You have my best wishes for a fruitful university career, & I think you have chosen an excellent institution. Two of my best friends are graduates of the U. of Wis.,[2] & both sing its praises in no faltering accents. Madison, too, is a delightful town according to all the accounts I've heard.

Most cordially & sincerely yrs—
H P Lovecraft

Notes

1. I.e., "Pickman's Model."
2. Maurice W. Moe and Alfred Galpin.

[11]   [TLS, JHL]

Sauk City, Wisconsin
13 September, 1926

My dear Mr. Lovecraft:—
I am progressing very nicely with THE SLEEPERS. I hope Wright will take it, but even if he doesn't I think GHOST STORIES will use it. As yet I have received only a file number for my three tales at GHOST STORIES. That's nothing definite.

I am greatly indebted to you for putting me on the trail of THE THREE IMPOSTORS; I am enjoying it immensely.

Although the University of Wisconsin school year opens next Tuesday, the twenty-first, I have made no preparations. I'm registering the coming Thursday, and I am planning to major in History, taking Ancient and Medieval the first year. My ultimate aim is to tack a Ph. D. and an LL. D. after my name.

Recently I stumbled across a volume of unusual tales in a volume, SHAPES THAT HAUNT THE DUSK, of Harper's Novelettes series, edited by W. Dean Howells and Henry Mills Alden, copyright 1891–1907. The tales concerned very commonplace supernatural themes. I am quite certain that the book is out of print, so I am going to attempt to purchase the book, breaking the series. I doubt my success in the endeavour, but there is nothing like trying. The authors in this volume are not very familiar: Georg Schock, Richard Rice, Howard Pyle, Madelene Yale Wynne, Harriet Lewis Bradley, Hildegarde Hawthorne, M. E. M. Davis, F. D. Millet, E. Levi Brown, H. W. McVicker. I've heard of only the third and sixth in that list.

Have you ever read Charles Kingley's HYPATIA? I'm going to read it; I've been informed that it is rather weird. Just recently I was presented with Shelley's FRANKENSTEIN. A new addition to my collection of the weird, that.

Very cordially yours,
August W. Derleth

[12] [ALS]

10 Barnes St.,
Providence, R.I.,
Septr. 27, 1926

My dear Mr. Derleth:—

I found your letter upon my return from a two weeks' trip which included the Philadelphia sesquicentennial, New York, & a coach ride through the ancient villages of Connecticut.[1] Was very glad to hear of your progress on your tale, & certainly hope you can place it to advantage. *Ghost Stories* has just rejected my "In the Vault" without reference to two others I submitted with it. Glad you find "The Three Impostors" enjoyable, & congratulate you on your acquisition of "Frankenstein", which I have in a rather oldish edition. I read "Hypatia"[2] some 25 years ago; but while recalling much richness in the historic colour of the Alexandrian age, do not seem to associate the volume with intense weirdness. However—you can't do ill in reading it.

You are fortunate in coming across "Shapes that Haunt the Dusk", & I certainly hope you may succeed in getting a copy for yourself. I shall make an effort to get access to this volume somewhere. Am surprised that Howells was concerned in a venture like this, since ordinarily he was old-womanishly opposed to the really gruesome & terrible. He made an absurd apology for including Mrs. Gilman's "Yellow Wall Paper" in an anthology he edited.[3]

By this time I trust you are duly entered at the U. of Wis. Your choice of studies would seem to be a wise one, & I trust you will pursue you curriculum till your name becomes the leader of a formidable procession of degrees.

With best wishes,

Most sincerely yrs—
H P Lovecraft

Notes

1. HPL's wife, Sonia, had asked him to come back to New York as she was in town

for two weeks. HPL was there 13–25 September.

2. By Charles Kingsley. HPL owned Kingsley's *The Heroes; or, Greek Fairy Tales for My Children* <1856> (Philadelphia: H. Altemus, 1895; *LL* 499).

3. William Dean Howells included Charlotte Perkins Gilman's "The Yellow Wall Paper" (1892) in his anthology *The Great Modern American Stories* (1920). In the introduction (p. vii) he said of it: "It wanted at least two generations to freeze our young blood with Mrs. Perkins Gilman's story of *The Yellow Wall Paper,* which Horace Scudder (then of *The Atlantic*) said in refusing it that it was so terribly good that it ought never to be printed. But terrible and too wholly dire as it was, I could not rest until I had corrupted the editor of *The New England Magazine* into publishing it. Now that I have got it into my collection here, I shiver over it as much as I did when I first read it in manuscript, though I agree with the editor of *The Atlantic* of the time that it was too terribly good to be printed."

[13]   [TLS, JHL]

823 West Johnson Street
Madison, Wisconsin

4 October, 1926

My dear Mr. Lovecraft:—

I located your letter in my veritable mountain of all kinds of mail when I went home this week end.

I have sent in THE SLEEPERS and am awaiting an answer from Wright, due today if I calculate correctly. I have also done a short sketch about the "little people", called THE MILL WHEEL, which I am going to try on WEIRD TALES.

GHOST STORIES rejected all three of the tales I sent them, one at a time. I find the magazine goes though an inconceivable amount of "red tape" before either finally accepting or rejecting a story. I'm going to try a short prime story of mine on FLYNN'S,[1] though without much hope of having it accepted.

My address is now 823 West Johnson Street, Madison, Wisconsin, although any mail addressed to Sauk City, will reach me just the same.

I finished THE THREE IMPOSTORS, and I'm ready for more of it. I purchased Machen's THE HILL OF DREAMS for a minute study of his style. Just before I came in this morning I visited a book store and came across Sir Oliver Lodge's RAYMOND, OR LIFE AND DEATH, in the abridged two dollar edition, just like new, for ten cents![2] Of course, I procured it at once, together with Joseph French's latest anthology of tales, GHOSTS, GRIM AND GENTLE. This latter book contained one of the most humorously entertaining ghost stories I have ever read, THE CANTERVILLE GHOST by Oscar Wilde.

I managed to purchase SHAPES THAT HAUNT THE DUSK from the lady who owned it. The poor old woman was almost frightened when I told her that the book contained ghost stories. She didn't even read it.

I am now entered at the U. of W. I changed my course slightly, cutting out Medieval History in favour of Botany, and passing an English 1a test by an Excellent mark, I was enabled to take up English 2a; now I am carrying one sophomore subject.

I just bought the latest WEIRD TALES, and I am rather disappointed in it. I was especially piqued by Frank Belknap Long's tale, THE DOG-EARED GOD, for he is capable of much better work. E. Hoffman[n] Price hasn't surpassed either THE RAJAH'S GIFT or THE SULTAN'S JEST by his THE PEACOCK'S SHADOW. THE CITY OF SPIDERS wasn't bad, but Munn's WEREWOLF OF PONKERT surpasses it by far.[3]

Very cordially yours,
August W. Derleth

Notes

1. *Flynn's* (1924–28), later titled *Detective Fiction Weekly* (1928f.).

2. Sir Oliver Lodge's *Raymond* (1916) is a book claiming that Lodge had established contact with his son Raymond's spirit after his death in World War I. Lodge had once been a respected physicist, but destroyed much of his reputation with this book and others expressing credulous belief in spiritualism.

3. FBL, "The Dog-Eared God," *WT* (November 1926); E. Hoffmann Price, "The Rajah's Gift," *WT* (January 1925), "The Sultan's Jest," *WT* (September 1925); H. Warner Munn, "The City of Spiders," *WT* (November 1926), "The Werewolf of Ponkert," *WT* (July 1925).

[14]   [ALS]

10 Barnes St.,
Providence, R.I.,
Octr. 11, 1926

Dear Mr. Derleth:—

I note your new address with interest, since it seems to be very near the quarters (830 W. Johnson) occupied by a very brilliant young friend of mine (Alfred Galpin, now an instructor in Northwestern Univ.) during his college days five years ago. From what he used to say, I think you will like Madison very much.

Hope Wright will like "The Sleepers", & that you'll try him with "The Mill Wheel". Tales of the "little people" in the Machen manner always interest me, & I hope you'll let me see yours in MS. if W.T. doesn't accept it. I am still waiting for a verdict on the longish tale—"The Call of Cthulhu"—which

I sent in a week or two ago.[1] *Ghost Stories* has rejected two of my tales and will probably reject the third, but I rather expected that. To land anything with them, one would have to study a special technique suited to the crude minds of half-baked readers. Since the pay is 2¢ per word, I may yet try it! Good luck with tale at *Flynn's*!

Glad you got poor old Lodge's "Raymond" for a dime—it may, at a charitable estimate, be worth almost that! I haven't read it, but fancy it is more a mass of delusional details on spiritualism than anything really exciting. There's nothing more flat than the pitiful seriousness of those who actually believe in the supernatural. I've always heard about "The Canterville Ghost", but never read it. As a rule, I find *humorous* ghost stories rather insipid; Brander Matthews' "The Rival Ghosts" & Frank R. Stockton's "The Transferred Ghost" being cases in point. I shall be interested to hear more of "Shapes That Haunt the Dusk." Let us hope it fully justified the dear old lady's fears!

I've been too busy on a special revision job to read the latest *Weird Tales*, but young Long showed me "The Dog Eared God" in MS. several months ago. It is not one of his best, yet far from his worst. Fiction is to him only a means of corraling cash—he is a poet & aesthete, & has put his real soul into the thin volume of verse he issued (at a doting aunt's expense) last winter.[2] He's a great boy, all told, & ought to make his mark in literature sooner or later. I shall go over "The Peacock's Shadow" & "The City of Spiders" with great interest & not too exalted expectations.

Your changes in curriculum are doubtless well-advised, & I am glad you are able to take advanced English. I hear through Victor E. Bacon[3] that you are only seventeen years old—which is truly a remarkably early age to be entering college & writing stories as good as yours. At this rate, you won't delay very long before producing impressive results!

With every good wish,
Most cordially & sincerely yrs—
H P Lovecraft

Notes

1. FW rejected the story, but when he later asked to see it again he accepted and published it.
2. FBL, *A Man from Genoa*. The book was financed by his aunt, Mrs. William B. Symmes.
3. Bacon was an amateur journalist and formerly Official Editor of the United Amateur Press Association (1925–26).

[15]   [TLS, JHL]

823 West Johnson Street
Madison, Wisconsin

15 October, 1926

My dear Mr. Lovecraft:—
                    Just received your letter after coming in from a quiz
in Botany. Yes, 830 West Johnson is just across the street from where I am. I
like Madison all right, but I prefer Sauk City. Strange, preferring a town of
1200 to a city of 50,000, isn't it?
     Wright took THE SLEEPERS at once, but he rejected THE MILL
WHEEL. He pointed out to me what was wrong with it, and I can easily see
now that it is unworth[y] of WEIRD TALES. A friend hinted that it resem-
bled one of Blackwood's tales, JOHN SILENCE, or A PSYCHICAL INVA-
SION. I read the tale and my story does hint at it very much; so much that I
am glad that Wright didn't take it. I am sending you the manuscript. Wright's
main objection was that it lacked convincing qualities. If you can make this
thing into a convincing tale go ahead and use it. Wright also accepted an old
story of Mr. Schorer's and mine, THE BLACK CASTLE, which he had rejected once before. However, I didn't revise it.
     Let me know how you come out on THE CALL. Yes, I believe one must
conform to the vulgar style of GHOST STORIES. Have you done anything
of late for WEIRD TALES? I might add that I enjoyed your essay in DRIFT
WIND.[1]
     I certainly received a severe jolt when I read what you said in your letter
about those who actually believed in the supernatural. I have a very learned
friend, a lady whose intellectual qualities have reached a high degree of perfection, who firmly believes in the supernatural—not in spiritualism, but in spir-
itism. There is a great difference, she asserts. Mr. Schorer, the co-author of
THE ELIXIR OF LIFE and THE MARMOSET, was the percipient of a telepathic ghost of myself projected to him in the wee-small-hours, during a period
in which I was critically ill last May. Nothing can shake my belief in the latter
possibility. A young lady once came to me and accused me of keeping her
awake from twelve to one, one night. She stated that she had been soundly
asleep, when suddenly she was awakened. She thought constantly of me, for an
hour; she distinctly heard the clock strike one, and then she dropped off to
sleep again. Now at the hour she mentioned I had been thinking about her in
connection with an affair she had had with a young man for whom I entertain a
dislike[.] The affair, (although it had no reason to concern me) annoyed me exceedingly, and I was puzzling over a way to acquaint her of the fact that the
young man was not the kind of company she should have. This is only one instance in many. Telepathy, I presume. I might add an odd instance that occurred to my grandmother, still living. If you laughed at this tale while she told

you, she would wither you with a glance. I laughed once, so I know.

One o'clock in the morning of a certain day in November many years ago, my grandmother awoke from a sound sleep, feeling an unquenchable thirst. She got up, slipped on a dressing gown, and started to go down stairs. As she reached the first landing she looked downward and saw clearly outlined in the light from the moon a whitish figure, an exact replica of my grandfather, who she had left in bed behind her. She stood for some time looking at it; it started to move slowly toward her and disappeared. *A year from that date* my grandfather was challenged to a duel to death by an enemy of his who had sworn to "get" my grandfather. My grandfather accepted, and shot his enemy through the heart! Of course he was imprisoned for this act, and one year from the date of his imprisonment, *two years from the date* that my grandmother had seen the "ghost", at one o'clock in the morning my grandfather died in prison. Can you explain that?

Yes, I am but seventeen years of age; I'll be eighteen next February 24. V. E. Bacon had asked me to be secretary-treasurer of the N.A.P.A., and I've accepted his offer, though I won't say for how long. Hoping to hear from you soon, I am very cordially yours,

August W. Derleth

Notes

1. "The Materialist Today."

[16]   [ALS]

10 Barnes St.,
Providence, R.I.,
Octr. 19, 1926

My dear Mr. Derleth:—

I am *not* surprised that you prefer Sauk City to Madison, for I am also fond of the quiet atmosphere of smaller places; in fact, I can't picture anything more delightful in America than one of the quaint colonial seaports on the New England coast, which have been sleeping almost unchanged a century & more. If I weren't attached to Providence by nativity & lifelong residence, I'd like to live in ancient Marblehead, Mass. I regret the growth of my own town to something like moderate metropolitan stature, (pop. 267,918 in city limits; Metrop. district as a whole, 580,631) it having been decidedly more provincial & overgrown-village-like in my youth—although it had a population of 175,597 in 1900. What I love are the antiquities—the old pre-Revolutionary houses & the quaint crooked streets winding up the ancient hill that rises precipitously above the river (or head of Narragansett Bay.) Antiquarianism, I might say, is my leading hobby; & I spend absolutely all my spare cash on trips to old colonial towns like Boston, Philadelphia, Newport,

Bristol, Concord, Salem, Marblehead, Newburyport, Portsmouth, &c. to absorb architecture & atmosphere. Providence, though, has sections as quaint as any of these other places; & I only hope that the devastating hand of modern "progress" will not ruin it too completely before I die.

Glad to hear that Wright took "The Sleepers", as well as "The Black Castle". He rejected my "Call of Cthulhu", as the accompanying note will ruefully testify. That was almost a novelette, so I regret the cheque I shan't get for it! I have another new yarn—"Pickman's Model"—which I shall probably try soon on W.T., for I don't imagine *Ghost Stories* would consider it.

I read "The Mill Wheel" with much interest, & would advise its redevelopment with more emphasis on *atmosphere*. Take Machen rather than Blackwood as a model—Blackwood has absolutely no style except by accident now & then, & sometimes "flops" pitiably. Don't stress the immediate events so much as the whole weird background—latent horror lurking just outside the edge of the known. Let the 'little people' be barely hinted of in terse, furtive whispers, & lead up to the momentary appearance of the evil troll face by the most careful climactic stages. The main thing to avoid is too brisk & matter-of-fact a tone. That's what spoils much early work in the Gothic manner, & makes Walpole's "Castle of Otranto" amusing rather than terrifying. Thanks for the offer of the plot—but I really think you'd better save it to tinker with at your leisure. One's own ideas have a certain vividness which makes it a shame to waste them on another!

As to the supernatural—I simply believe the way I think the evidence of Nature as analysed by science points. I am no crusader, & am well content to let others believe as they choose—even that *Drift Wind* article was prepared solely at Coates' insistence from a private letter not meant for publication. I am aware that many persons of cultivation believe in weird things, for *general* culture offers no especial argument against the spirit world. It is only when one begins to compare & correlate different sciences, & investigate the illusion-forming & memory-twisting qualities of the human brain, that one finds it impossible to continue in supernatural faith.

These "telepathic projections", by the way, do not necessarily involve the supernatural; since the principle of thought-waves in the ether is a distinct possibility. I have heard many accounts of these things, & do not wish to speak too dogmatically against their reality; but am inclined to think that most of them result from an unconsciously doctored memory coloured by subsequent suggestion. A, for example, thinks frequently of B. On one special occasion B conjures up a particularly vivid image of A—either dreaming or waking—& tells A about it. A is impressed—& his memory unconsciously emphasises the thoughts he had of B at the moment B says he saw him. If B gave the *wrong* hour for his vision, A would "remember" having thought of him at exactly that hour. This unconscious action & illusion of the memory is very hard to credit or understand at first, but psychologists are very familiar with it, & can cite more striking cases—known as such—than any of the laymen who have encountered the apparent phenomenon of telepathy.

The case of your grandmother is highly interesting, & recalls many of the most famous family legends of history. One has, of course, to study these instances at first hand before venturing a real opinion on causes; but it is very probable that many of the earlier details were unconsciously moulded after the occurrence of the later events. Real coincidence doubtless played its part, but an *approximate* tallying of dates often becomes an *exact* one through revised memory, while repetition heightens the drama & supplies the colour & corroborative detail. Still—when science changes its conclusions, I'm ready to change with it. I've no personal preference either for or against the existence of a spirit world; & being intensely devoted to the weird as an aesthetic conception, would be only too glad to see it added to the domain of actuality!

I am indeed glad to hear of your acceptance of the U.A.P.A. Sec. Treasurership. We need competent officials badly, & it has been most regrettable that the present younger generation has not taken hold as enthusiastically as former younger generations did. Amateur journalism has magnificent possibilities, & I hate to see it in a state of decadence.

With every good wish—

Most cordially & sincerely yrs

—H P Lovecraft

[17]   [ALS]

10 Barnes St.,

Providence, R.I.,

Octr. 25, 1926.

My dear Mr. Derleth:—

Well—here is "Cthulhu"—& I only hope you won't be too greatly disappointed with it. I can see how Wright must consider it slow, but don't feel disposed to change it any. I have my own methods of developing horror in a cumulative way. I'll have to ask you to return this MS., since it is the only one I have. Others have not been very conscientious about returning the carbons which I lent them.

You have certainly had enviable luck in bookbuying, & I hope you will find your eight volumes well worth the half-dollar. I think I read "The Jungle"[1] in an incredibly remote past, though I cared comparatively little for it. These excited sociological harangues are not art—propaganda is never art—& I am too much of a cynic to be anything more than bored by the indignation of those who look for "justice" in an absolutely meaningless & blandly impersonal cosmos that sizzles from nowhere to nowhere. Sinclair is fluent, though, & he might be an artist if he worried less about the poor oppressed under dog & all that sort of thing. I'm glad you have Dunsany, & that you are on the trail of "The Pale Ape". This latter has some potent matter indeed, & gives about the cream of Shiel's products. You may have to pay more than the 8/- in the end through customs charges. That seems to be usually the case with foreign importations, though the present bargain is well worth it, & will still be a good bargain after all charges are paid.

As to the supernatural—there is no harm in each person's believing whatever his appraisal of the evidence before him prompts him to believe; & no lack of dignity in changing opinion when data warrants it. Edison's views on matter & energy have always been somewhat fantastic,[2] hence I am not wholly astonished to hear of a leaning on his part toward supernaturalism; but I doubt if his belief is very much like the unscientific conceptions of the outright spiritualists. I'll look up that Forum article[3] if I get time, though just now I'm utterly rushed to death with revisory work. As if it weren't enough to have a desk piled high with mundane duties, one client[4] wants me to come to Detroit for a week & do some daily personal collaboration with him—a proposition which I'll certainly sidestep if it can be managed without danger of the poorhouse!

Well—I hope "Cthulhu" won't bore you. Some time I'll let you see other unpublished junk of mine if it would be of any interest to you. I think I've sent you only "The Nameless City".

With all good wishes—
Most sincerely yrs—
H P Lovecraft

Notes

1. By Upton Sinclair. The novel is a graphic account of the meat packing industry in the Chicago stockyards.
2. The great inventor Thomas Alva Edison (1847–1931) was also an adherent of spiritualism.
3. H. Carrington, "Is Psychical Research Science?," *Forum* 73, No. 1 (January 1925): 73–78; or O. J. Lodge, "Spiritualism and Religion," *Forum* 74, No. 2 (August 1925): 184–93.
4. I.e., Harry Houdini.

[18]   [ALS]

10 Barnes St.,
Providence, R.I.,
Octr. 31, 1926

My dear Mr. Derleth:—
                    I am very glad that you like "Cthulhu", for I keep fearing that advancing years may take something out of the vitality of my stuff. My *technique,* I think, is better than it was when I was young; but one always suspects that despite this *mechanical* improvement there may be a parallel slackening of the tension & vitality of one's work as one slips out of intense & wondering

youth into stolid & cynical middle age. Dunsany, for example, doesn't write the stuff now that he wrote twenty years ago. I'd give any amount if he—or somebody—would evolve another set of yarns like "A Dreamer's Tales"!

Only about half of my stories have appeared in W.T., & if you'd enjoy seeing the others I'll be glad to lend you the MSS. Enclosed is the latest of my efforts[1]—which I haven't submitted to any publication as yet. I guess I'll try it on Wright in the end. A full list of my yarns—such as I have thought worthy of saving from destruction—is as follows:

*The Tomb	*The Cats of Ulthar
*Dagon	*The Temple
Polaris	*Arthur Jermyn (pub. as "The White Ape")
Beyond the Wall of Sleep	Celephaïs
*The White Ship	From Beyond
The Doom That Came to Sarnath	Nyarlathotep (prose-poem)
*The Statement of Randolph Carter	*The Picture in the House
*The Terrible Old Man	The Nameless City
The Tree	The Quest of Iranon
	*The Moon Bog
Psychopompos (in rhyme)	*The Unnamable
Herbert West—Reanimator	*The Festival
*The Outsider	The Shunned House
The Other Gods	*The Horror at Red Hook
*The Music of Erich Zann	*He
*Hypnos	In the Vault
*The Hound	Cool Air
The Lurking Fear	The Call of Cthulhu
*The Rats in the Walls	Pickman's Model.
The Silver Key[2]	

*published in or accepted by W.T.

You might return this list, checking off any titles you wish to see—or crossing out those which you have read. One or two of those named may not be available, but most of them are.

I trust that "The Pale Ape" may arrive without mishaps. Your other bargains are certainly encouraging, & I envy you your sight of "Melmoth the Wanderer". It is unobtainable at the libraries in Providence, N.Y. & Brooklyn. You'll find some good Wells material in the new magazine *Amazing Stories,* which specialises in reprints,—which reminds me that you *must* read "The Island of Dr. Moreau" in the last two issues; a truly *loathsome* thing now wholly out of print as a book.

I've recently begun reading the work of Sir H. Rider Haggard *for the first time*. "She" is very good, & if the others are at all commensurate, I have quite a treat ahead. I suppose you've seen most of these—or doesn't the younger generation follow Haggard as he was followed of yore?

With all good wishes,

Most sincerely yrs—

H P Lovecraft

Notes

1. I.e., "Pickman's Model."

2. This title was added later in blue pen by AWD.

[19]   [ALS]

10 Barnes St.,
Providence, R.I.,
Novr. 7, 1926

My dear Mr. Derleth:—

Glad you found the new tale worth reading. I'll try it on Wright in the next batch & see what he thinks of it. Your verdict on the current W.T. seems to me very just—for I must say that nothing except "The Metal Giants" struck me as thoroughly worth reading. That verse of mine[1] was part of a personal greeting to Wright on a Christmas card last year, but with the omission of the final stanza of the original it became available for publication. I shall be interested to see your tale, "The Black Powder", & trust that when completed it may win editorial approval.

Janvier was certainly rather forehanded in ordering books without your authorisation! It will teach him a lesson if you don't take the items involved. As to "Melmoth"—of course it drags in places, like all the interminable novels of its time; but it seems to me to hold a certain convincing kinship with horrors beyond the veil which we find lacking in its predecessors—such as "Udolpho", "The Monk", &c. Glad you've read "Moreau". Frank B. Long Jr. started it when he was 8 years old, but his mother thought it was bad for his nerves & wouldn't let him finish it! In later years he could not find a copy, & only just now—at the age of 24—has the reprint in *Amazing Stories* enabled him to gratify the excited curiosity of his infancy. My expectations of Haggard are not so high that any disillusion will be very painful. I can see that he is essentially a "best seller" hack, but fancy he is fairly good as hacks go. I'll keep your recommendations in mind.

Enclosed are "Beyond the Wall of Sleep" in a carbon most inexcusably but economically written on the backs of old letters (as Pope wrote his Iliad translation!)[2] & "The Lurking Fear", as published in a positively beastly but now happily defunct magazine called *Home Brew* in Jan.–April, 1923. This tale was modelled in conformity with the demands of the magazine, & has melodramatic climaxes at the ends of the instalments which do not meet my artistic approval. I shall some day rewrite it as a single & continuous tale. Pardon the misprints—always giving me the benefit of the doubt when confronted with evidences of apparent incoherence or illiteracy. Unfortunately I haven't any copy whatsoever of "The Shunned House", the last one having gone to W. Paul Cook, who means to print it in his coming magazine *The Recluse*.[3] As to a book of my stuff—the idea has been broached to me, & one of the business backers of W.T. says he is going to show certain things of mine to publishers; but I don't really think anything will come of it. My natural style is not a popular one, & when I try artificially to meet popular demands I invariably trail off into utter inanity & dulness. Of my own stuff I have no favourite tale though I think "The Hound", (1922) "The Tree", (1920) "The Terrible Old Man", (1920) "From Beyond", (1920) "The Moon-Bog", (1921) "The Unnamable", (1923) "He", (1925) & "In the Vault" (1925) are the poorest. The enclosed "Wall of Sleep" is pretty bad—& was written in 1919. I notice that I wrote most stories in 1920.

As for autographed likenesses—like many another lover of the beautiful who is personally as homely as hell, I detest having formal photographs taken. I haven't had one since 1915,[4] when I was 25, but here's a wretched postcard snapshot which I was wheedled into having taken last year at Coney Island. It looks like me—for at my stage of middle life a year doesn't extensively change one—although I don't think my actual expression is quite as savagely determined as this wide-eyed presentment would seem to imply! By the way—I wouldn't mind seeing a view of you if you have such a thing to spare. ¶ Sincerely & cordially—H P Lovecraft

Notes

1. "Festival" (published as "Yule Horror").

2. Indeed, HPL composed *The Dream-Quest of Unknown Kadath* on the backs of some of AWD's letters.

3. "The Shunned House" did not appear in *The Recluse,* and Cook printed it to publish as as a small book (see letters 82f). However, the book was not bound until 1961, when AWD obtained the printed sheets and distributed the book through Arkham House.

4. This is his famous *United Amateur* portrait; see frontispiece in *An H. P. Lovecraft Encyclopedia.*

[20]   [ALS]

10 Barnes St.,
Providence, R.I.,
Novr. 12, 1926

My dear Mr. Derleth:—

I am very grateful for the two interesting portraits, & read the explanatory matter with due appreciation. Surely your literary colleague is a strict aesthete indeed to have such objections to eyeglasses! I might mention that I hate the damn things myself from the point of view of *comfort*, & that since the taking of the view sent you, I have largely left them off. I don't see so well at a distance, but the cloudier definition doesn't make me dizzy or headachy as it used to do. Now I only wear glasses at lectures or the theatre, where clear sight of distant objects is imperative.

As to the tales—I couldn't publish "The Lurking Fear" in a magazine again, I fear, since its former publication might create some legal complication. When I spoke of revision, I meant one for the benefit of myself—& friends on the manuscript circuit—alone. Here are four more things of mine, including a rhymed tale of whose crumbling MS. I must ask you to be very careful.[1] I *abhor* typing, & since this is my last copy, I am treating it very tenderly in the hope of prolonging its life.

"In the Vault" is not a favourite of mine, but I send it to see whether you agree with me in considering Wright's avowed ground of rejection foolish. He said it was *too horrible* to "sit well" with the censors—which impresses me as sheer nonsense in view of the equally horrible stuff by myself & others published constantly without protest or interference.

As for W.T. covers—I agree with you thoroughly. All the alleged "art" work is indescribably vile, & I feel lucky whenever Wright is merciful enough to leave the beastly stuff off my effusions. The first "artist" they had—Heitman—was intolerably commonplace. Then they had a half-decent illustrator named Brosnatch—who did the cover you like. Now, however, they have a poor devil called Olinick, who is even worse than Heitman.[2] The stiffness of his human figures is ludicrous—the only people he could draw well are the inhabitants of a morgue—& his range of poses and expressions makes Egyptian murals look like photographic realism!

I own Shiel's "Zaleski", but cannot get very deeply excited over it. It consists of three medium length tales—none of which impressed me as "The House of Sounds" did. Shiel inclines toward extravagance, superficiality, & attempted cleverness—the faults of the '90s. I think I said that the H. of S. was rewritten from an earlier tale in which the author's characteristic faults appear.

By the way—I enclose a cutting (which please return) about a forthcoming book which gives me high anticipations. I certainly hope I shall be able to get hold of it when it is issued!

Your United suggestions are good, & I hope you'll get them before the membership. Latterly it seems almost impossible to maintain any widespread interest or even to correlate effectively the work of the faithful few who are interested. I once prepared an amateur Who's Who for a year book which never appeared—but that was in 1917 & the personnel is almost entirely different now.[3] A bibliography of published *books* would be sadly slender—but a list of outstanding contributions to the amateur press would be valuable indeed. Have you many old amateur publications? I might put you in touch with a few old-timers who perhaps could spare you some typical specimens.

> Sincerely & cordially yrs—
> HPL

Notes

1. "Psychopompos: A Tale in Rhyme" (1917–18). The poem appeared in the *Vagrant* but was rejected by *WT*. The eventual appearance of this rejected item, and many others, in *WT* after HPL's death was due to the efforts of AWD.

2. "Heitman" did the cover of the May 1923 *WT*; Andrew Brosnatch the covers for November and December 1924, January–November 1925, and January and March 1926; G. O. Olinick did no covers, only interiors.

3. See "A Request."

[21]   [ALS]

> 10 Barnes St.,
> Providence, R.I.,
> Novr. 19, 1926

My dear Mr. Derleth:—

How can I thank you sufficiently for that carbon of Psychopompos! I am flattered that you found the thing worth typing, & infinitely glad of the duplicate. That other copy wouldn't have survived many more trips—at least, its last page wouldn't! Wright rejected "Psychopompos" on the ground that such long verse was against the magazine's policy—which no doubt it is. These cheap magazines have an unbelievable veneration for precedent! If I ever type "Sarnath" I'll see that you have a copy. I did type it once, but that MS. is in the hands of the man (J. C. Henneberger of Chicago, connected with W.T.) who says he is trying to get my stuff placed with some book publisher. Enclosed are two more things of mine, both rejected by W.T. for no stated reason except mediocrity. I don't like "From Beyond" myself, but fancy that "Cool Air" isn't so bad. I'll be interested to hear how you like "Prince Zaleski". It's fairly clever, but when you get "The House of Sounds" you'll see how much better Shiel can do when he takes the trouble. I've never read Wells' "War of the Worlds", though I mean to some time. His tales, to me, lack a certain imaginative charm—their fantasy is too calculated & scientific, & and undercurrent of social satire impairs their convincingness.

Yes—that "Outsider" illustration was about as good as anything yet offered by W.T. as a pictorial heading.[1] Other stuff by the same artist, however, was very commonplace. I wish they'd use some of the drawings of Clark Ashton Smith of California, who really catches the essence of the grotesque & fantastic. He is a remarkable character—poet & artist alike—& ought to be known better than he is. An article on his work by a chap named Wandrei in Minneapolis will appear in the next *Overland Monthly*[2]—which reminds me that I am sure you would like to own Smith's weirdest book, containing the really epoch-making poem "The Hasheesh-Eater". It is called "Ebony & Crystal", & the author sells it himself for two dollars. Address Clark Ashton Smith, Box 388, Auburn, California. Smith was a protege of George Sterling, & will be tremendously cut up by the news of Sterling's suicide last Wednesday.[3]

For old amateur papers, try Harry R. Marlow, 360 Palmyra St., Warren, Ohio. I think he has a good assortment for distribution. And speaking of amateurdom—I mentioned you to the quaint & lovable editor (age 74) of *The Tryout*, and he asked if you would care to send any short tales (700–1000 words) for publication in his homely little paper. If you have any bits that you'd care to see in print without pay, send them on to *me*, & I will see that they are properly proofread. The amateur editor in question (C. W. Smith, 408 Groveland St., Haverhill, Mass.) is a notoriously poor typographer, but gives me proofreading privileges on all material contributed through my mediation.

Glad to hear that your play is acquiring a wider fame! By all means let as many organisations as possible present it, for at this stage of your career publicity is an important asset.

With every good wish, & unbounded thanks for that copy of "Psychopompos", I remain

Most cordially & sincerely yrs—
H P Lovecraft

Notes

1. B. Goldschlager illustrated "The Outsider" for *WT*.

2. DAW, "The Emperor of Dreams," *Overland Monthly* 84, No. 12 (December 1926): 380–81, 407, 409; rpt. *Klarkash-Ton: The Journal of Smith Studies* No. 1 (1988): 3–8, 25.

3. George Sterling, the California poet, CAS's friend and mentor, died by his own hand on 17 November.

[22]   [ALS]

10 Barnes St.,
Providence, R.I.,
Novr. 26, 1926

My dear Mr. Derleth:—

Glad you found "Cool Air" decent in spite of Wright's dictum. I'm getting near the end of my accumulated fiction now, & can't find any MSS. to send except two new ones, which you won't like because they represent my more Dunsanian style. "The Silver Key", I may add, is not in its final form; but will shortly undergo an extensive amputation of philosophical matter in the early part, which delays the development & kills the interest before the narrative is fairly begun.[1]

I feared you wouldn't find "Zaleski" such a treasure, & am sorry you paid as much as $2.75 for it. You will not, however, be disappointed in "The Pale Ape". I certainly hope your dealer will hustle up & send it soon—there seems to be no valid reason for further delay. You will like Clark Ashton Smith's poetry, & I only wish you could see some of his bizarre drawings & paintings. I'll send you the Wandrei review of his work in the next *Overland* when I get it—I'm asking Smith to send two copies, one to keep fresh for my files, & one to lend to such persons as are interested.

Thanks exceedingly for the items to go in Tryout.[2] The editor needed copy very much, & will be fervently grateful for these piquant bits. It's safe to say that the waste basket will not form their acquaintance.

With 57 items to your credit you are certainly well launched in the literary arena. I count only the 30-odd tales listed in a former letter to you, for I don't consider my verses & critical essays worth including in any list. Many tales I have destroyed as below even my most charitable standard, & I'm not sure but that this fate awaits the long fantasy I am concocting at this moment.[3] You needn't worry about your "Night Rider" appearing at a disadvantage beside my "Red Hook". The latter is one of the poorest things I ever perpetrated; having been written with the magazine in mind, & being therefore pervaded by a cheapness & atmosphere of crude melodrama which quite alienates my aesthetic sense. I shall never do another thing like that—unless I need the money damned badly!

With every good wish, & hoping that the enclosed will not bore you too desperately,

I am

Most cordially & sincerely yrs—
H P Lovecraft

Notes

1. HPL never did revise "The Silver Key." The story was based on HPL's visit to an-

cestral sites in Rhode Island in mid-October, which he described in detail to numerous correspondents.

2. "Dawn," "The Splinter," "The Figure with a Scythe," and "Sixteen Years on Death."

3. *The Dream-Quest of Unknown Kadath* (completed 22 January 1927).

[23]   [ALS]

Friday [3 December 1926]

My dear Mr. Derleth:—

I was delighted to hear that you like the "Strange High House", for that is by all odds my own favourite among my recent yarns. The two elements in all existence which are most fascinating to me are *strangeness* & *antiquity*; & when I can combine the two in one tale I always feel that the result is better than as though I had only one of them. It remains to be seen how successful this bizarrerie can be when extended to novel length. I am now on page 72 of my dreamland fantasy, & am very fearful that Randolph Carter's adventures may have reached the point of palling on the reader; or that the very plethora of weird imagery may have destroyed the power of any one image to produce the desired impression of strangeness. This tale is one of picaresque adventure—a quest for the gods through varied & incredible scenes & perils—& is written continuously like "Vathek" without any subdivision into chapters, though it really contains several well-defined episodes. It will probably make about 100 pages—a small book—in all, & has very small likelihood of ever seeing the light of day in print. I dread the task of typing it so badly that I shall not attempt it till I have read it aloud to two or three good judges & obtained a verdict as to whether or not it is worth preserving.[1]

I was greatly interested in your list of tales, & would like to see some of those which you have starred in ink of one colour or another. I don't know which to choose first, but will select at a guess the following—picking them merely by their titles:

The Garden of the Dead	The Lost Continent
The Grotto	Shadows

After that I'll let you pick some to send—provided, of course, that you have the MSS. at hand & that their transmission is perfectly convenient for you. I trust that your dramas may all develop successfully, & that your new tales—now under construction—may surpass your brightest expectations. "The Black Powder", "Beyond the End", & "The Undead" sound highly alluring. Vampirism is always a fruitful theme—do you recall "The Return of the Undead" in W.T. a year ago? That was written by a friend of mine, Arthur Leeds, then of N.Y. but now of Chicago.[2]

This time I can't enclose any tales because I have no further MSS. available. If Cook ever prints "The Shunned House" I'll see that you get a copy of the magazine to keep, & after some other MSS. are returned I may have a few copies of other things to send. Meanwhile I hope to see some tales of yours, & trust there will be no inconvenience in sending the ones I have indicated.

With every good wish,

Most cordially & sincerely yrs—

H P Lovecraft

Notes

1. As predicted, HPL never typed the novel and it was not published in his lifetime. AWD included it in *Beyond the Wall of Sleep* (1943) and serialized it in *Arkham Sampler* (1948).

2. Arthur Leeds, "The Return of the Undead," *WT* (November 1925).

[24]　　[ALS]

10 Barnes St.,

Providence, R.I.,

Dec. 11, 1926

My dear Mr. Derleth:—

I am very grateful for the sight of the three tales enclosed, & consider them all truly good in their various provinces. "The Grotto" is a prose-poem of undoubted merit & poignancy, & reveals a command of language which speaks well indeed for the development of your style. "The Piece of Parchment" sustains the interest very well, but lacks a close knitting of the incidents. For example—the existence & disappearance of the niece Allegra has, so far as I can see, no visible bearing on the plot as a whole; & in a short story every detail ought to be a factor in the building up of the climax. One might say, too, that the denouement is not sufficiently a surprise—nothing developing to give the reader's mind a wrench or sensation of unexpected revelation. But the tale is excellent, & the incident of the *wax* particularly potent. By the way, though—*parchment* was not used for common writing as late as the 18th century. Ordinary paper reigned supreme then as now. "The Pacer" is the best of all three as a *story*, its atmosphere being full of genuine dread & suspense. The idea is splendid, & all I could suggest would be a little touching up of the ending—the reservation of something particularly cataclysmic for the very last line. You might have the dying man hear the pacing descend the stairs & enter the room, & have *something* brush invisibly past the spectators. Then a death struggle might occur, *& the livid marks of a strangler's hands appear on the throat of the doomed Brent.* But don't let me be too finical. It's a fine tale, & Wright is an ass if he rejects it.[1]

As to my stuff—I'm afraid you won't see "The Shunned House" till Cook prints it, for he has my absolutely only copy. But it isn't important enough to worry about. I haven't done anything whatever about the weird fiction article since completing it last July. As I said, I have heard of a rich source of new material in Providence, but have not felt like bothering about it just yet—being more in the mood for writing tales. The Randolph Carter novel won't amount to much, but it will at least afford me practice in more extended fictional composition. By the way—I am eager to see your new Nibelung piece.[2] The theme ought to be infinitely fruitful to the fantaisiste.

I am now in touch with Clark Ashton Smith's friend, Donald Wandrei of St. Paul, Minn., & find him a delightful enthusiast in the field of the weird. It interested me to learn that he is planning to write a history of supernatural fiction—& if he does, I may not bother to elaborate mine. I hope his article on Smith in the December *Overland* will not excite ridicule—as I said before, it is the least bit sophomoric & effusively over-enthusiastic.

I saw "Ben-Hur" last September,[3] & found it intensely powerful. My liking for broad scenic & architectural effects made me appreciate the settings very much, while my lifelong admiration of Rome & her warlike civilisation gave me many a thrill as the legions & their imperial eagles marched across the field of view. Speaking of the cinema—it is my deepest regret that I never saw "The Cabinet of Dr. Caligari",[4] which everyone tells me had more of the truly weird & fantastic than any other film ever made.

Congratulations on your acquisition of "The Pale Ape"! You certainly have not only Shiel at his best, but one of the great weird stories of all time.

With every good wish,
Most sincerely yrs—
H P Lovecraft

Notes

1. See further letter 95.

2. Unidentified.

3. *Ben-Hur* (MGM, 1925), directed by Fred Niblo; starring Ramon Navarro, Francis X. Bushman, and May McAvoy. Based on the best-selling novel (1880) by Lew Wallace.

4. *The Cabinet of Dr. Caligari* [*Das Kabinett des Doktor Caligari*] (Germany, 1919), directed by Robert Wiene; starring Werner Kraus and Conrad Veidt. Distributed in the U.S. (1921f) by MGM.

[25]   [ALS]

10 Barnes St.,
Providence, R.I.,
Decr. 16, 1926

My dear Mr. Derleth:—

The stories in your latest batch are very interesting, & I am sorry that Wright will not consider any adaptation of the "Piece of Gold" plot for W.T. It seemed to me very rich in atmosphere & fantasy. I would certainly advise further revision, with perhaps a greater emphasis on the atmospheric element; & I hope that your easy-going collaborator will find the time & energy to furnish such auxiliary work as you may desire. I think "Symphony" is very good[1]—much on the idea of "The Second Generation" by Blackwood, & hope it may ultimately find favour in some editorial eye. "Dawn" certainly strikes the modern note—illustrating very well the staccato effects over which most of the younger generation have run wild.

As to the new W.T. cover—only its predecessors could possibly have calloused my soul to the point of unprotesting tolerance![2] The only decent thing in the issue, aside from such shorter features as your tale, is "The Last Horror"—which is truly *clever,* though more quasi-scientific than weird. I have long planned something of that sort myself, though of psychic rather than physical cast—an attempt on the part of an educated negro to project his personality & secure the tenancy of a white man's body through the arts of voodoo.[3]

Too bad we both missed "Dr. Caligari", for it was by all accounts the best fantastic cinema ever produced. I have heard that the original negative is in such poor condition that no fresh prints can be made, but hope that its fame may some day lead to its reproduction with new actors & duplicate scenery. The one weird film I did see was "The Golem",[4] based on a mediaeval ghetto legend of an artificial giant. In this production the settings were semi-futuristic, some of the ancient gabled houses of Prague's narrow streets being made to look like sinister old men with peaked hats.

I'm glad "The House of Sounds" wears well with you—as I was sure it would. It is surely a classic, & an excellent example of the good results of revision. If you want to see the flamboyant first version, (whose title I forget) look up the book of short stories called "Shapes in the Fire"—although this volume is not worth buying.

I have at last received the *Overland* from Smith containing Wandrei's review of his weird poetry. The thing is wretchedly misprinted—indeed, the whole magazine has a vile typography hinting of marked decadence since its period of international fame. In the same issue is a posthumous review by George Sterling of our fellow-United-Member Samuel Loveman's book "The Hermaphrodite",[5] in which the printer renders the name Loveman as "*Tweman*", & gives the line

Whose footfall loosed Olympian splendour
as
Whose *football* loosed Olympian splendour!

I've just read final (I hope!) proof for "The White Ship", which will appear in W.T. soon. That's the last thing of mine accepted, but I've sent in "Pickman's Model" & am awaiting results. When convenient let me see some more of your work—pieces which you yourself consider the best & most representative.

With all good holiday wishes,
Most sincerely yrs—
HPL

Notes

1. These do not appear to have been published or to survive. ("Symphony" may be the same as "Symphony in Gold.")

2. The cover illustration by C. B. Petrie, Jr., is for the first installment of John Martin Leahy's serial "Drome."

3. Cf. *CB* 108: "Educated mulatto seeks to displace personality of white man & occupy his body"; 109: "Ancient negro voodoo wizard in cabin in swamp—possesses white man." These entries date to roughly 1923.

4. *The Golem* (UFA [Germany], 1920), directed by Paul Wegener and Carle Boese. HPL based his commentary on Gustav Meyrink's novel in SHL on his viewing of the movie.

5. George Sterling, "Rhymes and Reactions," *Overland Monthly,* 84, No. 12 (December 1926): 395.

[26]   [ALS]

10 Barnes St.,
Providence, R.I.,
Decr. 25, 1926

My dear Mr. Derleth:—

Some of my loaned tales came back last week, hence I am able to send along three more which you have not seen. Of these I least like "The Tree". "Polaris" was written in 1918, before I knew anything about Dunsany, & is interesting as a case of unconscious parallelism of manner. "Celephaïs" dates from after my introduction to Dunsany, & I will leave to the critic the question of just how much of the style is due to Dunsany's influence, & how much to my own independently similar cast of imagination.

I am not surprised that you found "John Silence" interesting, for some of the tales shew Blackwood at his second-best if not best. I thought the first & last the poorest, & gave first place to the one about the French village where everybody turned into cats & celebrated the witches' sabbath.[1] As to "The Second Generation"—I'm hanged if I can remember just what collection it's in, but fancy it's either in "Day & Night Stories" or "Ten-Minute Stories".[2] The only sure way to find it is to look through the tables of contents of the various short story collections. Blackwood's unevenness is really astonishing, & alienates many of his less patient readers. Often I wonder how anyone can write such drivel—("The Extra Day", "The Wave", &c) & then I come upon something like "The Listener", "The Willows", or "The Wendigo" & take it all back. But certainly he has no *style* at all. Whenever he is powerful it is by sheer accident—or from the intrinsic force of his theme.

I shall be glad to see more tales of yours when you are again near your stock of supplies. Meanwhile I am expecting to look over the work of another young author with whom I have lately come into correspondence—the Donald Wandrei of St. Paul, whose published review of Smith's weird verse I will lend you if you have not been able to get the *Overland* containing it. Wandrei says he has written a tale called "The Chuckler" which forms a sort of answer to my "Statement of Randolph Carter", & is planning a bibliography of fantastic fiction.[3] Another young man—a Bernard Dwyer, living somewhere in rural N.Y. State—has likewise written me lately, saying that he also writes weird tales. So altogether it looks as if the fantastic field were not wholly an abandoned one!

My novel has been going slowly of late on account of other work & reading, & is now on page 87. I shall be glad to be done with it, for it is really only practice work in a fuller medium, & I am anxious to handle some other themes.

You were wise not to buy "Shapes in the Fire", though two items in the thing are worth *reading* if you ever come across the volume. One is the original & meretriciously florid version of "The House of Sounds", (under a title which I have forgotten) & the other is a brief & noxious thing called "Xelucha". On the whole, Shiel is distinctly mediocre.

With all good holiday wishes, I remain
Most cordially & sincerely yrs—
H P Lovecraft

Notes

1. The first story is "A Psychical Invasion," the last "The Camp of the Dog." The story HPL favored was "Ancient Sorceries."

2. "The Second Generation" is in *Ten Minute Stories*.

3. DAW, "The Chuckler," *Fantasy Magazine* 4, No. 1 (September 1934): 26–27. DAW did not publish the planned bibliography, but *MTS* contains a lengthy catalogue of weird fiction volumes he owned.

1927

[27]   [ALS]

10 Barnes St.,

Providence, R.I.,

Jany. 2, 1927.

My dear Mr. Derleth:—

Glad to hear you found the tales readable—& you agree with me in preferring "Celephaïs". In the novel I am writing I use some of the scenes mentioned in the earlier story—these are adventures, for instance, on the cold desert plateau of Leng, & an escape from the windowless stone monastery of the high-priest not to be described. I'll be glad to see your new tales when you get them in shape for transmission, & am sure they will prove highly creditable.

"The Empty House" is a book of short stories of which I think only one or two are much good. "The Lost Valley" is also a collection of indifferent merit as a whole, but *one* of the tales—"The Wendigo"—is worth the price of the entire volume![1] It tells of a horror that stalks in the Canadian North Woods. Your reaction to "The Pale Ape" is about what I thought it would be—& precisely like my own.

Yes—of course one ought to know general literature in addition to one's special field, but I don't believe one need to purchase widely if one has access to a good library. It is especially unwise to load oneself too heavily with modern books—comparatively few of which are likely to last, or to take any important place in the development of letters. I think that for general literary background one had better begin with the classics of Greece & Rome in standard translations, later following the high spots of English literature as outlined in some suitable manual, & subsequently adding some salient items of Continental literature. The moderns, of course, ought to be skimmed over as a matter of duty in acquiring a sound perspective on contemporary trends—& it is interesting to watch the growth of their particular mental habits & stylistic mannerisms, beginning with the French decadents & spreading as the present wave of philosophic & aesthetic unrest gains force. This chaotic type of expression will always be historically interesting as marking a definite period in the evolution of thought; though I do not believe it constitutes art in the truest sense, or deem it likely to contribute toward the main stream of our literature. You can get a fairly good bird's-eye view of literary modernism by reading Ben Hecht's "Erik Dorn" for prose, & T. S. Eliot's "The Waste Land" for what purports to be verse. The keynote of the modern doctrine is the dissociation of ideas & the resolving of our cerebral contents into its actual chaotic components as distinguished from the conventional patterns visible on the outside. This is supposed to form a closer approach to reality, but I cannot see that it forms any sort of art at all. It may be good science—but art deals with beauty rather than fact, & must have the liberty to select & arrange according to the traditional patterns which generations of belief & reverence have marked with the seal of empirical loveliness. Beyond or behind this seeming beauty lies only chaos & weariness, so that art must preserve illusions & artificialities rather than try to sweep them away.

Hoping you will have an enjoyable programme of studies ahead of you during the coming college session, I remain

Most cordially & sincerely yrs—

H P Lovecraft

Notes

1. Both by Algernon Blackwood.

[28]   [TLS, JHL]

823 West Johnson Street
Madison, Wisconsin
[between 3 and 10 January 1927]

My dear Mr. Lovecraft:—

I am sending, as I promised, my two latest skits, DEATH OF AN OLD MAN and THE DANCE OF DEATH. The first is quite pointless, but quite the better of the two; the second is trite, but I have no desire to change it.

I got a letter from Algernon Blackwood the other day. He informs me that he himself has no copy of either THE EMPTY HOUSE or THE LOST VALLEY, but he has put me in touch with a London dealer that might have them. He notes that his best works might soon be reissued if everything goes well. I have heard and read much of THE WENDIGS; in fact, my ideas of that story are the chief reason for my wanting THE LOST VALLEY.

I've been acquiring quite a few books of late .. all two dollar editions for prices ranging all the way from .75 to .45. I bought Wilkie Collin[s]'s WOMAN IN WHITE for .35; S. H. Adams' THE PIPER'S FEE for .47; Leo Tolstoy's ANNA KARENINE [*sic*] for .50 (by the way, have you ever read this book? What did you think of it?); Hall Caine's WOMAN THOU GAVEST ME at .50; Gerald Bullett's THE STREET OF THE EYE, Conan Doyle's ADVENTURES OF SHERLOCK HOLMES, and Stephen McKenna's THE OLDEST GOD at .75. This latter book is reviewed as being a decidedly weird thing and I anticipate reading it. I mustn't forget to mention that excellent mid[d]ling-classic, Beatrice Harraden's SHIPS THAT PASS IN

THE NIGHT at .25.

Your suggestions as to accumulating a library are like many others that I have received. I know it isn't a good idea to purchase much of the moderns. I intend to gather together all of the Modern Library. I shall look up Ben Hecht's ERIK DORN.

And after all this, what do you think of the last WEIRD TALES? I wrote to Wright and suggested attempting a plain cover with a list of the feature tales centered.[1] One story, THE UNEARTHLY, was abominable; anyone in the "know" so to speak realizes that the trick that the Egyptian magician performed was done by thought images and mild hypnotism; therefore there would be no motive in destroying the camera film, for it would only register the magician and the boy somewhere, and the magician could easily explain his trick, winning the money anyway. Most of the remainder of the stories were quite well done; though I can't say that I went wild over Seabury Quinn's tale.[2]

Hoping to hear from you soon, I am, very cordially yours

August W. Derleth

Notes

1. AWD's *Arkham Sampler* (1948–49) and *Hawk and Whippoorwill* (1960f.) sported simple, plain-text covers, much as discussed here by HPL.
2. Don Robert Catlin, "The Unearthly"; Seabury Quinn, "The Man Who Cast No Shadow," *WT* (February 1927).

[29]   [ALS]

10 Barnes St.,
Providence, R.I.,
Jany. 11, 1927.

My dear Mr. Derleth:—

I read your new sketches with much interest, & like both of them. At this stage of your literary evolution these prose-poems form an excellent kind of practice for you; permitting you to exercise yourself in atmosphere, colouring, & precise rhythms & mood-values without the dragging responsibility of a plot or the annoying obligation of conforming to this or that popular fictional model. The more of them you write, the more will you absorb pleasantly & unconsciously those fundamentals of real literary expression which distinguish a true artist from a mere mechanical modeller of stock images, situations, & phrases.

It interests me exceedingly to learn that you are in touch with Algernon Blackwood—& rather surprises me to hear that he lacks at least two of his own books. I still have enough vanity left to desire a full quota of my major printed efforts. The issuance of a new edition of Blackwood would be a very welcome event indeed—although opinions would differ on just what constitutes his best material. By the way—that story is THE WENDIGO—not "Wendigø". My beastly handwriting again! It is truly a powerful tale, & I'm not sure whether or not the superstition it describes is a real one in northwestern Canada.

Your recent book bargains all sound very fortunate, & I hope their digestion may prove altogether pleasant & culturally profitable. I read "Anna Karenina" years ago, but can't say I cared greatly for that or for anything of Tolstoi's. To my mind, Tolstoi is sickeningly mawkish & sentimental, with an amusingly disproportionate interest in things social and ethical. Of course, that is typical in a way of all Slav literature; but other Russian authors show far less of this sloppiness in proportion to their genius & insight into character. If you want Russia at its best, try Dostoievsky, whose "Crime & Punishment" is a truly epic achievement.

I agree with you that a plain cover for W.T. would be a merciful relief from the crudities & distortions now prevailing, but fear that the bulk of crude readers would never accept anything so conservative.

In the recent issue I found your "Volga Boatmen"[1] very interesting, & of the longer tales liked "The Church Stove" & "The Atomic Conquerors" the best. "The Church Stove" is really a magnificent *conte cruel*, with all its parts admirably fitted, balanced, & developed. "The Unearthly" was, of course, a very crude & minor attempt.

Long has just written a very weird novelette about a nameless thing produced by protoplasmic metamorphosis,[2] which I hope sincerely Wright will accept. W. is still debating with himself & friends about accepting "Pickman's Model", but I can see he doesn't care much for my later stuff. "The White Ship" will appear next month.

As to Quinn's tale—I find all his later work insipid. He has fallen victim to the popular magazine style, & has given himself over wholly to a background of weakly cheerful stock characters & situations which neutralises & ruins whatever of original horror he manages to get in the development of his plots. It is too bad, really, for he is normally an excellent writer—absolutely void of crudity or immaturity, & thoroughly master of his language & imagery.

With every good wish—

Most cordially & sincerely yrs

HPL

P.S. Just noticed your tale in Tryout. Too bad the editor feminised your collaborator's name from Marc to Mary!

Notes

1. Published as "The River."

2. FBL, "The Man with a Thousand Legs," *WT* (August 1927).

[30]   [ALS]

10 Barnes St.,
Providence, R.I.,
Jany. 20, 1927

My dear Mr. Derleth:—

I liked "The Child" very much—its atmosphere gathers very effectively, & we feel that something strange is in the air when the child says with such emphasis that she *cannot* fall down the well. As you suggest, this tale has more "point" in the way of connected plot & denouement than some of the more frankly prose-poetical studies, & will probably please a wider circle; but that is no argument against the intrinsic merit of the others. My advice would be to keep on writing both kinds!

Your book bargains all sound very tempting—& I am sure that at this rate you will soon have an exceedingly formidable library—if indeed you haven't one already! In these latter years I haven't felt able to invest very heavily—both on account of initial cost & lack of space—but once in a while I pick up something which positively can't be resisted.

Wright's "jury"[1] seems to be still deliberating "Pickman's Model", & I can't say that I'm very much interested—except from a baldly financial point of view—in the question of whether he takes it or not! "The White Ship"—a prose-poem—will be in the coming issue, out Feby. 1. I shall welcome the new cover artist,[2] & can feel sure at least that he can't be any worse than those who have hitherto messed up the magazine. The worst artist, all in all, that W.T. has had is the present designer of headings—Olinick. His wooden automata & freak faces nearly transcend the limits of my patience! Long hasn't sent in his story yet, but decided to make some alterations that I advised. It combines good construction with popular treatment, & ought to have an excellent chance of landing with Wright. "The Outsider" must have sounded interesting with a professional elocutionist's art to conceal its defects. A good reader can do much to redeem a tale—in N.Y. when I presented a new tale to the small group of which I was a member, I always liked to have a certain person—James F. Morton—read it because of his technical proficiency in delivery.

About Oscar Wilde—it seems to me that he forms a prominent point in the history of literature without having been supremely great himself. He embodied with peculiar thoroughness & assertiveness the general aesthetic tendencies of his period—the reaction of the later XIXth century against Victorian pompousness & tastelessness—& has come to be its symbol; but when one analyses what he actually wrote one finds more of cleverness than

of real genius, & more of accomplished mannerism than of truly compre-
hensive & penetrating vision. The type of paradox of which he was master is
really more of a mechanical trick than an artistic form, & even his weirdest &
most exotic effects are not without a touch of that *mechanical* element—the
mere calculated cataloguing of things with glamorous names—which must
always be distinguished from the genuine wonder & strangeness of those
whose eyes really catch the overtones of marvellous individual worlds of colour & fantasy. He was always too conscious of himself to be really great,
though he undeniably did succeed in producing a vast amount of *almost* great
material. His comedies rank with the best comedies of manners in our language—he was the last lineal heir of Sheridan—whilst his fairy tales are assuredly most exquisite bits of prismatic marvel & musical prose. I think I like
"The Fisherman & his Soul" best of all. "Dorian Gray", too, is a notable
tour de force, though it has about it a studied smartness which detracts from
its power as a tale of the unreal. But in almost all of these fields—except, of
course, the light comedy—he is excelled by the real masters; & I had any day
rather have Dunsany's "Dreamer's Tales" than Wilde's "Happy Prince" or
"House of Pomegranates". Wilde's poetry is not very seriously considered
nowadays, since it forms so obvious an echo of earlier work, especially Swinburne. Nevertheless I can read it with pleasure, & find a genuine charm in
such things as "The Sphinx". Altogether, literature would not like to spare
Wilde; although he is not one of those giants whose products stand on their
own intrinsic merits. Curiously like his mental & moral antithesis Dr. Johnson, he is more of an *influence than a creator*, for he certainly did impress certain types of idea very strongly on his generation, notwithstanding that the
generation was already inclined to such ideas. Many living writers would
have been vastly different had not Wilde preceded them, so that I suppose
on the whole he will always be regarded as more or less of a landmark. And
since publicity & notoriety were always his ruling passions, I presume this
status would satisfy him as well as that more solid fame—the fame of a Shelley, Keats, or William Blake—which comes from original artistic accom-
plishment. As a man, however, Wilde admits of absolutely no defence. His
character, notwithstanding a daintiness of manners which imposed an exterior shell of decorative decency & decorum, was as thoroughly rotten & con-
temptible as it is possible for a human character to be; a fact which is
unfortunately established beyond mere rumour by the reluctant testimony of
those toward whom he practiced no concealment. So thorough was his absence of that form of taste which we call a moral sense, that his derelictions
comprised not only the greater & grosser offences, but all those petty dis-
honesties, shiftinesses, pusillanimities, & affected contemptibilities & cow-
ardices which mark the mere "cad" or "bounder" as well as the actual
"villain". It is an ironic circumstance that he who succeeded for a time in being the Prince of Dandies, was never in any basic sense what one likes to call

a *gentleman*. Of course Wilde's imprisonment was a mistake, for no good is ever accomplished by arousing dramatic publicity over mere degradation & degeneracy which calls for the alienist rather than the policeman. But that is no valid whitewash for the degenerate in question, so that it is hard to feel much charity or affection toward the bloated, dissipated, & diseased old high-liver who virtually rotted to pieces & exploded in "Valdemar" fashion on that grey winter day of 1900. No—there's no use in idealising poor Oscar, although it is equally futile to deny the undoubted influence he wielded, or the undoubted merit, in their own peculiar class, of the distinctive writings which he produced.

With every good wish, & congratulating you again on "The Child",

I remain

Most cordially & sincerely yrs—

H P Lovecraft

Notes

1. Unknown. But see HPL to DAW, [2 August 1927]: "after due deliberation & grave consultation with E. Hoffmann Price, Wright has very properly rejected my 'Strange High House in the Mist,' as not sufficiently clear for the acute minds of his highly intelligent readers" (*MTS* 138).
2. C. C. Senf. Actually, HPL cared little for Senf's work.

[31]　　[TLS, JHL]

823 West Johnson Street
Madison, Wisconsin
22 January, 1927

My dear Friend:—

I certainly was interested in your paragraph on Oscar Wilde. My reaction to him is much the same as your own; though I must admit, that, while not actually idealising him, I have attempted to use his works as a sort of model. Your statements regarding his character were reiterations of what I have constantly heard from those who undertake to argue with me concerning him. I believe that Wilde was much misunderstood. He was undoubtedly a victim of early repression; this common fallacy caused him to become a homosexualist while a young man—a practice which he continued until his unfortunate imprisonment. From a homosexualist he became a profligate of the worst sort; in this stage he wrote DORIAN GRAY, and it is only too evident to the knowing observer that Dorian Gray is Oscar Wilde, himself. DE PROFUNDIS, the most bitter thing that I have ever read, also reveals his homosexualism. I agree with you in saying that DORIAN GRAY is too real to be truly classed as unreal. I have never read THE FISHERMAN AND

HIS SOUL; the last fairy tale that I read was THE BIRTHDAY OF THE INFANTA. I regard THE BALLAD OF READING GAOL as one of his best, if not his best, works. It is quite true that Wilde's fame rests in his being a transitional author.

Your liking of THE CHILD enheartens me: I am going to send it at once to Wright. Some weeks ago I sent him DEATH OF AN OLD MAN as an experiment, but I haven't heard from him regarding the tale as yet.

Mr. Schorer didn't mind the misprint of his name in TRYOUT as much as I did; he says that the magazine is too insignificant to mind a thing like that.

Recently I acquired W. H. Hudson's GREEN MANSIONS in the Modern Library edition and Carroll's ALICE IN WONDERLAND in the same edition. I've been wading through Dickens' CHRISTMAS STORIES: I always enjoy A CHRISTMAS CAROL, but I do not care very much for THE CHIMES and THE CRICKET ON THE HEARTH. As a change I read Floyd Dell's MOON-CALF, which pleased me immensely. I am just about to begin J. S. Fletcher's THE TIME WORN TOWN; it looks interesting for light reading. My next addition to my library is to be Niccolo Machiavelli's THE PRINCE. After that follows THE GHOST BOOK (Machen, Blackwood, Bierce, de la Mare, and others) edited by M. Asquith. I read Tolstoi's ANNA KARENINE, keeping your criticism in mind: I found it just as you warned, mawkish and ridiculously sentimental.

By the way, I lent my copy of THE OUTSIDER to my English instructor without comment; she returned it, remarking that she thought it to be the best approach to Poe that she has seen.

Very cordially yours,

August W. Derleth

[32]   [ALS]

10 Barnes St.,
Providence, R.I.,
Jany. 25, 1927

My dear Derleth:—

You make no mistake in using Wilde's work as a stylistic model. His style was as close to absolute perfection as any human style can be, & is admirably adapted to fantastic & imaginary writing. When one declines to place him in the very first rank of genius it is merely because he did not have the very first class of visions & conceptions to 'back up' his style— but that is nothing against the style itself. "Dorian Gray" is undoubtedly a transcript of Wilde's own mental life, (the strange French book mentioned as an influence being Huysmans' *A Rebours*) but not of his external aspect, since he was always rather gross & hulking in looks, & later became repulsively fat & flabby & oily to the sight. "The Fisherman & His Soul" is exquisitely exotic—you can find it in the Modern Library edition of Wilde's fairy tales. "Reading Gaol" is probably his greatest poem—the least artificial & imitative. As to W's character—it is probably understood about as little—or as much—as that of any social offender. Of course there is a cause for any departure from a normally adjusted emotional life, but if we fail to blame one we must fail to blame all—or vice versa. In reality both praise and blame are futile, since there are no absolute standards in a meaningless cosmos; but we may at least adopt the empirical standards we inherit, & consider all acts in the light their harmony or inharmony with the social & biological legacy of our particular race & culture. This has at least the merit of tallying more or less approximately with our natural preferences & prejudices. Wilde's derelictions were of course the result of some variant or other from the normal in his heredity or early life, & perhaps repression played its part. But others have undergone equal & greater repression without any such repellent results. Heredity also did not favour Wilde. His father was a notoriously gross old reprobate, & his mother a mincingly romantic & innocently silly creature. The combination was a bad one, & poor Oscar reaped the fruit. His brother William was a very exasperating & unamiable character—a journalistic hack of no especial distinction, & very unlike the scintillant master of paradox.

I hope Wright will take "The Child"—& I fancy he will, since you have had pretty good luck with him on the whole. He has just accepted "Pickman's Model" as a result of his jury's deliberations, & I shall continue to try any less imaginative flights upon him. The other day I finished my novelette—which came to 110 pages—& have provisionally named it "The Dream-Quest of Unknown Kadath".[1] Heav'n only knows how I dread the typing! Meanwhile I'm writing a new tale in more horrible & less fantastic vein—something with a Providence setting. I'll let you see it when it's done & typed.[2]

Your library certainly grows, & bids fair to become a very well selected aggregation. I read Dickens in youth, but could never like him on account of his grotesque sentimentality. Maybe he'd seem different to me now—I guess I'll try him again in some spare moment. J. S. Fletcher used to amuse me, but detective fiction bores me after a while. The best detective tales I've read in a decade are two by Eden Phil[l]potts—"The Grey Room" & "The Red Redmaynes". Long has just sent me an American Mercury—guess he thinks the Old Gentleman needs modernising! There's quite an article on Herman Melville,[3] whose "Moby Dick" I respected more than I enjoyed, & whom I must know better some day.

Glad to hear that "The Outsider" has received commendation. I very nearly destroyed that thing before publication because I felt that the secret of the ending was prematurely given away.

With all good wishes—

Most sincerely yrs—

H P Lovecraft

Notes

1. HPL's A.Ms. for the novel bears seven possible titles.

2. *The Case of Charles Dexter Ward*. Like *The Dream-Quest of Unknown Kadath*, HPL never typed it, and it was published only after his death, through the efforts of AWD.

3. F. L. Pattee, "Herman Melville," *American Mercury* 10, No. 1 (Jan. 1927): 33–43. Pattee later reviewed HPL's SHL in *American Literature* 18, No. 2 (May 1946): 175–77. HPL owned his horror novel, *The House of the Black Ring* (1916; *LL* 679).

[33]   [ALS]

10 Barnes St.,

Providence, R.I.,

Feby. 9, 1927.

Dear Mr. Derleth:—

Yes—there is an English translation of Huysmans' "A Rebours", (Against the Grain) & I believe it is considered a very good one.[1] It is quite recent—three or four years ago—but I can't recall either publisher or translator. I read it & thought it excellent. Huysmans shewed the aesthete & decadent at his extreme development, & his work has really become a classic of its kind—the definitive epitomisation of the neo-hedonistic philosophy of the 'nineties. Huysmans wrote other things—"La Bas", a novel of Parisian Satan-worship, "En Route", which pointed out Catholicism as a solution for modern aesthetic & philosophic problems, & many more that I forget, or haven't read. He himself—an underpaid government clerk—became a Catholic, as did so many of the decadents.

You shall surely see my novelette when it is typed, but I can't tell when that will be, for I dread the job & have many things to do before. The later tale—with its antiquarian background—is coming out longer than I expected it would, & is now on page 56, with a possibility of 25 or more pages to come. In a way, this is better practice work for long-fiction composition than the other story was, since the atmosphere of realism & verisimilitude makes necessary a closer knitting of elements & a more careful linkage of incidents. In general I'd call both these tales self-educational rather than creative attempts.

I am interested in your tale "Pomegranates", & trust that its development in both forms may be successful. Hope also to hear that Wright has accepted your earlier sketches. You'll shortly notice in W.T. two stories by a young friend of mine—Wilfred B. Talman—which I think are rather good. "Two Black Bottles" will probably be the first to appear.[2] Talman lives in the old

Dutch-settled country west of the Hudson, & knows the old legends & super-stitions of the Ramapo Hills very well.

So Phil[l]potts uses a pseudonym in addition to his own name![3] Thanks for the tip, which I may follow later. I don't know how well he manages to sustain the excellence he achieved in "Grey Room" & "Red Redmaynes".

Your library additions sound very well-chosen. I've seen reviews of Tarkington's "Plutocrat", & have recommended the book to many aesthete friends who seem over-inclined to ridicule the "solid citizen" type. I admire the aesthete sufficiently, but I also respect the constructive man—be he military, governmental, or commercial—who makes possible the tangible physical civilisation out of which aestheticism grows. Personally I'm far enough from the solid, useful type—but I don't let my point of view become biassed by subjective considerations.

I hope you can induce your new acquaintance to send drawings to W.T.—he couldn't help being an improvement over the present staff—especially that atrocious Olinick. In the current issue I think "The City of Glass" is the best tale, with "Evolution Island" as a second. Both are gratify-ingly imaginative though poorly written. It is unfortunate that craftsmanship & inspiration are not always parallel. Technically, Seabury Quinn leads all other contributors, but he is becoming drearily tame & hackneyed.

With all good wishes—

> Most sincerely yrs.
> H P Lovecraft

Notes

1. HPL had read this edition before acquiring his own copy in the 1930s.

2. Wilfred Blanch Talman, "Two Black Bottles," *WT* (August 1927), revised by HPL. The other story (not revised by HPL) was probably "The Curse of Alabad and Ghinu and Aratza," *WT* (February 1928).

3. In some of his early works, Phillpotts used the pseudonym "Harrington Hext."

[34]   [ALS]

> 10 Barnes St.,
> Providence, R.I.,
> Feby. 20, 1927

My dear Mr. Derleth:—

Yes—Joris-Karl Huysmans (not Huysman) was a highly inter-esting character. He was a descendant of the old Dutch painter Cornelis Huysmans on his father's side, & French on his mother's side. Of all the ex-treme decadents he was probably the greatest, & his *A Rebours* has been jo-cosely called "The Bible of the Nineties". As to Catholicism as a solution for the symbolist's or decadent's aesthetic-philosophic problems—you will find that an enormous number of the aesthetes of the nineties really did find in the rich colour & ancient ritual of the Roman Church a peace & sense of satisfaction they had not found elsewhere. It appears to me likely that the dominant element in their choice was a realisation of the ultimate futility of thought—i.e., of logical analysis & criteria of absolute truth. They envisaged life purely as a congeries of sensations pouring in upon them, & believed that the only value in any systematic interpretation or commentary concerning life was its power of satisfying the emotions & the aesthetic sense. In short, they submerged philosophic in aesthetic problems. Now with this point of view it is easy to see why the Catholic church, with its invitation to surrender responsibilities & accept as a guide a very ancient & beautiful symbolisation of all simple human feelings & aspirations, would be likely to appeal strongly to this intellectually disillusioned & beauty-loving type of artist. These men saw in the church a supremely poetic—even a dramatic— conception of man & his relation to infinity, & felt that its rich & ancient ceremonies formed the most perfect of all glorifications of the vital phases of man's emotional experience—the only branch of experience which they considered valid or significant. If you have found it otherwise, it may be either because your reaction to life is less wholly aesthetic than theirs—or because your type of aestheticism is different—or because the Catholic church in America may lack some of the maturity of ritualistic development which it has in Europe. At any rate, there is no denying that thirty years ago aesthetes flocked to Catholicism in large numbers; the converts including Huysmans, Arthur Machen, Aubrey Beardsley, Francis Thompson, & dozens of others whose names I've heard mentioned but whom I can't recall. It seems to me—an atheist of Protestant ancestry—that Catholicism is really an admirable faith for those artists whose taste is wholly Gothic & mystical without any mixture of the classic or the intellectual. It is the inheritor of ancient & beautiful rhythms of thought, cadence, & gesture which thousands of years of human feeling have woven symbolically & expressively around the various significant points of mortal experience; & as such it cannot help having a profound & genuine artistic importance & satisfyingness. It is the oldest continuously surviving poem of life that the races of Western Europe possess, & as such has an authority which no other one system of symbolic expression can claim. It seems to me that if one is to have anything so extrarational as religion of any sort, the Catholic & Episcopal systems are the only two sects with enough roots & anchors in the past to make them worthy of the affiliation of an artist. The life which they express is the natural, simple life of elder times, before the spread of industrialism & scientific discovery began its present transformation & destruction of society. No religion could express more, because all religion is a traditional art form dependent on a simple & continuous heritage. The future civilisation of mechanical invention, urban concentration, & scientific standarisation of life & thought is a monstrous & artificial thing which can never find embodiment either in art or in religion. Even now we find art & religion completely divorced from life & subsisting on retrospection & reminiscence as its vital material. There is no really *contemporary* art which expresses the scene & deeds & feelings of to-day as the art of other periods expressed the scene & deeds & feelings of those periods. We have entered a definite decadence, & must live our imaginative lives in the past. Life as flowing today has not enough links of gradual development from the simpler life that moulded our race to inherit anything of true aesthetic potentiality.

Wright is certainly determined to have glibly superficial 'tales with a twist' or nothing! He has accepted Long's new tale at last, but only after forcing Long to delete a very dramatic & effective incident which struck his limited imagination as "chimerical"! I shall be greatly interested in the growth of your novel. My new tale of antiquarian horror seems destined to become very like a novel, for I am now on page 96 with much still to be said.

Your library seems indeed to be faring well. De Gourmont's "Night in the Luxembourg"[1] was hailed when it appeared as one of the most significant philosophic fictions since Gautier's "Mlle. de Maupin". It surely embodies the neo-paganism & hedonism which many envisage as the social & intellectual order of the future, & it may be that for France it forms a species of prophecy. I do not think, however, that so purely classic & Gallic a system can have a wide or lasting appeal to those bred more closely in the Gothic tradition. The Northern races are too ingrainedly mystical & mediaeval in inner mental habits to accept whole-heartedly the frank cynicism & fleshly philosophy of the Latin.

No—I haven't seen the latest *Amazing Stories,* for I dropped it last month after deciding that the standard reprints were getting too few to make it worth buying. However—if it is as good as you say, I guess I'll get this one more issue at least. Wells is indeed discouragingly uneven—& all of his tales lack a certain mystic delicacy that one finds in Machen. He is too much of a scientific intellectual to be a master of the unreal.

Your dramatic & musical opportunities have been very fortunate; & will, I trust, be followed by others equally good. I go out very little myself lately—drama doesn't interest me as it did ten or twenty years ago, & music is unfortunately outside the circle of my most sensitive appreciation. Providence has good art exhibitions—I enclose a folder which you need not return. The view on the cover is that seen westward from the steep ancient hill on which I reside. The marble dome of the R.I. State House rises in majesty, & in the foreground there is faintly visible the belfry of old St. John's—1810. The original painting is highly impressive.[2] Last Thursday night I went to hear the Irish poet Padraic Colum lecture on modern poetry.[3] He proved a very fine & intelligent speaker, & most of his views seemed to coincide pretty well with my own.

    With every good wish—

            Most cordially & sincerely yrs—

                    H P Lovecraft

Notes

1. HPL had read *A Night in the Luxembourg* in the autumn of 1923 (see *SL* 1.250).

2. Rhode Island State House (McKim, Mead & White; 1891–1904), at 90 Smith Street, overlooking downtown Providence. St. John's Episcopal Church (1810) at 275 North Main Street.

3. On 17 February 1927, HPL heard Padraic Colum (1881–1972) speak on "Contemporary Poetry": "Colum started by denying that such a thing as 'contemporary' poetry exists, & shewed very clearly that the ideas & life of the present period are as yet artistically unformulated. We live on memories—& I think that is all we can ever live on now, since mechanical invention has so appallingly divorced us from the soil & from those conditions of our forefathers around which the aesthetic feelings of the race are entwined" (HPL to CAS, 18 February 1927; *SL* 2.104).

[35]   [ALS]

                                        March 2[, 1927]

My dear Mr. Derleth:—

            Well! I've just finished my second novelette, & it came to 147 pages before I could give it a decently rounded finish. As you say, this & its immediate predecessor could well be joined as a full-size dual book—if there were anyone willing to publish it! W. Paul Cook talks of printing my "Shunned House" as a single thin volume, but I don't know how much beyond the talk stage it will ever get. He wants my history of weird fiction for immediate use, so I suppose I'll have to type the damn thing as it is—without the additions I wished to make.

    Huysmans could explain the aesthetic side of Catholicism better than I—especially in the book "En Route". I *think* that Long owns a good translation of this book, (I know he lent me the one I read) hence would advise your writing him if interested. Too bad you can't get "A Rebours" locally. If it's in the Providence library (which I doubt) I've half a mind to get it out & lend it to you by mail, if you'd like to participate in such a flagrantly extra-legal procedure.

    Yes—Wright's suggestion to Long was very typical—but the promise of $85.00 has placed the young author in a very conciliatory state of mind! I've just bought the new *Amazing Stories* which you spoke of as having good material, & am now looking forward to a chance to read it.

I'll send your friend's poem to Tryout,[1] & trust he'll use it. He doesn't favour material by non-members of the organised associations, but if I say it's a possible recruit he may overcome his scruples.

"The Ghost Book" sounds alluring—are the stories very new, or do they contain any familiar ones? Of course the well-known names argue semi-classics. Which of De la Mare's is represented?[2] His best—from the horror standpoint—is "Seaton's Aunt", although he has done other splendid things of the sort. I haven't read the others you mention—but really would like to follow good old Sherlock into his modern exploits. I dropped him about 1908 or so, but suppose he has been very active since then. As for Wells—he is flagrantly uneven. He has done good things, but trades shamelessly on his reputation & peddles some abominable drivel & hack stuff.

I am no more a student of art than you, but like you enjoy such exhibits as please me both in subject-matter & technique. I'm not aesthete enough to go wild over a picture for its technique alone. I saw the original of that Island of Death[3] at the Metropolitan Museum of N.Y.—& believe me, it is a first-rate inspiration for a weird tale, as you can judge from your reproduction. As for Abbey—you ought to see his Holy Grail frescoes in the Boston Public Library![4]

With every good wish,
Most sincerely yours,
H P Lovecraft

Notes

1. Unidentified.
2. Lady Cynthia Asquith's *The Ghost Book* (1927) contains Algernon Blackwood, "Chemical"; Hugh Walpole (1884–1941), "Mrs. Lunt"; L. P. Hartley (1895–1972), "A Visitor from Down Under"; and Walter de la Mare, "A Recluse." HPL revised SHL to include mention of all the stories except Blackwood's. See letter 96.
3. "Island of the Dead" ("Die Toteninsel") (1880) by the Swiss painter Arnold Böcklin (1827–1901). The painting is at the Metropolitan Museum of Art in New York.
4. Edwin Abbey (1852–1911), illustrator and mural painter, *Quest for the Holy Grail* (1890–1902), Boston Public Library.

[36]   [ALS]

10 Barnes St.,
Providence, R.I.,
March 11, 1927.

My dear Mr. Derleth:—
My history of weird fiction will be in a magazine—the first issue of a semi-amateur venture to be called *The Recluse*. It will, however, be virtually a small book; since it runs to 72 pages of double-spaced typing, & is di-

vided into ten chapters. Cook may later republish it as a book, after I have done some more research & enlarged it considerably. The typing was a hellish job—Gawd only knows how I'll ever get my 110-page & 147-page novelettes in shape without wearing myself into a martyr's grave! You are right—"The Shunned House" *is* a short story coming to 24 double-spaced pages. The "book" which Cook intends to make of it will be a very thin volume, uniform with the little books he has already published—Long's poems & Loveman's "Hermaphrodite". It will not be issued for a very long time—for Cook has another item (a prose-poem by Loveman, "The Sphinx", in the style of Flaubert's "Temptation of St Anthony") on his programme ahead of it.[1] If the weird history does not appear in print soon, I'll lend you a carbon of the MS.—now lent to Long. By the way—Long has had two stories of his re-printed from *Weird Tales* in British anthologies of weird fiction. "Death Waters" appears in "Not At Night", & "The Sea-Thing" in "More Not At Night".[2] These collections, he tells me, (he's only just received copies himself) are very good, & I shall ask him for the loan of them.

Glad you can find "En Route" in Madison. Parts of it will bore you, but you must read it as a philosophical & aesthetic document rather than as a story. Huysmans is a great figure—there is no question about that. He summarised a certain aesthetic attitude better than any other one person, & was an exceedingly potent influence on later writers of his school. You will find "A Rebours" worth going to a good deal of trouble to get—though that, of course, is more philosophy than fiction. Huysmans was not a lover of the story for its own sake.

I'd like very much to see "The Turret Room" when it's ready, & hope Wright will take it. I liked the March *Amazing Stories* very much—especially Merritt's "People of the Pit". Stribling's story was a finer piece of work, but the element of humour detracted from the atmospheric tension, hence I can't say I liked it quite as well as the other.[3]

I wonder what Machen's "Munitions of War"[4] is like? Yes—De la Mare's "Riddle" is the best of all collections of his tales if I recall aright. I think it's the one that has "Seaton's Aunt"—also a couple of other good ones—"The Tree" & "Out of the Deep". His newest collection "The Connoisseur & Other Tales" has about two "top-notchers"—"Mr. Kempe" & "All-Hallows". Wells's "Dream of Armageddon" was pretty good if I recall it rightly. Is it the one where the leader takes a vacation in Italy while things go to pieces & a terrible conflict develops, ultimately engulfing him? Very vivid descriptions, I seem to remember.

Your recent reading certainly shows a rapid capacity for assimilation! I don't try to keep up much with the new things. Do you know the old weird writer J. Sheridan Le Fanu? Someone has lent me a book of his, & I'm going to sample it shortly.

With every good wish,

Most sincerely yours,

H P Lovecraft

P.S. Yes—Smithy says he'll use your friend's poem.

Notes

1. Cook published the one-act play many years later in the *Ghost* No. 2 (1944): [19]–41, and also as a separate book. He had published FBL's *A Man from Genoa* and Loveman's *The Hermaphrodite* in 1926.
2. FBL, "Death Waters," *WT* (December 1924); rpt. Christine Campbell Thomson, ed., *Not at Night* (1925), pp. 96–111; "The Sea-Thing," *WT* (December 1925); rpt. Christine Campbell Thomson, ed., *More Not at Night* (1926), pp. 202–16.
3. A. Merritt, "The People of the Pit," *Amazing Stories* (March 1927); T. S. Stribling (1881–1965), "The Green Splotches."
4. Machen's "Munitions of War" is in Asquith's *Ghost Book*.

[37]   [ALS]

10 Barnes St.,

Providence, R.I.,

March 16, 1927.

My dear Mr. Derleth:—

Most certainly you shall have a *Recluse* with my weird tale history. I don't know just when it will be out, but it will probably be some time this spring. The two collections containing Long's tales are called, respectively, "Not At Night" & "More Not At Night". As soon as I ascertain the publisher I'll let you know. I own a copy of "La Bas" in translation, but it has been lent for a year to someone who has forgotten to return it. I'll try to hustle him up—& when I get it back I'll be glad to lend it to you. It was suppressed soon after publication, & is really nauseously disgusting; but is worth reading on account of the information on French Satanism in the '90s & the historical account of the famous sadist Gilles de Retz—the latter data said to have been supplied to Huysmans (who hated research) by Remy de Gourmont.

The "Lost Valley" quotation sounds good, but I don't know about the "Empty House" at $3.50. I seem to recall only one really good story in the latter collection. Yes—Hearn is one of the great stylists of our language, & in addition a master of the weird. Have you read his "Fantastics"—written in New Orleans—& his volume of Japanese ghost stories called "Kwaidan"? You can't afford to miss either of these. Glad you've found de la Mare acceptable. The novel "The Return" has a thread of bizarrerie which ought to appeal to you—& have you read his poetry?[1] "The Listeners" is quite unforgettable. I'll tell you about Le Fanu when I've read "All In the Dark"—but I don't think he'll prove anything marvellous.

I won't bother you yet for that "Ghost Book", since I am faced with more reading than I can ever get through. Thanks for the offer, just the same. I've not seen the new *Amazing Stories*, nor *Weird Tales* either—but I shall buy the latter. I read "The Time Machine" years ago. It's better than most of Wells' fantasy—yet has the same scientific coldness & social satire. Fortunately it isn't a long book. Congratulations on "The Turret Room"—Wright has a lucid interval now & then! The theme is very well handled indeed. (But did you know that Gloucester is one of the Dukedoms restricted to Princes of the Royal Blood? There are several such, like Albany, Connaught, Cumberland, Clarence, York, &c.) I will send "Dawn" on to Smith in my next letter, & believe he will be glad to use it.

You are certainly ambitious in your decision to continue the Sherlock Holmes tradition![2] Doyle will probably feel rather complimented, & will undoubtedly write you some sort of acknowledgment. I shall take pleasure in looking over the tale—for it's nearly if not quite twenty years since I last saw a Sherlock Holmes story. What, I wonder, is the full list of those since the "Return of Sherlock Holmes"? I think I've only read one or two (published about 1908) since then. Wasn't there a novel issued about 1912? I meant to read it but never got around to it.[3]

With all good wishes,

Most sincerely yrs

H P Lovecraft

Notes

1. De la Mare's poetry is collected in *Songs of Childhood* (1902; as by Walter Ramal), *Poems* (1906), *The Listeners and Other Poems* (1912), *Poems: 1901–1918* (1920), *Poems* (1926), and other collections.

2. AWD wrote a series of stories, which ultimately comprised seventy-eight works, about the investigator Solar Pons.

3. HPL refers to the last of four Sherlock Holmes novels, *The Valley of Fear* (1914).

[38]   [ALS]

10 Barnes St.,

Providence, R.I.,

March 26, 1927.

My dear Mr. Derleth:—

Well—you certainly are going in for Huysmans de luxe! I mean to get an "A Rebours" translation some day, though I shall wait till a more favourable financial opportunity presents itself. When I summon up the energy, I'll try to get "La Bas" back from my Brooklyn friend—hoping to Heaven that he hasn't lost it through a forgetfulness even more complete than mine was until I thought of the matter the other day! I know the Dauber

& Pine bookshops well—in fact, the amateur-journalist poet Samuel Love-man is the principal rare book expert connected with the place, being the sole compiler & editor of their somewhat ambitious catalogues. The firm is a sound & reliable one, though they overwork Loveman frightfully. The Blackwood investment is a good one—I always stand up for Algy, though Long combats me steadily on this point, ignoring all of Blackwood's fantastic insight through disgust at his weakness of style & lack of the selective faculty. I am giving Blackwood extreme praise in my brief history—which has, by the way, now advanced to the proofreading stage; so that you will probably see it within a month or two. I'm not yet sure whether Cook means to publish it all at once or serially.

Hurrah for Olinick's farewell! Brosnatch was the best in the long run, & is probably as good as they can hope to get for what they are willing to pay. I don't know Rankin, but Senf is probably a fair draughtsman if he did the heading as well as cover design for the new Cummings serial. It's hard work, though, finding anyone with a real mastery of the bizarre in pictorial art. I wish they'd let Clark Ashton Smith do a job or two.

I've not read "The Monk & the Hangman's Daughter"—is it any good? The fables, I think, are not true specimens of the weird. I've almost forgotten what they are in the eight years since I glanced at the volume containing them. All agree that the cream of Bierce will be found in the two collections of short tales—"In the Midst of Life" & "Can Such Things Be?" I have read both, but own only the latter—which is the predominantly supernatural vol-ume.

The Sherlock Holmes stories I have read are as follows:

A Study in Scarlet	The Hound of the Baskervilles
The Sign of the Four	The Return of Sherlock Holmes
Adventures of Sherlock Holmes	An odd (& rather mediocre) pair or
Memoirs of Sherlock Holmes	series of tales appearing about '08.[1]

I shall keep in mind the names of the newer ones. What are some of the titles of the "Tales of S.H."?[2] I don't seem to recall hearing of that series. Good luck with your continuation—& may the mantle of greatness fall upon you! I have a fine old copy of "The Castle of Otranto" with the "long s". As a story, it is likely to evoke more chuckles than shudders nowadays, but to its own less jaded & sophisticated generation it was a revelation of Gothic terror & mystery. They took it seriously, imitated it, & developed its atmosphere to such an extent (yet with such basic fidelity to the original in setting & spirit) that we may consider it authentically the father of all Gothic romance both in England & in Germany; & by this same token the grandfather of all horror fiction of today. I treat this point at some length in the outline which you'll see shortly. You will find "The Turn of the Screw" rather mincing reading, but the author certainly achieves a persistent strain of lurking menace which triumphs over all the foibles & fussinesses of the style. Speaking of James-es—do you know the weird tales of the living writer Montague Rhodes James? If not, you surely have a revelation ahead of you! "Kwaidan" & "Fan-tastics" will emphatically repay your notice. I only wish Hearn had written more of this material!

As to your birth control debate—I'm afraid I shall have to line up on the enemy's side so far as the present age of civilisation is concerned; for al-though the custom perhaps marks the advent of a more or less artificial & decadent social order, it is none the less necessary as an emergency measure to keep the decadence from sinking to a still more painful degree of chaos. And the decadence itself is something no mortal or group of mortals can avert—being an aging of our Western culture as natural & inevitable as the aging of an individual, & perfectly analogous to the senility & decline of all preceding civilisations. Have your read Oswald Spengler's now celebrated work "The Decline of the West", whose first volume was lately translated into English? You will find there much sound & bitter sense regarding the slackening of the cultural fibre of the dominant Aryan race during the last century or less. The normal evolution of a human stock presupposes a cer-tain amount of struggle with nature & with enemies in which the weak & in-ferior will be unable to survive, & will disappear in sufficient quantities to prevent exhaustion of food supplies & to ensure the perpetuation of the species through its able & more vigorous specimens. Modern civilisation, however, has developed a sentimental protection of the weak which ensures the survival of the inferior as well as the superior; so that unless something equally artificial* is done to counteract the tendency, we shall be overrun with the unlimited spawn of the biologically defective & incompetent. For the competent, on the other hand, birth control has become a grim & abso-lute necessity; since the industrialisation of the social order has made it abso-lutely impossible to rear a large family in a comfortable & enlightened manner without a far greater fortune than the majority of moderately com-petent, decently-born, & well-bred people possess. There is no use at all in expecting the tastefully-living but non-wealthy middle-class citizen not to practice birth control. As long as he knows he never can bring up ten chil-dren decently, he is going to stick to one or two or three & see that they *are* brought up decently. For him the matter is an intensely practical one, no matter what he may think in vague theory. The better classes, then, are out-side the argument. With them birth control is an accomplished fact, & it will

---

*And remember that birth control is no more artificial & contrary to Nature than the peace-policies & sentimental coddling of the weak which overpopulates the world and makes it necessary.

always be so. Meanwhile, since the reproduction of good blood is so artificially cut off, shall we allow bad blood to multiply unchecked through ignorance, till the spawn of weak & unfit stock forms the bulk of our population? My answer is emphatically *no!* To hell with principle—our first duty is to save the fundamental biological quality of the race! ¶ With every good wish—Most sincerely yrs

H P Lovecraft

P.S. Have you read that fascinating mass of cosmic eccentricity called "The Book of the Damned" by the scientific crank Charles Fort? I have just finished it, & surely there never was a more gloriously provocative source-book of breath-taking notions about the earth's relations with Outside Things. Fort is a personal friend of the Weird Tales writer Edmond Hamilton, & has given the latter the ideas for most of his tales.

Notes

1. Some of the Sherlock Holmes tales collected in *His Last Bow* (1917) appeared in the U.S. in *Collier's Weekly*. HPL may have seen "The Adventure of Wisteria Lodge" (15 August 1908; as "The Singular Experience of Mr. John Scott Eccles") and "The Adventure of the Bruce-Partington Plans" (12 December 1908).

2. There were a number of pirated American editions of the Sherlock Holmes tales entitled *Tales of Sherlock Holmes,* containing miscellaneous stories from the Holmes canon. HPL is probably referring to the volume published by Grosset & Dunlap (New York) c. 1911.

[39]   [ALS]

Saturday [2 April 1927]

My dear Mr. Derleth:—

You'll find "A Rebours" no disappointment—a veritable text-book of aestheticism carried to a reductio ad absurdum. The organ of perfume that plays fragrant symphonies—& a hundred other details—go to make up a memorable summary of the attitude of the decadent 'nineties. Hope I can get "La Bas" for you eventually. "The Book of the Damned" is published by Boni & Liveright, & is still in print. It first appeared in December 1919. While much like other effusions of scientific cranks in its general tone, it represents a far higher cultural level, & opens up some very provocative vistas.

"The Willows" and "The Wendigo" Long freely admits to be great stories—among the greatest horror tales extant—though he has no use whatever for Blackwood as a whole. He & I rather quarrel about Blackwood, for despite the latter's unevenness, occasional inanity & didacticism, & outrageous overproduction, I still consider him as one of the finest fantaisistes in all literature. There is a type of vision & an understanding of the human sense of the unreal in Blackwood which I have never found elsewhere, so that I can excuse him for any amount of dulness or bad writing.

Good God! If you've only read *four* Bierce tales, you have the treat of your life yet ahead of you! Would you like me to lend you my "Can Such Things Be"? I shall certainly get "In the Midst of Life" when the Modern Library issues it. The four you have read are quite excellent & typical, but there are easily twenty others just as good. "The Death of Halpin Frayser" in "Can Such Things Be" has been called by the critic Frederic Taber Cooper the most unutterably ghastly piece of fiction in the literature of the Anglo-Saxon race.[1] One of my favourites—from "In the Midst of Life"—is "The Suitable Surroundings". This is a horror-story *about a horror-story.*

Thanks for the Sherlock Holmes data. Some day I'll get around to that catching up. I saw "The Bat" as a play,[2] after dozens of persons had extolled its weird qualities, & was wearied to yawning by its mechanical unconvincingness. Writing of the definitely "popular" grade has lost its appeal for me; for this type of composition almost invariably lacks atmosphere, & has such visible marks of merely clever workmanship that its net effect is superficial & unstirring. The latest *Weird Tales* is a horrible example—absolutely nothing in it could hold my attention a second. You have a treat ahead in Montague Rhodes James. Beyond question his best book is his earliest—"Ghost Stories of an Antiquary". Next in order of interest is "A Thin Ghost & Others". James is an eminent antiquarian, & much of his erudition strongly colours this fictional side-line of his.

I used to know *Secret Service* long before you were born. It certainly did have ingenuity, although the level was by no means uniform. Different writers were employed, all using the same pseudonym. These five-cent novelettes with coloured covers were a great juvenile institution in my day—invariably forbidden by parents & teachers on vague general principles. Besides *Secret Service* there were dozens of other weeklies—*Nick Carter, Pluck & Luck, James Boys, Frank Reade, Liberty Boys of '76, Brave & Bold,* &c. &c. Nowadays they are being collected as rare items in public libraries—& modern parents would be glad if their children would read anything so naive & harmless!

With all good wishes,

Most sincerely yrs

H P Lovecraft

Notes

1. See Frederic Taber Cooper, "Ambrose Bierce," in *Some American Story Tellers* (New York: Henry Holt, 1911): 331–53. Cited in SHL.

2. *The Bat* (1920), a three-act play by Mary Roberts Rinehart and Avery Hopwood, based on her novel *The Circular Staircase* (1908); HPL stated that it "made me drowse back in

the early 1920s" (*SL* 4.154). It was later made into a film (United Artists, 1926).

[40]   [ALS]

April 8, 1927

My Dear Mr. Derleth:—

As to book prices—I think you ought to be able to get "Ghost Stories of An Antiquary" even now at much less than four dollars, unless it has lately gone out of print. I may be behind the times, but it seems to me that the current edition sells for something around $2.00. If, however, the edition in question is the *old* one, with several illustrations, (none are included in the new one) then I guess the value is a fair average. I shall get that book some day—& in time, "A Thin Ghost". The tales I liked the best were "Count Magnus", & "The Treasure of Abbot Thomas" in G.S. of an A., & "An Incident of Cathedral History" in the Thin Ghost.[1]

The Weird Tales whose dulness I deplored was the April one; but the new issue is nothing to brag about either, taken as a whole. The cover-design story is a crime[2]—& well shows Wright's new policy of featuring extravagance & unusualness of conception at the expense of literary merit. Your tale "The Black Castle" is very good—& the serial "Drome" is far from dull despite a wearisome conventionality of conception & absence of artistic atmosphere & treatment. The one strong point of "Drome" is its visual pageantry. I was glad to note the absence of Olinick work—the unsigned headpieces look to me like Brosnatch. Let us hope for the best regarding Rankin.

Well! with your collection you certainly ought to be an authority on Old & Young King Brady! I had no idea the series was continued as late as two years ago, for I haven't seen anything of the sort since 1904 or 1905. I knew, however, that the Nick Carter tales had been reprinted in book form. To hear that Nick is still alive in the magazine you mention is news indeed, & makes one feel that the old days are not so far off after all! Does he still have his traditional assistants Chick & Patsy? They were great helps back in '02 & '03!

Dime novel collecting is getting to be very popular these days. There is a whole era of nickel weeklies *before* the period I know, & many men who were boys in the '70's & '80's delight in getting files of "Old Sleuth" & "Old Cap Collier". I never read any of these, but suppose they were much the same in essence as the tales of my slightly later day. Since the latter still survive after a fashion in magazines, I wonder if the former will be given a chance for revival?

The last *Amazing Stories* was wretched, but since "The Moon-Pool" is coming I guess I'll have to postpone my discontinuance for three issues more. I read that in the *All Story* nearly a decade ago,[3] & admired the first part (originally a separate complete novel) more than any other popular weird tale (i.e., of cheap magazine grade) I had ever read. It has the real thing in the way of atmosphere. Merritt could be a marvellous fantaisiste if he would stop catering to common taste.

Sherwood Anderson[4] must have been quite a lecture attraction. I respect his attitude toward art very much, although I abhor his style & am bored to death by his themes. An autograph of his is no mean possession!

I have not read "The Flame of Life", although bought a copy a couple of years ago as a present for a young aesthete. D'Annunzio is certainly a vivid phenomenon—I admire his colourful patriotism, which certainly saved Fiume for Italy.[5]

Wishing you good luck with your new tale, & trusting to see it either in print or in MS.,

—Most sincerely yrs—
H P Lovecraft

P.S. Long has shewed some of my stuff to the well known critic Vincent Starrett, & the latter speaks very kindly of it.[6]

Notes

1. I.e., "An Episode of Cathedral History."

2. Donald Edward Keyhoe, "The Master of Doom"; cover by C. C. Senf.

3. "The Moon Pool," *All-Story Weekly*, 22 June 1918 (*LL* 17). The novel version was reprinted in *Amazing Stories* (May, June, and July 1927).

4. Sherwood Anderson (1876–1941), American writer whose best-known work was *Winesburg, Ohio* (1919).

5. In 1915, D'Annunzio, then living in Paris, returned to Italy to urge his nation to join the Allies against the Germans in World War I. He himself joined the army as a volunteer. After the war, he was outraged by the Allies' failure to wrest the province of Fiume from Austria and led a private army there; he held the province as an independent state from September 1919 to January 1921, when his forces were driven out.

6. For HPL's letters to Starrett, see *Letters to Samuel Loveman and Vincent Starrett*, edited by S. T. Joshi and David E. Schultz (West Warwick, RI: Necronomicon Press, 1994).

[41]   [ALS]

Friday [15 April 1927]

My dear Mr. Derleth:—

Thanks very much for the glimpse of "East India Lights". I can't imagine why Wright returned it, but he is past all explaining anyway. If I had any criticism to offer, it would be merely that the spectral warning theme is a bit old—but Wright uses still older themes without compunction, & you have surely given the tale enough atmosphere to make it individual. In my own tales I try to avoid the employment of usual *motives* & *values*, & to present flashes of an *outer* or *deeper* cosmos in which all natural laws, standards, feelings, & purposes are entirely without relation to those of the familiar universe. You will see this somewhat plainly exemplified when I send you a copy of my latest effort, "The Colour Out of Space".

Yes—one hopes for the best in connexion with the future numbers of W.T. There will at least be one or two things by Long & Munn to redeem it from utter banality. I don't have my W.T. bound, although I have so far saved the complete file through mere habit. The thing isn't really worth keeping permanently as a whole, & sooner or later I shall throw my file away after extracting the few stories which really deserve preservation. I took the *Golden Book* until last September, but finally saw that I'd never have time to keep up with it. I recall hearing of the *Famous Story Magazine,* & am interested to learn that the *Golden Book* took it over. Constantly growing files become a burden when one's space is limited, & I can't pretend to keep nearly all that I buy. So far I have kept *Amazing Stories*—& shall buy at least the two next issues in order to get the complete text of "The Moon-Pool" in its revised form, which I believe is markedly inferior to the original version appearing a decade ago in the *All-Story.*

Interested to hear that Mr. Carter still enjoys the whole-hearted coöperation of his ancient colleagues! Yes—*Tryout* is a mess, but good old Smithy is a rare character none the less. It does no good to read the proofs—I carefully corrected the title "The Decay of Lying",[1] but you see what ultimately got before the readers!

Just now I'm making a very careful study of *London* by means of maps, books, & pictures, in order to get background for tales involving richer antiquities than America can furnish. It is really a very fascinating pursuit, for I am doing it in a thorough, gradual way involving a minute following of the town's historic growth from a thatched Celtic village on piles. The knowledge I gain will help me appreciate to a greater degree all those authors who lay their scenes in London, & I shall certainly never need a guide if I am ever fortunate enough to visit the place! If there's anything I hate, it's writing about a locality without an adequate knowledge of its history, topography, & general atmosphere; & I don't wish to make this blunder in anything I may concoct with an Old London setting.[2] What I write will probably begin in Roman times—something will *survive* in one way or another.

> With every good wish—
> Most sincerely yrs—
> H P Lovecraft

Notes

1. Rulh [*sic*] K. Miller, "Artistic Lying," *Tryout* 11, No. 4 (April 1927): [3]–[7], mentions Oscar Wilde's "The Decay of Lying" (1889), printed as "The Decade of Lying."

2. This bit of research may have led to the writing of the fragment known as "The Descendant."

[42]   [ALS]

April 23[, 1927]

My dear Mr. Derleth:—

Well, you *have* evolved a splendid yarn, & no mistake about it! Really, "A Matter of Sight"[1] excels anything else of yours which I have seen, & has a maturity of form that forestalls all need of apologies for the author's youth. Your constant practice in composition is bearing fruit—& I shall look ahead eagerly to future products of your pen. This tale—with its fine modelling & absolutely unanticipated (yet eminently justified) climax is certainly miles above the *Weird Tales* grade, & I will see if there is any amateur journal of imminent issuance able to do it credit. When you join the National association the *National Amateur* will be a good place to have things appear, although I believe the present editor[2] is said to favour official & social rather than literary matter.

No—I haven't read "The Sun Also Rises"—in fact, I've almost ceased to look over new books, since my interests are becoming more & more definitely antiquarian. But I can imagine what the characters are—since the radical literary or other expatriate has become quite a fixed type in the last few years. It is a dreary kind of cattle which makes me rather tired—the Greenwich Village herd on a slightly exaggerated scale. Convincing conversation is a very hard thing to achieve, & if the author has done it he deserves much credit. Which reminds me that you seem to be developing the element of dialogue very capably yourself. I have seldom used this form of presentation myself, since all my tales are conceived with extreme objectivity and detachment.

Years ago I read several things by Edgar Wallace[3] and J. S. Fletcher—the former mostly as magazine serials—but find myself unable to get interested in their narratives nowadays. A book can't interest me unless it has enough convincing atmosphere to give me an actual visual picture—& fiction of the popular type does not seem to be able to do this in these jaded days of my old age. Your recent purchases all seem to be bargains of the most encouraging sort—but at this rate you'll soon have to make some extra outlays for shelving & library space!

I'm enclosing my latest tale for perusal & return—asking that you take especially good care of it (not but what you always take good care of MSS!) since this is the copy which will be submitted to the professional press. Long expresses a very kindly opinion regarding this effort, but I have my doubts regarding its marketability. It is really an atmospheric study rather than a closely-knit short story. I've not yet begun to use the London material, & perhaps I shan't for a long period to come. These impressions must have time for assimilation & incubation. Yesterday I took a long scenic walk—like those Machen describes in his autobiographical volumes[4]—& picked up a number of images which I may or may not use later on. Among other things I discovered a horrible new slum in a railway district—whose existence I had never before suspected—& beheld some of the most fiendish alleys of grey dimness & foetid decay that the imagination can conceive.

With every good wish, & congratulating you again on "A Matter of Sight", I remain

Most cordially & sincerely yrs—

H P Lovecraft

Notes

1. Of this story AWD has written: "It may be set down here for the record that *A Matter of Sight* was written on a wager from an instructor in Sophomore English at the University of Wisconsin that I could not write a story of which she could not guess the ending. The stake was an A rather than a B grade in the course, and, fortunately for me, she did not guess the ending" (*NLW*, p. x).

2. Jacob Moidel, Official Editor of NAPA (1926–27).

3. Edgar Wallace (1875–1932), prolific British writer of mysteries and thrillers.

4. See *Far Off Things* (1922), *Things Near and Far* (1923), and *The London Adventure* (1924).

[43]   [ALS]

April 29[, 1927]

My dear Mr. Derleth:—

I'm sure your teacher is right in thinking $25.00 none too high a price for your new story, though of course *Weird Tales* makes no pretence of paying on a basis of merit. This might be a good time to agitate the question of better remuneration—when you have such an excellent specimen to back you up.

You're undoubtedly correct in predicting that Wright will have little use for "The Colour Out of Space". I shall probably try it on him as a matter of routine,[1] but do not expect the thing to achieve the dignity of fully professional print. I will surely let you know where it appears if anyone does take it—which same also goes for any other stuff I may have printed. I'll see that you get "The Shunned House" when Cook issues it in book form.

I've read "The Celestial Omnibus",[2] & think you'll find the first story—about a passing of the Great God Pan—the best of the lot. The rest incline toward benign whimsicality rather than downright bizarrerie—though the title story is very appealing. I own Maurice Level's "Tales of Mystery & Horror", but am not exactly an enthusiast about them. For the most part they are not weird tales in the strictest sense, but rather what the French call *contes cruels*— sharply startling, physically gruesome bits in which the "kick" is obtained through suspense, poignant tantalisation, & maddening frustration. I have not seen "Those Who Return"[3]—is it good? I imagine that Level could do very well with the actually supernatural if he tried.

I shall take pleasure in seeing both of your new stories when they are ready. The second, in particular, sounds promising to me! Your historical research will no doubt be interesting even if laborious. To my mind the question of relative importance simplifies itself at once by narrowing down to Caesar & Alexander, for Napoleon cannot compete with either of these in the enduring effect which they left through extending the area of the highest civilisation. Of these remaining two, Alexander was probably the more spectacular & appealing, & his work was truly titanic in creating an Hellenistic world which retained the vital culture of Greece long after Athens herself was effete. But I think the palm must really go to Caesar—for it was he who brought civilisation to that western world which is our own, & who engrafted the heritage of antiquity upon those new & vigorous race-stocks which were destined to supplant the Mediterraneans as masters of the globe. Alexander merely extended Hellenism to races already decadent—Eastern races which have not sensibly influenced the growth of European culture. Even without him Hellenism would have reached us through Rome's conquest of the Grecian world. But Caesar's work was vital & essential. He brought classical culture to those best adapted to its utilisation & perpetuation. Of course, nations & influences are always greater than individual men. Rome would have conquered the west, Caesar or no Caesar. But it remains a fact that Caesar served as the active agent of this important movement, & that no one could possibly have been better fitted than he for the responsibility.

  With every good wish,
    Most sincerely yrs—

     H P Lovecraft

Notes

1. HPL did not in fact submit the story to FW but instead submitted it directly to *Amazing*. See HPL to CAS, 15 July 1927 (ms., JHL): "As for 'The Colour Out of Space'—Wandrei tells me that *Amazing Stories* doesn't pay well, so that I'm sorry I didn't try *Weird Tales* first." In the end, *Amazing* paid HPL ¹/₅¢ a word for the story. When FW learned that HPL had gone to *Amazing*, he increased his payments to HPL from 1¢ to 1¹/₂¢ a word.

2. By E. M. Forster. The first story is "The Story of a Panic," about Pan.

3. Also by Level.

[44] [ALS]

                May 6, 1927

My dear Mr. Derleth:—

      I read both of your new tales with a great deal of pleasure, & believe that each is a fine specimen in its way. You are perhaps right in considering the "Melodie"[1] the better of the two as a finished product—it is assuredly very powerful with its high tension & convincing atmosphere of smoky sordidness, & suggests such a world of drab & beautyless horror as we find in Frank Norris's "M︠c︡Teague". But after all I think the *idea* in "A Question of Habit" has greater possibilities of stark, cosmic fright & strictly original development. I'd advise you, after using the MS. as it is, to elaborate it somewhat; providing hints of a real-life counterpart of the pictured lamia, & containing a climax of more visibly & dramatically cataclysmic nature. The idea is a big one, & ought to have treatment to match. You can make it sufficiently unlike James's "Mezzotint" or Blackwood's tale of the Chinese boatman's picture[2] to fulfil all the demands of perfect originality. Yes—I decidedly like both of the new tales, & shall await the future ones with interest. I think this new material is well worth a place beside "A Matter of Sight".

I have never read Thomas Mann, although I have heard of him incessantly for the last two or three years. I think I saw that "Borzoi 1925" book on a shelf once, but didn't have time to go through its pages. A study of Machen by Shiel is surely an interesting item![3] I've seen many pictures of Machen, & agree that he has a very fine face. He looks as mediaeval as he feels, & indulges in the harmless affectation of wearing his now white hair rather long, after the dominant manner of the Middle Ages. I do not recall ever seeing a picture of De La Mare, but am interested in what you say. He lectured in Providence a year or so ago, (although I didn't get to see him) & auditors complained that his voice was too faint to carry beyond the first few rows of benches. I have not read anything by Knut Hamsun, although I am not deaf to the echoes of his mounting fame.[4] But if you want a good weird tip—get the *early* work of the now degenerated *Robert W. Chambers* & see what a mystagogue he used to be! The best book to look for is "The King in Yellow"—1895.[5]

It must be interesting to hear in person from Algernon Blackwood. I am giving him very favourable mention in my history of the weird tale, although conceding those defects which place his work below the top level of conscious artistry. I finished reading the proofs of this article yesterday, & am now wondering just how much of the text Cook will use in his first *Recluse*.

If this epistle be more than ordinarily devoid of sense, pray lay it to the nefandous toothache I'm fighting at this moment! I had a dental appointment yesterday; but today the left side of my face is most daemoniacally swollen, so that I shall have to telephone the D.D.S. for an immediate emergency session. A dragging burthen like this almost robs one of the power of intelligent concentration!

With every good wish—

Most cordially & sincerely yrs—

HPL

Notes

1. "Melodie in E Minor."

2. "The Man Who Was Milligan," in *Tongues of Fire*.

3. M. P. Shiel, "Arthur Machen," in *The Borzoi 1925: Being a Sort of Record of Ten Years of Publishing* (New York: Knopf, 1925); rpt. as "On Scholar Artistry: (The Writings of Arthur Machen)" in *Science, Life and Literature* (London: Williams & Norgate, 1950).

4. At the time, AWD was reading Knut Hamsun's *Growth of the Soil*. Hamsun had won the Nobel Prize for literature in 1920.

5. Robert W. Chambers was primarily a writer of popular fiction, but he did write several notable works of weird fiction, chiefly early in his career.

[45]   [ALS]

10 Barnes St.,

Providence, R.I.,

May 16, 1927

My dear Mr. Derleth:—

Wright's procedure seems very characteristic—but why not try "A Matter of Sight" on Edwin Baird, *former* editor of W.T., who is starting a new magazine which welcomes all sorts of tales? I think the address is 1050 N. Clark St., Chicago, though I haven't it by me. He has just accepted two stories of Long's, & I have sent him six to look over[1]—though I haven't heard from him yet. I'm not sure just what sort of a market there'd be for a high class weird magazine. Plenty of material could certainly be obtained—but it's a question how widely it would circulate. Wright sees that the way to enlarge his circulation is to aim lower & lower in the mental scale.

I shall read "Rebirth" with interest when it's done. Yes—I know Chambers' "King in Yellow" is hard to get now, but if I were you I wouldn't pay too high a price. After all, only the first five tales are the "real stuff". "The Maker of Moons" & "In Search of the Unknown" are other early Chambers material worth picking up if one doesn't have to pay too much for them. Your recent accessions all sound substantial—of them all I have read—& possess—only "Pendennis". Thackeray was certainly one of the novelistic titans of all time—standing with Meredith in the forefront of 19th century analysts of life.

Good idea of yours, having your short tales bound.[2] My own MSS. are in frightful disorder & decrepitude, but are likely to remain so, since the dread of typing is one of my paramount passions. It's still a question whether my two novelettes will ever reach typed form at all!

The toothache, fortunately enough, succumbed to treatment—though my dental siege is not yet over despite the five appointments I have had. Two other molars needed attention—which I gladly accorded them, lest neglect make them protest as the offending one did! You have my sympathy anent your own visitation of pain—it must have been like my state a week & a half ago!

I've just been lent four books which I shall read as soon as possible—"Vampires & Vampirism" by Dudley Wright, "Lilith", by George Macdonald,

"The Thing from the Lake", by Eleanor M. Ingram, & "The Valley of Eyes Unseen" by Gilbert Collins. I'll let you know later whether or not they're any good. I also have H. Warner Munn's MS. of "The Werewolf's Daughter", which he means to try on Wright. I shan't read that till after the next W.T. comes out—containing "The Return of the Master", which precedes it in the trilogy of the Werewolf of Ponkert. At present I'm rushed with revision work & haven't as much time for reading or writing as I'd like. An author really ought to be financially independent, so that he need neither cater to the commercial field in his writing, nor expend his time & energy on other pursuits. However, of the two evils, catering & outside work, the latter is by far the lesser evil. That at least does not impair the artistic sincerity of the small amount of writing one *does* do. I have more respect for an honest plumber or truck-driver who writes to please himself in his spare time, than for a literary hack who extinguishes his own personality in a servile acquiescence to the puerile & artificial demands of an ignorant herd.

    With all good wishes—

        Sincerely yrs—

          H P Lovecraft

Notes

1. HPL to DAW, 6 May 1927: "He is founding a new magazine open to all types of fiction, including 'that manuscript which others have rejected.' I've unloaded a good half-dozen Wright rejects on him, & am awaiting results" (*MTS* 97). Possible submittals include "The Call of Cthulhu," "In the Vault," "Cool Air," "The Nameless City," "From Beyond," and "Beyond the Wall of Sleep." The magazine was never published.
2. AWD's bound mss. survive to this day, and are in the possession of his estate.

[46]   [ALS]

                            May 22[, 1927]

My dear Mr. Derleth:—

        "Rebirth" is really a splendidly written tale, & perhaps stands first among the works you have so far produced. It is well handled, the setting is good, & the conversation is for the most part facile & spirited—even if touched here & there by obvious earmarks of the 1890's. The ending is both dramatic & logical, & the whole piece has the convincing unity of scene, action & manner which one may call atmosphere. The language shows increasing sureness, though here & there a passage might be improved by a technical emendation or two—as in that at the top of the fourth page, where you say "the change that he himself could offer only a weak diagnosis of". That prepositional ending is awkward, & ought to be changed. If you find a certain stiltedness in the form "the change of which he himself could offer only a weak diagnosis", you might say "the change which he himself could only weakly diagnose". If the piece has any one outstanding fault, it is a possible touch of the lecture-room manner here & there, as evidenced in a visible carefulness to be scientifically complete & accurate. Of course one has to be clear in presenting an obscure & unfamiliar subject, but it is better to be too little encyclopaedic than to be too plainly didactic. Let the story tell itself as much as possible—i.e., let the psychological principles show themselves in visible words & events rather than in direct & literal scientific statements. However—this is a relatively minor point, & does not obscure the very real merit of your close & vivid mental analysis. The mood of this tale approaches serious literature—& it is really a pity that you did not hit upon a theme more susceptible to public reception, since general sentiment almost closes the recognised avenues of expression to such portraits of abnormal pathology.

I trust that Baird may favourably receive your tales. He has not yet answered my note or acknowledged my MSS., but has taken two stories of Long's. He was more hospitably disposed than Wright to my work when he edited W.T., although not so prompt in payment or so businesslike in general.

As to typewriters—mine is in fiendish shape, although it could be put in order if I wanted to stand the expense. It is a prehistoric non-visible Remington, bought—as a rebuilt machine—in 1906, & is the only typewriter I have ever owned. Those old fellows were built not merely to last a lifetime, but to hand down as heirlooms from generation to generation!

The copy of "Vampires & Vampirism" loaned me—the property of C. [*sic*] Warner Munn—*is* an American edition, published by David McKay, 604–8 South Washington Square, Philadelphia. It was printed in Edinburgh—but I suppose the McKay imprint makes such an edition technically American. I've had no time to read the others which I mentioned, since revisory work has well-nigh swallowed me up; but Long writes that he is sending me still another item, which he considered the most unutterably terrible book ever written. It is called "The Purple Cloud", & is by our old & provokingly uneven friend M. P. Shiel, of "House of Sounds" fame. Your reaction to Maurice Level is about what I thought it would be—I had a chance once to get another book of his, but did not improve it.

As to your choice of subject-matter—your own taste is all that can determine such an element properly, hence the only advice another ought to give is that you follow the road which you tend to take most naturally. I don't think that realism is passing permanently, for there must be a type of writing to fit every type of mind; but the dominant popularity of all forms is recurrent. The best policy for an author is to forget the fashion altogether & write what is in him.

With every good wish,
Sincerely yrs—

H P Lovecraft

[47]   [ALS]

May 28[, 1927]

My dear Mr. Derleth:—

Like a bottled MS. cast into the sea by a doomed mariner, I send forth my last missive before tackling a Gargantuan job of prose revision which will leave me either mad, white-haired, or damned surprised! Moriturus te saluto.[1]

Yes—"Rebirth" was really a splendid piece of work, & I hope you can some day run across a semi-private magazine or review or something which will consider its publication. If you don't care for the money element you might try it on W. Paul Cook, Box 215, Athol, Mass., whose coming magazine, *The Recluse,* is to be a semi-amateur venture of high quality. He is especially anxious for unusual & unhackneyed material, & might take a fancy to the tale—although of course I can't predict another's moods in advance. It is *The Recluse* which is to print my long history of weird fiction.

Your new stories are both good from a popular standpoint, & ought to succeed with some professional magazine or other. Contrary to your own opinion, I think that "The Nature of the Evidence" has the greater possibilities—more cleverness & originality—although it is in a less finished state as it stands. The general situation in "Across the Hall" is by no means new to literature. In these & other tales beware of *spelling.* The words which occur to me just now are those which ought to be as follows:

coroner	fidget	
defendant	laborious	(u omitted in this compound, even by most conservative orthographers)

Hope you'll have good news from Baird. I haven't heard yet, but can afford to let him take his own time. I have a notion he'll reject most or all of my stuff.

"Vampires & Vampirism" proved an excellent source-book. Nothing literary—just data—but valuable as a field for ideas. "The Purple Cloud" was magnificent, despite a perceptible weakening or letting down of the tone in the latter half. Shiel is the most maddeningly uneven writer alive—part genius, & part banality. This book was both written & published in 1901—by Chatto & Windus, London—& I greatly doubt if any later edition exists.[2] It deals with vague Black Powers & White Powers battling for the earth's supremacy—how the former were released by the visit of a man to the frightful lake & carven column at the North Pole, & how all the human race save him & one other were thereupon wiped out with prussic-acid vapour. But it is in the *details* that the power lies. Ugh! What pestilential death-ships & dead cities! This book is worth buying if you can possibly get it.

Your recent acquisitions all sound good. I haven't read Hearn's "Some Chinese Ghosts", but can assure you that his *Japanese* weird collection called

"Kwaidan" contains some real terror. I don't care for Hardy, despite his impressive reputation. There is an overtone of the mawkish about him, & his sane view of the universe is spoilt by the owlish seriousness with which he takes it. I agree with George Moore that "Tess of the D'Urbervilles"[3] is rank melodrama.

I haven't decided whether or not I'll get my W.T. file bound. I hardly think it's worth it, & would be much more inclined to accord that honour to *Amazing Stories* on account of the standard reprints. By the way—you ought to add Paul Suter's "Beyond the Door"[4] to your W.T. list of distinguished mention.

> With all good wishes,
> Most sincerely yrs
> H P Lovecraft

Notes

1. "I who am about to die salute you."

2. Shiel published a radically revised version of *The Purple Cloud* in 1929, but HPL does not appear to have read it.

3. The British novelist and critic George Moore spoke disparagingly of Hardy's *Tess of the D'Urbervilles* in the article "Half a Dozen Pictures at the Academy," *Speaker* No. 186 (23 July 1893): 73–74, and elsewhere.

4. Paul Suter, "Beyond the Door," *WT* (April 1923).

[48]   [ALS]

> 10 Barnes St.,
> Providence, R.I.,
> June 3, 1927

My dear Mr. Derleth:—

That revision job still engulfs me, but now & then I take brief recesses in which to scribble notes or read odd items. I'm doing the non-typing part in the open air—on a delightful park-like embankment that overlooks all the picturesque roofs & ancient steeples of the lower part of this hilly town.[1]

I shall be delighted to see your "Symphony in Gold" when it is done. Your style shews a steady growth in power, scope, & finish, & I feel sure that you have some very notable results ahead of you. Too bad your instructor dislikes the weird—but of course everyone has his personal preferences. Those preferences ought not to affect one's judgment in giving scholastic marks, though. In professional revision I always try to be eminently fair toward good work which bores me to death on account of the subject matter or type of treatment.

I never heard of the *Two Worlds Monthly*,[2] for modernistic literary movements have virtually no interest for me. I've never bothered to read "Ulysses"[3] & never intend to—although young people tell me that it's almost a literary bible in the new generation. I have, however, some acquaintance with de Gourmont's stuff—dating from the days when I had more or less of an interest in philosophy.

Yes—I think *Amazing Stories* ought to be worth binding. I must get the new issue, which ought to be out by this time. The new *Weird Tales* ought to be out, too—I think Long's new story is in this issue,[4] with a design by Rankin of which Long showed me the original drawing. How are you preparing your own stories for binding—in typed MS. form, or typed on both sides of smaller pages in imitation of book printing? When I was young I used to type & bind books myself—in a somewhat clumsy & juvenile way.

But I must get back to my task, or I shall be swamped completely. This is the dullest job of its size that I've had in five or ten years!

With all good wishes, & hoping in due time to see your "Symphony in Gold",

I remain

Most sincerely yrs

H P Lovecraft

Notes

1. I.e., Prospect Terrace off Congden Street.

2. Samuel Roth's *Two Worlds Monthly* published an expurgated, pirated selection from James Joyce's *Ulysses* (September 1925–September 1926).

3. Joyce's novel, published in Paris in 1922, was banned in the U.S. until 1933. HPL mentioned having seen extracts of the book, probably in the *Little Review* (1918f.). In "The Omnipresent Philistine" (1924), HPL acknowledged *Ulysses* as "significant contributions to contemporary art."

4. I.e., "The Man with a Thousand Legs."

[49]   [ALS]

June 9[, 1927]

My dear Mr. Derleth:—

Yes—I received the same sort of letter from Baird, & have told him he can take all the time he likes so long as he doesn't lose the MSS. I'm curious to see what sort of magazine—if any—he'll publish when the last of the year comes around.

Trust the examinations will all turn out well, & that you can start for home with an easy mind. Possibly your German test will come out all the better for your not having studied yourself into a worry about it!

Yes—I have heard of the chaotic, impressionistic style & daring content of "Ulysses", & don't doubt but that it is highly typical of the dominant school of ultra-moderns. Five or so years ago it was the height of fashion to have read it, & almost the equivalent of a peerage to own a copy—but I never became ambitious enough to investigate its vaunted merits. I have never perused the inimitable Miss Stein,[1] either, except in very brief reprinted extracts.

Amazing Stories & Weird Tales for the current month are at last in my archives. I see that Long's story was postponed—though it is announced in the list of coming attractions. Yes—the illustrations have improved beyond all comparison. Rankin is the best yet—in fact, the only decent artist so far—& his illustration for the Long tale is exceedingly good. I saw the original of that.

"Symphony in Gold" will be welcome when it appears. The bound volume must surely be a fascinating piece of work—& I envy you the copious illustrations. Most of all, I envy you the ability to draw yourself; for I have no talent at all, yet would like to perpetrate a few nightmares in light & shade to accompany my verbal horrors.

Still at the extra revising—though I took a day off Tuesday to accompany James F. Morton (whose name you've doubtless seen in amateur papers) on a geological trip around this state—collecting minerals for his museum in Paterson. The curator of the local museum[2] & a young man from the college accompanied us; so that, the day being good & the luck fair, the excursion was really a most delightful interlude. Now, though, I must make up for it!

With all good wishes,

Sincerely yrs—

H P Lovecraft

Notes

1. Gertrude Stein (1874–1946), American expatriate writer whose writing emphasized sound and rhythm over sense. AWD had been reading her *Three Lives*.
2. William Bryant of the Park Museum in Providence. (A single letter by HPL to Bryant is extant at JHL.)

[50]   [ALS]

June 17[, 1927]

My dear Mr. Derleth:—

That was certainly bad luck about the history examination, & seems to emphasise the fact that formal academic courses sometimes stress the non-vital at the expense of the vital. In history the only important things are sequences & influences—not the numerical date of a happening, but its relation to other happenings & forces & to the civilisation or civilisations involved. One would think, to read the prefaces of some modern textbooks, that most people realised this truth nowadays; but when it comes to the test of pedagogical application the old standard of rote memory seems to hang on persistently. Here's to its early death!

The two good stories in the current weird tales are Hugh Irish's "Mystery of Sylmare" & "The Edge of the Shadow"—especially the former. That has real atmosphere & subtlety. Munn also does well—he has a fluent command of style & situation, & will make quite a figure if he'll steer clear of the best-seller style. I trust that some of your new or revised tales will have some luck with Wright.

Glad you've secured some more Huysmans material—I haven't seen this collection, though I noted a review or two. Rops was a marvellous decadent artist—I'd like to see more of his work than the few meagre specimens I've chanced upon.[1]

I saw "The Sorcerer's Apprentice"[2] reviewed about a month ago, & have been meaning to look it up at the library. From the review I got the idea that the horror is more psychological—in a pathological sense—than supernatural in the truest weird-tale sense. It seems to centre around some manifestation of witchcraft.

I have the Modern Library edition of Wilde's poems—very good edition, it seems to me. Sabatini & Hutchinson[3] haven't extensively appealed to my predominantly fantastic soul.

I've now found time to get at my borrowed books. MacDonald's "Lilith" has some fine dream-passages, but is ruined by allegory, Victorian didacticism, & namby-pamby. Eleanor M. Ingram's "Thing from the Lake" is a really good story—with a genuine thread of horror despite best-seller form. I'm now in the middle of Gilbert Collins' "Valley of Eyes Unseen"—which is an exciting adventure story of a lost nation of classic Greeks—the real old Hellenes—in the midst of the mountains of Thibet. I haven't yet arrived at the supernatural part.

I hope I can get some time for writing next week—but the chances are that some of that damned revision will tie me up!

With all good wishes—

　　　　Most sincerely yrs—

　　　　　　H P Lovecraft

Notes

1. Félicien Rops (1833–1898), Belgian painter, printmaker, and leading fantastic artist.

2. By Hanns Heinz Ewers.

3. Rafael Sabatini (1875–1950), author of adventure and historical fiction novels and stories. Arthur Stuart-Menteth Hutchinson (1880–1971), Italian-born British novelist.

[51]   [ALS]

June 24[, 1927]

My dear Mr. Derleth:—

Too bad you didn't read "Sylmare" as a whole. It started off badly, so that anyone reading only the first part would be apt to form an unfavourable bias. Munn's new manuscript comes to 92 pages, though Wright will probably cut it down as he did the other two. I wish Munn wouldn't concede quite so much to the popular taste—he seems to have leaned farther in this direction since his first spectacular success.

By the way—my young friend & correspondent Donald Wandrei of St. Paul, Minn. (whose work you will see in W.T. beginning next month) called at the W.T. office last Tuesday while passing through Chicago on a hiking trip East.[1] He found that Wright & Sprenger[2] are the entire staff—czars, readers, editors, & office-boys—& spent a very pleasant day from 10 a.m. to 5 p.m. in their company. He says Wright is an admirably pleasant chap to meet. Rankin, the new illustrator, called in during the day, & displayed every evidence of promise & capability. Wandrei saw the heading for "Pickman's Model" & thought it excellent—I haven't seen it myself. I hope Rankin works through to the cover design pretty soon—the present "artist" Senf has no sense of the fantastic whatever.

I hope "Rebirth" will have luck—but am afraid the *Mercury* demands a more angular & prosaic modernism of style; a sort of general copying of the Mencken manner & attitude. It's years since I've seen a copy of *The Dial*—does it keep on in the manner of the early 1920's?[3] I fear that *The Recluse*'s delay means leisurely work rather than heavy & scholarly editing. To the best of my knowledge it's all set up, but awaiting a favourable opportunity for press-work. Cook is manager of the printing plant of the *Athol Transcript,* and has heavy duties which leave him all too little time or energy. It's a wonder he can do as much amateur & semi-amateur publishing as he does. I hope your agent plan will succeed. It stands to reason that a man whose profession is knowing markets will be able to find more openings than one whose profession is knowing literature. The stories you mention for submission seem very good choices.

I hope I shall have a chance to see "Down Stream".[4] The other day I read Dunsany's new book, "The Charwoman's Shadow", & was distinctly disappointed. There is vast charm & beauty in the tale, but something of the old Dunsanian magic is missing. Here's hoping the old inspiration of Pegāna will come back! The other day a friend of mine picked up "Melmoth the Wanderer" for $6.75 at Dauber & Pine's in N.Y.—a matter concerning which I am properly envious. It was a 3-volume edition.[5]

I hadn't heard of the educational colony at Sauk City. It must be both a pleasure & a bore to you, according to mood or circumstances! Once in a while one finds an intelligent teacher—the best one I know is Maurice W. Moe of Milwaukee, a graduate of your own university.

No—I haven't read the much-discussed "Elmer Gantry".[6] Lewis is a didactic essayist, not an artist, & I can't get interested in his human documents. The new book is probably truthful but overdrawn—& will no doubt help out the author's finances very nicely. But theology is too dead an issue with me to give me any emotion one way or the other.

With best wishes—

Most sincerely yrs—

H P L

[On envelope:] P.S. Hurrah! "The Colour Out of Space" has just been accepted by "Amazing Stories"! Just heard from Vincent Starrett, who likes the tales I sent him.

[On flyer for books by Everett McNeil:] The author of these books is a member of our gang in N.Y. Keep him in mind if you ever want to buy a present for a youngster.

Notes

1. DAW actually was hitchhiking his way east to see HPL and others.

2. William Sprenger, business manager for *WT*.

3. It was in the *Dial* that HPL first read Eliot's *The Waste Land*.

4. By J.-K. Huysmans.

5. This likely was W. Paul Cook, who gave HPL a three-volume edition of *Melmoth* in January 1933 (see letter 299).

6. A novel about religious fanaticism by Sinclair Lewis.

[52]   [ALS]

Thursday [30 June or 7 July 1927]

My dear Mr. Derleth:—

I saw the advertisement of White's "Lukundoo", & wondered what the other tales were. He has done some fairly good things in the book line, & I was rather surprised when I saw him in W.T. Have you read his long historical novel of some five years ago—"Andivius Hedulio"? That is the best modern evocation of old Roman life which I have ever seen, bar none. Nothing makes me more weary than the attempts of the average ignorant writer to portray classical antiquity. They make a mess of manners, customs, architecture, & geography, & display an almost imbecilic obtuseness when it comes to coining proper names—none of them know how to employ the Roman system of praenomen, nomen, & cognomen right, nor realise the subtle changes in dominant gens names & usages which began to affect nomenclature as the age of the Antonines advanced. But White escapes all this. He is a teacher of Latin & Greek in a boys' school in Baltimore, & knows the ancient field minutely. His pictures of Roman life are absolutely correct in atmosphere & detail, & reproduce the feelings & point of view of the period as well as the externals. With him there is none of the sickly romanticism one finds in things like Davis's "Friend of Caesar", or the wishy-washy Christian propaganda pervading such things as "Quo Vadis".[1] Another good book of his is "The Unwilling Vestal". His favourite period is the empire under Marcus Aurelius or Commodus—a period of incipient decay much like our own. These Roman tales are not weird, but in another book White has several that are. This latter is called "The Song of the Sirens & Other Stories". He has also written some modern tales dealing with South America. As a plot-builder he is naive & unsatisfactory, being given to extravagant adventure. His characterisation is also conventional. But in the capture of difficult atmospheric touches he is unrivalled. He makes Rome live again—indeed, "Andivius" is almost an encyclopaedia of later Roman antiquities.

Sorry "Rebirth" didn't land—but as I said, it will not be easy to place a tale so delicate in subject-matter. I was quite astonished at the acceptance of my "Colour Out of Space", & fancy it must have been due to the camouflage of pseudo-science which I applied near the beginning—the laboratory jargon connected with the analysis of the meteor fragment. I don't know when it will be printed, but naturally I shall be on the lookout. The cheque ought to be very respectable, since the text covered 32 pages.

Your local summer colony surely gives you an excellent chance for studying mankind in many of its modifications! I'm glad the commercial contingent has a healthy veneration for the genus auctor—too often the prosperous plutocrat is inclined to despise that unfamiliar & unenterprising animal! Well—after counting up results I think I can return the compliment by expressing a deep veneration for any sort of business man!

You are fortunate in being paid for labour intermittent enough to permit of poetry & correspondence between times! I'd like to find a pea factory around here, & knock off the revision grind! Some alternation—to brew brine for the peas in one instant, & wring poetic brine from your readers' eyes in the next!

With every good wish,
Most cordially & sincerely yrs—
H. P. Lovecraft

Notes

1. By Henryk Sienkiewitz.

[53]   [ALS]

July 12[, 1927]

My dear Mr. Derleth:—

Yes,—you certainly ought to read the Roman novels of Edward Lucas White. I think the best order would be the "Unwilling Vestal" first & "Andivius Hedulio" next—following the chronological order. Yes—I saw new Sherlock Holmes notices, & believe Holmes dies at last—permanently, & not in the tentative fashion of the 1890's.[1] I'll have to read all the later Holmes material some day—but Heaven knows when it will be!

I'd like to see your new story. Wright—probably impelled by his conversation with Wandrei—has just asked to see my "Cthulhu" again. I've sent it along, but have no idea it will be accepted. I also put in a couple of others for luck—& without any extravagant hopes.

I haven't read the new W.T. yet, but am glad to see two of my friends represented. I prepared the plot sequence & climax of that Talman story myself, although T. did all the actual writing & conceived the idea. He knows Ramapo local colour very intimately, having been born & lived all his life in the village of Spring Valley N.Y., just at the edge of that region. Talman attended Brown University in Providence, & since his return to N.Y. has been attending the meetings of our old "gang" in the metropolis—Long, &c. He is very quick at picking up atmospheric & technical points, & ought to be quite a success professionally. Wright has accepted a good deal more of his stuff. But the way—Long's address is *823 West End Ave., New York City.* You had better write him in my care, though, unless you can catch him before the 19th, for on that date his whole family will depart for a month & a half's motor tour of New England & Canada. They are having all their mail sent to me, & I am going to forward it weekly to their various temporary destinations as announced later. Yes—his "Man with a Thousand Legs" is really excellent.

Speaking of vacation activities—I am certainly on the brink of some active entertaining & sightseeing guidance! Tonight young Wandrei will arrive for two weeks, & on the 19th James F. Morton will be here for five days. Then on the 21st Long & both his parents will come for two or three days en route to Cape Cod—giving me a party of five all at once. I shall be very interested in meeting Wandrei, who is truly a first-rate writer—only 19, & through with his 3d year at the U. of Minnesota. You doubtless saw his story announced in the new W.T. It will be interesting to shew him the "Pickman's Model" district in Boston!

Your book purchases excite my envy as usual, but my purse won't admit of competition. My only recent acquisitions are Haldeman-Julius Blue Books—which are nothing to laugh about, at that![2] There's nothing on earth better for casual reading on trips than a stack of these little fellows—you can carry a whole library, properly distributed, without bulging out your clothing.

I shall be looking for "The Turret Room" next month. "Pickman's Model" will come in October. Wandrei's tale will probably be in the same issue with yours,[3] & I think you'll recognise it as having a touch of genius. ¶ With best wishes,

Sincerely yrs

HPL

Notes

1. The last Sherlock Holmes collection by Sir Arthur Conan Doyle, *The Case-Book of Sherlock Holmes,* was published in 1927.

2. Emanuel Haldeman-Julius (1888–1951) began publishing his "Little Blue Books" in 1919 to make classic works of literature available at a low price, typically five or ten cents each. The books (more than one thousand titles—some original—on myriad subjects) were widely popular, and by 1949 more than 300,000,000 had been sold.

3. AWD's story appeared in the September 1927 issue of *WT;* DAW's "The Red Brain," appeared in *WT* (October 1927), his first appearance therein.

[54]   [ALS]

July 26, 1927

My dear Mr. Derleth:—

What I have read of Sheridan Le Fanu was a great disappointment as compared with what I heard of him in advance—but it may be that I haven't seen his best stuff. I don't know "Uncle Silas", but the thing I read (I can't even recall the name) was abominably insipid & Victorian. So Holmes isn't dead after all? Glad to hear it! It was only from a sort of review or editorial that I gained the impression.

I shall want to see all your new tales. "Cthul[h]u" encountered good luck this trip—accepted, & at an increased rate which Wright is now giving me, so that it will bring me in $165.00. Wright may also take "The Strange High House", though he rejected "The Silver Key". I also learn to my great pleasure that the British "Not at Night" anthology which reprinted two of Belknap's tales has used one of mine—"Red Hook"—in its third issue.[1] This will bring enough of a royalty to keep me in postage stamps if Belknap's experience be any criterion. "Pickman's Model" & "The Red Brain" will both appear in the October issue. I shall be looking for your material in future numbers.

Wandrei arrived on the 12th, & proved to be the most congenial person I have met in years. He is gifted to the point of absolute genius, & of amply commensurate scholarship. In personality he is infinitely attractive, & has won the admiration of all who have met him. He is very slender, dark, & 6 feet 2 inches tall. He will be at the U. of Minn. next year—his senior year—but you are not likely to see him at any sporting event, since he is bored to death by athletics & all forms of competition. He is still here, but will leave on Friday for Athol, Mass., where he will visit W. Paul Cook. Later he will stop to see Bernard Dwyer (a weird artist of great power) in West Shokan, N.Y., & after that he will return home to St. Paul—stopping again in Chicago to see Farnsworth Wright.

As for other guests—on the 19th there arrived James F. Morton, plus the entire Long family; while on Saturday I was honoured by the presence of W. Paul Cook & H. Warner Munn, who motored down from Athol. Munn is a fine, sturdy young fellow of 23, who has just received a gold medal for heroism in saving a man from drowning. This was my first sight of him. Naturally, activities have been many; & have included trips to Boston, Newport, Salem, Marblehead, & various woodland scenes around Providence. In Boston I was pained to find that all the ancient wooden houses around the "Pickman's Model" district have just been torn down.

Most of my guests have haunted the local bookshops assiduously— Wandrei is at one of them now. I am less diligent in this direction; since I really don't care for books, but only for the ideas & images behind them. If the text is clear & correct, I don't care anything about the binding or edition; & had as lief have a little blue book as anything else.

With all good wishes,
Most cordially yrs—
HPL

Notes

1. Christine Campbell Thomson, ed., *You'll Need a Night Light*.

[55]   [ALS]
Thursday [4 August 1927]

My dear Mr. Derleth:—
I shall be interested to know of your final opinion of Le Fanu, upon reading through "Uncle Silas". James is such a good weird author himself, that he ought not to champion an inferior colleague—but one never can tell about the critical judgment of creative artists.[1] I must obtain "Ghost Stories of an Antiquary" myself, for it's probably the best of James's collections. I have "A Warning to the Curious", but don't think it's equal to the earlier books. The prices you paid were surely reasonable enough! You are lucky to have the Blackwood autographs. I haven't a single book of Blackwood's, though I mean to get "John Silence", "Incredible Adventures", & "The Listener".

Well—after taking "Cthulhu", Wright has just rejected "The Strange High House in the Mist". I've forgotten the name of the British firm that issues the "Not at Night" anthologies, but Wright could tell you quickly enough. It's like an average publisher to choose a writer's worst tale for particular preference. "Red Hook" was so poor that I hesitated in sending it to Wright in the first place, but he thought it was one of my best!

I read your playbill with great interest, & don't envy you the task of drilling your company. Active administrative duties always bore me frightfully, & I'm sure that if I ever wrote a play I would leave its production & acting to other & more energetic hands. Here's wishing you a brilliant success!

Wandrei left Friday morning for Athol, where he confabulated with W. Paul Cook & H. Warner Munn. He has now gone on to West Shokan, N.Y., & is exchanging weird reminiscences with the weird artist Bernard Dwyer. Thence he will return home to St. Paul, stopping again in Chicago to see the Wright outfit. I've advised him to include Sauk City in his itinerary, but he tells me that it all depends on favourable "lifts" from motorists, & Sauk City is rather off the main trunk lines toward the Minneapolis region. If you're ever in Madison these days, though, you have a good chance to meet one of my best friends—Maurice W. Moe of Milwaukee, who is stopping at the University Y.M.C.A. He is putting in the summer helping Prof. Sterling A. Leonard edit a new series of high-school classics—for with the years he's become quite an authority on the subject of educational examination. He is an English teacher in the Milwaukee West Division High School—one of the few really intelligent teachers alive. Drop in on him if you have the chance— he'd be cordially delighted to see you. If you ever get to Chicago you'll have some interesting conversations with Weird Talers. Wandrei says that Wright is a splendid chap, & there is quite a little circle centreing around him—E. Hoffman Price, (a West Point man & ex-officer who can speak *Arabic*) Otis Adelbert Kline, Robert S. Carr, (a young fellow who has just made almost a fortune through a sensational novel) the artist Rankin, &c. &c.

Well—I must cease & get to work. Revision is piling up, & I have a new job in the form of editing the posthumous poems of a recently deceased bard.[2] Did I say in my former letter that Cook & Munn came down July 23d & 24th? Munn is a fine young fellow, blond & burly, who has just won a gold medal for saving a man from drowning. ¶ All good wishes—

Sincerely—HPL

I've just fallen for Maurice Level's second book—"Those Who Return"—for 35¢. Also paid a dollar for Scott's "Demonology & Witchcraft", which I've wanted for years. My guests led me into bookshops, & the temptation was too great!

Notes

1. M. R. James contributed to the revival of Le Fanu's work by editing a collection of stories, *Madam Crowl's Ghost and Other Tales of Mystery* (1923).

2. HPL edited the posthumously published collection of the poetry of John Ravenor Bullen (1886–1927), *White Fire* (1927), *White Fire,* financed by Archibald Freer of Chicago. For the book's preface, HPL revised his essay "The Poetry of John Ravenor Bullen" (1925) to reflect Bullen's decease.

[56]   [ANS][1]

[Postmarked Gloucester, Mass.,
1 September 1927]

After America's greatest fishing port, it'll be homeward bound. Have had a marvellous trip!
Regards—HPL

Notes

1. Front: 3. The Universalist Church, built 1806, Gloucester, Mass.

[57]   [ALS]

10 Barnes St.,
Providence, R.I.,
Septr 5, 1927.

My dear Mr. Derleth:—

As you have doubtless seen from my cards, I have been taking a rather extended & diversified vacation in search of the archaic & the picturesque. Now I am almost paralysed with the accumulation of work which I found awaiting me on my return—but even so, the outing was worth it.

I first visited W. Paul Cook in Athol—an exceedingly pretty little town of 10,000—& was taken by him on some glorious side-trips to scenic & historic regions, including ancient Deerfield, & the hills & lakes of Vermont & New Hampshire. At West Brattleboro we called on the poet Arthur Goodenough, who is a quaint, old-fashioned farmer living obscurely among his ancestral hills. I am only the second amateur journalist he has ever met in person—& he has never seen a city. After leaving Athol, I took a lone jaunt to various colonial regions; stopping at YMCA's & doing some very intensive sightseeing wherever I went. At Portland I visited both of the Longfellow houses, took side-trips to ancient suburbs, & made one long excursion to the White Mts., where I ascended Mt Washington on the cog-wheel railway. Coming down the coast, I did justice to ancient Portsmouth & Newburyport; crossed over to Haverhill to call on good old Smith, the Tryout man, (who will be 75 in October, but who hasn't aged a jot in the five years since I saw him last) & edged across to Gloucester via Ipswich & Essex. Gloucester is the last of the old New England fishing ports, & I revelled in its incomparable colour—including such suburbs as quaint Rockport & cliff-splendid Magnolia. I then worked south through Manchester & Beverly to witch-haunted Salem, (my "Arkham") spent an afternoon in fascinating Marblehead, (my "Kingsport") & finally returned home via Lynn & Boston. I reached here Friday night, but have done nothing save battle well-nigh hopelessly with my accumulations of work.

About James—I'll admit that "A View from a Hill" is a fine story—also the one about the Saxon crown.[1] But so far as average contents goes, I can't compare the newer book with the one containing such things as "Count Magnus" or "The Treasure of Abbot Thomas". At Cook's I saw the two "Not at Night" anthologies, & asked the name of the publishers. It is *Selwyn & Blount.* I trust your new tales will all take form successfully, & hope to see them when they are completed. Glad they play was a triumph—but I wouldn't work that hard for any guerdon!

I haven't had time to read "Those Who Return". Dreiser's "American Tragedy" is undoubtedly one of the few important American books of recent years—though I haven't read it, since I don't care for realism, & have given up reading for culture's sake.

Sorry you can't get to Chicago—although you might not like it once you were there. My young friend Wandrei of St. Paul detested it so vehemently that he refused to stay a second night. Illinois is a very ugly state—the scenery gets flat & monotonous south of Wisconsin.

Well—now I must get to work! Heaven only knows how I'll ever dispose of the staggering programme before me!

With best wishes—

Sincerely yrs—

H P Lovecraft

Notes

1. I.e., "A Warning to the Curious."

[58]   [ALS]

10 Barnes St.,

Providence, R.I.,

Septr 13, 1927

My dear Mr. Derleth:—

I'll say it was a great outing! I'm lucky if I ever see another such—though next year I hope to do Cape Cod & the south-of-Boston region in the same way.

Too bad Wright returned your story—but what can you expect of a man who accepts & prints things like "The Bride of Osiris" & "The Dark Lore"?[1] He cut several lines from Wandrei's "The Red Brain".

Glad you've laid in some good library additions—you'll certainly have to enlarge your shelf space soon! Dostoevsky is really one of the titans among all novelists, so you can't make any mistake in accumulating him. Personally, I can't really get the Slavic slant, emotionally or subjectively—it has to be a matter of external observation with me—so I don't specialise in this sort of reading. I don't believe I ever read "The Brothers Karamazov", though I did digest "Crime & Punishment", & recognised the magnitude & power of the work.

As to James' "View From A Hill"—the central idea seems simple enough to me. Old Baxter made his lenses by filling the spaces between curved glass discs with some hellish psychic fluid obtained from the distillation of the bones found on Gallows Hill, whereby he could see everything that those hanged men were able to see in life—the old Fulnaker church tower as it used to be, & so on. This device he used in obtaining all his historical & antiquarian data, till the dead men finally became exasperated, & despatched a ghostly party to arrest him & hang him on the ghostly gallows whose material frame had so long ago vanished. The procedure being an unholy one, it ruined the black magic of the glasses to carry them inside a consecrated church, as Fanshawe innocently did. The influence of the sacred place dissolved the spell, & turned the evil distillate in the lenses from necromantic transparency to inky opacity. In general, the story is a very good one—undoubtedly the best in its volume.

I trust that your meeting with Mr. Weissenbaum may introduce you to many absorbing literary fields & congenial friendships. So you know Chicago—I've never been there, but would surely like to see it some time. One can never judge a place from one person's opinion—Wright loves Chicago as much as Wandrei hates it!

By the way—if you want a quintessential thrill of supremely authentic & atmospheric horror, read the new play "Goat Song", by Franz Werfel, (translation pub. by Doubleday, Page, & Co. 1926) which H. Warner Munn has just lent me. It's truly a great artistic achievement, with a development & denouement savouring of extraordinary genius. The scene is laid amongst the Slavs beyond the Danube—the Dracula country, as it were—toward the end of the 18th century. I believe it attracted much attention when put on the stage last year.

With all good wishes—

Sincerely yrs—

H P Lovecraft

Notes

1. By Otis Adelbert Kline (*WT*, August–October 1927) and Nictzin Dyalhis (*WT*, October 1927), respectively.

[59]   [ALS]

Octr. 1[, 1927]

My dear Mr. Derleth:—

I was very glad to hear of your safe re-entry into the University, & of the well-assorted programme of subjects you are following. Your course seems to me exceedingly well balanced, & I am sure you will enjoy it thoroughly.

"An Occurrence in an Antique Shop" impresses me very favourably, & I can't say that I object to the alleged indefiniteness. Curiously enough, the one suggestion I might be tempted to make would tend toward *greater* indefiniteness—i.e., I would not have Clavering actually *see* the cutlass in the sailor's body, but would have him detect some faint, half-intangible evidence that it *had been* there. Perhaps the heavy coating of dust could be curiously absent *from the carven cutlass alone*—& perhaps something about Morrison's death could suggest wounding. As for any possible element of greater *definiteness*—I wouldn't change the main action at all, but might introduce a retrospective glimpse of some marine tragedy in which Morrison had figured.

Wandrei's "Red Brain" is an excellent sample of his average output. He is really a highly remarkable youth—a poet & fantaisiste of the very first order, yet only 19 years of age. This autumn he begins his senior year at the U. of Minnesota. Why don't you drop him a line? I am sure he would be glad to hear from you, & encouragement always cheers a beginner. His address is 1152 Portland Ave., St Paul, Minn. By the way—Frank B. Long has just completed a novelette of which *I* am the hero.[1] In his tale, my monstrous & blasphemous stories draw down formless, nameless *things* from outer space which leave me a blackened, distorted corpse on the floor of my room!

Your recent purchases & reading all seem commendably substantial. I have been atrociously busy, but have managed to skim through a few weird volumes lent me by W. Paul Cook. "The Worm Ouroboros", by E. R. Eddison, is a real work of art—gorgeous fantasy & singing prose—which everyone ought to read. "The Three Eyes", by Maurice Leblanc, has a splendid idea ruined by commonplace treatment. "Atlantida", by Pierre Benoit, is exceedingly well-written, but has more of the adventure than of the weird element. I am now about to read "The World's Desire", by Haggard & Lang.[2]

I shall be glad to see your "Symphony in Gold" when it is done. For my part, I haven't written a story since last March, since revisory matters weigh me down to the exclusion of nearly everything else. By late autumn, however, I hope to work up some plots I've long had in mind. Meanwhile here's an old phantasy which you've not seen before. I didn't have the energy to type it, but Wandrei puzzled out the handwriting of the rough draught & generously made me this legible copy.[3] Please return it—I may try it on Wright later on. There is a certain naivete & allegorical namby-pamby about the thing which I wouldn't be likely to duplicate today—but this was written six & a half years ago, when Dunsany was my dominant influence.

   With every good wish—

        Most cordially & sincerely yrs

           HPL

Notes

1. FBL, "The Space-Eaters," *WT* (July 1928).
2. *CB* 141 contains an extract from *The World's Desire*.
3. "The Quest of Iranon."

[60] [ALS]

            Saturday [8 October 1927]

My dear Mr. Derleth:—

    I'm sure Long will be glad to lend you the MS. of his new tale if Wright doesn't take it. It seems to me, though, the kind of thing which Wright might favour. Time will tell.

  Of the books I mentioned, Leblanc's is the very poorest! You must somehow get hold of a copy of "Ouroboros". It is really literature—which is perhaps the reason that the author is unknown.

  "Iranon" is not among my best things, but embodies a mood and manner definitely obsolete with me. It is too *directly* Dunsanian—one really ought to consider such imitative things as mere exercises incident to the incorporation of a new influence into one's style. "The Silver Key" & "Strange High House" show this element in its finally absorbed state.

  I shall be glad to see your "Symphony in Gold", & shall follow with keen interest in your future use of Sauk City as literary material. I thoroughly agree with the old settlers in their urging, for I truly believe that every creative mind is the essential outgrowth of its own native soil, & that no material is quite so perfectly adapted to it as the rich colour & background of that soil. You will notice that I put much of my own New England into my tales—& if I ever type my longest novelette you will see an enormous amount of historical atmosphere connected with my native town—the retrospective part involving certain events in Providence between 1692 & 1771.

  I must read something by Thomas Mann, although in general I no longer attempt to keep up with the moderns. Also, I shall try to see the cinema you mention[1]—though I never attend films nowadays, & don't even keep track of the names of pictures & performers of the present. The last film I saw which was any good was "The Thief of Bagdad"[2]—three or four years ago. That had a really Dunsanian touch in its Arabesque scenic setting.

As to concerts—I fear I can't give you any advice; since music represents almost a blind spot in my aesthetic development. I have absolutely no taste, & don't think it worth while to make the usual pretence to such. Not that I don't like to whistle a lively tune—but that my emotional grasp of music is just about as profound as the typical messenger-boy's grasp of literature as represented by the Nick Carter Weekly!

I wouldn't worry about uncreative laziness if I were you—there's no object at all in grinding out vast quantities of material. A few choice things are what the artist should strive to produce. At your age, absorption & correlation are of far more permanent importance than expression. As for *The Recluse*—my advance copy came last Tuesday morning, & if you don't soon receive yours you might drop Cook a line. The magazine makes a really fine appearance. Incidentally, I expect to see Cook tonight, since he spoke of driving down from Athol for the week-end.

With all good wishes,
    Most sincerely yrs—HPL

P.S. Long has just moved to 230 West 97th Street—four blocks from his old home.

Notes

1. I.e., *Metropolis* (UFA, 1926), directed by Fritz Lang; starring Alfred Abel, Gustav Frolich, Rudolf Klein-Rogge, and Brigitte Helm.
2. *The Thief of Bagdad* (United Artists, 1924), directed by Raoul Walsh; starring Douglas Fairbanks, Snitz Edwards, and Julanne Johnston.

[61]   [ALS]

                                                    Friday [14 October 1927]
My dear Mr. Derleth:—
                        I'll surely keep you posted on the fate of Long's tale—I don't think he's sent it yet, since he spoke of touching it up a bit.

Yes—"The Worm Ouroboros" is the book I mentioned. It has the singing quality of a Saga & the fresh, pristine colour of an epic. Really, it is quite unique among modern productions, & makes one want to read the author's other work—"Styrbiorn the Strong". I strongly advise you not to miss the Worm if you can possibly get hold of a copy.

As to your work—again I'd urge you not to worry about it, since long lacunae exist in the production record of virtually every truly imaginative author. This has been impressed on me anew by a life of Hawthorne ("The Rebellious Puritan" by Lloyd Morris) which I read last week. The best way to produce fine work is not to give a hang whether you write or not. Then, spontaneously, you will occasionally sit down & reel off something of poignant merit—because it will represent the natural crystallisation of a store of authentic images which actually demanded expression.

I shall get around to Mann sooner or later, & shall remember the item—"Death in Venice"—which you recommend for first perusal. I've read the Sinclair "Uncanny Stories" but didn't care much for them, since they lacked a certain cosmic sense which I find essential to fictional enjoyment. Cabell I admire but don't enjoy. His touches of satire & grossness display a mood very far removed from that on which my imagination feeds. Of his work I don't recall reading more than "The Eagle's Shadow", "The Cream of the Jest", "Jurgen", "The Line of Love", "Figures of Earth", & one or two others I can't place . . . . . & of these I retain only the vaguest & most academic of recollections. *Irony* doesn't amuse me. De Gourmont I used to enjoy as a philosopher but not as a fiction-writer. Maugham I've never read, though many have urged him upon me. James's "More Ghost Stories" will please you, though they don't average quite so high as the first collection. The best items, I fancy, are "The Stalls of Barchester Cathedral" & "The Tractate Middoth".

Wandrei spoke of hearing from you, & I imagine his letter has reached you by this time. He is really a most remarkable youth, as you will realise with double keenness when you've seen his contributions to *The Recluse*.[1] W. Paul Cook is now about to issue a book of his collected poems, which may cause quite a sensation when it appears. *The Recluse*, by the way, is probably at your home. I think you'll find it a magazine of unusual merit & interest.

I've just been reading up some books lent me by Cook—Thacher's "Ghosts & Superstitions", Yardley's "Supernatural in Romantic Fiction", Vaughan's "Hours with the Mystics", & Eino Railo's "The Haunted Castle: A Study of the Elements of English Romanticism". Only the last-named item is of great importance, but that ought to be read by every student of Gothic horror. It is astonishingly exhaustive & analytical, & furnishes a background quite essential to a clear understanding of the earlier tales of terror—the Walpole-Radcliffe-Lewis-Maturin cycle.

Glad that letters alleviate your ennui. You may hear from a new correspondent shortly—a picturesque young Frenchman named Jean Recois, in New York, who is intensely interested in weird literature. He got in touch with me through the "gang" in N.Y., & I've given him the names of all the weird enthusiasts I know.

With all good wishes-

Most cordially & sincerely yrs—

HPL

Notes

1. DAW's contributions to the *Recluse* consisted of the story "A Fragment of a Dream" (pp. 18–21) and the poem "In the Grave" (pp. 76–77; later titled "The Corpse Speaks").

[62]   [ALS]

Friday [21 October 1927]

My dear Mr. Derleth:—

You won't be disappointed in "Ouroboros"—it certainly is the real stuff, & I hope that cheque will materialise amply & soon. I'd like to see that story "The Tenant" some time. Is the magazine to which you sent it the one of which Robert Sampson is editor? He rejected my "Cthulhu" on the ground that it was "too heavy" for his airy & popular publication.[1] "Cthulhu", by the way, will appear in the *February* W.T. (out Jan. 1) if Wright's present plans hold good. Hope your latest Holmes tale will develop to your satisfaction.

Very odd that your *Recluse* hasn't come—better drop Cook a line, & I'll do likewise myself. I expect him down here some time next week, & shall add a personal & oral admonition if the mails have not by that time served their purpose. You may have read most of the things mentioned in my article, but on the other hand you may get a suggestion or two which will repay your wading through the desert of 25,000 words.

You leave me far behind in the matter of current reading! I've never seen "Amos Meakin's Ghost,"[2] & shall be interested to hear how you find it. It's very difficult to find really authentic weirdness in a popular best-seller—I only know one or two which seem, in contemporary jargon, to 'pack a real kick'. Your method of titling the bound volumes of *Amazing Stories* is surely ingenious enough—& I feel very much flattered by your choice of a caption for the latest one! The magazine's name is certainly rather shabbily melodramatic & out of keeping with the atmosphere of a grave scholar's library.

I've now finished that history of Gothic fiction which I spoke of—"The Haunted Castle: A Study of the Elements of English Romanticism" by Eino Railo—& can recommend it very heartily to you. I see by a bill of sale accidentally enclosed that Cook ordered it of Richard Jaschke, London, & that it cost him $6.50. It is published by Routledge, & I doubt if there is an American edition as of yet. The author appears to be a Finn, connected with the University of Helsinki, Finland, but he writes like a native Englishman, & with a profound & sympathetic knowledge of the whole English literary tradition.

The last two or three days I've been busy enlarging my shelf space, for my library is slowly & insidiously outgrowing its former bounds. By annexing an alcove to the library area, & filling the shelves of the wider cases double, (less interesting books behind) I shall be able to take care of things for some time to come—but some day there'll have to be more cases .... hanging ones, since floor space is all fixedly preëmpted.

With all good wishes,
 Cordially & sincerely yours,
  HPL

Notes

1. HPL had submitted "The Call of Cthulhu" to *Mystery Stories,* ed. by Robert Sampson, but it was rejected c. May 1927.
2. By Wilbur N. Stine.

[63]   [ALS]

Friday [28 October 1927]

My dear Mr. Derleth:—

So Eddison has an article in a current magazine![1] I must look it up. There's lots of good stuff in Icelandic literature—Iceland always fascinated me prodigiously, for it presents a marvellously picturesque combination of subarctic mystery & splendid racial stock. Wandrei, by the way, has a friend who was born & bred there—a finely intelligent chap named Hjalmar Bjornson.

Too bad "The Tenant" came back, but I hope Wright will take it. I read "The Sleepers" in the new issue last night, & think it is really one of your best in elusive effect—the effect of terror lurking behind a commonplace background handled with naturalness & simplicity. Yes—I've also heard that England is a better market than America for weird material, but have never taken the time to investigate the different periodicals.

De la Mare's "Return" is indeed excellent—follow your instructor's advice & read it. Did you say you had or hadn't read both of the best short story volumes—"The Riddle" & "The Connoisseur"? I'm giving de la Mare quite a tribute in my article—which I've just asked Cook to be sure to send you.

Too bad the examinations didn't turn out as refulgently as you expected—but there's not much need to worry if you passed. Most of the material is only general background anyway, & the details would soon cease to stand out even if kept sharply to the fore during the quizzing season. That art lecture will no doubt be quite a notable event—Monet seems to be one of the presumably permanent figures of a generation not all of whose celebrities will be so popular a decade or a half-century hence.

Thanks for the reading tips—which I hope I'll have a chance to follow up sooner or later. Here's a list of Cook's latest purchases—which I can't guarantee as interesting from personal knowledge, but which I'll submit for what it is worth:

The Italian—Mrs. Radcliffe
Queen of Atlantis—Aubrey
Street of Queer Houses—Vernon Knowles
Here & Otherwhere—   "   "
Uncanny Tales—F. Marion Crawford
The Caravan & Sheik of Alexandria—Hauff
Out of the Past—Spurrell
The Secret City—Doke
Ghost Stories—Michael Arlen
The Weird o' It—Clive Pemberton

I don't think you've missed much by destroying your accumulated cheap magazines. I'm going to do the same thing with my W.T. file some day—after tearing out the few items worth saving. Possibly I'll follow your example & have this residue bound. Wandrei buys up all the old *Argosies* &c that he can find, & tears out the few desirable things for preservation.

Your new book purchases will no doubt confirm your qualifications for satirising the modernistic intelligentsia—I'm too old to keep up with such things, but let the young folks go their own way. I read more old things than new—have just tackled James Rhoades' translation of the Æneid,[2] which is by far the best English version I've ever seen. It gets the Virgilian spirit & literal wording to an extent surprising for pentameter blank verse, & is gracefully idiomatic as an English poem as well.

With best wishes—

Cordially & sincerely yrs—

HP—

Notes

1. E. R. Eddison, "The Sagas and Iceland of Today," *Bookman* 66, No. 4 (December 1927): 384–92.

2. Virgil, *The Aeneid*, translated into English Verse by James Rhoades (1841–1923) (London: Longmans, Green, 1906); later included in Rhoades's translation of *The Poems of Virgil* (London: Oxford University Press, 1921).

[64]   [ALS]

Friday [4 November 1927]

My dear Octavius Augustus:—[1]

Merciful Heaven! what a week's work! And you were complaining about non-productivity only a little while ago! I told you that this sort of thing is intermittent, & that one oughtn't to worry when the arid spells come. Such spells are even useful, in that they afford leisure for necessary reading. It's a pity when incessant writing puts a stop to the further expansion of one's mind & background of scholarship—as has happened in the case of one oldish plodder of my acquaintance. Wright's acceptance of three out of five of the stories is really remarkable luck, & ought to encourage you greatly in a business way even if it is not altogether an aesthetic index. I trust your more serious work will progress with equal success—though I can't manage to get interested in the overworked "sex question", whose present literary emphasis seems to me a more or less transient phase of cultural decadence based on a confusion of art's province with that of philosophy, biology, sociology, & medicine. I don't see anything of the "intelligentsia"—in fact, I've never been able to survey any of its members or assemblages without a certain mixture of disgust & amusement which does not encourage a cultivation of their acquaintance. So far as I can see, these clamorously self-conscious "rebels" & "intellectuals" are essentially a small group of more or less mildly degenerate & hysterical minds—what pathologists call "mattoids"[2]—surrounded by a much larger penumbra of merely colourless-minded followers who, being without ideas of their own, bask in the reflected romance of their unbalanced leaders . . . . . just as they would bask in the reflected sunshine & Babbitry of civic spirits & business promoters if chance had brought these influences, rather than the "intelligentsia" ones, to the fore.

So you are like Cook in having to *own* a book before you can enjoy it! Fortunately for my slim purse, I'm not afflicted with this inconvenient prejudice—else I would be a very ill-read person indeed! I have about 1500 books—including the sciences as well as literature—but these follow my own particular interests so closely (aside from some of the inherited volumes, retained for associations rather than enjoyment) that I wouldn't cover much general ground if I relied altogether on them. My only current acquisition is Bierce's "In the Midst of Life"—just issued in the Modern Library, & forming a very welcome companion to "Can Such Things Be"? which I've owned for the last five years. Yes—I've read Crawford's "Screaming Skull" in the collection called "Wandering Ghosts". I shall ask Cook to lend me "Uncanny Tales" if the floods haven't washed it . . . . or him . . . . away.[3] The current cataclysm centres quite near him, & I haven't had any word in over a week. I dropped him a line Tuesday. No—I didn't assume that you had destroyed your W.T. files, although I fear a volume of the really valuable contents wouldn't be at all ponderous. In the new issue I found more good stuff than usual. "The Canal" is truly fine—real terror woven into the inmost atmosphere—& "Bells of Oceana" comes close to packing a genuine kick. The Price tale is rather a disappointment—I fear he is beginning to write to order—supplying a touch of the popular.

I congratulate Wandrei on his poetic honours—the second, I think, that he has received. Cook is printing his book, & is trying to ensure its early appearance. As for the "moderns"—I sympathise with such of them as are free from affectation & charlatanism, for I suppose they are seriously trying to put into art some echo of the intellectual & philosophical chaos of the present era of decadence. But I simply can't be interested. They write too much—& their task of weaving beauty from the void may be an impossible one. Ten years from now will be soon enough to read such of them as may survive the test of time. ¶ Sincerely yrs HPL

Notes

1. HPL addresses AWD with a Roman name in recognition of his famous Roman dream (published as "The Very Old Folk"), which he described in detail in letters to DAW, FBL, and Bernard Austin Dwyer but oddly not to AWD.

2. The term *mattoid* was coined by Italian criminologist and physician Cesare Lombroso (1835–1909) in *L'Uomo di genio* (1888; Eng. tr. as *Men of Genius*) to denote those individuals halfway between sanity and madness.

3. Severe floods occurred throughout northern New England in early November—an incident HPL later used in "The Whisperer in Darkness" (1930).

[65]　　[ALS]

Friday [11 or 18 November 1927]

My dear A. W.:—

Your mention of this new magazine interests me intensely,[1] & I thank you very much for calling my attention to it. I have not seen it on the stands—has it started, or is it still in incubation? I shall send them some things at once & see what comes of it—probably "Strange High House", "Nameless City", & one or two others. Of course I can't tell just what they want till after seeing a copy of the magazine. Speaking of *payment*—beware of *Amazing Stories!* I haven't received anything yet for "The Colour out of Space", & shall have to make inquiries soon. Sorry your tales came back from Wright.

Your recent literary activity is indeed quite startling in its volume! I doubt whether the Shakespearian-sonnet question will ever be fully settled. Conjectures regarding the Dark Lady seem to waver betwixt Mary Fitton & the wife of the innkeeper Davenant—mother of the playwright Sir William Davenant, who used to like to hint at possible Shakespearian paternity.

I feel very complimented by the mouthpiece selected for my opinions in your "Intelligentsia Visit Heaven"![2] Let me see a copy of these satires some time. I've never bothered to read "Ulysses", but from the extracts I've seen I fancy your parody is well merited! As for the erotic—of course I realise that it's hard stuff to evade if one is in active social & intellectual contact with the "mad generation". It was so in the old Restoration age—minus the hypocritical veneer of science & philosophy—but reaction came later on.

As for *affectation*—I'm not fond of any kind, but hate *literary* affectation the worst, because it is more permanent & subversive in its essence. We can get rid of our personal affectations when we begin to see their absurdity, but our literary affectations are embalmed in cold print, & have perhaps ruined or at least vitiated what might have been our best work. When we go back to correct them, we sometimes find it's too late—youth & the creative fire have gone, after having been wasted in artificial triviality & impossible media. The only really perfect undoing of a piece of youthful affectation which I've ever seen is M. P. Shiel's revision of his own florid tale of the 'nineties into the incomparable "House of Sounds", in the 1900's. That is the exception which proves the rule.

But I'm no friend to personal affectation, either—although I know it's perfectly natural & perhaps absolutely inevitable to youth at one stage or another. It arises primarily from a lack of the sense of proportion—a thing of course mostly developed in later life—& in other cases from a subtle sense of insignificance or inadequacy, which seeks to counteract itself by attracting attention or being singular at any cost. The mature & really well-balanced man, I think, is disposed to be very plain & inconspicuous—relying on his quiet merits for a sense of importance, & understanding life well enough to prefer to view it as a properly subordinated spectator. I feel very certain that all of your amiable singularities will disappear one by one during the next decade. I also had my affectations at your age—mainly a sedulous cultivation of premature elderliness & sartorial antiquarianism manifesting itself in stiff bosom shirt, round cuffs, black coat & vest & grey striped trousers, standing collar & black string tie, &c—with austere & reticent mannerisms & speech to match. Now that is all over with, & I am the plainest of citizens. I don't consider the rabble worth shocking, & don't care to be annoyed by their notice. ¶ Cordially—HPL

P.S. I hope you'll enjoy the Chicago trip if you decide to take it. Give my regards to Wright!

Notes

1. *Tales of Magic and Mystery* (December 1927–April 1928).
2. Probably an intended follow-up to "The Case for the Intelligentsia" (apparently never written).

[66]   [ALS]

Nov. 29[, 1927]

Dear A W:—

        I was glad to hear from you, though sorry to learn that your Thanksgiving was marred by illness. Here's hoping you'll have a doubly pleasant Christmas to make up for it!

I have read the "Incident in A Roman Camp"[1] with great interest, & believe you are right in classifying it among your best products. If there are any points which I'd suggest touching up, they are perhaps the following:

(a) Give the Latin of the inscription. Such a simple phrase ought not to be unknown to anyone of ordinary education. You might have it read INTERITVS.EXTRA.SI.NON.INTRA. The word *interitus* is the best one to use for "death", since it is not so painfully common as *mors,* & has implications of *annihilation* & mystic disaster which the other lacks. It is also more suitable than *nex,* I believe, though the latter has specific implications of *violence.*

(b) Let the silver urn exercise an oddly disturbing influence over the narrator—also have other slight evidences of strangeness. Where he carries it under his coat, you might have him find a *burned spot* on his flesh—subtly burned, as with X-rays or radium & having a peculiarly disquieting, vaguely familiar shape. When he gets it to his study, strange winds might well sweep in at the window—& perhaps in the shadows of a far corner he will half-fancy he sees a wraithlike Roman face with its tight lips, beaked nose, & broad, low forehead.* A suspicion of Latin words in the distance would not be amiss, also. This, of course, on the assumption that the magic was of a generally pervasive character. If your idea is that of some entity directly imprisoned in the urn, you might have its liberation marked by other consequences than the death of Fielding. In a longer story you could have a series of disasters until the narrator stumbles on a formula which sends IT back into Its millennially archaic urn-prison. In general, it seems to me that something *besides* the disappearance of urn & locality ought to happen during the narrator's presence.

(c) Be a little clearer about Caerleon. You convey the idea that the spot is merely the site of a villa of Hadrianus, whereas—as you are probably aware—it was really an important Roman city & camp as far back as the time of Nero. Coins of Nero's successor, M. Salvius Otho, have been found in the ruins. Caerleon (corruption of *Castria Legionis*) was known in Roman times as *Isca Silurum,* & was the capital of the district called *Britannia Secunda.* It was the headquarters of the Second Augustan Legion, & had the important status of a *colonia civium Romanorum;* being a walled town with large amphitheatre, baths, Temple of Diana, paved streets, & bridge-connected suburb (*still* known as "Ultra Pontem") across the river. There were many fine villas, of course, in the neighbourhood—together with the raised camp of the legion which Machen immortalised in "The Hill of Dreams". There is a museum there, containing a marvellous wealth of objects (tiles, columns, Roman gravestones, vases, coins, statue-fragments, funerary urns, &c.) unearthed by archaeologists. According to Giraldus Cambrensis, Caerleon's "splendid palaces, with

---

*or the rather stormy, non-Roman face of Hadrianus if you want to associate the thing with him.

their gilded roofs, once emulated the grandeur of Rome". The place, in Arthur Machen's boyhood, had sunk to a mere village; & just now it is alarmingly threatened with a far worse fate—that of absorption into the expanding industrial city of Newport, Wales, as a grimy & dismal factory suburb. Newport has attracted an enormous population since the war, & is crawling ponderously up the Usk. Something really ought to be done at once to save Caerleon—the peerless Isca Silurum of old.

(d) If you want to bring Hadrianus in on account of his dark tactics & reputed fantastic dabblings, (you probably recall the strange things he constructed at Tibur) you had better place the scene near *York*—Eboracum, the seat of the Sixth Legion & the principal town in Roman Britain—which was the principal Ælian stamping-ground. Of course Hadrianus no doubt visited Isca Silurum many times, but it is unlikely that he ever stayed there for any considerable period. Eboracum was the big town, & residence of all important officials—whether emperors or governors. (praetorian legati) Any official building a rustic villa would have it up in Yorkshire rather than down in South Wales. Caerleon's importance was as a *local* metropolis. I am herewith returning your carbon, in case it may be useful to you. Let us hope that—whether in its present form or otherwise—the tale may ultimately find favour with Wright.

I shall have to get a copy of the new weird magazine—which, by the way, hasn't yet reported on the tales I sent in. I thought you'd become a James fan before long—there is a charm & piquancy & homely realism about his horrors which grows on one. "Barchester Cathedral" has been copied many times in anthologies. One of my favourites is "An Episode of Cathedral History" in "A Thin Ghost". I suppose you know that Dr. James is a noted antiquarian & palaeographer—a standard authority on mediaeval MSS. & cathedral architecture. There is nothing amateurish about the archaic element in his tales.

And so your library continues to grow! You will surely need a new building before long, as our Prov. Public Library does right now![2] I don't doubt but that your trip to Chicago was full of pleasant excitement—I can remember when going to Boston was a thrilling event; though nowadays my indifference to music & the drama makes me remarkably independent of metropolitan needs, my only goal in a large town being the museums. A week ago yesterday I heard a highly interesting lecture here in Providence—Sir Rennell Rodd on survivals of classic myth in modern Greek folklore.[3] I was astonished at the amount of ancient belief still persisting under thin Christian disguise amongst the remoter peasantry. Gods masked as saints still worshipped at their ancient shrines, the Fates, Charon, nymphs, satyrs, (now called *kalikanzari,* & having hideous attributes like those of Machen's "little people")[4] & so on. . . . They even put a coin as Charon's fee in the mouth of the dead, just as of old! Rodd said that nowhere so much as in Greece is a traveller reminded of uncanny spiritual influences. That ought to be a weird tale tip for any enterprising author with access to a shelf of travel volumes at the library.

As for affectations—I still think that in a decade you'll be finding out that they're not so necessary after all! If I'm still alive in 1937 I'll ask you about the matter.

With all good wishes
Most sincerely yrs
HPL

Notes

1. Published as "Old Mark."
2. AWD's personal library grew to 15,000 volumes.
3. HPL owned a copy of *Rose-leaf and Apple-leaf* (1882) by Rennell Rodd (1858–1941).
4. The *kallikanzari* are cited in "The Whisperer in Darkness" (*DH* 214).

[67]   [ALS]

Dec. 6[, 1927]

My dear A. W.:—

Well—have you got your *Recluse* yet? If not, don't fail to notify either Cook or me, because it's been mailed to you. Cook was here last Sunday & said he had positively covered all the lists I sent him—so if your copy isn't in Madison it's probably in Sauk City. Vincent Starrett—who has just received his copy—has written me very flatteringly about my article, & has asked for extra copies.

Glad you found my remarks on Roman Britain of interest. Your story nucleus is very fine, & certainly worth developing into a tale of considerable length. Curiously enough, your difficulty in writing *long* stories is in me matched by an equal difficulty in writing anything really short. I seem to think in terms of novelettes lately, & couldn't produce anything as brief as my "Cats of Ulthar" or "Terrible Old Man" if I wanted to today. Thus does a span of seven or eight years increase the garrulity of an old man!

Thanks for the glimpse of "The Tenant" & the revised "Occurrence in an Antique Shop", both of which I like immensely. I am especially partial to "The Tenant", which somehow holds just the right quality of hideous brooding menace, & reveals just the right amount at the end. Congratulations on the lucid interval which impelled Wright to accept it! I hope he'll take the amended "Antique Shop"—have you tried it on him? I haven't seen the new W.T., but can't get up much enthusiasm from your description! Neither have I seen the new *Amazing Stories*. I have, though, secured the first number of *Tales of Magic & Mystery*; & agree with you regarding both text & illustrations.

There seem to be at least *five* illustrators; two of whom surpass any W.T. artist—even Rankin—& one of whom has a Beardsleyan touch altogether beyond anything one would naturally associate with a cheap magazine. These I would classify as follows:

1. Commonplace—ill. of "The Black Pagoda"
2. Crayon style—ill. of "The Ghost Maker" & "Bullet Catching"
3. Fair outline drawings—ill. of "Mummy's Hand"
4. *Genuine grotesque genius*—ill. of "Devil's Darling"
5. ***Really splendid fantaisiste***—ill. of "Well of Wadi" & magazine's general frontispiece.[1]

I hope that you may ultimately place your "Broken Chessman" with Baird.[2] He might sometime form a good market for your various Sherlock Holmes tales. Too bad the *Wis. Lit Mag.* hasn't a higher standard. Wandrei's college Quarterly[3] is—or was—remarkably good of its kind, & had some highly unusual contributions. A change of editorship, howe[ve]r, augurs ill for it. No—I didn't know "The Moon Terror"[4] was out, although Wright said some time ago that it would be soon.

Cook brought me a stack of weird matter to read, of which I've so far finished "The Weird O' It", by Clive Pemberton, (only fairish) & "Ghost Stories" by Michael Arlen. (rotten) There now remain to be read two books by Vernon Knowles—"Here & Otherwhere" & "The Street of Queer Houses"—& two of Mrs. Radcliffe's old Gothic standbys—"The Romance of the Forest" & "The Italian". I've just made one of my infrequent additions to my library—five books, all on the subject of Greek & Roman antiquities.

Wishing you all possible luck & literary productivity—
Most cordially & sincerely yrs—
HPL

Notes

1. *Tales of Magic and Mystery* (December 1927): Peter Chance, "The Black Pagoda" (first of three installments); [unsigned], "The Ghost-Maker"; Bernard Perry [pseud. of Walter Gibson], "Bullet Catching" (first of two installments); Jack Hazlitt, "The Adventure of the Mummy's Hand"; Eric Jules, "The Devil's Darling"; Frank Owen, "The Black Well of Wadi."

2. "The Adventure of the Broken Chessman."

3. The *Minnesota Quarterly*, which published numerous stories, poems, and essays by Donald and Howard Wandrei.

4. By A. G. Birch et al. HPL's proposed collection (which he wanted to name *The Outsider and Other Stories*) was to follow *The Moon Terror*, but because the latter sold so poorly, HPL's book was not pursued.

[68]   [ALS]

Dec. 13[, 1927]

My dear A. W.:—

    I'm glad you received *The Recluse* at last. Cook was slow in mailing them, & several still report non-receipt, but I guess he means to get around to everybody in the end. I'll ask him to supply those whose names you send. Bless my soul! I scarcely thought my humble remarks on Blackwood & Dr. James would ever be likely to reach the august eyes of those Olympian dignitaries! I've never been in touch with the great, & they still remain more or less awesome & abstract figures for me. Your teacher seems to be more of a literary character than I had imagined. I hadn't heard of her book—but its subject would seem to qualify her as a judge of the fantastic.[1] Her opinions of your work, as you have mentioned them from time to time, have always seemed to me very sound; nor is the recent advice regarding your Britanno-Roman story an exception.

    Magic & Mystery has returned 3 of the 8 tales I sent them, & I expect the rest to come back before long.[2] Wright just sent me the advance sheets of Cthulhu, & I have so far noted only three misprints—all minor ones. I've read the new W.T. at last, & don't think it's as good as the one before. Unlike you, I didn't care for "The Golden Whistle". It's too mawkish & sentimentally "human" for a cosmic tale—you'll see from the next Eyrie (where a long extract from a letter of mine is printed)[3] that I have decided notions about the maintenance of a non-human alienness in stories of the outer abyss. "The Time Raider" wasn't nearly as bad as most strange adventure yarns of the sort, but was rather a disappointment to me because of the conventional "action stuff", & the unimaginative treatment of the awful mystery of time— Good God! fancy a couple of intelligent men cavorting about the fathomless future & glamorous past without becoming aflame with historical curiosity & imaginative awe! They land the Aztec in doomed Mexico & the Roman in the Eternal City of Tiberius' time, yet never so much as get out of the "time car" for a look around! There are other crudities—logical & otherwise—in the story, though the one brief account of Angkor & Cannell's first seizure is undeniably good. "In Amundsen's Tent" was *the* story of the issue, though the style is poor—as always with Leahy. "The Garret of Mme. Lemoyne" could be made into a good story, while "The Bone Grinder" has a splendid story-idea if anyone would only write a decent story around it. I haven't begun the Cummings item—I never begin a tale till I have it all complete before me.

    Your new reading sounds interesting—& I'd like to read your paper on Webster. No doubt you've read "The White Devil". I suppose "The Italian" is a bore—though there are those who say it's literarily the best of Mrs. Radcliffe's products. I shall at least skim over it for curiosity's sake. "The Romance of the Forest" is said to be unbelievably mawkish & lachrymose, but since it's here, I guess I'll see sketchily what it's like. I've read extracts from both in an anthology of Gothic literature edited by George Saintsbury.

Cook plans to issue about one *Recluse* per year—& is already considering contributions & cover designs for #2. H. Warner Munn will have some comments on popular contemporary weird literature, & Wandrei will later contribute a very full & scholarly bibliography of fantastic writing.

With all good wishes,

Most sincerely yrs

HPL

[Postmarked 15 December 1927]

[P.S. on envelope:] Just received the new "Not at Night" anthology—Selwyn & Blount, Ltd., 6 Duke St., Adelphi W.C.2, London, Eng.—with my "Horror at Red Hook" in it. This issue is called "You'll Need a Night Light". Your "Coffin of Lissa" is included—so I suppose you've also received a copy of the book.

Notes

1. Helen C. White, *The Mysticism of Blake* (Madison: University of Wisconsin Press, 1927; University of Wisconsin Studies in Language and Literature No. 23; Ph.D. thesis, 1924).
2. Besides "Cool Air" (which was accepted), HPL had submitted stories rejected by FW, including "The Strange High House in the Mist" and "The Nameless City," and probably "From Beyond," "Beyond the Wall of Sleep," and "In the Vault."
3. HPL refers to his celebrated letter to FW of 5 July 1927, *WT* 11, No. 2 (February 1928): 282 (*SL* 2.149–51).

[69]   [ALS]

Dec. 26[, 1927]

My dear A.W.:—

I feel about the same concerning "Red Hook" as you do anent "The Coffin of Lissa"—but that's the way with cheap magazines & anthologies alike! Odd that Wright hadn't spoken of your inclusion in 'Not at Night' before—he must have known months ago, for he told me about "Red Hook's" coming appearance as far back as last July. By this time you'll have seen the book, & I trust it hasn't proved a disappointment. We ought to get small cheques representing our respective fractional shares of the royalty in the course of a year. Speaking of annuals—I was prodigiously pleased to get a note the other day from the famous critic-anthologist Edward J. O'Brien—now living in Switzerland—asking me for a brief autobiographical note for his "Best Short Stories". [of 1928, I suppose, since I see 1927 now advertised] That is flattering recognition indeed—& the tale which earned it is undoubtedly "The Colour Out of Space", given the letter came in care of *Amazing Stories*.[1]

All but two of my tales are now back from *Magic & Mystery*—& I guess it won't be long before I see them unless the editor has lost 'em! I haven't seen the new issue—nor the new *Amazing Stories* either. One has to draw the line sometime & somewhere! Too bad your tales also came back. I hope to see that Webster essay eventually—it might make a good *Recluse* article later on. Cook, by the way, ought to be willing to exempt "A Matter of Sight" from his general copyright; & I trust you'll find him favourable to the idea. Glad to hear that *The Recluse* continues to excite approval in Wisconsin circles.

I am interested to hear of the link between Fremont & Sauk City, & will tell McNeil about it. Mac is a nice old boy—getting on in years now—& a native of your own state. Born in Stoughton & knows Madison well. I shall be eager to see your historical novel when it is done—I enjoy anything with the flavour of tradition.

Your rate of reading beats mine! My only notable recent bit is the "Monk & Hangman's Daughter"—which I began out of curiosity because I'm doing some revision for the man who collaborated with Bierce in writing it, but which I soon began reading for its own merits alone.[2] It is really a splendid piece of description & atmosphere—the wild mountains & salt-mine regions of Bavaria—& although there is nothing supernatural in it, there is an omnipresent atmosphere of dark weirdness which suggests at least the close proximity of the supernatural.

The book of poetry I've been editing has come out at last, & it surely does make a fine appearance. Cook did his duty on the mechanical end! Only wish the contents were worth it.

Trusting you may enjoy a uniformly pleasant holiday vacation—most sincerely yrs—HPL

Notes

1. "The Colour out of Space" was cited as a three-star story on the "Roll of Honor" in Edward O'Brien (1890–1941), *The Best Short Stories of 1928 and the Yearbook of the American Short Story* (Boston: Small, Maynard & Co.; New York: Dodd, Mead & Co., 1928). The story was not reprinted, but HPL's "[Biographical Notice]" appeared on p. 404. O'Brien's letter of 29 November 1929 from Gruyères, Switzerland, is extant among HPL's papers at JHL.

2. At the time HPL was revising "The Last Test" (orig. "A Sacrifice to Science"). He also revised "The Electric Executioner" and perhaps one other story for de Castro from his book *In the Confessional and the Following* (New York: Western Authors' Publishing Association, 1893).

1928

[70]   [ALS]

Friday [6 January 1928]

My dear A. W.:—

    Pleased to receive both your Chicago postcard & your letter. You certainly have been 'seeing life' at a more active rate than I ever tried to see it when I was your age! Glad you have "The King in Yellow", & hope you'll enjoy it. I'd like to get hold of a cheap copy myself. I paid a dollar for "Can Such Things Be" in N.Y. in 1922—a discarded library copy in good shape. The Clarke Poe is certainly an enviable item.[1] Ngghrrr! Is the Valdemar picture included? It's very odd that you haven't received complimentary copies of the Selwyn & Blount anthologies with your work in them, & I'm certain that it must be due to oversight. The general quality is nothing notable, & the format leaves much to be desired. Speaking of books—Wright has just sent me a free copy of that new W.T. venture—"The Moon Terror" &c—& I'm really quite charmed with its appearance. The paper is cheap, but the general makeup is undeniably tasteful. Rankin has an excellent jacket design.

    O'Brien isn't going to reprint the "Colour"—he merely asked for a biographical note. Of greater financial significance is W.T.'s decision to use one of my old yarns—"The Lurking Fear"—for reprinting at 'second serial' prices. It will haul me in $78.00 which I certainly didn't expect! And *Tales of Magic & Mystery*, after rejecting seven of my tales, has finally accepted "Cool Air". I shall be glad to see the promised reward, due next month.

    The book of poetry I've been editing is the posthumous work of the late amateur journalist John Ravenor Bullen, who died nearly a year ago. It is being financed by a wealthy Chicago man who desires to pay tribute to his memory & incidentally to help the family. All I had to work on was an unclassified batch of poems of varying merit; but I managed to classify, revise, & assemble them, & finally got them into shape for publication, with a biographical & critical preface of my own—largely a reprint of a United article written in 1925. Cook handled the publishing, & after many delays we have managed to turn out a de luxe volume of which we're properly proud. 86 pages 6 × 9 on art paper, with real photographic print of author's portrait—in sepia, on an impressed panel—as frontispiece. Bulk of edition in cloth of soft grey colour with paper labels—24 presentation copies in dark green leather stamped with gold—a work of genuine art. Cook has at last agreed to handle the distributing & selling end, & will probably charge $2.00 per copy. The poetry is perhaps a bit tame—but mechanically the book is a collector's item![2] Speaking of Cook—& *The Recluse*—he says it would be too much trouble to exempt an individual contribution from the general copyright he takes out, but that he will gladly waive all rights in an informal way & let you do what you please with anything you contribute. I've sent him "A Matter of Sight", & fancy he'll like it—& will use it unless you object to the copyright arrangement.

By the way—Cook wants the addresses of certain celebrities for the *Recluse* mailing list,[3] & I wonder if you can supply them? They are

H. G. Wells	Arthur Machen	Carl Van Vechten
A. Conan Doyle	M. P. Shiel	Charlotte Perkins Gilman
Irvin S. Cobb	Rudyard Kipling	Mary E. Wilkins Freeman (if still living)

What is Dunsany's best address—53 Lowndes Sq., London, or Dunstall Priory in Kent? Cook was glad of the Blackwood & James addresses you supplied.

Still paralysed with revision—worse job than I thought! And paralysed with the cold, too! I was out Monday morning & the low temperature about knocked me flat. Had to call a cab, & have been half dead ever since. I ought to live in Ecuador!

Yr obᵗ Servᵗ H P L

Notes

1. Edgar Allan Poe, *Tales of Mystery and Imagination*, ill. Harry Clarke (1919). HPL received his copy from RHB in January 1934. CAS received the book following HPL's death.
2. See letter 55.
3. Even though HPL had easy access to the addresses of his contemporaries, he never attempted to write them. Regarding the *Recluse* and HPL's essay, we have only James's response: "[HPL's] style is of the most offensive. He uses the word cosmic about 24 times. . . . What tosh . . . critics do write." M. R. James to Nicholas (Nico) Llewelyn Davies, 12 January 1928. Jack Adrian, "An M. R. James Letter," *Ghosts and Scholars* No. 8 (1986): 30–31. Arthur Machen's response can be gauged by his letter to DAW; see DAW to HPL, 27 September 1928: "I received a letter to-day from Machen, in which he mentioned your article and its hold on him" (*MTS* 227).

[71]   [ALS]

Friday the 13th [13 January 1928]

Dear A. W.:—

Thanks tremendously for those addresses, which I am at once relaying to Cook. Too bad Shiel can't be found—I wonder if a magazine sent to his publishers would be forwarded? Just now I'm looking for another & lowlier sort of address—that of the American Poetry Association, formerly of Milwaukee, of which one Clara Catherine Prince is the head. Bullen—whose posthumous book I am editing—was a member of that outfit, so I've got to look it up & send 'em a complimentary copy.

No—"Cool Air" hasn't been paid for yet, though I am promised a cheque by the middle of next month. *Amazing Stories* has just promised to remit before the end of this month—though I fear, from what everyone tells me of their rates, that it won't be a very impressive sum. Thanks indeed for the quoted puff of the "Colour". Good for old Middleton, whoever he is! I'll hire him for a press agent if I ever get the cash! I haven't bought A.S. for two months, but will have to get the new one just to see how them kind words look in printer's ink.[1]

I've just read your three new tales with keen interest, & for once in my life coincide with Brother Farnsworth far enough to say that "A Panorama to the West" is unquestionably the best of the three. However—the other two are far better than reams of the stuff which he accepts every day without hesitancy! If these two have any trouble, it is in lack of a *distinctive* turn—for both situations are of a general classification which has been used more than once before. I think that "St John's Wood"[2] excels "Moscow Road" in general interest & dramatic value, but it has some dubious London geography which needs to be straightened out before it would pass muster among close observers. In the first place, *St. John's Wood* is not a *street* but a *locality* in Marylebone, just west of Regent's Park, in the northern part of the town. There is, however, a **St. John's Wood Road,** & this ought to form the title of your tale. Incidentally—although St John's Wood was *once a suburb,* you could hardly call it that now. It is, one had perhaps better say, *toward the northern edge of the city.* The streets are continuous & integral parts of the compact built-up street system of London. Secondly, *there are no surface tramways at Charing Cross or anywhere else in the central part of London.* Everything is a subway system, (the Metropolitan Railway & the District Railway) called variously "the underground" & "the tube", & employing multiple-unit electric trains like those with which the Chicago Elevated must have made you familiar. There is an 'underground' station at Charing Cross, & also one (on the Metropolitan) at St[.] John's Wood Road. I don't know just what directions the trains take to get from Charing Cross to Baker St., but the route is probably rather circuitous. Baker St. is the station before St. John's Wood Road station. In order to give you a little touch of realism I'll copy a bit of Walter Besant's map[3] of the streets around St John's Wood Road. You can get an idea from this map of just what you would see getting out of the tube station. On the left, St John's Wood Rd. & Lord's famous cricket ground, where all the most famous cricket matches are staged. (Oxford v. Cambridge, Eton v. Harrow, &c.) On the right, at the open junction of four great roads, the handsome St. John's Wood Chapel, with churchyard now open as a public park with seats under the willow trees. The chapel, built in 1814, has a fine Ionic portico, & there are many old gravestones about it. The eccentric "prophetess" & religious

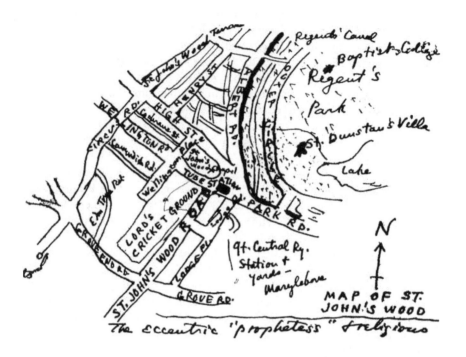

The eccentric "prophetess" of religious

fanatic Joanna Southcott, (1750–1814) whose silly secret box (supposed to hold portentous things & not to be opened till far in the future) was opened a couple of months ago, was interred in this churchyard, & the great painter Benjamin West lies in a vault beneath the church. On the right you will see the curving border of Regent's Park & the Regent's Canal, & behind are the great yards of the Marylebone Station. A walk out Albert Rd., to the right, along the park border, will take one to Primrose Hill, north of the park, whence one of the finest of all views of London may be obtained. It is well always to get a scene into one's mind like this. That's what makes for convincing *realism*. Use maps & guidebooks. Until *you* see the whole thing visually, you can't expect your readers to do so! Before you write your story finally, see how the *numbers* go on the road—whether there is a 7, &c. You might use St. John's Wood *Terrace* instead. (vide map) London street guides, if accessible at the library, would help you. "The Moscow Road" is good, but it might have more *atmosphere*. Don't make your style too light & brisk & snappy, & don't trust to quick-fire dialogue for scenic & atmospheric effects.

"A Panorama to the West" is splendid—really original in its combination, & the only spy-glass weird story I've ever seen except M. R. James's "View from a Hill". I think it surely is worth developing into a novelette, as suggested, & I hope you'll go to it whether or not Wright accepts the present version. You can use it again, legally enough, in a book, even if previously printed in a magazine. Veil your "elemental"[4] & its worship in as much darkly suggestive obscurity & as many hints of unhallowed pre-human antiquity as possible. Don't have the wall writing anything as human or familiar as Latin—let it rather be some vague, puzzling, geometrical symbol or set of symbols older than mankind; & let the horror come from its *identity* in the two cases of deserted house & skyscraper tower. I'll leave to your imagination the kind of symbol to devise—something darkly *geometrical* is probably the best thing, since the more *primal* & *unwholesomely archaic* a thing is, the more closely may it be assumed to embody those basic principles of *rhythm* underlying the constitution of matter & the operations of the cosmos. But I wouldn't have it Latin. There's no inherent horror in that—the only reason it is effective in a tale whose antecedent influences hark back to Roman Britain is that in this case it suggests the lingering influences of older worshippers. Where there is no clearly implied Roman worship in the background, it is well to be as abstractly cosmic & non-terrestrial as possible—or rather, in this case, as *un-human* as possible; for I assume that "elementals" are supposed to be terrestrial in their connexions. I can visualise the scene of the final catastrophe from the picture of the Tribune Tower which you sent me, & from having been in similar places myself—but let me suggest that you arrange your *topography* with care. No tower high enough to be a popular place of observation with an admission fee would have any kind of a view of a small, low building huddled on the ground below. I know, for I've been up in the Woolworth Bldg. in N.Y. (where the fee, by the way, is half a dollar!) time & time again. The surrounding terrain, except for neighbouring skyscrapers, is virtually no more than a small-scale panoramic map, & an individual house is simply lost. I know nothing whatever of Chicago, but would suggest that you arrange if possible to have the skyscraper not too high, & the accursed house on a *hill* which can bring it more on a line with the point of observation. And about the man's death—I think you could have that much more effective by bringing in the element of *fire*. That would have a symbolic & dramatic value. Let him be found in the tower burned to a crisp; or *better still,* let the body on the ground below be found to be *charred as well as crushed.* This final episode must be handled with care. For one thing, the *body itself* couldn't be seen except as a dot from the height of the tower; so that the *crowd* must be the object of visibility to those above. If I were you I'd change the climax to have the *charring of the body* the crucial incident. Something like this—beginning at p 5, line 4 from bottom:

Some distance away in Michigan Ave. a crowd seemed to be collecting, but it was too far off to be the falling-place of anything from this tower & platform. For a moment Miss Johns looked, then turned to a blackened scrawl on the wall close to the glasses. It was as if something had been singed there, leaving a charred deposit—and it was the same strange symbol which the caretaker had found in the burned-down house in North Clark St. There was no mistaking it, for the caretaker had drawn out carefully what he had seen.

Miss Pierce looked curiously at the brownish-black lines, so familiar & so horrible in their geometric precision.

"He must have had some torch or something," she said, "& burned this thing before he jumped. Those people were supposed to worship a fire spirit, & I suppose they had this writing as part of their ceremonies. You know you said the same thing was found in that house. When he found the house gone, he must have thought he ought to die. I can't think about it—it makes me sick."

But Miss Johns was not listening. She was watching the crowd which they had seen at first, & which had now gathered to astonishing proportions. Once in a while a roar as of awe or horror floated up from it; & at length a rift or lane appeared, permitting the passage of some vehicle to the centre. Then suddenly the awful import cane to her, & she fell back.

"Oh, my God!"

Miss Pierce summoned her courage & leaned forward. She followed Alice Johns' pointing finger.

"Look, Miss Pierce, that *must* be where he landed. What else could that crowd be? But he couldn't have *fallen* there; he couldn't even have *jumped* there. Something must have *thrown* him—yet there was no one else up here!"

The two women shuddered & turned, & quietly entered the tower. They looked at the glasses focussed on the ruins of a house in N. Clark St. Then, saying nothing to the elevator boy, they went down to the ground level to see what the crowd was really about.

It had begun to break up when they left the lobby of the building, & little groups of people were talking in whispers as they walked along. Three men had paused near the building as if to bid one another good-bye, & scraps of their hushed conversation could be caught now & then. The woman listened.

"I never saw a body so smashed up before. It was frightful. I wish to God I'd never seen it—it'll never get out of my head!"

"But Joe, didn't you see the *face*—you ought to thank Heaven you didn't! It was not only the *expression*—that was bad enough—but it was distinctly *charred*, as if the fellow had walked through a fire."

"Do you suppose that had anything to do with the blinding flash of light they spoke about—the flash right here in the T——— tower just before the man fell? Of course he couldn't have fallen from there, but there might have been some queer electric or ether-wave connexion with wherever he fell from. You never can tell in these days of radio."

"Well—you chaps saw enough, I guess, but you'd better be glad you didn't see what I did. You know I was toward the front when they lifted him, & his clothing crumbled off in that queer way. I saw his back & side—& the *marks* there. We'll hear about that in the papers."

"What marks, Al? I didn't hear anybody speak of them."

"I guess nobody wanted to speak of them. I hardly do. Can you imagine what the print of a giant hand or paw a foot or two across would be? I'm too damned imaginative, I suppose, but these things get on my nerves. Great parallel lines, two or three feet long. *And they were burned in black an inch or two deep!*"[5]

———

No—I don't think you 'got soaked' in the purchase of "The King in Yellow". I'd give two dollars for a copy any day. Wandrei was lucky, & got one in N.Y. for $1.25. He saw another at the same price, too—which I'd have asked him to get me in an instant if I'd known of it. Chambers' "Maker of Moons" & "In Search of the Unknown" have fine spots, also—especially in the first two stories in the latter.

"Can Such Things Be" is a great book. Did you say you also had "In the Midst of Life"? I obtained that in the Modern Library last autumn. I'm doing revision for a man once closely associated with Bierce, hence feel rather in touch with the dour old fellow. Have you read "The Monk & the Hangman's Daughter"? It seems rather hard to get, & is in none of the N.Y. libraries. Providence has a copy, so I'm going to flout library regulations & get it to lend to Long.

Glad you find Cook's copyright arrangement all right. I haven't heard from him since sending him "A Matter of Sight", but feel quite sure he'll want it. It is really a fine tale, with one of the most effective climaxes I've yet come across.

Bless my soul! but I feel flattered by your citation of my article in your Webster paper! That's the second time I shall have been collegiately used, for Wandrei tells me that he has entered me as an official bit of supplementary reading in reporting on his course in the Gothic novel.[6] Glad your friend & preceptor like *The Recluse*. All verdicts seem pretty favourable, & I don't blame Cook for feeling rather good about the whole venture. He certainly did get together as fine an amateur magazine as I've ever seen.

I've read some of M. R. James's antiquarian material—especially a fine illustrated work on certain old cathedrals which Cook lent me.[7] Many fail to realise that James has written ghost stories, though these latter become better & better known each year.

The cold spell has gone, thank heaven, but I am so overwhelmed with work that I haven't had a chance to get out of the house. I'm helping Cook attend to the distribution of the Bullen book—which takes more time than I thought it would. Glad you're having vernal weather—ordinarily I know that your part of the world is much colder than hereabouts, since at Providence the thermometer has never been below -3°, & does not fall below +20° or +25° more than ten or fifteen days in the course of a whole winter. This is plenty cold enough for me, though—so much so that I virtually hibernate from December to March. I'd spend the winters south if I had the money. Everyone says I ought to live there, considering my sensitiveness to cold, but I'm too much attached to my native soil to live anywhere else. However, had I been born in a still colder place, such as Canada or the Mid West, I would have *had* to forfeit ancestral scenes through sheer self-preservation!

So you're one of the buoyant army of hatless youth! In my day things were different, & the sun of heaven never shone down upon my uncovered locks!

With all good wishes, & hoping you haven't found my story suggestions a bore, I remain

Most cordially & sincerely yrs—
H P L

Notes

1. Eugene S. Middleton, letter to the editor, *Amazing Stories* 2, No. 11 (February 1928): "How anyone can criticize unfavourably 'The Colour Out of Space' by H. P. Lovecraft is beyond me. It is of that superbly fascinating type of stories like 'The Willows' by Blackwood and 'The Thing from—Outside.' It easily ranks as one of the best ten stories ever published in *Amazing Stories,* and is wellnigh perfect, both as to plot, technique and ending. Now, if H. G. Wells could make anything as worthwhile as 'The Colour Out of Space' he *would* have something to brag about."

2. Alternatively titled "The Charing Cross Horror," but ultimately published as "The Tenant at Number 7."

3. In Sir Walter Besant (1836–1901) and James Rice, *Sir Richard Whittington, Lord Mayor of London* (New York: G. P. Putnam's Sons, 1881; *LL* 83).

4. This "fire-elemental" seems to be a precursor to AWD's Cthugha.

5. This scene appears in "A Visitor from Outside" by AWD and Mark Schorer, pp. 432–33. The passage as revised by HPL does not appear in the story, but it is not known if AWD rejected HPL's suggestions, if AWD never revised the story, or if the story was an early draft.

6. DAW, "The Imaginative Element in Modern Literature," *Don't Dream* (Minneapolis: Fedogan & Bremer, 1997), pp. 361–65.

7. M. R. James, *Abbeys.*

[72]   [ALS]

Friday [20 January 1928]

Dear A W:—

      Your two essays are really splendid, & I shall send them at once to Cook. I have no doubt but that he will want one or both for *The Recluse*, for they combine good style & graphic data in a finely felicitous manner. Thanks, by the way, for your all-too-generous reference to my attempts in your final footnote. I wish indeed that I might be able to justify it! Speaking of Shakespeare's sonnets, have you heard the theory that the Dark Lady was the wife of the innkeeper Davenant—mother of the dramatist Sir William Davenant, who claimed a Shakespearian paternity with somewhat doubtful taste & without securing any vast amount of credence? I heard it in a lecture by Will Irwin about four years ago,[1] but don't know how well it has stood the test of time.

      Glad my London data was of value. London never had surface trains in the congested sections, 'busses & the underground taking care of all the public traffic. The last few years have seen a similar banishment of street cars from the heart of Boston, & it is only a question of time before New York will follow suit. Even Providence—the trading centre of an unusually populous area—has talked at times of the same thing, though it has not come to pass as yet. Glad W.T. has taken another collaborated effort[2]—you certainly manage to land an encouraging proportion of your work! I shall re-read "The Tenant" with keenest interest—that is surely a first-rate tale, & I congratulate Wright on the lucid interval which impelled him to take it. I also hope to see, in time, some finely revised versions of the "Incident in a Roman Camp" & "Panorama to the West".

      I've never seen "The Devil's Dictionary";[3] but don't fancy I'd be wildly enthusiastic about it, since I'm past the age where smart cynicism & epigram interest me. But "The Monk & the Hangman's Daughter" is really splendid, & I hope to get a copy some day.

      So you're still a dramatist & producer? I trust your 1928 offering may prove a success in every way, & envy you the energy which enables you to tackle such propositions & enjoy them! I trust you will send me your essay on art later on—I'm really quite interested in the theory of aesthetics.

      Wandrei's book of poems is nearly done now, & I trust you won't miss seeing a copy. It will probably create more or less of a major sensation amongst his associates at the U. of Minn.

      With all good wishes,

        Most sincerely yrs—

          HPL

Notes

1. HPL to Lillian D. Clark, 30 March 1924: "Last Tuesday I attended the Writers'

Club, where I heard an exceedingly acute address on Shakespeare by the celebrated Will Irwin, who had enough new material to teach something to even the most erudite of his hearers. As casual anecdote I may remark that at the general breaking-up it was my fortune to be helped on with my overcoat by none other than the distinguished speaker himself . . . to whom, however, I refrained from offering a tip!" (*SL* 1.336).

2. Apparently "Riders in the Sky."

3. By Ambrose Bierce.

[73]   [ALS]

[late January 1928]

Dear A. W.:—

     I'm glad you've been having some acceptances lately, & hope you won't be at all discouraged by the concomitant rejections. At your age, & with your hasty & voluminous mode of writing, I don't think 16 out of 100 is such a bad record. You could probably increase the percentage—& probably will do so—by adopting slower & more thorough methods; not trying to write so much, but trying to make what you do write exquisitely perfect in detail & atmosphere. A story ought to be lingered over—to be lived through vicariously, as it were—by the author; so that each scene is sharply limned in his own consciousness, while all the little niceties of incident, mood, & language are polished up to something like ideal smoothness & accuracy. That is not, perhaps, the "spirit of the times"—but it would pay many a young author to forget all about the times for a while in the interest of those standards of good literature which are ageless, & eclipsed only now & then by waves of barbarousness & decadence. I have great hopes of the rewritten tales—especially the Roman & fire-elemental ones—& am eager to see them in their metamorphosed aspects. I'm sure Wright will like them—especially the one laid in his beloved Chicago.

     As to the "Devil's Dictionary"—I don't doubt but that it's very clever of its kind, but I merely don't care for the genre any more. That sort of thing wears thin—for when one's cynicism becomes perfect & absolute, there is no longer anything amusing in the stupidity & hypocrisy of the herd. It is all to be expected—what else *could* human nature produce?—so irony annuls itself by means of its own victories! Once utterly disillusioned, we turn to the realistic & unhumorous study of the scene in an objectively scientific light, or else weave new & conscious illusions in the spirit of phantasy. However—I shall undoubtedly read the D.D. when a copy stumbles under my nose all of its own volition. Personal interest in Bierce would be enough to make me do that.

     I've just read one of the minor Gothic novels—"The Horrors of Oakendale Abbey"[1]—which Cook lent me. It is a watery imitation of Mrs. Radcliffe, published in 1797, & is ineffably tame, artificial, & inane. It was interesting to peruse it in the original edition, with long s's & all.

I'm not surprised at the high mark given your Webster paper, & feel sure that Cook will welcome it enthusiastically. I don't know whether to congratulate or commiserate you on your Victorian course. Personally I don't like the 19th century, but I know it produced some marvellous literature—much finer literature, as a matter of fact, than the 18th century, of whose general aspects I am so overwhelmingly fond.

I guess you won't be disappointed in Wandrei's book. It's almost done now, though probably it won't appear for another month.

With best wishes—Yr most obt Servt HPL

Notes

1. By Mrs. Carver.

[74]   [ALS]
                                                        Tuesday [31 January 1928]
My dear A. W.:—
                        I read the revised Roman tale with very keen interest, & believe it is greatly improved by the changes & amplifications. I hope Wright will take it; but if he doesn't, there is really no reason to give it up as lost, since the idea is good enough to warrant still further work on it. You could make the Roman antecedents more definite—introducing in some way an account of a Britanno-Roman sorcerer & his shunned & detested villa—& could give to the ancient magic a somewhat clearer characteristic pattern which the modern sequel could duplicate. In such a "flash back" you might have your wizard a man of mixed Roman & Celtic blood. Give him a Roman praenomon & gens-name, but a Latinised Celtic cognomen—such as Marcus Vitius Galgacinus or Caius Ostorius Vindemarus. He will thus inherit both Druid magic, & such dark eastern lore as filtered into Rome from its Oriental provinces. In writing out your inscription, it would be better to give the "U" of INTERITVS. the "V" form, which most commonly served for both in Roman epigraphy. You ought to read Arthur Weigall's "Wanderings in Roman Britain". I haven't seen the book, but enjoyed some of the component chapters in newspaper-article form before the book was published. It isn't obtainable in Providence at present, though Weigall's other book "Wanderings in Saxon Britain" sells here for $3.00. I want to own both some time, for one really ought to have all possible data on the remote sources of the existing Anglo-Saxon culture. There are many weird opportunities in such research—especially as connected with the worship of the local Britanno-Roman deity *Sylvanus Cocidius*, who seems to have been a kind of British Pan, at once venerated & feared by the rural population. Altars to him have been

found at many places, especially in the north, where the frontier garrisons camped.[1]

I am interested to hear of the destinations of your other MSS., & hope that Wright will take all of those sent him. If he doesn't accept "A Panorama to the West" in extended form, I shall be very much disappointed. There's no explaining his moods, though—he's just rejected a splendid story by my young friend Talman,[2] whose "Alabad, Ghinu, & Aratza" you may have noticed in the current issue.

I haven't seen *Tales of Magic & Mystery* since the first number, but don't feel that I've missed much. Let me know when my "Cool Air" comes out, for they may not send me a copy. I hope you'll land with them as well as with Baird—nothing like repeated trying!

Vincent Starrett's present address—his third since he began writing me—is *940 Buena Park Terrace, Chicago, Ill.* He seems a very pleasant sort, & although I haven't seen any great weird work of his, his taste in such matters is generally just & sensitive.

At last I've finished the hellish job I had on my hands—the first which I've done for old Danziger, collaborator in "The Monk & the Hangman's Daughter". Now I hope I can get a second to breathe in! Best wishes—HPL.

P.S. Let me know if you come across the address of that American Poetry Association, formerly of Milwaukee. I can't find it anywhere.

Notes

1. Sylvanus Cocidius is mentioned in *The Case of Charles Dexter Ward* (MM 138).
2. Possibly Talman's "The Wyvern."

[75]   [ANS]

Feby 9[, 1928]

Dear A W:—

        Did you receive your revised Roman story back? I am rather worried, since at least two non-deliveries have been reported in connexion with mail which I sent out on the same day! I have a fear that all that day's batch has somehow been lost in the local P.O., hence as soon as I check up on all the items I remember, I mean to file a "tracer" & see if the trouble can be located.

I certainly hope the tale—& the letter with it—will turn up eventually. Meanwhile let me know conclusively whether it really did fail to arrive.

Hastily—

        HPL

[76]   [ALS]

Sunday [12 February 1928]

My dear A. W.:—

Your letter happily dispels the postal doubts expressed in my postal card—& I am glad to know that "Things We Know Not Of" is safe home. Evidently every item in that day's mail did not get lost, although three or four seem to be gone conclusively. Too bad Wright returned it—but let us hope it will meet a better fate some day when expanded & particularised. I didn't know you were incorporating "A Panorama to the West" in "The Chicago Horror". You have a great idea there, & I wish Wright could be made to see it! He's a curious critic, so that I always feel the element of chance as a dominant factor in acceptances or rejections. The recent story of Talman's was his first fully independent venture to appear—for I shaped the synopsis of "Two Black Bottles" myself from his basic idea. He is gradually developing as an unassisted craftsman—though Wright has just rejected a fine new tale of his. Yes—Wandrei told me about the acceptance of his sonnets,[1] & I shall surely welcome their appearance in print. I haven't had time to look at the new W.T., but want to re-read "The Tenant" shortly.

Your reading, as usual, seems very sound & timely; & I regret I can't even begin to keep pace with such a programme. I've just read "Lazarus", by Henri Beraud—a remarkable study of a vivid phase of madness—& "Witch Wood", by John Buchan, which treats of the workings of the witch cult in 17th century Scotland. The things I most wish to get hold of now are "The Dark Chamber" by Leonard Cline, "The Place Called Dagon" by Herbert S. Gorman, & the new Dunsany book—"The Blessing of Pan."[2] My library has increased only through the "Lazarus" aforementioned—a gift from Long—& "The Monk & the Hangman's Daughter", given to me by the old fellow who claims to be the principal author of it. His controversy with Bierce over the primary credit for this little masterpiece will be further elaborated in the forthcoming book of memoirs which I may revise. Meanwhile he has—on the strength of a letter written in 1900 in which Bierce seems to acknowledge his own lesser participation—persuaded the present publishers of the book (A. & C. Boni) to omit the Bierce preface in future editions & substitute an explanatory note of his own. Personally, I think that both Bierce & Danziger-de Castro take too much credit. From internal evidence I'd say that all the strength of the book came from one who was both an artist & intimately acquainted with the wild Bavarian countryside described. This points to the original German author, Prof. Richard Voss of Heidelberg, from whose tale I feel certain de Castro did no more than make a literal translation. Having seen his own crude fiction, I'll guarantee he never wrote a story like that!

Long has just lent me a couple of books which I'm about to read—"Memoirs of a Justified Sinner" by James Hogg, (the Ettrick Shepherd) & "The Barge of Haunted Lives" by J. Aubrey Tyson. I read the latter in the *All*

Story Magazine over twenty years ago, but shall be glad to go through it again. Probably, though, it will impress me less today.

With best wishes—

most sincerely & cordially yrs

HPL

Notes

1. Ten of DAW's sonnets were published in *WT* under the heading *Sonnets of the Midnight Hours* between May 1928 and March 1929. DAW had notified HPL of their acceptance in a letter dated 31 January 1928.

2. When AWD came across HPL's description of *The Dark Chamber* in his "List of Certain Basic Underlying Horrors Effectively Used in Weird Fiction" (see item 52, *CE* 2.173), he assumed it was a plot HPL had conceived, and thus used the description as the genesis of the "posthumous collaboration" "The Ancestor" (1954).

[77]   [ALS]

Saturday [18 or 25 February,
or 3 March 1928]

Dear A. W.—

Wright will certainly have to be broken in on longer stories from you! Keep it up—he'll capitulate sooner or later! I reread "The Tenant" in the current issue, & was just as favourably impressed as I was the first time. A fine story—& the best in the issue so far as I've read it. That "Eighth Green Man" was a curious mess. Something could have been done with the basic idea & atmospheric setting if the author had been even half-way competent; but as it is, the result is abysmally crude & chaotic. Good luck with your Baird play—& with the later ones, which I presume are intended for the same destination.

I'm looking forward to "The Dark Chamber". "The Place Called Dagon" sounded promising in the reviews—& interested me because I know the geographical setting in central Massachusetts. As you say, though, it may disappoint me. I saw an advertisement of Priestley's "Old Dark House" the other day, & think I shall try to get hold of it soon.

Glad you find time for the old amidst the new—Mark Twain is never stale—but what a capacity for rapid-fire absorption you have! I think I told you I read "Goat Song" last summer. Don't miss it—it has a marvellous atmosphere of menace.

Almost paralysed with fresh revision just now—may have to turn some over to Long.

Best wishes—

Most cordially & sincerely yrs

H P L

[78]   [ALS]

March 11[, 1928]

My dear Mr. Derleth:—

The publishers *didn't* send me a copy of the magazine with "Cool Air", but I condescended to buy one. I haven't read it yet, & don't feel in any hurry to do so. The frontispiece is the best thing about it. Whoever does that work is the best weird tale illustrator in the magazine field today— wish W.T. could lure him away from his present berth! "Cool Air" only brought me $18.00. I haven't counted the words, but fancy this rate is only half or ¾ as much as the normal W.T. rate.[1]

I have just received a card from the library saying that "The Dark Chamber" is being reserved for me, & expect to have it tomorrow. From all accounts, I fancy it is the season's best weird output; hence I am all expectancy for the coming treat. Cline, the author, is all through with his trial now. He pleaded guilty to *manslaughter* & got off with one year's imprisonment because of justifying circumstances—the victim having been unduly attentive to the author's wife.

Your reading list, as usual, staggers me with its amplitude. What most excites my envy is "The Wind in the Rosebush", which I have been vainly trying to get for the last decade. It is not in any library in Providence, Brooklyn, or New York City—though I don't think I've tried Boston yet. One story from it—"The Shadows on the Wall"—is in the "Lock & Key Library"[2] which I own; & it was this which made me anxious to see the rest.

The Modern Library indeed makes a good appearance, though I haven't bunched my volumes together. My shelves are all arranged by *classes,* hence the units of any one "library" like the Modern or Everyman's are all scattered about. Now & then a group naturally comes together, but not often. In general, my shelves are a tough-looking mess, with dilapidated old volumes clearly in the majority. I'm no bibliophile, but merely seek what is in the various tomes irrespective of their mechanical makeup or condition. I seldom buy a new book—my only lavish orgy of the kind being when J. C. Henneberger (former owner of W.T.) paid off his back debts to me in 1924 with a $60.00 order on Scribner's instead of a somewhat lesser amount in cash. I was in New York then, so did my marketing in person, Frank B. Long accompanying me to help choose. I took everything of Machen's in stock, made my Dunsany collection complete, & put the rest of the order into books on Georgian architecture & colonial antiquities. It was a great afternoon![3]

I trust that all your current literary productions may develop well. I am utterly swamped with revision, & don't know when I'll ever be out of the woods. I just fixed a *weird* story for a client in Kansas City, so if you ever see a tale in print called "The Curse of Yig", you'll know that I came damn close to writing the whole thing.

Sincerely yrs

HPL

Notes

1. "Cool Air" has roughly 3,440 words, and so the rate was ½¢ a word, well below what *WT* was paying HPL.
2. "The Shadows on the Wall" by Mary E[leanor] (Wilkins) Freeman is in vol. 9 of Julian Hawthorne's *Lock and Key Library*.
3. See *SL* 1.355–56.

[79]   [ALS]

Tuesday [March 20, 1928]

My dear A. W.:—

I am interested to hear of the new editorship of *T of M & M*, & wonder if it would be of any use to re-submit any of the stuff which Gibson rejected.[1] I trust that some of your material may land—though only Heaven knows what can be the selective principle among editors who print the sort of junk which forms ⅞ of both W.T. & its new contemporary! Let us hope, too, that a little emendation will place your detective story with Baird.

"The Dark Chamber" is *magnificent*—a work of art from start to finish, & the greatest continuous prose-poem of macabre morbidity that recent American literature can boast. It is truly *lyrical* in tone, & builds up with an exquisite selectiveness of detail an atmosphere of almost incredible distortion & malignity. If it has any faults, they are the dual ones of diffuseness of background-building incident & preciosity in the choice of singular & allusive words—but these points become negligible when the astonishing power & excellence of the whole are considered. The creeping terror of Richard Pride's quest for an ancestral memory behind humanity—behind life itself—becomes a breathless & ominous reality to the reader. Ugh! The *odour* toward the last—& the madness of the sinister hound Tod, who seems to share his master's soul! Don't miss this tale—& if you must needs *own* all the books you read, rest assured that your cash will not be misspent in securing it! Long says "The Place Called Dagon" is very poor, but I mean to read it just the same. Meanwhile I see that our magazine friend A. Merritt—of "Moon-Pool" fame—has come out with a cloth-bound novel entitled "Seven Footprints to Satan".[2] I want to see it—along with Priestly's "Old Dark House", Dunsany's "Blessing of Pan", & a new one Belknap tells me about—"The House of Dr. Edwardes" by Francis Beeding. I hope to glimpse that "Wind in the Rosebush" some day. I think you'll find the famous Hoffmann rather a disappointment—as I did when I got hold of his work after an expectant longing for many years. It is *grotesque* rather than convincingly & seriously terrible—being the prototype of some of Poe's attempts to combine levity with sombreness.

I trust your new London book—plus your monocle—will give you all the atmospheric verisimilitude & geographic colour you need for your neo-Holmesian narratives. I must investigate Father Brown—who has so far remained a stranger to me.[3]

With all good wishes,

Most cordially & sincerely yrs

HP

Notes

1. Walter B. Gibson (1897–1985) was editor of *Tales of Magic and Mystery* from December 1927 to April 1928 (a cover was printed for the May 1928 issue, but the magazine did not appear). The magazine folded before a new editor could take the helm.

2. *Seven Footprints to Satan* (1928) serialized in the *Argosy* from 2 July to 1 August 1927.

3. I.e., the Father Brown detective stories of G[ilbert] K[eith] Chesterton (1874–1936).

[80]   [ALS]

April 2[, 1928]

My dear A. W.—

"Coleman's Shoulder" is splendid—full of genuine atmosphere—& I strongly hope it will see print eventually. Your teacher's suggestion is good, unless it means a definite abandonment of the *possibility* of supernatural action. Don't go to that length—leave a *horrible doubt* in the reader's mind. That's the secret of an effective terror-tale.

I also enjoyed "The Lost Ghost"[1] very much. Do you wish it back? If so, it is safe. I had not read it before, & was tickled by the authenticity of the New England dialect. Miss Wilkins caught the characteristic idiom of our lower middle classes with admirable fidelity, & her work forms a really valuable historical record now that the dialect is disappearing beneath the onslaught of schools, radio, immigration, & changing ideas & ways of life. In many a backwater village you will still hear some of the older people speaking in much the same manner as Mesdames Meserve & Emerson. I certainly must get hold of "The Wind in the Rosebush" some day.

I shall look for your new stories in W.T. My "Lurking Fear" will appear in June,[2] with an art heading so pleasantly indefinite that it does not especially belie anything in the tale. I trust that Br'er Farnsworth may have a good time in Texas.

I'll pass the word around concerning "The Dance of Death", & may invest myself—although there are others of Blackwood's works which I want more. I mean to get "Incredible Adventures", "John Silence", & "The Listener &c." What is Blackwood's newer work like? I hope he doesn't tend to get mild & insipid with age, as Dunsany does. Dunsany will be fifty next July.

Which reminds me that I've read "The Blessing of Pan". It is full of poetry & music, & winds up in an exquisite vision of delicate beauty, but it has not the strength & substance of early Dunsany work. I have also read Gorman's "Place Called Dagon"—which is rather puerile & poorly written; but which held my interest because of the authentic New England colour & certain isolated bits of weird atmosphere whose merit is undeniable. I advise you to read it. Also re-read Tyson's "Barge of Haunted Lives", which I hadn't seen for over 20 years. It is clever but superficial & artificial.

Thanks for the *T of M & M* tips. As for "7 Footprints to Satan"—I guess I won't bother with it. An *Argosy* detective tale isn't my idea of anything much! I'll look up the Belloc-Chesterton thing[3]—although it seems to me some review said it was *humorous*. My idea of a perfect cipher is a humorous "weird" tale.

I'm going to read James Hogg's "Memoirs of a Justified Sinner" as soon as I can get a spare second to call my own. Belknap is wild over it, & Wandrei thinks it has some magnificent passages of cosmic terror.

Best wishes—

Most cordially yrs—

HPL

Notes

1. By Mary E. Wilkins Freeman.

2. HPL did not make the revisions he always claimed he would make before allowing the story to be reprinted following its appearance in *Home Brew*. The story was not reprinted until after his death.

3. *The Haunted House.*

[81]　　[ALS]

10 Barnes St.,

Providence, R.I.,

April 19, 1928

My dear AW:—

Your new tale is delightful—full of a genuinely poetic quality—& I surely hope that Wright will feel more leniently disposed toward it than he did toward my "Strange High House in the Mist". The central setting suggests some sort of shrine like the one in Dunsany's "Secret of the Sea"—though on a rather different basis. The Sime illustration for that tale always fascinated me. Glad my comment on "Coleman's Shoulder" did not disappoint the judgment which caused you to wait for it before starting revision. I hope to see it in print yet. This reminds me that I liked your collaborated tale in the current W.T. very much. It has real atmosphere—& even caused me a dream on the night after I read it! Bacon of the UAPA also liked it exceedingly. Thanks, by the way, for permission to retain the Wilkins story. If you don't find the tale among your effects I'll be glad to send it back at any time.

I think your choice of Blackwood tales is very good. You're making no mistake in getting "The Dark Chamber". Belknap has just read it, & is as wildly enthusiastic over it as I am. It is a genuine work of art. Your other recent purchases give me the usual & appropriate vertigo. I don't see how you young folks have the energy to imbibe so much in such little time! I must look up Wilder[1]—although I make no attempt whatever to keep abreast of contemporary fiction. I don't believe I'll look very hard for "Seven Footprints", but Belknap tells me that "The House of Dr. Edwardes" is pretty good. That van Dine thing ran in *Scribners*,[2] which my aunt takes, but I wasn't interested enough to wade through the instalments. I can't get interested in detective fiction any more, much as I used to like it in my youth.

I may be obliged to go to New York next week—though I'm not yet sure—& if I do I shall be glad to see Belknap. Just now revisory work is piling up asphyxiatingly—I wish I could depend on placing enough original work to let me out that devastating grind!

Wandrei's book is out at last, & I think Cook has produced a job which does ample justice both to himself & to the poems. You may have seen most of the verses before, but print gives them an added attractiveness.

With best wishes—
    Yr most ob^t Servt
      H P L

Notes

1. Thornton Wilder's *The Bridge of San Luis Rey* (1927) won the Pulitzer Prize for 1927.
2. S. S. Van Dine [pseud. of Willard Huntington Wright (1888–1939)], "The Green Murder Case," *Scribner's Magazine* (January–April 1928); New York: Scribner's, 1928. Van Dine was the creator of the fictional detective Philo Vance.

[82]   [ALS]
Temporary Address for use   395 East 16th St.,
during the next 3 weeks or so[1]   Brooklyn, N.Y.,
                                May 2, 1928.

My dear A W:—
        As you will observe, I am on alien soil just now—circumstances having forced me to be in the N.Y. region for quite a little spell. I don't welcome this sojourn, since I hate N.Y. like poison; but there remains

at least the mitigating fact that I am staying in the one real oasis of old-time leisurely life which the urban area contains—the former village of Flatbush, now technically absorbed by Brooklyn, but still preserving its separate wooden houses, green lawns, & back yards, shady, quiet streets, & other signs of healthy small-town atmosphere which the rest of N.Y. lost long ago. It is pretty well protected by restrictive agreements among property-owners, hence is not likely to be engulfed in the mongrel welter of the metropolis for many decades to come. To hear the silver chimes of the churches on the still air of a vernal Sunday morning, & see the decorous householders straying reposefully along under the delicately-leaving trees, one could scarcely suspect that the din & chaos of 42nd street are only a half-hour away on the subway. There is nothing of New York here—& you may depend on it that I visit the actual metropolitan foci as seldom as possible! During the nine days I have been here, I have only once been above ground in mid-town Manhattan. When I'm not sticking close to Flatbush, I'm to be found in the upper Manhattan or Riverside Drive section where our young friend Frank Belknap Long lives. Later on I shall do some antiquarian exploration, but there'll not be much of novelty to see. I came to know the whole region so painfully well during my two years of residence—1924–26—that nothing has much of a "kick" for me now. I shall be damned glad to get back to colonial Providence & its ancient steepled hill! However, I'm going to improve my presence 200 miles west of my natural habitat by making this the season for exploring such ancient places as lie beyond in this direction. Before I go home I mean to visit Philadelphia & Washington again, & perhaps fare as far south as Richmond & Williamsburg, in Virginia. I want above all things to have a chance to explore the colonial towns of Annapolis & Alexandria—& Williamsburg if I can.

I must look up the *Golden Book*—I took it at first, but found I didn't have time to read it. The other things you mention will also go on my list. Do you know anything about a book called "The Dark God",[2] lately advertised?

Wandrei's book is truly excellent. Cook—who called on me a couple of days before I left home—says that there is one bad misprint, but I haven't found it yet. Cook is now making a book of my story, "The Shunned House", & is having Belknap write an introduction . . . . or rather, *allowing* him to do so at his own request. Personally I think introductions to such small brochures are silly & cumbrous, but Cook & I don't wish to discourage the literary enthusiasm of as promising a youngster as Long. Cook, by the way, is convalescing finely, though still a bit shaky.

It's about time for Brother Farnsworth to be back now, & I surely hope he'll be favourably disposed toward the tales you are sending him. I must try to get some stuff of my own to him soon.

I haven't read Pater's "Concept of Beauty", though I'm really quite interested in the theory of aesthetics from an ignorant layman's point of view. I have always meant to read up on the subject more thoroughly, but something always sidetracks me.

>With all good wishes—
>>Most sincerely yrs—
>>>HPL

Notes

1. HPL was visiting his wife Sonia at this time. They had married in 1924 and divorced in 1929 (although HPL never signed the final divorce papers). HPL finally mentioned to AWD in 1931, after five years of corresponding, that he had once been married.

2. By John Chancellor.

[83]   [ALS]

>395 East 16th St.,
>>Brooklyn, N.Y.,
>>>May 8, 1928.

My dear A. W.:—

I'll let you know all about "The Shunned House" when it appears. Proofs haven't come yet, so I imagine Cook isn't rushing it any. Knowing his usual leisurely ways—& knowing how much work he has on hand just now—I don't anticipate very quick results. Long is going to write a brief preface—although I detest prefaces as a general thing.

Congratulations on your new work! I wish I could snatch the time from revision to do a few original things myself! Hope you have good luck with the novel—I shall be interested to hear of its development as it gradually takes form under your hands.

I've just bought the new *Weird Tales,* but haven't had time to read it yet. Generally speaking, it's a dreary affair from month to month—though not so bad as the other allegedly weird magazines. Hamilton is a pretty good writer on the whole.[1] He undoubtedly derives his cosmic predilections from Charles Fort—the eccentric author of "New Lands" & "The Book of the Damned"—whose admirer & protege he is. This afternoon I heard that the literary editor of *Amazing Stories*—C. A. Brandt—wants to get in touch with me while I am in N.Y. I don't know what proposition he has to make, but I'm not forgetting that his skinflint firm paid me only $25.00 for a story as long as the one for which W.T. gave me $165.00!

You have my sympathy regarding "David Copperfield". Dickens bores me painfully, & I wonder how I ever had the patience to read him through in youth! I think the only two Dickens tales which I ever really enjoyed are "Barnaby Rudge" & "A Tale of Two Cities".

So far I haven't been in downtown New York much, hence have not been exposed to many bookshop temptations. To date I have bought only two books—Adlington's Apuleius & Burnaby's Petronius,[2] which I have long wished as items in my modest classical library. I got these volumes—perfectly new, & normally priced at $2.50 each—at one dollar apiece; a bargain which, like beginners' luck in gambling, may lure me into further indulgences in the dangerous domain of bookbuying.

The old gang had a well-attended meeting last Wednesday, & expects to have another tomorrow night. With Long, Talman, & myself, there will be three W.T. writers present. Quite a conclave. We expect to have as a guest the rising poet Clifford Gessler of Hawaii—editor of the Honolulu Star-Bulletin.[3]

With all good wishes—

Most cordially & sincerely yrs—
H P L

Notes

1. A possible reference to Edmond Hamilton, "The Dimension Terror," *WT* (June 1928).
2. Lucius Apuleius (2nd century C.E.), *The Golden Asse of Lucius Apuleius,* tr. William Adlington, anno 1566 (London: Chapman & Dodd, [1898]; *LL* 38); T. Petronius Arbiter (1st century C.E.), *The Satyricon of T. Petronius Arbiter* (Burnaby's Translation, 1694), intro. Martin Travers (London: Simpkin, Marshall, Hamilton, Kent, [1923]; *LL* 688).
3. Clifford Gessler (1893–?), author of *Kanaka Moon* (New York: Dodd, Mead, 1927).

[84]   [ANS][1]

[Postmarked Grand Central Annex, N.Y.,
date obliterated, 1928]

My dear A W:—

Here's hoping you'll come through with all your examinations successfully—as I'm sure you will. I trust, too, that you'll enjoy your call at the House of La Follette.[2] You're certainly picking up material for a first-rate political novel! The note from Miss Gale[3] is good evidence of your growing assimilation into the world of recognised authors—I guess it'll suggest its own answer when you come to study it more closely. Wisconsin seems to be quite a haven for the literary! I shall await your contemplated new tale with great interest. You young people surely do have unlimited energy! I shall have to shelve revision & write a story myself pretty soon! Trust you'll have good luck with the play, & that its reception will fulfil all your expectations & justify all your labour. ¶ I shall be moving on tomorrow—not directly to West Shokan, as I had expected, but to Vermont for a week first; a friend having invited me with an urgency not to be denied. While there, I expect to get in touch with W. Paul Cook—since Athol isn't so very far off. I shall no doubt drop you cards from various places of interest. Glad you're back home for a spell, & will wager you'll enjoy it. ¶ Regards—Sincerely,

H P L

[On front:] This is one of the rural villages near N.Y. which my exploits have been covering.

Notes

1. Front: Panorama of Richmond. Staten Island, N.Y.

2. HPL refers to the powerful Wisconsin political family that included Robert M. La Follette (1855–1925), U.S. Senator (1905–25) and Progressive candidate for president in 1924; his elder son, Robert M. La Follette, Jr. (1895–1953), U.S. Senator (1925–46); and his younger son, Philip F. La Follette (1897–1965), governor of Wisconsin (1931–33; 1935–39).

3. AWD published a biography of Zona Gale (1874–1938), *Still Small Voice: The Biography of Zona Gale.* He dedicated his novel *Wind over Wisconsin* to her.

[85] [ANS][1]

[Postmarked Brooklyn, N.Y.,
19 May [1928]

My dear A. W.—

Glad to hear of the further acceptance, & hope that the other tales may also find favour. Wright is giving you quick verdicts—two of my clients sent him stories almost 3 weeks ago without having any results yet. ¶ Belknap & I are putting a revision advertisement in Weird Tales.[2] ¶ I must look into this matter of *Mystery Stories.* I recall your saying recently that Sampson (who rejected "Cthulhu") is no longer editor. ¶ Just now I'm being pestered incessantly—in person & by telephone—by that old duffer who wants me to revise his Bierce memoirs.[3] He wants me to waive advance pay & accept a promise of a share in the profits—but I'll be eternally damned if I do! I'll see $150.00 hard cash before I'll lift a pen on the job! ¶ Belknap is now writing an introduction to my "Shunned House", & I fancy the book will be ready in a couple of months. You'll see a copy as soon as it's out. If cash holds out, I may be starting on my Southern trip soon.

Yr ob^t H P L

Notes

1. Front: Soldiers and Sailors Arch, Brooklyn N.Y.

2. FBL and HPL placed the following ad in the August 1928 *WT:*

Frank Belknap Long, Jr.——H. P. Lovecraft
Critical and advisory service for writers of prose and
verse; literary revision in all degrees of extensiveness.
Address
Frank B. Long, Jr., 230 West 97th St., New York, N.Y.

3. I.e., Adolphe de Castro.

[86]   [ANS][1]

[Postmarked Brooklyn, N.Y.,
c. mid-May 1928]

Dear A W:—

Well—I'm glad that Wright took at least *one* story! Cook has just sent me "Shunned House" proofs, but I haven't yet had time to read them. Rushed beyond words! Yes—Cook will have more *Recluses*, & one or the other of your essays will probably be included. Good luck with the Black Narcissus[2]—I can always appreciate the desirability of a good, generous cheque! I'll let you know what Brandt says when I look him up. Certainly, I'm not going to stand for starvation rates again! I dropped Amazing Stories several months ago—Weird Tales being now the only magazine of its kind which I take regularly. You ought to come to N.Y. & look up the gang some time. Had a great motor trip with Long last Friday.

Sincerely yrs

HPL

Notes

1. Front: Soldiers and Sailors Arch, Brooklyn N.Y.
2. "The Adventure of the Black Narcissus."

[87]   [ALS]

Saturday [19 or 26 May 1928]

My dear A W:—

Glad to hear of your two successes with W.T. Just now I'm rather elated to see that two of my revision clients have landed very substantial stories with Wright—thus giving my critical services quite a practical testimonial. Watch for them & see if you can recognise my style—"The Last Test", by Adolphe de Castro, & "The Curse of Yig", by Zealia Brown Reed. I am quite eager to see your new tale—in the manner of "Coleman's Shoulder"—& hope you will not fail to lend it to me when it is finished.

I'm not exactly surprised to hear that *Tales of Magic & Mystery* has entered the long night of oblivion, but hope that the chief staff artist will eventually drift over to W.T.[1] He's too good to be lost! Too bad Baird proved adverse after so much indecision. He's even worse than Wright—having used the same vacillating policy repeatedly in connexion with Belknap's stories.

Good luck with "Vanity Fair" & your Pater essay. I read "Marius"[2] many years ago, & was greatly impressed with its importance as a study in philosophy & aesthetics. I'm sure your political satire will be interesting—your personal acquaintance with some of the figures will add to its piquancy & convincingness. The historical novel, too, promises to be highly important—& I surely hope that you can make good arrangements for its publication after it is finished. It ought to command wide interest throughout your region—& beyond.

I've been detained around here longer than I expected to be, but have managed to have a fairly good time notwithstanding. Have made several excursions to scenic & historic regions of late, including one to the Washington Irving Country—Sleepy Hollow, Tarrytown, Sunnyside, &c. There's a fine old Dutch church thereabouts—built in 1685—of which I'll enclose a postcard picture. In New York City the most interesting thing I've seen lately is the birthplace of Theodore Roosevelt, now equipped as a museum. I'll enclose some descriptive matter which may interest you. The upper rooms, fitted up in the Victorian manner, remind me exceedingly of my own birthplace as I first remember it.

With all good wishes,
Most sincerely yrs—
HPL

Notes

1. Earle K. Bergey (1901–1952).
2. William Makepeace Thackeray, *Vanity Fair;* Walter Pater, *Marius the Epicurean.*

[88]   [ANS][1]

[Postmarked Brooklyn, N.Y.,
2 June 1928]

Yes—literary acceptance is surely a matter of ups & downs! Here's hoping the ups will predominate increasingly in your case. Don't expect too much of Collier's—the standard magazines are almost beginner-proof. ¶ As I have said before, the versatility & energy you display in organising theatrical ventures certainly form something very enviable indeed. You must have unlimited patience & enthusiasm alike! ¶ I surely wish you the best of luck with your historical novel—& know it will amply justify all the keen interest lately displayed in it. Slow, painstaking workmanship & gradual condensation form an ideal policy. ¶ I'm sure your "A" on the Pater essay wasn't as undeserved as you fear. No doubt you adopted the right course concerning "Vanity Fair"—though an astonishing number of critics persist in calling it one of the few great novels of our literature. I can imagine the feelings with which your essay was received! ¶ My antiquarian tours continue. The old house shown on this card is within the legal limits of N.Y. City. Wednesday I shall go up the Hudson to see a friend who has just landed a piece in W.T.[2]
Sincerely—
H P L

Notes

1. Front: Old Perry Estate showing Old Bucket Well Elmhurst, L.I., N.Y. [HPL's note:] Central portion built in *1661*
2. Bernard Austin Dwyer, "Ol' Black Sarah" (verse), *WT* (October 1928).

[89]   [ANS]

[Postmarked Athol, Mass.,
c. 18 June 1928]

Visiting a connoisseur of the weird at Athol, & making some splendid side trips into historic country. Have seen historic Deerfield, & have been in Vermont & New Hampshire as far north as Lake Sunapee. The country all around here is exquisitely mountainous & scenic.

Regards—H P Lovecraft

H Warner Munn
    W. Paul Cook

Cook is about to send you a famous paper of his, dated some years ago, a National Amateur for July 1919.[1]

Notes

1. Although this issue of the *National Amateur* (41, No. 6) is dated July 1919, Cook did not publish it until roughly two years later, apparently shortly after the NAPA election in the summer of 1921. Thus, it contains HPL's "The Picture in the House," written in December 1920, and "Idealism and Materialism—A Reflection."

[90]   [ANS][1]

[c. mid-July 1928]

Dear AW—I think "The Lilac Bush" is splendid—masterly in its suggestiveness & restraint. Keep it up! Did you say that Wright rejected this? If so, he is a greater ass than I thought him. Good luck with the newer material. ¶ I knew you'd like "The Dark Chamber". Cline will be out of prison in a couple of months, I am told; & has meanwhile "got religion" & become a Roman Catholic. ¶ I must see both "Lukundoo" & "The Dark God". Meanwhile I have read Hogg's "Memoirs of a Justified Sinner" & Esther Forbes' new "Mirror for Witches". Haven't had time to read the new W.T. at all. ¶ Congratulations on the cheque from *Mystery Stories!* I must try them with material soon. ¶ "The Shunned House" is all printed but not yet bound. Belknap contributed an excellent brief introduction. ¶ Am still on the move. After visiting Vermont I spent a week with Cook in Athol, & another week with other friends in rural Mass. Then I went over the Mohawk Trail & down the Hudson, & have since explored Philadelphia, Baltimore, (where I saw the grave of Poe) Annapolis, & Washington. Am getting nearly broke now, so will be home soon. Yr obt Servt

HPL

Notes

1. Not postmarked. Front: Carpenters' Hall, Philadelphia, Pa.

[91]   [ALS]

Home Again
July 25[, 1928]

My dear A. W.—

I read "The Deserted Garden" with much interest, & hope that it may eventually find editorial lodgment in some form or other. It is perhaps not as compactly finished as some of your other tales, but nevertheless has fine atmospheric material in the central portions descriptive of the garden. The early parts, I would be inclined to say, are a little too cheerfully matter-of-fact to harmonise with the main action; & if I were you I would not retain the elementary didactic paragraph inserted for Wright's benefit. I would also make the denouement & ending less diffuse & explanatory—let the actual climax be more cataclysmic & less anticipated. Also—I'd try to find another marvel to serve as climax, since the mark of the goat-hoof has been rather famously used by E. F. Benson in "The Man Who Went Too Far".[1] But I repeat that the atmosphere of the middle of the story is very fine, & I surely hope that you will continue working on it. If I were you I'd spend more time on the nicer points of the style—avoiding slightly awkward constructions such as split infinitives & frequently repeated pronouns. It might add to the story's power to omit the touch of jauntiness inherent in the ceremonious repetition of the hero's full name & title every now & then.

I'd like to see you new tales when they are available, especially the one which you compare with "The Lilac Bush". The idea of a book of your collected stories is a good one, & I hope you & Cook can advantageously arrange for such a thing. Unfortunately I can't give an idea of his publishing prices, since I am not paying for "The Shunned House". This venture is all Cook's own—I would never pay a cent to get anything of mine published, since I don't believe there's any profit in it, & I'm too old to care about seeing my name in print. Cook had the idea that he wanted to publish "The Shunned House", & is doing it despite my solemn warnings that he'd better not unless he wants to lose money. It's all his funeral—& I really don't know how much it is costing him. I think the book of Belknap's poems cost $125.00, whilst the larger volume of Bullen's posthumous poems came somewhere around $500.00. A book of the length you intend, if not especially ornate in format, ought to be about $500.00 or somewhat less if done at Cook's very low prices.

"The Shunned House" will not be bound & issued for some time, since Cook has a paid-in-advance job which comes ahead of it. Just how much per copy he will charge I really don't know. It ought not to be more than a dollar, though I fear he won't meet expenses unless he charges more.

I shall look for your new tales in coming issues of W.T. Wright has asked to see my "Silver Key" again—though I greatly doubt if he'll accept it after all. It is frankly non-popular in nature, & I never at any time fancied he would care for it.

My trip is now a thing of the past, & as I look back upon it three things stand out as definite "high spots"—the crowded green hills & brook-haunted glens of Vermont, the colonial charm & quaintness of Annapolis, Md., & the awesome hush & mystery of the *Endless Caverns* at New Market, Va.[2] Did I send you a booklet about the latter? If not, let me know & I will quickly do so. These caves are an inspiration to any lover of the fantastic & the macabre—& especially so to me, since I had never before seen a cave despite the reams I have written about the gruesome secrets of the nether world. At last I have seen the real thing—& I can assure you it was no disappointment.

Most cordially & sincerely yrs—

HPL

Notes

1. See letter 267.

2. HPL recorded his impressions of his 1928 travels in the essay "Observations on Several Parts of America" (1928).

[92]   [ALS]

10 Barnes St.,

Providence, R.I.,

August 4, 1928.

My dear A. W.—

I am enclosing the booklet of the Endless Caverns, & also the Haldeman-Julius book containing Benson's "Man Who Went Too Far". Please return the latter, since one can never be sure of the permanence of some of these H-J items, & I might be unable to get another copy. If I were you I'd try to get one for yourself—I think it's Benson's best tale except "Negotium Perambulans" & "The Horror-Horn".[1]

Thanks in advance for "The Oldest God"[2]—which I've read, & which Belknap owns, but which I wouldn't mind seeing again. The thing as a whole was a bit namby-pamby in its ethicality & allegory, but there are some excellent passages & moments of atmospheric suspense.

Your new acquisitions all sound good, especially "They Return at Evening".[3] I've seen several reviews of the latter, & have been intending to look it up. I believe that better weird writing—subtler & more convincing—is being done today than at any other time in literary history; hence I am always eager to come across a new production in this line.

I shall be glad to see your various new tales when you have available copies. Yes—I fancy that Wright's willingness to take "The Silver Key" (which he has just formally accepted at $70.00) is due entirely to the tone of his correspondents. He sent me a copy of the September "Eyrie" which formed quite a floral garland for my unworthy & insignificant self.[4] I have at last snatched the time—through a high-handed neglect of other tasks which may cost me added labour in the end—to attempt some more writing of my own; & am now on the 22nd manuscript page of a long short story to be called "The Dunwich Horror". The action takes place amongst the wild domed hills of the upper Miskatonic Valley, far northwest of *Arkham,* & is based on several old New England legends—one of which I heard only last month during my sojourn in Wilbraham. In construction, it is one of the *double climax* sort—& I am now working on the second & final horror. It is not quite so restrained in tone as "The Colour Out of Space", nor yet so flamboyant as "Randolph Carter" or my earlier work in general. It belongs to my realistic rather than to my prose-poetic group, & is so horrible in conception & incident that I rather fear Wright may be afraid to print it, as he was my "In the Vault". If he does take it, it will bring a gorgeously gratifying cheque; for the whole thing ought to make almost 30 typed paged when done.

I had a call Monday from young H. Warner Munn of Athol, our fellow-contributor to W.T. He was passing through Providence in the course of a motor trip, & stopped most of the day. In the late afternoon I piloted him for about 20 miles of his course toward New York, leaving him at the quaint village of East Greenwich & coming back by trolley. In N.Y. he will look up Wandrei (who is rooming only 2 blocks from my old place at 169 Clinton St., scene of "The Horror at Red Hook") & Belknap also if the latter is home from his own trip. Incidentally, when Munn & I were in Eddy's book shop Monday, (this Eddy is uncle of the C. M. Eddy Jr. who writes for W.T.) we met the venerable Joseph Lewis French, editor of the anthology "Ghosts, Grim & Gentle". He is a quaint, peppery-voiced old codger of 70.

With every good wish, & hoping you will like "The Man Who Went Too Far", I remain

Yr most oblig'd & ob[t]

HPL

Notes

1. Both stories are in Benson's *Visible and Invisible;* the former in included in *WK.*

2. By Stephen McKenna.

3. By H. Russell Wakefield.

4. In "The Eyrie," *WT* (September 1928), W. H. Wakefield, Donald G. Ward, Alvin V. Pershing, L. D. Kingery, and H. F. Scotten discussed HPL's "The Outsider," "The Call of Cthulhu," and "The Lurking Fear."

[93]   [ALS]

August 12[, 1928]

My dear A. W.—

Glad you found the Benson tale worth reading. Those titles in "They Return at Evening" sound very alluring to me—I prefer non-committal, non-sensational titles as a general rule; especially when the stories are themselves subtle & elusive in their weirdness. I shall certainly get the book as soon as it reaches the local libraries, & anticipate an exceedingly pleasant session with it. The author is surely a man to be watched in future, & I hope his macabre vein is still far from exhausted. I noted the other day a review of a new book of twelve connected short stories by John Buchan, called "The Runagates' Club" & described as distinctly weird. Buchan's literary past does not altogether recommend him, but "Witch Wood" is in his favour. I think I shall look the thing up, though I doubt whether it will ever get as far as the pages of that hypothetical second edition of my weird story article.

I note your programme with much interest, & sympathise greatly concerning the obstacles you have encountered as a dramatic producer. It is hard enough, I imagine, to stage a performance even under the most auspicious conditions; while the addition of obstacles forms nearly a last straw. But I am sure you will triumph over all disasters, & come out in the end with a successful season behind you. The various vaudeville numbers will doubtless form an attractive seasoning for the main drama—you seem to have selected & arranged them very cleverly.

Yes—I read the programme advertisements with great appreciation, & regret that I dwell so far from such a centre of uniformly high quality & efficient service. Pardonable pride & metropolitan assurance are no monopolies of the thickly populated centres, & such a balanced array of healthy & growing industries may be said to indicate an economic soundness prophetic of that prosperity which is the forerunner of aesthetic maturity & cultivated leisure.

I finished my story Tuesday night, & am now struggling with the loathsome task of typing the damn thing. It will probably make all of 50 double-spaced pages, & I hope Wright will look favourably upon it.

With best wishes for the play &c—

Yr most & obᵗ Servᵗ

HPL

P.S. "The Oldest God" came safely. Many thanks!

[94]   [ALS]

August 20, 1928

My dear A. W.—

I have just read the two stories—which I return herewith—& like them both very much. On the whole, I think I prefer "The Whistler", whose climax has unusual force & originality. The other is very well written, though the main idea has been used quite frequently before. It seems very odd that Wright returned them, for they are infinitely better than the majority of the stuff he prints. I note that you prefer the dialogue form as a medium of expression—a circumstance which perhaps indicates that you are a playwright at heart. I myself am the exact opposite. My purpose in writing a tale is to delineate a certain visual picture or crystallise a certain atmospheric effect—in which human beings are only incidental "properties". For this mode of conception or presentation, straight narration is the only—or at least the most—fitting form; hence I adhere to it quite largely in most of my effusions. My new story has more spoken material than any I have written for a long time—since I use the alarmed stories of rustics as a medium for describing the hideous presence which lumbered about Dunwich after a certain being was killed. You'll see this tale eventually—whether in print or otherwise . . . . . probably otherwise.

Your meeting with the La Follette scion must have been somewhat interesting—& I trust he duly appreciated the theatrical material presented to him. I am glad to hear, by the way, that the programme went off successfully; as indeed I felt sure it would do. I feel confident, likewise, that you obtained equal success with the show "on the road". Here's wishing you a substantial financial profit in addition to the artistic glory!

I've been too busy with old material to look up "They Return At Evening", but I am still eagerly anticipating it. I may purchase it if I like it upon perusing it at the library. I shall also set down on my list "The Beast with Five Fingers".[1] Just now I am reading "The Elixir of Life", by Arthur Ransome, one of several books lent me by W. Paul Cook. While there is considerable vapid romanticism in it, a pall of genuine horror hangs over the setting; & I do not hesitate in pronouncing it distinctly worth perusal. I have also read lately those old Radcliffe standbys—"The Italian" & "The Romance of the Forest"—neither of which is really weird according to my standard.

Wright sent me proofs of the last few tales I had in W.T.—for which I was rather grateful, insomuch as it enabled me to prevent some of the little misprints which occur in nearly all the earlier stories. I don't like the proofreading process intrinsically, but I am willing to undergo it for the sake of its results.

With all good wishes—

Most sincerely yrs—

HPL

Notes

1. By W. F. Harvey.

[95]   [ALS]

Friday [31 August 1928]

My dear AW:—

          I like "The Pacer" exceedingly—it is really one of the best
things you have done so far. The atmosphere & suspense are very convincing, & the denouement is powerful enough to justify the elaborate preparation. If Wright doesn't take it, I shall believe that his recent lucid interval was
a phenomenally brief & insubstantial one. As for a criticism—as usual, I'd
suggest your taking a little more pains regarding the fine points of style—
precise selection of words, avoidance of repetition, skilful management of
rhythm & tone-colour, &c. &c. Be careful about the spelling, too—you have
the name JONATHAN a bit off, & also NON-EXISTENT. Now as to the
actual structure—the most obvious fault is having the grave distinguishable
as a *mound*. If Brent had wished to conceal the body he certainly wouldn't
have raised a *mound*—the conventional symbol of a grave—over his victim's
place of interment. And mounds don't sprout of themselves above inhumed
corpses! The best way to suggest a grave is to have a spot where the grass
does not grow well—a spot shaped something like a man. That likewise suggests the essentially horrible & unholy nature of what lies beneath. One
other thing—you are aware, I suppose, that fastidious technicians frown on
the delineation of incidents which leave no survivor to tell about them; since
a story seems much less convincing when it flatly contradicts all conceivable
possibility. Careful authors always avoid killing off all the witnesses or destroying all the evidence of a given scene or happening—for if all record is
lost, how is the teller of the tale supposed to know about it? Eminent authors sometimes violate this canon, as Poe did in "The Masque of the Red
Death"; but it doesn't pay a modern author to copy such exceptional cases.
Now you have no way to explain how you know what Larkins saw or what
his actions in the death scene were. Could you have him call somebody up
on the telephone toward the last, & gasp out an account of what was confronting him?[1] Could you have him attempt to photograph the thing & have
the negative developed afterward?[2] Could you have him try to scrawl a last
message to the world?[3] Something like that is really necessary if the story is
to be perfect. Lastly—I'd use a little more care, detail, & *striking novelty &
originality* in describing the monster. I spent enormous pains thinking out
Cthulhu, & still more in devising the two blasphemous entities that figure in
my new "Dunwich Horror". It's a good thing to work *slowly & carefully*, &
never to set anything down until you can see & feel it poignantly & realistically yourself. My advice to all writers is to cut out all "dash" & jauntiness
with a relentless hand; using instead a quiet, deadly objectivity *& seriousness*
of tone, & a careful & scholarly attention to plausibility & accuracy of detail,
which will serve in the end to build up a haunting atmosphere of convin-

cingness & realism. But don't mind these trifling remarks on details. It's a fine story, & Wright will surely take it if he has any sense.

As I have said, I congratulate you sincerely on the recent acceptances, & hope such events will keep up frequently in future. You may be amused to hear that a bit of my prose[4] is going into a child's 7th grade reader published by Macmillan & edited in your own college town of Madison. No—it isn't a *horror,* but an extract from a letter describing Sleepy Hollow, used as a local-colour note to Irving's celebrated classic. It was written to my friend Moe, who is collaborating on the reader series with Profs. Moffett & Sterling A. Leonard;[5] & he thought he'd like to see it in the books. Finding Moffett & Leonard willing, he chucked it in—so I shall live in after years on the tongues of babes yet unborn. Exegi monumentum aere perennius &c![6] ¶ Best regards—H P L

Notes

1. Cf. HPL's "The Statement of Randolph Carter" (1919) and "The Dunwich Horror" (1928).

2. Cf. HPL's "Pickman's Model" (1926).

3. Cf. HPL's "Cool Air" (1926).

4. "Sleepy Hollow To-day," an extract from "Observations on Several Parts of America."

5. Harold Y. Moffett and Sterling A. Leonard were textbook writers. See also letter 126n3 re Leonard.

6. "I have reared a monument more lasting than brass." (Horace's prophetic assessment of the value of his poems, *Odes* 3.30.1.)

[96]   [ALS]

Thursday [6 September 1928]

My dear AW:—

I shall be interested to hear of the fate of "The Pacer" after its collaborative emendation. It is a good story, & I'm sure I don't see why Wright rejected it—as if there were any reason to expect consistency in that estimable dictator! I shall look forward to seeing "#7"[1] in print—as well as the others scheduled for later dates.

"Carnate Crystal" in the current W.T. is something of a tragedy. The idea is splendid—more or less of what I was groping for in "The Colour Out of Space"—but the craftsmanship is so naive & inartistic that most of the effectiveness is lost. I agree with you that "The City of Lost Souls" is the best thing in the issue. Munn's effort—I read the whole tale in MS. a year ago— has romantic facility, but to my mind he seldom achieves real *weirdness.* He is, though, a very capable writer, & ought to have quite a future ahead of him. Wright tells him that his collected "Ponkert" tales will form the third book of a W.T. series beginning with "The Moon Terror"—my own tales forming the second. Personally I'd wager that much time will elapse before W.T. publishes any more volumes. I wonder if you noted the verses "Ol' Black Sarah", by Bernard Dwyer. He is an excellent correspondent of mine, & a man of genuine fantastic talent both in writing & in drawing. Wright has so far rejected all his prose offerings.

I shall at once put "Death in the Dusk" on my list.[2] And incidentally—what was that other book you recommended in addition to "They Return At Evening"? I've been trying to find your letter mentioning it, but don't succeed. I don't know when I'll get time to do any reading. I'm so rushed now that I fear I'll never finish the books Cook lent me. I'm on the Asquith anthology of ghost tales now—the best things in it so far being Blackwood's "Chemical", L. P. Hartley's "Visitor from Down Under", Walpole's "Mrs. Lunt", & De la Mare's "A Recluse".

I haven't sent "The Dunwich Horror" to Wright yet, but both Belknap & Dwyer speak very encouragingly of it. I must pack it off pretty soon, & get the question of its fate over with. If it doesn't land, I'll send you the rejected MS. at once.

With best wishes—

Most cordially & sincerely yrs—
HPL

Notes

1. "The Tenant at Number 7."
2. By Virgil Markham.

[97]   [ALS]

Friday [14 September 1928]

My dear A. W.:—

I hope to hear favourable news of "The Pacer", as well as of the new story on which you & your colleague are working. The plot of the new one sounds promising—I always like those tales that hint of the survival of strange local influences. Your other literary efforts are surely multifarious, & I trust a fair percentage of them may win favour amongst the editors. What is this new Macfadden thing like? His *Ghost Stories* represented about the nadir of banal cheapness. Is that thing still running? Apropos of detective stories— I've just come across as striking a *forerunner* of the type as Voltaire's "Zadig." It is one of the brief tales in "The Sheik of Alexandria" by Wilhelm Hauff, (1802–1827) & is entitled "Abner, the Jew Who Saw Nothing".[1] In this little sketch the Jew describes precisely a horse & a dog that he has never seen— using the approved Sherlockian method of footprints, strands of hair, & similar bits of obscure evidence.

I've heard nothing yet about that proposed volume of my tales—that is, nothing except the allusion Wright made in writing to Munn—hence don't anticipate any early appearance—if indeed any appearance at all! Naturally Wright would be grateful to you (& so would I if there's any cash in it!) for any such stimulation of its sale as you could effect around Madison if it ever does really come out. I haven't sent "The Dunwich Horror" yet. Incidentally—I told Wright a year ago, when he was discussing the possible book, that I thought the best title would be "The Outsider & Other Stories".[2] He seemed to agree about it. The title for Munn's book ought to be "The Were-wolf of Ponkert".

Wright was as puzzled as you over the de Castro-Danziger riddle when "The Last Test" reached him. The fact is that Gustav Adolf Danziger & Adolphe de Castro are one & the same individual, the somewhat flighty & eccentric scribbler having changed his name in 1917 in deference to the popular Germanophobia of the period. He is a strange old bird—half Pole & half Jew, educated in the German universities, & a resident of San Francisco during early manhood. He is not, properly speaking, an *author* of "The Monk & the Hangman's Daughter", & neither is Bierce. The novel is a German one, by Richard Voss of Heidelberg, & its original name was "The Monk of Berchtesgaden". De Castro merely translated it—with some omissions—into wretched English, & Bierce turned the wretched English into decent English. Bierce & de Castro both acted like absurd credit-hogs about this tale—indeed, if it weren't for his desire to minimise Bierce's part, de Castro would never be calling attention (as he is doing in his unpublished Bierce memoirs) to the half-forgotten original source. He is now quarrelling with the Boni firm over the credit & copyright, & has tried to persuade W. Paul Cook to publish a new edition with Voss's full text translated & with the illustrations used in the first (Chicago 1893) edition. I did a lot of revision for de Castro—& so did Belknap—last winter & spring, including "The Last Test" which was an unutterable mess to start with. Belknap & I later negotiated about the revision of the coming Bierce book, but the old fox wouldn't come to any decent terns, so we gave him up as a nuisance. He is one of those "big talkers"—trying to impress the world as a potent international figure on the "inside" of all historical crises of the last 40 years. In his way, though, he is both harmless & amusing. I took him to one of our "gang" meetings last May & he made quit a hit!

I'll read "The Fourth King"[3] if I come across it, though I don't go in much for detective material nowadays. Lawrence's "Rocking-Horse Ghost"[4] was rather good. I've read almost nothing of his despite his fame. Was the book you recommended "The Beast with Five Fingers" by Harvey? Belknap recently recommended Housman's "All Fellows & the Cloak of Friendship".

Best wishes—

Most sincerely yrs—H P L

P.S. *The Recluse* is delayed by Cook's other duties & misc. homestead moving, (he bought a farm near Athol) but is by no means abandoned. Munn has just finished an article for it.

Notes

1. Wilhelm Hauff, "Abner, der Jude, der nichts geshen hat," in *Der Scheik von Alessandria und seine Sklaven* (1827), translated as *The Sheik of Alexandria and His Slaves* in *Tales by Wilhelm Hauff*, tr. S. Mendel (1866), among other volumes.

2. AWD and DAW used this title for the collection of HPL's stories that they published in 1939.

3. Apparently *The Fourth King* by mystery writer Harry Stephen Keeler.

4. HPL meant Lawrence's "The Rocking-Horse Winner."

[98]   [ALS]

Thursday [27 September 1928]

My dear A. W.—

"Death in the Crypt"[1] certainly does sound interesting, & I hope to have a look at it presently. At last I've sent "The Dunwich Horror" to Wright, & am—without undue suspense or excitement—awaiting his reply. I'll lend you the MS. as soon as it comes back—but oh! what a cheque those 48 pages would bring if by any miracle it were to land!

I don't believe I could ever place anything in a Macfadden magazine— I'm not versatile enough—but why don't you try it? The first person seems to me the easiest of all persons to write in—so cursedly easy that one has to be on guard against monotonously using it all the time. I steered clear of it in "The Dunwich Horror", yet even so found myself psychologically identifying myself with one of the characters (an aged scholar who finally combats the menace) toward the end.

Your correspondent's side-light on Wright is highly illuminating. Though myself a teetaler who has never tasted liquor, I feel tempted to unearth a local bootlegger (& God knows Providence's Italian quarter is a miniature Chicago of hootch, gang wars, & rackets!) & send Brother Farnsworth a case of synthetic brilliancy! Or—cautious thought—maybe it is the dry, sober spells that are the lucid intervals! Actually, Wright has a great deal to combat in the form of ill health. He has described his trouble to me—a kind of creeping palsy or paralysis called "Parkinson's Disease", which has no known cause, but which threatens to cripple his right hand in future. A friend & physician of his believes he can cure it in the next five years, but Wright (who is past 40) is dismally doubtful & apprehensive. I hope he will come out of it all right, for he really is an admirably amiable, conscientious & honourable person despite his limitations in critical judgment.

No—I didn't notice the "Not at Night" advertisement you mention.[2] Bold plagiarism of titles—but I suppose it's a different anthology. I must look it up.

Which reminds me that I have at last read both "They Return at Evening" & "The Runagates Club". In the former, I think the atmospherically best story is "The Red Lodge", though much is to be said for "He Cometh & he Passeth By", "And He Shall Sing", & "The Seventeenth Hole at Duncaster". The style is a little too matter-of-fact & knowing to produce much of a weird effect—too smart & humorous to contain any subtleties or undertones. Wakefield has copied the M. R. James method, yet has not found James's inner secret of macabre convincingness.

"The Runagates Club" has only three really weird stories in a total of twelve. "The Green Wildebeest" is excellent. "The Wind in the Portico" is a splendid example of our favourite Britanno-Roman survival theme. "Skule Skerry" is a masterful northern atmospheric study, but cruelly, barbarously ruined by a rational explanation.[3] I'd advise you to get the book at the library for the sake of these three items—though I'd scarcely recommend its purchase.

With best wishes,
Most cordially & sincerely yrs
H P L

P.S. I trust Madison seems pleasant after so long an absence. I know just what the town looks like now, for my pedagogical friend Moe sent me an admirable panoramic view of it last summer (how I hate to say "*last* summer"!)—clipped from The Chicago Tribune's rotogravure section. A delightfully attractive lakeside city!

Notes

1. AWD and Mark Schorer, "The Occupant of the Crypt."

2. Edited by Herbert Asbury. The book contained HPL's "The Horror at Red Hook" and AWD's "The Coffin of Lissa," both of which had appeared (as did other titles in the book) in Christine Campbell Thomson's "Not at Night" anthologies. The book was published illegally; see letters 114–15.

3. HPL listed all the Wakefield and Buchan stories mentioned here in "Books to mention in new edition of weird article" and addressed them when he revised SHL.

[99]   [ALS]

Octr. 5, 1928

My dear A. W.—
        Tough luck about "The Pacer", but you're wise in not tinkering with it to suit Wright. It never pays to mix in any ideas save your own. Suggestions are all right when you have the privilege of weighing them & ac-

cepting only those which your own judgment backs up—but don't take anybody else's advice when you really have a strong feeling that your original version is the proper thing. Dollars to doughnuts that Wright will accept "The Pacer" later on without change. That's his way.

Incidentally—he has just accepted my "Dunwich Horror" at *$240.00*; the largest sum any story of mine has ever brought. The MS. runs to 48 pages—no padding, but merely one of the sort of tales that require gradual unfolding.

Sorry your college work is delayed through a technicality. The course sounds very good to me. Are the *education* items due to pedagogical or professional ambitions on your part? Yes—I suppose Madison would pall in time if one were naturally restless. In my own town I am very settled & satisfied. Providence never bores me—for it is a city of extreme landscape beauty & quaint antiquarian charm—& I hope to live all my days & die here, where I was born. *Other* cities, however, *do* bore me after a time if seen continuously. New York & Brooklyn have become such an intolerable monotony that I never want to see the damn places again. Boston is good for about two weeks. Philadelphia & Washington are the only *large* cities I really like, though there are small ones—quaint, ancient places like Newport, Salem, Marblehead, Newburyport, Portsmouth, Annapolis Md., Alexandria Va., & so on—where I could stay on indefinitely almost as happily as at home. My only taste of the Middle West has been a visit of 2 weeks & 3 days in Cleveland six years ago. I liked the city exceedingly, though it had not much to offer my antiquarian side.

As for prohibition—I'm beginning to doubt its value myself, though I was originally an enthusiastic advocate of it. If anything could totally get rid of liquor, it would be a good thing—but the question is whether the present attempt has produced any results comparable to the harm inflicted. However, I'm for Hoover—I think he is the abler man generally, & that the Republican party represents the most basically sound governmental principles. My real *interest* in politics is virtually nil.

As for "Not at Night" anthologies—your mention of the Asbury book coincides with special timeliness with a note just received from *Weird Tales'* London agent. Selwyn & Blount have failed, & no royalties can be paid their authors before next March. Another company has taken over the sale of the remaining books—but I fancy that the new "Gruesome Cargoes"[1] will end the series unless this Asbury person finds a way to take over its good-will.

Oh, yes—the Wakefield book by far eclipses "The Runagates' Club". As I told you, the latter has only three really weird tales. But don't miss "The Wind in the Portico".

Belknap has just written a hellish new story of the 4th dimension—"The Hounds of Tindalos". I hope Wright will take it, though one can never be sure.

With all good wishes—

Most sincerely yrs—
                                    HPL

Notes

1. The contents of *Gruesome Cargoes,* ed. Christine Campbell Thomson, were primarily previously unpublished, unlike the previous volumes in the series.

[100]   [ALS]
                                    Lincoln Woods
                                    Friday [12 October 1928]

My dear A W:—
            Once again I am penning my day's correspondence in my beloved woodlands—now unbelievably gorgeous with the colours of autumn, yet today blessed with the genuine burning heat of summer. I haven't seen any official reports yet, but I'll wager the mercury stands nearer 90° than 85° this minute. And to think of the hideous cold a little way ahead! But anyway, I'm making the most of decent weather while it lasts—doing all the work I can in the open . . . . Just this moment the sun came out from beneath a fleecy cumulus cloud & struck such sparks of gold from the iridescent foliage that I was almost moved to gasp aloud in an aesthetic ecstacy. If you want to know what beauty is—sheer abstract loveliness raised to the nth power—just ramble through a rural New England landscape in October!

            Glad to hear of your success with the new magazine, & hope you can keep on contributing. Your versatility will pay you well—for the detective-story market is a vast one, & much more eager for MSS. than the weird market. Once you get on the right side of a few editors, you ought really to have a very steady line of cheques coming in. Yes—I've heard that the scarlet confession sheets pay enormous prices, but believe that they require a certain knack—a sort of inner comprehension of the psychology of the lowest stratum of tabloid-hounds—which regular authors aren't likely to have. I never tried them, but if I could land $1000 per tale, I'd confess in the most sensational way to any crime in the decalogue! God! Suppose the world knew what lies buried beneath a certain ancient house I once inhabited! In the night . . . . IT comes knocking . . . knocking . . . . But no—I suppose they don't care for the weird touch!

            Here's hoping the magazines will save you from pedagogy—though a good dependable salary is a darned fine thing to fall back on now & then— would that I had one myself! I think you'd get a great deal of benefit from Oxford—you're a quick & encyclopaedic assimilator, & the experience wouldn't be lost on you. Many of my own progenitors were Oxonians—the latest in direct line being my father's maternal grandfather. I'd relish seeing Oxford myself—as an antiquarian—to say nothing of the rest of Old England. I vow I'll get to London some day, if my next move has to be to the poor house.

In the matter of politics—I don't go much with the younger crowd. I'm more interested in keeping the present 300-year-old culture-germ in America unharmed, than in trying out any experiments in "social justice". Smith,[1] to my mind, is a direct exponent of the newer-immigration element—the decadent & unassimilable hordes from Southern Europe & the East whose presence in large numbers is a direct & profound menace to the continued growth of the Nordic-American nation we know. Some people may like the idea of a mongrel America like the late Roman Empire, but I for one prefer to die in the same America that I was born in. Therefore I'm against any candidate who talks of letting down the bars to stunted brachycephalic South-Italians & rat-faced half-Mongoloid Russian & Polish Jews, & all that cursed scum! You in the Middle West can't conceive of the *extent* of the menace. You ought to see a typical Eastern city crowd—swart, aberrant physiognomies, & gestures & jabbering born of alien instincts.

I'm sure you ought to have received royalties from the Not-at-Nights. Belknap has had many cheques for the two tales of his that were reprinted. Better ask Wright about it.

Regards—

　　　　　Sincerely yrs—H P L

P.S. The lower the sun gets, the mellower the light—& the more gorgeous the many-coloured foliage. *Some* day!

Notes

1. Al Smith, governor of New York and Democratic candidate for president in 1928.

[101]　　[ALS]

　　　　　　　　　　　　　　　　Lincoln Woods
　　　　　　　　　　　　　　　　Octr. 17, 1928
My dear A. W.—

　　　　I hate to tantalise you after your rain-blighted quest of autumnal rusticity, but can't help remarking that this is my third successive day in my favourite woodland—each one as fair & summer-like as last Friday! The beauty of this region is beyond description—the outer fringe is typical New England farm country of a century & a half ago, whilst the heart of it goes back to the primitiveness of Indian times. I'm now seated on the edge of a rocky bluff that beetles high above a woodland lake—with a deep, mysterious forest glen on my left, & the autumnally colourful slope of a majestic wooded hill on my right—beyond the small lake. Ahead & behind the forest slopes rise gently—huge rocks cropping out through the leaf-carpeted soil, & all the great trees gaudy in their transient rainbow-hues. Not a human being is in sight—only birds & squirrels—& a mysterious wind rustles the leaves & sends some of them earthward in sibylline gusts. Any man who stays voluntarily in a city on a day like this must have something the matter with him! It certainly is a piece of phenomenally exceptional luck for a town the size of Providence to have a region as primitive & unspoiled as this within a fifteen-minute trolley ride of the business centre.

Well—I've just finished "Those Who Seek", & consider it a genuinely good & absorbing tale. Its revelation lives up to the promise of the preparation—there is no let-down—& that is the most important thing about a weird tale. If I had any criticism to make, it would be that the narration is a little too *diffuse*. You might get to the disappearance of Arnsley with a little less wealth of incident. I also question the advisability of having Phillips notice the left-handed nature of his picture so soon. The actual discovery of a circumstance like that would so stun any ordinary man—& a painstaking artist would know there could be no mistake—that he could not drop quickly back to the normal manner as you have Phillips do. Better defer the discovery somehow for a revelation near the very end. I'd also take a great deal of time & care in re-arranging the details & hints that prepare one for the facing of the mystery. The slab is a good beginning as you have it—only I'd place it earlier. Let the artist & Arnsley be at the abbey when the story opens, & have the remarking of the inscription by Phillips the first incident. Don't let Arnsley be ignorant of it—despite your current grudge against the language. In the first place, any English gentleman's son—presumably a public-school product—would know a simple phrase like that. In the second place, in real life Arnsley would certainly have discussed the whole business with his father years before. By the way—the matter of the *building* is a bit vague. If the present abbey is so *old*, no one today would be likely to know what the previous building looked like. Better have Phillips draw some salient feature which existed within the memory of man, but which was torn down 100 to 200 years before by a populace enraged & frightened by something they had witnessed in connexion with it. If you intend to convey any idea of possible *Roman* origin, don't have *Romanesque* architectural details. Romanesque is the debased-Roman style current in the Dark Ages—what is called "Saxon" in Great Britain. After Phillips's remarking of the slab, let Arnsely recall the sinister tales his father has told. Let this recalling turn his mind to the idea of literally following out the inscription & searching for a crypt. Don't let any mode of opening the crypt be discovered *or even thought of* before Phillips & Arnsley *sleep*. Let Phillips *dream* of the way it is really opened—& let him find that Arnsley (having presumably dreamed the same thing) has actually entered that way. Don't make the incident of the shadow so spectacular. Invent some detail that was *not* in Lord Lord [*sic*] Leveredge's tale, but which is verified later by Father Richards. Also—give a fairly detailed account of the abbey's supposed history. Say it was founded as an abbey by the Saxons in such & such a year—that in so-&-so A.D. the Danes besieged it, but that the besieging party *was never heard of again,* &c. &c. Mention a gruesome incident connected with its destruction by Henry VIII, & so on. Don't give so much space to experiments on the moving of the slab—but have the black figure glimpsed at the moment of some unusually violent attack on the supposed portal. Your central scene is OK as it stands. The mumbled ritual is good. Also—what was found later. Meanwhile don't let Phillips realise quite what he has painted. Assume he has noted the extra detail in the canvas as found upon his return to consciousness, & that he is curiously puzzled thereby—whence his act in bringing it to Father Richards. Have the main talk with the priest occur *before* the picture is shewn, & let Father Richards refer to the features in the original building which are not there now. As he describes them, have Phillips give a start of surprise & produce the picture. Then let the priest start as well, & produce from a cabinet an old engraving precisely paralleling the Phillips painting. This is a good nucleus for the climax.

The foregoing are just impressionistic notes jotted down as I let the story sink in—take 'em or leave 'em, as you like. I'd say the main fault of the tale is a kind of careless construction—looseness & diffuseness of development, & haste & carelessness of characterisation. Go slower—& more thoroughly. Do some more elaboration if you choose. If you want to play up Fate & the inevitable, you could have Arnsley the descendant or reincarnation of one of the old Roman cult members who betrayed his fellows to the governor of the province & caused the temporary stamping-out of the rites. If you do this, make him *curiously Roman-looking*—broad forehead, aquiline nose, firmly set mouth, thick neck, short stature, & so on. But anyhow, there's great stuff in the tale, & as it stands it towers high above the W.T. average. Hope Wright will take it—you never can tell. I fancy his use of certain words & terms as grounds of rejection is merely automatic habit—thoughtless parrotism & unconscious rubber-stampery. He only knows he doesn't think a piece would please his Quinn fans & Nictzin-Dyalhis-hounds, & seizes the first conventional word that comes to mind.

"Bascom Hall" sounds rather interesting to me, insomuch as all my summer mail from my friend Moe had a Bascom Hall return address in the corner. That's where he toiled with Leonard & Moffett on the Macmillan readers. I wonder if he saw any of the *revolting subjects* in the night! Let me see the tale if Wright doesn't. Also your assorted "Deaths".

Sorry you & the language of the Augustans are on the outs. I think the old pedant is to blame, for I can't conceive of anyone's not loving Latin if it is properly presented to him. I dote on it—& so does Arthur Machen in its softened mediaeval forms.

So "Gruesome Cargoes" isn't taken from W.T.! Maybe they wouldn't have failed if they'd stuck to their good old source! Hope you get some royalties from the defunct S & B in the end.

Best wishes—

Yr most ob^t Servt H P L

[102]   [ALS]

Thursday [25 October 1928]

My dear A. W.:—

"165 Bascom Hall" is a splendid short tale, & I really haven't a single suggestion to offer concerning it. Its only possible vulnerable spot is the fact that there is no survivor to account for our knowledge of what Jones saw—a point I also noticed in connexion with one part of "The Pacer"—but I am not inclined to be a stickler about this detail. Poe used a similar licence in "The Masque of the Red Death", & it is found in several later authors of standing, including A. Conan Doyle. The tale as it stands seems to me highly adequate—& the climax is highly original in its mention of the *twisted faces* of the specimens. Dissecting-room tales are of course not new; but if Wright has previously printed anything with a climax like that, it must have been torn out of any copy of W.T. which I've seen! Your English teacher's endorsement was certainly not unmerited. Thanks for the glimpse— I return the tale herewith.

You are certainly fortunate in securing the book-reviewing opportunity— I wish I could stumble across such a chance myself![1] To draw on all the standard publishers for the pick of the season's best books is surely a privilege to be envied. I imagine the reviewing itself doesn't take much time or energy. The hardest part is no doubt the avoidance of those stock phrases & forms of presentation which have come to form a special reviewers' patois.

Congratulations on the Latin-English deal whereby you & your colleague will reap equal intellectual profit. Next year I trust your Latin education will be in the hands of a pedagogue less arbitrary & crotchety than the present ogre.

Glad to hear your "Black Narcissus" will be published reasonably soon, & that the W.T. items are also due for an early appearance. Wright's views on the "Antique Shop" are certainly picturesquely contradictory! I never heard of anyone else so prone to sudden & inexplicable reversals of opinion. I didn't know that Wandrei had run up against this characteristic also.

It seems to me that Wright said something once about the "rights" of my stories, but I was too poor & negligent a business man to pay much attention to it. Anyway, I was supposed to get something for the "Not at Night" reprint. Belknap writes that the collapse of S & B has 'cost him precisely thirty dollars'—& he adds that Wright has commenced to beat him down on the price of stories. His splendid new "Hounds of Tindalos" has been accepted at considerably less than a cent a word. I suppose Brother Farny will start in on me next.

Let me know what the contents of "American Ghost Stories"[2] is if you get your review copy. It may be all familiar material, but then again there may be some less known piece which will form a revelation to most of us.

With best wishes—

Yr most oblig'd, most ob^t Servt

HPL

Notes

1. AWD had been publishing book reviews in the *Wisconsin Literary Magazine,* a university publication, since early 1927.

2. Edited by C. Armitage Harper.

[103]   [ALS]

Friday [2, 9, or 16 November 1928]

My dear A. W.:—

I don't think your luck with the weird tale has been *extremely* bad, as such things go, though it doubtless seems so to you at the time. Possibly you may get a larger ratio of acceptances with the detective story—in which case it would of course pay you to specialise in that field for the present. Let me know where to find the "Black Narcissus" & I'll join the laudatory chorus. It has often occurred to me that a shrewdly businesslike author with connexions in various parts of the country could really make himself a very important & much-demanded figure by means of such a shower of favourable letters—directed to all the magazines where his work appears. Wright is certainly guided almost entirely by his Eyrie mail. Good luck with your "Retired Novelist"[1]—I'm ready to praise that too if it lands.

Yesterday I received a letter from a man in New York named T. Everett Harré, who says he is compiling an anthology of the "world's best" weird & unusual stories. He wants to reprint "Cthulhu", & will pay me $15.00 for the privilege. Since I doubt if I could dispose of second rights at any better figure, I'm inclined to look favourably on the proposition; but it awkwardly happens that "Cthulhu" is also one of the tales which Wright wants to use in his contemplated collection of my stuff. I gave Wright the option on it—but that must have been a year or more ago, & nothing has been done toward issuing the book. Wherefore I am now asking Brother Farnsworth just what he does intend to do & when, if ever, he intends to do it. If he has no immediate intention of using "Cthulhu", I'll revoke my option & accept Harré's fifteen bucks; but if he really shews a desire to hang on to it, I'll advise the anthologist to take "The Colour Out of Space" instead. The "Colour", by the way, received a "three-star" or Roll of Honour classification in Edward J.

O'Brien's annual short story list in the *Boston Transcript* for Octr. 20. I suppose his book with the biographical note about me will appear shortly. If the note is in any way ample, I guess I'll buy a copy.

Old Adolphe de Castro has turned up again, & is pestering Belknap & me with dubious revision propositions. He says the *Century Co.* has just accepted his Bierce book, which is surely interesting if true. He claims to have just returned from a European trip.

Your book-reviewing proposition certainly looks like a good thing! Here's a tip—based on a review in last Sunday's *N.Y. Times* which set me all atingle with expectancy.

> THE SHADOW [*sic*]-THING, By H. B. Drake.
> Macy-Masius, The Vanguard Press, N.Y. City.
> $2.00.

If this is as good as the review indicates, I advise you to put in an early application for it! I certainly must get hold of it somehow.

Glad you're going to have some good musical opportunities. Madison seems highly favoured with first-rate talent.

Best wishes—

Most sincerely yrs

H P L

Notes

1. "The Adventure of the Retired Novelist."

[104]   [ALS]

Friday [23 November 1928]

Dear A. W.:—

Congratulations on "Reading Gaol"! You are vastly to be envied—I shall have to find some paper to do reviews for! Yes—I'll have to find the Vassos-illustrated "Ballad" in some local shop.[1]

Sorry you were disappointed about the censored book. My commonplace tastes are a good thing for my purse—for as a matter of fact I wouldn't give half a dollar for any work ever suppressed either in England or America! Except, perhaps, Huysmans' "La Bas" with its Black Mass information. I did own that, but the wretch to whom I lent it sold his library & included it in the bargain by mistake!

Glad "The House on the Highway" has landed at last. Cheer up—"The Chicago Horror" & "Moscow Road" will get in print some day! I think I'll drop a tactful word to Wright about Rankin. He ought to brace up—a good man slipping is a more annoying phenomenon than an absolute total loss like

Olinick of golden memory. As for "The Shunned House"—Cook has been so upheaved this autumn that I really don't know when he will get the thing bound & issued. It's all printed. He bought a farm last September & started moving out into the country on a large scale. Then he found he couldn't get heating installed in time for winter, & had to take temporary quarters in Athol. Thus seesawing back & forth betwixt town & country, & rushed to the limit with his regular work, it's no wonder he can't get time for his side issues. I expect him down here before long—although he has to keep postponing even that brief outing.

Yes—I guess Macy-Masius would be a good firm to try with weird material, since they seem to be handling so much of it. I must, though, give Wright the first chance with the collection of tales. He continues to express a wish to handle it, & he has—despite all his limitations—been at all times so considerate & honourable in his dealings with me, that the least I can do is to give him the initial option. That is what I said only the other day to a friend of mine connected with the *Sat. Review of Literature,*[2] who wanted to use his pull among publishers to get my stuff a hearing.

Lately came across some more weird book titles which sound promising. They are—

> Blind Circle—Renard & Jean
> The Last Devil—Toksvig.

Signe Toksvig contributed a very poor story to W.T.,[3] but the reviews seem to speak well of this volume.

Some time soon I am going to Boston to see the new wing of the art museum there. It is devoted to architectural interiors from 1493 to 1801, & is said to be so representative that it makes the Metropolitan Museum's American wing retreat as a back number. This is right in my line, & with the museum so near at hand (an hour by train—two by 'bus) I mean to take early advantage of it. It opened yesterday.[4]

Best wishes—
Sincerely—H P L

Notes

1. Oscar Wilde, *The Ballad of Reading Gaol,* ill. John Vassos (New York: Dutton, 1928). AWD's review of the book has not been found.
2. See letter 105.
3. "The Devil's Martyr," *WT* (June 1928).
4. HPL did not actually get to the museum until January 1929.

[105]   [ALS]

Monday [3 or 10 December 1928]

Dear A. W.—

I also noticed the *Times* review,[1] & was delighted to see your tale singled out for mention. It is amusing how people become famous for writing which they themselves despise. The old poet Campbell was always referred to as "the author of 'Pleasures of Hope'"—a didactic effusion of youth which he heartily detested in later life. It may be thus with you & "The Coffin of Lissa". It rather tickled me to see this Herbert Asbury claiming *editorship* of a book which he merely took as he found it—but maybe he changed the punctuation in some of the tales. I suppose "Red Hook" must be in it— & if so, I am wondering if I ought to get any royalties. Maybe I'll write the London agent Lavell[2] & see. Your autograph plan is very good, & I trust the "editor" will accede to it. Surely I'll be glad to decorate the gift copies with all the chirography which may be desired. I'd like to see the volume anyway, to get an idea of its mechanical appearance.

While it is far less easy to market book MSS. than individual tales, I see no harm in your trying a collection on Macy-Masius.[3] The selections you have made seem to me excellent, & I surely hope the tales will "land". The favourable *Times* review of "The Coffin of Lissa" ought to count in your behalf. Here's hoping some fortunate accident will cause Macfadden to take "The Pacer".

As for my stuff—I know the W.T. imprint won't mean much, but one can't go back on an early promise—especially to a person as honourable & considerate as Wright has always been toward me. The *Saturday Review* friend who wants to market my stuff is the same Vrest Orton who drew the *Recluse* cover design & who got Wandrei his job at Dutton's. I shall give him a collection to market *after* Wright has either issued his book or conclusively decided not to. Wright later plans to issue Munn's werewolf tales as a book—& did I also mention that this new anthologist Harré has been approaching Munn about "The City of Spiders"?

Many thanks for your friendly mention of me in reviews—but I fancy it'll be some time before the general publishing world clamours for my material. Incidentally—what are the tales in "American Ghost Stories"? Anything I'd be likely to have overlooked?

The Janvier catalogue mention quite inflates me with a sense of classic importance! I think I'll have to write for three or four copies to give away. Such is senile vanity. Thanks for the transcript of the text. Cook wrote me that the item had appeared, & seemed rather critical of Janvier for putting a personal gift—as the *Recluse* was—on sale. By the way—Cook says he means to bind "The Shunned House" soon, so that you may see it before the new year. It will, of course, be some time before he issues a second *Recluse*.

Thanks for the novel tip. I'll pass up "Blind Circle" & look for "The Last Devil". The other day someone lent me "The Strange Case of Miss Annie Spragg",[4] & I found it disappointing as weird material though good as a novel.

  With best of wishes—
    Most sincerely yrs
      H P L

P.S. W.T. is surely getting to be rotten pay. Old De Castro hasn't yet received his $175.00 for "The Last Test", & tells Belknap he intends to draw a draft on the company.

Notes

1. [Unsigned], "Horror Tales in the Nth Degree" [review of *Not at Night!*], *New York Times Book Review* (25 November 1928): 36. The reviewer notes: "'The Coffin of Lissa,' by August W. Derleth, is brief, vivid and with a dramatic climax." HPL's tale is not discussed.

2. Charles Levell, *WT*'s British agent.

3. AWD's first collection of weird stories, *SD*, was self-published in 1941 under the Arkham House imprint. Macy-Masius was an imprint of the Vanguard Press, which in 1930 approached HPL about possibly doing a book. The venture came to nothing.

4. By Louis Bromfield.

[106] [ALS]

                   Decr. 14[, 1928]

My dear A. W.—

    I shall have to appoint you as my Official Announcer of Public Honours! Thanks for the news about the O. Henry Memorial volume[1]—I'll try to get a look at it in some bookstall, even if I don't buy it. This fame business would be rather expensive if it were followed up—O'Brien's book $2.50, the Asbury "Not at Night" perhaps $2.00, & the O. Henry thing I don't know how much! It pays a poor man to cultivate modesty! I've just wondered, though, if Long & I oughtn't to get some royalties from the Asbury affair. We kept our book rights, & Selwyn & Blount have either paid or promised a legitimate return—even posthumously. How come this Asbury person git so much fo' nuffin'? But then—Gawd knows I'm no business man. Your account of the new "Not at Night" sounds very attractive, & I may yet fall for it. The copies to be autographed have not yet come, but I'm prepared for quick action when they do. Asbury's geographical mistakes are somewhat amusing. Really, I'll have to emigrate to the States if there's a chance of getting well known over there some day! Beastly fog, this—I can hardly see St. Paul's dome from my Bloomsbury upper window as I write!

I shall be eager to see your new tale—I think I said once that most aesthetes seem to find a curious fascination & inspiration in the mystic atmosphere & ritual of the ancient Roman church, with its countless survivals from the Middle Ages & from pagan antiquity. I hope you will be able to place it professionally, even if not in as finical a medium as the *Dial*. Good luck with "The Seventeenth of February"—I know the cheaper magazines dote on crude details, & I'd dish 'em up myself if I knew how to concoct such things in the popularly desired manner.

I had heard—& read in reviews—that "Annie Spragg" was more or less indebted to the celebrated "Bridge", but did not know to what extent, not having read the earlier & more famous production. Still, I don't think the touches of *weirdness* in "Annie"—the excavated Priapus, & the suggestion that Cyrus Spragg (with his suspicion of Indian or French blood) was an avatar of that deity—could have been culled from the literary luxuriance of the Thornton Wilderness. However, I surely do mean to read the "Bridge" sooner or later. I'll add "Dr. Garine" to my list of circulating library desiderata—& you can let me know whether the new Keeler product is worth a glance.[2]

Heaven only knows when Cook will bind "The Shunned House"—so let us hope that your friend & collaborator's birthday does not fall too early in 1929! I may be able to slip you one copy for nothing—I think Cook will allow me a few for gift purposes—& you can purchase the other from Cook. He is assuming all the expense, & will handle all the business end. I shan't accept any returns from him till he is fully reimbursed for his outlay. *Then* we'll share profits—if any. You're welcome to the autographs—ink is only 10¢ a bottle! But don't count on their acquiring a market value. One O'Brien biography doesn't make an author!

I've just heard again from the new anthologist Harré, who has been ill for several weeks. He asks advice about what old-time specimens to select, & I am giving it with pleasure. The book will be published by the Macaulay Co. Rather a trashy & obscure house, isn't it?

Well—best wishes, & let me know if you find any more public notices of me!

Most cordially & sincerely yrs—H P L

Notes

1. Blanche Colton Williams (1879–1944), ed., *O. Henry Memorial Award Prize Stories* (Garden City, NY: Doubleday, Doran, 1928). HPL's "Pickman's Model" was awarded a third-rank rating.

2. Boris Sokoloff, *The Crime of Dr. Garine*; Harry Stephen Keeler, possibly *The Voice of the Seven Sparrows* (1928), *The Spectacles of Mr. Caliostro* (1929), or *Thieves' Nights: The Chronicles of DeLancy, King of Thieves* (1929).

[107]   [ALS]

Thursday [20 December 1928]

My dear A. W.:—

Thanks for the advance data on O'Brien's annual! Really, I am quite astonished at the space he gives me. Sent him a bunch of facts & told him to chose what he liked, but I never expected he'd retain so much. Bless my soul, but I feel quite like a public personage! I suppose I shall have to buy the book when it appears—it's not every day I get such a boost toward immortality! Yes—I surely hope O'Brien will include the "Black Narcissus" in his next year's survey. It might do no harm to have somebody send him the magazine containing it, although I suppose he gets most periodicals himself. He must have an appalling ocean of stuff to wade through. If he makes any money out of his book, I'll say he earns every cent of it! I'll be glad to secure *Dragnet* & give your tale a royal sendoff when the time comes. Letters seem to be the big critical determinants with all small-fry editors. I've noticed how the W.T. readers seem to take to Wandrei—& am glad to hear that it's securing him a better market. I am, incidentally, delighted to learn of his commercial good fortune. I don't think he had secured this berth when he last wrote me. Dutton's is a very miserly firm in many ways. They publish the juvenile books of my quaint & venerable friend Everett McNeil, & pin him down to vile starvation contracts. I hope Wandrei will be able to help good old Mac by pushing the advertising of his books. Hitherto the company has been very negligent in this matter, so that poor Mac's royalties have been woefully meagre.

I note with interest your account of your various fictional enterprises—& marvel how you can manage to work on so many tales at once. I have to live in one story until it is evolved to completion. Working on another would break the mood & ruin the atmosphere. Here's hoping that some of your resent stories land with Wright, & that he pays you for current tales before long. My "Silver Key" will appear next month—& I hope the promised $70.00 will soon follow. Wright sent me the advance sheets—it has a Rankin vignette depicting one of the bearded & finny Gnorri that live in the seas of that region whither Randolph Carter went. Rankin is turning from broad crayon effects to thin line drawings, & I don't like the result at all. He is falling off atrociously—an effect which W.T. seems to have on all its artists & near-artists. Ah, me! Is the soul of Rankin to be buried in a grave beside the soul of Brosnatch?

Wright released my "Cthulhu" very graciously, saying he would use "The Dunwich Horror" instead in the book he still intends (so he says) to publish. Thanks for your propaganda work—but I'm not counting very much on the appearance of the volume. I have now told Harré he can have "Cthulhu" for his new anthology—though that may be merely a chimerical plan which will never come to anything.

Whether or not "The Shadow Thing" would be disappointing I'm sure I can't say—but I'd like to see it just the same. Have you heard of "Nightseed & Other Tales" by H. A. Manhood? An advertisement of it looks alluring.

Best wishes—

Most sincerely yrs—H P L

[108]   [ALS]

[H. P. LOVECRAFT
10 BARNES ST.
PROVIDENCE, R. I.]

Decr. 26, 1928

My dear A. W.—

I trust the books safely arrived—& not too late for appropriate Yuletide use. I remailed them immediately upon their arrival last Friday—the 21st—& was rather worried about the lateness of the date. I think Asbury might have been a bit prompter. There was, of course, no time to send them back to N.Y. for Belknap's signature; but I am sure he would be glad to add his autograph at any time that any of the final recipients care to send their copies to him for such a purpose. His address, as possibly you know, is *230 West 97th St., New York City.* I thought the appearance of the volume delightful, but did not care much for Asbury's slighting reference to the artistic & scholastic merit of the contents. I was tempted to answer his slur about scholarship by pointing out that his own lordly erudition was not sufficient to detect & delete the mispunctuation which destroys the sense of the quotation from Delrio—the comma after *tali* which the British anthologist stupidly copied from the original misprint in *Weird Tales**. I'm not sure yet whether or not I'll but the book. Belknap has put in an order for a *used* copy at the nearest Womrath Library—since they sell books rather cheap after withdrawing them from circulation.

I read "The Peace of the Cardinal-Archbishop"[1] with great interest & admiration, & do not think you are wrong in considering it the best of your productions, to date. It has richness of atmosphere conjoined to great delicacy & subtlety, & would probably meet with no misinterpretation on the part of those to whose level of taste & discernment it is addressed. I'd like to see the others of the triad, even though you think them distinctly lesser in merit. Too bad the "Peace" didn't land with the *Dial.*

The fateful 25th having passed into history, I'll try to secure *The Dragnet* & peruse your "Black Narcissus". And of course the editor shall hear of my

---

*In the copies sent to you, I have carefully scratched out the intrusive comma with a penknife.

profound admiration for the latter! I trust that all your other tales may be finished in due time—your skill in quantity production is quite beyond me!

My anthological suggestions to Harré have not been dissimilar to yours, though he was particular in stressing his policy of excluding all *well-known* material. He has got in touch with Wandrei, & has received much help from that scintillant youth.

I may pick up that "Golden Book", although "The Wings of Horus" does not form one of my favourite Blackwood items.[2] As for "The Connoisseur"—yes, I advise you to snap it up! "Mr. Kempe" & "All-Hallows" are alone worth the price of the volume! Your other purchases all sound sensible & contemporary. I lately read the Proust book in the new Modern Library translation, & believe that the author is really an important aesthetic figure. His mastery of *imaginative association* is almost unique. I must look up the new Masefield item, with its weird "Hounds of Hell".[3]

With best wishes, & the hope that your had a jovial Christmas to be followed by a felicitous New Year, I remain

Yr most ob^t Servt—

HPL

Notes

1. AWD submitted "The Peace of the Cardinal Archbishop," along with "Old Ladies," to the French literary magazine *This Quarter* in August 1931.

2. Algernon Blackwood, "The Wings of Horus," *Golden Book* No. 48 (December 1928): 725–35.

3. John Masefield (1878–1967), "The Hounds of Hell," *Enslaved and Other Poems* (London : W. Heinemann, 1920); rpt. in Masefield's *Poems* (New York: Macmillan, 1925).

1929

[109]   [ALS]

[H. P. LOVECRAFT
10 BARNES STREET
PROVIDENCE, R. I.]

Jany. 12, 1929

Dear A. W.—

    I am indeed relieved to hear that the books arrived in time for effective use! I had feared they were meant for remailing—which would of course have entailed a hopeless lateness. Thanks for the postage—I've forgotten myself how much it was, for I didn't intend to bring in a bill!

    I'll be glad to see your two new sketches as soon as you have them in permanent & transmissible form. Your work is undoubtedly improving steadily; & with the mellowness of later years, & an increasing attention to the details of craftsmanship, you ought certainly to produce some widely recognised material eventually. You do well in keeping your art-work & your popular magazine work in separate mental compartments, & preserving an inviolate wall between.

    I obtained *The Dragnet* a few days ago, & read your "Black Narcissus" with much interest. I also read one or two of the other tales in order that I might speak of them in my letter to the editor. Then I penned my epistolary tribute— & I don't think you could possibly find any flaws in the unbroken panegyrical strain. I wish I had saved a copy for you—but you can read it in the magazine if Brother Hersey sees fit to dignify it with printing. I began by faintly commending "The Black Bag", & then I worked up to my climax. Among the things I said was that "Solar Pons" ought to take his place among the standard detectives of fiction.[1] If you can get 25 or 30 letters of equally encomiastic tone, you'll be well launched on your career as a popular magazine idol!

    As for "Narcissus" itself—of course I am no judge of detective fiction, but it seems to me that the story is a fine specimen of its kind. The plot is clever, & with an adroit element of real surprise; whilst the conversation & flow of narration proceed with admirable smoothness & naturalness. My points of criticism would be confined to the most trivial details of local colour—details so trivial that they are scarcely worth citing.

    For one thing—I doubt very much whether the staid & stately *Times* has extras with scareheads and photographs. Better make it the *Daily Mail* if you want sensationalism. Another thing—I don't believe the U.S. Westernism *slicker* is used in England at all. It isn't even used here in the Eastern U.S., although we know what it means from reading of it in Western writing. We say "raincoat". I don't know what the preferred British usage is, but you might pick it up from the clothing advertisements in British magazines. "Waterproof coat" sounds appropriately ponderous & insular. Still another point involves *general probability*. Are presentation greetings & names usually inscribed on *kitchen knives?* Finally—do you think that the relatives of a financier prominent enough to be listed among large losers ought to be quite so lowerclass & Cockneyish as you represent Missus 'Enery Clymer to be? Possibly some or all of my suggestions are unjustified, but you can consider them for what they are worth in preparing the tale for book publication. I was pleased to note the increased accuracy of your London geography.

I liked your amplification of "An Occurrence in an Antique Shop", & believe the tale is now in its best possible shape—easily worthy of book publication. I also (as I think I told you when I saw the MS) like "Melodie in E Minor" exceedingly—& agree with you that Wright's subtitling is singularly infelicitous.[2] Best hopes for your tales now with Wright! The new W.T. is, on the whole, somewhat below its none too impressive average. As you remark, the mania for undraped ladies in the "art" department has come to be an unmitigated nuisance—especially since they are lavishly supplied where the text explicitly calls for something else. You'll recall that Rankin made ample-bosomed wenches of my *male* orgiasts in the Louisiana swamp scene of "Cthulhu!" I suppose Wright thinks the custom has a sales value. Edmond Hamilton has come dangerously near writing himself out of late—I couldn't even begin to get interested in his utterly mechanical & conventional "Star Stealers". Quinn is getting to be a pest—but a profitable one, no doubt. The worst thing about him is that he must *know better*—for he is clearly a man of wide knowledge & cultivation, with a keen brain when he chooses to exercise it. I haven't attempted the Colter oeuvre—I never read a serial until it's done—nor have I tried to plough through the Nichols serial. Ernst made a mess this time, but I've seen better stuff of his. Only a few months ago he had a haunted house tale—"Beyond Power of Man"—which shewed *real imagination* despite a very inadequate use of his idea. "The Three" is really fine, brief thought it is. "The Ghost Ship" is trite & disappointing. I can see the imitative element in Wells' "Brass Key". "The Highwayman" didn't excite me much—& the pseudoarchaism is ridiculous. Worrell's effort is a vast disappointment, for he wrote a splendid thing—"The Canal"—only about a year ago. I second your opinion anent Harlow & his bits of useful information! I read "The Tall Woman" in an anthology some time ago, & believe it must be a really powerful story in the original Spanish. The idea has infinite capabilities. Of the verse, I thought the opening specimen "Ghosts of the Gods" very mediocre, but liked the Wandrei & Howard offerings. Wandrei's coming tale is excellent—I read it in MS. a couple of years ago.[3]

Yes—singular as it may seem for a conservative old gentleman—I found Proust a truly remarkable artist. Whether I shall follow up "Swann's Way" with others of the sequence remains to be seen, for I am very indolent about such matters; but anyway, I add my senile tribute to the chorus of esteem which proceeds from my sprightly juniors. It seems to be a standard French idea to attempt the large-scale portrayal of broadly representative cross-sections of life, & Proust well carries on the tradition so auspiciously begun by Balzac. It would be hard to find anywhere such an authentic & exhaustive exploration of the human consciousness.

Last week I had a pleasant & unexpected visit from my poetic friend Samuel Loveman, & was able to shew him the quaintnesses & antiquities of my beloved Providence for the first time. I then accompanied him to Boston, & introduced him to the historic reliques of that ancient metropolis. Last of all we explored witch-haunted Salem & incredibly archaic Marblehead—so that all in all my guest may be said to have received a very vivid condensed course in Colonial atmosphere & colour. Upon my return home Sunday night I was knocked flat by a devastating cold, from which I am still suffering.

With best wishes—

Yr most obt Servt—

H P L

P.S. I enclose a few postcard echoes of last week's trip.

Notes

1. Mignon Eberhart, "The Black Bag," *Dragnet* 2, No. 1 (February 1929): 7–61. HPL's letter about AWD (see Appendix) ironically was published under the heading, "One for the Black Bag"; doubly ironic since he confessed HPL had not even read "The Black Bag."
2. Presumably HPL refers to the subtitling of "An Occurrence in an Antique Shop," which read "Strange Was the Death of the Antiquary," a play on James's *Ghost-Stories of an Antiquary,* rather than "'Melodie in E Minor'" ("A Five-Minute Ghost Story").
3. "The Shadow of a Nightmare," *WT* (May 1929).

[110]   [ALS]

[H. P. LOVECRAFT
10 BARNES STREET
PROVIDENCE, R. I.]

[c. 21 January 1929]

My dear A W:—

By this time you will have received my letter which crossed yours of the 16ᵗʰ—& which I addressed to Sauk City, forgetting the date of reopening of your institution of learning. Shortly after mailing that document I received the enclosed from *The Dragnet*—which is certainly rather melancholy news! However, even if this magazine does go the way of all wood pulp, it is a good thing that my letter reached the editor; for he still seems to control quite a chain, any link in which is potentially a market for you.

Congratulations on "The Pacer"! I'm sure it's only a question of time before Wright will take the other three—though his delirious comments on "A Matter of Sight" do not encourage the belief that this final acceptance will be due to genuine appreciation. Brother Farnsworth's blindness to subtleties is probably what makes him a good commercial editor. Sometimes it provokes one, yet sometimes it works rather conveniently, as in the case of my "Unnamable", which he certainly wouldn't have accepted if he'd suspected what it was all about. I hope Price's comment on your "Antique Shop" will be printed in the Eyrie—though possibly it was an oral one, which will consequently escape immortality. Anyway, I have an idea that you'll succeed more & more with W.T. placements.

I haven't the faintest notion when "The Dunwich Horror" will appear—indeed, I haven't been paid yet for "The Silver Key"! I feel greatly complimented by your eagerness to read the tale, & with the characteristic reaction of tickled vanity am sending a carbon of the MS. under separate cover for your perusal & return. I trust you won't find it a sad example of an old man's failing faculties. I shall be glad to see your "Deserted Garden" in print. Keep it up—& you'll fast become as regular a standby as the peerless Seabury Quinn!

Your book purchases are certainly a record haul, & I especially envy you the De la Mare items. I've never felt able to afford personal ownership of all my favourites, but some day I want to lay in Blackwood, De La Mare, & James items to an extent at least comparable with my Machen & Dunsany shelves.

I trust that the proposed censorship of the Hall book[1] may not be adopted—assuming that the volume really is a serious work of art whose theme was not chosen for sales-promotion purposes. The whole problem of censorship is a highly complex one—so much so that I am still frankly neutral concerning it. I don't think the abstract right to suppress a book ought to be wholly abrogated by the government, yet it is obvious that some means must be provided to distinguish between authentic art—or science—& commercial pornography if the process is to be other than ridiculous.

With all good wishes, & trusting that "Dunwich" may prove at least a *mild* soporific, Yr obt Servt

HPL

Notes

1. Radclyffe Hall, *The Well of Loneliness,* a pioneering novel of lesbianism.

[111] [ALS]

[H. P. LOVECRAFT
10 BARNES STREET
PROVIDENCE, R. I.]

Jany 21—[1929]
Afternoon

My dear A W—

Just received your latest note, & have decided to include my reply in the letter I finished an hour ago. Hope you'll land the "Chicago Horror", as well as the other items you have sent. Your new "Adventures" sound alluring—whilst many an anticipatory shudder is aroused by the titles "The Wind" & "Death in the Crypt"!

Your proposed thesis is surely an ambitious one,[1] & I shall see that your list circulates among all who would be likely to have items to add to it. I'll send in a list of my own—if I can think of any—with my next letter. Just now all I can do is to suggest that you'll have to drop poor Fitz-James O'Brien—who was killed in the Civil War![2]

Oh, wait, though—you must add one more *Shiel* item at all hazards! "The Purple Cloud" is an absolute masterpiece despite a weak, romantic ending—a novel, & a thing of nightmare! Also, you ought to have the Shiel collection called "Shapes in the Fire", which contains "Xelucha". (also the florid prototype of "The House of Sounds".) Of moderns, don't omit John Buchan's "Witch Wood" & some of the tales (notably "Skule Skerry") in "The Runagates' Club". And how about Herbert S. Gorman's "The Place Called Dagon"? Then there are the two books by Vernon Knowles—"Here & Otherwhere" & "The House of Queer Streets."

Altogether, the persons who can help you most are W. Paul Cook, Wandrei, & H. Warner Munn. I advise you to write them all—Munn's address is *Fire Station #1, Athol, Mass.* They form, collectively, a virtual encyclopaedia of recent weird fiction. Munn can tell you especially about magazine stuff—like A. Merritt's "Moon Pool". It is, by the way, very flattering of you to include my stuff—provided I get anything published in permanent shape at the time you go to press.

Here's wishing you luck with Rankin's "Pacer" design. I suppose the length of the story ensures you one. Personally, I'd rather my tales had no designs; for rarely does the "artist" express my imagery exactly.

My cold is waning encouragingly, & I've been outdoors once. Sorry you've also been under the weather. Yes—you must get around New England way before long & let me shew you some of my cherished antiquities. Think of seeing Arkham & Kingsport!

Best wishes—

Yr obt Servt—

H P

Notes

1. Published as "The Weird Tale in English Since 1890" (see Appendix).
2. Fitz-James O'Brien (1828–1862), whose most famous works are "What Was It?" and "The Diamond Lens." Both were reprinted in *WT,* the former also in *Ghost Stories.*

[112]   [ALS]

[H. P. LOVECRAFT
10 BARNES STREET
PROVIDENCE, R. I.]

Feby. 1, 1929

My dear A W:—

I am indeed glad to hear that you found something of merit in "The Dunwich Horror", & that its unusual length—for a short story—did not alienate your interest. Your friend's reaction, too, is very pleasing—for I always try to achieve a realism of atmosphere by adhering to absolutely commonplace nature *except* where my one thread of supernaturalism is concerned. My great complaint against most weird tales is that they annul their own effect through careless artificiality & romantic unlifelikeness. Incidentally, I have just received advance sheets of "The Dunwich Horror", (with minor misprints) & am told it will appear in the April W.T.—out one month from today. Rankin has done well with the design—it is quite in his old-time spirit!

It was interesting to hear of your new professor's acquaintance with "Not At Night"—& flattering to learn his opinion of "Red Hook." I can't like that yarn at all, myself, & wouldn't be inclined to place it first even in the Asbury compilation.

As soon as I'm out of the toils of a revision job now engulfing me, I'll see if I can send you some more suggestions for your coming thesis. I know that Cook, Munn, & Wandrei can help enormously with this venture; & trust you will fully avail yourself of their aid.

Your library is certainly becoming highly impressive. In this new list of additions are many that I never heard of—including the Munro, Wharton, McSpadden, Oliphant, Blashfield, Funk, & Peattie items.[1] Are any of those worth my looking up with reference to a possible 2nd edition of my article? I guess I'll see how many of them are procurable at the local libraries.

I'm eager to see your new tale "The Wind", with its whippoorwills & fireflies.[2] I derived these items from my sojourn of last summer in Wilbraham, Mass., where an astonishing number of weird legends still linger. That belief about the whippoorwills is a serious matter with Wilbraham rustics, whilst the fireflies near where I visited are profuse to a degree I never saw elsewhere. I'll never forget the display they staged over a marshy meadow one evening early in July. It was like the descent of an electrified galaxy to earth!

I'm sure the "Black Buttons" will be interesting, & trust that at least one of the re-submitted tales will land with Wright. It seems he has been ill—he speaks of his return from a sanitarium. Glad the *Dragnet* is to have a successor, so that the effect of my epistolary masterpiece won't be lost.

I've just lent my weird notes, cuttings, & commonplace-book to young Long, who complains that he's wholly run out of ideas! With me the problem is just the other way around. I have ideas & plot-germs to burn, but lack the time & energy to write them up. We both ought to envy you, with your facile & untiring productivity.

Best wishes—

Yr most ob^t Servt—

H P L

Notes

1. See letter 290.
2. AWD obviously lifted the whippoorwills from "The Dunwich Horror," just read. They became something of an obsession with him over the years.

[113]   [ALS]

Feby. 8[, 1929]

My dear A W:—

The packet arrived safely, & I have been reading your stories with much interest. All are excellent, & seem to me to indicate that you are squarely on the high road to an ultimate fictional success—commercial as well as aesthetic.

"Three Black Buttons"[1] is admirably well-wrought, & quite revives for the moment my long-defunct interest in detective fiction. The suspense is very genuine, & the revelation comes as a real surprise. There is a moment earlier in the tale where one half-suspects Simmons, but that is long past when the final denouement breaks.

"Spring Death" is really finely poetic—& it would take a more sophisticated reader than I to see any element of burlesque or satire in it. Why not try it on Cook for *The Recluse?* All I can possibly criticise is the single expression *From where* in place of *Whence*. Isn't that a trifle cumbrous??

"The World is Mad" ought to be very salable as a Christmas story—I presume you'll try it on the magazines in July or whenever the proper Christmas fiction season is.

"The Seventeenth of February" is vivid enough, but a bit theatrical & incomplete. It seems to need rounding-out—& unless it explains why the narrator is exempted from the general death, it ought to record his fear of coming death as he writes. I would have Momsen a lineal descendant of the murderer, though unknown even to himself. Let him be drawn curiously to the house, & make him feel vaguely that he has known it of old. Have him, for instance, try unconsciously to walk through a door which was sealed up in 1827 & of which only later examination gives any hint. When the death comes, let some hint of *finality* be given—as if Momsen were the true avatar of the murderer, & the one the ghost had sought to reach all along. Have an air of dread lift perceptibly from the place, & intimate that there will be more deaths. Incidentally—you might have Feb. 17 a date which Momsen has *always* dreaded—& which he notes as a vast "coincidence" when he hears the history of the house. And by the way—the Hudson isn't in *New England*. It belongs to a region of entirely different colonial architecture & traditions.

"The Missing Tenants"[2] is good, though the actual ending is somewhat foreseen as soon as the demented Roland is mentioned. Incidentally—"bug" isn't used as a general term for "insect" in England, it being confined to common vermin only.

Thanks for the tips. I'm late for *Mystery Stories*, but I shall surely get the dollar "John Silence" when it appears. It's absurd that I don't own a single Blackwood tale—I must eventually have "Incredible Adventures" & the collection containing "The Willows".

With best wishes, & thanks for the generous glimpse of your work—
            Your most obt Servt—
                  H P L

Notes

1. Published as "Two Black Buttons."
2. "The Adventure of the Missing Tenants."

[114]   [ALS]

                                                        Feby. 15[, 1929]
My dear A W:—
            Too bad the tales didn't land this time—but they may the next! Good luck with the second shipment. On the whole, you fare pretty well with Wright—I don't know of anyone else but Quinn who keeps up such a record of consecutiveness. The other day I heard from "Francis Flagg", (Henry G. Weiss) author of "The Chemical Brain" in the January issue. It seems that he knows someone I know—Walter J. Coates, editor of *Driftwind.* "Flagg" appears to be a bright young man—his story was certainly

above the average. Yes—I read the new W.T., & found it no worse than the average. Your "Deserted Garden" surely compares well with anything else in the issue. I think you have picked the best tales about as I would myself—"Rat" & "Tindalos." Something *could* be made of the subject-matter of "The Immortal Hand" by a real writer, & I thought "The Sea Horror" was going to be good until it began to settle down to the usual Hamilton formula. Whitehead was below par. He *can* write a splendid tale when he chooses, but this time the popular-fiction convention had him aesthetically bound & gagged. That's what got Quinn. Notice how much better he was in the old days, as shewn by "The Phantom Farmhouse".[1]

Yes—I shall look up the Wharton & possibly the Munro material. And I hope still to get hold of a copy of Mrs. Wilkins-Freeman's "Rosebush" collection at some library. I haven't even begun to read the amount I ought, but I trust I can get the time & energy next summer. This reminds me that I have at last perused the meteorically famous "Bridge of San Luis Rey". It is surely a brilliant & well-knit piece of work, but I can't help feeling that it is a trifle mechanical & *consciously* "artistic". Its exaggeration of human emotions & emphasis on unusually warped types gives it something of the nature of grotesquerie & removes it from the convincing current of actual life. After all, I am a pure *realist* in my tastes the moment I turn aside from the domain of phantasy. Romanticism impresses me as merely an elaborate form of absolute zero. Heretical as it may sound, I believe that Bromfield's "Annie Spragg" (which you consider a San Luis derivative) is a better & sounder—more vivid & vital—piece of work than the Wilder specimen. It has a firmer grounding in familiar experience, & wastes less time on the mechanical devices of stage pity & stage irony. It is more concrete—more a natural growth—& has an infinitely more visualisable scenic setting. Let the academic dons—including Prof. Tunney—say what they will, I stand by my naive opinion as an ignorant layman & vote for Bromfield & his Annie!

Glad to hear that you plan more work in the "Spring Death" vein. You get far closer to real aesthetic expression in work of this sort than you can ever get whilst following the popular-fiction pattern demanded by Wright & his ilk. Your Wisconsin definition of "New England" was certainly a new one to me, although I've known & corresponded with many a son of the Badger Free State! New England represents one definite historic enterprise & one definite set of *mores* & traditions, whose western limits are the boundaries of Connecticut, Massachusetts, & Vermont. Beyond this line the culture comes from very different sources & waves of colonisation, & the divergence in customs, folklore, thought-habits, dialect, tastes, & architecture is obvious even to the untrained observer. There are really *three* basic Northern cultures—New England, New York, & Pennsylvania; with many intermediate fusions, of course. ¶ Best wishes—Yr most obt

HPL

P.S. Wright is going to sue Macy-Masius for printing (under an invalid contract) the contents of "Not at Night", & wants Long & me to let him include us among the complainants. I think I'll let him—I surely wouldn't mind some extra royalty!

Notes

1. Seabury Quinn, "The Phantom Farmhouse," *WT* (October 1923; rpt. March 1929; in *WK*).

[115]   [ALS]

Feby. 25[, 1929]

My dear A W:—

Thanks for the additional pages of vernal decease, which very ably carries on the atmosphere established in the earlier section.[1] I shall indeed be very glad to keep in touch with the later parts as they are evolved— who knows but that this may be the beginning of something as eventually important as the Proust cycle? I realise the difficulties of anchoring such a chronicle to earth, but imagine you will find an effective & graceful way of managing it. I have often thought of attempting a task slightly analogous to this—namely, the delineation of that vague dream-life of wonder & beauty which one mentally reconstructs around the isolated high spots of aesthetic experience after their actual realistic setting & prosaic interludes have receded far into the past. Such a record would not be confined to childhood alone, although it would include a good deal of childhood. In principle this would be much like what you are doing, though in my hands it would probably be more remote from reality, & more coloured with a fantastic background not truly mnemonic at all, but rather of the nature of sheer imagination. I know of Burke only by reputation. Is he really worth reading?[2]

Hope you have good luck with the new & revised tales, & that Baird will like the "Black Buttons" as well as I did. Wright is paring down his prices discouragingly—he has just accepted a new tale of Long's at considerably less than a cent a word, which compares very badly with what he used to pay Long.[3]

I knew you would be surprised at my comparative estimate of the "Bridge" & "Annie Spragg", but that's the way the two strike me. Certainly, the Wilder product is more brilliantly written—but to me the brilliancy is artificial & geometrical at bottom. I have graduated from the state where manner seems more important than matter—though naturally I prefer a good style when, caeteris paribus, there is a choice. Anyhow, both books are good, & I'm sure I don't begrudge Wilder his representation in the Modern Library. Is the "Cabala" in your opinion comparable to the "Bridge"? The title seems to promise *weirdness*, though I think I recall one reader's warning me that it is not weird.

As for Wright's lawsuit—I suppose the rights sold to Selwyn & Blount were British rights only, so that reprinting in the U.S. is illegal. Wright said something about a defective & unauthorised contract which Macy-Masius had made with somebody named Jeffries—but I couldn't quite get the drift of the situation, since the explanation seemed to assume my possession of information which in truth was never given me. However, I wish Wright luck, & hope that Belknap & I can get something out of it. Too bad you relinquished all rights on those older tales of yours which are represented.

A new correspondent of mine has recommended an author named Geoffrey Dennis, who he says greatly resembles M. P. Shiel. Ever hear of him? He also recommends the novel "Chalk Face", by Waldo Frank.[4] Dear me! There is too much weird material in the world for one indolent old man to keep track of!

With all good wishes,
Yr most ob^t Servt
H P L

Notes

1. The genesis of AWD's semi-autobiographical novel (variously titled *The Early Years* or *Evening in Spring*) is extremely complex and requires further investigation. AWD revised and recast it, incorporating and discarding much prose, between 1929 when he first began work on it and its publication in 1941. HPL read AWD's many revisions of the ms.

2. See letter 262.

3. FBL, "The Red Fetish," *WT* (January 1930).

4. Geoffrey Dennis, British author of *Harvest in Poland* (1925), a novel about the future of Europe expressed in supernatural terms.

[116]   [ALS]

Friday [8 March 1929]

My dear A W:—

Your new venture promises to be a rather ponderous one for a young writer, insomuch as it dips into metaphysical subtleties & still-unsettled philosophic-scientific questions which might well perplex the gravest & most profound of scholars. I have myself often been fond of speculating in a laymanlike way upon aesthetic theory, & it is my belief that *art* is a very complex matter, with diverse roots drawing upon sources as widely separated as abstract rhythm or symmetry, & certain types of imaginative association which vary with the individual & the civilisation. The two extremes are connected, however, by the essential identity of *rhythm* with *repetition*—the latter being the crux of the matter of imaginative association. Art must cause certain nerves in the brain to *repeat* a former pattern. It is this fact which makes it impossible to separate the whole body of aesthetics from tradition, as some moderns would like to do. *Morality* I consider also a compound—practical expediency, plus aesthetics. It is of course a variable thing, depending on the age, race, & civilisation, but would seem to be too naturally connected with tradition to admit of sudden changes on the part of any one culture-stream. The question of literary censorship need not really be connected with anything so basic as a nation's moral code. It concerns, rather, a nation's custom or technique in applying its moral code. As I have said before, I don't think any genuine work of art ought to be censored— yet commercial pornography would certainly become a very ungraceful nuisance if not constantly discouraged. It seems to me that very few works of major art have ever been permanently suppressed—so that the "problem of censorship" is really a far less important matter than most of the eager younger generation at present imagine.

I will look up "The Cabala" when I get a chance. Meanwhile I am rather anxious to see Prof. Kittredge's new book on witchcraft. I saw a review of an interesting-sounding book in last Sunday's N Y Times[1]—about a lost world of horror under the Antarctic ice. It is—"The Greatest Adventure", by John Taine, Dutton, $2.50.

Wright is certainly not much of a paying proposition—though I hope his low rates will not cause you to stop writing such weird matter as your own inclination may impel you to write. Heaven knows, I wrote weird stuff before I ever thought it had the remotest chance for publication; & shall probably still be writing it long after the collapse of the present mystery fashion has closed the market again. Bought the new W.T. last Monday, but haven't had a chance to look at it yet. Not that I harbour any bright expectations! No further word from Bre'r Farnsworth about the litigation.

With best wishes—

Yr most obt Servt
H P L

Notes

1. [Unsigned], "Dragon's Brood" [review of *The Greatest Adventure* by John Taine], *New York Times Book Review* (3 March 1929): 9.

[117]   [ALS]

March 14[, 1929]

My dear A W:—

I am sure your coming articles will be of great interest, however much you may decide to limit their cosmicism of scope. Here's wishing you luck with *Plain Talk*[1]—of which I'll try to get a glimpse when your friend's article appears. The nature of art or beauty is something which has always interested me, & about which I have always been prone to speculate now & then in amateurish fashion. My latest ebullition in this line was a year ago last August, when an article on the basis of beauty appeared in H. L. Mencken's column of the *Chicago Tribune*,[2] & my friend M. W. Moe of Milwaukee (who is in Madison *summers* about as much as you are *winters!*) replied to it. My own position was about half-way between those of Mencken & Moe, & I could not resist outlining it somewhat at length to the latter. Enclosed (please return) is the text of the whole controversy, which I send for your possible amusement. Read the newspaper cutting first, then the yellow sheets, & lastly the white sheet. No doubt you'll have many points of disagreement with all three!

Good luck with all your story ventures! Your musical tale surely takes the prize for extensive revision, the only ones of mine comparable in that respect being "The Picture in the House" & "The Nameless City." I shall still look for weird specimens now & then, & hope that Wright may have a tardy glimmering of reason anent "A Matter of Sight". What a plethora of magazines there are! I never heard of the *London Aphrodite*[3] but hope it takes your "Cardinal Archbishop".

If I read the Taine book I'll tell you about it, but I probably shan't see it unless it accidentally falls my way. I tried to get the cheap new "John Silence" edition yesterday, but couldn't find it at the shops I tried. I may send to Dutton's for it. I must look up some of Montague Summers'[4] stuff—I hear he well-nigh believes in witches & suchlike himself!

Your new paragraph of aesthetic reminiscence appeals to me with especial strength—since as you know, I am an enthusiast about ancient houses & streets, & the innumerable signs & symbols of generation-long continuous habitation which linger in the soul of an old town. I have no use for a modern city with garish, atmosphereless new buildings, & broad, unimaginative gridiron-ranged streets. A town is a real town to me only if it have houses with histories—houses that appeal to one's retrospective fancy & sense of pageantry. It must, too, have narrow, curving hill streets, & frequent little courts where grassy patches, moss-crusted bank walls, occasional former farm-buildings tell mutely of the countryside that used to be—200 years ago. You ought to come East & let me show you around. Pre-revolutionary houses are common, whilst in Salem & elsewhere I can point you out ancient, peaked dwellings dating from the middle 1600's & now going on 300 years old.

Yes—I've had bulletins about Old 'Dolph's Bierce book, & Belknap has seen one review. We are anxious to see whether or not he has removed the preface Belknap wrote.[5] If he has, he's a damned old scoundrel & hypocrite!

Today is the 3d of a delightfully warm spell. Yesterday was so magnificent that I took all my work out to the woods in spite of the mud.

Best wishes—

Yr most ob^t Servt

H P L

P.S. Don't know when I'll ever get time for another tale. It takes longer to write a very brief story than to write a longish one.

Notes

1. *Plain Talk* (1927–38) was a monthly literary and political magazine published in New York (later Washington, DC).
2. H. L. Mencken, "Aesthetic Note," *Chicago Sunday Tribune* (7 August 1927). HLM's column ended in January 1928.
3. A bi-monthly magazine published from August 1928 to July 1929.
4. Montague Summers (1880–1948), British editor, ecclesiastic, and occult scholar; author of *The Geography of Witchcraft* (1927), *The Vampire: His Kith and Kin* (1928), *The Vampire in Europe* (1929), *A Gothic Bibliography* (1938), and others.
5. The book contains a preface signed "Belknap Long."

[118]   [ALS]

[c. 22 March 1929]

My dear A W:—

Let us hope that Wright's delay about your two tales is a favourable sign—& that a convenient paucity of fillers will cause them to "land" at last. Congratulations on the Hersey acceptance[1]—which I hope will be followed by more. If Hersey takes the advice I gave him in my letter, he will make a steady feature of Derleth material! Evidently you are getting a finely solid start in the detective line—a line which has immensely remunerative possibilities. By the way—did I say that I liked "A Dinner at Imola" very much? It is a very effective bit, & ends up without any letdown. Too bad you are receiving only ten dollars for it. No—I haven't been paid for "Dunwich" yet, nor do I expect to be before *May 1st* according to W.T.'s new policy as observed in recent instances. Two months after publication is evidently the present practice, & the company seems rather prompt & consistent in adhering to it. That is really all right when one gets used to it—you always know when to look for your pay, & can calculate matters accordingly.

I shall get that dollar "John Silence" sooner or later. The other Blackwood books I most wish are "Incredible Adventures", & "The Listener & Other Stories" (containing "The Willows")—though I wouldn't mind having "The Centaur" & "The Lost Valley" (containing "The Wendigo") as well. Your Blackwood shelf, I imagine, is rather well filled. It's odd that I don't own a single Blackwood item despite my fairly full Machen & Dunsany sections.

As for the aesthetic controversy—of course, if one is not a materialist I suppose there are all sorts of mystical interpretations of beauty which can be indulged in. But I see no sensible reason for going beyond the authentic, objective, & test-capable evidence which our contact with the perceptible universe provides—hence have to confine my fantastic subjective flights to weird fiction. I guess that Mencken item was pretty widely syndicated, so you probably saw it somewhere even if not in the *Chicago Tribune* whence Moe clipped it.

By the way—the publication of "The Dunwich Horror" has just earned me a curious & interesting letter from an old lady in Boston, a direct lineal descendant of the Salem witch Mary Easty, who was hanged on Gallows Hill Aug. 19, 1692. She claims to have heard some strange traditions handed down in the family, & to possess certain powers of peering into the future which she cannot explain. A quaint old soul, apparently—I shall write & see if any of her "inside" witch traditions have fictional value. She wants to know whether Dunwich & Arkham are real places, since they don't appear on ordinary maps of Massachusetts! Incidentally—the author of "The Chemical Brain" (Jan. W.T.) has just asked me whether or not the *Necronomicon* is a real book!

Glad to hear that spring is striking Wisconsin, too. The warm weather keeps up here, & all the lawns are crocus-spangled. I haven't, however, been able to repeat my woodland excursion as yet. Clark Ashton Smith writes that the northern California spring is well under way, with a profusion of varied flowers & all the customary magic of awakening Nature. I am vastly relieved to see winter go—I can't bear the cold, & really feel alive only from about May to September.

Well—best wishes, literary & financial alike.

Yr most ob^t hble Servt

HPL

Notes

1. "The Adventure of the Missing Tenants."

[119]   [ALS]

All Fool's Day [1 April 1929]

My dear A W:—

Congratulations—a thousand times! You certainly have struck "pay dirt" at last, & bid fair to outdistance all the rest of the gang financially. I wish I could do it—I'd a thousand times rather write detective tales than revise—but I'm afraid I haven't the knack. Long tries to concoct popular fiction, but it never seems to get accepted. Hope my letter to Hersey did have something to do with the recent acceptances—but it couldn't have done the trick if your material had not been up to the standard. Surely, I'll be glad to furnish another panegyric—remind me to buy *Dragnet* on the first of May. And let's hope for the best regarding Brother Farnsworth & his filler needs. You certainly manage to keep busy—stories plus college themes plus "Spring Death". I shall, as I intimated, be particularly interested to see that part of the latter which deals with the atmosphere of houses & towns.

That Wells volume surely will make an ideal addition to one's library[1]—I rather like the series of one-volume collections, for it enables one to economise space admirably. I haven't any as yet, but Long has Shakespeare, De Maupassant, & one or two others. It surely is good news about Shiel[2]—watch me snap up "The Pale Ape" & "The Purple Cloud" when the chance comes! I hope the new stuff will be as good as the old—too often these veteran authors peter out & get insipid toward the last. Shiel is a curiously uneven cuss—his best work is marvellous, & his worst work equally marvellous—in the other direction! I think he has created the most extravagantly inane of all fictional detectives—"Cummings King Monk."[3] Someone said once that Shiel is rumoured to have a drop of negro blood, although he is generally supposed to be of Irish origin. The drop, I believe, was supposed to have come in through a West-Indian ancestor.

Yes—I may call on that venerable & genial witch-descendant before long. She is certainly the epitome of thoughtfulness & generosity—no sooner had I chanced to mention casually my long desire to read "The Wind in the Rosebush", than the good soul sent it along as an unsolicited loan—she having owned it these 25 years, ever since it was published!

Next week or the week after—or very possibly the last of this week—I may see "the gang" en masse for the first time since last June; for despite my hatred of New York my good friend Vrest Orton has at last induced me to visit him in the colonial farmhouse he has hired in Yonkers, on the northern rim of the metropolis. Probably I shan't stay more than 2 or 3 weeks—& I'm undecided whether I'll combine this trip with further travel or save the latter for the summer. I would like to get up the Hudson to see Dwyer.

Old De Castro's book received a scathing review in the N.Y. Tribune[4]— I couldn't help chuckling at it! Long & I haven't seen a copy yet, so we don't know whether he included Long's preface or not. If he didn't, he's a damned old reprobate!

Well—best wishes & keep up the good work!

Yr most obt Servt

HPL

P.S. The other day I picked up a marvellously vivid book as a 39¢ remainder—a study of Nero entitled "The Bloody Poet", by Desider Kostolanyi. It is a very keen analysis of the artistic temperament.

Notes

1. *The Outline of History.*

2. HPL may have been referring to *Here Comes the Lady,* a new collection of stories by M. P. Shiel. Shiel's earlier work was also being reissued in revised editions by Victor Gollancz at the time. A radically revised edition of *The Purple Cloud* appeared in 1929.

3. AWD eventually published, after long delay, Shiel's *Prince Zaleski and Cummings King Monk* (Sauk City, WI: Mycroft & Moran, 1977). Shiel's letter to AWD was published in John D. Squires, *M. P. Shiel and the Lovecraft Circle.*

4. Lewis Mumford's review of *Portrait of Ambrose Bierce* in *New York Herald Tribune Books* (24 March 1929): 1, stated that the book "is full of pretentious judgments and in general has an authentic air of unreliability."

[120]   [ANS][1]

[Postmarked Yonkers, N.Y.,
13 April 1929]

In such a desperate whirl of visiting around N.Y. that I can't cope with correspondence save with postcard replies! Shall be here for 2 weeks more—address me in care of *F. B. Long—230 W. 97th St. N.Y.C.* ¶ Congrats on the Hersey placements. You surely are landing big! Wish I could do so well! Somebody had given me a letter of introduction to the editor of *The Red Book,* & I shall call on him, though probably nothing will come of it.[2] Expect to see Wandrei Monday. If Hersey does start a weird magazine he can surely count on me for contributions! ¶ The Kostolanyi book is really fine—a searching study of the artistic temperament. Glad you heard from Miss Hall—you must have been glad of such recognition from one whose work you admire. ¶ Your new Spring Death instalment is splendid—I can enter right into it. Keep it up & be America's Proust! ¶ Am having a pretty good time despite my dislike of NY as a place of residence. What irony that most of my closest friends live in a town I can't endure! But it's good to visit the old gang once in a while—we expect to hold an old-time meeting next Wednesday [evening].
Best wishes,
Sincerely
HPL

Notes

1. Front: Brooklyn Bridge, New York City.

2. T. Everett Harré had given HPL a letter of introduction to Arthur McKeogh, editor of the *Red Book,* and HPL went to see him toward the end of the month; but he rightly concluded that "I don't think McKeogh of the Red Book can use any of my stuff, for the tone of his magazine is very different from mine" (HPL to Lillian D. Clark, 30 April 1929 [ms., JHL]). See further letter 121.

[121]   [ANS][1]

[Postmarked Paterson, N.J.,
24 April 1929]

My dear AW:—Glad to hear that you have read "Annie Spragg" at last—I thought you had done so before. I stick to my verdict that it beats "The Bridge"—it is the "philosophy", heavy, ostentatious, & superficially popular, which alienates me from the Wilder opus. Clever & mechanically finished, I concede—but lacking in the prosaic colour & background which mean real life. My young host F. B. Long has just read "Annie Spragg", but has not read the "Bridge" as yet. We'll see what he has to say when he does—as he means to do. Yes—of course the weird element adds to my liking for "Annie". ¶ Trust your vacation has proved pleasant & that you will soon have some more "Evening in Spring" material to shew. The gang here all congratulates you on your Hersey detective successes—we can't begin to do as well. Last Monday I had a talk with Arthur McKeogh, Asst. Ed. of the Red Book, but it merely convinced me that nothing of mine is adapted to his type of magazine. Long may do better. I've seen Wandrei several times lately—he's doing very well at Dutton's. Tomorrow night the whole gang meets at 230 W. 97th, & a great time is expected. Today is a decent & sunny day—a rarity for this spring! Best wishes—Yr obt Servt—HPL

LATER—Long & I are going to Paterson to see our genial fellow-gangster James F. Morton. Looks like quite an outing.

Notes

1. Front: Washington Arch, New York.

[122]   [ANS][1]

[Postmarked Richmond, Va.,
4 May 1929]

Greetings from the birthplace of the nation! Am having a great trip to end my season of vacationing. Stopping in Richmond, & taking side trips to all the colonial places within reach. Williamsburg is great, & it is impressive to tread the storied soil of Jamestown. Going broke, so may have to cut my trip short before seeing all I want to see. Had hoped to stop in Washington & Phila., but probably can't. May have to cut out my Dwyer visit, too—can't tell about that as yet. I like the South best of all of all places outside New England—it is summer down here, all the greenery being out. Visited the Poe shrine in Richmond yesterday—will send you a card of it.
Regards—HPL

Notes

1. Front: Jamestown Church Tower and Communion Service.

[123]   [ANS][1]

May 10[, 1929]

My dear A W:—

Well, here I am in ancient Kingston, home of our friend Bernard Dwyer. It's a great old town—full of village atmosphere & ancient stone houses despite its 30,000 population. Had a great trip through the South—Jamestown, Yorktown, Williamsburg, Richmond, Fredericksburg, Washington, &c—then back north via Philadelphia. You can imagine how much antiquarian colour I absorbed! Now I've crossed back through NY & had a lift to Kingston in the Longs' car. From here I go to Albany & across the Mohawk Trail to Athol for a session with Cook—then home at last for another indefinite period of seclusion. The sparse, delicate leafage of the northern spring seems odd after the summer-like greenery of the South, but this vernal landscape has a loveliness all its own. Purple Catskill foothills loom up in the distance.

Congrats on Wright's acceptance of "Across the Hall"—he'll take the others later on! Hope the revisions turn out well, & that "Mater Dolorosa" will be a success. No hurry about "Evening in Spring"—the slower & more naturally you evolve it, the more poignant & authentic it will be.

As for your Rowfant purchase & the express charge which has impressed you so unfavourably—I could not repress a slight smile in view of the fact that this is the shop of which Samuel Loveman, author of "The Hermaphrodite", is half-owner! However, I can assure you that it isn't he who attends to the sordid details of the business end. *He* is the rare book expert, & a detestable little rat of a partner conducts the commercially administrative side. If you don't think you received a square deal, why not write Loveman at his home address, 78 Columbia Heights, Brooklyn?

Dwyer is a delightful chap, & I like him exceedingly. Great burly fellow 6 ft 3 in tall & broad to match, but highly strung & imaginatively sensitive. He has great stuff in him, & I hope his literary career will not be hampered by meagre financial circumstances. I shall stay here till Monday—then for Athol, Cook, & home.

Regards & best wishes—
    Yr obt Servt H P L

[Envelope postmarked Kingston, N.Y., 16 May 1929:] P.S. Belknap has finished "San Luis Rey" & agrees with you in preferring it to "Annie Spragg".

Notes

1. Composed on two postcards: Front No. 1: K. 49. Kingston, N.Y., Old Senate House by Night. Front No. 2: Bird's Eye View, Rondout, Looking West, Kingston, N.Y.

[124]   [ANS]¹

[Postmarked Athol, Mass.,
16 May 1929]

Greetings from a conclave of weird enthusiasts! My trip is ending up as gloriously as it began. After Kingston I explored the ancient Dutch & Huguenot villages of Hurley & New Paltz with their venerable stone houses, & then went up the Hudson to Albany. This morning I took the train back to my native New England, & am now in the congenial atmosphere of Athol, in the office of the Recluse Press. At the end of the week Cook & I shall go to Providence together—thus ending the most extended & glorious trip I ever took in my life.

Yr obt Servt HPL

H.P.L. will be here some days and we will explore a bit. He says no damage was done by my neglect of your letter of last winter. W. Paul Cook

---

Cook & I are going to get together very soon & make up a list to send you. Best of luck. MUNN

Notes

1. Front: New Arch Bridge, Main Street, Athol, Mass.

[125]   [ALS]

10 Barnes St.,
Providence, R.I.,
May 26, 1929.

My dear A W:—

Home again at last! It was a great trip, but I'm glad to be back for all that—for Providence is exquisite in the late spring. I do most of my writing outdoors in warm good weather—today I am on a rustic riverbank which I have known ever since I could walk—& which has not changed a particle in the 35 years & more since then.

Glad to hear of your renewed activity, & of the new Wright acceptances. Wright's amenability to repetitive bombardment is quite amusing, & I have no doubt but that all of your tales will land in the course of time. Trust your luck will be equally good with the detective tales. Your thesis on the history of this form must be highly interesting & well-informed—& much more popularly acceptable than the alternative topic you were forced to abandon!

Glad that Shiel is proving a generous & pleasing correspondent—I am wondering just how effective this second attempt at a revival of his work will prove. He has produced some astonishingly fine material, but is sadly uneven as a whole.

I am still hoping that I can write a few tales during the summer, though just now other duties oppress me to annihilation. Reading up a month & a half's accumulated papers & magazines was more of a job than it sounds!

Munn has had a strange submarine tale accepted by *Amazing Stories*, & I imagine it's well worth watching for. And don't forget to look for Long's "Black Druid" in some future W.T.[1]

With all best wishes—

Yr most ob^t Servt

H P L

Notes

1. Munn had no story in *Amazing Stories*. FBL, "The Black Druid," *WT* (July 1930); in *SNM*.

[126] [ALS]

Wednesday [5 June 1929]

My dear A W:—

Well, I'll be damned! Wright's methods of acceptance & rejection recede farther & farther beyond me the more I hear about them! And what has the good soul against poor Einstein! As for me—I have a sort of dislike of sending in anything which has been once rejected, so for the present I fancy I'll wait till I have something new. If Wright asks for any of the older stuff, he's welcome to it—but I don't like to push my things forward. Silly attitude, no doubt, but old men will be old men! Incidentally, I'm going to send Wright a tart note if he doesn't ship me the May copy of W.T. for which I paid almost 2 weeks ago. I lost mine while travelling, & sent Wright 25¢ in stamps for another—but that's the last I've heard. The letter couldn't have gone astray, since it bore my return address.

Good luck with "Old Hanson", "The Chicago Horror", & "Mr. Faversham". I must take a look at the new Shiel book.[1] Meanwhile I have lately read "Death in the Dusk" by Virgil Markham, (hopelessly artificial & conventional, yet with an horrific moment or two) "Chalk Face" by Waldo Frank, (cumbered with philosophy, but magnificent in its conception of the individual's relation to the external world) & "The Man Who Was Born Again", by Paul Busson.[2] (an excellent picaresque piece, with overtones of weirdness) I am now about to go over the weird short stories of A. Conan Doyle—as many as I could round up in W. Paul Cook's private library. Some of them I know, some of them I've read & forgotten, & some of them I seem never to have seen at all. It is quite possible that my opinion of Doyle as a weird writer will measurably increase within the next week or so!

As for extra copies of my "Outsider" & "Rats"—I regret very much that I haven't any such wholesale supplies as you need, & that I don't know of anyone who has. The best I could do would be to land you my sole detached copies—one apiece, in printed form, & with the "Rats" in a state of imminent disintegration. Too bad I can't supply the desiderate quantity—but this is all I have! However, I guess the stuff isn't worth writing up, after all!

Glad you've secured the autographed volumes from "We" (as I understand the neurotic William Ellery[3] is called by his intimates to distinguish him from the pedagogical "Say"—Sterling A) character, & a figure of real importance in American letters. Many of the "gang" admire him with particular intensity—especially our ex-member Alfred Galpin, who studied under him. This Galpin is the youth who roomed at 830 West Johnson St.—a neighbour of yours, save for a mere decade of the illusory element called time.

Yes—I'll tell Long to watch for "Pacer" "Lilac Bush", & "M. of S." I'm not sure but that Munn did send Wright his undersea yarn before *Amazing Stories* finally took it. He'll probably get more than he would have under the Gernsbackian regime, though perhaps not as much as W.T. would pay. If I produce any future material which could possibly be interpreted as pseudo-scientific, I shall probably try it on A.S. after W.T. rejection. Then there is, of course, a third & last resort—the new thing which Gernsback has just started.[4]

Old De Castro has popped up again—asking why I don't quote him prices, as I promised, on that proposed revision of his old printed tales. Alas, I must get busy! The old fox says he's had an accident & been ill four months, which may or may not be so. He gently intimates, in his fulsome way, that his Bierce book wouldn't have received such a critical drubbing if I had revised it—but that wouldn't get him anywhere if he expects I'll do his new revision in the nebulous terms which I rejected for the Bierce job!

Sorry that the heat has oppressed you—that's what a *cold* wave is doing to me right now! As I may have said before, we are opposites on the temperature question, since I definitely belong to the tropical fauna. The hotter it is, the better I like it & the more work I can do—I was at my best last week when the mercury touched 92°. But cold lays me out completely. I can't use my hand for writing under about 73° or 74°, & can't even think under 70°. Real outdoor winter cold—anything under 25° or so—is beyond my power to endure at all. I nearly collapsed to unconsciousness winter before last at 14°—had to be helped into a convenient restaurant, & was good for nothing for a week after that. It gets my respiration, digestion, locomotion, equilibrium, & everything else! The really ideal temperature for me is about 80°.

With best wishes—

Yr most ob^t h^ble Servt

H P L

Notes

1. M. P. Shiel, *How the Old Woman Got Home* (1928); *Here Comes the Lady* (1928); or *The*

Last Miracle (1929).

2. Later presented to HPL by AWD (see letter 160).

3. William Ellery Leonard (1876–1944), professor of English at the University of Wisconsin (1906–44) and author of *The Locomotive God*, which describes his distance phobia.

4. *Science Wonder Stories*, begun in June 1929 and retitled *Wonder Stories* in June 1930.

[127]   [ALS]

June 16[, 1929]

My dear A W:—

  I shall try to obtain *The Dragnet* on my next trip downtown, & will ask some of the gang to comment on your "Missing Tenants". It will interest me to see what changes you have made—I think I recall liking it even in the original form. Glad you have received a favourable notice—the writer will undoubtedly be glad to hear from you. You surely are getting to be a Hersey fixture. Belknap sent Hersey a tale & it was promptly returned!

  Wonder how long before Wright will take "The Chicago Horror"—it's quite an amusing game; like golf—see how many shots it takes to achieve a stated objective. It's all nonsense saying that Einstein has nothing to do with the 4th dimension—for he makes *Time* virtually that. Wright does love to quibble about words in matters of scientific definition. Yes—he sent me his wedding announcement. Poor fellow! And he had so many good qualities! Ave atque vale—requiescat in pace—if he can! Maybe I will try "The Nameless City" on him some time—but I certainly *shan't* re-type it! I'd rather write a dozen stories than type one—Hades, how I hate machines! If I don't get my May W.T. soon I shall break in on the Farnsworthian honeymoon with a brief but urbane reminder. I don't want any permanent gaps in my W.T. file as long as I try to keep any file at all.

  I used to own "Round the Fire Stories",[1] & can't imagine why I ever let it go. Yes—in the Doyle collection Cook lent me I recognised many of the old familiar tales, though there were a few I had not seen before. Doyle doesn't affect me as powerfully as he did 25 or 30 years ago. In those days I got a real shudder out of things like "J. Habakuk Jephson", "John Barrington Cowles", "The Ring of Thoth", & so on, but now I seem to sense the mechanics & the essential naivete. Doyle lacks some vague quality of mystical potency which Blackwood & Machen & De la Mare possess. But he is a good author for young readers, & I can see why he impressed me so strongly in the golden age of the 90's & early 1900's.

  The autographed poem volume was surely an honour. Odd that the author refuses to read MSS.—but perhaps they remind her too much of routine collegiate work. Good luck with your Rats & Outsider search—if you think the tales are worth it!

  I fancy that in this pleasant weather you are glad to be back in Sauk City again. I take my work outdoors nearly every day—sitting on the same lovely wooded river-bank which has been my favourite haunt since infancy, & which has changed not at all in all those long years. The way to defeat the sense of time is to cling close to unaltered early haunts. Amongst those forest paths I know so well the gap between the present & the days of 1899 or 1900 vanishes utterly—so that sometimes I almost tend to be astonished upon emergence to find the city grown out of its fin de siecle semblance!

I shall have a three-day guest Sunday morning—my fellow-gangster James Ferdinand Morton, whom Belknap & I were going to see in Paterson that day when I dropped you the postal—written en route—which you couldn't decipher.[2] We expect to do considerable exploration both antiquarian & mineralogical. I had hoped to have Cook & Munn down from Athol at the same time, but it now appears that they must postpone their trip a week or more. Hope you can get around this way sometime!

Best wishes—
H P L

Notes

1. By Sir Arthur Conan Doyle.
2. Letter 121.

[128]   [ALS]

[before 22 June 1929]

Dear A W:—

I can imagine your pleasure at being back in native scenes during these genial days, though I didn't know you found Madison so repugnant in its proper season. Most U. of Wis. graduates whom I know seem to think rather well of the old erudition-mart!

Wright, I fancy, is slowly coming to the surface; insomuch as I've just received the long-delayed back number of W.T. Hope you'll soon hear from him, & that you'll have several more of his typical reconsiderations to report. Regret to hear of *Murder Mysteries'* demise, but trust that the Hersey market will still remain expansive enough to accomodate all your products. I shall shortly get to the reading of the "Missing Tenants", & will see that somebody sends the editor a glowing critique. Your rate of production is beyond me— here's hoping you can keep it up to maximum financial advantage! But don't neglect the artistic side, as represented by your Proustian reminiscence.

You hopelessly outdistance me likewise in bibliothecal accumulations. At this rate you will have but little need for public libraries—which is a fortunate exemption if one can afford it.

I have lately had as a guest the genial James F. Morton, & have enjoyed shewing him some of my favourite ancient villages. Now I am expecting W. Paul Cook & H. Warner Munn for a briefer though no less pleasant call. Work has suffered amidst social distractions; but I hope to buckle down shortly, get the worst revision items cleaned up, & finally try my hand at one or two new tales.

    With all good wishes—

Yr most obt Servt

HPL

[129]   [ALS]

July 8, 1929

Dear A W:—

    Both shipments duly arrived, & I have perused all the items with keen interest & pleasure. I return them herewith—thanking you sincerely for the glimpse. "The Wind" is splendid, taking rank among your best work. Whilst the actual denouement is not a new device, the style & incidents surely supply all the originality which could be asked for. The intimations of cosmic overtones—Music of the Spheres, as it were—are highly effective, & I really cannot suggest any possible improvement. The atmosphere is adequate & haunting—of the sort which most poignantly appeals to me—& the style is unusually good; being that simple, direct, yet delicately shaded kind of utterance which will probably become your characteristic prose manner when your writing has fully mellowed & matured. "Old Hanson" is excellent, too. Though of a fairly familiar ghost pattern which you use not infrequently, it has a homely sincerity of atmosphere which gives it real strength. Beyond a doubt, your work has grown perceptibly during the past year. It has an increasing substance & convincingness, & you are rapidly discarding that early touch of *jauntiness* & quasi-assurance which tended to make some of the older stories seem mechanical & slightly superficial. "He Shall Come" is surely a dramatic & effective use of the devil motif, & compares well with any devil-tale I seem to recall. There is no doubt about the stranger's identity—indeed, the openly described imprint of the cloven hoof leaves almost too *little* doubt for the reader who relishes subtle suggestion. I would be inclined to *hint* rather than *state* the presence of the hoofmark—indeed, I think it might be well to have the phenomenon so bafflingly *indefinite* that even the priest entertains only a *horrible suspicion*. I would give the whole proceeding an air of phantasy & mystical nebulosity, toning down what is conventional & prosily theological—& also what is rather extravagant or grotesque; i.e., the physical ascent & vanishment of His Satanic Majesty in the sky. That shooting upward has just the least hint of the Gothic extravagance of the naive early horror-writers—as when Walpole in "Otranto" has the magnified form of the good Alfonso shoot up to the bosom of St. Nicholas amidst appropriate thunderclaps. Make the dissolution of the fiend more subtle—more a sort of *evaporation**. There is plenty of room for dramatic effectiveness in this—you could have strange intermediate distortions & changes (or suggestions of changes) of form as in the death of Helen Vaughan in Machen's "Great God Pan".

But it's a fine story, never fear! Even as it is, it ought to make W.T., & in somewhat subtilised form it would undoubtedly take a gratifying artistic rank. I enjoyed the O'Brien article[1] very much, & agree with your conclusions so far as my reading of O'B. permits me to do. I can see that my acquaintance with this author is sadly rudimentary—I have never, for example, seen "The Lost Room", "The Pot of Tulips", "The Wondersmith" or "The Bohemian"—& I wish I knew where I could get hold of a volume of his collected tales.[2] I fancy I would find "The Lost Room" particularly appealing. Your history of detective fiction interested me exceedingly, for I used to follow Sherlock Holmes with tense interest. Some day, for old times' sake, I must read the later Holmes stories. I have never read the Father Brown material, for it appeared after my zeal for sleuths had abated. Gaboriau[3] I read in youth, but he never appeared to me even comparable to Doyle.

By the way—I re-read the "Missing Tenants" with interest in *The Dragnet*, & Belknap has agreed to write Hersey a letter of praise. Hope this market will always prove receptive to your work. Did Hersey print the letter I wrote him about the "Black Narcissus"? I'll tell Cook not to use "A Matter of Sight".

Your bibliothecal additions seem very apt—I have heard "Wolf Solent"[4] praised to the skies as a sort of second "Wuthering Heights."

Weird Tales has seemed not quite so bad as usual for a couple of issues. I wonder if the E. F. Benson stuff is really fresh or merely reprinted? Of the indisputably original matter "The Death Touch" by Chester L. Saxby & "The Shadow Kingdom" by Robert E. Howard stand well among the longer yarns as your own contributions do among the shorter ones. I haven't finished the latest issue yet. Of all the tales recently published, Thatcher's "Last of the Mayas" is beyond a doubt the worst.

I am just now confronting a damnable revision job from old De Castro[5]—the Bierce satellite & biographer—who has made delay impossible by paying in advance! Consider me, then, as lost in chaos & woe for the next couple of weeks. It is like what I did for him in 1927–8—doctoring up some fictional junk he wrote in 1893. The old boy is going abroad on the 10th, & wants the work delivered while he is in London.

With best wishes, & thanking you again for the glimpse of the MSS., I remain

---

*Introduced, of course, *suggestively* and *indefinitely,* as it might have been an hallucination or imaginative symbol on the cleric's part. There is room for immense atmospheric subtlety at this point.

Yr most obt hble Servt

H P L

P.S. I've just finished the new W.T. Your "Old Mark" has been immeasurably improved by revision, although I think the new title does not apply to the central theme as well as it might. The "hero" is not Old Mark, but Old Mark's hideous familiar.

Notes

1. Emery Barnes, "Genius and Dandy: A Forgotten Master of the Short Story," *W. John O'London's Weekly* No. 293 (15 November 1924): 258.

2. Fitz James O'Brien, *Poems and Stories of Fitz-James O'Brien* (Boston: James R. Osgood, 1881), or *Collected Stories* (New York: Boni & Liveright, 1925).

3. Emile Gaboriau (1832–1873), nineteenth-century French mystery writer, novelist, and journalist, one of the pioneers of the modern *roman policier*. In his own time Gaboriau gained great popularity, but when Sir Arthur Conan Doyle created Sherlock Holmes, the international fame of his detective Lecoq declined.

4. By John Cowper Powys.

5. Presumably "The Electric Executioner."

[130]   [ALS]

July 20, 1929

My dear A.W.—

I read both of your new products with much interest, & think the "Evening in Spring" instalment remarkably vivid. As a lover of the sky, I noticed the astronomical portion with especial pleasure, & hope you will be sure to check up your facts correctly—as regards hour & season. Have you ever noticed anything *green* about Venus? I can't say that I have, & if there's anything about it in ordinary text books I must admit that I've forgotten it. Also, I trust you realise that the two *Dippers* & the two *Bears* are *identical,* so that you will not list both Dippers & Bears. More—no doubt you realise that the Pleiades are an *autumnal* cluster which does not rise in summer till midnight or after. And still more—Betelgeuse is of course a characteristic *winter* brilliant, which wouldn't appear till near dawn at the aestival season your account suggests. Better make sure of your stars through use of a revolving planisphere, if any such is accessible to you. "July Macabre" is good as far as it goes, but I think it lacks substance a trifle. If I were you I'd have more of a history develop regarding the child—that she was drowned in the well—& when—& why—&c. I can see the basis for Wright's criticism of this & the "Wind", although of course he generalises too extensively in the matter.

Sorry, by the way, that the "Wind" came back—but probably Brother Farnsworth will take it some time. He has just asked for my "Strange High

House in the Mist" which he rejected almost three years ago, but it is now too late. I let Cook have it for *The Recluse*,[1] & it would be very poor taste to ask him for its return—thus implying that he can have only such things as nobody else wants. In answering Wright I've suggested that he can use "The Nameless City" if he cares to. Incidentally, my miserable old tale "The Hound" is to be re-printed next month—a typical instance of Wrightian taste in selection!

I hope your book will duly come to pass in time, & think the tentative se-lections you mention are quite wise. It will interest me to see the final version of "He Shall Come". So Farnie chose the title "Old Mark", eh? I might have known it!

With such a strong recommendation, I shall indeed make an effort to procure & peruse Father Brown, & have no doubt but that I shall find him much above the ordinary level of fictional detectives. He & the more recent Philo Vance are two famous sleuths whom I know so far only by reputation! Some day I shall read the rest of Sherlock Holmes—there must be consider-able of a later date than my final perusals. Incidentally, my dipping into Doyle's weird material continues in a desultory way. Occasionally I recognise a yarn as something I have read in youth, & then will come something I don't seem to recall. "Lot 249"—the best thing I've struck so far—is quite a puzzle. Is it one of "Round the Fire Stories"? The *name* has always been familiar to me, yet when I read it it seemed absolutely new. How on earth could I ever have forgotten such a tale if I had read it before?[2]

Glad the "Narcissus" letter appeared. I don't recall reading "The Black Bag" through, but thought I'd mention it first to make my letter seem less obviously a Pons-puff. I've done the same in the outline which Belknap will send in—mentioned another story without having read it!

Great weather lately, & I've been doing all my writing in the open. Have varied my trip today, & am at Roger Williams Park—one of the largest & fin-est formally laid out parks in the U.S.—on the southern rim of the city. Did I tell you that I had a visit from the amateur journalist Victor E. Bacon last week, & that I took him to some of my favourite antiquarian haunts—Newport & Pawtuxet? Trust you're enjoying good weather & seeing some-thing of the countryside.

Best wishes

Yr most obt Servt

H P L

Notes

1. "The Strange High House in the Mist" and six sonnets from *Fungi from Yuggoth* (1929–30) were to appear in *Recluse* No. 2. The story reached the proof stage, but the poems did not. The issue never appeared.

2. "Lot No. 249." HPL described the story in "Weird Story Plots" and the rev. ed. of SHL.

[131]   [ALS]

July 29[, 1929]

Dear A W:—

 I think I'll shew Cook that "Evening in Spring" material. Do you want to supply any freshly revised copy, or is it all right to send along what you have furnished me in instalments? I haven't had a line from Cook since he & Munn were down here a month ago, & don't know when he'll ever get out that *Recluse*. There's no hurry, I imagine. Poor chap—I can appreciate his rushed state just now with especial poignancy, now that I'm overwhelmed with such a flood of revision. Another item on my feverishly jammed docket is a textbook on poetic appreciation by your fellow–U. of Wis–er Maurice W. Moe of Milwaukee. All I am doing is supply examples of certain metrical forms & give advice & comment on certain exercises. The thing is magnificent just as it stands, & I hope to Hades Macmillan will bring it out.[1] I wish you could meet Moe sometime—he was in Madison this summer for the reunion of his class of '04.[2]

 I am interested to hear of your work on your MSS. Wright told me to send "The Nameless City" along for a second consideration, & I have done so. Heaven only knows what the verdict will be. Perhaps he'll use "The Strange High House in the Mist" after Cook prints it—of course the *Recluse* will reach only a handful of people, none of whom are of the W.T. clientele.

 "Lot No. 249" does not concern real-estate, but applies to a *freight-shipment*. An oblong box. No—nothing murderous—only an Egyptian mummy . . . . . . *but* . . . . . I do not own the volume it's in, but have it here as a loan from Cook. It is one of a series of reprint volumes published in 1922 & 1924 by John Murray, London, "Murray's Fiction Library." The Doyle short-story miscellany (exclusive of Sherlock Holmes) comprises six volumes, titled as follows:

> Tales of Ring & Camp
> Tales of Pirates & Blue Water
> Tales of Terror & Mystery
> Tales of Twilight & the Unseen
> Tales of Adventure & Medical Life
> Tales of Long Ago.

The standard-edition volumes from which these tales are drawn are, according to the publisher's statement, "The Green Flag", "Round the Fire Stories", "Round the Red Lamp", "The Last Galley", "The Captain of the Polestar", & "Danger". There are also a few hitherto unpublished tales. "Lot 249" is in "Twilight & the Unseen". I could vow I've always known the title, yet never seem to have read the story till this time. These Murray volumes are priced at 2/- each.

 From your description, I don't think I'd care for Philo Vance. I hate these laboriously whimsical & artificially mannered fiction-heroes—they are so mechanical that they lose all touch with reality & become grotesque bores. I fancy Vance is, on a somewhat maturer level, about what Jules de Grandin is on his elementary plane. But I must look up Father Brown before I totter to the tomb.

Haven't been able to take any real trips lately—too damn busy—but have enjoyed the woods & fields as usual. I've read of your midwestern heat-wave, & duly sympathise from your point of view—although as I've told you, I never find it too hot. When it gets *cold*, it is I who need the sympathy. I couldn't possibly live through the winters of your section. Rhode Island's cold is almost too much for me, though you wouldn't call it anything at all— seldom under 20°, almost never below zero, & absolutely never below -3° within the history of the local weather bureau.

Well—best wishes—

Yr most obt

H P L

P.S. I'll sub-lend you Cook's volume containing "Lot 249" if you'd care to see it.

Notes

1. *Doorways to Poetry* (never published). Cf. *SL* 2.253, 255; 3.10, 13, 55, 129.
2. For the occasion, HPL wrote the humorous poem "An Epistle to the Rt. Hon[ble] Maurice Winter Moe, Esq. of Zythopolis, in the Northwest Territory of HIS MAJESTY'S American Dominion" (1929), recounting his memories of 1904. *Zythopolis* is Lovecraft's coined name for Milwaukee, meaning "Beer-town" (from the Greek ζύθος). Moe apparently printed the poem in a booklet prepared for the class of 1904, but this item has not been located.

[132]   [TLS]

Sauk City, Wisconsin
30 July, 1929

Dear H. P.,

Wright just returned the revision of THOSE WHO SEEK and 165 BASCOM HALL with the following:

"I like THOSE WHO SEEK in some ways, but it does not seem to click yet. I am unable to put my finger on the defects, but I sense that they are there. Specifically, the ending seems to be flat." Of the latter story, he says it lacks adequate motivation.

Can you suggest revision hints for these tales—having just revised them, I'm loath to go over them again, naturally, without something definite to work on.

Sincerely,

August W Derleth

[133]   [ALS, written on letter 132]

[2 August 1929]

It's hard to think of exactly what "Those Who Seek" needs, though perhaps the term "general tightening-up" would not be amiss. Have a tenser, more brooding *atmosphere* from the very start—less normality & cheerfulness of tone—*less conversation*. Have evil reputation of abbey *hinted at* more vaguely. Let Phillips's dream be *less specific & clear-cut*—stressing, as high spots, the location of the aperture & the appearance of the greenish-black Thing. Don't have Phillips hear chanted prayer *after he is awake*, & don't have him *actually see* anything down the opening. Just blackness—a stench—& a final *scream* which sends him fleeing & shatters his equilibrium. *This is the true actional climax*, so compress all subsequent material to the very limit. Have Arnseley's body found as stated. Also retain picture incident. That is especially good. Let Fr. Richards' comment be *very brief* & somewhat awed. Have him speak of the monster-picture first, then have Phillips shew his painting—& have its archaism recognised. The last paragraph is excellent as it is—the query of doubt as to who placed the inscription.

As for "Bascom Hall"—have the incidents preceded by the arrival of a strange figure on the campus—a pasty, unwholesome, glassy-eyed man who walks like an automaton & asks (in a curiously repulsive & hollowly gelatinous kind of bass voice) for permission to inspect the laboratory & the corpses stored for dissection. He claims to be a surgeon specialising in certain anatomical fields, & indeed shews vast surgical knowledge; but is highly obnoxious to those around him, inspiring an inexplicable sensation of dread. One student (young Valens) thinks he bears a singular resemblance to a noted physician who died 50 or 75 years previously, & who in life was devoted to odd theories about the union of body & soul. He is present when Jones makes a bad & clumsy mistake in dissection—*cutting out the tongue of a corpse unnecessarily*—& gives the youth a look of malevolence which many remember for a long time. Actually, of course, *he is a dead man*—the long-dead mystical physician himself—kept together & animated by strange arts, & intent on organising the dead of the world into a revolt against dissection in colleges &c. Mention certain earlier disarrangements in laboratories reported by the press—indicating the Dead Thing's arrival in America. Have Jones *deliberately lured* to Bascom Hall—the corpse steals his notebook & deliberately forges a note in a friend's handwriting, telling him the book may be found in the fateful room. Handle the lecture scene slightly more subtly. Don't have quite so many plain descriptions of the content of the lecture. Let a haze of vague indistinctness & mounting terror surround the whole business. Put *atmosphere* above everything else at this point. *Intimate* things rather than *saying* them.

When Jones is found, *let his tongue be missing.* Have it assumed that he bit it off in his fright, but let the *clear-cut nature of the severance* be widely wondered at. You might also have something found in his hand—clutched in his death-struggle. *The hand & wrist of a skeleton*—presumably some medical specimen he had been using, but pronounced by experts to be *very old.*

Well—here we are! Hope my comments may be of some slight use. Am knee-deep in work—including preparation of that poetry-manual by your fellow-Wisconsinite of which I think I spoke. Monday I'm going to take a vacation—trip to the celebrated "Wayside Inn" in Sudbury,[1] now owned by Henry Ford. Near though it is to Providence, I've not yet seen it—on account of the lack of transportation lines.

¶ Good luck & Best Wishes—
HPL

N.B. Noted your reference to U of Wis Memorial Union with especial interest, because my friend Moe has just been raving about it. His class of '04 had its principal reunion exercises there.

Incidentally—the *Saxons* never practiced *Druidic* worship. That was *Celtic.* Our ancestors worshipped Odin, Thor, Alfadur, & the Northern gods.

[On envelope:] Your material just came—I'll look it over as soon as possible. Wright has just re-rejected "The Nameless City"—he said the readers violently disliked "The Silver Key", & therefore. . . . .

Also, he says that the successors of the late Selwyn & Blount are going to issue another anthology of W.T. stuff, & intend to include "Pickman's Model."

Notes

1. Chronicled in "An Account of a Trip to the Antient Fairbanks House . . ."

[134]   [ALS]

Aug. 13[, 1929]

Dear A W:—

"The Door" captivates me exceedingly, & if Wright doesn't take it he ought to be deprived of his editorship! That last paragraph is a little puzzling—for how does anybody know that the hero was "drowned in the pool" unless the physician who sent him back to the cabin inferred it? Would it not be more probable if his mere *disappearance* were reported? Of course the pool would eventually be fruitlessly dragged, because the doctor would tell his story & the whole case would be remembered. It would even be said that Dunbar murdered Bruce & later committed suicide in remorse. But at first the general impression would merely be one of disappearance. The 'bus driver saw him get off—but nobody ever saw him again! As you say, the tale is really one which ought to go on & on. The doctor ought to become interested & after a tentative opening of the door ought to be impressed enough to undertake strange & thorough investigations—perhaps calling in some sort of "John Silence" for aid. Then there ought to be a final revelation or *intimation* of some kind—suggesting forbidden avenues between different systems of dimensions, or ordinarily sealed corridors into inconceivable reservoirs of infinity. But of course if the very brief "storiette" length is desired, I suppose it is all right to end where you do. At any rate, it's a fine story, & I hope it will appear in print soon.

Yes—Harré's anthology is supposed to have my "Cthulhu" in it, & I think it also contains Belknap's "Space-Eaters." I had a note from Harré the other day, saying that the Macaulay Co. were about to send me a free copy—but it hasn't come yet. The cheque—only $15.00—is slated for later transmission. I wouldn't be at all surprised if the new Not at Night annual had a goodly quota of your material. I trust that I may get a free copy, as I did of the issue containing "Red Hook".

Your list of acquisitions is as impressive as usual—& I am sure you will find the Doyle material welcome. These one-volume editions are a boon to those with limited space—I wish I could afford to get them all, & do away with the multi-volumed bulk of many of the authors now on my shelves! A friend of mine is doing this, & now has Poe, de Maupassant, Shakespeare, & many others in one-volume form. I've seen reviews of this new Coates book[1]—which doesn't sound very alluring to me. I met Coates—a pleasant, red-headed, youngish chap—in 1924, when that glib faker Henneberger (then of Weird Tales) was in N Y trying to get contributors for some silly humorous-verse magazine he was trying to found. Coates is a very intelligent & prepossessing person, & displayed an expert antiquarian knowledge of New York's colonial districts which quite captivated me—since my own interest in that field was considerable. I think we exchanged one or two letters, but later I lost track of him. Now & then I've seen articles of his in the N Y Times or Tribune. Neale's "Great Weird Stories" doesn't sound very alluring, either. So you never read Machen's "Shining Pyramid" till now! I wish I had some good unread Machen material to look forward to!

I shall shew Cook the "Evening in Spring" material & see what he thinks about using some or all of it. He ought to take to it very enthusiastically! I haven't heard from him in over a month, but fancy he's still among the living.

Last week I had a marvellous antiquarian trip, including the oldest house in New England (the Fairbanks house in Dedham, built in 1636 & forming the oldest frame building in America) & the celebrated "Wayside Inn" at Sudbury, built in 1686. Later this week I may join Belknap for a few days on Cape Cod, where he & his parents are stopping after their motor tour of Quebec. I've never seen the Cape, despite its relative proximity to Providence.

Best wishes—

Yr obt Servt

H P L

Notes

1. Robert M. Coates, *The Eater of Darkness*, a burlesque of the mystery novel.

[135]   [ALS]

Tuesday [20 August 1929]

My dear A W:—

Well, I got back Saturday from my four days at Onset, & found the usual delirium of work awaiting me. Belknap & his parents had invited me to join them at this last pausing-place on their long summer motor trip, & I was very glad of the refreshing outing. Onset is a rather sprightly beach resort of no especial quaintness, & outside of giving me my first aëroplane ride, (an exhilarating experience!) furnished no especial kick. But it is within easy reach of a very historic maritime region, so that side trips afforded all the colonial colour needed by my antiquarian soul. The ancient wharves & waterfront of New Bedford formed the high spot of the excursion; for although I had often been in the town before, I had never thoroughly explored it. This time I missed nothing—seeing among other things the old Seaman's Bethel on Johnnycake Hill mentioned in Melville's "Moby Dick", & the marvellous whaling museum with its realistic half-size model of the barque *Lagoda*. Other trips were to points on the lower arm of Cape Cod—where I found Sandwich the most interesting & attractive of the various ancient villages. The colonial windmills of the region were also of extreme interest. I was glad to see Belknap again—his party come through Providence on their return, & I was able to shew him the Harré anthology which had arrived during my absence. The company were very generous, & sent me *three* copies free. It is very good on the whole; but I was sorry to see Belknap left out, & think that Harré ought to have acknowledged the important aid given him by Wandrei in the matter of research & selection. Also, I had hoped to see Munn's "City of Spiders" included. However, I'm very glad to have the book; for much in it is new to me, besides a great many tales which I have read, but have not possessed in permanent form. By coincidence, I have also just received as a gift a copy of the Asbury "Not at Night" volume. This "Omnibus of Crime"[1] volume sounds rather good, & I find I have not read half of the items listed. I shall surely try to get hold of it. Thanks exceedingly for quoting the contents.

Good luck with your own work! It will interest me to see the ultimate version of "Those Who Seek" & "They Shall Rise in Great Numbers,"[2] & I hope Wright may decide to use them in the end. Hope, too, that "The Door" may meet success on its second trip out. You are certainly able to keep a lot of things going at once! I shall try to get hold of the September *Dragnet* & inspect your "Broken Chessman." You are lucky to be able to write detective stories, & thus have two markets open to you. Meanwhile I trust "Evening in Spring" may develop as powerfully & gracefully as it has been doing.

I am about rushed to death just now—& your fellow–U. of Wis.–adherent M. W. Moe is largely responsible; insomuch as he is hurrying me on the revision of his poetry textbook. Another possible source of congestion may likewise come from your alert & active commonwealth—a temporary job of magazine-editing, with its subject situate in Wauwautosa. [*sic*] This job concerns the *American Poetry Magazine*; whose editor, one Clara Catherine Prince Homan, is in arrears to the printer for nearly a thousand dollars. If she doesn't come across soon, this printer is going to attach & seize the magazine—publishing it himself until she pays up. And if this comes to pass, he wants me to edit the damn thing during his custodianship! I've said that I would if necessary—yet I rather hope I shan't have to. It would be a frightful burden just now! ¶ Regards & best wishes—

Yr obt Servt
HPL

Notes

1. Edited by Dorothy L. Sayers.
2. AWD and Mark Schorer, "They Shall Rise."

[136]   [ALS]

On a high wooded bluff
above a broad river a
mile west of my home—a
spot unchanged since I
haunted it in infancy.
Septr. 4, 1929

Dear A W:—

Congratulations on the acceptances! Wright is surely an adept in the calisthenics of taste! Glad "The Tenant" will appear in the new Not at Night[1]—possibly the "Antique Shop" will get into some other anthology. Macaulay Co. sent my $15.00 cheque over a week ago. Honest, even if not precisely munificent!

I shall have to look up the new Wakefield book.[2] I think I said I bought the first one last spring in N Y, when I found it on a remainder counter for half a dollar. I hope all the Shiel items will be included in the dollar series. I want "The Pale Ape" & "The Purple Cloud", though I wouldn't give much for any of the others. I was disappointed at Harré's not including "The House of Sounds" in his anthology. The tale he did use has a certain extravagance in proportion to substance which the longer yarn escaped.

Sorry the heat has adversely affected your health. I thrive on it—& am utterly knocked out by the cold. Today & yesterday were delightful sizzlers, & I have made the most of them by taking my work & reading to those ancient meads & groves which I have trodden since youth—good material for an "Evening in Spring" sort of reminiscence. Last week I took an all-day trip into the idyllic countryside of Western Rhode Island; covering a region endeared to me by hereditary memory, insomuch as it is the place where most of my maternal ancestors dwelt in the 18th & early 19th centuries. I visited a number of ancient family homesteads, & two family burying-grounds—at which latter I continued a task begun three years ago, of copying all the *epitaphs* of my progenitors. Worked on Phillipses this time, getting back to my great-great-grandfather Asaph, whose old slate slab bears a doleful weeping willow, & the touching lines

> The sweet remembrance of the just
> Shall flourish when they sleep in dust.

Before winter I shall make another trip—to an older burying ground far south of this one which I have never seen—& get the epitaphs of Asaph's father (d. 1807) & grandfather (d. 1746)—both named James. Then later I shall renew my hitherto vain search in Newport for the grave of Michael, the elder James's father, who croaked in 1686. After that I shall tackle Mike's old man—the Rev. George—whom the wind colic[3] bumped off at Watertown, Mass. in 1644. And then I'm out of luck unless I can dig up a trans-oceanic ticket; for George's pa Christopher, & all of Chris's predecessors, are planted in & around the ivied parish church of Rainham St. Martin's, in the hundred of Gallow, Norfolk, Old England. But I guess the American epitaphs alone would make quite a book, considering that this Phillips line is only one of many whose units are cached beneath the waving grasses of rustic New England! The scenery of the region I hunted through last week is as idyllic as anything in Virgil or Theocritus—green stone-walled meadows, shadowy woods, gnarled sloping orchards, brooks gliding through forested ravines or winding sinuously through lowland postures, lines of low hills with vistas of far purple horizons, quaint farmhouse gables rising above neighbouring crests, white belfries embowered in distant valleys—all the properties, in short, of the typical landscape of the pastoral bard. With an ancestry steeped in such topography, it's no wonder I'm a devotee of scenic rusticity & congenital hater of metropolitanism!

Trust your factory activity won't sap too much of your energies from literary pursuits. It can't be as bad as revision—for it doesn't demand any such concentration of the consciousness on annoying & repulsive matters outside one's real interests. At worst, it only takes your time & physical energies. I wish I could get something like that to do—for it's the encroachment of work on one's *mental* independence & energy that I resent. You will no doubt enjoy Chicago—large cities are all right until you have to live in them! Too bad so many of your friends—including your chief collaborator Schorer—will be in distant parts.

> With best wishes—
>
> > Yr most obt Servt
> >
> > H P L

P.S. I lately showed Belknap a good many of your MSS., & he was most favourably impressed. He said he could feel an *intelligence* in your writing which is absent both from Wandrei & from Clark Ashton Smith.

Notes

1. Christine Campbell Thomson, ed., *By Daylight Only*.
2. *Others Who Returned*.
3. Pain in the bowel due to extension with air or gas.

[137]   [ALS]

friday [13 September 1929]

my dear e. e. cummings—[1]

so the exigencies of the machine age have driven you into the modernistic style! fie upon such slavery to wrought steel! how blessed, in contrast, is the freedom of the 18th century wherein i spiritually dwell—a good goose-quill makes caps as easily as small letters, & if one can't catch a goose, a good wing-feather from a hen will do!

long saw several of your tales—indeed including "a matter of sight", & likewise some of the detective yarns. he also saw certain parts of "evening in spring." his opinion is worth something, so I think you are quite justified in being pleased. i wish you could get east & see him, as well as other members of "the gang", in person. i shall look for "scarlatti's bottle" in the next w.t.— & thereafter for the later acceptances.

i'll have to get hold of that wakefield book soon, & this norwegian collection[2] sounds interesting, too! i like the atmosphere of the far north for horror, (perhaps because all cold weather is an acute horror to me) & respond to things like "the house of sounds" & "skule skerry" with shudders of exceptionally heavy timbre. just now i am about to read a rather rare modern book in the greek spirit by a pseudonymous author—an ex-curator in the british museum— who uses the name of "compton leith". it is called "sirenica", & from extracts cited to me i must say i never saw finer contemporary prose. my friend & client m. w. moe of milwaukee is sending me a copy as a gift, & if you haven't seen it but wish to, i'll be glad to lend it to you. the prose is of the rhythmical, semi-poetic sort. yes—i imagine i'd enjoy de la mare's "ding dong bell" if it delves into antiquarianism & epitaphs. i like de la mare in almost any mood except the vapid whimsicality which he occasionally achieves in "broomsticks".

i'd like to see your wisconsin scenery, which i've been told is the finest in the middle west. you escape the monotonous prairies, i believe, which devitalise the scenery of illinois & other places to the south. the scenery of new england has, for its keynote, a sort of settled restfulness & quiet beauty; a great luxuriance of vegetation uniting with a gently rolling terrain studded with rocks to achieve a high degree of variety & loveliness without ever breaking into violence. it approaches the landscape of old england more closely than does any other american scenery. added to this natural setting are the ancient white farmhouses, gnarled orchard trees, narrow, winding roads, rough, low stone walls, & embowered village steeples & belfries which the hand of pastoral mankind brought in the first two centuries of colonisation, & which have blended harmoniously & almost indistinguishably with the landscape to form a highly characteristic & reposefully lovely type of scene. on every hand calm, long-seated, & wisely adjusted life is suggested—the net effect being more old-world & european than anything else south of french canada on this continent. of course the fringes of cities are now spoilt by cheap bungalows & tawdry mechanisation, but the back woods sections off the state roads retain a marvellous amount of the pristine colonial charm. these remarks apply mainly to *southern* new england. in *northern* new england we see the same *type* of landscape features on an enhanced scale—with a ruggedness which now & then (as in the white mountains & some parts of vermont) ascends into positive grandeur. northern new england is likewise much less vitiated by modernism & mechanisation.

trust you'll enjoy "dracula"—though i believe the play doesn't include the best parts of the novel. never having read the original "fu manchu", the cinema wouldn't have disappointed me[3]—though i seldom find much of merit in the cinema. i never go unless dragged by someone else—so that i doubt if i've seen ten performances in the last year.

as for expatriation—admitting the complete dulness of conventional american life, i have often wondered whether things are very strikingly different in those european regions so eagerly sought by dissatisfied aesthetes? it is true that the main intellectual streams of the older nations are sounder & mellower & more intelligent—less hog-ridden by the nightmare illusions of speed, commerce, machinery, & material wealth & luxury—than ours; but just how much of that basic advantage appears in the thousand small contacts & incidents of every-day life, remains to me a question. it seems to me as if an independent & self-sufficient man might get along quite as comfortably in america as anywhere else—exchanging ideas with the few who are like him, & letting the feverish, babbittistic majority go to the devil in their own way. certainly, one couldn't escape the sight of fools, both in & out of governmental office, in europe or anywhere else! so i am rather a favourer of home soil, where one has the benefit of accustomed scenes & childhood associations which one would miss elsewhere.

i must look up that blackwood item in the magazine.

with best wishes—

yr obt servt

hpl

p.s. wandrei has resigned his dutton job in disgust with commercialism, & is now engaged in the writing of a tale of age-old horror![4] he may visit providence this autumn.

Notes

1. HPL parodies the tendency of poet e. e. cummings (Edward Estlin Cummings, 1894–1962) to write poetry in virtually all lower-case letters, and thus presumably AWD's unintentional imitation of him because of a malfunctioning typewriter.

2. HPL may be referring to Jonas Lie's *Weird Tales from Northern Seas*, translated by R. Nisket Bain (London: Kegan, Paul, Trench & Trübner, 1893). Lie (1833–1908) was a leading ninteenth-century Norwegian writer.

3. *The Mysterious Dr. Fu Manchu* (Paramount, 1929), based on *The Insidious Dr. Fu-Manchu* (1913) by Sax Rohmer.

4. I.e., *Dead Titans, Waken!*, published as *The Web of Easter Island* (Sauk City, WI: Arkham House, 1948).

[138]   [ANS][1]

[Postmarked Providence, R.I.,
September 20, 1929]

Thanks immensely for the delightful landscape views. That harvest field especially appeals to my pastoral soul, & makes me hope I'll be able to take that western Rhode Island trip at the peak of autumnal picturesqueness. I know that Wisconsin has some exquisite scenic material—the United Amateur Press Association once held a convention at the Dells of the Wisconsin, & sent me the most alluring & tantalising array of pictures. By this time you're no doubt en route for Madison—which is not at all bad for scenery if pictures tell the truth. I had a good rural outing last Monday, but since then there's been a cold wave which keeps me crouching over the gas heater. You had *your* suffering in the hot weather—but *my* days of trial & anguish lie ahead! Best wishes—
HPL

Notes

1. Front: University Hall and Manning Hall, Brown University.

[139]   [ALS]

Septr. 26, 1929

Dear A W:—

Hope you'll receive the Wakefield book eventually—surely the lackadaisical shop that caused so much delay is a good place to change from! Such indifferent service is often provoking—though at my age I'm not especially impatient about such things. I am too much of a cynical sceptic about the value of speed to adopt a quantitative chronological standard. Thus while I can sympathise with you in the matter of the telephone, I can't imagine myself getting at all excited in a similar way. I hardly ever use a telephone, although there's one in the quiet house where I room. I take more pleasure in barriers interposed between myself & the modern world, than in links connecting me with it. I like to remain abstract, detached, neutral, indifferent, objective, impersonal, universal, & non-chronological—if you know what I mean. The whole ideal of modern America—based on speed, mechanical luxury, material achievement, & economic ostentation—seems to me ineffably puerile & undeserving of serious attention. My policy is to glide along quietly in the slow, restful backwaters of the world, where the familiar ways & thoughts & scenes of yesterday remain to lend the illusion of significance to a cosmos & life-process actually without purpose or meaning. My one unceasing question to the external world is simply: "What is anything?"—& I don't get any answer which would indicate the wisdom of adopting modernity's high-pressure life in preference to the more leisurely ancestral programme. The only conceivable value in existence is the satisfaction of the emotions; & if the elder ways will accomplish this as well as—or better than—the newer ways, then I'm all for the antique stuff! Of environment in general I ask only two things—a visual beauty, scenic & architectural, of sufficiently traditional quality to have poignant significance to me; & a quiet unobtrusiveness complete enough to allow my subjective imagination to function unhampered. I don't give a damn how bourgeois the circumambient population is, so long as a place is visually aesthetic & atmospherically restful. I can write letters when I want to exchange ideas. The two sorts of environment that would stifle me are the modern metropolitan & the *unpicturesquely* rural or village type. New York, I know from experience, asphyxiates me; & I don't fancy I'd be much better off in a flat Kansas farm or in a booster-ridden Iowa hamlet or small town. But New England fits me like a glove—since it has all the necessary beauty & quiet, besides holding all my childhood memories. I'd very much like to *see* Europe, & spend months in England, France, Germany, Spain, Italy, Greece, Constantinople, & Egypt—for I love travel, & need the imaginative stimulus of new impressions now and then. But I can't picture myself not wanting to get back to Providence after a while. My roots are here, & all my sense of natural orientation is based on local geography.

I shall be delighted to see your bright young friend & collaborator Schorer whenever he can get around.[1] It's only an hour's train ride, & about

2 hours' 'bus ride, from Boston to Providence—& the 'bus route, over the ancient Boston Post Road, is very attractive. Round trip 'bus fare is only $2.00. Tell Schorer to drop me a note or postal heralding his visit, so that I can be sure to be home. There's plenty of interesting stuff around Providence to show him—all the more interesting because the ancient & historic East is new to him—& he couldn't find a more willing guide than Grandpa H P! Hope I shan't bore him to death! I'll send full instructions for meeting me—or getting up to #10 Barnes—when I learn of his prospective advent.

"Dracula" was here a year or more ago,[2] but I passed it up. I'll go if it comes again, although I got bored by the drama as a whole over a decade ago. Glad that *Dragnet* still yields seasonable cheques—I've advised Long to go after that market, but I don't think he has your skill in the weaving of apt detective plots. By the way—his address is 230 West 97th St., New York City.

I am much interested in your choice of weird tales for thesis subject-matter, & believe I am more or less in agreement with the selective principle you employ. Of your first list, the only items which didn't give me the most supreme sort of kick are "A Dream of Armageddon" & "A View from a Hill." Wells never achieved enough *atmosphere* to give me a real emotional reaction, no matter how vivid the *events* he relates. As a James item I'd prefer "Count Magnus" to "A View from a Hill". And I'd add to any first-choice list Machen's "The White People". I'm enclosing a recent list of weird favourites compiled by Belknap (please return) which may be helpful as indicating the findings of a very acute & very independent & unbiased critical sense. I think he is right in listing "Halpin Frayser" above "Carcosa" amongst Bierciana—also in counting Blackwood's "Wendigo". Whether any of my junk belongs in such distinguished company remains to be seen. Of late I've been acquiring an increasing dissatisfaction with my products—especially the earlier ones—so that I'm almost glad Wright seems to have given up the book idea. There is a quality of cheap melodrama—extravagance, floridity, unrestraint—in my style, which needs ironing out, although it has decreased of itself since my "Hypnos" & "Hound" period. Still—I'm far from proud of the 30-odd items which stand on the books against me. Whether I can ever produce better work, or whether an attempt to civilise the style would cramp & denature the imaginative content, yet remains to be seen. But at any rate, the revisory hack work which I hate so bitterly has really not been without its positive value to me—for it has built up by degrees a severer & severer critical standard, which I naturally apply to my own stuff as much as to that of others. Now to get some time to grind out some junk based on that newer standard! Belknap's choices agree with yours in a good many cases, I see—as well as with my own. Of the items in your second list, I'm not sure that I've read one; ("The Blackthorn Gallows"—by whom?)[3] whilst one other, "The Woman at Seven Brothers", (is it a lighthouse story by Wilbur Daniel Steele?) lingers at the back of my head as something perused & half forgotten a decade ago. The

"Horseman in the Sky" isn't much of a *weird* tale—but rather a *conte cruel* like Maurice Level's. I think that Atherton "Striding Place" at the end of the Harré book ought to have a prominent place. "The Dead Valley", by Ralph Adams Cram, is another good thing. Further de la Mare items are "A Recluse", "All Hallows", & "The Tree"—& from Wakefield I'd cite "The Red Lodge" & "And He Shall Sing".

You mention a *new* book I spoke of, but I've forgotten that I did mention any. Do you mean W. Compton Leith's "Sirenica", which your fellow-Wisconsinner M. W. Moe lately gave me? That is not a new volume, but a reprint of something written perhaps a decade ago. It is not weird fiction, but a long-drawn essay of exceedingly Hellenic thought & style; & is remarkable for being cast in the finest rhythmic prose which either Moe or I have seen in aeons. It is quite uncommon; the British edition being small, & the Mosher reprint which I have being limited to 450 copies. Let me know whenever you care to see it, & I'll shoot it along as a loan.

I'll be glad to see the scenic snaps you speak of sending—for as you know, I greatly appreciated the postcards of kindred theme. I wish the New England rural landscape were adequately covered in postcards—I think I've sent you some from time to time, but I'll have to take views myself in order to shew the exact feel & quality of the scenery.

Best wishes—& tell Schorer to drop around here if ancient sights & ancient men don't bore him!

Yr obt Servt

H P

[P.S. on enclosed postcard:⁴] Just recd. yours of the 23d. Glad all the enrolling bother is over! Hope your Professor's weird discoveries won't turn out disappointing. That new Hutchinson anthology sounds good⁵—wonder if the firm is going to specialise in the weird? No—of course this collection can't be ours. That will be all W.T. reprints, & will probably have some (now woefully hackneyed) title connected with nyktophobia. I am saving your list of book titles for reference—all sound good, & may the gods grant me time to get at 'em some day! Just now I am making a bold effort to keep awake over an old Victorian novel which some damn'd misguided oaf recommended to me as "weird"—J. Sheridan Le Fanu's "House by the Churchyard." I had been disillusioned before by Le Fanu specimens, & this one about clinches my opinion that poor Sherry was a false alarm as a fear-monger. His reputation doesn't stand up under examination, & I shall cut him out of any possible 2nd edition of my historical sketch.

¶ Just now I'm nearly paralysed by a new bunch of revision from a guy in Chicago!⁶ Yr obt H P

[Note on reverse of HPL's bookplate, attached to postcard:] What do you think of my new bookplate? The colonial doorway motif typifies the atmosphere of old Providence, as well as my general antiquarian tastes. It was designed by Wilfred B. Talman—some of whose stories in W.T. you may recall

Notes

1. Such a meeting does not appear to have taken place.

2. HPL alludes to the play version of *Dracula* (1924) adapted by Hamilton Deane. A revised version by Deane and John Balderston opened in New York on 5 October 1927.

3. E. E. Speight, "Blackthorn Gallows," *WT* (September 1925).

4. Front: Windings of the Trail and River. Mohawk Trail, Mass. [Note by HPL on front:] New England scenery!

5. Probably Cynthia Asquith, ed., *Shudders*.

6. Lee Alexander Stone, who did not pay his bill (see *SL* 3.170–71).

[140]   [ALS]

Octr. 6[, 1929]

Dear A.W.:—

Regarding your inscription for "Death in the Crypt", I'd say, offhand, that the general cast seems quite all right, although a detail or two needs changing. In the first line, considering the whole arrangement, I'd advise *hic* instead of *qui*. I think it is perfectly possible to use *insto* intransitively, & *hic* seems to convey the desired sense best of all. Use your own judgment, though. In the third line my first thought is that you must say *hoc*, not *hunc*, since *feretrum* is neuter. And on second thought I fancy you'd better say *sepulcrum* instead of *feretrum* if I recall the scene correctly. You want to suggest a *tomb*—a permanent resting-place—instead of a movable *bier* for transporting a corpse; & *feretrum* (whose derivation from *fero* is obvious) most exclusively & emphatically suggests the latter. *Sepulcrum* being likewise neuter, let the *hoc* suggestion stand. In short, I'd have the inscription thus:

CVIVS. PASSVS. HIC. INSTAT.
CVIVS. MANVS. DESCENDIT.
HOC. SEPVLCRVM. VT. TANGAT.
EI. CERTE. MORIENDVM. EST.[1]

The only other suggestion I could make, would be to consider the casting of the *halt & descend* verbs in the *future* tense—i.e.—whose step *shall halt* here, &c. In that case, naturally, you would want to say INSTABIT. & DESCENDET. But use your own judgment. Good luck with the tale!

Yes—Wandrei's St. Paul return was surely sudden, & I regret that it annulled that Providence visit to which I had been looking forward. But I fancy it is the best thing for him. Home is one's ideal setting if one is to develop one's best attributes, & New York is no place for a white man to live. The metropolis is a flurried, garish dissonance of aimless speed & magnitude, hybrid & alien to the core, & without historic roots or traditions. It is an emotional & aesthetic island—& a desert island in the long run. A man belongs where he has roots—where the landscape & milieu have some relation to his thoughts & feelings, by virtue of having formed them. A real civilisation recognises this fact—& the circumstance that America is beginning to forget it, does far more than does the mere matter of commonplace thought & bourgeois inhibitions to convince me that the general American fabric is becoming less & less a true civilisation & more & more a vast, mechanical, & emotionally immature barbarism de luxe. But there's a good deal of the elder atmosphere left, & we may enjoy it while it lasts. Providence is the place for me—& St. Paul for Wandrei. It is well to be a Ulysses now & then, but every Ulysses must have his Ithaca.

I trust that Long & Wandrei will give you clear & succinct verdicts on your submitted list of tales. As for me—I'll do what I can, though I haven't all the texts before me, & my reading of some of the items is of very ancient date. Had you not deleted "The Outsider" from your list, I would have repeated my objection that much of the apparent force of that narrative is due to a climactic arrangement amounting to little more than a meretricious mechanical trick. The crux of a really fine story is much deeper & subtler than that.

    The Willows. This is, I think, the finest weird story ever penned by human hand. It is *perfect*—the loneliness of the river scene, the instability of the sandy, low-lying islet, the odd marine object just glimpsed, which *may have been* an otter, the subtle atmosphere & portents, the footprints, the damage to the canoe, the visual impressions half-glimpsed—& best of all, the absence of any anticlimactic final explanation. I have not this tale at hand, & last read it five years ago.

    The House of Sounds. Superlatively fine despite its obvious derivation from the H. of Usher. The *atmosphere* is *utterly unsurpassed in all fiction*—the chill horror & desolation of the dark, cryptic north, & the lashing, half-sentient, abyss-born waters. The north & the waters .... the waters & the north. .... I know of no parallel in this field save Buchan's recent (& deplorably anticlimactic) "Skule Skerry"—& Buchan probably got his atmosphere from Shiel. The tale itself—the curse, the brazen tower, the *measured* doom, & the unholy *listening*—is tremendously potent, & lives well up to the general atmosphere. Deserves a place on any list of the 12 best. I don't own this, & last read it 5 years ago. Have you ever read Shiel's crude prototype of this story (I forgot the title) in the volume called "Shapes in the Fire"? The change from that to the final version is a study in intelligent revision.

The White People. One of the greatest of all supernatural tales, & a work of tremendously accomplished art. Easily the foremost case of the use of the witch-cult & Roman-Britain motif. The *subtlety* is magnificent—only about a fourth of its readers ever realise what the essence of plot & climax is. The use of an artless child-narrative as a medium of narration is a stroke of genius, & the occasional reference to witch-cult secrets—Aklo letters, Voorish domes, &c.—has an enormously suggestive potency. The buttressing of the main narrative by episodic digressions is admirable, & the sinister figure of the nurse is well & sparingly drawn. Then comes that central marvel of the whole tale—that stupendously fine *landscape description* connected with the child's journey into the hills. Never have I seen more of malign sentience woven into the natural world—& so cunningly & convincingly woven. The climax, of course, is a masterpiece of elusiveness—& so ingeniously foreshadowed by the window & finger anecdote at the beginning. Machen never wrote a finer spectral tale than this—& of all his general writings I think that only "The Hill of Dreams" excels it. I own the book, but it's lent at present, so that I have to speak from 5 year old memory.

Count Magnus (infinitely finer than "A View from A Hill") This tale does not really belong in the "Willows" & "White People" class, yet ought surely to be among the best 12. James gains a certain laconic force through his matter-of-fact style of narration, yet there is an inevitable sacrifice of atmosphere. He never did better than this, though he came near it in "The Treasure of Abbot Thomas" & perhaps "An Episode in Cathedral History." The atmosphere of legend gives this tale an excellent background, & the landscape contributes much. Cryptic hints of a "Black Pilgrimage" add greatly; while certain clever touches like the tomb-carvings, the unlocked & fallen padlocks, &c &c. are very effective. It is a master-stroke to have the narrator flee *before* he sees what is issuing from the tomb. There is no final let-down. The ship's passengers—indefinite number, cloaked man, &c—furnish a good item; & the grim ending is appropriate. This is certainly one of great weird tales of all literature, although as I have said, it doesn't quite reach the best Blackwood or Machen or Poe level—& perhaps not that of "The House of Sounds". Don't own it, & last read it in 1926.

The Shadows on the Wall A very fine story, but doubtful of membership in the *utterly best* class. The tensity & restraint of the atmosphere are admirable, & the incidents are cleverly devised & arranged. There is some powerful & realistic character-drawing here; & the way the various members of the family react to the unnatural phenomena is splendidly suggested. If any limitations exist, they are such as arise from an overapplication of homely realism to a point where cosmic mystery seems impoverished—or perhaps this sense of impoverishment springs from the baldly simple & essentially mundane nature of the marvel delineated. There is *no room* for the more poignant sensations of *cosmic outsideness*. But it's a great tale— genuine literature. I have the text before me as I write.

The Yellow Sign—A very fine piece of work, with a well-nigh unsurpassed atmosphere of heavy, vividly present, & eldritchly stifling *nightmare*. Certainly deserves a place among the best twelve, since its suggestion of *cosmic outsideness* & malign backgrounds *behind life* is of extreme potency. Finely managed throughout—the gangrenous change in the painting after the appearance of the watchman, the description of the man himself, the anecdote of the bell-boy, the dovetailing nightmares, the talisman with the sign that is not of earth, & the book whose perusal is madness & terror. The last touch is masterly—"that man must have been dead for months!" I have the text before me as I write.

An Inhabitant of Carcosa. A splendid & artistic piece of work, & one suggestive of vast marvels & unholy aeons; yet to me somehow lacking in the atmospheric overtones which the nature & magnitude of the theme demand. Just a trifle too facile, mechanically. A trifle too dependent on the punch of an artificially clever climax. This plot is now woefully trite, but I'll give Bierce credit for being among the earliest users. As you know, this tale forms the germ of Chambers's "King in Yellow" idea. If you want to see Bierce at his real best, turn not to this but to "Halpin Frayser". I have the book before me as I write.

The Monkey's Paw. A melodramatically vivid & on the whole extremely powerful tale, probably deserving a place among the 25 or 50 best, if not among the dozen best. The tensity of the moment in which the dead son, in his mangled state, appears to be knocking at the door below, is hard to surpass. What keeps this story from actual *greatness* is its mechanical cleverness. It is too glib—to dependent on artifice—& not thoroughly permeated with that deep fibre of vague cosmic suggestiveness & profound abnormality which characterises supernatural literature of the first rank. Haven't the text here, & last read it in 1924.

Seaton's Aunt Very fine—may perhaps claim a place beside Blackwood & Machen, & certainly belongs in the best twelve. This tale has infinite subtlety & atmosphere, with hints of lingering forces of evil clustered about the vampiric old lady. Is in a subdued key which makes it less instantaneously striking than the typical Machen tale, but grows on one as one reflects upon it. Haven't the book, & last read the story in 1926.

A Dream of Armageddon A very effective story of its kind, with the element of time well handled. Magnitude & fatality—even majesty—can be glimpsed in the stupendous aerial combat scenes, & it ought to rank high with the "scientifiction" devotee. As weird art, however, it is distinctly lacking atmospherically—there is no subtle, elusive, cosmic profundity or stealthy, abnormal adumbration. Does not, in my opinion, belong with best 12. I last read it in 1923.

The Upper Berth.[2] Very fine. Belongs near if not in the best twelve. Has a stark, physical horror, mixed with the spectral element, very seldom surpassed—culminating in the hand-to-hand tussle with . . . *It.* The close quarters in which the action occurs, & the consequent *nearness* of the monstrous thing at every phase of the narrative, are especially notable. The jaunty, cheerful introduction detracts from the net power of the tale, but the latter half is so good that this incongruous note can be condoned. The story's real lack of greatness proceeds from the absence of any profoundly abnormal & original idea behind the horror. The mere ghost of a dead lunatic is "old stuff", so that there is a perceptible let-down toward the end. Not enough laws of the universe are broken to make the story really *tremendous.* We miss the *cosmic outsideness* which all profoundly great weird fiction must possess. Therefore I can't class it, good as it is, with Machen's & Blackwood's best. I have the text before me as I write.

"The Dead Valley" occurs in the anthology called "Ghosts, Grim & Gentle", (1926) edited by Joseph Lewis French. It is very subtle & fine, & I shall mention it in any possible future edition of my historical sketch. It seems to me that I've heard of other weird tales by Cram—& if so, I want to see them some day. The same mediaeval mysticism which motivates his exquisite Gothic architecture has this minor & less known outlet in literature. As for "The Blackthorn Gallows"—I've just looked it up in my files—not without some perplexity, since its date is Sept. *1925* & not 1926 as indicated. It is indeed an excellent story, & incomparably above the level of its surroundings—I recalled it perfectly upon re-reading—but I'd hesitate before singling it out for mention in a list of masterpieces. It is effective—as nearly all tales with animated corpses are—but has a sort of mechanical cleverness which saps at its vitality. In the last analysis it is probably supposed to have a rational explanation—that is, the visit & summons of the corpse was a conscience-vision, while in reality it was the mob of villagers who seized & hanged Martin. The clever thread of doubt is that created by Widow Gregory's curse, & her threat to send her son's corpse after Martin. One is left to wonder whether his vision was due to any long-distance spell from her. Now this sort of elusive ambiguity, developed with neatly dovetailed incidents, is very good technique; & the sort of thing which instructors in short story courses praise to the skies. But in my sober opinion, it is not the highest form of art. Artifice can never be quite that. Real art has a greater *simplicity*—no trickiness—& gains its appeal through a concentrated force & vividness which conveys the illusion of reality. Contrast this story with "The Willows"

& "The White People" to see what I mean. But that's not saying the story isn't good. It is—& for *Weird Tales* it is truly remarkable!

Glad you like the bookplate. It's none too large for my taste—indeed, I've seen specimens considerably larger. Talman is rally a fine decorative artist as amateurs go, though he doesn't excel in imaginative drawing as Clark Ashton Smith & Bernard Dwyer do. I'm rather pleased & amused to hear that Wright has been using "Two Black Bottles" as a model, insomuch as I planned the entire action & denouement myself. Originally the thing was called "*Three* Black Bottles", & had a vast amount of superfluous & loose-end material. I took it in hand & made a fresh synopsis—inventing the picture of the lumbering thing seen against the rising moon, as well as the evidences of disturbance from beneath in the parson's grave. I also invented the antecedent references—the background of diabolism & the origin of the hellish sexton. But I didn't do any of the writing—the phraseology is all Talman's. He had, I think, two more stories in W.T.—with which I had nothing to do. He is now a reporter on the N.Y. Times.

By the way—if you want to see a new story which is practically mine, read "The Curse of Yig" in the current W.T. Mrs. Reed is a client for whom Long & I have done oceans of work, & this story is about 75% mine. All I had to work on was a synopsis describing a couple of pioneers in a cabin with a nest of rattlesnakes beneath, the killing of the husband by snakes, the bursting of the corpse, & the madness of the wife, who was an eye-witness to the horror. There was no plot or motivation—no prologue or aftermath to the incident—so that one might say the story, as a story, is wholly my own. I invented the snake-god & the curse, the tragic wielding of the axe by the wife, the matter of the snake-victim's identity, & the asylum epilogue. Also, I worked up the geographic & other incidental colour—getting some data from the alleged authoress, who knows Oklahoma, but more from books. As it stands, the tale isn't bad according to W.T. standards; though of course it is absurdly *mechanical* & artificial. I have no regrets at not being the avowed author. I got $20.00 for the job, & Wright paid Mrs. Reed $45.00 for the completed MS.

Sorry the new Wakefield book doesn't equal the first—but I'll read it anyway if the local bibliothecae have it. I don't recall the title of the Chambers tale—"The Messengers"[3]—but if it's in the volume "In Search of the Unknown", I must have read it. That, the K in Y, & "The Maker of Moons", are the only 3 weird Chambers items I know of.

Wright hasn't formally notified me of an abandonment of that book plan, but I take his silence—plus the issuance of the Kline volume[4]—to mean that it's really off. I shall feel free to send my stuff around if I choose, but am in no hurry about it—& am too busy to attend to it now anyway. I don't think there'd be any cash in it. I may have quite a professional link with your state if certain plans go through. A friend of my friend Moe is thinking of establishing a publishing house for pedagogical books, & if he does, he will have me do all the revising. This is the bird in Wauwatosa who prints the Am. Poetry Magazine. Incidentally—speaking of professionalism—Harré has secured some hack work for Long to do—a job he would have given Wandrei had the latter stayed in N.Y.

Shall be glad to see the scenic snaps. Yes, I had imagined Wisconsin scenery not radically dissimilar to that of New England. ¶ Best wishes—

Yr most obt

H P L

P.S. Shall be delighted to see Schorer at any time. Did you say his course is post-graduate work at the Law School, or was that a mistaken impression of mine? He has a pleasant town to live & study in—I'm tremendously fond of quaint, old-fashioned shady, sleepy Cambridge, although I'm not stuck on Boston. My younger aunt lived in Cambridge 20 years—right near the college—so that from frequent visits I came to know the place almost as well as Providence. It has a subtle atmosphere of its own that grows on one.

Notes

1. This is how the inscription appears in the final version of the story (*CM* 257).

2. By F. Marion Crawford.

3. "The Messenger," *Ghost Stories* (November 1929). In *The Mystery of Choice* (1897).

4. Otis Adelbert Kline's *The Port of Peril* (Chicago: McClurg, 1930; originally a serial in the *Argosy*, as "The Fatal Messenger") was advertised on the back cover of *WT* for November 1929, apparently leading HPL to think that *WT*'s parent company, the Popular Fiction Publishing Co., had published the book.

[141]   [ALS]

The Quinsnicket Country
6 miles north of Providence
Octr. 21, 1929.

My dear A W:—

Let me thank you with the utmost sincerity for the generous batch of landscape photographs you so kindly lent—& which I shall return, packed very carefully, in tomorrow's mail. At this moment I am appreciating them in the least invidious & most appropriate manner possible—namely, viewing their transmitted beauty in the midst of the glowing, first-hand, autumnal beauty of the finest landscape vista in New-England! I am seated on a hillside—on the browning turf beside a road which spirals down before me to an eastward valley with a blue, glimmering mere at its bottom. The descent is undulant & variegated, with picturesque granite outcroppings, gay-foliaged trees, & rambling, old-fashioned stone walls here & there. On my right is the edge of a forested ravine with a brook at the bottom whose placid coursing I can just hear. In that ravine—now out of sight, but to be visited by me later in the afternoon—are the picturesque ivied ruins of an ancient mill which I knew in youth . . . . . raw material for some future "Evening in Spring" study of my own! On my left the ground sharply ascends in a series of graceful slopes now dotted with the sheaves of harvest-time, whilst peeping through the gnarled trees of red & gold hillside orchards are the time-stained gables of two venerable farmhouses—the Richard Comstock house, built in 1670, & the Benjamin Arnold house, built in 1732. But most fascinating of all is the panorama straight ahead, across the pool-bottom'd valley. There the opposite slope arises in the distance, rich with autumnal foliage, & shewing through the treetops the sun-gilded roofs & steeples of far-off Saylesville—an old-world prospect which carries the fancy back to Old England & the peaceful meads & vales along the Thames & Wye & Avon. Truly, I do not know of any landscape on earth which more appeals to me than this. It satisfies almost every major longing in my imagination. The charm could not possibly be captured by photography—& I would give nearly everything I possess for the power to draw or paint it. I have frequented this region since youth; & about the time you were born, tried to capture its charm in a long piece of 18th-century verse called "Quinsnicket Park"—whose sonorous heroic couplets emulated the Muse of Tickell in his "Kensington Gardens" or Denham's in "Cooper's Hill."[1] But it would take a vastly better artist than I to turn the trick! Just to give you an idea of the general topographical layout before me, I'll append herewith a crude diagram:

But oh, Hell! What's the use? You'll simply have to come East & see it for yourself! Well, anyway, you can see that I'm very much in a mood to appreciate the Wisconsin landscapes! Truly, I was tremendously glad to see all the views, & am strengthened in my conviction of Wisconsin's extreme beauty. I shall doubly appreciate "Evening in Spring" through having had visual glimpses of the regions involved.

. . . . The afternoon sunlight is getting golden & glamourous now—I wish you could see the way it catches that distant village steeple! . . . . . .

About the stories—yes, I dislike mechanically clever tales because I feel an omnipresent atmosphere of spuriousness & insincerity about them. I choose those with an element of cosmic outsideness, because I believe that this element is really the only form of the supernatural which can be used without a suggestion of flatness, grotesqueness, & falsity. Only in the direction of the outside can our sense of *mystic spaciousness* & *expectant adventurousness* be titillated to the fullest extent. The field is far richer—though of course it is possible to do very poor work in it. A bad artist can make *anything* flat, tame, & trite! On the whole, I can't pick any real flaws in your choice of 12 best tales. It is really very hard to find 12 first-raters by different authors.

Glad you voted for "The Curse of Yig". As soon as I finish my current De Castro quota I shall tackle another incident-germ ("plot-germ" would be too flattering a designation!) of Mrs. Reed's, producing a story which will be virtually my own. I hope (mildly, because I'll get my $20.00 anyhow!) Wright will take it when it's done.[2] His verdict on "He Shall Come" is even more than usually stupid—about on a par with his dictum that my "In the Vault" is too ghastly for his delicate & tender-souled readers!

Hope you'll come to satisfactory terms with *Manuscripts*—regarding both prose & poetry. "Small Town in Autumn" & "Rain in October" both strike me as admirable—sincere, specific, concrete, & poignant, & with an admirable suggestion of wistful mystery. I certainly advise you to continue poetry-writing, for you have the genuine material. If I had any criticism to make, it would be, first, that you have some conventional archaisms, inversions, & expressions (*o'er, drop now their leaves, touch of you*, &c) which are hardly suited to contemporary verse; & second, that possibly the necessities of stress do not fully justify the arbitrary irregularities of line-arrangement involved. I am a strong advocate of the *rhythmical prose* form for many elusive poetical images & ideas; & it seems to me that a fine stylist can manage his rhythms better without typographical interruptions. Breaks & stresses *suggest themselves*, without any aid from the printer, in really fine poetic prose. But all these are really minor points. The poems are in truth splendid, & I am extremely glad to have seen them. Here's hoping the editor of *Manuscripts* will like them as well as I do!

Hope you can stand the Macfadden hack work—Belknap landed one tale with *Ghost Stories*, but could never manage to repeat.[3] I couldn't make that magazine if I tried a century! Has Belknap told you of the hack work he is now doing for T. Everett Harré? Harré was going to have Wandrei do it, but Wandrei thought St. Paul looked better than Manhattan grubbing!

Well—that glamourous sun is sinking, & I'll have to move on if I want to glimpse that ruined mill in the ravine! Getting cold, too—I'm glad I carried a waistcoat along in my bag of books & papers! Fear the warm spell won't last—but it has been great for the past week. Last Wednesday & Friday I took long walks under the mystical Hunter's Moon—it was especially fine Friday, when one might clearly understand what Flecker was thinking of in describing "burning moonlight" in his "Hassan."[4] It just occurs to me that I've never seen this present landscape by moonlight. I'll have to come here some evening when the full moon is high enough to strike the valley.

On my way out here this noon I laid in a new stock of picture postals. Here are a few—& a thousand pardons if I've sent 'em before. That Betsey Williams cottage (built 1770) is a typical New England gambrel roofed farmhouse, & gives quite an idea of the pastoral, old-time atmosphere I love.

Well—regards & good luck, & renewed thanks for the landscape glimpses. Will return 'em tomorrow. Do you want the coloured view from the newspaper, too?

With best wishes—

    Yr most ob^t Servt

    H P

Notes

1. HPL alludes to the poetry of Thomas Tickell (1686–1740) and Sir John Denham (1615–1669).

2. The story was "The Mound," rejected by FW but published (as abridged by AWD) in *WT* after HPL's death. The story was not published in complete form until 1989.

3. FBL, "The Man Who Died Twice," *Ghost Stories* (January 1927).

4. The phrase "burning moonlight" does not occur in James Elroy Flecker's *Hassan,* but the phrase "blazing moonlight" is found in a scene description in Act V, Scene II. See *Hassan* (London: William Heinemann, 1922), p. 179.

[142]   [ALS]

                10 Barnes St.,

                Providence, R.I.,

                Novr. 8, 1929

Dear A W:—

    The various envelopes duly arrived, & I am indeed grateful for the captivating landscape glimpses. That colour-process is finely adapted to the reproduction of autumn views—I wish some of our local papers would adopt it! I can see that Wisconsin scenery has not, indeed, been overrated; for apparently it wholly escapes the monotony of the more southerly Middle West. I must see the region some time. It would certainly be a tragedy if your beloved hills were spoilt by summer cottages, & I hope fervently that the current rumours are unfounded. Surely, if you have the cash to do it, the wisest thing would be to buy up the land for a future estate of your own! I am unusually fortunate in the fact that all the choicest spots of my youthful stamping-grounds are part of the local park system—hence destined for perpetual preservation in their primal state. There are one or two exceptions, though, which I never cease to mourn—notably an idyllic ravine near my birthplace; now filled in & covered with streets & houses. My greatest regrets are for the quaint old streets of my youth—reliques of Colonial days into which "progress" gnaws as insidiously as a horde of rats. This autumn a whole row of ancient brick warehouses along the waterfront is doomed—& I am in a gravely melancholy mood thereat.[1]

As for mechanically clever tales—they may be all right for those who like them, but for me they have no more interest than the tricks of a vaudeville juggler—though of course there are many who like vaudeville jugglers! I prefer art—something which is half a reflection of reality (be that reality objective or subjective) & half an emanation of the artist's personality. One "Willows" is worth a carload of "Monkey's Paws"! About your poems—if you don't defend 'em, what can another say? Your retrospections always shew a keen poetic sense, & it's too early to say just how this faculty will shape itself in your ultimate expression. Rejections don't mean much.

Glad to hear of your various fictional placements—I never heard of the magazine *Detective Trails* before. Hope I can get down town before it's off the stands—just now my nose is at the revisory grindstone. I just received a semi-amateur sheet called *The Western Rustler* with some of your work in it.[2] Thanks—since I assume you are responsible for its arrival. Trust you'll have favourable reports from *Manuscripts* & *Ghost Stories*. Your recent bad-weather work sounds alluring, & I hope to see some of it shortly. The other day Belknap had a caller who would have amused you—a gross, fat braggart[3] who claims to be a friend of Wright & Henneberger & Vincent Starrett & all the W.T. crowd. He says Wright makes $8000.00 yearly from W.T., & that he cynically explains his underpayment of authors by saying "Why pay them more? They can't place such tales anywhere else!" This adipose being then went on to boast how he makes $15,000.00 per year by "writing for the pulps"—i.e., the cheap, wood-pulp printed magazines—& of how he despises an artist or literary man or anyone who does anything except make money. He stayed at the Long's till 4 a.m., talking a continuous blue streak; & Belknap says he has scarcely yet recovered! Such is a typical plutocrat of popular literature. He mentioned your friend Hersey, saying that "he used to get $12,000.000 [*sic*] a year from Hersey alone."

Your new literary material all looks good to me, although I'd suggest that "The Shuttered House" lacks definiteness & motivation. What's the idea—is the madness of Carlotta a residue from that of Mark & Elva, [& if so, why the coincidence of *both* Mark & Elva going mad?] or are all three madnesses due to some malign quality in the house—or its shutters & garden wall? And if the latter be the case, what *is* the source of the malignity? The story can't become a story in the fullest sense till you have given more of a hint of this than my unsubtle brain is able to discover. But the atmosphere is excellent, & I hope you'll keep the MS. for future amplification if Wright doesn't take it as it is. That reminiscence of trees & lights is delightful, & reminds me of the fantastic visionings induced throughout my life by certain landscape, architectural, & light-&-shade effects. The "Inversion of Hay" is good realism, but I can't see that such sensual-clinical matter belongs in the same realm as imaginative evocation. However, since the Proustian model sets the precedent—& since the imaginative life of the hero must receive considerable colouring from such experiences—I suppose at least a moderate amount of this stuff belongs indispensably in the narrative as a matter of scientific accuracy. It is too early to give an impartial verdict on the status of this promiscuous eroticism in which the younger folk wallow; since we cannot yet tell whether it be the precursor of a permanent change in erotic standards, or whither it be a mere episode like the morals of the Restoration era. If permanent, the only criticism which can be legitimately applied is against the *furtiveness* of the newer manner of life—a furtiveness which practices a code that it hasn't the guts to announce openly & explain in an historical & scientifically sociological way. One can condone the code of the open rebel or innovator more than that of the mere back-alley cat!

Glad you like Belknap's verse—& I'm sure he'll excuse your delayed remittance. He is crowded to the wall with revision, just as I am, but his venture in hack-writing exploded with the suspension of Macfadden's *True Strange Stories*. Did you notice in *Time* (which I think you take) what trouble Harré is having with some of his "ghost-writing"?[4]

I'm just finishing Hervey Allen's "Israfel: The Life & Times of Edgar Allan Poe", which I picked up as a remainder for $2.98. A great biography really, though in a somewhat careless style. It is the best exposition of the world of the '30s & '40s that I have yet come across.

Haven't taken any outings lately—too cursedly busy, & weather not warm enough to lure me out in defiance of all obligations! Leaves are getting sere & scarce, alas! What I want to do now is to get my working programme under control & write a few stories!

Good luck & best wishes—

Yr obt Servt

H P

P.S. Is the new Doyle book, "The Maracot Deep", any good? And what of the new Blackwood novel?[5] I assume that your literary omnivorousness makes you familiar with both of these contemporary items.

Notes

1. See letter 148.
2. I.e., "The Matchboy."
3. This was Armitage Trail, pseud. of Maurice Coons (1902–1930), author of *Scarface* (1930).
4. Harré was quoted as saying "It's a tough business, this ghost-writing" in the unsigned article "Liberty Liberties?" *Time* 14, No. 16 (14 October 1929): 71.
5. *Dudley and Gilderoy: A Nonsense.*

[143]   [ALS]

Tuesday [17 November 1929]

Dear A W:—

Thanks tremendously for the additional landscape view. Autumnal splendour hereabouts is now passing into autumnal bleakness & greyness; so that pictures like this begin to have the quality of wistful retrospection. If I ever get out to Wisconsin, I shall certainly ask for no better scenic guide than yourself—for your taste & capacity in rural aesthetics need no further demonstration than that set of snapshots, & your selective eye for colour-gravure items!

I think I get your point about "The Shuttered House" now, & am sure that with suitable polishing you can make a work of art of it. Wright, though, may be hard to convince regarding its subtleties—for he is a great stickler for prosaically diagrammed perspicuity! Your bulk of recent work quite paralyses me, & I trust that such of it as goes to "the pulp" may encounter a remunerative reception. The shorter items you mention, however, are probably of the most significance in relation to your literary career. I hope you can manage to spend next year in Europe, as suggested by your advisers—for certainly you would be able to absorb a vast amount of background which you could put to instant & advantageous literary use. I wish I had the cash to travel more myself—every time I visit a distant place I get filled with new visual impressions which persist in my head tenaciously; combining & re-combining with other mnemonic images, & forming the basis of hundreds of fresh & fantastic dream-landscapes & architectural vistas. I wish I could *draw* the stuff I get in this way—for of course only a small proportion of it has a logical place in prose fiction. A trip to Europe would outfit me with a lifetime stock of image-elements—& some time I hope I can take such a thing.

I haven't had time to read the December W.T., but can easily believe your verdict on it. I'll look for "The Shuttered Room" when I get at the magazine. That Walpole item has been recommended to me,[1] but I never got around to reading it. I hope I can manage to read "Look Homeward, Angel"[2] & the Asquith anthology in time—but bless my soul! I couldn't drink in books at your rate if I spent all my time trying!

As for Poeana—Krutch's study, while keen & able, is not a biography. It is, rather, an attempt at tracing the sources of the Poe mood & explaining the tales & poems in terms of the man. Hervey Allen's "Israfel" is an actual biography, explicit & documented, relating the objective events of the poet's life in copious detail & chronological order besides indulging in the usual analytical estimates & psychological speculations. It is subsequent to the Krutch book, & praises the latter considerably—agreeing perhaps 75 to 80% with Krutch's conclusions.

The other day the literary editor of the local *Journal* had a discussion in his daily column about the weirdest story ever written—& his choices were so commonplace that I couldn't resist writing him myself & enclosing transcripts (with my own tales omitted) of your & Belknap's lists of best horror tales. He wrote back asking permission to discuss the matter publicly in his column, mentioning you, Belknap, & myself by name—& I have told him he may do so. I'll send you whatever appears in print about us.[3]

Clark Ashton Smith has started writing weird tales as well as poems, & Wright has accepted several of them. He does pretty well, & is of course infinitely above the W.T. level. I've just read the carbon of his latest—a lamia-tale entitled "The End of the Story".[4] You'll soon see it in print.

Best wishes—

Yr most obt Servt

HPL

Notes

1. Hugh Walpole, *Portrait of a Man with Red Hair*.

2. By Thomas Wolfe.

3. B[etrand] K[elton] Hart (1892–1941) mentioned HPL several times in his column, "The Sideshow," in the *Providence Journal*: 101, No. 280 (23 November 1929): 2; No. 281 (25 November): 2; No. 286 (30 November): 10. See Kenneth F. Faig, Jr., "Lovecraft's Own Book of Weird Fiction," *The* HPL *Supplement*, No. 2 (July 1973): 4–14.

4. CAS, "The End of the Story," *WT* (May 1930).

[144]   [ALS]

Sunday [1 December 1929]

Dear A W:—

I am tremendously interested to hear of the authoritative judge to whom you referred our Jacobean argument! His verdict is a marvel of judicial tact which satisfies both sides—for you, who like a *well constructed* story, are told that "A View from a Hill" is the *better-proportioned*; whilst I, who like a *vividly & spontaneously conceived* story, have his assurance that more of his creative satisfaction went into "Count Magnus"! So we're both right—& so is Montague Rhodes James. Let me know of any more high spots which you may decipher in his letter through later research.[1]

Yes—"Shudders" sounds like the best single book of the cited lot to tackle, though description of "The Gold Point" is not wholly unalluring.[2] Some one has lent me "Vain Oblations" (1914) by Mrs. Katherine Fullerton Gerould, with the recommendation that it is weird. I shall see soon what I think of it.

Your own work is bewilderingly voluminous, as usual. I hope I shall see some of it in time, though I can't get around much to the magazine stands in this diabolically cold weather. I don't see how you do so much. My chief—& sufficiently submerging—occupation is concocting what will pass as a tale by the author of "Yig", though it will really be altogether my own, as woven around the merest non-plot suggestion. It is getting to be almost a novelette— & I'll be curious to see how you like it if it ever gets into print. The provisional name is "The Mound". When that's off the books, I shall refuse further major revision jobs till I can write some *acknowledgedly* original stuff of my own. Meanwhile—amusingly enough—I have slightly relapsed into my ancient versifying habit, & have ground out some weird jingles for Wright to reject.[3]

Here are at least two of the cuttings connected with the *Providence Journal* discussion—there will be three if my younger aunt arrives with some promised duplicates before I seal this epistle. I can't go out myself in weather like this—the thermometer's down to about 14°, & Friday night I nearly collapsed from the cold. You can keep any of these cuttings which you'd really like to add to your files—though you might send back for further lending any that would otherwise reach the waste basket. In case I don't get the third one, I'll mention that it is mainly a flattering review of "Cthulhu"—on which "B. K. H" stumbled in the Harré book without my ever having told him I wrote fiction. The odd kick is that he once actually happened to room in the building at 7 Thomas St., which I describe as the quarters of the artist Wilcox. But a much more personal kick which I got out of the item was the discovery, through allusions made therein, that I have "made" the three-star O'Brien group a second year in succession—"The Dunwich Horror" being thus honoured in "Best Short Stories of 1929", which I haven't yet seen. Since "Dunwich" was the only tale of mine that appeared in 1929, I hardly expected O'Brien to pick it! In the course of his column, "B. K. H." (Bertrand K. Hart) threatened to arrange with the local ghouls & wraiths to send a monstrous visitor to my doorstep at 3 a.m.[4]—& I am acknowledging his threat in the following lines—

The Messenger
— to B K H —

The Thing, he said, would come that night at three
From the old churchyard* on the hill below;
But crouching by an oak fire's wholesome glow,
I tried to tell myself it could not be.
Surely, I mused, it was a pleasantry
Devised by one who did not truly know
The Elder Sign, bequeathed from long ago,
That sets the fumbling forms of darkness free.

He had *not* meant it—*no*—but still I lit
Another lamp as starry Leo climbed
Out of the Seekonk†, & a steeple chimed
Three—& the firelight faded, bit by bit.
Then at the door that cautious rattling came—
And the mad truth devoured me like a flame![5]

In a recent number of his column B. K. H. speaks of a recent Providence visit of the eminent author & critic John Cowper Powys, & tells how that discerning person calls your precious "San Luis Rey" "a bit of pastry"![6] Get that, young man! I'm rubbing it into Belknap, one of whose idols Powys is. ¶ Best wishes

—Yr obt Servt

HP

P.S. I enclose another cutting about a delightful Providence hill vista.

P.P.S. Note that B. K. H. shares my own view anent "Armageddon", although I hadn't told him a word about my opinion!

[On envelope:] ***Extra!!***

Saturday's Sideshow is quite given over to your work—I've just learned about it, but haven't got one to send now. If Hart hasn't sent you one himself I'll do so. The column is getting to be quite a gang organ. He mentions "The Outsider"—but just notice that this has never formed an O'Brien choice.[7] O'B gave "The Picture in the House" 2 stars in 1924, then 3 stars in 1928 & 1929 to "Colour" & "Dunwich" respectively.

Notes

1. M. R. James to AWD, 13 November 1929 (ms., SHSW).

---

*St. John's—dating back to 1723—very spectral.
†River bounding Providence on the east.

2. Charles Loring Jackson, *The Gold Point and Other Strange Stories.*

3. HPL refers to "Recapture," "The Ancient Track," and "The Outpost" (the last actually was rejected because of length--only eight lines longer than "The Ancient Track," but too long to fit on a single page).

4. B. K. Hart, "The Sideshow," *Providence Journal* 101, No. 285 (29 November 1929): 12.

5. HPL's poem appeared in B. K. Hart, "The Sideshow," *Providence Journal* 101, No. 288 (3 December 1929): 14.

6. B. K. Hart, "The Sideshow," *Providence Journal* 101, No. 277 (20 November 1929): 2. Powys had said "a trifle of pastry."

7. B. K. Hart, "The Sideshow," *Providence Journal* 101, No. 285 (30 November 1929): 10.

[145]   [ALS]

Saturday [December 7, 1929]

Dear A W:—

Here is the rest of the Sideshow stuff. It was probably my mistake that the 1890 limit on your weird tale list was not emphasised; but as you see, the second printing of your list sets things right. It was rather amusing to receive so much notice in my own town, for hitherto my feeble attempts & their echoes have been prone to flutter mainly in distant places. Of those cuttings, the one about your work is for you to keep anyway—& you can keep the other two if you have any especial use for them. Thanks, incidentally, for your kind words to B. K. H. I fear you overestimate my products, but it is pleasant to have them thus overestimated by an acute & widely read young critic!

Well, well—so the O. Henry volume also takes a look at my lowly 3d-class work this year![1] I haven't much respect for this concoction, since its choices are largely governed by the popular commercial short-story tradition; but it is amusing to be mentioned, none the less. I do have respect for O'Brien, though; for throughout his 15 years of anthologising he has consistently adhered to a standard of real art value in making his choices. One may not agree with all his selections, but there's no denying that he works from sound principles, & with a commendable degree of sensitiveness. As for "Outsider" & "Rats"—oughtn't it to make you suspicious of your choice to reflect that these immature trick tales are also *Farnsworth Wright's* favourites? I agree with you about "Erich Zann"—indeed, I am not sure but that I like it best of all my tales—but I draw the line at "Rats" & "Outsider"!

As for Powys & the eternal "Bridge"—you are right in not letting one eminent person's opinion unduly influence you, but I must protest that familiarity with the literature of any *one* period—be it modern, Elizabethan, or anything else—is no test at all of a critic's ability to judge a work of art in general. Genuine art is absolutely timeless; & if a man have an adequate amount of general taste & classic literary background-knowledge, he is just as well able to pass on any given work whether or not he be erudite in the special products of the decade in which it was written. Indeed, a lack of this special familiarity is often an asset rather than a liability, since we can never study a thing impartially until we can separate it from the transient & the local, & get it scaled against the background of the whole main stream. Our opinions about immediate things are always distorted & confined by novelty & imperfect perspective—as we can easily see by comparing our *present* estimate of the books of a decade ago with the temporary estimate we made when they were new. Of every generation's products, a few survive—but how many critics ever pick the correct few *at the time*? Therefore I'd say that a man is a better critic for not clogging his taste & numbing his sensibilities with an excess of the minor work of any one period. True, he ought not to *neglect* any one period disproportionately, any more than he ought to overfeed his mind on any one. The real critic is non-chronological & balanced—& knows Langland & Surrey & Peele & Suckling & Waller & Thomson & Shenstone & Blake & Southey & Arnold & Swinburne & Masefield & T. S. Eliot in equal measure; knows, that is, the whole field, evenly & equally, & without the lumpy nuclei & lacunae of unevenness which spoil the judgment of the modernistic & the immature. He sees the landscape before him, without being swallowed up in the obscuring woods of any minute part of it. Heaven knows *I* don't belong to that ideal classification. Indeed, I'm no critic at all, but just a plain citizen who knows what he likes & what he doesn't like. But that's my idea of what a critic is. Of our gang, there's only *one* who really comes up to this standard—& that's the stout & genial James Ferdinand Morton. As for tenacity of opinion—it's well to be no weathercock, but my *theory* is directly opposed to your own. I think all opinion should be wholly *provisional,* & subject to revision when new data or new emotional experiences connected with standard-forming tend to amplify the base from which one's original view was obtained. My own opinions—so far as I am qualified to hold any—do not change often or mercurially, yet they do change in some cases when added knowledge, maturer judgment, or enlarged association-factors warrant it. I can look back, indeed, at two distinct periods of opinion whose foundations I have successively come to distrust—a period before 1919 or so, when the weight of classic authority unduly influenced me, & another period before 1919 to about 1925, when I placed too high a value on the elements of revolt, florid colour, & emotional extravagance or intensity. My present position is as unlike either my first or my second, as the second was unlike the first—& may very conceivably be followed by others of equal differentiation. None of these phases has implied any revolutionary repudiations or upsets of my general bulk of tastes & views; but all have meant minor changes in the *stress* of my preferences, aversions, & indifferences. And so with my opinion of any one work of art. I don't often execute a complete reversal of judgment, but the "curve" of my exact regard is not always a straight line. In time I may like the "Bridge" more—or perhaps less—than I do now. As I said, I do like it very much even at present, but simply do not give it the extreme rating in relation to other works which some enthusiasts do. Probably my love of the weird does prejudice me in favour of "Annie Spragg"; yet my chief basis of comparison does not concern weirdness at all, but revolves wholly around the undeniably cheap philosophic sententiousness of "The Bridge"—an obvious & conscious attempt to be "cosmic", yet with no better tools than a conventional & sentimental use of the illusion of teleology. This sort of thing needn't kill a book—but it makes it less meritorious than a book which is free from the defect.

Yes—I know that chapter in "Peter Whiffle",[2] which I read years ago when it was new. I found it an extremely clever & entertaining book, & am glad it is reprinted in the M. L. I'd like to see the new James tales—indeed, I must get hold of that "Shudders" soon. I'll pass on any data I hear of—although you're much more likely to get hold of novelties than I.

Your recent activity is quite paralysing, & I surely hope it will bring you an adequate financial return. I have the January W.T., & will try to get the Dec. *Dragnet* if it isn't off the stands. Appropriate letters to the respective editors may be expected. Your "Matter of Sight" is really the best thing in the Jany. W.T.—& I'll say so if I can do it without offending Belknap. His "Red Fetish" was written 5 or 6 years ago, but held by Wright for some cryptic reason. It has too much of the glib popular-magazine convention about it to suit me. As for the issue in general—my objections to the cover are (a) that it shews a man with a full beard in a clean-shaven age, & (b) that it shews diamond-paned casement windows in a house supposed to be of middle-Georgian date. But it's no worse than the story it goes with. My god! What linguistic mush Quinn concocts to represent the speech of the 1750's!!! It would be a prize-winner but for a particular "howler" in the same issue—that hilarious botch about Capt. Kidd's ghost. *That* thing is *unbeatable.* O gawd! O Montreal! Did you "get" the fancy diction—& the long ride *from Newgate to London*? Good Night!!! Hamilton has the usual formula—I wonder when he'll invent a new one? Always the hazardous destruction of the great machine at the last moment.

I'm still hoping to get at a new tale by the new year. Meanwhile I'm glad you regard my metrical vagaries kindly. Wright has just taken two—"The Ancient Track" & "Recapture". Here's another that he turned down on acct. of length. Please return it. ¶ Best wishes & regards

Yr oblig'd obt Servt.

HP

P.S. Watch for Clark Ashton Smith's new *stories* when W.T. begins to print them. "Satampra Zeiros"[3] is pure Dunsany!

Notes

1. "The Silver Key" was a "story ranking second."
2. By Carl Van Vechten. HPL probably refers to ch. 10, about Arthur Machen.
3. CAS, "The Tale of Satampra Zeiros," *WT* (November 1931). It was rejected on its first submittal, and so CAS's creation, Tsathoggua, first appeared in print in HPL's "The Whisperer in Darkness."

[146]   [ALS]

Sunday [15 December 1929]

Dear A W:—

Glad you enjoyed the additional Sideshow material. It's really a surprisingly brilliant column—better than any other I've seen in any paper—& I wonder how Hart can keep it up so unflaggingly. He seems to be one of those persons with unlimited energy & erudition like yourself!

As for Outsider & Rats—it makes one feel important to have them so profoundly debated in a learned thesis, though I can't seem to vary my opinion about them. Equal differences of opinion, however, have existed about far more genuine works of art! Regarding criticism in general—I guess your canons & methods are sound enough at bottom, though twenty more years of life may shift some of the emphases. All artistic appraisal is perplexingly vague & difficult, & there isn't any one critic alive whose verdicts could properly be endorsed 100%. Powys—whom I mentioned lately—has a disconcertingly explosive & subjective method of evaluating literature; though it is one which appeals tremendously to young Belknap.

Yes—I fancy Quinn pretty nearly reached his nadir in that recent effusion. Upon my soul, I don't see how he *can* grind out such pap, for some of his early work shews him to be undoubtedly a man of some taste & learning, & infinite technical cleverness. It is clear that his work for W.T. no longer means anything in the way of serious art to him. Your estimate of the tale is good—though I fear its effect on Brother Farnsworth will be annulled by several dozen scrawls of opposite tenor from the herd of illiterates forming the magazine's main clientele. The matter of *padding* reminds me of the fact that this is one thing I never need to do—since my manner of telling a tale always runs to such length that great restraint is needed to keep it within short story bounds.

Did you get "By Daylight Only" free, or did you have to buy it? I haven't seen a copy, & had no idea it was out, although Wright lately sent me a cheque for $21.25 to cover "Pickman's Model." Where does one get it? I'd sort of like to own it, since I'm represented therein. I hope the Blackwood volume has "The Willows" & "The Wendigo".[1]

Your two recent poems sound very prepossessing to me, & indicate the growth of a lyrical faculty which ought to turn out some fine work. "Runing" seems a very reasonable coinage, & surely no more of a departure than other poets have made in other directions. This verse has a hauntingly pensive quality, & the only objection I can think of is a tendency toward stock phraseology in one or two places—notably the expression "in all their splendour". In the few metrical attempts I make, I try like hell to get rid of this tendency—which as you probably know, I once had in a very acute form owing to my lifelong predelection for 18th century style.

Well—at last I've begun doing something to relieve the shelf congestion in my library. Lacking any more floor space, I've obtained three small bookcases to set on top of previously existing low cases—building up in skyscraper fashion, as it were. But these three do no more than barely accomodate the surplus heretofore scattered over the floor. I shall need to devise still further expedients if I expect to have anything like really orderly spaciousness. This arranging-siege makes me glad I'm not such a titanically large-scale collector as yourself. How do you manage to accomodate all your books—great shelves reaching to the ceiling? ¶ Best wishes—

Yr obt H P

Notes

1. Algernon Blackwood, *Strange Stories*. The volume is a selection from Blackwood's earlier collections. It includes "The Willows" but not "The Wendigo."

[147]   [ALS]

[week of December 22, 1929]

Dear A W:—

I was delighted with your two new sketches, & hope eventually to see the other recent serious work whose titles you cite. These sketches have a genuine poetic content—sincere emotional expression—& show that careful recognition & analysis of subtleties in mood & impression which is the one real contribution of the present age to literature. As I said when I first saw the "Evening in Spring" sections, I may try to do something of the sort myself some day—although the results I'd obtain would be antipodally different from yours. The idea of impersonal pageantry & time-&-space-defying phantasy has always—quite literally from the very dawn of consciousness—been so inextricably bound up with my inmost thought & feeling, that any searching transcript of my moods would sound highly artificial, exotic, & flavoured with conventional images, no matter how utterly faithful it might be in truth. What has haunted my dreams for nearly forty years is *a strange sense of adventurous expectancy connected with landscape & architecture & sky-effects*. I can see myself as a child of 2½ on the railway bridge at Auburndale, Mass., looking across & downward at the business part of the town, & feeling the imminence of some wonder which I could neither describe nor fully conceive—& there has never been a subsequent hour of my life when kindred sensations have been absent. I wish I could get the idea on paper—the sense of marvel & liberation hiding in obscure dimensions & problematically reachable at rare instants through vistas of ancient streets, across leagues of strange hill country, or up endless flights of marble steps culminating in tiers of balustraded terraces. Odd stuff—& needing a greater poet than I for effective aesthetic utilisation.

I'd like the address of the place you got "By Daylight Only" if you have it conveniently at hand. I'm too broke to buy it now, but sooner or later I'd relish its presence on my shelves. I'm still waiting for O'Brien's 1928 annual to reach the cheap second-hand market, so that I can pick up a copy of my "official biography" without unbecoming extravagance! Too bad you let Wright have all rights on "The Tenant". I got $21.50 for the use of "Pickman's Model"—the arrangement in this case being one outright payment instead of the dribbling royalty system used in connexion with the earlier "Not at Nights".

Your new book titles sound apt & impressive, as usual. I read "The Worm Ouroboros" a couple of years ago, & was immensely taken with it. It has a magnificent spirit of phantasy, & not enough satire to spoil the effect. The bound volumes of your own work must be very convenient. I largely let my stuff go to the devil—chucking all my duplicate MSS. & W.T. tear-outs into one large tin box & leaving the rest to the gods of chaos. As a result, I have a hell of a search every time anybody wants to borrow any particular manuscript!

Just now I am wretchedly melancholy over the destruction of some ancient local landmarks which did more than anything else to preserve the quaint, colonial character of downtown Providence. I enclose an illustrated article describing them—which I'll ask you to return at your convenience. I've bombarded local editors with protests against this vandalism—the last of which, in verse, I'll shew you when it comes back from the Journal.[1]

I was delighted to receive your recent likenesses, & agree that the distinct & normal one is the best. Belknap appreciated those you sent him—& I trust will reciprocate with a snap or two of himself. I wish you could persuade him to shave off or wipe off the alleged moustache or marks of stolen jam (one never can be sure which) on his upper lip!

Best Christmas wishes—

Yr obt Servt

HP

Notes

1. The letter "Retain Historic 'Old Brick Row,'" and the poem "The East India Brick Row."

[148]   [ALS]

[c. 27 December 1929]

Dear A W:—

I shall indeed be glad to see the new sketches, & agree with those who wish you could publish a collection of this material. You pen is so prolific that I am sure you will have a sufficient quantity of text before you know it—although of course this kind of product comes more slowly than the facile fiction you construct for "the pulp"—to quote Belknap's assertive caller.

Your European trip—a kind of "wanderjahr", as the phrase goes—will undoubtedly be a splendid thing for you, & will give you imaginative nourishment for years to come. I only wish I had the cash to do likewise! Let us hope your problem of personnel will adjust itself acceptably & practicably—why not persuade some nice old lady to go along as chaperon? If I were seeing a region for the first time I'd want to go absolutely alone, so that I could proportion the all-too-precious sightseeing time exactly according to my own tastes & caprices. No two people want precisely the same itinerary & scale of emphasis; so that unless cash & leisure are unlimited, somebody must be a martyr in all save solitary travelling.

If I get "By Daylight Only" it will probably be from the Argus—whose catalogues have reached me regularly for many years. What is their price? Not much more, I imagine, than the ultimate cost when ordered from England, if all the duties & incidentals be counted in. Munn—represented by "The Chain"—tells me he has a copy; & I am asking him whether or not he had to pay for it.

The loss of those landmarks still has me in a state of melancholy. The waterside facade is still standing, & the sense of tragedy one has in viewing it is tremendous. I enclose what I wrote on the subject—please return. It surprises me to hear that Sauk City has buildings as old as 1836, & I hope that you have local historical societies interested in the preservation of at least some of them. The early lore of the Mid-West must really be very dramatic & interesting, & I wish it could be better known to the country at large. How about that historical novel on which you were working some time ago? Illinois, I am told, (& the town of Delavan in that state was settled by kinsfolk of mine) has many old farmhouses of the traditional New England pattern, built by the first Yankee settlers & reproducing the ancient, simple constructional forms to which they were used at home.

Yes—Little Belknap calls the thing he wears a moustache. He has been coddling it for a full decade—ever since he was about $17\frac{1}{2}$—& in that interval it has gained some 7 new members & about 0.3 millimetre in collective length. Under certain conditions of illumination it is visible to the naked eye quite plainly, & camera lenses of sufficient speed & focus will register traces of it upon long exposure. He who can induce its sanguine young bearer to abolish it, will perform a service for contemporary aesthetics, & deserve well of his countrymen! But the kid is a great little poet for all that, & you'll make no mistake in presenting your friend & collaborator with a copy of his "Man from Genoa." I wish he could have another book, for his later work is more mature than these semi-juvenilia. Watch for his "Dagoth Wold" in W.T.[1]

I certainly hope you can stop in Providence before your European trip. Really—a taste of American antiquities is almost a necessary bit of background for the proper appreciation of Europe's remoter antiquities. It will delight me to shew you all you have time to see—not only Rhode Island, but that utterly incomparable north-of-Boston region where the decay of industry has left everything in a fairly Colonial condition—the "Arkham" & "Kingsport" country. Too, you ought some time to see the antiquities of the Middle-Atlantic & Southern regions. In N Y you must make Belknap show you some of the historic things—I'll tell you, or him, what.

The other night I was moved to pen a weird sonnet sequence which I shall soon try on Wright. Here's the MS. for a preview—please return.[2]

Best wishes for 1930—

Yr obt Servt

H P

Notes

1. FBL, Jr., "The Horror on Dagoth Wold" (verse), *WT* (February 1930).

2. I.e., *Fungi from Yuggoth*. The contents of this particular ms. are unknown. HPL modified the sonnet sequence in 1936, when R. H. Barlow intended to publish the sequence as a booklet, to include "Recapture" (November 1929) to make a total of thirty-six stanzas. He circulated copies of *Fungi From Yuggoth* as a sequence consisting of only thirty-three sonnets, holding back "Evening Star" and "Continuity" to be the concluding poems in the event that he later might write more sonnets as part of the body of the sequence (see letter 154). The ms. sent to AWD must have contained fewer than thirty-three sonnets. The extant A.Ms. of the poem contains the notes "Dec. 27, 1929" and "14 sonnets 196 lines." Another note states "16 additional sonnets—Dec 28, 1929–Jany 2 1930." "Evening Star" and "Continuity" were not composed until 4 January 1930. See further letter 149.

1930

[149] [ALS]

[early January 1930]

Dear A W:—

    Thanks for the generous array of recent works—a magazine in itself! You are certainly getting toward a place where your sketches ought to be eligible for the standard magazines—you have the faculty for extracting significance from the commonplace which they dote upon. Of the various items I think that "The Old Lady"[,][1] "The Strauss Waltz", & perhaps "Houses at Night" are the most solid & subtle & generally meritorious. For one of your few years you have an extraordinary insight into the pathos of age & loneliness, & can symbolise & illustrate it splendidly. Of the two weird tales I think "The Laughter" is the more powerful. In the other one, by the way, you oughtn't to call James "Mr." if he is a *baronet*. A baronet is an *hereditary knight*, & bears the title "Sir"; so that your hapless hero is properly *Sir Hilary James*. If I were you I'd brush up somewhat on British usage—you are so fond of British settings for your tales. Another thing—your 18th Century archaism in the 1727 note rather overshoots the mark, though not so badly as Quinn's in last month's *Weird Tales*. I wonder why so many authors, despite a presumable knowledge of Addison, Pope, Swift, De Foe, Arbuthnot, &c &c., persist in foisting a kind of quasi-Elisabethan diction on the 18th century! The entry you cite ought to go something like this:

> "This year—1727—at Quarter-Sessions, was Condemn'd for Poaching by Sir Guy James, Bart., one Hamish Inness of yᵉ village; who being convicted, was hang'd upon yᵉ Knoll, & dying, lay'd this Curse on Sir Guy's line: that it shou'd end in yᵉ seventh Generation hence, when he, the said Inness, wou'd come to the Heir then living & hang him in his thirty-seventh year from ye same Tree. This yᵉ condemn'd sware (as he said) by yᵉ Branches of yᵉ Inverted Cross, by the Arm of Gallows-Tree, & by yᵉ All-knowing Trinity."[2]

As you may know, the form "yᵉ" (used because the Saxon letter for *"th"* looked something like a "y") was employed *in handwriting only*—interchangeably with "the"—& was pronounced *"the"*, just as if spelt in the common manner. Incidentally, though—if your hero is the *heir* of Lᵈ Furnival, why is he not himself Lᵈ Furnival instead of Sir Hilary James, Bart.? Possibly you had better cut out the 1727 peerage in order to be consistent. Another thing—your weird tales would be more powerful if told without the element of aimless jauntiness appearing in such mannerisms as the repetition of the full name & title "Sir Hilary James" over & over again whenever referring to your central character. What a weird tale needs above all else is *straight-forward simplicity*—devoid alike of bombast, humour, mannerism, & affected kittenishness. *Objectivity* is the keynote unless a fantastic or vaguely dreamlike atmosphere is to be used. But your tale is excellent, none the less, & I heartily hope that Wright will take both it & "The Laughter."

I feel flattered at your taking a copy of "Brick Row"—though I can't agree with your view as to line 8. The omission of the first *and* would be good prose, but would form a jarring note in this particular place. *Flowers* here has its colloquial monosyllabic value.[3] As for the sonnet you dislike—#10—I've had my doubts about that, too, because its appreciation depends upon a familiarity with the actual customs of the "Hell's Kitchen" slum in New York, where bonfire-building & pigeon-flying are the two leading recreations of youth.[4] To one unacquainted with the region & its *mores,* the sonnet would inevitably have a tendency to seem pointless. That ought to give it an excellent chance with Wright, judging from the majority of the "poems" he uses. I've ground out about 20 more of these things, & shall see what Brother Farnsworth has to say of them.

As for *affectations*—you'll outgrow your present liking for them when a wider perspective of life gradually reveals them to you as inane, shoddy, & essentially irrelevant—like the jigsaw ornaments on houses of the 1880 period. Most of us go through an egocentric & affected period around twenty—my especial penchant was being austere & dignified, & wearing black ties, white bosom shirt, black coat & vest, & grey striped trousers like my grandfather. I thought that was being highly conservative—& even went as far as high standing collars, round barrel cuffs, silver-headed walking stick, & heavy mosaic cuff-buttons that my grandfather bought in Italy . . . . St. Peter's on one, & the Forum on the other. But I came out of it before long, & nowadays dress & act just as plainly & quietly as possible. The only people who let their affectations stick to them in later life are small-calibred & emotionally immature folk—perpetual adolescents, or tawdry self-advertisers like the late Elbert Hubbard[5] with his flowing tie & locks. A genuine adult knows that there is no point or sense at all in calling attention to himself. He does his work, & lets that speak for him. Attention gained by cheap advertising is unwelcome rather than welcome to the mature mind. Just as every part of a Greek temple fits harmoniously into the design of the whole without calling individual attention to itself, so does a gentleman wish to become a quietly harmonious part of his natural background—eliminating crude assertiveness & self-dramatisation, & recognising how small a part any individual plays in the massed scheme of things. When a man really has something to do, or something to say, he has no inclination to indulge in irrelevant side-issues like theatrical rigging-up & exhibitionistic strutting. He gets his kick out of what he is creating—or out of the objective aesthetic or intellectual experiences which make him create. Only the sterile or juvenile mind finds its main kick in exploitation of the person or of the ego. But of course we all have to be young once. I'm not blaming you yet—but I do think that little Belknap-rascal is about old enough to wipe that fuzz off his lip, get a real man's haircut, & settle down as a serious creator! God knows I was all over my posing period at his age!

My opinion of the recent W.T. coincides with yours. You & Guy de Maupassant stand alone & preëminent amongst the fictional contributors. I really think the magazine is getting worse, if possible, than it used to be. Edmond Hamilton's devotion to his one formula is getting to be more than a mere joke—it is as irritating a repetition as the torture of dropping water! And E. Hoffmann Price, real colourist & Orientalist though he is, has become thoroughly cheapened & popularised. "Behind the Moon" is simply wasted space except for a colour-touch or two connected with the vegetable-men—although the earlier serial "Skull-Face" really did have some fine touches. Robert E. Howard could be a real writer if he would throw the popular romantic convention overboard & just be himself. I hope I shan't be too badly disappointed in the announced serial by Paul Ernst—from whom I seem to recall some very decent work. Pretty soon I expect to get around to some story-writing of my own—but I need plenty of continuous leisure to do that. Hasty junk is just as well unwritten. I shall be glad to see "The Pacer" in print. Has the text been changed since I saw the MS. last? I'll probably purchase "By Daylight Only" from the Argus. It ought to be worth a dollar & a quarter!

With best wishes, & renewed thanks for the return of the MSS.—

Yr most obt Servt

H P

Notes

1. Possibly the same as "Old Ladies."

2. In this passage, and certain others in subsequent letters, to evoke a sense of archaism HPL used the "long s" typical of eighteenth-century orthography.

3. The line reads: "Which gives us flowers and mountains and the sea."

4. The original draft of "X. The Pigeon-Flyers" of *Fungi from Yuggoth* was named "Hell's Kitchen."

5. Elbert Hubbard (1856–1915), American author, publisher (whose Roycroft Press promoted hand craftsmanship and fine books), and proponent of rugged individualism.

[150]   [ALS]

[mid-January 1930]

Dear A W:—

Thanks exceedingly for the Chambers story,[1] which is really quite good. It seems to be one of a series, of which the others ought to be interesting. Do you know what book it's from? Too bad Chambers left off weird work—he certainly had a genuine special talent in that direction. I suppose I've missed some good reprints through not keeping up with *Ghost Stories*, but I can hardly take a dozen magazines merely for the sake of a few occasional items. Thanks also for the landscape views. I must see your state some day! That old rail fence idyll is one of the most charming vistas I've glimpsed in ages.

Respecting archaisms—oh, yes, I know that y^e & y^t were thus printed in the incunabula period, but I was talking about the Early Georgian Age. It is odd that so few people seem to have a correct "feel" for the easy swing of Georgian prose. Nine-tenths of the popular authors foist the fumbling Jacobean or Elizabethan idiom on to any dialogue laid before 1800! M. R. James, though, has the correct tempo—as becomes a professional antiquary.

Your sympathy with lonely old age is indeed remarkable, & I shall be much interested in seeing "The Gold." Your other new products, too, sound interesting in their respective directions; & I hope they may meet the approval of the editorial fraternity. Have you seen the new pseudo-scientific magazine *Astounding Stories*? It appears to be a pallid imitation of *Amazing Stories*, & ought to form an additional market for anyone able to meet its demands. There is one tale in it by a *Providence* writer—Hugh B. Cave. I don't know anything about him, but his versified attempts frequently appear in the local papers.

By the way—my "Brick Row" got such a favourable public response that the *Journal* editor wrote me a very pleasant letter. Wish the thing might have appeared sooner—though of course it couldn't really have saved the old buildings. Another recent thing which rather tickled me was a favourable mention of my tales in William Bolitho's column in the *N Y World*[2]—although it was spoiled by the coupling of my name with that of the amiable hack Otis Adelbert Kline! Speaking of hacks—Belknap's new fat friend blustered into the Long apartment the other night waving an 18-month contract with the Pathé cinema firm which will yield him the average sum of $25,000 per annum. "Man, Man!" he shouted to Belknap, "do you mean to say that with your genius you aren't making at least $15,000?" This animal is named Trail, & is only 26 years old. Did you ever come across his name in "the pulp"?

Your recent library additions sound very prepossessing—but gawd! where can you put so many books!?!!? I must get hold of one or two Blackwood items myself—my first choices being "Incredible Adventures", "John Silence", & anything containing "The Willows." But when one is near good public libraries one doesn't have to own everything.

Just had an invitation to go up to Northern Vermont, but had to decline because of my susceptibility to cold. I can't stand anything under about +20°, & would be a corpse in ten minutes in the climate of Montpelier. But it was hard work resisting the temptation—for the crowded hills of Vermont must be magnificently weird & impressive amidst the death & desolation of snowy silence.

Well—best wishes, & let me see some of your new material when it's ready.

> Yr obt Servt
>
> H P

Notes

1. "The Mask," *Ghost Stories* (February 1930). In *The King in Yellow.*
2. In his article "Pulp Magazines," *New York World* (4 January 1930): 11, William Bolitho remarks: "In this world [of pulp writing] there are chiefs, evidently. I am inclined to think they must be pretty good. There is Otis Adelbert Kline and H. P. Lovecraft, whom I am sure I would rather read than many fashionable lady novelists they give teas to; and poets too."

[151]   [ALS]

[late January or early February 1930]

Dear A W:—

    I have read "Walking in the Moonlight" with extreme interest, & think your own regard for it is eminently justified. It has the modern virtue of sincerely attempting to get beneath surfaces & trace actual impressions, associations, symbolisations, & moods—& it appears to me to succeed in a very substantial degree. It ought to be included in "Evening in Spring"—which will certainly be a monumental work when it is done. I hope you'll take your time about finishing it—giving it a thorough polishing, & balancing the parts in such a way as to produce a thoroughly integrated & artistically symmetrical whole. I'm going to send the MS. for Belknap to see—& I'll tell you his opinion.

    Descending to the ridiculous—I'll ask whether or not this fat blustering Trail's praenomen is *Armitage*. Probably it is—for mediocre stuff of the sort you imply is exactly the kind of thing to bring in vast loads of cash. I don't pretend to understand the world of low-grade professional writing—it has laws & conditions of its own, & surely yields rich dividends to the callous & fortunate beings who can find a place therein.

    That Blackwood book looks distinctly worth having, even though a more judicious selection of stories might have been made. I can see how you might be bored with a good deal of Brother Algernon's work—for he has produced incredible amounts of insufferable namby-pamby—but can't follow you when you extend your ennui to cover such things "A Descent into Egypt." I liked that—& I don't care who knows it! I can understand very sympathetically what Algy is trying to do—& although he necessarily does it imperfectly, I still think he does it a damn sight better than anybody else so far. Certainly,

I'm out of the running despite my most earnest attempts! What this objective is, is to capture those elusive & indefinable sensations tending to create illusions of disordered dimensions, realities, & time-space elements, which all sensitive & imaginative people possess to a greater or lesser degree. Naturally, this is a full man's sized job—& I don't know of anybody else who has had the guts to tackle it seriously. You ought to sympathise very keenly with the process, because it is really a phase of the very ideal you follow—the modern wish to get beneath artificial patterns & track down subtle impressions & gradations of mood. Those who treat of man's sense of the weird in the traditional objective way—following ready-made conceptions of the supernatural & presenting their material integratedly, narratively, & from the outside—are only superficial dabblers so far as actual psychological expression is concerned, no matter how artistically their products may be modelled. Even Machen & Bierce don't get far in this direction. Poe tried to, but lacked the especial temperament. I try to, & have the temperament to know what I'm trying, but I lack the skill to convey anything of value to the reader. Blackwood—because he plunges right in & isn't afraid to make a fool of himself now & then—has gone farther than any of us. No one else has ever managed to express or suggest just what he has expressed & suggested when at his best—& such an unique victory is more than enough to atone for the slush & drivel of "The Extra Day", "The Garden of Survival", "The Wave," & such pathetic though well-meant junk. If I could have written "The Willows" & "Incredible Adventures", I'd feel that I'd justified my existence, & wouldn't worry about any future work. Yes, indeed—I'd be damned grateful for your old "John Silence" . . . . . & for "Incredible Adventures", too; although if you're sensible you will eventually decide not to discard the latter. That one book is worth all the tales M. R. James ever wrote or will write!

So that Chambers tale came from "The Maker of Moons"![1] So much for an old man's memory! I read that book 4 years ago—& can't recall a trace of this material!

Best wishes—

Yr most obt

H P

P.S. I see that Lafcadio Hearn's "Kwaidan" is reprinted in the dollar Riverside Library. I shall try to get it.

Notes

1. AWD is in error. See letter 140n3.

[152]   [ALS]

Feby. 18[, 1930]

Dear A. W.—

Well—you certainly set the old gentleman a good-sized job in the matter of that list of W.T. stories! Did you think I could *remember* all that assorted & casually skimmed material extending back five or six years? Well—as it happened, I was interested enough to get out my complete file & set the mnemonic cords twanging again, with the result that I am able to give you some comment after all. It brought back old times to go over the ancient stuff, & in general I found my hazy original opinions sustained by these second glances. My verdicts seem, in general, to coincide fairly closely with your own—it having being my tendency to cross out certain things which you include, rather than to add things you do not include. I have, however, made a few such additions. Of course this is all sheer personal opinion, for you to take or leave at your own option. Heeding your admonition, I have not tried to pass verdicts on my own stuff; although I doubt if I'd include "The Hound" or "The Terrible Old Man" in any select list. I also have my doubts about "Red Hook", & think that "The Lurking Fear" needs a very thorough re-writing in order to be worth anything. "The Moon-Bog" is another dud, & "The Tomb" & "The Temple" are nothing to brag about. "Hypnos" is on the borderline—at present it bores me profoundly. Of all my tales I half-believe I like "Erich Zann" the best. After that come "Dunwich", "The Colour out of Space", "Ulthar", "Nameless City", "Cthulhu", "Arthur Jermyn", (White Ape) & perhaps "Dagon". "The Hound" is the worst piece of mine to get into print. Looking over the whole contents of W.T., one's final impression is that of a devastating desert of crudity & mediocrity, relieved by a very few oases. The high spots that impress me are Suter's "Beyond the Door", Humphreys' "The Floor Above", Arnold's "The Night Wire", Worrell's "The Canal", Burks' "Bells of Oceana", & Leahy's "In Amundsen's Tent".[1] Those things have the *atmosphere & suggestion* which spell power.

I'll suggest to Belknap that he lay off the deific titles—though possibly his "Elephant God"[2] caption is only tentative, since he often changes titles at the last moment. As I read over his older tales yesterday, I was impressed by the extent of his progress since 1924 or 1925. In those days he had some of the tricks & affectations of the popular-magazine tradition, as exemplified by favourite words & phrases; but he is shedding these as he matures. I shall be interested to know what you think of Clark Ashton Smith's prose work when it begins to appear in ample quantity. He is writing many tales, & if Wright doesn't reject them all, (as he did the best one!) you will see some remarkable specimens.

Possibly nothing will come of the Badger proposition,[3] but there's no harm in seeing what it does amount to. I agree with you that it is better not to attempt publication until some firm is willing to assume the financial risk itself. As for the amount of material available—of course, if a book were to be *weird only*, you wouldn't want to wait for more tales; but even now you have a good stock of MSS. if you could mix the serious non-weird things with the weird MSS. I hope, incidentally, that you will succeed in that *Ghost Stories* placement. Their rate of pay makes them an admirable market, though I doubt if I could ever suit their requirements. Wright's new magazine ought to be an excellent thing for you, though it probably wouldn't pay any more than W.T.

Yes—I wish I had the energy & imagination to write some of the myriad tales that are floating around in my head, but I'm not good for much in winter! Hope the spring will limber me up a bit, as it generally does. If I can ever get through another damn northern winter, I shall marvel at my endurance. Much as I love my native New England soil, I may have to migrate south some day—to some old city like Charleston, S.C., St. Augustine, Fla., or New Orleans—unless some unexpected windfall enables me to *travel* in the south between November & May while still retaining a strategic base & aestival habitat in Old Providence. I wish to Gawd I had been born in a climate fit to inhabit!

Well—I hope to enclosed annotations will be of some use to you. I shall want a copy of your critical & bibliographical magnum opus when it is done.

Best wishes—

Yr most obt hble Servt

H P

Notes

1. J. Paul Suter, "Beyond the Door" (April 1923; rpt. September 1930); M. L. Humphries, "The Floor Above" (May 1923; rpt. June 1933); H. F. Arnold, "The Night Wire" (September 1926; rpt. August 1934; in *NS*); Everil Worrell, "The Canal" (December 1927; rpt. April 1935; in *S&D*); Arthur J. Burks, "Bells of Oceana" (December 1927; rpt. April 1934); and John Martin Leahy, "In Amundsen's Tent" (January 1928; rpt. August 1935; in *S&D*). HPL may have been instrumental in having these tales reprinted; now gathered in Douglas A. Anderson, ed., *H. P. Lovecraft's Favorite Weird Tales: The Roots of Modern Horror* (New York: Cold Spring Press, 2005).

2. FBL's "The Elephant God of Leng" was published as "The Horror from the Hills," *WT* (January and February/March 1931).

3. Richard G. Badger was a publisher in Boston, known for publishing the work of poetical novices.

[153]   [ALS]

Tuesday [25 February 1930]

Dear A W:—

Thanks tremendously for the pictures—I wish our local Sunday Journal would adopt colour in its rotogravure section! The page of "Zero on the Farm" gave me some appropriate shivers. The scenes look much like my own New England—& I suppose the temperatures are about like those of that Vermont region to which I had to decline a January invitation! Brrrr!! .... but the sketches are really admirably done. I shall keep this page with the scenic views in my files.

As for Blackwood—I still hold to my settled view, while freely admitting that he often wastes words, repeats himself, & flounders generally. His *style* has been corrupted by journalistic influence, & is not to be taken seriously in any way. What *does* matter about him is his *insight* & *subject-matter*. He gets at psychological subtleties & profundities that others wholly overlook. Nobody claims that he gets at them in the best & neatest way they could be gotten at. The point is that he gets at them at all—which is more than anybody else has ever done. I shall be the first to cheer—& to praise beyond Blackwood—any future writer who combines Blackwood's insight & sensitiveness with the Machen-like craftsmanship which we all admit Blackwood does not possess. But in the interim I award Algy the palm which is his, as it were, by default.

I hope that material of yours lands with *Ghost Stories,* for their paying conditions surpass those of Brother Farnsworth. Apropos of "The Bridge of Sighs"—see the enclosed which just arrived from our friend Victor E. Bacon. It seems that I am not the only one in good old New England to appreciate your work! This Badger, I have heard, makes authors finance their own work; yet if you have the cash I suppose you could do worse than deal with him. I gave Bacon your address—or rather, informed him of the continued effectiveness of the one he has.

I like "Just a Song at Twilight" very much. If that's a typical specimen of your new weird material, I'm sceptical about your 'falling off'—indeed, I imagine the decline is in your special interest rather than in your ability. It certainly seems to me that the average quality of your contemporary weird output is greatly above that of your tales of several years ago—in workmanship, at least.

By the way—Wright tells me he is about to launch another magazine,[1] devoted to "stories which are truly strange & unusual in plot." All subjects will be included—even weird stuff now & then. I don't suppose this opening will mean much to me, but it ought to mean a new market for one of your versatility. I just received an $11.00 cheque for "The Ancient Track", & now I'm up against the job of revising a newly typed MS. of "The Rats in the Walls" for reprinting in the June issue. Incidentally—Wright has just accepted one of the tales I've been revising. Watch for "The Electric Executioner", by Adolphe de Castro. I started a tale of my own yesterday[2]—a Vermont horror that brooded in the hills—but after three paragraphs a god-damn rush revision order hit me! I think the gods are against my ever writing anything more!

I'll transmit your regards to Little Belknap. The kid's working on a novelette of horror—"The Elephant God of Leng"—which ought to be pretty good.

Best wishes—

Yr obt Servt

H P

Notes

1. Probably *Oriental Tales,* which began publication in October–November 1930.
2. "The Whisperer in Darkness."

[154] [ALS]

Monday [3 March 1930]

Dear A W:—

       "The Gold" is splendid—I hasten to return it as requested, & am very grateful for the glimpse of it. It is full of a masterfully drawn shadow & pathos, & certainly ranks among your best work. Your command of the psychology of lonely old age is really extraordinary.

I'm sure your thesis will interest me, serious or not, & hope to see it in due course of time. Have you any plans for publication? If professional markets seem unlikely, you might see if Cook wouldn't like it for some future number of "The Recluse."

It is always amusing to hear of Wright's rejection-&-acceptance tactics! Hope "The Portrait" won't be malformed too badly—my own rule is to allow no alterations whatever in MSS . . . . take 'em as they stand, or reject 'em! Of the 33 "Fungi from Yuggoth" which I wrote & sent around, Wright has taken 10, & the *Providence Journal* five more. The *Journal* pays modestly, but of course the W.T. batch will bring me $35.00—not so bad for a few random verse trifles! I reached page 4 of my new tale when some more rush revision hit me. Good night once more!

The Bishop Murder cinema has come & gone without attendance on my part, but at your recommendation I'll try to see it on its second run.[1] Belknap has urged me to read the book, but I thought the film would probably ruin whatever merit there was in it. I have not followed the various "Van Dine" productions, because the first one rather wearied me (as far as I read) in *Scribners.*

Your new Solar Pons oeuvre promises to be a piquant & ponderous affair, & I trust will be proportionately remunerative. I wish I had the gift for grinding out such material instead of doing revision—but we are such as the gods have modelled us! As for Fu Manchu—I have never read any of these tales, & wonder whether they have anything of merit in them. So far, Rohmer has interested me only with "Brood of the Witch-Queen".

After some hellish cold, New England is basking in what amounts to be a premature spring. Thank gawd while it lasts! I think I shall knock off indoor work this afternoon & get out somewhere in the open—taking along a port-folio of letters in an effort to answer some of them from a woodland seat.

Best wishes—& renewed congratulations on "The Gold".

Yr most obt

H P

Notes

1. *The Bishop Murder Case* (MGM, 1930), based on the detective novel (1929) by S. S. Van Dine.

[155]   [ALS]

[late February 1930]

Dear A W:—

I think the "Pacer" revision in the March W.T. was very good, & wish the changes in "The Portrait" were equally in the right direction. Unfortunately, there is more than one kind of revision! I have not yet seen the new W.T., though I suppose it is out. No doubt its level is about the same as usual—about the same as it will always be so long as Wright is at the helm. The damned fool has just turned down the story I 'ghost-wrote' for my Kansas City client, on the ground that it was too long for single publication, yet structurally unadapted to division. I'm not worrying, because I've got my cash; but it does sicken me to watch the caprices of that editorial jackass! I'll bet ten bucks he turns down the first really signed story I send him, too; notwithstanding his insistent urging that I write one. Which reminds me that I'm now about 10 pages into that new Vermont horror—the writing of which is constantly interrupted by other matters. One of the things Brother Farny won't like about that is a decidedly long letter by one of the characters—but I've decided that this is the best way to introduce the main action, & if he doesn't like it he can reject it as he did "The Nameless City". I am through with doing things to suit anybody else.

Yes—I shall try to see both book & cinema of the Bishop Murder Case. With such a galaxy of favourable opinion—you & Belknap—I cannot but be assured that the thing is truly notable.

Your list of favourite books interested me greatly—especially since I haven't read more than half of the volumes in question. I would have to think hard before selecting a compact "desert island" library, but I could probably patch up some sort of a list in the end. Of the items on your list, I think that "The Hill of Dreams" is the only one which would appear upon mine. Other choices of mine would be the complete tales & poems of Poe, the complete works of Dunsany, Machen's "House of Souls", Blackwood's best tales, a complete set of "The Spectator", Pope's, Thomson's, & Moore's poems—Milton & Keats—probably Baudelaire—much of Hawthorne—something of

Balzac & de Maupassant—some form of Homer & Virgil—good histories of Greece, Rome, England, & the United States—a geography & atlas—a good encyclopaedia—some works on the folklore & antiquities of New England & Virginia—& some art books or other volumes giving plates of old furniture, classic & Georgian architecture, & the sculptural masterpieces of Graeco-Roman antiquity. I think I would like a full set of Hogarth engravings—which I have, I am glad to say.[1] Yes—& I would want a good work on astronomy, one on chemistry, one on geology, one on biology, & one on the history of philosophy. Quite a different collection from yours, but one which would express my own natural tastes & interests without affectation. I am not by nature a marked aesthete or litterateur, but merely a dilettante in life & a seeker after certain impressions & mental stimuli . . . . mostly impressions & stimuli based on a sense of historic pageantry, of adventure & discovery in the unknown, & of the anti-natural defeat of the laws of time, space, matter, & energy. If books can give me these things, well & good; but I am more interested in the things themselves than in the manner of giving. I value direct experience more than art—the latter being only a means to an end. But since one doesn't encounter much of the weird or cosmic in direct experience, or have personal access to many different historic periods at once, I have to depend on art a good deal. Sympathy on the blizzard—& hoping for real spring!

Yr obt

H P

P.S. Clark Ashton Smith has just made me a present of some fragments of *dinosaur bone*. How's that for a relique? Parts of an entity 20 feet high that lumbered through the fungoid morasses of California & Lemuria 50,000,000 years ago!

Notes

1. *The Complete Works of William Hogarth.*

[156]   [ALS]

[after 5 March 1930]

Dear A W:—

I have now read the April W.T., & can pensively agree with you about its quality. Your own tale, assuredly, would be far better without the added sentence. And the rest of the contents, save for Belknap's "Icy Kinarth", is negligible. I didn't even care for the reprint—which is an item I've seen several times before. This month even the good writers fall down—especially Whitehead, whose tame story contains my pet abomination; quasi-Elizabethan dialogue engrafted on to a relatively modern period—the year 1818. Good god! Haven't those birds *any* sense of chronology? A man of Whitehead's cultivation simply *must* be familiar with the conversational prose of 1818—which is not greatly different from our own singular idioms—for there are scores of plays, genre essays, letters, verbatim records, &c. &c., that anyone can't help having come up against. There is absolutely no excuse for hauling in 16th & early 17th century "romantic" language where the modern age is concerned .... & anything after the Restoration belongs essentially to the modern age. The thing is simply a cheap & abominable literary convention—like the stage convention of giving Civil War plays with civilian costumes (swallowtail or full-shirted coats, great beaver hats, high stocks, & even ruffled shirts!) ranging anywhere from 1830 to 1850 instead of with the correct stiff shirts, string ties, cutaway coats, stovepipe hats or low-crowned derbies, &c. of the actual 1860's. One doesn't have to be a finical pedant about such things, but if anyone pretends to write at all, there are certain congruities & general backgrounds which he ought to know as a matter of course, & which he ought to make some approximate effort at adhering to. Whitehead's "artist" is only a trifle less inept than he—his design being evocative of the middle 18th century. Speaking of designs, though, I think that Senf has nobly redeemed himself in the splendid border he has given Belknap's "Kinarth." This once he has outranked Rankin—for surely that glamorous cliff with the malignly populous sky is the realest of the real stuff! Belknap is tremendously pleased, himself—& I am reminded of the opinion of Bernard Dwyer, expressed over a year ago, that there really is some marked ability to Senf at bottom.

The dinosaurian reliquae have come—small crumbling fragments, & no room-filling ribs or collar-bones! Not so very much to look at, yet monstrously evocative of primordial visions. Through what grotesque swamps in forgotten lands may that curious behemoth not have splashed!

Most certainly my hypothetical "irreducible minimum" library is a conservative one—for is not the complete structure of anything more vital & important than the mere subsidiary outgrowth which forms the latest wing? Most certainly every successive age contributes something to the whole; & the present period has made several very valuable additions in the way of psychological analysis—distinguishing apparent thoughts & motives from real, rectifying the details & orientation of many values, more minutely tracing the ramifications of thought, &c. &c. &c. But of course this is of real value only when added to the antecedent mass; & in the end does not bulk very large in relation to the whole. Much of "modernism" is of course merely a specific nomenclature for things which have always been recognised. To assign a preponderant importance to recent work, or to waste one's time in trying to wade through all its minor manifestations at the expense of general literary perspective, is a highly grotesque mistake which many young persons make. They have ahead of them a rude awakening from their dream that any kind of "new world", sharply differentiated from that of the past, exists. Actually, an immense amount of flashy modern stuff is of no more permanent value than

Victorian trash. The present as well as the past has its characteristic sentimentalities, insincerities, mob-delusions, & meaningless fashions—indeed, we may say that any one age in history is merely one phase of human folly & delusion as distinguished from other equally fatuous & deluded phases. No one age is much better or more significant than any other; & certainly, the world has never been so genuinely civilised as during the Hellenic period—say about 400 B.C. As for the Bible—I know it is in spots a work of major literary value, & that its historic influence has occasionally been extreme—nowhere more than in my own New England. I have about a dozen assorted hereditary copies myself—both complete & New Testament only—which extend back to an Edinburgh imprint of 1795 with the long s, & which I keep for sentimental value & for the ancestral signatures on the various flyleaves. But the fact remains that the book & its atmosphere & associations really have very little personal interest for me; so that I could hardly put it on a list of indispensables. Such a list, remember, is based not on intrinsic merit but on more individual appeal. No great names merely for their sound—I think I didn't even list Shakespeare, & when I said Homer I really meant only the Odyssey. I could do admirably without the Iliad.

Glad your novel is done. I'm still stalled on p. 26 of my Vermont horror. Revision . . . revision . . . revision . . . . & only last week that old bird de Castro had the nerve to ask me to give a *free* second revision to a tale which editors didn't like—& which I warned him in the first place that they wouldn't! Did he get it? He did not! The thing I shewed him where & how to get was off! Your "psychic" sensations were no doubt interesting—but I confine such thrills to paper, myself. And I know how much you must have enjoyed the Sauk City drive. I have been out into the open two afternoons so far—but it isn't warm enough for me yet. March 5th I heard Joseph Wood Krutch lecture on Poe, but he didn't say anything more than he did in his book published in 1926. He has a nervous manner—hangs on to a desk & sways as if he were going to vault over it.

With best wishes—

Yr most obt hble Servt

H P

[157]   [ALS]

Wednesday [19 or 26 March 1930]

Dear A W:—

"The Sand" is a splendid story—full of an *atmosphere* which some of your earlier tales didn't have in such abundance. I think it would go all right as it is—it is certainly too good for any Macfadden rag—though in a second version you might have your characters broach the idea of vampirism with a little more subtlety—a little more wonder, & sense of the utter cosmic incredibility of what is to be hinted. As you doubtless realise, the main fault of most popular weird tales is that they take their supernatural element too much as a matter of course. Now in supplying this added emotional element, I think you have an excellent chance to dispose of your other plot problem—the corpse of the unfortunate sportsman which would presumably become a local vampire unless *treated*. Have his bloodless state widely discussed in the village, & let the parish priest—whom you could represent as a profound student of mystic lore; a sort of Montague Summers—darkly hint of things beyond common speculation. Let him persuade the townsfolk to have the corpse *treated*—or burned, which is equally effective as a vampire-exorcism—& thus eliminate any aftermath from your plot. After relating this, go on to tell about the stranger on the boat, & the biter who was murdered. Then, on page 14, let the matter of vampirism be *openly* broached for the first time—in an awed, hesitating, indirect way beginning with a reference to what the priest had the townsfolk do to the sportsman's body. Avoid by all means such blunt, matter-of-fact statements as "That fellow animated his own corpse." But even as it is, it's a fine story, & I certainly hope it finds congenial placement in the end. I enjoyed the local colour tremendously—& for vividness' sake got out my Sauk City pictures from the scenic files where I keep them. I could easily visualise the terrain! Thanks, by the way, for the new views. Wisconsin is certainly New England's rival in the matter of landscape!

Thanks immensely for the Hersey tip![1] I think I shall send him "The Nameless City" & perhaps one or two others—although I fear none of these has the popular appeal demanded by the "pulp" press. The remark about interplanetary stuff, though, sounds encouraging. It's time now for somebody to write a tale of a voyage to the new 9th planet discovered at the Lowell Observatory. As for *Astounding Stories*—I am taking this address again from your letter, though Belknap says he has not seen any new copies on the stands since January. Do you suppose they've failed? By the way—here's an odd thing. Clark Ashton Smith just had a pseudo-scientific tale rejected by *Science Wonder Stories* on the ground that it was *too technical!*[2] I thought the technological atmosphere was their specialty! This incident almost tempts me to send them something some day. Your new work sounds interesting—& I shall watch for "The Whistler."

Your appraisal of contemporary literary work is very interesting—& looks to me (judging by such of the items as I have read) very sound & cautious. I think it has an excellent chance of coinciding fairly well with the verdict which posterity will render when it appraises the multitudinous products of the present. If any phase is neglected, I would suggest that it is the phase which deals with the more ultimate phases of human disillusion regarding values. I would include "The Modern Temper" by Joseph Wood Krutch, & "Erik Dorn", by Ben Hecht.

Thanks for that alluring "Turn of Screw" jacket. The Sideshow column (in a sketch which incidentally mentioned me) called attention to its M. L. reprinting, & I rather think I shall buy it later on.[3] My only recent book purchase is Durant's "Story of Philosophy" in the Star Dollar Books.

Decently warm today—if it keeps up I shall take some work out to the woods & fields. I long to get embarked on that Southern jaunt!

Best wishes

Yr ob[t]

H P

Notes

1. AWD may have mentioned that Harold Hersey had become the editor/publisher of *Ghost Stories* with the April 1930 issue.

2. Probably "Marooned in Andromeda," *Wonder Stories* (October 1930).

3. B. K. Hart, "The Sideshow," *Providence Journal* 102, No. 66 (18 March 1930): 12.

[158]   [ALS]

Wednesday [2 April 1930?]

Dear A W:—

    I shall be very glad indeed to see your new Proustian novelette, & will furnish whatever critical comment my sluggish faculties may be able to think of. Some day you will doubtless assemble all your reminiscent sketches into an organically developed whole—but it would be just as well to experiment with separate units first, & see what the chances of publication are.

Meanwhile I hope your success-percentage in "the pulp" will remain high. I note the data on various magazines, & am glad that *Astounding Stories* is still going. What, by the way, is the present address of *Amazing Stories*? Before long I may try some old MSS. on some of these scattered markets—especially the new Hersey venture you spoke about.

Glad you found "In Search of the Unknown"—but bless my soul, you oughtn't to give away as good an item as that! That has some damned fine stuff toward the beginning . . . . ugh! I can hear *The Harbour-Master* flopping around now! Still—if you're resolved to get rid of it, I'm sure that 10 Barnes will be more appreciative than the average waste-basket! Which same goes for the other items. I read & enjoyed "The Man Who Was Born Again", but have never seen "The Last Devil." Glancing again at your letter, I see that you have a duplicate of the Chambers book. Well—that's more like it!

Commiserations on the weather—& especially on that inopportune snow! R.I. hasn't gone to such extremes, but even so, I've had very little incentive for any outdoor excursions. About the middle of the month—say between the 15th & 20th—I expect to get started on my annual antiquarian exploring expedition; beginning with a visit at Belknap's, but later including a southerly terrain beyond the utmost limits of any previous wanderings. When I get back to my favourite R.I. rural haunts, they will be clothed in all the glamour of mid-May. Thanks, by the way, for those delectable landscape views. The Norwegian village must be ineffably quaint—it seems to have an exotic architecture with the Scandinavian touch. In New England, the immigrant elements have brought relatively little of their own architecture; since for the most part they settle in houses already existing, & merely copy the current machine-age cheap bungalow models when they do build anything. They have a sort of mania for concrete-block construction—in Rhode Island, at least. The most striking exceptions I know of are in Providence, where the Italian element (tremendously numerous, wholly concentrated in a district all its own, & of relatively high grade as compared with the Italian groups in other Eastern cities) has built at least five splendidly impressive churches, all in the pure Italian manner with half-Byzantine arcades, tiled roofs, & lofty campaniles. One of them crowns a hilltop in the most spectacular way—its golden cross catching the sunset light in a manner to stir the imagination.[1] There is nothing like this in any other American city I know of. Does Wisconsin have much genuine Scandinavian architecture? Since so much of the Scandinavian settlement was genuine colonisation—that is, first occupancy of virgin territory—it seems to me that this ought to be more the case than in the East, where the newcomers have merely filtered into a region with an existing civilisation & architecture. Sweeping down the cost from French Canada, America has just about *six or seven* really indigenous architectures, of which two or three are no more than traces. English extends from Maine to New York, whilst Western Long Island & the Hudson Valley have a Dutch background. The French Huguenots in this region seem to have left no traces architecturally—even their solid colony at New Paltz (which I visited last spring) being of purely Dutch design. From New Jersey to Pennsylvania English again prevails, but in the latter state there is much authentic German architecture—some going back to 1680 or so—as well as a curious trace of *Welsh* influence manifested in heavy eaves & cornices carried around gable ends. There is also a faint *Swedish* trace remaining from the early Delaware colony. This latter is shewn in steep roofs & needle-point spires. Southward from here English again reigns until the *Spanish* touch in St. Augustine, Fla. appears. Turning westward, the former Louisiana territory along the Mississippi is full of typical French forms—with a subtle coating of Hispanicism left from the years when Spain owned the territory. Balconies, arcades, & other Latin elements enter into the architecture of towns like New Orleans, Mobile, Natchez, & so on. I must see all this some day—though I can't do it this spring. Then, when one gets to Texas, the solid Spanish belt is encountered—culminating in really Spanish towns like Santa Fé, N.M.

Your programme is surely crowded enough! From what I hear, the cinema must be picking up lately—I must see what these new talking pictures are like. I am in the final stage of my spring rush. Got to page 32 of my tale, but am stalled again!

Best wishes—& send the novelette when it's ready.

Yr obt hble Servt

H P

Notes

1 HPL refers to St. John's Catholic Church on Atwell's Avenue (now destroyed), used as the setting for "The Haunter of the Dark" (1935).

[159]   [ALS]

April 9, 1930

Dear A W:—

Your novelette duly came, & I have read it with the closest attention. Truly, it is a splendid piece of work, & I can scarcely give an honest opinion of it without seeming to flatter. I knew from your isolated, fragments that you had the real stuff of literature at your command; but now that I see some of these arranged in a proper organic relationship, my opinion takes an additional upward soaring! There is profound & subtle beauty, splendidly modulated in the sequence of dream glamorous pictures. You have a keen & sensitively selective eye for details & sensations & images, as indeed I realised before. Now I see that you are equally felicitous in arranging these things in a significant, revelatory, & aesthetically satisfying form. It seems to me that you are coming to handle words & sentences more & more skilfully & adequately—you will recall my mentioning, in years past, that carelessness in this field (repeated words, sentences of doubtful trimness, symmetry, & compactness, &c. &c.) was one result of your over-voluminous writing which ought to be corrected a bit. Time, I imagine, is supplying this correction—for this novelette has passages of beautiful & musical language as well as of poignant imagery & convincing emotion. There is no mistaking the right of the piece to be considered as serious literary expression. I don't know of anything turned out by any of our group which has a clearer claim to substance & authenticity. Keep this up, & you'll be on the map of the major writing world before many years are past!

Replying to your specific questions—yes, indeed, the sketches all have the feel of genuine life & sincerity about them. They create a scene & atmosphere with solid reality in every part—even though it be that ethereal reality which depends on mood & subjective vision for its palpable outlines. You are obviously not trying to give a cross-section of the entire lives of the characters in all their complex humanity. What you are doing is to trace a certain line of emotional activity in them—& in this you succeed with admirable completeness. Most certainly I find all three characters clearly outlined—visible & psychologically realisable. Though each one represents a temperament & emotional life antipodally different from my own at their age, I can detect the earmarks of truthful portrayal throughout the story. There is an impression of authentic life—a feeling that some sort of key is furnished to the fumbling & ambivalent thoughts & motivations of a vast proportion of actual adolescents whom one has observed. I really lack the power to give any specific suggestions for improvement. To suggest that the characters—or at least the boys—are not quite typical of the majority would be quite irrelevant, for art is not concerned with the quantitative. It is for each artist to furnish one stone for the general mosaic which is literature's reflection of the universal. Certainly, this is a marvellously fine piece of delving into the obscure associative imagery & emotional overtones of a certain part of the stream of consciousness of a certain type of introverted & somewhat hyperaesthetic youth. I can see the differences in intention from the Proust & Joyce schools of fiction, & think on the whole that your attempt is somewhat more conservative than the latter's. You preserve a certain coherence & integration, & exercise a measurable degree of selectiveness despite your departure from the superficial & the conventional. It flattered me to note your reference to "Randolph Carter"—but let me remind you that at the conclusion of that horror it is *Harley Warren—not* the narrator Randolph Carter—who is subterraneously announced as dead! I am herewith returning the MS. to Sauk City with what I trust will be adequate promptness. Again let me offer my praise & congratulations. You have the real stuff, & with the progress of time it seems to me overwhelmingly probable that you will produce literature of a major calibre. Keep it up, Son!

Thanks for the address of *Amazing Stories*. I doubt if it would be of much use to re-submit my rejected stuff to Wright, for he briskly re-rejected "The Nameless City" when I sent it in a few months ago. I located the *American Poetry Magazine* some time ago—in fact, I found it was printed by the same firm that handles the book tests of my friend Moe. I must investigate this Day of Judgment novel.[1] One more item on my list of "must reads".

The new W.T. didn't impress me very favourably aside from the stories by yourself & Smith. "The Land of Lur" is really an atrocious hash—an ignorant tyro running amuck with a copy of Poe in one hand & Roget's Thesaurus in the other! Everil Worrell is unbelievably maudlin & mawkish, & Pendarves doesn't shake clear of mediocrity at any point. Wright has just rejected some more splendid stuff by Clark Ashton Smith. No wonder the magazine stays commonplace, with all the really original stuff turned down!

I trust you'll have a pleasant vacation amidst your vernal native landscape. My trip will begin in a little over a week if present plans hold. At Belknap's till the 1st of May, then southward through a colourful succession of ancient cities culminating in historic Charleston. You'll receive cards from me as I thread my carefree antiquarian course.

With best wishes, & hoping that "The Early Years" may achieve a professional placement worthy of its merits, I remain

Your most o^bt h^ble Servt

H P

Notes

1. Leo Perutz, *The Master of the Day of Judgment*. Cf. *SL* 4.91.

[160]   [ALS]

[mid-April 1930]

Dear A W:—

Bless my soul, but your library certainly is having a renovation! Don't be too rash with the eliminations—you might regret some of the items too late! Thanks tremendously for the ones you suggest sending me. I don't own a single one of them—though I have read the Chambers, Marsh, Busson, & Blackwood volumes with appreciation & admiration, & the Stoker volume with more mildly favourable sentiments. Belknap will envy me possession of "The Man Who Was Born Again", for he is tremendously enthusiastic about it. Another friend of mine is infatuated with "The Beetle"[1]—though he owns it himself & will therefore be exempt from invidious pangs.

I am glad my remarks on "The Early Years" proved encouraging, & can assure you they were well-considered & sincere. You have some great stuff in that MS.; & in conjunction with the other series or fragments mentioned, it ought to form the beginning of your really permanent work. I shall surely await the publication of all these things with the keenest interest.

At last I am beginning to get caught up with my programme of work, & hope not to have to cart too many jobs along on my trip. According to present indications I shall start on Thursday, April 24th, staying at Belknap's for a week or more, & then starting out with the Longs when they make their annual Atlantic City trip. At their farthest-south point I shall bid them adieu—& then, sing ho for the South! Charleston or bust! I'll drop you postcards from along the route.

Best wishes—

Yr most ob^t h^ble Servt

H P

Notes

1. By Richard Marsh.

[161]   [ANS, JHL][1]

[Postmarked Charleston, S.C.,
29 April 1930]

Revelling in the most marvellously fascinating environment—scenically, architecturally, historically, & climatically—that I've ever encountered in my
life! I can't begin to convey any idea of it except by exclamation points—I'd
move here in a second if my sentimental attachment to New England were
less strong. Glorious room at the Y. with harbour, town, & sub-tropical verdure vistas. Will stay here as long as my cash holds out, even if I have to cut
al the rest of my contemplated trip. Wait till I write you in more detail! This
steeple (over) is the choicest object in my window vista.

Regards—

H P

Notes

1. Front: St. Michael's Church, Charleston, S.C.

[162]   [ANS, JHL][1]

[Postmarked Richmond, Va.,
7 May 1930]

Behold the earthly paradise upon which I have just stumbled! This series of
gardens fairly takes my breath away. I don't believe there's another such thing
open to the public in the U.S. It is Poe's "Domain of Arnheim" & "Island of
the Fay" all rolled into one! I can't believe I'm awake! As you may know, to
me the quality of *utter, perfect beauty* assumes *two* supreme forms or adumbra-
tions—one a mass of city roofs & spires against a sunset, glimpsed from a
distant height; the other, the experience of walking through ethereal & en-
chanted gardens of exotic delicacy & opulence, with carved stone bridges,
labyrinthine paths, marble fountains, terraces, & staircases, strange pagodas,
hillside grottos, curious statues, termini, sundials, benches, basins, &
lanthorns, lilied pools of swans, & streams with tears of waterfalls, spreading
gingko-trees, & drooping, feathery willows, & flowers of a wild, bizarre pattern never beheld on land or beneath the sea . . . . . Well, Sir, this garden almost *wholly fulfils* ideal or adumbration No. 2.!!! ¶ Hate like hell to move
northward, but fear I shall have to do it tomorrow. Via longa, pecunia brevis![2]

Regards—

H P

Have spent 2½ solid days in this garden!

Notes

1. Front: Japanese Garden in Maymont Park, Richmond, Va.

2. "The road is long, money short"—a parody of the Latin tag *Ars longa, vita brevis* ("Art is long, life is short").

[163]   [ANS, JHL][1]

> [Postmarked Richmond, Va.,
> 10 May 1930]

Greetings from Poe's home town! It was like pulling a tooth to break away from Charleston, but stately old Richmond makes the transition less overtly painful. I miss the palmettos & live-oaks, (for Richmond's really in the North except for social & political ties) & find the relative scarcity of niggers queer! ¶ Am making a systematic round of sites connected with Poe—after some research at the public library. I found some good material in the Mary E. Phillips biography—the one published in 1926 but at once eclipsed by Hervey Allen's "Israfel." Just now I am loafing in old Capitol Park—where Poe used to walk—& now going down to the long-deserted Southern Literary Messenger office at Maine & 15th Sts. ¶ My aunt writes me from home that she has forwarded a letter of yours to me in care of Belknap before she got my Charleston forwarding address. I'll find, read, & answer it in about a week, when (reluctantly enough) I hit N. Y. Gad, but how I dread the sight of that damn'd mongrel vortex. The South, I vow, is the only place for a gentleman to live!
Yr ob[t]
H P

P.S. I finished my new horror tale in Charleston.[2]

Notes

1. Front: Old St. John's Church, Broad and 25th Sts., Richmond, Va.
2. "The Whisperer in Darkness" proved only provisionally finished. HPL subsequently revised it after receiving suggestions from FBL and Bernard Austin Dwyer. It was definitively completed on 26 September 1930.

[164]   [ALS]

> At Belknap's—
> May 24, 1930

Dear A W:—

This hasty scrawl will probably be sadly inadequate—but you know how limited writing opportunities are when one is visiting. I am coping with a huge stock of mail forwarded from home. I regret leaving the mellow & traditional South, but am having a pretty good time here—vising museums & confabulating with various members of the old gang. We shall hold one of our regular old-time meetings Monday night—at Wilfred B. Talman's, which is only just around the corner from the depressing Brooklyn dump where I vegetated from Jany. 1925 to Apr. 1926. The other day Belknap & I explored the new Roerich Museum (which is right near his place, at 103d St. & Riverside Drive) for the first time,[1] & were fairly knocked out by the exotic impressiveness of the paintings therein displayed. Doubtless you know of Roerich—the Russian who has captured the mystery of remote & forbidden Thibetan uplands in art of a highly strange & original technique. His admirers have erected this museum to house his work—& to promote certain Oriental studies sponsored by him—an honour very rarely accorded any living artist.

I was glad of the chance to read your two new tales, & think that both are truly excellent. Glad that Wright had the sense to take at least one of them, & hope he'll take the other later on. It was surely a singular coincidence that "The Bishop Sees Through" should so closely resemble an earlier tale, but I think the type is common enough to remove the possible imputation of plagiarism on the part of the uninformed. The idea is handled with great skill & convincingness, & the only flaw I can find is your use of the title *"Count"* as something existing in England. You are so fond of British settings that you really ought to brush up on points of British custom & nomenclature! There is no such title as "Count" in England, the exact socio-legal equivalent being *Earl.* Thus you ought to have spoken of your spiritualist as *the Earl of Ruthven-Margold* or *Lord Ruthven-Margold.* The *wife* of an Earl, however, *is* referred to as a *Countess;* this being a vestigial remnant of the old Norman usage before William the Conqueror's nobleman became Anglicised, & thus before the Norman "Counts" became English "Earls". You would refer to the husband & wife as *the Earl & Countess of Ruthven-Margold,* or as *Lord & Lady Ruthven-Margold.* As for "The Lady Who Wouldn't Stay Dead"[2]—that is an excellent tale, & Wright is a damn fool to reject it. I'll wager he missed the irony conveyed by the circumstance that a *real* white moth (as implied by the fact that Blake's *friend* could see it) was the final agent in luring Blake to his death.

Thanks tremendously for the news that Hersey has bought the Macfadden *Ghost Stories.* Belknap is quite excited about it, & I shall certainly submit a goodly quote of rejected material—including my favourite "Nameless City." You ought to find it quite a market for your own things—for Hersey is evidently a great appreciator of your work.

As for my new tale—its tentative name is "The Whisperer in Darkness". It is slow-moving & atmospheric, & comes to 58 pages, 8½ × 11, of my longhand—which combination does not argue well for Wrightian acceptance. I hesitate to make the gamble of typing it until I can get a few responsible opinions on it. About "The Shunned House"—Cook is still holding the printed sheets in unbound form, & is the only one who can decide its future. And concerning a collection of my stuff—I may try some publisher some time, though I don't feel the least haste in the matter. I agree that Wright has no further claim upon my stories, since he clearly has no intention of publishing them.

Well—more later & at present best wishes. Belknap sends his regards. Yr
obt Servt

H P

Notes

1. Nicholals Roerich (1874–1947) was a Russian painter and writer who had spent
several years in Tibet and become a Buddhist. The Roerich Museum in New York,
now at 317 West 107th Street, was a favorite haunt of HPL's. Roerich's paintings par-
tially inspired *At the Mountains of Madness* (1931).
2. I.e., "The White Moth."

[165]   [ANS, JHL][1]

[Postmarked Kingston, N.Y.,
4 June 1930]

Greetings! Your new tale is great—I shall speak of it again in answering your
letter. Still on the move—have ascended the Hudson to Kingston & am enjoying the sunlit countryside with that price of artists, Bernard Austin Dwyer.
Next move—Athol & Cook. ¶ I wish you'd lend Dwyer a copy of "The Early
Years"—he would be able to appreciate its delicate charm to a singularly
thorough degree. Regards—H P

I greatly enjoyed *The Return of Miss Sarah*.[2] Would be glad to see your other
work, as H.P.L. tells me it is splendid.

I would be very glad of a letter from you 292 Fair St. Kingston, N.Y.
Bernard A. Dwyer

Notes

1. Front: Old Senate House, Built 1676, Kingston, N.Y.
2. I.e., "The Return of Sarah Purcell."

[166]   [ALS]

En route—

Kingston, N.Y.,

June 7, 1930

Dear A W:—

As you have doubtless learned through the joint card from Dwyer
& myself, I duly received both your recent communications—one forwarded to
N.Y., the other to Kingston. The new stories are utterly splendid—"The Panelled Room" being about the best weird thing you have written so far—& I

can't think of a single criticism to apply to them. Both Belknap & Dwyer share my enthusiasm for "Miss Sarah", & Dwyer (for Belknap has not seen it) is still more admiring in his reaction to the "Room." That really has a marvellously hideous suggestion, & the handling of the plot element is tremendously clever. I wouldn't be surprised if, in time, something of your more serious side—the "Evening in Spring" & "Early Years" side—began to permeate your macabre fiction; making a synthesis of the most effective possible sort. Again let me congratulate you on this recent pair of triumphs—here's hoping Wright will take both in some temporarily inspired moment!

My "Whisperer in Darkness" has retrogressed to the constructional stage as a result of some extremely sound & penetrating criticism on Dwyer's part. I shall not try to tinker with it during the residue of this trip, but shall make it the first item of work on my programme after I get home—which will no doubt be in less than a week now. There will be considerable condensation throughout, & a great deal of subtilisation toward the end. You shall surely be among the first to see it when it does finally emerge from its scaffolding.

Your remarks & extracts in connexion with the weird story thesis excite my utmost interest, & make me all the more anxious to see the completed product in some form or other. I still stand by my original position regarding *cosmic outsideness*, & shall take pleasure in seeing what arguments you bring to bear against it. You ought to shew a copy to B. K. H. of the Providence Journal in view of his unusual interest in the subject. The final choices for discussion which you cite surely have much to recommend them, though I can't agree in all cases. "The Yellow Wall Paper" is a great tale, but to me it lacks just that final touch of "outsideness" necessary to make the top grade; nor can I work up a really first-rate enthusiasm for "A View From a Hill" or my own "Outsider" & "Rats". I'd think twice about "The Upper Berth" & "The Shadows on the Walls", [*sic*] though I'm wholly with you regarding "The Yellow Sign", "Halpin Frayser", "The Monkey's Paw" (?), "Seaton's Aunt", "Count Magnus", "The White People", "The House of Sounds", & "The Willows." The specimen paragraphs you give seem to indicate a prose form worthy of the scholarly content.

Your new book shipment seems to contain some highly desirable items—though I found the Arlen stories dull when Cook lent them to me some years ago. I own Benson's "Visible & Invisible". What is this "Screaming Skull" by one *Horler*? I thought F. Marion Crawford wrote that tale. I think I have read F. Britten Austin's collection, though it didn't get me very excited. Of the Wyllarde item I never heard before.

My trip continues to be delectably interesting. Despite my dislike for New York, Belknap & the gang made my 2 weeks there very pleasant. We had several meetings of the old crowd, & naturally covered all the principal museums. Of the latter there is now a new one which I think would interest you very much—the Roerich Museum at Riverside Drive & 103ᵈ St—up in

Belknap's general neighbourhood. This is wholly devoted to the strange & mystical paintings of the Russian artist Nicholas Roerich, who draws his inspiration & scenic subjects from the daemon-haunted uplands of forbidden & half-fabulous Thibet. Some of these things have a bizarre, cosmic, & eerily two-dimensional quality which allies them wholly with the land of dream as opposed to the objective world—so that they make a tremendous appeal to any lover of outré *outsideness*. I'll enclose a card which very inadequately suggests the quality of this material.

Just now the beauty I'm revelling in is that of the American rural scene. Monday I start across the Mohawk Trail for Athol & home. ¶ Best wishes—

Yr obt Servt

H P

P.S. My gifted host Dwyer will insert a note of his own in this envelope. You ought to know him—an aesthete of rare sensitiveness & discrimination, with the most delicate fantastic imagination I have ever seen. He would appreciate your "Evening in Spring" & "Early Years" more than anyone else I know of. Wish you could lend such MSS. to him.

[167]   [ANS, JHL][1]

[Postmarked Athol, Mass.,
11 June 1930]

Home to New England after a pleasant week with Dwyer. Am staying in Athol with H. Warner Munn. Cook still looks a bit seedy after his midwinter breakdown, but is improving all the time. New Recluse partly finished, but won't be out for months. Weather doubtful, but hope to get some rural trips before I go home Sat. or Sun. Last night Munn took Cook & me in his car to a splendid woodland glen & rock waterfall—Bear's Den—which I saw once before in 1928. All along the way I revelled in the distinctive New England scenery—the narrow winding roads, rocky rolling pastures, stone walls, great elms, squat farmhouses & sheds, & other things one finds nowhere else. ¶ Had a great ride on the Mohawk Trail yesterday. It's great to be back in good old New England again! ¶ Dwyer shewed me your study of "The Krafts",[2] & I believe it is a truly fine & penetrating piece of work. There is both pathos & cosmic irony—& good character-drawing to boot. Keep it up! Best wishes—

H P

Notes

1. Front: In Between the Mountains, Mohawk Trail, Mass.
2. Unidentified.

[168]   [ALS]

June 20, 1930

Dear A W:—

Home at last! It has been a great trip, & I don't regret it even in the midst of my struggles with the work which has piled up on me despite my efforts to have things forwarded for attention en route. But it's good to see familiar sights again after nearly two months; & I revel in the contemplation of the ancient streets, & neighbouring woods & fields, that I have always known. I had a good week in Athol with Munn & Cook, though the latter's illness pained & alarmed me. The nervous breakdown of last January was severer than I had suspected, & on top of that have come a bad spell with chronic appendicitis. Cook ought to have had his appendix out 20 years ago, but refuses to do so because of a morbid dread of the surgeon's knife which amounts almost to a positive psychosis or "phobia". His seizure of last week alarmed the doctor exceedingly, & almost keyed himself up to the operating-point; but a later subsidence of pain caused him to falter again, so that he is still dragging on as usual. I fear that one of his seizures will be the end of him if he doesn't brace up & get rid of the offending organ. He has a Recluse in press—almost half done—& I understand that it will include a great deal of your material—such as your essays on Webster, Shakespeare's Sonnets, &c. He also says that the edition of my "Shunned House" has gone to the binder's in Boston. Munn is doing good work of its kind—though it runs more in the direction of historical romance than toward the actually weird. I've seen his latest tales, & believe that Wright has made no mistake in accepting them. Just now he is in the throes of moving—to a delightful hillside home on the semi-rustic fringe of Athol. Henceforward his address will be *168 Bliss St.* During my Athol sojourn I saw a vast amount of fine scenery. I think I described "Bear's Den" on a card to you. Later on Munn shewed me Doane's Falls—a series of rock cascades in a wooded gorge which would be famous if a few travellers were to give it a writeup. And there's still more for me to discover on future trips, I am told. Let me thank you, by the way, for the latest specimens of Wisconsin scenery. I surely must see your region some day!

Glad to hear that "The Early Years" have gone off to Dwyer. He will appreciate work of this kind to a profound & poignant extent, for his sensitiveness to subtle impressions is acute & phenomenal. There is in Dwyer a tremendous amount of genuine aesthetic material, which will come out in a slow, gradual, & painstaking, but ultimately important way. His artistic methods are as yet largely groping & subconscious, but their simplicity, sincerity, & motive-force are all in their favour. He needs to read & practice more, & with proper encouragement will do so. I do not know anyone with a richer or more fertile fantastic imagination than Dwyer. His responsiveness to the symbolic overtones of things; & his keen feeling for those implications of the cosmic & the unreal which reside in certain effects of atmosphere & arrangement, are such as to suggest Arthur Machen & Algernon Blackwood at their best. I'd like to see a book of his some day, illustrated by himself.

Your own new work sounds marvellously interesting, & I am sure "The House of Macht"[1] will turn out to be a very substantial thing. I hope to see it eventually. You rate of production quite dumbfounds every member of our group who hears about it—Belknap in particular was overwhelmed by such evidence of a mental & physical endurance beyond anything we are familiar with. Of course Wright would reject "The Panelled Room" & "The Return of Miss Sarah"—but perhaps persistence will overcome his obtuseness, as many times in the past. His admission concerning his beloved clientele is indeed refreshing! Good luck, too, with "The White Moth".

I hadn't heard about Wright's new "magazine of Orientales", but shall look for it with interest. I saw the Herseyised *Ghost Stories* at Dwyer's, but found it apparently full of left-over Macfadden material. Wright has just forwarded a scholarly & interesting letter from the W.T. author Robert E. Howard, concerning my "Rats in the Walls".[2] I think I shall write Howard shortly, for he seems to be an exceptional chap. I like some of his work very much, though he makes too many concessions to the popular fiction ideal.

As for my tale—I shall get to work on its re-writing as soon as my present chaos of accumulated work is cleared up. I don't know whether it'll be much good or not, but at any rate it will be better than the present version. About "The Strange High House"—Wright asked for that himself about a year ago, but I could not let him have it since I had given it to Cook for *The Recluse*. It would hardly have been courteous to recall another thing from Cook after submitting it to him—& I did so recall "The Outsider".

I am indeed anxious to read your thesis, & hope you will send me a copy as soon as you have one conveniently available. My stand on *cosmic outsideness*, however, is likely to remain unchanged; for I feel that this element is eminently necessary to produce a macabre thrill of the very first water. "The Yellow Wall Paper" & "The Shadows on the Wall" are excellent of their kind, but the sensation they produce is a tame & secondary one as compared with that produced by "The Willows", "The White People", "The House of Sounds", or even (in my estimation, at least) "The Yellow Sign".

Glad your examinations came out well, & hope you'll always have plenty of favours at your disposal around examination season! I am assuming that you will continue next year in post-graduate work in order to get the advanced degree necessary for collegiate pedagogy.

Have lately heard from a man named Bailey, evidently of the U. of N.C., who mentions you & says he is preparing an historical study of pseudo-scientific fiction.[3] I can't help him much outside the domain of the weird, but am referring him to the blbilographically omniscient Munn. Best wishes—

Yr obt Servt

H P

Notes

1. I.e., "The Head of the House of Macht."

2. REH's first letter to HPL does not survive, but it launched a voluminous correspondence that ended only with REH's death in 1936.

3. One letter by J[ames] O[sler] Bailey (1903–1979) to Lovecraft, dated 16 June 1930 (ms., JHL), survives. Bailey eventually published *Pilgrims through Space and Time: Trends and Patterns in Scientific and Utopian Fiction* (New York: Argus Books, 1947), the first academic study of science fiction.

[169]   [ALS]

[c. 26 June 1930]

Dear A W:—

I don't think you need to worry about your Sauk City rate of production! Three tales a week would be prolific for anybody else—& it never does to force matters. Don't fall into the false psychology of speed-&-quantity standards, which has made contemporary commercial America a feverish expanse of greedy barbarism instead of a civilisation!

I knew Dwyer would appreciate "The Early Years", because he has a particularly fine & sensitive imagination—delicately responsive to the value & symbolism of elusive moods & memories. Work of this type will stimulate his own creative processes—he ought to read more of it, as I am telling him.

I can imagine the boredom of a commencement ceremony, though the 94° in the shade would be welcome rather than otherwise to me. The hotter it is, the more braced up I am—& conversely, the cold wilts & congeals me into mental & physical helplessness. You are rather lucky, I think, to have that canning factory so handy to step in & out of when you need some extra cash. I wish I had something of the sort at my disposal.[1]

Naturally I am looking forward to your thesis with the keenest of interest, & wish it could be published at an early date. Have you thought of any markets for it? Of course you realise that if you don't want to market it professionally, Cook would look upon it as a godsend for his *Recluse*. It would fall directly in with his plan for a series of articles on the bizarre in fiction.

I have had another very pleasant letter from Bailey of N.C., & hope that Munn can give him the aid he needs. There is surely room for a work of his sort, & he seems very earnest & thorough in his plans. I wish him luck!

Morton's visit was a highly pleasant event, & included many rural trips of interest. We walked for the first time over the new Mount Hope Bridge, (between the Bristol peninsula & the island of Aquidneck on which Newport is situate) which was opened last October & is the 7th longest suspension bridge in the world, & took a delightful boat trip to Newport—as our joint postcard doubtless apprised you.[2] Newport is a great old place, which you must see when you make that long-planned Eastern trip. It represents the *early* 18th century just as Providence represents the *later* 18th century. While there, Morton & I walked out to the famous Hanging Rocks, where in 1732 Dean (later Bishop) Berkeley used to sit & write on the MS. of his celebrated "Alciphron; or, the Minute Philosopher". Berkeley's home—Whitehall—is a fine old Georgian mansion some distance northward; but on this occasion we had not enough time to visit it.

As usual, I am doing my work in the open fields & woods every warm & pleasant afternoon. I am undecided whether or not to attend the Boston convention of the National Amateur Press Association. It would be faintly enjoyable—& I would like some excuse to visit antiquarian scenes around Boston—but my cash is so low that all expenses are just now to be discouraged.

Best wishes—

Yr most obt

H P

Notes

1. AWD worked at a canning factory managed by Will Schorer, Mark Schorer's father, to supplement his income. His "Factory Afternoon" is a humorous work of fiction about working in the canning factory.

2. Non-extant.

[170]   [ALS]

July 13, 1930

Dear A W:—

The Boston convention was unexpectedly successful & interesting, with a phenomenal attendance of old-timers. Those present were optimistic enough to predict a general amateur renaissance during the coming year—though that doubtless involves some overconfidence. Naturally I made the most of Boston's antiquarian side, & took side-trips to ancient Salem, Marblehead, & Quincy. Altogether it was a distinctly festive week. I regretted Cook's absence, but he has only just emerged from the hospital. He is going to Vermont next week, & it is quite possible that I shall go along with him.

Wright's acceptances & rejections are as amusing & paradoxical as usual. Talman called on him personally last month, & wrote a very interesting account which I'll send you after I've answered it. Apparently Wright's health is not so good as when Wandrei saw him in 1927. He has a peculiar disease of the nerves allied to palsy.

Thanks for the reading recommendations, which I am filing for reference & shall copy for Dwyer. Hope I'll have time to go through the list eventually.

Your thesis is just what Cook wants for *The Recluse,* & I shall at once write him about it. I am sure he will be eager for it if there is no hurry about its publication. He is keeping the coming issue in an unformed state, awaiting the final parts of Munn's article. I shall suggest that he get in touch with you directly.

Had another letter from Robert E. Howard, who seems to be a really profound student of Celtic philology & anthropology. I wonder that a scholar of his calibre makes so many concessions to popular taste. He has a theory that the early Irish legends contain a greater substratum of truth that we are commonly inclined to concede. His middle name, apparently resurrected from Celtic dawns, is *Eiarbhin. Robert Eiarbhin Howard* . . . . can you beat it?

Your landscape descriptions are highly alluring, & I know that the sunset touches will add prodigiously to the force of your reminiscent sketches. I think I have several times mentioned that *sunset* always forms the background of my own most poignant imaginative vistas; & I really do not think that any other visual phenomenon of nature has quite has much potency & universality of appeal. I shall be very anxious to see "At Sundown" upon its completion.

With best wishes, & hoping to see your thesis when Brother Farnsworth thinks he has assimilated it sufficiently, I remain

> Yr most obt Servt
> H P

[171]   [ALS]

[mid-July 1930]

Dear A W:—

Yes, indeed—I fancy you would find material for many pictures in ancient Salem & Marblehead! There are advantages in personally taken snap shots, but cards are cheap & easy to get, & when one has seen the places personally it does not take much to set the imagination working toward their recapture. Since writing you I have been to old Newport again—& I surely think that no place excels it in conveying the image of an old Yankee coast town. It is quainter & more obviously maritime than Salem, & not so internally dead & externally showmanlike as Marblehead.

"Body of the Moon" is great stuff, & it was typically asinine of Wright to decline it. Too bad you have to type more copies of the thesis—I wish it could get published from the first MS., so that a printed supply might be available. Wright's remarks are what might have been expected. I hardly recall "The Supreme Witch",[1] & am not sure whether I bothered to read it through.

Your prescription for amateurdom is a good one, but it would take an organising genius to induce the languid & scattered personnel of the institution to carry it through. There are so many fixed habits & customs in the thing as it has gradually bungled along & shaped itself, that it would take months of reorganisation to put over a truly reconstructive policy—if indeed it could ever be done.

Thanks tremendously for the envelope of Wisconsin landscapes. Your scenery is delectable, & has many points in common with that of New England. Just now I am enjoying scenery of a sort, insomuch as (pursuant to my general policy of outdoor aestivation) I am writing this from a bench in Providence's largest port.

Helm C. Spink, Official Editor of the N.A.P.A., has just been in this city, & appreciated the architecture & landscape very much. He is from Indiana, & when I took him down the bay to Newport I was astonished to learn that it was his first boat trip.

Dwyer spoke with vast enthusiasm of your "Early Years" & other material, & I have copied for him the reading suggestions you sent. Here's hoping that both he & I may have opportunities to go through the volumes mentioned—or at least a fair proportion of them.

With best wishes, & eagerly awaiting the arrival of the thesis, I remain

      Yr most oblig'd, most ob^t Servt
      H P

P.S. In "Body of the Moon"—p. 1—don't you think that "*thine eyes*" would be more euphonious & idiomatic than "thy eyes"?

Notes

1. G. Appleby Terrill, "The Supreme Witch," *WT* (October 1926); rpt. January 1935 and March 1953.

[172]   [ANS, JHL][1]

                          [Postmarked Providence, R.I.,
                                       31 July 1930]

Thanks for the glimpse of the thesis! You do it an injustice in your latest estimate, for really it is excellent as a whole. Individual dissent from some of your dicta—such as your relative estimates of various minor writers like myself—is of course possible; but the design of the thing is admirable, & it certainly covers valuable ground not covered before. The bibliography alone is a notable piece of work—& I can't conceive of Cook's not being enthusiastic over it. I shall send the thesis to him at once for perusal; with instructions to return it carefully either to you or to me if he does not print it. Shiel ought to like the book, since he receives such favourable treatment therein. Hope he is interested enough to read our tales—it would seem odd to have one's stuff read by a recognised master in the same vein, whom one has known of for years! ¶ Am absorbing landscape material every fair afternoon. Have just explored a wooded river bank only 6 miles from Providence which I had never seen before, although I had known of its existence for some time. ¶ As for the thesis—don't condemn it hastily! If you want to revise it at leisure before calling it definitive, all very well—but the main design is eminently sound & worthy of preservation. Thanks again for the privilege of perusal. Best wishes—

HPL

Notes

1. Front: College St. to Market Sq. Showing Hospital Trust and Chamber of Commerce, Providence, R.I.

[173]   [ALS]

Ten-Mile River Woods
[14 August 1930]

Dear AW:—

　　　　Commiserations on the bum finger—which I trust will mend in due time. Evidently you do your typing in the correct professional way. I use forefingers only—have for 24 years, since getting my first & only standard machine—& Belknap uses *only one finger*—his right forefinger, which hops over the keyboard with a supernatural rapidity I could never hope to parallel.

Best wishes for the Cossacks[1]—Wright will probably take it in the end. Don't let your enthusiasm for "The Early Years" wane. It's good, sound, sincere stuff, even though you may produce more finished work in late & more experienced periods. Glad Wandrei likes it—Dwyer had told me of his enthusiasm. Dwyer is usually a very fair instinctive critic in fields involving delicate imaginative overtones, though one may not always agree with his relative estimates of stories. I disagree with him—& with you & Wright as well—in attaching importance to my "Outsider" & "Rats". His estimate of the "Dewer" cover was based on technical qualities of draughtsmanship rather than on any real imaginative fertility & appropriateness—at least, I so gathered from his oral comments during my sojourn in Kingston, when he & I bought our copies of the issue in question. This month's cover is worse still—although last month's wasn't so impossible.[2] The new format is generally an improvement. I haven't read anything in the new issue as yet—though I can well imagine that the Suter reprint tops the list for quality. That was a notable tale—I singled it out for especial praise upon its first appearance over 7 years ago[3]. Yes—I think Belknap's "Visitor" was originally one of the "god" series. He is rather fond of it, though to my mind it has too much irrelevant jauntiness picked up at second hand from Montague Rhodes James. I see by the Eyrie that Klarkash-Ton, High-Priest of Tsathoggua,[4] is receiving his due from the readers—which is a very pleasing thing. He surely has developed a marvellous prose facility—I've just read several new MSS. of his, some of which Wright has accepted.

Rearranging your library & accomodating all the new accessions must be a rather arduous & perplexing business. I don't see how you find room for so many books! Belknap doesn't pretend to have a personal library—just a few favourites on a single set of shelves, & the public library for serious consultation. I occupy a middle ground—harbouring a few standard old-timers & reference works—perhaps 1000 in my room, with 500 more stored here & there—but making no attempt to keep up with the times or have any full or representative collection in any direction. Be careful about discarding any items which you may want later on—I've sometimes regretted things I've eliminated. But as I said, I shall of course be grateful for those cast-out items which you positively think you'll never want again.

I continue my open-air pursuits, & am writing this in the northerly river-bank region which I discovered a fortnight ago. The warm weather exactly suited me, though I dare say the majority found it somewhat excessive—as I would find cold weather. Ugh—how I dread the thought of coming autumn! It's too cold for me now.

Well—now I must get to work! Hope to hear next time that your finger is all well. I'll tell you what Cook says of the thesis when I hear from him. Don't belittle it—it's good stuff!

With best wishes—

Yr most obt h^{ble} Servt

H P

P.S. Am going to Onset tomorrow to share the last phase of Belknap's outing. Wish the weather were warmer!

Notes

1. "The Cossacks Ride Hard."

2. *WT* (July 1930), cover by C. C. Senf, illustrating Seabury Quinn, "The Bride of Dewer." *WT* (August 1930), cover by Hugh Rankin, illustrating Harry Noyes Pratt, "The Curse of Ximu-tal."

3. See HPL's letter to Edwin Baird, published in *WT* (September 1923): "I like *Weird Tales* very much, though I have seen only the April issue. . . . 'Beyond the Door,' by Paul Suter, seems to me the most truly touched with the elusive quality of original genius . . ." *H. P. Lovecraft in "The Eyrie,"* ed. S. T. Joshi and Marc A. Michaud (West Warwick, RI: Necronomicon Press, 1979), p. 15.

4. I.e., CAS.

[174]   [ANS][1]

[Postmarkeded Onset, Mass.,
16 August 1930]

Greetings from Cthulhu & the Visitor from antique Ægyptus! Circulating around Cape Cod betwixt bursts of rain, & assimilating various specimens of Novanglian antiquity. You ought to get around here & absorb landscape impressions!

H P

Greetings and best wishes from sea-splendid Cape Cod. I intended to answer your letter of 3½ years ago much sooner—but shall endeavor to redeem myself presently. FBL Jr.

Notes

1. Front: 106. The Oldest Windmill on Cape Cod., Mass.

[175]   [ALS]

Seekonk River bank
[late August 1930]

Dear A W:—

Yes—if the coming winter finishes me, I shall surely have had a well-filled final summer! The Cape Cod trip was exceedingly pleasant, & I was glad to see Belknap again. He is now back in NY. Incidentally—Wright has just accepted a long novelette of his at a price of $270.00.

Glad to hear that "The Early Years" & "Evening in Spring" find so much discriminating favour—as indeed I was sure they would. Both must certainly achieve publication some day—though naturally they will not be as easy to place as cheaply popular material would be.

Sooner or later I am sure that the Cossack detachment will capture the garrison at N. Michigan Avenue! Glad "The White Moth" landed—& I shall welcome the sight of "Mrs. Bentley's Daughter". As for the Dewer cover—naturally, opinions must differ. I am no art connoisseur, so that I can have no intelligent opinion. All I can say is that neither that nor any other Senf cover ever impressed me very strongly!

It's odd, but Belknap is very fond of his "Visitor from Egypt". He puts it above "The Black Druid" & "The Space-Eaters", though I can't see where comparison is possible. There's no accounting for tastes, & the best creator is often the worst critic.

No hurry about the books—& again let me urge you to exercise caution in discarding. Don't chide yourself for your vacation—what is existence for except to spend in the most pleasant & restful way?

I am getting the worst of my revision cleaned up, & hope to tackle original stuff shortly—but of course one can never be sure of one's programme. Am just now reading the Book of Mormon.[1] It is really an admirable weird tale!

Best wishes, & hopes for a warm & scenically colourful autumn!

Yr obt Servt

H P

P.S. Speaking of a well-filled summer—I have just learned of a cheap excursion to *Quebec,* a quaint & ancient place which I have longed to see all my life, & believe I'll finish the season by blowing myself to it. This will mark the first time I shall ever have been out of the U.S., & it will certainly give me a kick to tread at last the still loyal soil of that British Empire which gave me all my blood & traditions, & to which my inner spirit has never ceased to be loyal despite the secession of the Rhode Island colony on May 4, 1776. Quebec, founded in 1608, is the oldest American city north of St. Augustine & the Spanish region, & according to Belknap (who has been there recently) is the quaintest place in the Western Hemisphere. It is really not far from New England, & I have been intending to make the tip for ages. Will drop you a card from there.

Notes

1. HPL wrote to Walter J. Coates, editor of *Driftwind:* "I've waded through the Book of Mormon, and find it—despite much cleverness and occasional vividness—pretty thin and imitative stuff." *Driftwind* 7, No. 1 (July 1932): 13; rpt. *Uncollected Prose and Poetry,* ed. S. T. Joshi and Marc A. Michaud (West Warwick, RI: Necronomicon Press, 1978), p. 45.

[176]   [ANS][1]

[Postmarked Quebec, Canada,
2 September 1930]

Gad, what a place! It defies my powers of description! Never saw such a town before outside of dreams! Mediaeval or Richlieuian France preserved for the observation of posterity! I wish I could do a month's continuous sightseeing here. As it is, I am mastering the city pretty well, though only skimming the adjacent terrain. Am now on the heights of Levis across the river, looking at the magical skyline of Quebec, with its silver spires, in the sunset of a marvellous day! I'll tell you more of Quebec later.

Best wishes—

H P

Notes

1. Front: Sous-le-fort Street, Quebec, Canada.

[177]   [ALS]

[early to mid-September 1930]

Dear A W:—

Well—it certainly *was* a trip to be envied! Never have I seen such a thing as Quebec before outside of dreams! What a town! Antiquity & beauty enthroned to an extent I never thought possible in the Western Hemisphere. All my former standards of urban loveliness & picturesqueness vanish after my sight of this citadel-crowned marvel. I'd give anything if I could spend every summer of my life there. It is the utter summation & embodiment of the living past. Imagination can devise nothing more marvellous than the sunset view from the citadel over the pointed roofs, silver spires, & stately verdure of this fragment of old Bourbon France. I enclose a picture of the oldest house—the so-called Montcalm headquarters, built in 1674. On the way home I stopped off at Boston & took the all-day boat trip to Provincetown, at the tip of Cape Cod. This was not exactly anticlimax, since it involved an important experience for me—viz., my first sail *out of sight of land*. The sensation was very provocative to the imagination, & I can't recall a more impressive thing than approaching Boston Harbour at sunset—watching the grey headlands, lighthouses, & outlying islands loom up out of misty nothingness.

As for being "marooned"—you can't beat my record there! In youth my ill health precluded all travel, & I never spent a night outside my Providence home from October 1901 to July 1920—a little matter of nineteen years! No wonder I am on the move nowadays, making up for lost time. But the hell of it is, that although I now have the *health* to travel, I no longer have the *cash*; so that I have to content myself with these all-too-brief & all-too-seldom jaunts. I don't know whether I'll ever get to the Old World—though I'd hate to die without seeing England.

I haven't had time to read the new W.T., but will get around to it in a week or so. No—I don't see anything in the Keller stuff. It is impossible to make a comic story truly weird. Wright's dicta transcend all my powers of divination & interpretation! First he rejects something of Smith's or mine as "too utterly weird & fantastic", & then he objects to something of yours as "not weird enough"! I have never been able to discover *any* sort of consistent standard by which the fellow forms his judgments. Utter caprice seems to govern his entire policy. Well—I'll wager he'll take "Miss Sarah" after a few more sendings!

Haven't touched my "Whisperer" yet, but shall do so as soon as I dispose of the stuff piled up during my Quebec absence. Later on I hope to concoct some more original stuff, also. I'd like to see "Death Walker" & the revised "Shuttered House." Hope they'll both land somewhere in time. Clark Ashton Smith has just been asked to do a long series of interplanetary tales for *Science Wonder Stories,* but is reluctant to pin himself down to a business deal with that shifty Gernsback unless he sees a good slice of cash in advance.

Well—now to work! Best wishes.

Yr ob^t h^ble Servt

H P

[178]   [ALS]

Open fields near the River
[mid- to late September 1930]

Dear A W:—

I duly enjoyed your recent letter & enclosed cutting—the latter being especially appropriate at this moment, since I am sitting in the glow of a warm autumnal sunset amidst the ancient & unchanging woods & fields which I have known & loved & wandered through since infancy. I surely thank heaven for the fortuitous circumstances which have preserved such a generous & glamourous slice of the primal countryside so close to the thickest part of residential Providence. Beginning on the south is a long stretch of metropolitan park land. Then, contiguous with this (or just across a reedy salt creek) is the park-like domain of a sanitarium which admits the public except on Sunday.[1] Then, piecing out still farther northward, is the scenic expanse of Swan Point Cemetery—the borders of which are sheer countryside without graves, kept thus for aesthetic embellishment. Farther north still—over the city line in Pawtucket—is still another river-bank cemetery; but this is not so beautiful. The net result of all this is the preservation of a splendidly rural series of river-bluffs, wooded ravines, & meadows for a space of at least 2 miles along the shore & extending considerably inland. Its ownership & conditions are fixed, hence it has been the same throughout my life & is always likely to stay so. I can shed the years uncannily by getting into some of my favourite childhood haunts here. In spots where nothing has changed, there is little to remind me that the date is not still 1900 or 1901, & that I am not still a boy of 10 or 11. Images & ideas & perspectives of that period flood up from subconsciousness with amazing vigour & volume, & do much to prove the relativity & subjectivity of time. Sometimes I feel that if I went home to my birthplace & up the steps, I would still find my mother & grandfather alive, & my old room & things in accustomed 1900 order.

At this moment the setting sun is throwing the long shadows of great, ancient elms across a broad, level stretch of silent greensward. At the far side is an old New England stone wall covered with ivy, & beyond it a line of trees marks the course of a venerable curving road—half-deserted now that newer trunk roads have cut if off as a line of through traffic. In suggestions of a magic annihilative of natural laws & material spatial & temporal restrictions, this scene & hour would be hard to beat. And I know that the columnist-celebrator of "yellow banks" would amply appreciate it!

I must see some of this "Saki's" work.[2] Yes—Wright is true to form! And you ought to see the tale of Talman's he has just refused! Talman, by the way, has just left the N Y Times to accept an editorial post on the 4 trade publications of the Texas Oil Co. Larger salary & an office on the 19th floor of the world's tallest building. I trust it is a wise move. Which leads me to express the hope that your own possible opening may materialise. I didn't know that Wandrei was getting so influential among the publishers of his native terrain! By the way—Dwyer has just let me see a letter he received from our fellow-contributor Henry S. Whitehead. It seems that W. is quite bitter at Wright's caprices—the latter having rejected his best tales. Smith has wrung pay for "Andromeda" out of Gernsback,[3] & is going ahead with the series—more because he wants to write the tales than because he expects to profit by them. And incidentally—I'm finishing the "Whisperer" at last, in odd seconds snatched from other things. I'll let you see it before long—if I can survive the damn typing.

You surely must get in some travel sooner or later, & this region is the very best spot you could pick. It will delight me to serve as an antiquarian guide in both the Providence & Boston zones whenever you can arrange to get around—& I certainly hope you can do it next summer.

Glad your friend & hero has had political success this year. He & his brother seem destined for long & full careers of public service.

Best wishes—

Yr obt h[ble] Servt
H P

[P.S.] Accept my sympathy anent the tooth! My last dental tinkering was in 1927, but grumblings from a lower molar make me fear for the future!

Notes

1. This is Butler Hospital, where HPL's father (1898) and mother (1921) died.
2. "Saki" was the pseudonym of H[ector] H[ugh] Munro (1870–1916), who was noted for his humorous but sardonic short stories.
3. CAS's "Marooned on Andremeda" appeared in *Wonder Stories* (October 1930).

[179]   [ALS]

[c. 16 October 1930][1]

Dear A W:—

Exceedingly glad to hear you've secured the Fawcett position, & am sure you can fill it brilliantly. With your surplus energy one doesn't need to worry about your having time to continue your own writing. I trust you will find the scene of your new labours congenial despite its evidently sub-arctic location, & hope it has some landscape touches comparable to your accustomed Sauk City scenes. Thanks very much, by the way, for that excellent view of the bridge & its surrounding terrain. It makes "Evening in Spring" increasingly concrete & vivid.

I felt sure you'd like Wandrei, & am glad to know that his novel of ultimate horror seems so promising. When it is done I hope he can find a market for it—though I imagine a novel is much less easily placed than a short story.

I haven't yet seen the current W.T., but am not expecting anything startling from it. Howard proves to be a very interesting correspondent, & I believe he has it in him to produce much better work than any we have seen. He has spent most of his life knocking about ranches & boom towns in Texas, & defers more to popular standards than a more sedentary & reflective person might. In blood he is about 90% Celtic Irish, & he has an encyclopaedic knowledge of weird folklore quite in keeping with the traditions of that imaginative race.

Well—I finished "The Whisperer" last week,[2] & sent the carbon to Clark Ashton Smith with instructions to pass it on to you. If I receive your new address I'll notify him—though I imagine all Sauk City mail will be safely forwarded. I hope the thing won't bore you—it turned out longer than I had expected, & came to 69 pages of typing. I haven't much hope of its acceptance by Wright, insomuch as he appears to harbour a vast prejudice against long stories unless they be by popular-styled authors. Now I am finishing up one more "ghosting" job—after which I hope to snatch time for several short tales of my own, Pegāna willing. I wish I had the energy of you young fellows!

With best wishes for you in your new setting & amidst your new tasks—
　　　Yr obt hble Servt
　　　H P L

P.S. Later

And now the books have come! Bless my soul, child, but you have provided Grandpa with a whole winter's reading! How can I thank you sufficiently? Some of these things are items I have always wanted—& I was actually on the point of buying "The Turn of the Screw" in the Modern Library. As it is, the only duplicate is "They Return at Evening"—which I shall pass along, with your compliments, to either Belknap or Dwyer. I am tremendously glad to have such things as "John Silence", (my only Blackwood) "The Beetle", (which I read years ago with admiration) "In Search of the Unknown", (gghh! Will I ever forget *The Harbour-Master?*) &c. &c. &c. And some of the things I know nothing about look astonishingly tempting. At any rate, pray accept an old man's profoundest gratitude & most voluble blessings! Oh, yes—& some of the magazine extracts seem highly promising.

Again thanking you most profoundly—
Yr oblig'd & ob^t
H P

Extra!

Wright has just accepted "The Whisperer" for $350.00. Not so bad. Will appear as 2-part story in June & July issues. He adds that Everil Worrell will probably become associate editor very soon.

Notes

1. Envelope postmarked 16 October 1930. Addressed to 3203 Lyndale Ave. S., / Apt. 3 / Minneapolis, Minn.
2. HPL had completed the final draft of "The Whisperer in Darkness" on 26 September; by "finished" he presumably means he had prepared the typescript.

[180]   [ALS]

[late October 1930]

Dear A W:—
                    Of course, I know the new position must involve much drudgery & repellent dealing with cheap things in a cheap style; but at least it's a good anchorage for a while, & a financial asset which many a young writer may well envy. If Wandrei's accounts be accurate, the Twin Cities are far from a repulsive place to exist. He spoke once or twice of the mystic— almost cosmic—sky effects when the atmosphere gets filled with a peculiar sort of dust from the prairies.

Yes—by all means let Wandrei see the "Whisperer" & keep it as long as he likes. I hope it won't strike its readers as too hopelessly tame & flat & long-winded. I'm now awaiting the verdict of Klarkash-Ton, Emperor of Dreams & High-Priest of Tsathoggua. By the way—I've just seen the MS. of his new tale "A Rendezvous in Averoigne",[1] which Wright has accepted, & can assure you that it's a masterpiece of sinister colour. When Smith lets himself go, he can produce marvels, so that Wandrei's hero-worship of him is not a bit misplaced. Has Wandrei shewed you his books of verse—"The Star-Treader", "Odes & Sonnets", "Ebony & Crystal", & "Sandalwood"?

Again let me thank you for that all-winter reading supply! For Heaven's sake forget the express bill. I'd have paid nearly as much for one book alone—& I actually *was* on the point of getting "The Turn of the Screw" in The Modern Library—as I did for the whole batch of 18+! But I appreciate your offer, & commend your liberal spirit!

Robert E. Howard's address is *Lock Box 313, Cross Plains, Texas.* I think you'll find him very interesting—a human encyclopedia of Celtic antiquities. Klarkash-Ton's is *Box 385, Auburn, California.* He, too, is eminently worth hearing from. No—Long & Dwyer aren't exactly return-mail correspondents, but then—very few people are! Not many have your inexhaustible energy, & in most cases correspondences have lapses of weeks & months without any alarm or impatience on either side. Long, by the way, thinks your productive energy almost superhuman. When I mentioned your average of fiction-production once, he was simply aghast at a quantitative standard so far—abysmally, incalculably far—beyond anything his imagination could grasp as pertaining to the mortal species of *homo sapiens!*

This Welsh play[2] sounds interesting, though 20 bucks is rather a good price to pay for anything not supremely notable! I'm sure I'd stop & think a bit before laying out that sum even on the infamous Necronomicon of the mad Arab Abdul Alhazred! Let us hope it holds all the dark Druidic sorcery of Machen's ancient Gwent countryside .... & that it's in the English language, unless you happen to have studied Cymric at some period of your erudite & chequered career!

Yes—I hope I can grind out quite a batch of weird stuff during the coming winter, though one never can tell. At present I am doing something frankly recreational—reading up on the history of New-France as background for a travelogue of Quebec.[3] I shan't feel comfortable till I get some echo of that trip on paper—not, of course, for publication, but merely to help me crystallise & codify my own impressions. That town,—& Charleston S.C.—formed my two biggest kicks of 1930; giving me a greater imaginative stimulus than anything else since my first sight of ancient Marblehead, Mass.

Best wishes, & cordial regards to Wandrei when you see him. Tell the young rascal to drop Grandpa a line!

       Yr oblig'd obt Servt

          H P

Notes

1. CAS, "A Rendezvous in Averoigne," *WT* (April–May 1931).

2. Unidentified.

3. HPL eventually wrote "A Description of the Town of Quebeck" between October 1930 and January 1931.

[181]   [ALS]

                              All-Hallows [1 November 1930]

Dear A W:—

       I don't wonder that exile in a strange arctic land induces nostalgia—but am glad that Wandrei & others help to palliate it. The expanded "Evening in Spring" surely sounds most promising, & I shall read it with the greatest interest & appreciation upon its completion. Klarkash-Ton's poetry will, I think, be a very stimulating revelation to you. You may balk at occasional extravagances, as some fastidious-minded critics do; but all in all I think you will see in the work a genuinely poetic revolt against the intolerable limitations of time & space. By the way CAS has finished reading my "Whisperer in Darkness" & will shortly forward it to you. I don't know that it amounts to much—but it means 350 bucks at any rate. I shall be interested to see what you & Wandrei truly think of it.

Have just heard more from Howard—a highly interesting character, & *much* superior to his work. He has a poet's sense of the epic sweep of Texas life & history, & really ought to link up more with this native & lifelong soil of his. Perhaps he will some day—I shall certainly encourage it.

I hope eventually to have a sniff at the new Onions opus—& am meanwhile quite excited at the thought of a new De la Mare volume.[1] Really, some of the latter's things seem to me to represent nearly the high-water mark of weird writing—to belong almost if not quite in the "Willows" class.

Glad the Welsh drama didn't prove a disappointment. I didn't know but the actual soil-born literature of Wales might be less picturesque & appealing than the kind of thing a gifted & imaginative Anglo-Welshman would write retrospectively from a London garret. But what interests me is this new de la Mare item. I have not seen it reviewed, hence I assume it is not yet published in America, or likely to be in any public library as yet. Still, I shall be on the watch. The element of *time* means nothing to me, & I shall enjoy it equally whenever Fate gives me a chance to get hold of it. If de la Mare has equalled "Seaton's Aunt" or "Mr. Kempe" he has surely been doing well! He lectured in Providence some years ago, but I did not hear him. Those who did were disappointed, for they say he has a small squeaky voice scarcely audible from any but the front seats! The best writers are not always the best speakers. I heard Dunsany in 1919 from a seat so near that I could almost have touched him[2]—& although he has a very pleasant & mellow voice, his delivery is wholly without dramatic values & inflexions. One could hardly realise that he was the *author* of the work he read—for it sounded more like the amiable drone with which a bored father reads a fairy tale he does not relish or appreciate to his small son.

The other day I read some of the rejected MSS. of our fellow-contributor Henry S. Whitehead, (1159 Broadway, Dunedin, Fla.) but did not have occasion to differ from Wright as extensively as I had expected to differ. One tale, though, really was fine, & Wright ought to have taken it. It brought up the West Indian locale & character marvellously well, & had an exceedingly clever climax. I shall be interested to see more of his material.

Well—I trust you're becoming well acclimated to the new job. If it seems grating, reflect on the fortunes of our fellow-contributor Talman, who is editing a group of trade magazines for the Texas Oil Company!

Best wishes & regards—
Yr obt h^ble Servt

H P

Notes

1. Oliver Onions, *The Painted Face;* Walter de la Mare, *On the Edge.*

2. HPL saw Dunsany at Copley Plaza in Boston on Monday, 20 October 1919. Cf. *SL* 1.91–92.

[182]   [ALS]

Friday
[c. 7 November 1930]

Dear A. W.:—

Glad to hear that you have had a taste of home & the hills. It's a good thing to be near enough to renew contacts occasionally. I can imagine how welcome the accustomed landscape must have looked—even though I dare say the scarlet & gold have by this time given place to bare boughs. It's too cold now to give me much enjoyment in the outdoors. October marks pretty much the end of my active season.

Glad to hear that "Evening in Spring" is coming along well—I recall the fragments about street lights & nocturnal trees. When the MS. is done, I surely want to see it. Klarkash-Ton will undoubtedly appreciate "The Early Years", for he is highly sensitive to delicate impressions. I'll shortly send you a letter of his in which he speaks of the aesthetic & pseudo-mnemonic impressions to which he is subject—impressions corresponding to my own sense of adventurous expectancy in certain sunset scenes, & my feeling of tantalising & alluring quasi-recollection when confronted by certain architectural & landscape effects. You must read his poetry sooner or later—it is infinitely superior to any prose he has produced so far. And tell Wandrei to shew you some of his bizarre drawings & paintings. At one time his art interests threatened to swamp his literary endeavours! The story Wright boasts of accepting—"A Rendezvous in Averoigne"—is indeed a very fine vampire tale, full of haunting & convincing atmosphere. I have just read it in MS. As for my Whisperer—I fancy the trouble is not so much that you read it in two instalments, as much that I wrote it in many instalments—some of them separated by long intervals. Whenever I do that, the result never satisfies me. My own objection to the tale is vague. It is not lack of plot—for I utterly despise plot as a cheap mechanical device—but is rather an impression that the intended effect, that of an out-reaching & in-sucking horror manifest in ever-tightening coils of bondage, is not perfectly realised. I made a mistake in tackling so large an order in a busy period when I could spare so little continuous time. It is better to do short complete things all at once when one cannot put in continuous & uninterrupted labour day after day. Well—I trust the thing won't bore Wandrei too badly. I have told him to send it directly back to me, which will save you the bother of forwarding.

Your mention of the contents of "On the Edge" interests me vastly— though I could swear I have already perused "A Recluse" in some anthology.[1] Isn't it about a traveller overtaken by storm or darkness or something, who puts up at a country house whose master vaguely disquiets him? Doesn't he rise in the night in response to ominous impressions—so that in the end he is very glad to get away from that accursed & daemoniac spot? I'll look around in my notes to see if I recorded it for future mention in a possible 2nd edition of my weird fictional article. One reason this tale stood out in my memory was that, at one stage, I feared the guest was going to find a mask or other articles lying around which would prove his host no human being at all. This, of course, would have forestalled the idea which had been lying fallow in my own commonplace-book since 1919,[2] & which I used at last in the Whisperer.

By the way—how's this for coincidence? While I was writing the last paragraph the Whisperer came back from Wandrei! He seems to like it well enough[3]—probably because his own cosmically sensitive mind supplies whatever I failed to embody in actual words. I shall be eager to see his novel when it is done—also the long poem about the black northern forests which he contemplates.

In course of time I hope to see your new W.T. work—all of which I trust Wright will accept. If he doesn't take the Chicago Horror I shall "cancel my subscription"—for after all these years my curiosity respecting it has mounted to fever heat! Is it not an amplification of that tale involving a leap from the Tribune tower?

Have just received an exceedingly cordial & chatty letter—with picture enclosed—from Henry S. Whitehead. He invites me down to Florida—& I wish to Gawd I had the cash to go! Evidently he is a delightfully good fellow—of early middle age, apparently.

. . . . Have just dug up my annotation about de la Mare's "Recluse". I *did* read it—& it was in "The Ghost Book" by Cynthia Asquith (1927). But I must see "On the Edge" by all means.

Best wishes—

Yr ob^t h^{ble} Servt

H P

Notes

1. "A Recluse" was first published in Cynthia Asquith's *The Ghost Book.*
2. Presumably *CB* 69: "Man with unnatural face—oddity of speaking—found to be a *mask*—Revelation."
3. See *MTS* 263 for DAW's comments on "The Whisperer in Darkness."

[183]   [ALS]

Nov. 14[, 1930]

Dear A W:—

I hope you will be cautious about giving up a well-paying position—though of course with your youth & ability it would be only a matter of time before you secured another. All paid positions are necessarily distasteful—until one can work up into something like an editorship of Harper's or the Am. Mercury—but they have to be endured with grim fortitude. I'd feel lucky if I could get one myself! Still—you know better than I do how the conditions at Mystic compare with the limits of your endurance. It is certainly not wise to plug along in a *too* repugnant rut. But things may change perspective by the first of May—for habituation sometimes works wonders.

"When the Leaves Fall" sounds highly promising. It is refreshing to see how effectively [you] manage to get your dreams & impressions into usable form, instead of merely speculating how you will—or may—use them at some distant day! I shall of course be eager to see "Evening in Spring" when it is done.

Smith's "Offering to the Moon"[1] suffers from the haste imposed by a too-heavy production programme. If he would go more slowly, his prose would have more of the mellowness manifest in his early verse. Also—he has been too much prodded by cheap editors who urge more "action" & less atmosphere. "Satampra Zeiros" is a delectably Dunsanian thing which Wright was an utter fool to reject.

Alas for the Chicago Horror! That really deserves a printing—on the ground of perseverance all apart from its intrinsic qualities. I shall enjoy a look at the new weird material you mention—continuing to wonder how you can turn so much out in addition to all your other engrossments!

Glad you're sharing the genial weather. I'm too objective & background-seeking to go in for shirt sleeves, but leave off my waistcoat whenever the thermometer justifies it. Unfortunately a pressure of tasks has kept me indoors this past week—but today I am preparing to break bounds & get a look at the melancholy & bare-bough'd countryside. All too soon my hibernation will begin in earnest!

As for shocking the community—I don't believe you create any very deep-seated horror, for at your age one doesn't expect the extremes of conformity. It's the years which will later on cause you to ask what the use of singularity is. At your age I cultivated hoary senility—black coat & striped trousers, hard-boiled bosom shirt, black string tie, silver-headed cane, & so on! But I do hope you forgot to take the *monocle* along to the Great City![2] Enclosed is a very timely view from last night's paper, shewing that youthfully academic individualism is by no means confined to the virile Middle West—even our effete Yankee scions having their own brands of salad-day revolt!

Wandrei's moods of cosmic melancholy are curious, but I guess they're bound up in the same nervous organisation which gives rise to his cosmic prose & poetry. Now & then the absurd limitations of human life—time, space, matter, & energy—seem to get too much for him, so that he has to push aside reality for a while & work up the endurance to stand another dose of it. I recall how, when he was here in 1927, we had quite a conclave of literati—H. Warner Munn, W. Paul Cook, James F. Morton—in the old woodland ravine where I used to roam in infancy; & how in the midst of conversation Wandrei was moved by an impulse to climb the bank away from the mundane throng & stretch himself out on the ancient moss—alone with the fauns, dryads, & Outer Presences. A great kid, all told—his "Something from Above" pleased me immensely, although (as he explained) the very conventional ending was a tacked-on concession to our prosaic friend Wright. I'm anxious to see the novel of which this story is a fragment.[3]

Well—best wishes, & think hard before giving up a good job! I'm gratefully ploughing into the outer edges of my stock of winter reading!

   Yr obt h[ble] Servt

    H P

Notes

1. CAS, "An Offering to the Moon," *WT* (September 1953).

2. Cf. AWD's "The Monocle of My Great-Grandfather."

3. "Something from Above" (in *OSM*) was not in fact incorporated into *Dead Titans, Waken!*

[184] [ALS]

               Novr. 21[, 1930]

Dear A W—

   Recalling my own abhorrence of New York, I can't blame you for wanting to get away from large cities at any cost—yet I'm sorry it entails the relinquishment of such a lucrative post in your case. One thing in your favour is the ready way you manage to market your manuscripts—a point on which you have my perpetual congratulations. This reminds me that your "Pacer" will be companioned in the "Not at Night" anthology by Belknap's "Visitor from Egypt" & my own "Rats in the Walls"—the remuneration for each of which seems to be the same as yours.

   I can appreciate, too, the way an urban "intellectual" crowd must wear on your nerves after a time—although I can testify that the cosmic attitude is not necessarily either a pose or an attribute of sophistication. "Sophistication" is a mannerism for which I have not the slightest use—it being, essentially, just as meaningless as that more wondering & value-cherishing attitude toward the universe which it is meant to supplant—yet I have never in my life been able to think of human existence & experience as anything but a local, trivial, & more or less mocking phenomenon, or to look upon astronomical infinity ("outsideness", as I call it) with anything but a burning curiosity & fascination. It is no more a pose or mark of sophistication in me, than a child's curiosity about the moon is a pose or mark of sophistication. I have always had the attitude, & always shall. Time, space, & natural law hold for me suggestions of intolerable bondage, & I can form no picture of emotional satisfaction which does not involve their defeat—especially the defeat of time, so that one may merge oneself with the whole historic stream & be wholly emancipated from the transient & the ephemeral. Yet I can assure you that this point of view is joined to one of the plainest, naivest, & most unobtrusively old-fashioned of personalities—a retiring old hermit & ascetic who does not even know what your contemporary round of activities & "parties" is like, & who during the coming winter will probably not address two consecutive sentences to any living person—tradesmen apart—save a pair of elderly aunts! Some people—a very few, perhaps—are *naturally* cosmic in outlook, just as others are naturally 'of & for the earth'. I am myself less exclusively cosmic than Klarkash-Ton & Wandrei, in that I recognise the impossibility of any correlation of the individual & the universal without the immediate visible world as a background—or starting-place for a system of outward-extending points of reference. I cannot think of any individual as existing except as part of a pattern—& the pattern's most visible & tangible areas are of course the individual's immediate environment; the soil & culture-stream from which he springs, & the milieu of ideas, impressions, traditions, landscapes, & architecture through which he must necessarily peer in order to reach the "outside". This explains the difference betwixt my "Dunwich" or "Colour out of Space" & Smith's "Satampra Zeiros" or Wandrei's "Red World." I begin with the individual & the soil & think outward—appreciating the sensation of spatial & temporal liberation only when I can scale it against the known terrestrial scene. They, on the other hand, are able to think of wholly non-human abysses of ultimate space—without reference-points—as realities neither irrelevant nor less significant than immediate human life. With me, the very quality of being cosmically sensitive breeds an exaggerated attachment to the familiar & the immediate—Old Providence, the woods & hills, the ancient ways & thoughts of New-England—whilst with them it seems to have the opposite effect of alienating them from immediate anchorages. They despise the immediate as trivial; I know that it is trivial, but cherish rather than despise it—because everything, including infinity itself, is trivial. In reality I am the profoundest cynic of them all, for I recognise no absolute values whatever. All I want to do is to kick off the bondage of immediate time & space & natural law without losing touch with the particular corner of the universe in which I happened to be thrown. It is significant that

I always think of the cosmic gates of the sunset as glimpsed beyond the familiar spires & roofs & elm-boughs of the old Rhode Island country. If one is to step off into space, one must have a starting-point.

In matters of music, though, I would exasperate you more than Wandrei does—since I am absolutely without the first rudiments of taste. It is simply a blind spot with me, & I candidly recognise the fact. My aesthetic emotions seem to be wholly unreachable except through visual channels. Whenever I *seem* to appreciate a strain of music, it is purely through *association*—never intrinsically. To me, "Tipperary" or "Rule, Britannia" has infinitely more emotional appeal than any creation of Liszt, Beethoven, or Wagner. But at least I do not fall into the Philistine's usual pitfall of expressing contempt for an art which I cannot understand. I recognise & regret any limitation in enjoyment-capacity, & profoundly congratulate those more broadly favoured by Nature. But sometimes ignorance & incomprehension can exasperate more than intelligent controversial difference!

As for eccentricities & affectations—they undoubtedly arise from that same wish to expand the ego which lies back of nine-tenths of human motivation. The only trouble with such things is that they are crude & external & non-subtle, & do not constitute any true expansion at all as viewed by the mature mind. That is why they belong to youth, & are soon shed except by permanently childish types. They are absolutely meaningless & irrelevant in the light of any really adult perspective of the relationship of individual & universal—for independence & originality, as well as personal importance & ego-magnitude, are wholly matters of the mind & imagination; not in any way to be measured by bodily uniqueness or conspicuousness. There is no harm in a monocle if it pleases you, just as there was no harm in the toy locomotive you used to play with on the floor some 16, 17, or 18 years ago. But somehow or other the toy locomotive has ceased to be as relevant to your emotional life as it used to be—or at least, has ceased to be relevant in the same way—& in the course of time the monocle will likewise cease to be relevant. Eventually both the locomotive & the monocle will be placed on the museum shelves at the back of your memory, fondly regarded as reliques of days & moods that were. But don't give the monocle up now if you really crave it. Simply let Nature take its course.

Really, the question of what pleases one—what makes it worth while for each individual to endure the burden of consciousness for an average lifetime—is something involving the vastest psychological profundities. It all gets back to my perpetual query, "What is anything?" Accident has caused a certain momentary energy-pattern to coagulate for an instant in a negligible corner of limitless space. It calls itself "mankind", & has a certain number of basic needs arising from the chance conditions of its formation. Some of these needs are definite & satisfiable. Others are ambiguous, hazily defined, unrecognised, or actually conflicting. Amidst this confusion & conflict, what is the least futile & silly thing to do with oneself after the basic needs are attended to? Don't ask me—I gave it up long ago . . . . just as all realists have had to give it up ever since consciousness sharpened itself to the point of recognising the dilemma. Each person lives in his own world of values, & can obviously (except for a few generalities based on essential similarities in human nature) speak only for himself when he calls this thing "silly & irrelevant" & that thing "vital & significant", as the case may be. We are all meaningless atoms adrift in the void.

I shall take delight in seeing the new tales. Why not ask Klarkash-Ton about the "flaws" he thinks he found in "The Early Years"? He mentioned the MS. to me with the highest praise. I surely hope he will cut down his hack fiction programme before it "gets" him aesthetically, but fear the financial angle is a lure. He is very poor, & his success in placing this new stuff has been amazing. Wright alone has taken 13 tales within a year, & Wonder Stories is clamouring for his material.

I am positive you can do your best writing in Sauk City, & expect that "The Leaves Fall" will be a highly memorable production. All these delicately reminiscent works are potential parts of a long & significant emotional biography, & I look forward to seeing them published together & widely recognised some day.

Incidentally—I ought to adopt a very haughty tone these days; since the Macmillan Co. has made me, on a modest & unassuming scale, an official classic among classics! I told you that my friend Moe of Wisconsin had given a fragment of one of my "travelogues" to Prof. Sterling A. Leonard for use in connexion with Irving's "Sleepy Hollow" in Book II of the Macmillan Junior Literature Series, which he is editing. It was my impression that the thing was to be used as a note in the appendix, but the book came yesterday—& I was astonished to see my lowly contribution inserted as a full-fledged selection in the body of the text; on a parity with all the others, & with my name glibly included in the table of contents between Mr. Irving himself & Sir Walter Scott! Ah, me! Wright may reject my stuff, but at least, my name will achieve a mild & grudging kind of immortality on the reluctant lips of the young. Editing these school readers has its troubles. Moe did most of Book III—for high-school grades—but it now appears that the schools of overwhelmingly Semitised New York City will not use it because he included "The Merchant of Venice"! Oy! de perrents by de Bronnix dun't vant de teachings shood gedt pois'nal a'ready by deir sheeldrens! To such a pass has the supposedly Aryan western world come! Well—Moe & Macmillan's propose to solve the problem by preparing a special New York edition with "Midsummer Night's Dream" replacing the "Merchant". That ought to be safe unless representatives of the "good folk" & "little people" enter a protest that their kingdom is irreverently dealt with!

Have been hearing from Whitehead faster than I can answer him! Quite a boy! You may hear from him yourself before long, for he seems anxious to join the shadowy & unofficial "gang" composed of such W.T. veterans as you, Long, Dwyer, Smith, Wandrei, myself, & so on. He is exceedingly cultivated, & encyclopaedically well-informed. I envy anybody with his energy—as old or older than myself, yet just as full of activity & expectancy as any of you young fellows! He began writing in the year 1906.

I hope you will not have to pay for good autumn weather in the spring, as you fear. This has been a surprisingly fine fall hereabouts, though scarcely equal to 1928. Much of the warmth this month has been locally tempered by rain. My last woodland outing was just a week ago—but I may work in another tramp through the denuded countryside before the frost-daemon wholly shuts down. The one great thing about winter walks is the *sunset*. Nothing has quite the mystic beckoning effect of a gorgeous & apocalyptic sunset glimpsed beyond old steep roofs & bare boughs. ¶ Regards—

Yr most ob^t Servt

H P

[185]   [ALS]

Decr. 1, 1930

Dear A W:—

Your of the 24th proved highly interesting indeed, & I can easily see your point of view without feeling that my own is very seriously demolished. These differences are largely matters of emotional emphasis, & one position is just as sound as another. The only mistake one can make is to lose a sense of proportion & exaggerate the effects of one's position—whichever it be—until the result becomes (basically & subconsciously if not consciously) mere conspicuousness for conspicuousness's sake. It is easy to imagine a large amount of posing on both sides—one type of pose being just as absurd as its opposite. All that I try to do myself is to avoid artificial, irrelevant, & meaningless attitudinising in any direction—getting rid of juvenile self-consciousness, paying no attention to the surrounding world beyond wishing to be inconspicuous, (just as one pays attention to the weather & prepares accordingly to avoid suffering discomfort from heat or cold) & letting my contemporaries go to hell in their own respective ways whilst I go in mine.

About music—in connecting my blind spot with lack of wide musical contacts, one has to be careful in handling the element of cause & effect. Most certainly I recall the impressive names you list (when I recall them at all) merely as words on programmes which I have heard through & forgotten; but the facts that (a) I have not recalled music once heard, & (b) have not had the incentive to seek out music after an introduction to it, speak for themselves in a not uneloquent way. My mother was an amateur musician—piano & vocal—of no mean order, & in youth I was dragged to the usual round of concerts, including those of the celebrated Boston Symphony Orchestra—

but wholly without results. The enchanting effect of good music on me, while not wholly absent, is faint, temporary, & fragmentary. I am just as likely to detest a piece of good music as to relish it, & had rather hear a steam-riveter than Stravinsky & other damn moderns. When I was seven I took violin lessons & made good progress, but I very soon lost interest & began to hate practicing worse than hades. At nine I had a kind of nervous breakdown, & physicians thought I had better not be forced to practice any more—hence the world lost one of its greatest virtuosi! But the ultimate & conclusive test of my musical ineptitude lies in the fact that I am not merely indifferent to good music, but positively fond of cheap tunes. That is a decisive indication—just as a fondness for cheap literature is a better indication of literary ineptitude than is mere ignorance or lack of reading. In youth I gaily whistled the fleeting ditties of the rabble in unison with the man in the street, & had the usual Philistine liking for the operettas of Victor Herbert, Luders, Friml,[1] & the rest of the popular boys. That just about settles Grandpa as a musician, I fancy! Still—I have heard of persons cultivating music & other arts in their old age, so if you ever get around this way you can drag Grandpa into some phonograph shop & make him hear some of the classics that all well-regulated people ought to like. Maybe there would be some result, & maybe not. Of the pieces you list, I recall hearing the Liszt, Wagner, Tchaikowsky, Debussy, Stravinsky, Grieg, & Schumann items, though I couldn't cite a single bar of any of them at this moment. If I heard them played, I'd probably have about a 50-50 chance of recognising any one of them, although I'll be damned if I could tell which was which in nine cases out of ten. The only person I know who is as indifferent as myself to music is young Frank Belknap Long—although I have reason to suspect that the painfully emphasised taste of one James Ferdinand Morton is more a matter of cultural duty & pride than of spontaneous emotion. At the other extreme are Samuel Loveman (have I ever shewed you his poetry—or has Wandrei?) & Alfred Galpin—the latter a fellow-Wisconsinan of yours, who (though now teaching French at N.W. Univ.) has ambitions of becoming a musical composer.

As for affectations—I find myself curiously unable to alter my original view. Undoubtedly many of those who seek a short cut to ego-gratification in this way are blandly unconscious of the fact—until they look back on it after the lapse of a maturing decade or so. They *think* they don't care for what others think & say—yet why are they so anxious to dress up & pose for the benefit of others? If they don't care for others, why do they mingle with others so much? Is there any law against their staying home as I do? You theory of comfort doesn't hold quite enough water to float a good defence. It has yet to be proved that monocles dangling from the neck contribute greatly to one's ease & freedom, or that dressing-gowns are radically more convenient & comfortable for street & visiting wear than a plain, loose-fitting sack coat would be. If comfort be the object, why not simply wear a suit two or three sizes too large for you? In effect, that is what I do myself. I hate tight, smart clothes, & always get spacious, loose-fitting suits & roomy #8 shoes—of the plainest possible pattern. No, young man, you wouldn't rig up in public if you didn't have your eye primarily on creating a sensation & manufacturing an occasion for the use of your satirical gift! You really think *more* of public opinion (as shewn by your desire to outrage it at any cost) than most of us do, rather than less. That's sound modern psychology. And the most amusing thing is that you don't actually need to take this short cut to distinctiveness—since your real gifts are abundantly amply enough to enable you to stand on your own feet! But never mind—go ahead, & added years will take care of the rest.

Klarkash-Ton has repeated his praise of your work, & added that he sees an important literary future for you. I trust he'll shortly send you a more specific letter of criticism of "The Early Years." I want to see that Sauk City history when you finish it—that kind of thing is just in my line—& I agree that you can do your best work on it when home.

You have my sympathy about the coryza! Winter is here, too, & I was nearly all in from the icy weather of last week. ¶ Regards—

Yr obt Servt
H P

P.S.—I suppose Wright has told you the bad news about W.T.—that it is to retrench & become a bi-monthly,[2] thus cutting our market opportunities exactly in half. Hope this isn't merely the first step toward discontinuance! No more serials will be used—& the "Whisperer" will be published complete in one issue.

Notes

1. Victor Herbert (1859–1924), Dublin-born American composer of popular operettas. Gustav Luders (1865–1913), German-born American composer of *The Prince of Pilsen* (1902) and other operettas. Rudolf Friml (1879–1972), Czech-born American composer of *The Firefly* (1912) and other operettas and revues.

2. Only three issues were published on the bimonthly schedule, from February–March to June–July 1931.

[186]   [TLS]

Decr. 13. [1930]

Dear A.W.—

Well, you will observe that Grandpa is making an unaccustomed capitulation to the Machine Age today—the reason being that my left eye has been raising several kinds of hell lately, so that I am trying to make my daily pursuits as purely manual and non-visual as possible. I hate this damn machine, but it's better to stand the clatter than to have the sinistral optic tugging at its moorings as it has been doing. If possible, I want to evade the expense and bother of an oculistical consultation.

As for our discussion—I fancy I see your point at last, though I must still insist that the emotional motivation behind your predilections is essentially juvenile and based on an extremely flimsy, artificial, and illusory point of view . . . . . . as perhaps, indeed, you are entirely willing to concede. When I was a kid I loved to rig up in false whiskers and play pirate, soldier, outlaw, explorer, detective, and so on; deriving a distinct pleasure from the crude drama inherent in the act of impersonation. In other words, I was still so subjective and unperspectived that I could attach a distinct imaginative significance to the concrete personal aspect I presented. Later—in adolescence—as I have said before, I acquired the dignified old man complex and did my best to emulate my revered grandfather's sartorial scheme. But as I got along in my twenties, my perspective began to open up; and I realised how absurd it was to attach any especial imaginative significance at all to the way I looked. It became crude, as I now viewed it, to base any really serious imaginative vista on anything so local, fragmentary, concretely material, transient, and cosmically insignificant as my physical hulk or its trappings. Of course, the change was not complete, for no adult ever sheds quite all of his juvenility. For example, my love of the eighteenth century and instinctive subconscious placement of myself in a Georgian colonial milieu causes me to regard a clean-shaven face as the only natural plan of barbering for me. I would feel foolish and uncomfortable with anything else, because a clean shave goes with the architecture, literary style, and other things I am fond of. Yet this is only a vestige—so faint that I would have no inclination to bother with persisting in it if it were jarringly out of keeping with the conservative contemporary scene. Really, I suppose I'd rather wear a powdered periwig, knee-breeches, small-sword, and three-cornered hat than any other kind of outfit—other things being equal. That is the sort of thing which seems to me, in a languid, indifferent way, as my natural costume—the costume which goes with my tastes, preferential memories, and point of view. In childhood I actually did long for such an outfit—and was supplied with one through parental indulgence—but today the wish has evaporated to a mere perspective—I still feel that the eighteenth century is my natural setting, yet have no especial desire to express that fact in costume. Costume and personal appearance have ceased, except in the vestigial way typified by my clean shave, to be for me the vital symbols of my imaginative yearnings. And it is so, I think, with most adults. One takes pride in maintaining a certain standard of neatness and taste in one's aspect—I like my hair to be well cut, my suit pressed, my linen immaculate, my shoes blacked, etc. when I appear in public—but the motive is no longer the dramatic one of juvenility. The adult does not groom himself as a gratification for his imagination, because his imagination can no longer derive gratification from so non-subtle a symbol. This neat dressing of later life is really a bid for inconspicuousness rather then self-assertion. A gentleman has a certain sense of harmony in the scene around him—architecture, gardening, language, conduct, etc. etc.—and costume naturally becomes one of the minor accessories of that general harmonised scheme. One dresses to avoid self-consciousness, so that one may be free to enjoy the external world without distractions to one's vision. The penalty of falling below the standard is a feeling of awkwardness or out-of-placeness. Naturally, different scenes call for different ways of dressing, but instinct usually guides one to a sartorial scheme at once suited to the environment and lacking all artifices of self-conscious rigging. Only a fop or a convention-slave has really rigid dressing customs—beyond, of course, such matters as not wearing dinner-jackets on cross-country hikes and not wearing sweaters to the theatre—but the man of sense does not follow any such things as mere caprice or dramatic posing (to himself or others) when he puts his liberality into practice. For instance—I often walk down town in old clothes and disreputable shoes—things contrary to what I recognise as fitting—but it is not because I am "playing tramp" as I used to do in childhood, but merely because I am going for a ramble in the distant woods, and don't want to submit decent clothes to brambly ruination. Likewise—I do most of my writing around the house in a ragged old grey dressing-gown; but this is not because I base any imaginative conception of myself as a robed Eastern monarch or toga-clad Roman senator upon the circumstance of being wrapped in a robe. My reason is that it's more comfortable to sling such a thing on over a shirt than to put on a collar and tie and button up in a coat and vest. Naturally, if I receive any company other than my aunts I put on my collar, tie, vest, and coat—just as I shut up my folding bed and clean up any litter of loose papers that may be lying about. Nor would I find any particular point in going out on the street in the old gown— any more than going out in bath sandals or with a three-day growth of beard. You get the idea, I'm sure. To me, and I think to the average man of mature years, the element of concrete personal appearance has come to be recognised as something so local, and so unrelated to any basic reality or stream of universal events, that it has lost the power of dramatic symbolism which it possessed for the childish or adolescent imagination. It no longer occurs to the grown man to think of the details of his sartorial aspect as significant imaginative properties. Aestheticism in dress manifests itself simply as a desire to avoid disharmony—but the whole field of dress has come to occupy so reduced a place in the adult's external world, that he no longer finds its properties and modifications an adequate or usable medium in symbolising his imaginative yearnings. Those yearnings have so evolved that they are no longer translatable into the crudely concrete medium of personal decoration. No acts of rigging up and strutting can reach the evolved moods and motivations around which the emotional-imaginative life of a mature man centres.

He may dress up outlandishly for experiment once or twice, but he'll quickly find that it won't get him anywhere. It doesn't touch the spot—there isn't any kick in it. It doesn't mean anything—it is a dead language so far as expressing the adult's wistful outreaching for wonder and beauty are concerned. Much as I would feel vaguely at ease in a suit of knee-breeches, velvet coat with silver buttons, great silver shoe-buckles, three-cornered hat, and so forth, I know damn well that after having it on five minutes I would forget all about it and read or scribble along just the same as if I were in my regular junk . . . . . besides feeling like an ass if anybody caught me in the stuff. Clothes have ceased to be any adequate expression for my reaction toward the universe. When I want to play upon my feeling of membership in the eighteenth century I have to do it through reading, writing, or exposure to certain Georgian scenic and architectural vistas under certain atmospheric and lighting conditions. The mere crude detail of personal clothing wouldn't turn the trick any more. In other words, it is characteristic of an adult's psychology that he doesn't care so very much what he has on. The sartorial aspect has ceased to have the power of giving him either pleasure or pain, intrinsically. It doesn't mean a damn thing to him whether he has on a flowered robe or a tattered smoking-jacket or a plain shirt, so long as he can lounge around without any arm-scyes or stiff collar tugging at him. When he does dress, his anxiety is to be harmonious and inconspicuous—to blend with the scenes through which he is moving, expressing the same kind of taste which makes him have preferences regarding scenes. And of course the external public does count to some extent with the average person. It's simply a matter of common sense to avoid arousing hostility and ridicule when absolutely nothing can be gained thereby. It is perfectly normal for all save very introverted and self-sufficient types to derive a part of their natural ego-gratification from the good opinion of others in the environment of which they form a part. A sense of public approval—or at least, of less than public disapproval—is normally a distinctly comfortable feeling. One knows it means nothing cosmically—yet who carries his individualist theories so far as to invite a reputation for madness or idiocy or crudeness or ignorance or bad taste? I do not think anyone can honestly say that he prefers a reputation for inferiority to a reputation for superiority. He may think he does—or at least, think he is truly indifferent—but at bottom his apparent bid for recognition as an inferior is really a subtle bid (generally a futile and poorly based one) for some unusual form of recognition as a superior. The most I would say about indifference to opinion is that we may sometimes be really indifferent to the opinion of certain restricted classes greatly and obviously inferior to our own, either socially or intellectually. For example, I really don't give a damn what a Greek restaurant-keeper or a nigger stevedore thinks about me—or what, even, an aristocratically conventional and bigoted Victorian thinks. But I certainly would dislike to be a common butt of contempt or ridicule on the part of persons approximately like myself—average people inheriting the same traditions and forming natural points in my accustomed environment. This is largely because one person has absolutely no meaning in the cosmos unless related to some pattern. The feeling of harmonious placement in some pattern is vitally necessary to a normal person's feeling of contentment. On the whole, I'd say that the average man's dressing is motivated both by his innate sense of harmony and by his desire not to advertise himself as defective in the qualities usually reckoned superior among his own kind. That is, he does not wish to be thought crude in taste as to line and colour, negligent as to neatness, ignorant as to the ordinary customs followed by his own class for convenience's sake, and so on. Men of a somewhat cruder type add to this motivation a desire to display wealth, or at least, to advertise their removal from poverty. Women add the element of erotic lure, but men seem to do so only in adolescence, or at most, transiently—relying on other characteristics to attract the female. Boil down the average adult male motives for being well dressed, and you'll find that an innate sense of harmony or background-merging, plus a desire to appear superior in the eyes of his own class, will account for at least 95% of his incentive. We don't often dress for ourselves—as witness the unkempt habits into which profound recluses or men in exotic environments almost always fall. That is the psychology of "going native". It takes a strong sense of class—like that instilled into the British public-school type—to make a regular adult dress up, as for dinner, when there's no audience around.

That, then, is why I think you'll outgrow your present sartorial amusements. What is juvenile is the fact that such things are capable of giving you pleasure at all. Your lorgnette, robe, & alpaca overcoat correspond to my Jesse James whiskers and policeman's badge and cowboy hat of thirty years ago, and my boiled shirt and black coat and vest of twenty years ago . . . . . or to the powdered wig, silver buttons, and buckled shoes. And the fact that I wouldn't get much of a kick out of these things now, seems to me a moderately fair indication that you won't greatly cherish your pet personal scenery when you, too, get to be an old gentleman! All of which you will possibly concede with perfect readiness—allowing of course for the natural differences in temperament which cause our respective juvenilia to be of somewhat different type, and of a somewhat different extent of practice. Go ahead, son, and don't let the old folks spoil your good time! I'm merely putting my estimate on record for future reference—so that you'll see what a prophet Grandpa was after you've outgrown the golden mists of the late 'teens and early twenties.

About music—you are probably right in thinking that a fresh approach to the field, coupled with a sympathetic attempt to analyse certain compositions of high value but simple elements, might tend to open up to some extent the atrophied or undeveloped channels of appreciation. It is barely possible that my violin-lesson experience, in which the nervous strain of enforced practicing became such a nightmare, developed a definite hostility toward the whole idea of music in my childish mind—an hostility which sank into the subconscious when the lessons were given up, but which nevertheless lurked as a latent influence to colour all my future feelings and build up a wall of resistance (interpreted as indifference when no longer associated with compulsion) and callousness against the aesthetic appeal of music. The callousness exists only toward music presented to me *as music*— that is, as a serious matter associable with the violin-compulsion of the old days. Anything in the way of tunes dissociated from the serious-music concept is all apart from this blind spot—indeed, I confessed as an evidence of weak taste my fondness for the stray ballads of the hurdy-gurdy and music hall. Psychologists may speculate as to what my taste would have been but for the violin ordeal. It may be said, for one thing, that I had the purely mechanical elements of perfect *accuracy* and *rhythm* in connexion with the cheap tunes which I used to hum and whistle in my day. It is impossible for me to whistle out of tune, or to miss notes by sharping or flatting them. Whatever I do hum, I hum with the mathematical precision of a well-tuned piano. Rhythm, also. When, at the age of 11, I was a member of the Blackstone Military Band, (whose youthful members were all virtuosi on what was called the "zobo"—a brass horn with a membrane at one end, which would transform humming to a delightfully brassy impressiveness!) my almost unique ability to keep time was rewarded by my promotion to the post of drummer. That was a difficult thing, insomuch as I was also a star zobo soloist; but the obstacle was surmounted by the discovery of a small papier-mache zobo at the toy store, which I could grip with my teeth without using my hands. Thus my hands were free for drumming—whilst one foot worked a mechanical triangle-beater and the other worked the cymbals—or rather, a wire (adapted from a second triangle-beater) which crashed down on a single horizontal cymbal and made exactly the right cacophony . . . . much as does the ordinary trap-drummer's single cymbal attached to the bass-drum. I was surely a versatile and simultaneous musician in my day—and on my plane. Had jazz-bands been known at that remote aera, I could certainly have qualified as an ideal general-utility-man—capable of working rattles, cow-bells, and everything else that two hands, two feet, and one mouth could handle. Ah, me—the days that are no more! Seriously, though, I do not think that music could ever be a prime outlet for my imagination, no matter how urbanely my taste might respond to development if freed from the early violin-barrier. The fact is, that my imagination is almost wholly visual, so that nothing very far removed from the potentially pictorial could make a very big dent in me. I am what the psychologists call "eye-minded"—I had rather write or read than talk or hear, and simply cannot understand my aunts' fondness for lectures. I tell them that they are wasting time bothering to get ready and travel nearly a mile to the Brown campus or downtown to hear people orate (often indistinctly, and at a steady rate allowing for no pauses to suit taste) a string of words which might be assimilated much more rapidly, comfortably, and completely from the printed page. It seems astonishing to me that anyone could prefer any channel to the eye for the reception of impressions from the external world. Still, though, I can get the idea of music in the abstract. I always think of strange, delicate fragments of half-heard melody associated with the ethereal and visionary worlds of cosmic memory or sunset glamour—even though I can form no concrete impression of what those fragments are, or what they are remotely like. What I hate worst in music, I guess, is *definiteness*. I like it to remain vague and cosmic.

Yes—it certainly is too damn bad about W.T. Just what the real reason is, I'm sure I don't know; but perhaps at this depressed period people hesitate to plunk down a quarter every month, yet would hang on as readers if asked to do so less often. By alternating Weird with Oriental, Wright is (presumably) commanding two distinct publics, each of which will stand for a bi-monthly, but neither of which would stand for a monthly. In other words, the only way to keep on getting a certain market for a magazine every month, is to have two sets of buyers instead of only one; so that one group will buy one month, and another group the next. In order to do this, it is necessary to have one month's magazine aimed at a wholly different element from that whose purse has been exhausted by the purchase of the preceding month. And later, of course, better times might make it possible to restore W.T. to a monthly basis, and even have Oriental follow suit—thus creating a business greater even than the original one. It is a safe thing to have many irons in the fire—or at least, that is how Brother Farny probably argues. I doubt very much if the tertium quid—Strange Stories—ever takes concrete form . . . . . . but then, who can predict about anything?

Well, I hope you'll be able to meet the change by grinding out Orientales as facilely as you produce weird material. Give the Arabian Nights a rereading, and see what luck you have! I haven't an idea when the Whisperer will appear—but I'm glad it will be in one issue instead of two. Glad Klarkash-Ton's "Satampra Zeiros" has landed at last. Your policy of repeated bombardment may become a regular policy of the gang! What do you think of Belknap's "Horror"? One handicap is the alleged illustration perpetrated by that monumental ass Senf. Good Gawd, but can't the fellow read? Belknap clearly described the nameless hybrid thing that is Chaugnar Faugn—a thing only remotely and obscenely suggesting the elephant—and look at the pretty Jumbo-on-a-pedestal that our distinguished "artist" has provided for our delectation! I hereby retract all the kindly things I said of Senf after his one tour de force—the design for "Icy Kinarth".

Whitehead's analysis of "The Panelled Room" is certainly astonishing in view of his undoubted scholarship and excellent original work—but simply illustrates the truth that one's abilities are seldom evenly developed. When I come to think of it, I can see that Whitehead's merits are all of an order very distinctly removed from subtlety or fine shadings. He is urbane, erudite, and tasteful, and has a very fine sense of the pictorial and dramatic; but it is upon these things, and not upon true sensitiveness to hints and shadings and intricacies, that the appeal of his colourful West-Indian stories is based. He is just a trifle dependent on the usual. He writes in something approaching the popular-magazine formula, deals with actually existing folklore, and adopts the conventional angle in motivations and value-presentations. You've guessed wrong in one thing—he is a very fervent and enthusiastic *Anglo-Catholic*, like Arthur Machen and the later T. S. Eliot, as he has told me with specific emphasis in commenting on my own mechanistic atheism. There's another thing, too, which ought to make you and him congenial—and that is his belief in the reality of "occult" phenomena; a belief to which I think you confessed some years ago, even though you may have outgrown it now. You and he are quite alone among our "gang" in this particular. I think you'll like Whitehead better on closer acquaintance. He strikes me as an altogether delightful chap, though a bit inclined toward the obvious and the conventional, and now wholly free from a certain amiable egotism expressed in occasional citations of his Ph.D., and in not dissatisfied allusions to the various celebrities of his personal acquaintance—celebrities including Sherwood Anderson and Ralph Adams Cram.

I shall look for the cinema of "Tom Sawyer", even though my excursions into the outside world are not many at this time of year. I hardly ever go to a show unless dragged by someone else—indeed, the only cinema I've seen since my Onset visit with the Longs is "Journey's End"—a really fine piece of work. I have always admired "Moby Dick", but have so far seen neither of the films based upon it.[1] I hope they do not belie the spirit of the original too flagrantly—it is pathetic to see an author's fine conception ruined by cheapening and popularisation. I always think of "Moby Dick" when I am in New Bedford. The little Seaman's Bethel is still on its accustomed hill and devoted to its original purpose, notwithstanding the disappearance of whaling. The waterfront is little changed, and from the upper windows of the great whaling museum one may look out over much the same tangle of old roofs that greeted the voyagers of long ago.

I shall be glad to see any new tales you may have evolved—and likewise the History after its completion. Sauk City is fortunate in having an historian so sensitive to the colour and spirit of things, and I'll wager the book will be more of an epic of subtle forces—landscape and people, and their mutual reactions through slow-moving generations—than one is accustomed to look for among American local chronicles.

Well—this machine and the consequent non-use of my eyes seem to have made me garrulous today!

Best wishes, and hopes for a fruitful programme.

Yr Ob^t Servt

H P

Notes

1. *Tom Sawyer* (Paramount-Publix, 1930), based on the novel by Mark Twain. *Journey's End* (Tiffany-Gainsborough, 1930), directed by James Whale; starring Colin Clive, Ian MacLaren, and David Manners. The film is a drama of World War I. Of the two film adaptations of Herman Melville's novel *Moby-Dick,* the first (*The Sea Beast* [Warner Brothers, 1926]) is a silent, the second (*Moby-Dick* [Warner Brothers, 1930]) a talkie.

[187]   [TLS]

Saturn's Day [19 or 26 December 1930]

Dear A. W.—

I see your point of view in the matter of costume-playing, and do not think it conflicts with what I suggested in my earlier argument—namely, that this method of ego-expression is essentially juvenile because it attaches a disproportionate significance to the visible and immediate physical aspect of the expresser. Probably I was careless in using the term "artificial", for what I really meant was simply a degree of empiricism and superficiality which amounts to artificiality when viewed by the fuller-perspective outsider. Naturally, it is not artificial for the subject himself so long as it continues to give him authentic emotional satisfaction. Your difference from my own early love of rigging and playing is probably mainly that I demanded conscious and visible links betwixt my costumes and the images and trains of pageantry which they symbolised, whereas you are satisfied to let these links remain unconscious—so that you enjoy a given scenic setting without interpreting it in terms of an ego-drama. This may be allied to the predominantly visual quality of my whole imagination—a quality which makes me actually unable to feel any mood which cannot be defined in visual outline, or at least, in the mystical suggestion of such.

I certainly do not disagree with you concerning the essential solitude of the individual, for it seems to me the plainest of all truths that no highly organised and freely developed mind can possibly envisage an external world having much in common with the external world invisaged by any other mind. The basic inclinations, yearnings, and ego-satisfactions of each separate individual depend wholly upon a myriad associations, hereditary predispositions, environmental accidents, and so on, which cannot possibly be duplicated in any other individual; hence it is merely foolish for anybody to expect himself to be "understood" more than vaguely, approximately, and objectively by anybody else. For example, I am perfectly confident that I could never adequately convey to any other human being the precise reasons why I continue to refrain from suicide—the reasons, that is, why I still find existence enough of a compensation to atone for its dominantly burthensome quality. These reasons are strongly linked with architecture, scenery, and lighting and atmospheric effects, and take the form of vague impressions of adventurous expectancy coupled with elusive memory—impressions that certain vistas, particularly those associated with sunsets, are avenues of approach to spheres or conditions of wholly undefined delights and freedoms which I have known in the past and have a slender possibility of knowing again in the future. Just what those delights and freedoms are, or even what they approximately resemble, I could not concretely imagine to save my life; save that they seem to concern some ethereal quality of indefinite expansion and mobility, and of a heightened perception which shall make all forms and combinations of beauty simultaneously visible to me, and realisable by me. I might add, though, that they invariably imply a total defeat of the laws of time, space, matter, and energy—or rather, an individual independence of these laws on my part, whereby I can sail through the varied universes of space-time as an invisible vapour might . . . . . . upsetting none of them, yet superior to their limitations and local forms of material organisation. The commonest form of my imaginative aspiration—that is, the commonest definable form—is a motion backward in time, or a discovery that time is merely an illusion and that the past is simply a lost mode of vision which I have a chance of recovering. Now this all sounds damn foolish to anybody else—and very justly so. There is no reason why it should sound anything except damn foolish to anyone who has not happened to receive precisely the same series of inclinations, impressions, and background-images which the purely fortuitous circumstances of my especial life have chanced to give to me. But as I look at it, the very naturalness and universality of this solitude remove that condition from the more or less painful state called "loneliness", in the conception of which there is implicit some suggestion of preventable ill, out-of-placeness, or resentment-meriting defeat. The cosmic solitude which we all share may justly breed a mood of wistfulness, but hardly one of acutely painful "loneliness". However— very possibly you realise all this as fully as I do, and merely use the word "loneliness" to signify exactly what I mean when I say "cosmic solitude". It is well, in exchanging ideas, not to get tangled up in mere nomenclature, as we are too often apt to do. As a safeguard against this bothersome verbal sidetracking I have often said that we ought to discard all the traditional terms of philosophy; which differently-thinking ages have invested with so many conflicting overtones of meaning that they have almost ceased to stand for any definite realities. "Good", "evil", "pleasure", "pain", etc. no longer define any exact concepts; whilst the very names of the different branches of intellectual approach have some to raise meaningless and irrelevant distinctions and images. We ought no longer to use words like "philosophy", "science", and so on, but should adopt some fresh term like "cognition", which has not yet picked up any misleading or ambiguous associations.

Where I begin to disagree with you is the place where you allow your sense of solitude to conflict, through a false sense of consistency, with the common sense of pattern-placement. I find this a rather odd conflict, insomuch as it is hardly to be expected in one who objects to the wholly cosmic perspective of Wandrei and Clark Ashton Smith. Their perspective, of course, repudiates pattern-placement from an angle opposite to yours—arguing against it because they consider the ego too small to place, rather than too large to need a pattern—yet I should think that the grounds on which you reject their view would at least incline you to be distrustful of any view not attaching significance to certain external points of reference.[1] You require certain landmarks like your beloved hills and river-bends—and it is only a step from this requirement to the need of a certain alignment with the natural traditions and folkways of the social and geographical group to which one belongs. One does not have to take these traditions and folkways seriously, in an intellectual way, and one may even laugh at their points of naivete and delusion—as indeed I laugh at the piety, narrowness, and conventionality of the New-England background which I love so well and find so necessary to contentment. But however we may regard such a pattern intellectually, the fact remains that most of us need it more or less as a point of departure for imaginative flights and a system of guideposts for the establishment of the illusions of direction and significance. And experience seems to shew that the only way one can effectively use such a pattern, is to refrain from repudiating it so far as the lesser symbolic conformities are concerned. Of course exceptions exist, and you may very well be one of them; but for the average person there is a need for personal anchorage to some system of landmarks larger than the ego yet smaller than the cosmos-at-large—a system of anchorage which can supply standards of comparison in the fields of size, nature, distance, direction, and so on; as demanded for the fulfilment of the normal sense of interest and dramatic action. Probably everybody has to have such a system—the differences being in the way various people envisage and express it. Religious people seek a mystical identification with a system of hereditary myths; whereas I, who am non-religious, seek a corresponding mystical identification with the only immediate tangible external reality which my perceptions acknowledge—i.e., the continuous stream of folkways around me. I achieve this mystical identification simply by a symbolic acceptance of the minor externals whose synthesis constitutes the surrounding stream. I follow this acceptance purely for my own personal pleasure—because I would feel lost in a limitless and impersonal cosmos if I had no way of thinking of myself but as a dissociated and independent point. And my particular way of following it is simply that dictated by relative ease and a natural economy of energy. Logically, of course, this conception of linkage conflicts with the fact of each person's individual solitude. This one may not deny—but we know as a matter of experience that abstract logic is not very meaningful when applied to the complex and ambivalent emotions of our species. In actual practice, we can see that our solitudes are always modified by that vague community which springs from the never inconsiderable area where individual heritages overlap—that vague community arising from the similarity of sights, impressions, and experiences to which all the members of any given group have been equally exposed. It would be foolish to carry the theory of individuality so far as to imply that certain sights and impressions have not a special group-significance as well as a special individual significance. We know as a matter of common sense that if we confront four individuals—two Americans and two Chinamen—with any given object or impression apart from the barest of universals, we shall *not* have four equally different reactions. A grouping of reactions, as determined by community of heritage, will most certainly take place; so that although there will indeed be four separate responses, these responses will not all be equidistant from one another, but will tend to group themselves into American and Chinese reactions. For example—if we place these four men before a Gothic cathedral, emotional linkages will exist for both the Americans which the Chinamen cannot possibly share. It is true that each of the Americans will have qualities of vision which the other cannot share; but it is also true that they will collectively have response-tendencies wholly absent in the Chinamen. To take a more personal and less clearly cut case—I have said that my own vague imaginative world must necessarily seem like damn foolishness to anybody else. Well, it is also true that it will seem like much damnder foolishness to some racial-cultural groups than to others. If it is built primarily out of my individual personal experience-background, it is also built out of my racial-cultural background as a New-Englander, Englishman, and inheritor of Teutonic blood-and-folkway streams diluted with Celtic. Much of my mood is sheer Teutonico-Celticism, with rough parallels in the folklore and poetry of the Teutonic and Celtic races, yet almost without analogues in the psychology of, let us say, Latins. Certainly, I would seem much less like an ass to one of the northern races—used to shadowy concepts in the Gothic manner—than to a logically brilliant, hard-surfaced Frenchman, or a non-brooding, emotionally tempestuous Italian. It would therefore be silly of me to deem myself simply an individual equidistant from all other individuals. Clearly, I am hitched on to the cosmos not as an isolated unit, but as a Teuton-Celt—with large emotional areas which can be shared with Teutons and Celts but not with others. This being admitted, it is certainly natural that I should seek a sense of placement and stabilisation through conscious symbolic alignment with my own Northern people. Summing up this point—the fact is that our individual isolation, while enormous, is certainly not absolute; its shadowy degree of external linkage being such that we can neither call ourselves wholly free, nor feel that we are in any way fully understood. No person's world is more than fragmentarily shared by any other person—yet on the other hand no person's world is wholly free from material contained in the worlds of other persons. Complexity and chaos reign throughout the cosmos—as the quantum theory is beginning to make plain in a mathematical way.

Not being Rohmerically erudite, I didn't get Quinn's latest borrowing,[2] but certainly don't think he borrowed to advantage! It is no longer possible to take him seriously, for he has clearly ceased to have any object in writing save the quantitative production of salable material. He undoubtedly knows better, and would probably be the first to agree that his stuff is mere synthetic tripe—but that doesn't make the tripe in question any less wearisome to the victim who attempts to read it! Here's hoping Wright takes your Death-Walker—as he probably will after a few resubmissions, even if he doesn't now. Probably you have received his recent form-letter of apology for not paying immediate debts. Belknap is quite discouraged, and feels that the magazine is on its last legs; but I fancy it's about an even question, as it was in 1924 when the Baird structure collapsed and the present Farnsworthian Phoenix arose from the ashes. Yes—Munn does get into arid and sterile regions when he tries to hitch his romantic-adventure mood and technique to the domain of the weird. He is drawing the poor Master out to such lengths that one cannot keep track of the creature's nature and attributes—indeed, the impression is that he merely retains the supernatural framework as a matter of duty—or concession to Wright—whereas he really wants to write a straight historical romance. But the kid's young, and we can well afford to give him time. Let him get Ponkertian werewolves out of his system, and see what he can do with a fresh start!

As for Whitehead—you certainly have an uncanny faculty for getting exhibitions of dumbbellism out of him! No "use" going on with Evening in Spring, eh? Bless me, but what standards of utility are we facing? Perhaps the tale does not teach a high moral lesson, or fails to contribute to that mood of healthy optimism which underlies America's commercial expansion and mass-production! Is it possible that Henry van Dyke or Bruce Barton[3] would not find it stimulating and idealistic? Hell—I give it up. I didn't think Whitehead was as bad as all that, for he certainly shewed sound enough discrimination in commenting on certain of the standard weird authors.* The only point on which he may not be quite so bad as you think is the comparison with Sherwood Anderson. It is true that this bird's style and treatment of the external scene is widely different from yours, yet I do think that Anderson has a sort of sense of wistfulness—of the solitude and essential inarticulateness of the individual—which resembles your mood in essence, despite the clumsily groping way he tried to get it down on paper. However, I fancy it's almost a decade since I have read anything of Anderson's—for much as I appreciate his artistic sincerity, I must admit that he fails to amuse me. As for Anglo-Catholicism—for most persons who reach it

---

*You must admit that W's latest story is excellent!

from the more fully Protestant fold, I imagine it is largely a way-station on the way to Rome. That is, the psychology which drew them that far will probably draw them the rest of the way if allowed to take its natural course. Accordingly I'm not surprised to hear that Machen and Eliot are now 100-percenters in their Catholicism. It may have been I who originally told you that Machen was a Roman Catholic, for I thought so till about a year ago, when someone told me he was an Anglo-Catholic. Probably he was an Anglo-Catholic when he first left his ancestral low-church Protestant Anglicanism, and has completed the transition at a relatively recent date.

As for occultism—to me all the alleged evidences—admittedly impressive when marshalled by a Flammarion or Chevreuil[4]—seem very clearly due to the almost unlimited hallucinatory capacity of the human mind—a capacity which has never been fully recognised till recently. We now see how frequently our minds invent impressions from the uncoördinated chaos of material stored within them, and how easily we may construct unconscious fictions through the involuntary transposition of events in time, or their involuntary rearrangement to suit a preconceived pattern. All this, too, is associated with an habitual and imperious urge of the ego to transcend the limitations of natural law and achieve a sense of importance impossible amidst reality—an urge leading to the most surprising cases of delusion or even downright mendacity. We know, also, how specific myth-types persist and accumulate supposed evidence which on analysis is found valueless. To my mind, the seance-forces you have felt—including the fear—are simply delusive rearrangements of materials already stored in your mind—I could muster up the same impression under similar conditions—but that would not make them mean anything. Of course, these hallucinations follow natural laws—and the great strength of Blackwood is that he describes them with deep and sympathetic authenticity.

Well—more later.   Merry Christmas!   Yr obᵗ Grandsire   H P

Notes

1. HPL's debate with AWD at this time caused him to dub AWD a "self-blinded earth-gazer" (*SL* 3.295).

2. Seabury Quinn, "The Wolf of St. Bonnot" (December 1930), "The Lost Lady," (January 1931), or "The Ghost-Helper" (February 1930).

3. Henry Van Dyke (1852–1933), prolific American author and journalist criticized for superficiality and conventionality. Bruce Barton (1886–1967), advertising executive and author of inspirational articles and books such as *More Power to You* (1917) and *The Man Nobody Knows* (1925), about Jesus.

4. Camille Flammarion (1842–1925), French astronomer who became interested in occult phenomena and mysticism. HPL owned his book *Haunted Houses* (1924; *LL* 319). Léon Chevreuil (1852–1939), French painter, spiritualist, and author of *On ne meurt pas* (1916), tr. as *Proofs of the Spirit World* (1920).

1931

[188]   [ALS]

Jany. 16, 1931.

Dear A W:—

My tardiness in replying to your recent New Year epistle may have convinced you that I am emulating the desperate measures of our friend Cook—who after his nervous breakdown fled from Athol without claiming his tons of back mail at the P.O. or supplying any forwarding address! Things aren't, however, quite as bad as all that—though I *have* been staggering under the weight of an imperative rush job which made all correspondence temporarily out of the question. I have about 20 letters stacked up for attention right now—a goodly number of which (acting under the insidious influence of Cook's example) I have not even opened!

And today I have a fresh handicap—the accursed, daemoniac, goddamn'd *cold!* This past couple of days have almost broken Providence records, & it must be close to zero outside. The furnace can't get the house up to more than 64° or so—& since I can't perform legible writing under 76°, I am reduced to desperate shifts. A gas stove in the alcove is the present provisional solution—but the illuminating facilities here are so rotten that I fear my scrawl will sink below even its usual reprehensible norm. Why the hell any people but Esquimaux will persist in building cities in regions north of Lat. 30°, is more than I can understand or forgive. These hellish winters will drive me South yet, as I get along in years & lose resisting-power, despite my hereditary & childhood attachment to the peerlessly beautiful New England landscape. As for *your* climate, where sub-zero temperatures are commonplace events—I simply can't envisage its habitancy by human beings! When I think of organic beings surviving a winter in Minneapolis, Duluth, Quebec, Winnipeg, or some place like these, I feel convinced that they must either harbour a strain of polar-bear blood or be protected by some elder magic gleaned from the Pnakotic Manuscripts of immemorial Lomar![1]

Sorry to hear that 1930 was a financial off year with you—but so it was with nearly everybody, & you really are doing marvels with free-lance writing for one of your age. When you come to consider the miserable luck & niggardly returns of many fine writers (like Belknap, for instance) who have been struggling for years, you will appreciate the strides you have made even before attaining legal adulthood. Only a few lucky individuals, who have some miraculous rapport with the facile emotions of the illiterate herd, ever make really substantial money in "pulp" free-lancing. For the majority—& this includes the most genuinely sensitive artists—it is a perpetual struggle for starvation profits. The only saving thing about it is that the victims generally know what they're in for from the start, & adopt it only because it seems less unfeasible than other things. You are profoundly lucky to have a regular job—I'd give my eye-teeth for one. The other day I had a chance at a reading & revisory post—but alas! it was in *Vermont*, which made it physically out of the question as a year-round matter.[2] But I hope you will find 1931 more profitable than its predecessor. Probably you will—especially if you expand your markets. Meanwhile I think you ought to learn to live on less money— for a writer is never likely to be very well fixed, & the sooner he gets his regimen scaled down to actualities, the more comfortable he is. It can be done—for I've done it myself. Up to 1910 or 1915 there was no one more recklessly careless of expenditures than I—even though the big collapse in family fortunes had come as far back as 1904. My mother used to say that I was absolutely ruined as a handler of money, & utterly spoiled as an endurer of poverty. However—as things grew still worse, the old man did manage to scale down everything; learning little by little what might best be eliminated without interfering with atmospheric continuity & freedom of imaginative life. Today I get along with a maximum expense of $15.00 per week, not counting the reckless antiquarian trips to which I irresponsibly blow myself about once a year. And this is not any squalid getting-along either—indeed, I'd feel damn lucky if I could always be sure of the hebdomadal fifteen which makes the present standard possible. It is a matter of caution & deliberation in the selection & preservation of things, & in the judicious quest for lodgings at once cheap & in a reasonably select neighbourhood. In the course of years, by a system of trial & error, one learns what nourishing & palatable food is cheapest, & what system of clothes-choosing is likely to make replacements as far apart as possible. One learns, too, how to make public libraries serve instead of indiscriminate bookbuying. $15.00 per week will float any man of sense in a very tolerable way—lodging him in a cultivated neighbourhood if he knows how to look for rooms, (this one rule, though, breaks down in really megalopolitan centres like New York—but it will work in Providence, Richmond, or Charleston, & would probably work in most of the moderate-sized cities of the northwest) keeping him dressed in soberly conservative neatness if he knows how to choose quiet designs & durable fabrics among cheap suits, & feeding him amply & palatably if he is not an epicurean crank, & if he does not attempt to depend upon restaurants. One must have a kitchen-alcove & obtain provisions at grocery & delicatessen prices rather than pay cafes & cafeterias the additional price they demand for mere service. Of course, this applies only to the single man. My one venture into matrimony ended in the divorce-court for reasons 98% financial. But if one expects to be a man of letters one has to sacrifice something—& for anybody of reasonably ascetic temperament the interests & freedoms of imaginative & creative life more than overbalance the advantages of domesticity. $8.00 to

$10.00 a week will get a very good-sized room in the best of neighbourhoods in the smaller cities, & $3.00 per week sees me fully fed. My dinners cost about 25¢ each, (a typical one—¼ lb veal loaf at delicatessen, 11¢; ½ lb potato salad, 8¢. Cake for dessert, 2½¢. Coffee—using condensed milk—averaging 2½¢) & my breakfast-lunches perhaps 10¢—a couple of doughnuts, cheese, & coffee. This is all I would eat even if wealthy, & it is just as palatable as the average programme. I also use Campbell's soups, 10¢ per can, & other inexpensive accessories. Then of course, now & then one blows oneself to a good restaurant gorge. As for clothing—buy plain designs, be careful of them, don't wear them out around the house when you can just as well be wearing any old spare rags, & you'll be astonished at the length of time they'll last. The important thing is to choose suits & overcoats so plain that no changes of style will make them conspicuous. I have an old topcoat (now relegated to rainy-day use) which I bought early in 1909—probably before you were born. My regular winter overcoat was bought in 1915, & my present topcoat in 1917—in April, just after the National Guard doctors had denied me the honour of olive-drab habiliments.[3] Of my suits—I always have four, a good heavy, a good light, & a second-best of each weight—three were purchased in 1925, & the other (scarcely used as yet) in 1928. None cost above $25.00. (although the overcoats did, since they date from the fringe of my "better days.") If I hadn't been robbed of all my clothing in a Brooklyn burglary in 1925, I'd have some still more venerable costume reliques. *Laundry* is an item which perplexes the beginner in economy, but one soon learns to have everything but shirts & collars done at a cheap "rough dry" rate—& more, one gradually picks up a facility in home laundering. The only way I ever take my long trips with a single small valise is by doing a good part of my own washing in Y M C A lavatories & drying the results on chair-backs & opened dresser drawers. Shoe-leather wears fast, but the wise man can make splendid $6.60 replacements at a Regal store. I don't get shoes more than once in two years. And there are chain-stores like Truly Warner's where $3.50 will get you as good a felt hat as you could wish for—one, too, that will last a couple of years. For straws, the sagacious pauper waits till the end of a season before buying his next year's specimen. One solitary dollar got me my 1931 straw (easily a 3.00 one) last August. I picked up a good deal of this lore during my Brooklyn days, for at least two members of the "gang" there—Arthur Leeds & good old Everett McNeil, (dead now, but Wandrei remembers him) were in straits even more immediately dire than my own. They had worked out the problems of poverty before, & I gradually absorbed something of their spirit & methods. They were free-lance writers—& had found out what the game means to the average struggler! Poor old Mac is gone now—but Leeds has come on slightly better times, through his side-line of the drama. Do you recall his W.T. vampire story, "The Return of the Undead"?[4] I think you starred it for your bibliography. Good old Leeds—he used to be pushed from lodging to lodging for non-payment of rent, & his coats were always bursting out at the shoulders if he moved around too violently; yet I never saw him in any state other than the most immaculate neatness—for somehow he had enough "pull" with barbers to get haircuts on credit, & never began a day without his bath, shave, & donning of home-washed-*&-ironed* (this latter is beyond me!) linen. It was Leeds who tipped me off to the cheap Jew clothing joints around 14th St. & 8th Avenue—places handling assorted remainders from which a keen critic with plenty of time might eventually pick something fit for a gentleman to wear . . . . as a spare suit, in artificial light. He found a suit for *$5.00*, but I couldn't quite duplicate that. $14.00 was the best I could do—for one's last residual aesthetic scruples aren't easily conquered.[5] I have that $14.00 specimen still, for around-the-house wear. Not, of course, that one would deliberately choose a regimen of penury as close as this—but that it's damn useful to know how to wriggle along when one has to.

No harm having a whack at the Confession field, but I'm told that this form of hokum requires a special knack—so that many successful general writers fail to meet editorial requirements. The successful "confessor" must have an expert working knowledge of the subnormal psychology of the greasy rabble who read this kind of thing; & this knowledge, even when gained, isn't always easy to apply. A fellow named Belvin,[6] who has had considerable success in Macfaddening, gave me quite an idea of the game a couple of years ago; & from what he said, I judge that it is a science in itself. The practitioner must learn to harp on certain key-words whose repetition catches the crude interest of the undeveloped mind; & must adhere to certain conventions of mood, scene, & event-sequence which the herd expect in advance. It is a dismal & discouraging business for anyone with any degree of sensitiveness, & many (such as Belknap) find it absolutely impossible despite repeated attempts.

As for our recent argument—I did not ignore the theoretical essence of your position—& my own as well—regarding the essential uniqueness & cosmic solitude of the individual. I merely considered the point in a practical & empirical way, & estimated the natural motivation-reactions likely to result from such a condition as tempered by the ordinary background, philosophic reflections, & instinctive habit-patterns of the normal individual at different stages of his growth toward disillusioned maturity. The essential solitude of the individual does not explain any individual's specific wishes in certain directions. It explains his unwillingness to be bound by herd custom, & his desire to follow out any course his fancy may dictate; but it does not explain why that same fancy dictates the things it does. Certain wishes can be shown to be characteristic of certain ages or stages of mental & emotional development; so that the free spontaneous preferences of twenty may appear pointless & absurd in the light of the equally free & spontaneous preferences of thirty or forty or fifty. Now of course one may reply to this that the preferences of 20 are just as logical *for that age* as those of 50 are for that greater age;

no matter how much less they may coincide with the demands of unemotional reason, or with those of the group collectively. This is perfectly true in theory—being indeed so axiomatic that the individualist never even bothers to reaffirm it. The real point is, though, that our actual practical comfort cannot ordinarily be gauged by the fulfilment of merely theoretical demands. The unrestrained following of irrational caprice always involves a more or less painful clash—in practical, every-day ways—with the collective rationality & folkways of the community; so that the net result of free capriciousness, in terms of pleasure derived, is always negative *unless the caprice-gratifier is profoundly & genuinely convinced of the real significance & value of his caprices.* That is, the only thing which can offset the discomforts of environmental disharmony is a genuine sense that the disharmony has not been caused by a course of action too trifling to warrant such a clash. Here is where the age factor comes in. Normally, only the immature can attach enough importance to trivial externals to have any decided wishes concerning them. Only the immature think enough about such matters, in the course of natural existence, to consider them worth bothering about. Nugatory matters like that have too little real connexion with the quality of unique personality to excite the notice of the matured adult. Of course, they may form the principal world of the adolescent; & if so, there is nothing to do but let him go ahead until he naturally ceases to consider such matters of any interest or attractiveness. While they last, they are his genuine world, & he has as much right to them as the older man has to the attributes of his own imaginative world. There is no need even to establish a qualitative difference between the two worlds—indeed, if the *valid nucleus* of the older man's unique personality clashed as much with the general milieu as do the salient aspects of the youth's, he might well be justified in treating collective folkways so lightly as the young individual does. We may say, from a certain point of view, that the adult's greater natural harmony with the external world is simply a piece of good luck on his part—a sort of accidental compensation for other physical & emotional qualities which he loses as youth drops away. However—again using a purely practical & empirical measuring-rod—it seems clear that there *is* a certain basic reality about an adult's quiet individuality which a youth's freakish physical & objective exhibitionism lacks. To begin with, the very transience of the material exhibitionism is a thing to be reckoned with. More—even at its most flamboyant, this exhibitionism can seldom be said to constitute the real core of my high-grade youth's individuality. It exists visibly enough, but only as the temporary excrescence of an individuality whose inner substance is as apart from physical externals as the adult's individuality is. It is not the seat of the youth's differentiation from every other living individual. It is a phenomenon—not a noumenon. To say that the youth's sacrifice of this external capriciousness for the sake of environmental harmony is as violent an infringement of personality as the corresponding individuality-sacrifice (mental or imaginative) of an adult would be, is to quibble with mere words & abstractions. No youth, in normalising his surface demeanour, is even touching those centres of personality which a mature man would touch if he were to change his imaginative life from external pressure. True, the environment-harmonisation of the youth demands more *visible* change than the corresponding harmonisation of the man; *but the difference in actual change demanded, as reckoned in units of real personality, is vastly less than appears on the surface.* What the youth is asked to give up is not his solid individuality, but merely a temporary expression of individuality which he would give up of his own accord—from sheer lack of interest— in the course of a relatively short time. His unique nucleus—a thing far deeper than any accidental whim of external manners—is as untouched as that of the adult, of whom less visible change is customarily asked because the chief visible caprices have atrophied of their own accord through the processes of nature. Well, that's the way it is. As long as any line of freakish conduct or appearance—or rather, to avoid using any collective criterion, as long as *any specific line of objective conduct or appearance*—seems to a person a matter of any real importance, & worth the trouble of following out in the face of obstacles, he would surely be unwise in trying to suppress or alter it. That is, as long as the net result is pleasurable to him, he is beyond the reach of logical criticism. The point is, though—as I have brought out before—that such feelings of importance & sources of pleasure do not exist for mature men. It is the fact that one is amused by such things, or that one considers them substantial enough to form real personality-attributes, which stamp one as juvenile. The moment one becomes touched with emotional adulthood, this business begins to seem *too irrelevant & meaningless to bother with.* In such a case, accidental circumstances determine the way in which one drops the fads. Normally, as I have said before, the ways of the community form so sensible a line of least resistance that any average person finds it most profitable—in terms of personal comfort & pleasure—to comply *in the absence of any strong reasons for non-compliance.* But this aspect—which you consistently underestimate as a practical general factor—is by no means necessary. We may imagine an abnormal type whose mental comfort is—either through complete seclusion or through some philosophic perspective of overpowering intensity— wholly dissociated from all mental & social relationships with his fellows. To such an one, the opinions of the world do not count—nor do any traditional precedents have weight as such. Suppose this unique specimen has been addicted to tall hats worn with striped pajamas to baseball games, or facial combinations of one left-hand side-whisker & one right-hand moustachio. Let us say that he has found these things so contributory to his pleasure that their maintenance has proved worth his while, even in the face of occasional rough-houses at college & occasional titters from the folks along Main St. Perhaps this narrow-minded social pressure—so powerless to ruffle him mentally—has physically served merely to drive him to New York, where people in red whiskers & medals & Harding-&-Coolidge buttons sit on the steps of the Public Library unmolested & call themselves Jesus Christ or Gautama Buddha; or to Paris, where Gerard de Nerval led a live lobster through the streets, & Raymond Duncan still gets away with a Greek robe.[7] Let us say that he considers his external attributes so essential & natural a part of himself that their abandonment would seem a needless, foolish, & unmotivated step, & that he has found a milieu in which he is not physically persecuted by the crude & callous. So far, so good—but let us also say that he is really normal in mind, & not subject to the psychological retardation of specimens like Duncan, or the actual traumatic insanity of wrecks like de Nerval. In other words, let us assume that he has the capacity for healthy mental adulthood. Now what is going to happen when this bird gets to be about 25? Here he is in Paris, independent of physical pressure or public opinion, yet at 25 he is beginning to find that there's no fun in the tall-hat & pajamas—worn now to gatherings at the Rotonda, or to the Auteuil or Longchamps races—or in the left side whisker & right moustachio. These things don't mean anything any more; & even if he doesn't stop to ask why he ever adopted them, he now wears them only through habit, with just the same mental attitude that he'd wear civilised things if he hadn't been started the other way. Well—what now? No external pressure exists to encourage a change of ways, & the community's average seems to him no more normal than his own particular scheme. But it has simply ceased to be a factor in his imaginative life whether or not he presents any particular type of aspect apart from the physical eurythmy & general neatness which express a sound & superior organisation. What happens? Well, let us say that one day an apple-core thrown by a small American boy (in Paris for the first time) knocks off the tall hat in the Boulevard St. Michel, & that a passing omnibus runs over it. Let us say that the day is cold & windy, & that our hero does not wish to walk back to his lodgings on Montparnasse with hair blowing about. He enters a hat-shop & orders his usual topper, but none are in stock. Instead, the proprietor (ignoring his pajamas, for this is Paris of the Left Bank) offers him a neat & commonplace Fedora for 70 francs. Why not? The day is cold, the hat is not ugly, & the young man is now 25 & an adult. Done—a bargain! And M. Lemaire-Jeans, born Elmer Jones of Sheboygan, Wis., goes home in the first appropriate headgear he has worn since the individuality bug bit him in his high-school sophomore year. And so it goes. He is sleepy one afternoon at the barbershop, & a poster of a Folies-Bergere beauty on the wall has the chief attention of Monsieur le barbier. Result—he is given a clean shave by accident, the artist having taken his cue from the right cheek & left lip-half instead of the left cheek & right lip-half. Home he goes—too sleepy to be angry. And when he notices the change he asks—what of it? Next time he goes to the barber he doesn't bother to give all the elaborate directions he has usually given. What's the use? So in time M. Lemaire-Jeans sports a he-man's straight shave under a normal Fedora. Then winter comes again, & our hero once more applies himself to the task of getting red flannel underwear warm enough to make the pajamas wearable. This is getting to be a harder & harder job every year, as houses are better heated & primitive folkways changing. This year he has fiendish trouble—till finally an amicable linen-draper suggests that he buy a regular woollen suit of clothes—just for the cold weather, of course. Eh, bien—pourquois pas? And so at last friend Elmer is dressed like a man—& all from merely following the line of least resistance! About that time—purely from childhood habit & lack of interest in earlier poses—he begins signing his name Elmer Jones again. And when spring comes, & he needs lighter clothing, he merely asks for "something cooler"; & forgets to be annoyed upon being given a regular suit of summer clothes. Thus, as the years go by, Elmer gets to be quite a regular fellow against his will—when finally someone asks him why he doesn't go home, since there is no longer any reason for staying away. Great idea! And one day we see Elmer on the good old hills around Sheboygan, renewing the impressions of infancy in the garb of normal maturity, & doing better work on his poems than ever before, because his attention is no longer sidetracked on meaningless frills. He is no longer flaming youth—the hair under the fedora is thinner & the waist behind the woollen suit is thicker—but he doesn't feel the loss very keenly amidst the occupations of a mind at last matured & objectivised. He now finds the world of external dream a thing of interest; & if he ever mourns his lost narcissism, it is with a mere objective sentimentality not untinged with amusement. Ho, hum—what a world! As a last reply to a possible objection of yours, let me reiterate a point lightly touched on before—namely, that individual caprices regarding externals are not in any way less "normal" than collective standards. The only juvenile or abnormal thing is the tendency to regard *any* system of externals as important enough to warrant cultivation in the face of obstacles or natural inertia. It isn't that your basic position about the individual's importance is necessarily wrong. That may all be—the individual may be everything & the cosmos an illusory dream. It's all in the point of view. But I do deny that a bathrobe & monocle constitute the real individual! Wait till you're 25 & see if you don't agree with Grandpa!

As for Whitehead's lack of acumen regarding your work—it will amuse you to learn (if he hasn't already mentioned it) that he is by profession a *psychiatrist*—a doctor whose specialty is supposed to be the phenomena of consciousness, & whose grasp of imaginative subtleties ought to be correspondingly keen! Alas for consistency! After all, the sensitive amateur sometimes sees a bit more keenly than the academicised profesh! Whitehead, by the way, confirms my second rather than first belief about Arthur Machen's theology—insisting that Machen is still an *Anglo*-Catholic.

And speaking of mental borderlands—your reaction to my statement that occult "evidences" are basically results of man's hallucinative capacity is exactly what I expected. It is a neat duplicate of Whitehead's position, & part & parcel of the attitude which makes one a believer in the first place. But perhaps I ought to have been more specific in my *definition* of man's hallucinative capacity. I refer to the essentially subjective nature of all our impressions from the external world, & the easy way in which any of them may be altered, distorted, transposed, magnified, or suppressed by any modification in our receiving machinery—as when emotion, habit, inertia, or anything of the sort has a chance to operate. Only the rough similarity of our minds, & the reasonable freedom of our sensory apparatus from disturbing influences, make it in any way possible for mankind to have any one collective & stable conception of the external world—or any conception having a constant & symmetrical relationship to the actual entities forming the external world. With what fatal facility this approximate collectivity, stability, & actuality of reality-relationship of our informative apparatus can be disturbed by the least extraneous (usually emotional) interference, we may daily see in cases of clashing evidence from identical observation; divergent deductions from identical premises; spurious, transposed, & externally suggested memories; & so on. Our perceptive relations with reality are in truth of the most tenuous & uncertain kind, & can be relied upon only after a wide application of simultaneous observation & mutual checking. We "remember" what we have dreamed or had suggested to us. We distort transmitted legends & artificially evolve "first-hand" evidence. We invent "premonitions" of events after the events have occurred, & suggest others into confirming our claim of having had the advance premonition. We run through a confused variety of thoughts about a major interest, so that upon the appearance of a sudden development we look back to the especial phase of forethought correlated with it, (forgetting all the rest of the medley) & imagine we have made a prophecy. And more than all else, there is the constant rebellion of the emotions against the galling limitations of reality, which gives us a pathetic & ridiculous wish to deem the supernatural true. This wish biasses all our perceptions & judgments, warps our sense of proportion, causes us to confirm the most absurd delusions, & often drives us into a half-conscious mendacity regarding the matters at stake. We can see all this very clearly in the dogged persistence of certain specific myth-types. The formation of such specific myths is a very definite thing, & the mental phenomena by which they are upheld deserve the most careful study. Some get wholly exploded in course of time, but their destruction does not lessen the faith of human sheep in the myths still publicly undestroyed. Witchcraft—the number 13—god—ghosts—the ordeal by floating—&c. &c. But I am not one to ridicule the summary dismissal of inexplicable phenomena. Certainly, when any reported happening is more than the most obvious lunacy or fakery, it deserves scientific investigation. The basic principles of psychical research societies is wholly sound. However, when we come to study reputed occult phenomena, we smell a rat at once. They always conform to the local lore of the regions of their origin*, & reflect whatever view of the cosmos may be prevalent there. Mostly, they occur in connexion with hysterical & inferior persons of the type most likely to have hallucinations or devise phenomena for obscure emotional gratification. Analysis of almost any specific case reveals discrepancies of memory, evidence, & narration; & alterations in repetition; which virtually nullify it. In short, any given case of "occultism" generally comes under one of the following heads: (a) something which never occurred, but was evolved through traditional rumour, (b) something which did occur but was mis-observed & mis-explained, (c) something arbitrarily invented, (d) pure coincidence, & (e) combinations of any or all of these. Of course, this allows for scientific principles still undiscovered. ¶ Regards & best wishes—H P L

P.S. Here is a story of Klarkash-Ton's which he asked me to send you[8]—for later passing on to Wandrei & ultimate return to the author. Pretty good malign atmosphere & suspense in the early part—but toward the end the horrors get a bit grotesquely *visible* & familiar.

Notes

1. A reference to HPL's "Polaris" (1918) and in all likelihood the gestating *At the Mountains of Madness.*

2. Through his friend Vrest Orton, HPL had received an offer of regular revisory work for the Stephen Daye Press (Brattleboro, VT).

3. HPL tried to enlist in the Rhode Island National Guard, but through his mother's intervention was rejected for health reasons.

4. Arthur Leeds, "The Return of the Undead," *WT* (November 1925).

5. Actually, the suit cost HPL $11.95 ($9.95 for the suit plus $2.00 for an extra pair of trousers). See *Lord of a Visible World,* pp. 161–64.

6. Ashley Belvin, whom HPL first met in April 1929. HPL wrote of him to CAS: "the way this chap coolly analyzed the needs of the Macfadden publications was enough to make an hippopotamus shrink. I'll own that I was hardly civil to him when he suggested that I try to reach this market—for my stomach was turned nearly inside out!" ([25 December 1930], AHT).

7. Gérard de Nerval (1808–1855), French Romantic poet; Raymond Duncan (1874–1966), brother of dancer Isadora Duncan and a fervent advocate of classical dress.

8. CAS, "The Return of the Sorcerer" (orig. "The Return of Helman Carnby"), *Strange Tales of Mystery and Terror* (September 1931).

---

*We all have a sometimes irresistible tendency to twist impressions to fit preconceived ideas & beliefs.

[189]   [ALS]

Jany. 23, 1931

Dear A W:—

I read all three tales with a great deal of interest & admiration, & believe that—judging from the sample—"The Leaves Fall" will prove a worthy sequel to "The Early Years." The general development you outline seems very logical & effective to me, & the mood & atmosphere of this first chapter appear to carry out your intention admirably. If any critics feel an air of hyperexquisiteness & sentimentality at this point, I am sure that a consideration of the text in its complete setting would soon disabuse them of that impression. Certainly, your lyrical prose power shews no wane—& I agree with you that the sentence from the coming section—blossoms "like sifted snow in the moonlight"—is very vivid, delicate, & apposite. Of the two popular tales, I will shock you by saying that I personally preferred "Death Walker". This gave my imagination & pictorial sense a tremendous kick, despite the more carefully modulated structure of the other tale. But "The Sheraton Mirror" is very fine, too, even if of more usual & traditional cast, & with less for the fancy to bite into. The suspense develops excellently—& will do so still more after your contemplated revision. The atmosphere of fatality, & the apportionment of the degrees of revenge, are finely managed.

Your suggestions for a new ending to Klarkash-Ton's tale are highly effective, & I hope exceedingly that you will make them to him—& that he will act them.[1] I was not so specific in any constructive comment, though I pointed out what seemed to me the vulnerable spot. He has sent this to *Ghost Stories*, though I fancy the chances for acceptance there are rather slim. W.T. is his next logical market—but Wright may object to the extreme gruesomeness as he has done in similar cases. Incidentally, your news of the return of W.T. to a monthly basis is the first hint to that effect which I have received. Most assuredly, I rejoice! Probably those whom Wright consulted reacted so unfavourably to the bi-monthly idea that he decided it would not pay as a permanent policy. I hope, though, that my "Whisperer" will get one-part publication, as planned under the provisional new regime.

As for economy—I can see that you appreciate the fine points of the art! Your room-rent underbids mine—but this is of course because you have home headquarters elsewhere. I have to have a larger room in order to accomodate the surviving residue of my accustomed books, pictures, & furniture—for existence would be absolutely meaningless to me except amidst the familiar objects—tables, chairs, bookcases, paintings by my mother & elder aunt, clocks, bric-a-brac, &c—I have always had around me from earliest infancy. Likewise, I couldn't stand a decaying or inferior neighbourhood. 15 months at 169 Clinton St. Brooklyn fed me up on all the seedy, lower-middle-class atmosphere, which I care to include in one limited lifetime. I'd curtail food rather than rent.

As for the argument—of course there are factors in every personal perspective which can be elucidated only by the most minute analysis involving ideas of the universe, scales of values, proportioning of emotions, habits of selective attention & emphasis, & so on—so that many philosophic disagreements, like the present one, have roots not readily reachable by any ordinary appraisal & discussion. The one basic question, "what is anything"? has so many possible answers, that it takes a long time for anyone to make clear just how he is attempting to answer it—or upon what unconscious attempt at answering it he is basing his daily acts & moods. Certainly, a week of observation & illustration might do much more toward mutual clarification than could many reams of academic debate; & I hope that the future may develop opportunities in this direction. At the same time, I still think that with the passing of years your views will gradually shift in the direction of those moods which are generally regarded as mature. I am not pronouncing such moods mature on my own judgment alone, but am merely repeating what seems to be the consensus of opinion among those who have objectively studied the emotional-imaginative life of different age-groups, & have sought to classify the various typical attitudes with respect to permanence, relation to basic character-patterns, & adjustment to the proximate landmarks of external reality. But wait & see. Not everybody follows the same cycle, but I'll bet that at forty you won't be wasting your time & cash on things as irrelevant & charlatanic as palmists, seances, & kindred vestiges of the individual's & the race's naive childhood!

As for the "occult"—I don't see any reason to change my views concerning the relative probability of explanations of reported phenomena. When a report violently transcends the body of probabilities indicated by universal observation & comparison, the burden of proof is on him who advances it—& I can't see that the advancers of such things have so far sustained that burden very well, in view of what psychology has now shewn regarding the interpolations of wishful emotion, the popular acquiescence in suggested myth-patterns, the unreliability of observation, the mutability of report, & the dependence of the whole attitude of credulity upon a theistic-spiritual belief whose natural anthropological causes are now too clearly known to give the existence of such belief any evidential value regarding its reality. You ought not to be irritated by doubts of the reality of your mental images, since such doubts apply equally to *everyone's* mental images. I have had thousands of impressions of unreal phenomena—false memories, &c—& have given them the most careful study—almost invariably tracking down the real sources of the impressions, which often bear only a slight resemblance to the impressions themselves. I have likewise accomplished similar tracings of the bizarre impressions of others. There is no reason to suppose that any given human impression has any exact correspondence with any external reality. All that creates a favourable presumption, is a high degree of correlation with the impressions of others & the general body of repeatedly demonstrated fact. Aberrant impressions can be accepted only on probation. As for "God"—there is of course no *theoretical* barrier to the existence of a "cosmic intelligence", yet *absolutely nothing indicates such a thing.* On the contrary, the notion never arises except through traditional suggestions based on the mythical perspectives of primitive man. ¶ Well—so it goes.

Best wishes—H P L

Notes

1. It is unknown whether CAS adopted AWD's revisions, but he did write to AWD: "I re-wrote the ending of 'Helman Carnby,' much to my own satisfaction. The other one had been giving me the artistic jim-jams" (7 February 1931; ms., SHSW).

[190]   [ALS]

Last of Jany [31 January 1931]

Dear A W:—

Glad to hear of your literary plans—though sorry G. S. refused "Death Walker". I fear they'll never be much of a market for anything greatly outside the commonplace. Klarkash-Ton sent me a copy of the damn thing a few weeks ago, but amidst my feverish rush I haven't had a chance to see what it's like. Your selection of names for section-headings in your serious works is notably good. There is genuine poetry in virtually everything your choose. "Wind at Night", "Lanterns over the Marshes", & "Calling to the Stars" evoke pictures & determine moods even before one approaches the text—& the pictures & moods are the right ones to prepare the reader for what follows.

As for palmists—despite my precepts of economy, I fancy it was the waste of time rather then of money that I was deploring. At my time of life one doesn't squander the hours on non-essentials which do not amuse—& I can't conceive of palmistry's amusing an adult. It is too meaningless & irrelevant to hold one's attention. Folklore-study is interesting enough when vividly & piquantly presented, but I am not enough of a specialist to care for the long-protracted witnessing of specific demonstrations of mass-stupidity & intellectual squalor. I had as lief waste time on fake medicine-shows or fly-paper sales-talks in Chinese! But youth, I dare say, has a restless energy that age recalls but faintly. I suppose I always wanted to be doing something when I was young—though I couldn't even begin to compete with you. Nowadays I haven't any surplus energy to work off—indeed, I haven't enough to do even a tenth of the reading & writing I want to do—hence it's difficult to picture a supercharged personality. Latterly I am appalled at the shortness of time in relation to the things I need to get done—years slip by, yet my programme gets nowhere—hence I am trying to develop a policy of conservation which shall squeeze a few more senile products out of me. "Amusement" has only a dim & far-off meaning to the old man now—though I dare say my occasional antiquarian jaunts form a fair equivalent to your palmists & other diverting juvenilia.

Yes—you had mentioned your sale to the 10-Story Book,[1] & I surely congratulate you upon it. The sale of anything seriously written, especially if the theme be unpopular, is an occasion worthy of rejoicing. I seem to recall this magazine on the news stands thirty years or so ago, & did not know it had weathered the storms of time. There used to be several such small magazines, having a reasonable standard but paying low rates, where beginners of merit found a more than commonly hospitable reception. The Black Cat— The Grey Goose[2]—one wonders what has become of them all now!

Glad Baird continues to be receptive toward your MSS.—a good sign, whether or not the legal farce lands. You have so many irons in the fire that you're never likely to be out of print long! Whitehead—to whose other distinctions I find that of Reverend or ex-Reverend added—has just started a tale from an idea of mine which he is suggesting that I finish as a collaborated work[3]—but I may pass it up because of inability to do justice to the West Indian locale he has seen fit to choose. I am the sworn enemy of armchair exoticism, & believe in writing about things one personally knows—except of course in the case of Dunsanian phantasy or cosmic infinity. I hope I can get to a few tales of my own before long.

Well—best wishes, & good luck with the editorial barbarians!

Yr obt hble Servt

H P

Notes

1. Presumably "Two Gentlemen at Forty."
2. The *Black Cat* (1895–1923) was not in any sense devoted to the weird, but did feature a number of "unusual" stories. HPL admitted to buying it regularly (*SL* 5.227). The *Gray Goose* (1896–1909) was subtitled "A monthly magazine of original stories."
3. "Cassius."

[191] [ALS]

Sunday [8 February 1931]

Dear A W:—

Too bad "Death Walker" didn't land—& hope it won't have to be spoiled too badly in order to make G.S. Still, it's good to have new markets; & I congratulate you on this prospect as well at the R.D.T. opening. Your professional enterprise breaks all records so far as our general group is concerned! Glad you're making debt headway—& trust you won't run up any more.

No—I rather doubt whether I'll do any collaboration. Usually it's a drag on both authors concerned, so that the result is below the level which either might have attained alone. There are, of course, exceptions—cases where two writers may possess distinctly complementary special gifts or fields of erudition.

Good luck with the novel. I feel sure that you can, in the end, bring the unsatisfying parts up to the level of the preferred sections. But naturally, one cannot sustain the level of the peaks indefinitely. All extended works of art have their lacunae, which the mood exacted by the high spots helps to bridge over.

Hope I can get some new tales going before long. The rest of the programme is slowly clearing up—but one can never count on the morrow. Here, by the way, is an absolutely splendid imaginative flight by our friend C A S,[1] who asks me to forward it to you for transmission to Wandrei & ultimate return to Auburn. The Crater Ridge scenery is genuine local colour—Smith sent me a piece of stone from there which looks exactly like some nameless, pre-human idol.

> Regards—
> > Yr obt Servt
> > > H P

[P.S.] Haven't seen new W T, but Dwyer tells me it's good.

Notes

1. CAS, "The City of the Singing Flame," *Wonder Stories* (July 1931); in *OSM*.

[192]   [ALS]

Feby. 17, 1931

Dear A W:—

Welcome home! Too bad a good source of revenue evaporated; but in view of your distaste for the job, & your determination to leave in the spring anyway, I guess you need not let mourning interfere too deeply with your homecoming enjoyment. You will be able to write in much greater comfort, & with your new markets may not be much the loser after all.

Klarkash-Ton's "Singing Flame" lacked the concentrated emotion & utter unity of "Carnby", yet had imaginatively evocative powers which moved me perhaps even more. I think I said that the Crater Ridge region is a real one, & that CAS sent me a stone fragment from it last year which looks exactly like some pre-human eidolon. CAS says, incidentally, that he means to subtilise the conclusion of "Carnby". He has an excellent idea—which substitutes *sound* for sight.

Whether I do anything with that Whitehead tale depends on how eager he is about it—for I hate being churlish & uncivil. He says he has it all started, & that he has prepared some guiding notes on the chosen West-Indian background. His spontaneous affability is disarming—just now I am vastly indebted to him for the generous & wholly unexpected gift of Cline's "Dark Chamber." Am still trying to cut down on the revision, but agree with you that I need a business manager—or would if my junk were important enough to be a ponderable commodity. My lack of all practical calculative sense is such as to suggest the absence or early excision of a whole definite group of cells from my aged grey matter!

Your conclusions on the affectation question are not, after all, wholly unlike the view I myself presented—that some impulses are typical of youth whilst others are natural to maturity. You will recall that I didn't blame you at present, but merely wished to go on record as predicting a different outlook on your part a decade or less hence. Likewise, you'll remember that I confessed to several pompous affectations of my own when at your age. Well—I don't know that I look back on my boiled shirts & black ties of 1910 with any special degree of scorn, for 20 is 20. One cannot, however, avoid reflecting that these juvenile tastes are based on a definitely unreal perspective; so that one always wishes for the sake of his ego's philosophic reputation, that they had been outgrown a little farther back on the childhood calendar. No—I don't see but that your can-collection was just as logical as the cigarette-picture collections favoured by the young in my day, & as many another universally accepted hobby. So far as sense goes, the S.S.S. appears equally immune from criticism; though in my time such activities might have been censured on aesthetico-ethical grounds as being not quite in line with those canons of taste which favour reticence-respect, civilised incuriousness, & personal non-encroachment as the best-working special policies. I never acquired an interest in the peep-show contrasts & ignominies empirically classified as "scandal"—perhaps because of a cosmic perspective which felt no vast difference betwixt one sort of inane behaviour and another sort of inane behaviour on the part of terrestrial puppets. It is, though, undoubtedly necessary for any realistic novelist to take a more detailed view of society; & to learn not only the common habits of the people, but overt & concealed, but the common reaction of various types & groups toward those habits & concealments. I don't wonder it takes a formal 'deteckatiff' organisation to assemble such data—indeed, in the midst of my quiet & sequestered existence I have often wondered how, merely from reading & ordinary social contacts, novelists can come to know as much as they seem to do about the natural history, manners, & customs of homo sapiens.

But I may remark that I, too, was a detective in youth—being a member of the Providence Detective Agency at an age as late as 13! Our force had very rigid regulations, & carried in its pockets a standard working equipment consisting of police whistle, magnifying-glass, electric flashlight, handcuffs, (sometimes plain twine, but "handcuffs" for all that!) tin badge, (I have mine still!!) tape measure, (for footprints) revolver, (mine was the real thing, but Inspector Munroe[1] (aet 12) had a water squirt-pistol while Inspector Upham[2] (aet 10) worried along with a cap-pistol) & copies of all newspaper accounts of desperate criminals at large—plus a paper called "The Detective", which printed pictures & descriptions of outstanding "wanted" malefactors. Did our pockets bulge & sag with this equipment? I'll say they did!! We also had elaborately prepared "credentials"—certificates attesting our good standing in the agency. Mere scandals we scorned. Nothing short of bank robbers & murderers were good enough for us. We shadowed many desperate-looking customers, & diligently compared their physiognomies with the "mugs" in *The Detective*, yet never made a full-fledged arrest. Ah, me—the good old days! ¶ Best wishes—H P

Notes

1. Harold Bateman Munroe (1891–1966), who, with his brother Chester Pierce Munroe (1899–1943), was one of HPL's closest boyhood friends.
2. Ronald Upham.

[193]   [ALS]

Friday
[27(?) February 1931]

Dear A W:—

No—the old man isn't dead, but engulfed in a maelstrom of stuff to do . . . . & most inopportunely moved to begin the mapping out of a new story about hellish Antarctic horror.

Was tremendously sorry to hear of your nervous attack, & hope you'll avoid prolongations or repetitions by taking things easier for a while. There's no question but that you try to do too much. Repose & relaxation are arts worthy of your cultivation!

I'd hardly say that Klarkash-Ton's "Singing Flame" is the *most utterly* cosmic thing I've ever read; but as I told you, I think it is very notable in that way. You are right in giving Chambers's Yian-Hastur-Yellow Sign cult a high place amongst cosmic evocations.[1] Blackwood also hits the heights now & then.

As to the question of how far juvenile tastes are based on an unreal perspective—I can't see any reason for changing my original estimate. This question does not concern subjective worlds at all, but merely the plain world of objective forces & phenomena. It remains a fact that much of the child's world—as of the savage's world—hinges directly upon a definite ignorance of the events, proportions, cause-&-effect relationships, &c. &c., of the objective scene around him; & that a modification invariably takes place when this ignorance is abated. Therefore, the adult in looking back to his childhood cannot help associating the old perspective with the old ignorance; & feeling, in consequence, a slight amusement in recalling various typical interests & points of view of that period. Not that the old interests & points of view were not natural in their day, but that they were necessarily phenomena of an imperfect state of adjustment to the universe—that is, a *more* imperfect state then an adult's, for of course nobody has an adjustment other than fragmentary & more or less deceptive. We don't feel ashamed of childishness if it comes at the right period; but just as I said, we feel tempted to push it as far back in our careers as possible, & to be a trifle mortified if any marked illusions dependent upon ignorance have carried themselves over beyond adolescence. For example—I am myself definitely ashamed of the belated naivete of much of the stuff I wrote up to the age of 28 or 29; because it reveals the mental indolence which caused me to delay the sharp analysis of various fields of knowledge which did not command my interest. I would not be ashamed of such writing if I could pretend I did it at 18 or 19—but at 28 or 29 it piques my pride. Also—I suspect that much I write now is not as mature & well-balanced as one ought to write at 40½.

No doubt your S S S victims will have amply earned their place in the pillory! Trust the novel will develop successfully & convincingly. As for collaboration—though I've done it in scores of ghost-writing cases, I think I'll dispose of the Whitehead case by keeping things in the air till he writes the whole thing himself. That's the way Dunsany & Padraic Colum "collaborated" on "Alexander". Dunsany did one act & waited a while for Colum to do the next. Then when Colum didn't, he went ahead & did it himself. And so on until he had finished the entire play single-handed! Poor Whitehead, by the way, has been very ill with stomach ulcers—in a local hospital on a milk diet—& may possibly have to go to N Y for an operation.

Belknap tells me that somebody has been attacking his style in *The Editor*,[2] & fears that Wright may be influenced into restricting his market. Hope you'll say a good word to W. about "The Horror on [*sic*] the Hills" in order to counteract any adverse impressions.

Thanks tremendously for the clipped stories, which look highly promising. Shall digest them shortly. Best wishes—& ease up your programme for your nerves' sake!—

H P

Notes

1. Yian is mentioned in the title story of *The Maker of Moons;* Hastur and the Yellow Sign are cited in various stories in *The King in Yellow.*

2. E. Irvine Haines, "The Use of Ambiguous Words," *Editor* 92 (17 January 1931): 46–48.

[194]   [ALS]

March 24[, 1931]

Dear A W:—

No—not even yet is the Old Man quite in his grave! But I may be before I'm through with what lies ahead of me . . . . . . which is nothing less than a siege of typing probably extending to nearly 100 pages! May Pegāna give me strength! The job in question is the new Antarctic thing which I was resolving in my mind when I last wrote you. Upon beginning the actual composition, I found additional incidents crowding in on me like pseudo-memories; so that the text spun itself out to 80 pages of my crabbed & interlined script before I could conscientiously call it a story. Judging from precedent, those 80 will expand to 100 in double-spaced Remington work— making a novelette of 30,000 or 35,000 words. It is divided into 12 sections, & is capable of a major serial division in the exact middle.[1] If I land it any- where, it'll mean a marvellously welcome cheque—but with such length, the landing process won't be easy. It is entitled "At the Mountains of Madness", & treats of a hellish legacy from elder aeons amidst the eternal icy peaks of the polar waste—S. Lat. 76°10', E. Lon. 113°15'. In a sense, it might be called a sort of pale "scientifiction"—but on the other hand, it belongs to the "Ar- thur Gordon Pym" tradition. I mention Pym, & have something scream that hideous & cryptic word—*"Tekeli-li!"*

Too bad you find relaxation so difficult. I wish you could convince your parents how much better a judiciously irregular writing programme would be— & also, how marvellously well you have done for a writer of your age. Consid- ering the years which so many spend in getting any kind of a professional bear- ing, you must surely realise how unusual & promising your early progress is. But anyway, I am glad you have had *some* rest, & that you have been so success- ful in opening up new markets—especially the Parisian elite affair. Hope they take parts of "Evening in Spring" as well. The Midwestern, too, looks like a very promising magazine to break into. Whitehead is just now jubilant about landing a tale with Adventure which Wright recently turned down.[2] By the way—this will probably not be news to you, but correspondents are telling me that a new weird magazine is about to be founded by Harry Bates, editor of As- tounding Stories, & that he is already considering MSS therefor.[3] This ought to be something for you to investigate at once if you have not already done so. About that Editor article—I haven't seen it yet, & don't believe Belknap has; but I could tell from the relayed description that it must be stupid. Who is the author, anyway? My reaction to "The Horror from the Hills" is not unlike yours—in fact, I tried to get Belknap to change the latter half when I read it be- fore publication last spring—but he couldn't be convinced. It has really, though, made quite a hit—being praised by Whitehead, Howard, Flagg, Tal- man, Smith, Dwyer, & others who, if not eminent critics, are at least reasonably familiar with the popular weird story. Incidentally—Talman is about to meet the fecund & apotheosised *Seabury Quinn* in person for the first time this week. I shall be interested to hear of the meeting, & to learn what kind of a chap Quinn is personally. In my opinion he will probably prove very attractive & intelligent, since his work is clearly the hasty tongue-in-cheek hokum of a well-read & accomplished craftsman who knows better. It always has a smooth glibness & machine-made polish distinguishing it from the utter amorphous slush of Nictzin Dyalhis & other total losses.

As for the question of values—i.e., the content of the ignorant versus the sensitivity & dissatisfaction of the restless & inquiring mind—I doubt if much comparison is possible. The difference between a clod & a sage is like that between a bar of steel & the same thing made up into a watch—each is quite adequate in its place, & of equal value in a purposeless cosmos. Undoubtedly it is only a prejudice—though an inescapable one for the human mind, with the accidental shape it has—which considers the evolved & complex any more intrinsically valuable or "higher" than the simple. The clod, without keen pain on the one hand or keen pleasure on the other, probably averages slightly happier than the evolved man whose pains & pleasures are both increased—since under any possible set of terrestrial conditions the pain must increase more in proportion than pleasure under the influence of education & sensitisation. However—that is not to say that the evolved man could have obtained greater pleasure by staying primitive. This would be true in only a few cases. Usually the evolved man is the result of a natural & unavoidable dissatisfaction arising before emergence from the simple state. He is different by nature & to start with—& could only make himself more miserable by thwarting all the instinctive outreaching of his mind & aesthetic sense. And being such, he cannot help adopting his rate of emergence as a sort of empirical standard of value—& consequently looking back a trifle amusedly at his earlier & simpler & less well-oriented self.

Best wishes—H P L

P.S. That damn left eye is bothering again. May have to readopt full-time spectacle-wearing, though I hate to consider it. The cursed things irritate my nose & ears beyond endurance, & I rejoiced when I seemed able to get rid of them in 1925.

Notes

1. *At the Mountains of Madness*. HPL thought the novel could be serialized, and yet it was rejected because of its length and other reasons. When the novel ultimately saw magazine publication, it was published not in two parts, as HPL intended, but three.

2. Henry S. Whitehead, "The Black Beast," *Adventure* (15 July 1931).

3. *Strange Tales of Mystery and Terror* (September 1931–January 1933). HPL placed no stories with the magazine.

[195]   [ALS]

[late March or early April 1931]

Dear A W:—

Well—the story is finished, but the typing is a nightmare darkly looming ahead! I don't know how well others will like it—but in two or three weeks you'll have a chance to judge for ourself. Glad Klarkash-Ton has landed "The Singing Flame"—that really impressed me vastly. I have recently been hearing from the book editor of G. P. Putnam's Sons,[1] who asked me to submit some stuff for consideration as a possible book-form collection—but doubt if anything will come of it. I have finally bitten to the extent of sending the 30 tales which I had around the house in loose form, but will not do any copying from my files unless I am assured of strong acceptance-chances. Glad that your own encouraging openings continue, & hope that your can get around the requests for changes in your tales. Can't you do a little adroit juggling which will convey an appearance of change without actually changing anything basic?

I was told of this new Clayton-Bates magazine simultaneously by three or four persons—Henry G. Weiss (Francis Flagg), Whitehead, Talman, & I think someone else, though I can't be sure. Probably they read of it in some writers' magazine. I have shipped Bates a lot of old MSS., but expect the whole business back. I have also sent "In the Vault" & one other old MS.[2] to Hersey for G.S. consideration . . . . with similar expectations of rejection. Think I'll try "Strange High House" on Wright again now that W. Paul Cook doesn't seem to be in a position to issue The Recluse. But I'll have a hell of a time landing my new story on account of its length.

Sorry your debts still bother, but if you keep on economising you'll have them paid up before long. Your friend's visit will surely be a welcome event—& perhaps you can inoculate him with a bit of your surplus energy. You will discover sooner or later that energy such as yours is rather exceptional—indeed, I can hardly conceive of such a thing, & look at your list of products with unfeigned amazement. Not everyone, of course, is as played-out & listless as I; but the general average is as far below yours as it is above mine.

As for the issue of values—it is quite possible that confusion as to essentials may exist on one or both sides. When such ethereal imponderables are under discussion it is very easy to miss a fine distinction—or, on the other hand, to imagine distinctions which actually do not exist. Clarification of such issues demands a very prolonged, exact, & detached exchange of arguments.

Chances for my southern trip hang in the balance. I could make it if every delinquent client would pay up—but this is a bad year for promptness! Haven't quite broken hibernation yet—but before long the woods & fields will be worth a walking-tour. No doubt the same will shortly be true of your favourite hills—though I fancy your spring is a little later than ours. I wish I were down in South Carolina right now!

Best wishes—
Yr obt Servt
H P

Notes

1. Winfield Shiras of Putnam's had written HPL, probably at the suggestion of Henry S. Whitehead.
2. Probably "The Nameless City" or "From Beyond."

[196]   [ALS]

Friday [3 or 10 April 1931]

Dear A W:—

"In the Moonlight"[1] is an exquisite bit of impressions, & confirms my belief that your are producing more genuine literature than any other member of 'the gang'. I saw a previous version of this—I forget just how different—& have a strong sense of improvement in the present text, though I can't tell exactly where it occurs. The whole thing is full of delicate poetry & music—keep this up & you'll be a recognised literary figure before many years have flown! Sorry the serious work is having to pause for potboiling exercises—but with you, slow or interrupted progress is about as fast as the average writer's swiftest normal progress! I rather thought you'd find the agency a superfluity. Even the advance tips aren't so tremendously significant or valuable. Too bad Bates returned the four tales—but I felt sure he would prove hard to suit. These Clayton magazines seem to demand a certain fixed pattern of unctuous mediocrity. As a further test, I sent Bates "In the Vault" not long ago—his treatment of that being likely to complete the settling of the question of whether my stuff has much chance with him.

"At the Mountains of Madness" has a certain kind of cumulative horror, but is altogether too slow for the cheap artificial market. Your offer to type the thing quite overwhelms me with gratitude & appreciation—but bless my soul, Child, Grandpa could never impose on a busy young author like that!! Half of the pages are corrected, transposed, & interlined beyond all human legibility—so that it's very doubtful whether I can read 'em myself! I just got a brand new ribbon, & shall put it in the machine shortly, after a long-needed cleaning of all the type. Then the gods will decide when to give me the nerve to start the job—whether before or after such vernal wanderings as I shall be able to make. But all the same, I can't get over my appreciation of your offer! An old man's blessing upon thee . . . . & pray command me when any favours are in order at the other end! I described this tale to Wright, & he said that he is again taking serials; in reply to which I told him I would let him look it over as soon as it was typed. At the same time you will see the carbon.

I have asked for the return of all story loans, & hope the desiderate items may be among them—but am not very optimistic about Putnam acceptance. The Strange High House is even less than 5500 words long, since it barely exceeds 9 pages. That, with me, means a scant 3300 words. Wright has claimed to be paying me 1½¢ per word since 1927, though I never bother to apply arithmetic to his cheques.

Thanks tremendously for the Dunsany item. It has the true charm & poetry of Dunsany, though I rather prefer the naiver early things found in "A Dreamer's Tales." I shall keep this permanently in my file. That M R James tip sounds alluring.[2] Alas! Why did I buy the G.S. of an Ant. & Warning to the Curious separately!

Breaking hibernation at last, & have for three afternoons taken my work out to my favourite woods & fields. Trip still in doubt—complicated by sudden news from Orton that his Stephen Daye Press may have a piece of book-editing to be done which would require my presence in Brattleboro, Vermont![3] If the pay were good, I could not afford to pass this up—but naturally I am asking for tangible details before relinquishing plans & hopes for southern latitudes.

Hope to see your new weird tales, either in print or in MS. And again thanks for that generous typing offer!

Best wishes—

Yr obt hble Servt

H P

P.S. Assuming that "In the Moonlight" is for return, I enclose it with utmost admiration & not a little reluctance. ¶ I'll tell Flagg of your praise of his tales.

Notes

1. Probably "The Moon Is Fair Tonight."
2. HPL refers to the one-volume *The Collected Ghost Stories of M. R. James.*
3. See letter 219.

[197]   [TLS]

April 16, 1931

Dear A. W.—

Enclosed are some things—which you might return when you have noted them to the fullest extent of their possible usefulness—which shed considerable light on the new Bates magazine question. As you will deduce, it was undoubtedly a tip from a literary agency which informed Weiss of the coming venture—and by inference, that holds good for Whitehead and the others. I sent Bates four old yarns—"Sarnath", "Nameless City", "Beyond the Wall of Sleep", and "Polaris"—together with a request for information as to whether material of that sort would be totally unacceptable from its very nature. You will see his courteous reply—which only confirms my original opinion that nothing of mine could ever find lodgment in a Clayton magazine. The prospectus which he enclosed is virtually a duplicate of what Weiss had from his agency—and is obviously the thing which was originally sent to the agency itself. As one far more facile and adaptable than I, you might easily "make" this magazine, hence I would urge you to study the requirements with care.

Likewise, it seems to me that this agency would be worth looking into. I have had no experience with such things, but these letters seem to show a very alert and intelligent man, not without solicitude for his client's interests. If I had more MSS. to place, I really think I would patronise something of the kind. Many W.T. authors do, I am told. Of course, your own energetic alertness makes you an agency all in yourself; so that perhaps any such service as this would be a superfluity for you. Still, these people probably have a kind of pull with editors which makes them not altogether to be overlooked. If you use Weiss's name to introduce yourself, note that he wishes the "Flagg" pseudonym adhered to. He is, as I have mentioned, a victim of communistic illusions; and fears that his real-name authorship of much radical verse would make him unfavourably known in his own person to conservative business interests.

I don't expect anything favourable from Putnam's, but will surely let you know when they report and what they report. I had not known the usual time consumed by book readers in reaching a verdict. As it is, I have not sent "Outsider", "Erich Zann", and a few others because of lack of available copies; but some of these will be recalled from loans before long—and then (as I told the editor) I will send them along unless headed off by an unfavourable report.

Wright has accepted "The Strange High House" for $55.00—assuredly, a most welcome prospect, though I am sorry it is Cook's misfortune which thus enriches me. "The Shunned House", as a 60-page book with introduction by Belknap, lies all printed in the form of loose sheets in a bindery at Boston—and will probably continue to lie there until the binder uses the edition (250 or 300 copies, I forget which) to stoke his furnace. And to think I read the proofs five times, till absolutely not an error remained! Cook hasn't the cash to get the thing attended to, and I haven't either—and anyway, even if I did scrape up enough to get the thing bound, what would I do with it in the absence of any marketing or circulating organisation? What I wish I could do is to salvage about a dozen copies to get individually bound up as gifts for various members of the gang. Or if a small payment would get the loose sheets delivered just as they are, I suppose I could tuck them under chairs and tables for a while, till some decision could be reached regarding the mess. I am asking Cook more about the situation—though perhaps the wisest thing is to forget all about it. Wright rejected "The Shunned House" years ago, but

I am including it (luckily I had a set of proofs) in the Putnam shipment. Poor old Cook—he finds it quite impossible to secure new industrial affiliations in New England, hence is contemplating a move to Oklahoma, where one of the old-time amateur journalists (Paul J. Campbell) has oil interests and considerable pull. I can hardly imagine Cook amongst the ugly red clay flatlands and nightmare derrick forests of the southwestern oil belt—he who was born and reared amidst our green rolling fields, stone walls, orchard-embowered farmhouses, and white village steeples—but necessity is a hard master. At any rate, he has not gone yet, and I hope to see him down here before he makes any move of so radical a sort.

I shall be eager to see the completed "Evening in Spring", and hope that all of these impressions may some day receive collected publication in suitable form. I can sympathise about the history—which, by the way, I did not know you had finished. Don't let any text-slaughter be perpetrated if you can possibly help it—and I think it would almost be better to get the MS. back than to have it published defacedly and anonymously. The liberties of commercial illiterates with works of art and scholarship are past all excusing—just now I am watching to see how Dreiser comes out in his controversy with the cinema gang.[1] I hope he succeeds in barring any mutilated version of his work—though possibly anybody is to blame who submits material to interests as notoriously tradesmanlike, sub-philistine, and boorishly arrogant as the cinemas. Anybody dealing with such swine ought to know what to expect—and yet the lure of the dollar must sometimes be tempting.

Glad to hear that the Wisconsin landscape is awaking to its ancient glories, and hope the fire didn't harm any of the shy denizens. Rhode Island is showing parallel phenomena—even to extensive forest fires—though the latter, fortunately, do not approach any of my favourite regions. The southern trip still hangs in the balance—but will be welcome at any time, however late. I wish I could be enjoying the Charleston late spring right now—the gnarled live-oaks and magnolias must be flaunting their full luxuriance, while all the gardens blaze with glory beyond description. Even as far north as Virginia spring is fully under way. Leaves on the trees around Fredericksburg and Richmond must be long past the feathery stage—though Virginia can produce some damnably chilly days even as late as mid-May. For real balminess, one has to get down to the tidewater Carolinas.

Wandrei's new book arrived the other day, and I must say it is quite the most artistic piece of work I have seen for some time. The kid is a real poet, and his brother certainly has a tremendous share of fantastic talent. The mechanical makeup of the book, too, well matches the contents. This is a far cry from "Ecstasy", and certainly suggests promising developments ahead.

Just now I am "all in" from four solid days of a kind of labour even worse than typing—viz., the straightening out of my various files and dump-heaps after three years of neglect. They had reached a stage where either the heaps or myself faced the prospect of being crowded out of the room—hence the unwonted activity of one who never does anything unless driven to it. Now that the nightmare is over, and the salient cuttings and papers arranged in their proper boxes with some semblance of order, I am rather glad that I did it. For a little while I shall be able to find things when I want them.

With best wishes, and hoping that your reply from Coward-McCann will be of an unexpectedly auspicious nature, I remain

Yr most obt hble Servt,

H P

Notes

1. Theodore Dreiser's novel *An American Tragedy* (1925) was adapted for the screen by Samuel Hoffenstein and Josef von Sternberg (after an unwieldy screenplay by Sergei M. Eisenstein had been rejected by Paramount). Dreiser attempted to halt the release of the Hoffenstein-Sternberg adaptation, contending that it distorted the message of his novel; but the U.S. Supreme Court ruled that the film was a faithful adaptation and permitted it to be distributed. It premiered on 5 August 1931.

[198]   [ALS]

Temporary Address—
℅ Dudley C. Newton,[1]
Box 1294,
St. Augustine, Fla.
May 9, 1931

Dear A W:—

Well—did you think the old man was dead? Possibly receipt of the story—typing of which came near making me so—tended to disabuse you of the impression. I staggered to the end of that cursed job—which I did in a continuous day & night phrensy punctuated only by brief naps & siestas—just before hopping off on my long-wished & long-deferred trip; & about that time your letter arrived. In the subsequent rush I have had no time to write anything—but now I am settled down for a week or two in one of the most delightfully quaint & reposeful subtropical towns—the oldest city in the United States—which the imagination can conceive. The climate braces me up like a tonic, & I hate to think of ever going north again. I surely was made for the torrid zone! Charleston—though absolutely nothing can approach it for rich continuity of tradition & survival of 18th century life & architecture—is only an adumbration so far as real tropicality is concerned. There, I thought a few low palmettos & live-oaks with Spanish moss were remarkable. Here, one finds great palms overtopping buildings & creating a mystical haze of green twilight, & vast tangles of cypress & live-oak that dwarf anything in the Charleston region. Around me are the narrow lanes & ancient buildings of the old Spanish capital, the formidable bulk of ancient Fort San Marcos, on whose turreted, sun-drenched parapet I love to sit, the sleepy old market (now a benched loafing-place) in the Plaza de la Constitución, & the whole languorous atmosphere (the tourist season being over) of an elder, sounder, & more leisurely civilisation. Here is a city founded in 1565, 42 years before the first Jamestown colonist landed, & 55 years before the first Pilgrim set foot on Plymouth Rock. Here, too, is the region where Ponce de Leon fared on his vain quest of 1513. Varied fortunes—British rule 1763–83, sale to U.S. in 1821—yet much of the old Spanish architecture remaining. For the first time I am seeing structures built in the 1500's. The post office is the old Governor's Mansion—with unchanged exterior—built in 1591. At the north end of the narrow (19 ft) main street the ancient city gate still stands, though the rest of the walls are down. Nearly everything is built of coquina stone (small shells fused together in the sea) quarried from neighbouring Anastasia Island. A poor tourist season has made all rates comically low—the non-sybarite being able to get breakfasts for 10¢, dinners for 25¢ or 30¢, & *really good* rooms for almost nothing. I have a magnificent room in a fine section, with balcony fronting on the bay & giving a gorgeous vista of Anastasia Island, the great lighthouse, & the ocean beyond & how much to you think I pay? Don't call Grandpa a liar when I state that the price is exactly *four dollars per week!* It will be like pulling a tooth to break away from here—yet a week or two is my limit. I shall make a side-trip to Dunedin to visit Whitehead, since his invitations are too insistently cordial to admit of refusal. I feel sure I shall like him vastly personally. The trip down was made with a 2-day stopover at my beloved Charleston. From Providence to Charleston the bus ride took just 48 hours, & I stopped off at N Y to pay Belknap a call. He seems to be flourishing as usual. Charleston was chilly, but one gets the real subtropics here. Physically I am in my element. How can I ever endure the north again?

Sorry "The Early Years" came back. Perhaps the trouble with these fragments is that they are too *short* for feasible book exploitation. Why not wait till you have a complete trilogy of book length, & then offer it as a unit under a single carefully chosen title? I've had no new word forwarded from Putnam's—but managed to get some loans back for shipment to them—including "The Outsider."

I continue to appreciate your offer to type my tale—but alas, Child, you know not the tangled mess that a page of Grandpa's rough draughts generally is! Some day I'll send you one as a sample—*not* to be typed, but just as a horrible exhibit. I take much time in shaping the details of sentences, &c—constantly correcting on the MS.—& in the course of a tale I change early parts to correspond to new developments in the later parts. The resultant melange of deletions, substitutions, & interpolations is absolutely unintelligible to any eye but mine—& sometimes to mine as well! In typing that wretched 115-page thing (yes—it came to 115, as you've seen by this time!) I had several times to bridge gaps by new composition—tangles of labyrinthine cacography whose purport I could not possibly decipher. That is the hell of writing long stories—the thought of ultimate typing deters me, yet nobody but myself could possibly do it! Hope you found the tale at least partly worth the blood & sweat I put into the typing. I left the original copy with Long—all addressed to Wright—for him to read before its W.T. transmission, & he writes very flatteringly of it. Maybe he's only kidding Grandpa along, but the soft soap will help to break the shock when Brother Farnsworth gives it a curt turndown. I fear its length, if nothing else, is hopelessly against it—yet it couldn't possibly be shortened. My aim is to put the strange city across *with adequate emotional preparation & buttressing*—avoiding the fatal defect of the cheap weirdist in delineating such unearthly things with a nonchalance which makes them meaningless & unconvincing. Wright rejected Klarkash-Ton's "Testament of Athammaus"[2] *because of the element of cannibalism in it.* Gawd—can you beat it? This tale has both the virtues & faults of its type. Smith has the real goods, but he writes too damn much! Bates promptly rejected "In the Vault", but said that a better story of that kind would be rather in his line. I doubt whether I shall ever make a Clayton magazine—they obviously want something in a mood & vein essentially alien to anything which could be mine. Hope you'll have better luck with "The Shadow on the Sky" & "Death in the Crypt".[3]

It's highly noble of you to offer an Old Gentleman the two spare James volumes when you get your one-volume outfit—but think twice before buying a new book merely for the sake of two or three extra stories! Don't accumulate a library merely to give it away! Still—if you do discard the "Thin Ghost" & "More Ghost Stories" I can assure you that 10 Barnes is the most appreciative of all possible rubbish dumps!

Sympathy on the cold weather! It was devilishly chilly in the east lately, even as far south as Charleston—& here in St Augustine, according to report, before my arrival. Now, however, I have nothing left to desire in the way of weather. I feel so spry that it is difficult for me to act my age!

I was vastly interested by your reports of progress on serious work. The idea of theme-statement in the overture looks eminently sound to me. Every time I see one of your delicate impression-studies I am tempted to try something of the corresponding sort myself—but soon realise that my extravagantly cosmic natural imagination & archaic, heavy-handed style would make a sad mess of such business, betwixt them.

The Blackwood reprints look interesting—I simply must have "Incredible Adventures" & "The Willows" sooner or later. I hope hereditary taste governs the contents of the Colin de la Mare anthology! An uniform Machen would be a boon—I mourn the loss of my "Three Impostors" by fire while lent to Dwyer.

Your "Death in the Crypt" looks full of excellent possibilities—but beware of the unctuously conventional in setting. As for an *ending*—I'm rotten as a plotter, but here's what naturally pops into an old man's mind.

Hark back to mediaeval or ancient times for an appropriate legend. Perhaps a monk of the abbey sold himself to the devil, became a monstrous immortal or semi-immortal *Thing*, & had to be walled up with certain magic formulae. Let the liberated Thing flounder off across the fields toward the vast ancient cathedral in dimly revengeful quest of the archbishop responsible for Its confinement—the lapse of centuries being only hazily realised. The cathedral is still there, & the Thing enters & lurks. Arrange an appropriate diversity of deaths & horrors, & use the typical M R James cathedral atmosphere. You might have the priest-brother Napier finally end the Thing with a magic formula which the old monks did not know. Make him a kind of Rev. Montague Summers . . . . . . led to the special study of magic by reflection on the strange legends in his family. The end of the Thing can be made very vivid & colourful, & you might have a blood relationship betwixt It & the Lonsdale family. A tale like this ought to specialise in atmosphere & in pictorial effects. Be sure to give a haunting glimpse of It shambling across the moor in the spectral moonlight!

The Midwestern Conference magazine duly arrived, & I must congratulate you on its quality & appearance. Your article on the "intelligentsia" interested me tremendously, & I may say that I agree with a good part of it. I shall be eager to see the next article of the series—touching on the cult of simplicity.

Well—I guess I'll dislodge myself from this bench & do some more strolling around the ancient lanes of the 16th century Spanish capital. I haven't yet visited the oldest house in the U.S. (1565) & the neighbouring Don Toledo house. This is a great place, & a week or a fortnight will pass all too soon. I hope you can manage to get around here sooner or later.

Best wishes—& hope the "Mountains of Madness" didn't bore you to the point of exhaustion.

Yr oblig'd obt Servt

H P

Notes

1. An amateur journalist.
2. CAS, "The Testament of Athammaus," *WT* (October 1932).
3. Published as "The Occupant of the Crypt."

[199]   [ALS]

May 16, 1931

Dear A W:—

Well—I'm certainly glad you found so much to like about the "Mountains"; yours being the second opinion so far received. I think I told you that I left the Wright copy all addressed & stamped with Belknap for him to read & send on. He did, & expressed a very gratifying enthusiasm. But I fear that Wright will think twice before handling anything of such length. If I hear from Putnam's (not a word out of them since March so far) in any sort of favourable way, I may send them this thing & suggest the sort of book you mention—but of course that depends on what they have to say when they say anything at all. It's not a bad idea to call this Cthulhuism & Yog-Sothothery of mine "The Mythology of Hastur"[1]—although it was really from Machen & Dunsany & others, rather than through the Bierce-Chambers line, that I picked up my gradually developing hash of theogony—or daimonogony. Come to think of it, I guess I sling this stuff more as Chambers does than as Machen & Dunsany do—though I had written a good deal of it before I ever suspected that Chambers ever wrote a weird story! I feel flattered by your adoption of some of this background. Robert E. Howard is doing it, too.[2] In making your allusions don't forget Klarkash-Ton's accursed & amorphous *Tsathoggua,* whom I have adopted into our malignly leering family pantheon! I shall identify Smith's Hyperborea with my Olathoë in the land of Lomar.[3]

As for the "Mountains"—I think most antarctic books apply the term "fin" to the flipper or atrophied wing of the penguin. The things do not permit of flying, & have no uses beyond combative value & guidance in the water when diving & swimming. You can't call them "wings"—I don't think anyone has ever done so—& when the choice is betwixt "fin" & "flipper" I don't know any reason to prefer the one to the other. Sorry I raked in so many obscure words—I must be getting as bad as Klarkash-Ton, despite my professed adherence to simple prose. Or perhaps those recherché twelve were merely scientific terms connected with the mock-realistic description of Those Others & similar early finds. In that case, of course, you surely see that the ordinary rules of prose simplicity have to be abrogated where descriptions of this kind become necessary.

Now as to the end of the thing—of course I'm not satisfied myself, but I am very oddly unable to decide whether more or *less* definiteness is needed. Remember Arthur Gordon Pym. In my tale the shoggoth provides a concrete & tangible climax—& what I wished to add was merely a vague hint of further spiritual horrors—as Poe hinted with his white bird screaming *"Tekeli-li! Tekeli-li!"*. I wanted to leave the *actuality* of the glimpse very unsettled, so that it might easily pass off as an hallucination. Possibly I ought to have left it *vaguer still*—& then again I had an idea that the thing ought to be developed at full length—perhaps as a sequel to the present thing, or perhaps as an expansion of that thing to full book length . . . . with the Simon & Schuster request, received last January, in mind.[4] What the thing was supposed to be, of course, was a region containing vestiges of some utterly primal cosmic force or process ruling or occupying the earth (among other planets) even before its solidification, & upheaved from the sea-bottom when the great Antarctic land mass arose. Lack of *interest* in the world beyond the inner mountains would account for its non-reconquest of the sphere. But then again, there may have been no such thing! Those Others may well have had their superstitions—& of course Danforth was strangely read, nervously organised, & fresh from a terrific shock. . . . . . . Anyhow, what I did set down was a sort of weak compromise betwixt the two ways I vaguely & ineffectively thought it ought to be. At the moment, I can't think of anything better; but when (I don't even give myself a hopeful "if"!) Wright shoots it back I shall have plenty of time to ponder & amend. Anyhow I am grateful for the suggestion. Belknap's criticism was in a different direction. He said I had not clearly motivated the long sleep of the Cretaceous entities—yet I feel sure I came near to doing so in shewing how so many varied life-forms were washed into underground caves, & how Those Others had an ingrained toughness & cataleptic capacity which held them just short of actual permanent death. The sun, of course, revived them. Incidentally—apropos of my dragging in the Taylor-Wegener-Joly-theory of continental cleavage & drift—it gives me quite a definite pang to see by the papers that Wegener himself has virtually been pronounced lost on the Greenland ice-cap.[5]

I haven't seen "The Hunters from Beyond"—my latest glimpse from Klarkash-Ton being "The Letter of Mohaun Los".[6] Hope he lands "Helman Carnby" with Bates, for 2¢ per word is nothing to snicker at.

Needless to say, I read the fragment of your "Evening in Spring" introduction with the keenest interest & admiration. So far, I don't see anything I could possibly suggest in the way of improvement; for the existing text seems to start out to explain your position with admirable clearness & in the most appropriate possible style. Naturally I feel vastly flattered by the inclusion of some of my "Hastur" figures among your bookish memory-spots; & trust you won't let good fellowship interfere with accuracy in determining the proportion of these things to incorporate in the final version. I can see how difficult the task of formulating the material coherently & intelligibly must be, yet am sure that the reward will be worth the trouble. The introduction will certainly add tremendously to the value of the whole linked series—& I still hope that the entire thing can be published as a single volume.

It is certainly kind of you to remember the Old Man in disposing of your spare library items, & you could not possibly find a more appreciative recipient for M R James. These compact volumes do save shelf space, & if I had more cash I might go in for some myself. The number of authors so available seems to be constantly increasing. It cheers me to know that I can get "The Three Impostors" for a dollar, & I think I shall do so shortly. Is the new Wakefield book any good?[7] I have not bothered to look up the second, since somebody (you, I think) told me that it is largely mediocre as compared with the first one.

Good luck with "The Shadow on the Sky"! I surely do wish that our gang could get an entree into some 2¢ a word market. I shall probably try Bates with a few more before giving up Clayton attempts. Of all my stuff, he would probably most relish that sort which deals with the deepest, blackest, & most corpsily physical & material kind of horror—a sort, unfortunately, in which I tend to specialise less & less as I get older. Nowadays I can't get much of a kick out of mere rotting bodies in crypts, or cheap ghosts of entities connected only with this particular planet. I want *Outside* linkages, & hints at the actual temporary overthrow of the laws of time, space, & energy on a wide scale. Yes—Belknap & I also received $12.25 from Lavell for the Selwyn & Blount anthology business—& a free copy of the book is promised on publication.[8] My remittance was forwarded to St Augustine from home—& 75¢ of it is tied up in high-denomination stamps which I can't exchange & for which I have no use here!

You may well envy me this trip, for I can't recall any that I have enjoyed equally so far. This place braces me up like a tonic, although I can't say that any day yet has been as hot as I'd really like. I still shiver now & then around morning & evening, but noon leaves nothing to be desired. The ancient Spanish atmosphere is infinitely alluring, & I am picking up various fresh touches of colour every day. I have seen all there is to see of the ancient houses & streets, & have visited the most fantastic old cemeteries imaginable. And the subtropical scenery is a never-ending delight. I am now beginning to note exotic fauna as well as flora. In one long glassy lagoon (across which the Moorish domes & belfries of the great winter hotels & churches can be seen in silhouette like some half-dreamed city of the djinni out of the Arabian Nights) there are flying or leaping fish; & above the water swoop diving birds—kingfishers, perhaps—always on the alert for prey. Then again—on the shore near the ancient fort one often spies long-legged, long-necked wading birds—herons or flamingoes, perhaps—such as I never before saw outside a zoo. And my friend Newton tells me that sizeable flocks of *pelicans* sometimes congregate around the wharves—though I have seen none of these as yet. A few days ago I went over to Anastasia Island to see the vast alligator & ostrich farm which lies in a dense cypress swamp there—& it was certainly worth the price of admission! Tall trees casting a sinister twilight over shallow lagoons—funereal garlands of trailing Spanish moss—& the whole ground surprise alive with scaly, wriggling saurians, some of which are computed to be 300, 500, even *700* years old! Many of them may actually have seen Ponce de Leon or Pedro de Menendez!

I shall hate to leave here, but unless I get a heading-off letter from Whitehead I suppose I am scheduled to shift down & across to Dunedin next Thursday. Accordingly the probable place to address a reply to this epistle is ℅ Whitehead, 1159 Broadway, Dunedin, Fla. But I shall try to stop in St. Aug. again on the way north—just as I must stop in Charleston & (I hope) Richmond.

Did I tell you of the amusing freak who has looked me up through W.T.? A chap named William Lumley of Buffalo N.Y., who *believes in magic* & has seriously read all such half-fabulous tomes as Paracelsus, Delrio, &c. &c.— despite an illiteracy which makes him virtually unable to spell. He wanted to know the real facts about the Cthulhu & Yog-Sothoth cults—& when I disillusioned him he made me a gift of a splendid illustrated copy of "Vathek"![9] Good old soul! ¶ Well—best wishes!—H P

Notes

1. AWD was quite obsessed with Hastur. HPL himself mentions Hastur (a god of the shepherds in the work of Ambrose Bierce, a constellation and a human being in the work of Robert W. Chambers) only twice in all his fiction— in "The Whisperer in Darkness"—and only within lists of mythic names. AWD dubbed Hastur (an entity) "the Unspeakable," conceiving of it as an "air elemental." Following HPL's death, AWD, respecting HPL's demur of "Mythology of Hastur," merely substituted *Cthulhu* for *Hastur* and later coined the term "Cthulhu Mythos" as a convenient tag for HPL's pseudomythology.

2. REH's first Lovecraftian story was "The Black Stone" (*WT,* November 1931; in *SNM*).

3. CAS wrote a cycle of thirteen stories set in Hyperborea, a pre–Ice Age continent. HPL's Olathoë in the land of Lomar is found in his story "Polaris" (1918). In *At the Mountains of Madness* he speaks of "the great cold that . . . put an end to the fabled lands of Lomar and Hyperborea" (*MM* 73).

4. In May 1930 Clifton P. Fadiman of Simon & Schuster had asked HPL to submit a novel. HPL said he had no novel to submit but could send submit a collection of stories. Fadiman had replied: "I am afraid that you are right in that our interest in a collection of short stories would not be very vivid. I hope, however, that you will buckle down and do that novel that you speak of. If it is good, its subject will be a help rather than a hindrance" (quoted in HPL to Lillian D. Clark, 24–26 May 1930; ms., JHL). For the January request, see letter 200.

5. HPL was a supporter of the continental drift theory, at this time doubted by many geologists. The German geologist Alfred Lothar Wegener (1880–1930) became the theory's chief exponent: he delivered a paper in 1912 on the subject and then published a book, *Die Enstehung der Kontinente und Ozeane* (1915), translated in 1924 as *The Origins of Continents and Oceans.* The theory was developed by Frank Bursley Taylor (1860–1938) and John Joly (1857–1933).

6. "The Letter from Mohaun Los" (as "Flight into Super-Time"), *Wonder Stories* (August 1932); rpt. as "Flight through Time," *Tales of Wonder* (Spring 1942).

7. *Imagine a Man in a Box.*

8. Christine Campbell Thomson, ed., *Switch On the Light* (1931). Contains HPL's "The Rats in the Walls," FBL's "The Red Fetish," and AWD's "The Pacer."

9. By William Beckford.

[200]   [ALS]

> % Whitehead,
>
> 1159 Broadway,
>
> Dunedin, Fla.
>
> May 23, 1931

Dear A W:—

Your letter & myself arrived simultaneously at Dunedin. The trip down & across Florida was very pleasant, & has brought me to a region much more definitely subtropical than St Augustine. Dunedin is a very prettily planned & gardened residential town on a low bluff above the Gulf of Mexico, & it is only a few yards from Whitehead's front steps to the shore. Whitehead himself is absolutely delightful—a very prince of good fellows, whose solicitude as a host extends to such lengths as the bringing of an eye-opening grapefruit to my bedside each morning. He is—contrary to my previous assumption—rector of the small local Anglican church, & is a highly valued fixture in his community. He does a good deal of work with boys' clubs—last night he had a dozen kids from 9 to 11 over here, & they listened very politely when (at Whitehead's un-dodgeable request) I told them stories—such as the gist of "The Cats of Ulthar". He insists that I prolong my stay indefinitely, but I shall not impose on his spontaneous affability. His health has taken a slight upward curve, but is still very troublesome; so that he cannot remain standing for long continuous periods, & is obliged to rest in bed for a time each afternoon. He is 49 years of age, & now much thinner than the snap-shot sent to correspondents a year ago indicates. Apparently he is exactly my build, so that he wants me to wear his white drill tropical suits if the temperature rises spectacularly.

As for my tales—surely I intend to fix up some shockers for popular vending when I get the time. I have, indeed, half-decided to shelve a good deal of revisory work in favour of such attempts. Whether such a policy will yield financial results depends on fate & editorial caprice. However, I shan't try to carry the writing-to-order policy too far; for all my attempts of the kind in the past have been pitiable messes. "The Lurking Fear" is a sample. As to overdoing the "Hastur" idea—of course I realise the danger of this, & have dozens of notebook entries of a totally different character. The only reason these have been postponed in favour of the "Whisperer" & "Mts. of Madness" is that the plots of these latter veritably thrust themselves on my attention & demanded to be written first.

The Simon & Schuster request I spoke of was made first a year ago, when their book editor Clifton P. Fadiman wrote me (after noting my name in the O'Brien anthology) to ask if I had any book MSS. to submit—& saying he would give careful attention to anything I did submit. I replied that I had nothing of novel length, but would like very much to get a short story collection published—to which, however, he responded that they do not consider short story collections. That was all, except that in January or February Fadiman wrote again to remind me that S&S were ready to look over a novel whenever I might have one ready. With this receptive attitude on their part, I shall certainly send them anything of the kind I may ever grind out.

As for the relative length of "Arthur Gordon Pym" & my "Mountains"—I am no quantitative sharp, & haven't seen "Pym" in ages; but would lay a fairly heavy wager that "Pym" is *much the longer* of the two! Get out your Poe & make an estimate![1] I still feel undecided about the trouble with my ending; & will let a symposium of varied opinions decide the question. It interests me to know that you do not share Long's misgivings regarding the sleep motivation.

Sorry to hear that Sterling A. Leonard has been drowned—that will be a genuine grief to my friend Moe, who has worked closely with him for many years on various enterprises. He seems to have been an authority of national eminence in pedagogical fields, though laying no claim to creative authorship.

I'll have to get a look at this second (& third) Wakefield book, even though I do not go so far as purchasing it. I'd also like to get a crack at Fort's "Lo!"—despite the fact that it's probably no more than a repetition of the kind of thing in "The Book of the Damned" & "New Lands". Whitehead has just made me a gift of Paul Morand's "Black Magic", & has most thoughtfully obtained Seabrook's "Magic Island" from the public library for my benefit. It always takes some incentive like that nowadays to start the old man reading!

I shall be vastly interested to see your new tale, "Something from Out There". Don't fear that my "outside" yearning will lead me into the glib "Hul-Jok" stuff of Edmond Hamilton & his tribe.[2] If I ever handle other concrete orbs & regions of space, you may depend upon it that the entire approach, proportioning, & substance will depart utterly from all precedent. The fundamental fault of the interplanetary tale is that it makes no attempt at emotional authenticity & gives no adequate reflection of the terrific magnitude of the departure involved. The characters all react falsely & superficially to the events. A really good story of other worlds is yet to be written—but in such a tale the chief element would be the emotional experience of the voyager.[3]

Whitehead sends his regards—& by the way, his opinion of your work is really very high; even if specific criticisms have led you to assume the contrary. He appreciated especially your article in the Midwestern, & is as anxious as I am to see the second item of the series, wherein you deal with the cult of simplicity.

Glad to hear your spring season has reached its exquisite height. I am basking in the mist of full summer, with palms, bamboos, live-oaks, & the like growing luxuriantly on every hand. Still, after a time one would miss the great elms, modest lilacs, rolling hills, & rambling stone walls of ancient New England.

The great trouble with this region is its absence of ancient & traditional things. I would get fearsomely bored here after a time; though the climate suits me exactly. St. Augustine is as far south as I would be likely to find the archaic things I relish, unless I could get to the glamourous West Indies themselves. What Whitehead tells about the Virgin Islands fairly makes my mouth water!

The nearest large city to Dunedin is Tampa, & this has more exotic & subtropical suggestions than any other town I have ever seen. I do not, however, like it; for it is sprawling & squalid & without any buildings or traditions of great age. The streets are broad & the houses (except for a few jarring near-skyscrapers) low, & life moves at a commendably leisurely tempo. There are benches outside the shops of the busiest commercial section, & one may sit down & loaf indefinitely without exciting notice or opposition. Cubans are abundant, since cigar-making is the principal industry, & they give the place a Latin flavour of more recent assertiveness than St. Augustine's historic Spanish background. The tropical quality is enhanced by the quality of the sky & sunlight.

I wish I could get all the way down to Miami or even Key West, but fear I can't financially manage it. It irks me to think of being in the North again—yet the ancient hills of New England will be gorgeous when I do get there—about July 1st. My address for the next week or so, I fancy, will still be % Whitehead.

Best wishes—

Yr most obt

hble Servt

—H P

Notes

1. Poe's tale has 71,700 words; HPL's 41,500.

2. "The Oath of Hul-Jok," *WT* (September 1928) is by Nictzin Dyalhis.

3. HPL codified his ideas on the interplanetary tale in "Some Notes on Interplanetary Fiction" (1934).

[201]   [ANS][1]

[Postmarked Dunedin, Fla.,

May 25, 1931]

Well—this place may not look much like your beloved hill, but I'll wager it would set your aesthetic apparatus working if you ever get down here—especially if you saw it under the guidance of an host as ideal as my present one! Last night we saw the white tropic moon making a magical path on the westward-stretching gulf that lapped at a gleaming, deserted beach on a remote key. Boy! What a sight! It took one's breath away! ¶ Watch *Adventure* for one of the outstanding weird tales in American literature—"The Black Beast", by H S W. ¶ Yr obt Servt H P

Canevin likewise salutes his correspondent; wishes you were in on this, too. I'm planning to disrupt H P L's schedule sadly by keeping him a little longer than he'll stay!!

Best—H. S. W.

Notes

1. Front: Untitled photo of boat and trees.

[202]   [ALS]

Whitehead Rectory
May 29, 1931

Dear A W:—

Yes—Whitehead is clearly improving in health; a change being perceptible even since my arrival. He is gaining about 5 lbs. per week, & his doctor thinks all danger of an operation is quite definitely past. But of course he must still be tremendously careful about diet & activity.

H S is just about the perfect host, & one of the most spontaneously like-able persons I have ever set eyes on. He owns up frankly to that little streak of Philistinism which prompted the obtuse verdicts on your tales; & after some degree of explanation has freely admitted how un-subtle he was to "muff" that ending of the story where the child's recognition of the malign influence in a room formed the climax. As I pointed out to him how the child's recognition clinched the *actuality* of the curse the mother was attempt-ing to deny, he fully conceded that his previous failure to "get" the story was a clear case of deficient subtlety on his part. Also—I think I have shewn him what was the matter with his whole attitude toward "Evening in Spring"; so that his reaction on a second perusal would be altogether different. He is more open to reason than you would think from his views as expressed on paper.

Meanwhile his young friend & guest Allan Grayson of New York (who turns out to be a dental patient of Doc Long's—Little Belknap's father!) has formed a tremendous admiration for you & your work, & wants desperately to see your whole trilogy of "The Early Years", "Evening in Spring", & "The Leaves Fall". I hope very much that you will encourage the kid by sending him as much of this material as possible; (you've doubtless received his letter) for he is really a prodigiously sensitive & aesthetic child, (age 17) & shews every sign of developing into a writer with much the same attitude as yourself. You could not get a more genuinely appreciative reader than this beauty-hungry & impressionable youth. He was, Whitehead tells me, something of a sissy originally; but H S's judicious & considerate influence has gently knocked a good deal of the pose out of him. I like him extremely, & shall be glad to shew him St Augustine & Charleston if he decides to make his homeward journey coincide with my northward turn a week hence. He'll make him good material for the gang, too—I shall introduce him to Belknap when all hands are assembled in Manhattan next month.

Let me congratulate you & your colleague Schorer on the bright pedagogical prospects now opening out ahead—also on the Bates sale, which certainly augurs well for the future. Glad to know that Klarkash-Ton has also clicked with Clayton. Your additions to "Evening in Spring" sound interesting, & I am sure your opinion of the work as a whole is amply justified. How you can do so much—& all the other items, too—is a sealed mystery to Grandpa! Even with the added energy of Floridian air I could never even begin to swing such a programme.

Glad the new "Not at Night" is a decent specimen of its kind. I shall wait till the publishers send me a copy. Shall be very glad to see your "Pacer" between cloth covers, & hope you will be equally well represented in whatever 1931 volume the firm may publish.

Your environing atmosphere sounds idyllic indeed—& I imagine it must be equally beautiful in my own New England. But I'm not homesick yet, for the exotic fauna & flora around here keep me continually fascinated. For the first time in my life I get a real kick out of *birds*—species I've never before glimpsed except in a zoo. There are all sorts of waders—crested & uncrested—herons, cranes, flamingoes, & the like—which flutter & light in the rushes very near me as I sit reading or writing by the shore as I am doing now. Likewise non-marine birds of various patterns & vocal accomplishments, including a liquidly trilling variant of the whip-poorwill whose repeated cry comes thrillingly in the mystical dawn-hour when I sometimes drift briefly & incompletely out of slumber. Of the

charm of the vegetation I have already spoken—the palms, the moss-hung live-oaks, & the tall, smooth-boled long-leaf pines that stand out against a marine sunset like the trees in a mystical Japanese print. The *sunsets* here are enough to make poets of anybody—so that when the Grayson kid asked for an entry in his autograph album I couldn't resist pulling the following:

To A Young Poet

You haunt the lonely sand where herons hide,
    And palm-framed sunsets open gates of flame;
Where marble moonbeams bridge the lapping tide
    To westward shores of dream without a name.

Here, in a haze of half-remembering,
    You catch faint sounds from that far, fabled beach.
The world is changed—your task henceforth to sing
    Dim, beckoning wonders you could never reach!

Whether I'll succeed in getting down to Southern Florida still hangs in the balance. One more unexpected cheque might turn the trick! But I shan't do myself out of another week in St Augustine, & a full week in Charleston. Those are the places that satisfy my imagination with historic antiquities. Here, despite the naturally beauty & physiologically congenial climate, I'd get bored to death in the long run. Whitehead wants me to move down here, but if the winter chill ever does drive me South it'll probably be to St Augustine. By the way—you ought to see my costume at this moment. White drill suit, of the sort that Whitehead wears in the West Indies! Very comfortable on a really hot day, though I have to get into my own old grey woollen suit in the cool of the evening. Whitehead is *exactly* my build, so that his stuff fits me as though a tailor had made it to my measure.

Like you, I want tremendously to see New Orleans; though there is no possibility of my doing so on this trip. I have read a bit about it, so that when I do get around I shall know where to go.

Thanks exceedingly for "The Captain of the Pole Star",[1] which I hadn't read in 30 years. It has real atmosphere, & packed about 0.8 of its original kick upon re-reading. Also glad to see the occult catalogue—which ought to be of avid interest to my new "nut" friend Bill Lumley of Buffalo!

As for Wakefield's "Others Who Returned"—lately discussed by us—I am now, suddenly & unexpectedly, its owner. Whitehead gave me his copy the moment I mentioned not having seen it. I've read it about 3/4 through, & like "The Cairn", "Look Up There", & "Blind Man's Buff". But how Wright would pan Wakefield for his *indefinite* endings!! ¶ Best wishes—
           Yr obt Grandsire
             H P

P.S. I'll send you a Dunedin paper with an account of H S's new juvenile book (accepted by Putnam's) if I can get an extra.[2]

[Enclosure: Unidentified clipping, "Dr. Whitehead to Have New Book Published."]

Notes

1. By Sir Arthur Conan Doyle.

2. *Pinkie at Camp Cherokee.*

[203]   [ANS][1]

[Postmarked Dunedin, Fla.,
5 June 1931]

Whippoorwills? I'll say we have 'em down here! Exotic ones, too, with a liquid rolling note apparently more complex than that of their northern kinsfolk. I first heard them in the mystical dawn outside my window, & half imagined that they were voices calling across the ultimate void from Beyond. And we have *snakes* as well. A splendidly mottled one paid us a call on the front stoop yesterday, & H S made his visit a longer one by catching him & pickling him in alcohol for my benefit. I shall certainly prize this addition to my modest museum! ¶ H S has read your Early Years & appreciates it tremendously, while young Grayson is ready to place you in numero deorum! Your "People"[2] is **magnificent**—& all three of us here are unanimously shouting its praises. You've got the stuff in you, Son! Best wishes—H P

Great stuff, A. D. Grayson goes north to-night. He is full of your praises. H. P. is a *salamander.* Thought *I* was hardboiled. Florida weather often resembles the real Tropics, but H. P. is utterly immune to the hottest *Siesta* period. H. S.

Notes

1. Front: Sunset, Florida.

2. In *SL* 3.374, AWD identifies "People" as equivalent to *Evening in Spring.*

[204]   [ALS]

En Route
June 9, 1931

Dear A W:—

        Yrs. recd. just as I am about to hop off on an extension of my tour. A timely pair of revision cheques make me reckless—hence I plan to dart briefly down to Miami & Key West—the most southerly point in the U.S., & close to the real tropics. From Key West to *Havana* the jump is very brief, & will cause me to count my cash with a very wistful aspect—but I have no real hope of making this leap. If I did, it would have to be at the cost of eliminating all the long-planned stops on the way home—even my beloved Charleston.

Grayson & Whitehead both reacted very favourably to "The Early Years"—the former with a veritably ecstatic enthusiasm. We all—as my card has told you—went wild over your "People"; & Grayson has set you up as a sort of idol for emulation. He is a very bright kid, & means to live up to your ceremonially autocratic 10-day rule as best as a mere mortal can. He left for New York last week, & I imagine he & Belknap will be boon companions by the time I pass through there on my way home. I think I told you that—as coincidence would have it—he turned out to be one of the dental patients of Belknap's father.

I am greatly interested to hear of your plans for the amplified & unified "Evening in Spring" & hope you will find a way to devote a great deal of uninterrupted leisure to it. You plan for intensive collaborated hack work sounds very ambitious, & I hope it may bear much remunerative fruit. It seems odd to me that you can do more effective writing in another's presence, since it is just the other way around with me. I have to be alone & utterly quiet in order to concentrate on a difficult job—& I doubt if I could ever collaborate very effectively. Your joint programme of diversified mass production sounds quite stupefying to my feeble energies, & imagine the inclusion of the "scientifiction" field will widen your market tremendously. You are surely fortunate in being able to strike a popular tone so effectively. The weird items you cite have a very appetising air, even though they may be parts of your frankly pot-boiling arrangement.

That owl incident is certainly picturesque in the extreme, & emphatically deserves a place in "Evening in Spring". I hope your friendship with the feathered youngster will continue, perhaps to the extent of gaining you a new pet! A sparrow once lit on my head years ago, but that is a very pallid thing in comparison to Athena's bird of wisdom!

H S was interested to hear of your continued taste for juvenile material. You will probably enjoy his coming book. He is really a great chap, & I regret leaving here tremendously. Now that he is in closer rapport with your work I think you will find him a less unsatisfactory critic.

This new anthology sounds interesting, & I appreciate your mentioning my lowly scribblings in connexion therewith. I shall be glad to hear from the editor—though very possibly he won't take the trouble to look me up.[1]

Well—now to get on the move. H S sends his regards & says he will write as soon as he can.

Best wishes—

Yr obt Servt

H P

Notes

1. Dashiell Hammett, *Creeps by Night* (1931); it contains "The Music of Erich Zann."

[205]   [ANS][1]

[Postmarked Key West, Fla.,
11 June 1931]

Greetings from the most southerly point in the U.S.! Climate agrees with me even better than St Augustine's & Dunedin's. This is a really tropical region—balconied, chimneyless houses amidst lush palm verdure. The view from the hotel roof looks exactly like pictures of West Indian towns. Fine old place—founded 1822, & so completely isolated that it has preserved a picturesquely simple early-American atmosphere! Cubans are very numerous—overflow from Havana, which is only 40 miles away. Damn sorry I'm too broke to get across there—I had retained hopes until the very last moment—the Florida Keys are some of the most fascinating sights in the world—green, low-lying coral isles in a clear, green & blue tropic sea—exotic fish & shore birds—waving palms, & c. Hate to think of turning north again! Saw Miami but was not impressed. Too modern & urban for me. Best wishes & good luck with the high-pressure production programme. H P

Notes

1. Front: Bird's-Eye View. Showing U.S. Naval Station and Post Office, Key West, Florida.

[206]   [ALS]

St Augustine again
June 17, 1931

Dear A W:—

Back at the old Spanish capital—the most attractive place in Florida, all told. Only here does one get the perfect combination of scenic & architectural beauty with an unbroken tradition of 366 years. Vast live-oaks with Spanish moss—narrow streets & ancient walls—the old fort—& sweet cathedral chimes sounding across a shady, drowsy plaza.

You have by this time received my Key West card, telling of the marvellous charm of that utterly remote place & sadly recounting my financial inability to get across to Havana. I hated to return, but it had to be done. At

Miami I took a side trip to the Seminole village where the Indians trade furs with the city merchants. A depressingly squalid place of pole-framed huts with peaked, palm-thatched roofs & wooden platforms. The Seminoles (who have infusions of Spanish & nigger blood & look like Chinese or Japanese) are ineffably dirty & odoriferous, & wear loose robes made of bright cloth fragments sewn together. I also took a trip over neighbouring coral reef in a glass-bottomed boat which gave splendid views of the exotic tropical flora & fauna of the ocean floor—grasses, sponges, corals, fishes, sea-urchins, crinoids, &c. A diver went down & brought up a bucket full of sea-urchins for distribution among the passengers, but I restored mine to its native element because I had no means of preserving it. Miami is set in a wretched landscape—flat sandy barrens, too far south for the subtropical live-oaks & Spanish moss, & too far north for a natural tropic growth like Key West's. Wealth & landscape gardening, however, have managed to create an artificial tropic growth which in places is highly spectacular & impressive. The ride up the east coast to St. Augustine was in places very picturesque—affording occasional glimpses of the open ocean. I shall stay here till Monday night—then on to Savannah, Charleston, Richmond, Philadelphia, & N.Y. Lack of cash will probably prevent me from staying very long at any one place, hence my next forwarding address will be in Belknap's care—230 W. 97th St., N.Y.C. I hate to think of going north—but of course actual summer is now close at hand.

Glad to hear of your industrious labours. You call yourself lazy—but bless my soul! Your laziest is more active than my very peak of activity! In this Florida climate, though, I really believe I would have more energy than I have in the north.

Hope the new weird anthology hasn't proved a failure. Sorry "A Matter of Faith" has been returned—but landing with Bates is undoubtedly a very difficult process. Trust that some of the work now held will meet a happier fate.

As for W.T.—I must say that I thought the present issue rather dull. The main trouble with "The Venus of Azombeii"—which as a *weird* tale I liked better than "Hill Drums"—is that it follows a pattern of deadly hackneyedness . . . . the old H. Rider Haggard formula. Also, it mishandles the moon's motions—a crescent waning moon never *sets* just before dawn, since it is then always climbing in the east.

Well—here's wishing you luck with your programme. I have had an idea of starting a new story down here, but have not found any time so far. If I use the tropic setting for any kind of a tale, it will be one involving brooding mysteries on one of those low coral keys which lie in spectral desertion just off the shore.[1]

Best wishes—

Yr obt hble Servt

H P

Notes

1. This image, though in a New England rather than a tropical setting, is found in "The Shadow over Innsmouth," begun in November.

[207]   [ANS][1]

[Postmarked New York City, N.Y.,
1 July 1931]

Dear August,

H.P.L., Long, and I have just emerged from the Metropolitan museum of Art. It is the second museum in an after noon. Therefore I am, as can well be imagined, rather tuckered out. I received your letter containing your photo. I will write a letter acknowledging it as soon as I find a breathing space in this helter-skelter life of mine.

A. B. G.

All hail! Recd. your new stories, & will return them at the earliest possible moment. Wright has turned down my long new story—that damn fathead! Best wishes

—H P

Greetings and all good wishes from Dr. Little, Jr.

Notes

1. Front: Commands of Rigden Jyepo, Nicholas Roerich, Roerich Museum, New York.

[208]   [ANS][1]

[Postmarked Asbury Park, N.J.,
3 July 1931]

Oh, dear—back in the North again, as the collective card signed by Long & Grayson has told you ere this. My hosts have not yet given me a spare minute in which to acknowledge your letter & delightful tale—but have patience, & suspend the 10 day rule for once! Shall visit Talman next week, & then home at last. Probably can't get up the Hudson to see Dwyer. Expect to meet Seabury Quinn Monday. Am at Asbury Park with the Longs over the week-end. Don't care for the place, but the ocean saves it from utter banality. The North is pretty chilly after the South—especially today, with the frigid sea close at hand.

Best wishes—

H P L

Notes

1. Front: 1: Rough Surf, Ashbury Park, N.J.

[209]   [ALS]

Prospect Park, Brooklyn
July 13, 1931

Dear A W:—

Hospitality is a good thing, but it does play the devil with correspondence! By a malign coincidence, about 0.90 of everybody I know has drifted to (or was born in) the New York area; hence whenever I pass through the damned babel I am engulfed in a round of visiting which gives me scarcely a second to myself. Such has been the case for the past 2½ weeks. After spending half the time at Belknap's, I am now stopping in Flatbush (where I dwelt in 1924) with Wilfred B. Talman, but shall be on the move more or less homeward within another week. As you have seen from a postcard, I looked up young Grayson & have had some interesting conversations with him. His admiration for your work is unbounded, & he is about to pass "The Early Years" along to Belknap. It will do the latter good to read this piece of work; for he needs to learn something of your simple directness of style & authenticity of subject-matter. He has a fatal tendency to use thinner & thinner material & more & more artificial mannerisms. Wright rejected his latest story, & I fear I can see why—though I would hardly admit as much to Bre'r Farnsworth himself.

Speaking of rejections—see how gracefully our little friend has turned down "At the Mountains of Madness"! And to think I typed all those 115 pages! I honestly think I'll quit writing altogether—or at least, quit trying long enough to do more than occasionally jot down a few notes for my own edification. There is no demand whatever for serious work in the weird. I am confirmed in this attitude by the polite rejection my stuff has just received from Putnam's—who asked to see it in the first place. They hem & haw & try to give me an easy letdown, but I shall pay no more attention to them. I'll shew you their letter soon.

I am indeed glad to hear of your recent work, & hope you'll keep it up till your finances are in better shape. Congratulations on the probable Bates acceptance! I read all three of your enclosures with the keenest interest, & like "The Thing that Walked on the Wind" best of all. I recall praising it in an earlier form,[1] & think it is now even better. In a few marginal notes I have indicated what I think might be logical steps toward still further improvement. "In the Left Wing" has a real punch, & held my interest unflaggingly. It is, though, exceedingly conventional in many of its elements; whilst the language is painfully careless. I have indicated possible improvements on the margin, & Belknap has added a note or two. "Something from Out There" seems distinctly more diffuse & less poignant than either of the other two. Just what would help it most, I can hardly tell; but I might suggest an elimination of characters & possibly of narrative stages—a general tightening up, as it were. Toward the end, the tightening ought to be especially thorough. The *aspect* of the thing ought to be kept under cover till it looms up in one climactic moment; while the element of *pursuit* ought to be kept down lest something like the close of Belknap's "Horror from the Hills" be perpetrated. If possible, the final cataclysm ought to be condensed & speeded—merged with the climactic appearance of the Thing, & explained fully by the very briefest of newspaper items.

The plot for "The Horror from the Lake"[2] sounds splendid to me, & I feel sure that you & Schorer will do it justice. There is room for infinite brooding cosmicism, as well as for plenty of "action"—so dear to the Bates type of editor. Glad that my hints anent 165 Bascom are bearing fruit.

New W.T., except for rare high spots, seems even duller than its predecessor. I am now trying to get the July 15 issue of *Adventure,* which contains Whitehead's truly splendid "Black Beast".

Well—I'll be in Providence pretty soon now!

> Best wishes—
>> Yr obt
>> H P

Notes

1. Then titled "Death-Walker." Published as "Ithaqua."
2. I.e., "The Evil Ones" (variant titles include "The Horror from the Lake" and "The Horror from the Depths").

[210]   [ALS]

> Home—strange to say
> August 3, 1931

Dear A W:—

Still alive—even though dead according to the 10-day reply ukase of imperious youth! The combined hospitality of Long & Talman kept me in the metropolis till July 20, & the day after my return I became a host myself—welcoming the wandering James F. Morton to Providence & guiding him about for three days. Since then I have been vainly trying to catch up with accumulated reading & correspondence. A feverish vortex—but on the whole amply justified by the trip which occasioned it. It surely was a magnificent outing—May 2 to July 20, & extending as far south as the U.S. goes! Florida gave me the only continuous two months of physical comfort which I have ever experienced in the course of a long life.

I was glad of the chance of reading your new tales, & like them all—especially "They Shall Rise in Great Numbers." "The Horror from the Lake" was delightful, even though it had some stylistic carelessnesses such as repeated words, grammatical solecisms, & one case of erroneous Latin. (you ought to have your participle agree in number with its noun—Negotia perambulan*tia*) If any major change is called for, it might be in the direction of condensation; but heaven knows the tale is good enough—infinitely above the W.T. average—just as it stands. The events are very well handled. "Nellie Foster" is splendid, too, as a brief bit of realistic horror—forming a sort of bridge betwixt your weird work & your tales of the Wisconsin soil. (no red clay pun intended!)

As for Wright's reactions, as so interestingly transcribed in your letter—it almost nullifies the sting of his latest rejection to see his irrational & inattentive capriciousness so amusingly revealed on a large scale! Of all Boeotian blundering & irrelevancy! And what pointless censure of the introduction of Cthulhu & Yog-Sothoth—as if their use constituted any "infringement" on my stuff! Hades! The more these synthetic daemons are mutually written up by different authors, the better they become as general background-material! I *like* to have others use my Azathoths & Nyarlathoteps—& in return I shall use Klarkash-Ton's Tsathoggua, your monk Clithanus, & Howard's Bran.[1] Indeed, I shall tell Wright of my attitude when next I write him. You have not used the "Elder Ones" any more specifically than Smith uses them in "The Holiness of Azadérac" (where he speaks of "Iog-Sôtot" &c)—which Wright has taken. As for *phrasing*—Hell! can't the fool see that certain set expressions like "The frightful Nec. of the mad Arab A.A" are *definitely crystallised phrases* equivalent to single words or names? The fellow seems to have absolutely no *flexibility* or sense or proportion in his judgments—everything is measured literally & pedantically. And his "idolatry" of one whose stuff he repeatedly rejects is surely a damn peculiar species . . . . . much like the Christian "worship" of modern people whose deeds are direct contradictions to the precepts they pretend to follow. As for the resemblance of your "Horror" to Long's—the museum incident & the final campaign against the menace are undoubtedly what prompted Wright's comparison. What he forgot was that both of these things are standard weird situations common to half the output of the last decade. As if these were any *individual* imitation![2]

The other Wright faultfindings you cite seem to me equally pointless—especially the strictures on "The Thing that Walked on the Wind", a story which seems to me full of the highest possibilities. Also—only sheer idiocy or inattention could cause the actual occurrence in "Nellie Foster" to seem obscure. In general, Wright is tending more & more to use stock phrases like "not convincing" or "lacks motivation" in his rejections. Each of these phrases *can* have a meaning—but he uses them indiscriminately, & in many cases where they do not have any meaning or relevance. And the whole process seems additionally asinine when one looks over a copy of the magazine & sees the insufferable tripe which he *does* accept—& which, by implication, must exemplify what he considers "convincing", "well motivated", & so on. About date of payment—I received my cheque for the "Whisperer" a week ago. Evidently the present schedule provides for payments approximately a month after publication.

But I hope you won't let these stupidities deter you altogether from weird writing. Though your major field will probably be much broader, you nevertheless have a very distinct aptitude for convincing spectral creation; & it would be a pity if things like the Tcho-Tchos & Rigelian daemons were to remain for ever unchronicled.[3]

However, you are right in putting "Evening in Spring" & cognate works first among your products. These things seem to me the closest approach to serious literature yet produced by any of our group. Long was immensely enthusiastic over the specimens passed on by Grayson—& I trust you will not fail to give the more recent chapters an eastern circulation.

I trust you'll duly land "They Shall Rise" with Bates. He lately told me that he had let down the bars against "atmospheric" as opposed to "plot" stories. The only change in this splendid tale that I would suggest, is a little clearer outlining of the steps whereby the narrator remembers Brook from the old pamphlet. As the tale stands, he seems very tardy in recognising the *name*—which ought to be even more familiar than the old man's aspect.

Thanks exceedingly for the generous package—books, & the magazines with your clever tales. Is this Mind Magic any kind of a market?[4] I saw one on the stands, I think, last week. M R James, the Not at Nights, &c., were all most enthusiastically welcome. Sorry M R is through with weird writing—& hope I can get a glimpse of the additional tales in the collection some day.

I hardly expected anything to come of the Putnam business—all standard publishers are afraid of *really weird* material. I'll send you the turndown letter when Whitehead returns it. No word from the John Day Co., so I fancy they are not using "The Outsider." Just as well, for that is a rotten piece of rhetorical hash with Poesque imitativeness plastered all over it. Glad you like the "Whisperer" in print. I haven't read the magazine version yet, though dread of the misprints I shall probably find.

Sorry the heat oppresses you—I fancy I'd like your 100-in-the-shade days, though one of your winters would make me a candidate for the churchyard. I have been reading & writing in the open ever since my return home, & am even now on the wooded river-bank which I have haunted since infancy. But some of the evenings are getting too cool for me even now. That's the hell of a northern clime—the exquisite summer comes so late, & chills into autumn so early! But there's always a haven by the gas stove.

Best wishes—

Yr most obt Servt

H P

Notes

1. The Hyperborean god Tsathoggua had been introduced by CAS in "The Tale of Satampra Zeiros"; HPL cites it in "The Mound" (1929–30) and numerous other tales. (Smith's entity was first mentioned in print in HPL's "The Whisperer in Darkness.") AWD mentioned the evil monk Clithanus in "Something from Out There," "The Horror from the Depths," and "The Passing of Eric Holm," but HPL never used Clithanus in his own work. REH introduced the Pictish chieftain Bran Mak Morn in "Kings of the Night" (*WT*, November 1930); HPL cited "Bran" in a list of names in "The Whisperer in Darkness" (*DH* 223). Neither CAS nor REH intended their literary creations to be part of HPL's pseudomythology.

2. AWD's transcription of FW's letter does not survive; but see FW to AWD, 13 July 1931 (ms., SHSW): "THE HORROR FROM THE LAKE is obviously inspired by Long's story, THE HORROR FROM THE HILLS, and some of the early scenes in your story parallel Long's. This in itself would be sufficient objection to bar the story from Weird Tales. Also, your story does not have the distinction of style which is one of the charms of Long's story.

"But a more serious objection to this story is the fact that you have lifted whole phrases from Lovecraft's works, as for instance: 'the frightful *Necronomicon* of the mad Arab Abdul Alhazred,' 'the sunken kindom of R'lyeh,' 'the accursed spawn of Cthulhu,' 'the frozen and shunned Plateau of Long,' etc. Also you have taken the legends of Cthulhu and the Ancient Ones directly out of Lovecraft. This is unfair to Lovecraft. Robert Louis Stevenson once said that in the days of his apprenticeship to the writing craft he 'had played the sedulous ape' to different authors in turn. But you have not merely aped Lovecraft in this story—you have even lifted his wording. My admiration for Lovecraft's writing amounts almost to idolatry, and I cannot allow such imitation in Weird Tales. It is all right to use the legends as Howard and Smith have used them—a mere allusion to them; but your usage oversteps the bounds of propriety." AWD used this same argument to dissuade others from using HPL's literary ideas, though he himself continued to use them.

3. AWD introduced the Tcho-Tcho people in "The Lair of the Star-Spawn" (variant title, "The Statement of Eric Marsh").

4. AWD published only one story in *Mind Magic:* "Wraiths of the Sea."

[211]   [ALS]

August 10[, 1931]

Dear A W:—

    Everything arrived safely, & yesterday I sent "Alfred Kramer" on to Klarkash-Ton.[1] As you say, this tale is full of weak points & hackneyed devices—such as having had an ancestor of the hero present at various important events in history—& ought not to have the weakening framework of Forbes's incarceration & suicide. I think there ought to be a narrator equivalent to Forbes—so that the ultimate disintegration of Kramer can be suitably detailed—but the narrator ought not to usurp attention with events subsequent to the true climax. Also—there is a great deal of stock phraseology in the language. Reincarnation stories are such old stuff that it is difficult to give them any real vitality or originality—but with improvements & eliminations this specimen might be quite vivid. The Valdemar-like climax—with the added touch about the mask—is excellent

    Confound this Clayton for rejecting "They Shall Rise"! Glad to hear, though, that *Ghost Stories* has a new & presumably less obtuse editor.[2] Is the address the same—25 W. 43? To the best of my knowledge, young Grayson has "The Thing that Walked on the Wind"—together with two other recent weird things of yours. I wish I could think of the exact points I deemed capable of further improvement; but my weary old memory refuses to specify beyond the fact that these points mainly concerned the early part of the mounted policeman's report, & had something to do with the relation of the language to the emotional values inherent in the subject matter. You will no doubt find my pencil annotations, made at the moment of reading, when Grayson returns the MS. Glad to see "The Sheraton Mirror" & "Miss Sarah" again. The former still has the charm it had at a first reading, & the only general criticism I could make is that perhaps the climax is a little too *extended*— i.e., lacking in the elements of overwhelming suddenness & surprise. Of minor verbal points I might mention that tautological use of *already* (a mid-Western speech habit which has now reached New York, but which is still wholly absent in New England & the South) on p. 11, where the speech of Taliaferro ought to be simply this: "I overheard you talking days ago." To add *already* (which means *now, at this time,* or *at sometime past*) to this complete sentence is simply to repeat needlessly the idea contained in the words *days ago.* Another verbal point is your employment of the actually non-existent word *"stomped"* on p. 12. This may be a corruption of *stamped,* but in the place I doubt if the latter is demanded. I would say *tramped* or *went.* "Miss Sarah", as I said when I saw the first draught, is an excellent tale; & I hardly know whether I'd advise the contemplated change or not. Of course, the climax is a bit diffusive—like that of the Sheraton—but there is a distinct type of thrill in a tale where the horror-element is so shadowy & indefinite. Indeed, I'd be almost tempted to revise the thing *the other way around*—keeping all signs of the supernatural under cover until the very last. I'd have the niece merely think Miss Emmy was getting childish until the final scene when Sarah comes back to claim her own—& even then I'd leave the matter as a *horrible doubt*. Let the end be overheard in another room rather than visually seen . . . . . . & let Hannah half-doubt whether it actually was Miss Sarah's voice which she heard as she hastened to investigate. Still—your new alternative makes an exceedingly powerful story of another kind, so that I would hesitate to weigh the one idea against the other. One thing, though—the prose of Miss Sarah might well be surveyed for minor awkwardnesses—such as the plethora of "thens" at the opening of page 9. It pays to couch a good idea in a smooth & correct external form.

I shall read your new "People" instalment with the keenest interest when it arrives. Certainly, the completed "Evening in Spring" will be a piece of very keen, sincere, & solid art by the time it is all written & assembled. Let us hope, meanwhile, that your more popular material will find suitable markets. I envy you your persistence in the face of rejections—for under similar circumstances I acquire a sort of distrust for the merit of my stuff, & a concomitant disinclination to write more. Just now, for example, the effect of the combined Wright & Putnam rebuff is to cause me to abandon original attempts & undertake several revisory endeavours. I doubt if I ever get on paper even a fraction of what I want to say—& it may be that I am wholly written out, anyhow. By the way—I enclose the Putnam turndown for your perusal & ultimate return.

I agree pretty much with your estimate of the latest W.T., & continue to wonder what sort of policy it is that lets this stuff get by while scores of undeniably better items are rejected. Whiskey or Parkinson's Disease—I give it up! There was room for tremendous power in Howard's tale of the primal African tomb—& even as it was I got a fairly authentic kick. But he had to work in one of his beloved fights before he could get down to business with the spectral part. "Deadlock" had a vapidly conventional motivation, but was unusual among interplanetary tales in at least tying to give some adequate emotional atmosphere when the fact of being off the earth becomes known to the voyagers. In that detail it anticipates the crux of an interplanetary tale that I had once planned to write—though I would have deferred my revelation till the surface of some alien planet was reached. Quinn was about as usual—frankly concocting as much remunerative prose as possible around one or two stock ideas or situations. Lucky devil, to have such a stand-in with the readers—& thence with Wright!

No—I hardly fancy that *Mind Magic* would prove much of a market for me. But it is interesting to see how weird publications come & go.

Your library is certainly growing! Don't bother to type those James tales merely to shew me—though if you get a lending duplicate of the collection you might give me an early place on the circulation list. Incidentally—I surely appreciate your kindness in completing my set of M R's older tales!

Yesterday I sent along Klarkash-Ton's latest—"The Maker of Gargoyles", which Dwyer passed on to me. It is not bad in many respects—though derivative in certain essentials. In one way it anticipates a proposed tale of mine—about cathedral gargoyles found with blood on their jaws, (or perhaps in transposed positions) indicative of nocturnal wanderings on their part.[3]

Just got some duplicates from Talman of pictures he took of Belknap & me last month. Here's one for you—you need not bother to return it if your files have any niche well suited to such an item.

Am having the devil of a time trying to get a new fountain pen to suit me. This is the 7th or 8th that I've tried in the last 3 months—but I never can get anything that works just right. I must be getting old & feeble, so that any pressure fatigues me. May have to adopt a pencil—gawd knows!

Best wishes—

Yr most obt

H P

Notes

1. DAW, "The Lives of Alfred Kramer," *WT* (December 1932).

2. Harold Hersey remained the editor of *Ghost Stories* from April 1930 until its demise with the issue of December 1931/January 1932.

3. CAS, "The Maker of Gargoyles," *WT* (August 1932). Cf. *CB* 76: "Ancient cathedral—hideous gargoyle—man seeks to rob—found dead—gargoyle's jaw bloody"; 77: "Unspeakable dance of the gargoyles—in morning several gargoyles on old cathedral found transposed."

[212]   [TLS, JHL][1]

Sauk City

14 August [1931]

Dear H. P.,

Many thanks for the photograph of yourself and Belknap. You look much different from the picture of you that I had some years ago—you seem to have taken on weight. The features remind me distinctly of what the movie people imagine an astute Scotland Yard man looks like; vaguely similar to G. P. Heggie, who takes the part of Inspector Hayland Smith in the Fu Manchu pictures. I'll mail you and Belknap some recent pictures of myself when I get around to having duplicates developed. One of my friends here has made a snapshot of me into a postcard.

The Putnam letter hedges. What the man seems not to realize is that 5,000 copies of a collection of Lovecraft tales could be sold to W. T. readers alone, people who have read all the tales before. And a sale of that magnitude is not to be scorned by any publisher. Have you tried an agent? Maxim Lieber, Suite 1007, 55 west 42nd Street, NYC is honest; he doesn't charge a reading fee, and ships the mss. back at once if he thinks they can't be printed. You might try the collection on him, sending him what you sent Putnam's, and telling him about your popularity in W. T. (don't be too modest to blow your own horn), adding that I suggested him to you.

Glad you liked The Sheraton Mirror and The Return of Miss Sarah. I am now working on revisions of Laughter in the Night, and The Lost Path; will do final drafts of The Statement of Eric Marsh, (story of the Tcho-Tcho people), and The Tree at the Window. I have sent to Allan[2] for the stories; he has not written since 15 July, and while I do not apply the 10-day rule to people like yourself whose letters invariably have a good deal of meat to them, I must apply it to Allan and others like him, because what has gone on between us is of necessity so unimportant to me that I relegate it to oblivion after ten days; therefore a letter referring to something in this past correspondence always sends me to my files to look it up should it come later than ten days. All of which is very complicated, and perhaps foolish. But I must have my idiosyncrasies.

Address of Ghost Stories is 570 7th Avenue. Try them with something. Thanks for the tip on use of "already"; I was not aware of this as a colloquialism. Re stomped; Wright caught me up on that, but I understand that this perversion has come into good usage. Won't swear to it.

I wish I could be with you for a while. Perhaps my energy might serve to impress you sufficiently for you to undertake new and revisory work despite rejections. My attitude re rejections is largely the utterly self-confident one arising out of innate pride, the attitude that tells me I will eventually sell 4 out of 5 rejected stories to one of the people who has rejected them. Thus I have made up my mind to sell Wright The Thing that Walked on the Wind; and nothing will convince me that I won't sell it to him—saving only the accident of its purchase by Ghost Stories which will first see the retouched ms.

Have you seen the September Strange Tales? It is a better magazine than the September Weird Tales. Best in the issue is Smith's Halman Carnby tale, retitled, The Return of the Sorcerer; after that Burks' The Place of the Pythons, and Hurst's The Awful Injustice. Other Weird-Talers represented are the more versatile Ray Cummings (not a bad tale), and Victor Rousseau (usual psychic stuff).[3] The next issue, November, will have Cassius by Whitehead, and I think my Shadow on the Sky.[4] The October W. T. looks to me better than the September, for it will have your Strange High House and Whitehead's Black Terror, and Ham tells me it will also use my short short, The Captain is Afraid, which is better than the medieval tales used thus far in 1931. Those Who Seek will be in the January 32 issue, and perhaps one of the two still left will appear in the December or November issues. I am getting ready about 15 tales, old and retouched and new for Wright's eyes when he comes back from his vacation in 3 weeks.

I personally do not believe Mind Magic will last much longer, though the company publishing it is a 13 yr old concern.

Re The Maker or Gargoyles. I liked it, but the end was bad; I wrote Smith suggesting this revision—since the tale was obvious from the beginning, one of 2 things had to be done—either the stress on the gargoyles in the beginning must be cut and the tale subtilized, or else, and preferably (for it is well written) the maker should mount to the roof, already suspecting what he will see, then when he is confirmed, seize upon something and begin to destroy the gargoyles, tumbling them from the roof; then abruptly he is seized from behind, and with the gargoyles, crashes to the cathedral steps below. There he is found in the morning, by the bishop, who to his horror, sees that one gargoyle's claw is caught in the maker's clothes, and twisted in a way that he the bishop *knows* was not wrought in the original stone. This makes up for the obviousness in a way. I recently saw a newer and better Wandrei tale, The Tree-Men of M'Bwa,[5] which he should have no difficulty selling to either Bates or Wright.

I still remember a coral-reef story you were planning on doing; I await this. Why not do it with an eye for Bates? His idea is not too much atmosphere, or at least not so much that certain action is not obscured. His chief criticism of my work is that it lacks a series of climaxes, one growing out of the other, not enough plot, he says. I have designed The Statement of Eric Marsh for Bates, though I feel there's still too much atmosphere for Him.

People should have reached you by this time. I have sent the original to Paris, together with Old Ladies, another part, and The Peace of the Cardinal-Archbishop, to This Quarter. Another duplicate went out to Lieber, for his opinion as to whether it would be advisable to publish it in book form, adding of course 8 to 10 case histories, as has been 3 times now suggested.

Well, best wishes, and trusting to see a new tale from you before many days have passed. Thanks again for the snapshot.

As always,
August

Notes

1. Letters 212, 214, 217, and 218 are typed on stationery of the Midwest Conference Magazine.

2. I.e., Allan D. Grayson. See HPL letters 200f.

3. *Strange Tales of Mystery and Terror* (September 1931, the first issue): CAS, "The Return of the Sorcerer"; Arthur J. Burks, "The Pace of Pythons"; S. B. H. Hurst, "The Awful Injustice"; Ray Cummings, "The Dead Who Walk"; and Victor Rousseau, "A Cry from Beyond."

4. Whitehead's story appeared in the November issue, but AWD's appeared in that for January 1932.

5. DAW, "The Tree-Men of M'Bwa," *WT* (February 1932).

[213] [ALS]

Ten-Mile River Woods—
Aug. 18, 1931

Dear A W:—

"People" duly arrived, & I read it with utmost admiration—passing it on to Grayson with instructions for subsequent Long-Whitehead-Author forwarding. The parts I had seen impressed me as vividly as before, & those I hadn't seen were quite commensurate in their effect. You surely have a phenomenally keen sense of the drama of quietly tragic lives—& these sketches strike me as having the very essence of solid literature in them. While they would certainly fit splendidly into your magnum opus, I can also see the advantages of having them as a separate volume of more purely objective nature "Evening in Spring". It's hard to give advise in this particular—but let's see what your agent says.

Glad the snap interested you—both Belknap & I will enjoy seeing the new ones of you when they are ready. I've aged vastly since the 1925 view you have—though the scales don't credit me with any added poundage. Possibly the weight is differently distributed.

Long has received a Putnam letter much like mine in tone—he having submitted a collection after I did. I don't think I'll bother to peddle my stuff around—but thanks for the name of the agent. I'm passing it on to Belknap—& may patronise the gent myself some day.

Hope to see your new tales soon—those Tcho-Tcho people sound tremendously interesting! Trust Grayson won't delay in returning the MSS. he has. Thanks for the new address of *Ghost Stories*, to which I'll send something if I start any more writing.

As for linguistic matters—I don't think "*sto*mped" can be regarded as anything but crude dialect as yet. It's about in the class with "hain't", "agin", & such forms. Not *every* corrupt phrase or form of this year gets into next year's Standard Dictionary! The corrupt & tautological nature of an "*already*" which merely duplicates another word or phrase indicating time will be obvious on reflection. For example—in answering a certain sentence such as "You'll have to see Jones about that matter today", we can easily see what sentences do—& what sentences don't—permit of the word's use. If we say

"No—I've already seen him."

we use the adverb legitimately, as indicating the completion of the seeing *at some time past.*

But if we say

"No—I saw him yesterday."

we cannot legitimately tack on any more adverbs of time. It was *yesterday* that the seeing took place, & that's that. Only in colloquial mid-western speech (or recently, in New York City as well) could one hear so impossible a tautological rigmarole as

"No—I saw him yesterday *already*".

In New York the classes who employ this superfluous "already" tend to slur it over & make it a sort of unaccented, trailing-off suffix of the word it precedes—& with them it is almost invariably intruded at the very end of the sentence—thus:

"Naw—I seen um yess'uddy—u'ready."

Which reminds me—I cut out one such *already* from your "People" MS.— & also changed "*Oklahoma* Territory" to "Indian Territory" in one of the sketches. On second thought you will realise that during the Civil War period the name "Oklahoma" was unknown. It was first used in 1889 when the now white man's territory was carved out of the western part of the old I.T., & did not spread to the whole original I.T. area till 1907, when the two divisions were recombined & admitted to the Union as the State of Oklahoma.

Yes—if anything could arouse energy in a played-out old man, I am sure it would be the sight of a young dynamo like yourself—inexhaustibly producing new material of every sort with both hands—while pens clamped to your toes revise your older stuff for Wright's reconsideration! However—I fear Grandpa can never be a serious competitor! I rather agree with the Putnam man regarding one of his objections—for upon reflection I do think that Wright's incessant demand for primerish obviousness & explanatory stuff has insidiously & unperceivedly corrupted my sense of subtlety. I doubt if any junk which would be admitted to W.T. could also be published by a firm of the Putnam grade as a collection. My story-sense has been warped, unconsciously, to an essentially low-grade form . . . . as I began to realise a year ago when Dwyer pointed out the obtrusively explanatory nature of the Whisperer's *original* ending. I cut out most of the rawest explanation on his recommendation.

I must get *Strange Tales* before returning home tonight. Glad it is starting out so promisingly. Belknap has seen it & seems to like it fairly well. Good luck with your 15 new & retouched candidates for Farnsworthian favour!

Your suggestion for Klarkash-Ton's "Gargoyles" is excellent, & I hope he has the good judgment to adopt it. I'd like to see Wandrei's new M'Bwa tale—hope it gets published. I've abandoned the Florida story, at least for the present. Doubt if it would have amounted to much. For the time being, revision has me engulfed. Incidentally, though, I've heard from the John Day Co. at last, & they are taking my "Erich Zann" for the coming Dashiell Hammett anthology. My remuneration is $25.00. They are also taking Belknap's "Visitor from Egypt" at the same price. I'm glad they're choosing "Zann", for it is next to my favourite (Colour Out of Space first) among my stuff.

Hope "People" & your other MSS. find a welcome in Paris. You'll have a taste of genuine literary recognition before long—& it will be amply deserved!

Best wishes—

H P

[214]   [TLS, JHL]

Sauk City
Wisconsin
21 August [1931]

Dear H. P.,

Your most welcome letter brings me the first good news since I last wrote you, and serves to break the apathetic spell of a most trying and nerve-racking week. And that news is the acceptance of Eric Zann, in which I had enough confidence, and which I pushed enough, to type the whole thing out and send it to Day rather than send the magazine with the story in it. I am glad not only because it somehow justifies my pride, but also because the John Day Company has promised $10.00 for each suggested story chosen, and I suggested Erich Zann and also A Visitor from Egypt, though in this latter someone may have got ahead of me. At any rate, I should make ten out of it. And that will keep me in postage stamps all through September.

Your appreciation of People pleases me. I have about decided that it will be, with the addition of 8 cases, a book in itself; the epilogue and prologue will be added to, and the title changed to either A TOWN IS BUILT ON TRAGEDY or A TOWN IS BUILT. Which do you like better? The Providence of which I write so often stepped in last Saturday to give me what will be the concluding case history—Rose Brandon.

The so trying week began with a notice from Harold Hersey that Ghost Stories had been suspended; that was last Saturday morning, and it came just after I was assured that They Shall Rise would be taken. That afternoon coming home from down town, I learned that my old girl (Margery) had been literally booted from her home (by her stupid mother, who was incensed because the girl was again going with a Catholic—you remember The Early Years?). The day before I had talked with Margery, during which time she had told me (as I had long known) that she had been little better than a harlot for the last years, intimating that at bottom I was the fault for breaking up the puppy-love between us—which, while I knew was untrue, distressed me. That afternoon her mother spoke to me, confiding that Margery was about to turn Catholic, and get married to someone she was not too much in love with—an emergency measure because she had been kicked out and was too proud to come back, for which in a way I don't blame her. What distressed me was the suggestion that after a mother-dominated youth, her marriage might be unhappy.

And then it is said that nothing ever happens in a small town. In the same week happened other things not concerning me directly—a man I detest was fined three times for different offences, which I applauded heartily; the Federal officials conducted one of their biggest raids in years, and dumped almost 2000 quarts of good Sauk City beer into ye olde Wisconsin; my whispering campaign against the fool editor who mutilated my history script showed final results when he announced that he had lost heavily on it. Just as I went into battle against the Telephone Co. for a monophone, I am now going into the field against this man, and will not rest until he is forced out of business. I don't mind one or two insults from a man, nor even five or six, but such positively swinish conduct as his has been will always merit from me a punishment. Some time ago he called one of my friends a son-of-a-bitch and a bastard; the friend sued and collected a good sum. In April this man called me the same things; since then he has paid almost twenty times the sum he paid my friend in business lost through my undercover whispering campaign. He and his family are actually in straitened circumstances, but I am not one whit sorry for them, because his father has money, and the man is out here in this German town, admitting that he "Hates" Germans, yet desirous of making money off them, and at the same time trying to run the town, which no outsider can do. Thus he plays into my hands.

Your various corrections are noted, and for them many thanks. I was not aware of the Oklahoma Territory error; it was copied from a verbatim report taken by me from the lips of an old soldier who died last November.

Perhaps on the other hand, your company might cause me to hesitate a little and produce better things more consistently. Which would be good. But you should not abandon the Florida story; I look forward to it. I can well imagine how you would do such a story; don't disappoint me now. I, too, have just got two new plots worked up; one a ghost story; the other a horror tale about a thing in a warehouse—how definite!

Herewith the Tcho-Tcho story, The Statement of Eric Marsh; I don't like the story. Have you any suggestions for a better one? But then, the story is rotten, too. (Return to me)

as always,
August

[215]   [ANS][1]

[Postmarked Plymouth, Mass.,
24 August 1931]

Enjoying the oldest town in New England—what a place! You must get around here some day—I can tell from "People" that you have just the kind of a traditional sense to appreciate it.
Regards—
H P

Notes

1. Front: Site of the First or Common House in 1621, Plymouth, Mass.

[216]   [ALS]

Aug. 26, 1931

Dear A W:—
          Well—I didn't know that the anthological choice of "Erich Zann" was such a Derlethian triumph! Thanks & congratulations all in one— & here's hoping you get the 10 bucks . . . . though I haven't yet received the 25 due me. I don't envy you the job of typing out the whole tale—it's more

than I'd have done for myself or anybody else! But I am glad you chose Zann—which is one of my own favourites—instead of that damned "Outsider", which young J. Vernon Shea was pushing. I wouldn't be surprised if you landed 10 fish for the "Visitor" as well. That's a good yarn, though I'd have chosen "The Black Druid" or "The Space-Eaters."

I fancy you're right in making "People" separate, & of the two titles you have in mind I think the more concise one—"A Town is Built"—is distinctly preferable. It will surely be an impressive piece of work when completed, & I hope it may fare well professionally. One thing, though, occurred to me, that I forgot to mention. At the close of "Charlie Techmann" you have a presumably illiterate workwoman find a Napoleonic order among the effects of the dead eccentric, & *read it* before destroying it. Now how could this be when that order would almost certainly be written *in French**? It is difficult to think of a workwoman's knowing several languages unless French (perhaps left behind by the French-Canadian pioneers) was a common spoken language around Sac Prairie. How do you think you'll get around this?

I am certainly sorry to hear of the accumulated misfortunes of the past week, & hope that they represent a bunching of all the ills scheduled for the next few years, so that you may enjoy an immunity from such things from now onward! It is regrettable that your region should have lost as important a figure as Rose Meyer, but your incorporation of her history into "People" will at least give her a sincere & effective memorial. Too bad contemporary folkways don't permit you to get after that obnoxious editor by means of a real duel! However, I fancy that he will sooner or later find the town rather uncongenial & unprofitable if he continues his present policies. Someone ought to found a rival paper & take all his trade away!

No—small towns are certainly not lacking in events; & I fancy people are beginning to realise the fact rather widely, since such places seem to be chosen more & more for literary exploitation. They furnish an excellent setting— a sort of magnifying medium—for human tragedy; & often let primitive emotions stand out with especial clearness because of the absence of complicating artificialities.

Tough luck that *Ghost Stories* is to be suspended just as it obtained a civilised editor. Only the other day Klarkash-Ton was reporting the purchase of a new copy & remarking what he thought to be a slight trace of improvement. I certainly hope that some haven may be found, sooner or later, for "They Shall Rise."

"Eric Marsh" is great—do you mean to tell me seriously that that ass Wright rejected it? Good god! What in hades can he pretend to himself that his standard of judgment is? The tale has careless linguistic spots—the non-

---

*Or have you historic information to the contrary? ¶ Or would you wish to imply that Charlie had written the order himself in a grandiose moment toward the last?

existent word *onto* for upon, the use of *inconsiderate* where *inconsiderable* is meant, the use of *similar* (adj.) for *similarly* (adv.), &c., &c.—but in general is a really notable piece of work, with a genuine kick to it. As for a new title— how would "The City of Elder Evil" do? Or "The Lair of the Star-Spawn"? I'm not much for fancy titles, but I presume something on this order is what you're looking for. I shall undoubtedly use the Tcho-Tchos in some later story[1]—let Wright say what he pleases!

Had a great trip to Plymouth last Sunday—5½ hours for exploration, & found many quaint antiquities I had never unearthed before. A good deal of the once quaint waterfront has been turned into a park for the display of the justly celebrated Plymouth Rock, but the narrow, unpaved, sidewalkless, steep streets south of Burial Hill remain in about their 18th century condition. It used to be hard to get to Plymouth from Providence, but nowadays there are admirable 'bus excursions (only $1.75) every Sunday. I shall certainly go again.

Well—here's wishing you better luck for the days to come!

Yr most o^bt h^ble Servt

H P

Notes

1. HPL made brief reference to the Tcho-Tchos in "The Shadow out of Time" and "The Horror in the Museum" (by Hazel Heald).

[217]   [TLS, JHL]

31 August [1931]

Dear H. P.,

Your enthusiasm over Eric Marsh pleases me, but I cannot agree; I still think it's a lousy story. Maybe it was written too fast. I have adopted your title, The Lair of the Star-Spawn; many thanks. It's seldom that I'm at a loss, but my imagination is running down. Thanks too for the grammatical errors; the obvious result of great haste.

But thanks especially for jerking me up on the important point in Charlie Techmann re the note in French and the illiterate woman at the end; that must by all means be taken care of pronto.

I send you herewith the revision of The Thing That Walked on the Wind. I hope you like it. I have complicated it a little by having the reporting officer fall a victim also, hinting at a horrible pursuit by night, having the whole story, including the Norris report, appear in the statement of John Dalhousie, division chief. Re the one point you marked for extension I hesitated over; I lengthened it a little, preparing the ground a little more (beginning p 7 of this version), but I couldn't do this for long, since the nature of the report forbids it. Still, it is improved by this little addition. Bates now has this, the Lair of the Star Spawn, and an early story Red Hands (a time worn plot; stolen loot buried on an island, 3 crooks, 2 kill 1, he mentions the "red hands" guarding etc., 2nd crook kills third, and goes on; falls victim to peculiar plant life which falls upon him drawing his blood away leaving marks like gigantic red hands on his skin); Bates has held Red Hands unusually long, which surprises me.

A letter from the John Day (mentioning nothing of renumeration [*sic*] thus far, but a very nice letter), says that they are considering but have not yet finally decided on He Shall Come for the book. I personally do not think it will be taken. I did push Space-Eaters most, but they liked the Visitor of Long's better. I personally did not like Visitor because its best possibilities I felt were not brought out; somewhat the same fault was noticeable in the Black Druid, which I as well mentioned.

Yes, J. V. Shea wrote me; he seems a nice chap, and I wrote him a lengthy letter answering about 25 questions he had.

I recently wrote an hilarious short short called These Childless Marriages, satirizing our modern cult; it is all in telegrams. Eventually I'll send a duplicate to you. I have sent the thing to Vanity Fair; will send it next to the The Chicagoan, if V. F. rejects it.

Now I'm ready to start my new weird short, In the Junction Station.

as always,
August

[218]   [TLS, JHL]

31 August [1931]

Dear H. P.,

I knew there was something I had forgotten to write you in my previous letter of this date, and it was this: I wanted to ask you to push three of my stories— The Thing That Walked on the Wind, They Shall Rise in Great Numbers, and The House in the Magnolias—with Wright. Smith is doing the same; soon as he finishes with the House, I'll shoot it along to you. If you agree, shoot a letter along to him so that it is on his desk for him by 8 September, by which time my mss. will also reach him. Smith suggested that as the proof of a thesis advanced by him—that Wright is easily influenced by the judgments of others, and I'm perfectly willing.

Autumn has descended suddenly on Wisconsin. It despresses [*sic*] me a little—time flies so fast, I can get so little done. But the change from the one-tone colour scheme of summer to the brilliant colours of autumn is a welcome one. Yesterday I went on a long drive with a friend, and in the afternoon on a long hike, which was more to my liking. In many ways autumn is the prettiest time of the year; I notice this especially in its night odours. Still in the long run, it is evenly balanced by spring; the perfumes of the spring nights are more subtle, more vaguely suggestive; while those of autumn nights are more clearly defined, richer.

This year, largely because I grow more and more alert, notice more subtle things, I have seen more clearly than ever how vast the detail structure of the average small town life can be, how great is the attention given to detail. I think most small towners live in the past; I know I do, know I should not. I am escaping this a little, yet never shall entirely get away. I remember most of the early happiness of my childhood, recall especially anything (including living persons) who crossed my horizon at that time, regard those things now as links to the past, and am vaguely hurt when they are removed either by death or by some other means. It is a curious existence. Someday I will write a great novel about it.

as always,
August

[219]   [ALS]

Open fields near the River,
Unchanged since my childhood—
Sept[r] 2, 1931

Dear A W:—

The revised Wind-Walker is *great,* & I can't think of any structural improvements to suggest. All changes are in the right direction, & the whole thing is of just the proper tensity. I have just dropped a line to Wright (ostensibly to praise the new artist Doolin[1] who illustrated my "Strange High House", for log-rolling ought not to be *obvious*) in which this, They Shall Rise, & Magnolias are referred to as items which any well-regulated weird magazine ought to welcome. Incidentally, I have spoken my mind concerning his absurd objections to the general use of my synthetic mythology. Hope that between us Klarkash-Ton & I can land the items for you! Meanwhile I understand that Bates is getting more & more liberal . . . . having taken even CAS's "Door to Saturn."[2] I still insist that "Star Spawn" is a good story. You boys always run down some of your best things—here's Little Belknap vilifying a new sea-horror of his[3] which I swear is his best thing since the Black Druid! By the way, though—always be careful of your grammar. There are one or two debatable spots in the Wind Walker—especially this: "Robert Norris was one of the most thorough, the keenest men under my orders . . ." How would you parse that? Modern schools, I vow, don't teach the relationships of words as such things were taught when I was young! I'd have that read "Robert Norris was one of the most thorough, *one of* the keenest men under my orders . . ."

I certainly hope John Day will include "He Shall Come." If they took a tale of yours *on your own suggestion* would they give you the ten-buck suggesting-fee as well as the 25-buck regular remuneration? I wish to gawd they'd include Shiel's "House of Sounds"—the thing that (at my suggestion) Harré *almost* included in "Beware After Dark." I am really curious to know just what the volume will contain. Any standard stuff, do you suppose, in addition to recent & fairly recent magazine material?

And still your production factory grinds on! Ah, me the energy of youth! I shall welcome the sight of the new items, both weird & comic.

Bless me, what an arctic zone Wisconsin must be! Autumn colours as soon as *this?* We are still in full aestival green at this season in Rhode Island, & shan't have any really flaming woodlands for almost a month. All things are relative—we are arctic here compared to Charleston; but as compared to Vermont or Wisconsin, Providence is very temperate. Also, though, I may not be able to enjoy this temperateness unbrokenly; for that proposition to do a revision job in Brattleboro, Vermont, has come up again. I'd have relished the jaunt in July, but in September it's another matter. If I have to go, though, I'll make the most of the trip scenically—perhaps mapping a route through Western Massachusetts to include regions I have never seen. The job is to revise & proofread a book of about 500 pages—by a Dartmouth professor[4]—which the Stephen Daye Press of Brattleboro (managed by my friend Vrest Orton) is doing for the Dartmouth Univ. Press. It is the kind of a job I like—but I hope it can be arranged as a mail-order proposition. The nights get viciously cold in northern New England (& no doubt Wisconsin) at this time of year.

I may, though, welcome anything to take me away for a while—for the house is getting worse & worse upheaved by the installation of steam heat. I'm having to fight to get the radiator in a place where it won't knock my furniture arrangement all to hell—& even at best the upheaval & chaos will be damnable. I shall spend most of my time over at my other aunt's place during the worst of the bedlam—or even, perhaps, hire a quiet room somewhere for a fortnight or so.

What you say of the fascination of autumn is very true—& I have always felt it despite the menace of physical discomfort it brings. I love an abnormally hot October, when I can wander around through the prismatic landscape & imbibe the spell of the ancient harvest season without shivering. There is melancholy in it, but the accompanying beauty & sense of adventurous expectancy are so great as to make that quality forgivable. It is a season of almost weird retrospection, when one seizes on the unchanged objects & processes of nature—or of anciently ordered life—& half-imagines that the past which they typify is still present. The woods—the fields—the hillside orchards laden with fruit—the fields of sheavèd corn—the old stone walls overgrown with flaming vines—the barnyards heaped with brilliant pumpkins & other garnerings of the year—the acrid odour of smoke—the distant notes of horn & hound across the stubbled fields & dying meadows—all these things have a potent magic for one who has known the old days & the simple folkways of an immemorial culture not yet urbanised.

Like you, I tend to live more & more in the past—since Providence, though populous, has preserved a phenomenal number of rural & semi-rural oases which link it to its picturesque beginnings. It is really absurd to think of me as urban, despite the revelations of the census board concerning the density of the Prov. metropolitan zone. At this second I am sitting on an old New England stone wall under an ancient elm, with a squirrel chattering nearby & a lovely profusion of poison ivy (to which I am oddly immune despite a cuticular hypersentiveness in other directions) climbing among the mossy rocks. As far as my eye can reach (since a merciful line of tall elms cuts off the smart villas of Blackstone Boulevard) the archaic, unspoiled fields spread around—pasture land ahead & on my right, & a cornfield on my left across the road. It has been this way for 250 years—& may the gods keep it so (by virtue of ownership by large, conservative institutions) as many more! Behind me is the old gambrel-roofed Richard Brown house—erected 1750 & the second brick house (the very first is also standing in good shape down town) to be built within the corporate limits of Providence.[5] Yet I am only a mile from 10 Barnes St., & perhaps a mile & a half from the downtown skyscraper centre! And as I have said before, the Barnes St. neighbourhood on the crest of the ancient hill is itself a relique of village days, with a quiet atmosphere suggesting towns of 2000 or 3000 population.

I have never been able to live without the ancient woods & fields. My birthplace, though an urban house on a solidly built-up street, was just on the edge of the settled district—with a rural vacant lot next door, & the whole stretch of unchanged farming countryside (now all built up in streets) only a block away. Thus I have always been in close touch with the earliest phases of New England agrestic life—able to walk in a few minutes to fields & farmsteads 200 years old & still harbouring the typical dwellings & agricultural arrangements of the past. I say *always*, because a few such farms have managed to survive even to this day—one or two now entirely surrounded by city streets, though retaining everything unchanged—gardens, barns, byres, orchards, & livestock. The park system, moreover, has preserved a number of scenically lovely bluffs & mystically shadowy wooded ravines near the river—so that no place of traditional nature need remain unvisited by me. And sometimes, of course, I make for the still wilder country north of the towns. I represent the main-stream rural tradition of English life to an extent which the younger generation in large cities—Belknap, for example—cannot begin to understand. He has known at close range only paved streets & grey walls void of greenery—feebly relieved by the greyish, moth-eaten patches of alleged verdure in Central Park & along Riverside Drive. Poor little Sonny! He is so thoroughly cheated of the Aryan's normal rustic heritage that he doesn't even long for trees & flowers & meadows & orchards & old roofs embowered in vines!

All rural & architectural beauty have acquired for me a symbolic value, with bearings on my own personal past & on the vividly envisaged part of my family & race-stock. Certain collocations of scenic or architectural details have the most powerful imaginable effect on my emotions—evoking curious contributions of poignant images derived from reading, pictures, & experience. Old farmhouses & orchards move me about as profoundly as any one kind of thing I know—though general rural landscapes are also supremely potent. They give me a vague, elusive sense of half-remembering something of great & favourable significance—just as city spires & domes against a sunset, or the twinkling lights of a violet city twilight seen from neighbouring heights, always inspire a vaguely stimulating sense of adventurous expectancy. I hate to see the old things go. Just now my greatest loss has been the stable of my birthplace; for years in decay, though the house on its high terrace has been rehabilitated as a doctors' building. The old barn went down a month ago to make way for a modern dwelling, & it seemed as though half of my linkage with youth went with it—for it was my exclusive playhouse after financial decline wiped out our horses & carriages. My younger aunt felt desolate, too, for she had seen it built—it being newer than the house. Last month she recovered from the shattered walls the baking-powder tin with "historical data"—tintype, newspaper sheet, & "to whom it may concern" letter—which she had put in in 1881, for the benefit of future archaeologists. How melancholy—& how illustrative of the emptiness of human designs—that she should have to reclaim herself that which was intended for a remote posterity! Eheu, fugaces[6] . . . sic transit gloria mundi!

[—*Just at this second* a mournfully appropriate sound has floated across the fields in pensive timeliness. A sweet bell's notes—from the lich-gate of neighbouring Swan Point Cemetery, (where the last three generations of my family lie, & where I shall some day repose) tolling at the passing of a funeral cortege!]

I'll wager you will make a great novel out of your memories & feelings toward the past—though that's more than I shall ever do. The literary effect of old scenes on me is to make me wish to write old-fashioned pastorals in the 18th century mode that reflects my boyhood reading & predilections. For example—the other day, sitting on the ancient riverbank & looking into a splendid ravine, I simply could not refrain from reeling off stanzas within the atmosphere & imagery of that 1731 period which seems to much more real to me than the present. Here is the gist of what I did—

On An Unspoil'd Rural Prospect

How tranquil spread those sloping Meads
  That glow as Evening gilds the West,
And verdant from the River's Reeds
  Ascend to join the Beech-crown'd Crest!

Yon bosky Vale, where lily'd Streams
  Glide on to shadowy Glens unknown,
Seems drowsy with the ling'ring Dreams
  Of Ages happier than our own.

For here the Breeze with soften'd Strain
  Salutes a Scene of changeless Grace,
And Spring on Spring returns again,
  As to a lov'd, remember'd Place.

These Oaks and Elms seem echoing still
  To Pipes that bygone Shepherds play'd,
As, resting on this self-same Hill,
  They graceful scann'd the neighb'ring Shade.

Notes that cou'd please the Naiad Band,
  And charm the Dryads of the Wood,
Sound soft once more along the Land
  When Twilight looms on Solitude.

The winding Walls, that Vines enfold,
  The mossy Roofs beyond the Mere,
Shine antient, as the Sunset's Gold
  Recalls each long-departed Year.

Here the encumb'ring Weight of Age
  Its bitt'rest Force a while resigns,
For sylvan Spells reverse the Page,
  And bare the long-hid earlier Lines.

In aureate Floods o'er Grove and Field
  The vandal Æons sink from Sight,
Till Time and Change, dissolving, yield
  A Breath's Eternity of Light!

Well—this ought to suffice for one instalment of an old man's rambling. The golden light athwart this level field is exquisite—& the shadows of the elms are getting long. I think *very late afternoon* is the most mystical & glamourous part of all the day. I shall now start on a ramble designed to give a supreme sunset vista—with the marble State House dome & a Gothic church tower against the orange west.

Best wishes

H P

Notes

1. Joseph Doolin had also done covers for *WT* in 1925 and 1926.

2. CAS, "The Door to Saturn," *Strange Tales of Mystery and Terror* (January 1932).

3. "The Horror in the Hold," *WT* (February 1932).

4. Leon Burr Richardson, *History of Dartmouth College* (1932).

5. The Richard Brown house stands on the Butler Hospital grounds. It was actually erected in 1731.

6. The phrase is from Horace's *Odes* 2.14.1–2: *Eheu fugaces* . . . / *labuntur anni* ("Alas, the fleeting years slip by").

[220]   [ALS]

Another part of the same
River-Bank Countryside
—Sept[r] 5, 1931

Dear A W:—

Thanks! I had *not* seen that particular view of you before, & am highly grateful for it. You have no complaint to make to Old Lady Nature for the set of looks handed you! The rugged rock view is extremely impressive, & confirms my opinion of the scenic beauties of Wisconsin. I have duly mailed Belknap's card after completing the address—which is *230 West 97th St., N. Y. City*—& have given the little rascal a talking-to for not writing you. He has just finished a story (not yet titled) which *he* despises, but which *I* like.[1] It is about a couple of ships that sailed into another dimension & encountered the nameless marine denizens thereof. *They* feed on human brains, like the Space-Eaters. Those on the *second* ship escaped alive. It is better not to hint at what befel those on the *first* ship!

Damn Bates for his rejections! I know I'll never have a chance with him. Clayton, though, is the absolute limit. Babbittus Americanus Gigans! Well—anyhow—Wright is getting the proper psychological preparation for Wind-Walker & They Shall Rise in case they go his way. Shall enjoy seeing "The Junction Station."

Haven't had a second yet to read the new W.T., but it certainly *looks* vastly above the usual level. Doolin is a find—& I hope he doesn't peter out as Brosnatch & Rankin did. I was delighted with the sketch for my tale—which conclusively showed that Doolin had read the thing. Later on, though, he may tire of such heroic punishment as wading through the stuff—as the increasingly irrelevant Senf evidently did long ago!

I'm greatly interested in your revised relative estimate of my stuff—which agrees better with my own opinions than did your former classification, though being far from the scaling I would adopt. I haven't such a great love for the "Rats"—though I do think they best the damned rhetorical "Outsider"—& would probably put "The Colour Out of Space" first of all. Glad your opinion of "The Strange High House" has risen. I hadn't looked at it in five years, & was prepared to repudiate it along with my other pseudo-Dunsany hokum; but upon re-reading it the other day—with Doolin's view as an added attraction—I really came to the conclusion that it wasn't so damn bad as such things go. At any rate, I fancy it's the one solitary specimen of my Dunsanian ravings which has enough merit to warrant preservation.

Hope you have good Parisian luck with "People". Both that & "Evening in Spring" will be notable collectors' items some day, as marking the serious start of a substantial literary figure.

God damn the steamfitters (or the fate responsible for their presence) for making #10 uninhabitable! I simply *can't* work there while they are invading, & in the evening after they're gone I'm too goddam tired to type coherently. As a result, the typing of my present revision job is all held up, though the work itself is finished. Of course, I do everything but the typing in the ancient woods & fields.

Took a long, circuitous walk yesterday—including parts of Providence in which I had never set foot in all the 41 years of my existence. Saw two great wood-fringed ponds (on the city's southern rim, with dismal streets now pressing close) for the first time, & discovered two woodland dells (one a public park, & one the abandoned bend of a suburban highway whose modern tar-macadam course has cut off a corner) of the utmost glamour. Also climbed Neutaconkanut Hill (at the city's western edge) for the first time in five years—enjoying the magnificent dual view of town in the east & primal countryside on the west. May take another long walk today—it's only noon now. Best wishes—

Yr most obt h[ble] Servt

H P

Notes

1. FBL, "The Brain-Eaters," *WT* (June 1932).

[221]   [ALS]

The Old River Bank
—Septr 9, 1931

Dear A W:—

    "The House in the Magnolias" is splendid, & I don't regret the way I praised it to Wright before seeing it! In the course of reading I noticed the following points—which are of course trivial, but which Wright's characteristic pedantry might pick up.

    p. 7—you have the woman describe herself & family as *Haitian,* which conclusively implies nigger blood. *There are no pure white Haitians.* White persons living in Haiti are not citizens, & always refer to themselves in terms of their original nationalities—French, American, Spanish, or whatever they may be. The old French Creoles were wholly extirpated—murdered or exiled—at the beginning of the 19th century.

    p. 9—you have a *New-Yorker* notice the pronunciation of "Mr. Wheeler" as "Mistuh Wheeluh". This could not be, for almost everybody on the Atlantic & Gulf seaboard pronounces it *exactly like that.* The rolled "rrr . . . . ." is peculiar to the West & Middle West, or to districts whose original stock was Scotch-Irish rather than English. (N.H., Vt., Northern N.Y. State, parts of Penna., &c.) All over the East, as a rule, the "*r*" is silent (except as affecting the tone of the preceding vowel) in words like "car", "far", "water", "Mister", &c. &c. I pronounce "Mr. Wheeler" in such a way that it could be spelled "Mista Wheela" without affecting the accuracy of the sound-portrayal. So does Belknap—& Munn—& Quinn—& Whitehead—& everybody from Maine to East Texas. We would have to write "Mistirr Wheelirrr" in order to convey to our ears the ordinary mid-Western pronunciation. Thus what you take to be merely a *Southernism* is a general *Easternism*—this being also the usage in London & all the southern parts of England.

    p. 13—you speak of the face at the window as *pale,* & later as *dark.* This is the kind of trifle that gets Brother Farnsworth all stirred up! Better say *bloodless* instead of *pale.*

    pp. 20 et seq.—It seems to me that the narrator is not sufficiently affected, emotionally, by the realisation that zombis actually exist. One should react more violently to this stupendous disclosure of the violation of natural laws. Also, the conventional zombi-cure seems to be accepted a bit naively.

    p. 20—I have eliminated a typical Midwestern "already."

    p. 20—you have a Louisiana paper refer to a negress as "*Miss* Arabella Martin"—something utterly incredible. No Southerner ever applies the titles of courtesy—Mr. Mrs., or Miss—to any nigger—buck or wench, coal-black or high yellow. Old niggers are affectionately called "Uncle" & "Aunt", but not in news items. Just the name, & the specification "negro" or "coloured".

But that's about all. It's a darned good story—indeed, I think you are putting more of your seriously artistic side into your weird work than was formerly the case.

Which reminds me of young Shea, & your amusing exposé of his mis-quotation of the Old Gentleman. Bless my soul, what a boy! To say I didn't like "Wind Walker", when it's one of my favourites! So far as I can see, the child must have synthesized that verdict out of two casual statements of mine—first, that your weird work in W.T. does not represent your most serious vein; & second, that I do place M R James below Blackwood & Machen on account of his emotion-deadening *light touch* . . . *not* because of any *matter of fact realism*. I *value* prosy-sounding verisimilitude as a powerful fictional asset, & deplore only that semi-humourous *lightness* with which James (& Belknap as well) often impairs his best effects. So far, so good—but if your "Wind Walker" is in the light James tradition, then my "Whisperer" is a candidate for *College Humour!*[1] Good Gord—as if an objection to James covered the whole field of quasi-realistic weird work! But the child is young yet—& has plenty of time to harness that ebullient energy of his to better judgment. He is only about 0.6 dumb—look over the enclosed critical analysis of my work & draw your own conclusions. Quite a boy! How I wish I had a tenth of his sheer drive & exuberance!

As for Mencken—I thought I had said many a time that I think him a very sound critical influence; though of course admittedly insensitive in the domain of poetry, & perhaps not as valuable today as when the state of American "literature" absolutely demanded a drastic corrective. O gawd—those days of Harold McGrath, Anthony Hope, Winston Churchill, Charles Major, Meredith Nicholson, Stanley J. Weyman, Charles Felton Pidgin, & all the rest![2] Dear, dead old 1900!! Mencken, for lending heavy aid in cleaning up this mess of sticky insincerity, deserves unbounded credit. And if his manners are crude & at times slightly infantile, who shall blame him for such a foible? The sound sense & alert vigour of his mind, & the essential correctness of his philosophic position, remain above question. And who knows? He may be needed again as badly as he was in 1900–1910. After every age of good sense there comes a reaction in the direction of sentimentality & insincerity; & we have reason to believe that such lies ahead of us. A generation of neo-pietists & romantics, artificially blind to reality & to sensible proportions, is even now slightly in evidence—& but for wise restraint & ridicule, will soon be reviving all the absurdities of the loose-thinking past. Old Heimie still has work ahead—& I wish him luck on the major enterprise even if he does tend to clown a bit, & to bombinate in a void when legitimate targets are scarce! You can't take any one critic as a Lordalmighty of infallible authority—but in the sensible symposium of contemporary criticism H L is an ingredient who can't be left out. He, Lewis Mumford, Joseph Wood Krutch,[3] & others, all have indispensable functions to perform.

Yes—little J. Vernon surely does carry anti-clericalism to amusing extremes—but that's because he is only recently emancipated from supernatural delusions—& also because his father is a sort of nut on occult matters—theosophy, Rosicrucianism, & such truck. When his scepticism is mature, he will be indifferent to all the mythologies of the past—Nordic, Graeco-Roman, Christian, Hindoo, Buddhist, & all the rest—& willing to use any or all as aesthetic properties. I achieved indifference at a very early age—always finding something fishy in the supernatural pap of the Baptist Sunday Schools, & reacting from Christianity to Mohammedanism & Graeco-Roman paganism, respectively, as I read the Arabian Nights & Bulfinch's Age of Fable. Then when I struck natural science—chemistry, natural history, astronomy, biology, anthropology—I cast off the whole puerile mummery for good. I have had no belief in the supernatural since the age of 8, & have long ceased to resent such vestigial anthropological phenomena in others. I oppose religion only when it obstructs the natural intellectual & emotional expression of mankind, or interferes seriously with a rational social & political policy. I think the Bolsheviki in Russia are just as foolish in discouraging religion, as the Babbitts & sentimentalists in America are in encouraging it. Mythology is perfectly harmless except when mistaken for truth.

Doolin is certainly starting off well—I've have a mind to ask F W for the original of that "Strange High House" drawing. So he has been illustrating other magazines? I thought he was no novice. Now let's see how well he lasts.

Count on me to help in any way with your "Panelled Room" campaign. Log-rolling is quite effective until it is overdone. The same ones ought not to do the praising too often, or to praise things which are just like things they customarily condemn. Thus I had to hedge when Belknap asked me to land his latest Cuban story—rejected by Wright, & in my (& Talman's) opinion indisputably rotten. On the other hand, I'm stronger for Belknap's latest—"The Brain Eaters"—than he is himself, & will go the limit in recommending it to Wright. By the way—Robert E. Howard wishes the gang would speak a good word for his new story in Street & Smith's *Sport Stories*.[4] It is the first of a series, & the fate of the later ones depends largely on its public reception.

So you liked Grandpa's flight into the pastoral poetick past! Bless my old bones, but that's the sort of stuff I used to reel off by the yard in the good old days of complete invalid hermitage & archaistick dreaming. None of it was worth reading—just a melange of 18th century stock phrases—but it coöperated with my other forms of antiquarianism in supplying that thoroughly Georgian or Queen-Anne inner life which was essential to my imaginative contentment. I think I am probably the only living person to whom the ancient 18th century idiom is *actually* a prose & poetic mother-tongue . . . . . the naturally accepted norm, & the basic language of reality to which I instinctively revert despite all objectively learned tricks. To others, like Austin Dobson,[5] Georgianism is an elegant pose. To me, it is the natural, subconscious thing—other styles being the artificial acquisitions. How I used to grind it off—sententious philosophising & all!

> Yon sparking Streamlet, fed by swollen Springs,
> Leaps in the Sun, and o'er the Mountain sings;
> Thro' Meads below, the River flows along
> With greater Amplitude but less of Song,
> At length the Force of thankless Toil to feel,
> And strain incessant at the whirling Wheel.
> Thus with Mankind: the sweetest Days are first;
> From youthful Lips the Songs spontaneous burst.
> Maturer Years a graver Aspect give,
> And Men become more wretched as they live.[6]

And so on—& so on—that's the crap I was spouting when I was young Shea's age & long before. Here is a gem (part of an ode to the moon, personified as Diana) which I wrote when only eleven—

> Take heed, *Diana,* of my humble Plea;
>   Convey me where my Happiness shall last;
> Draw me against the Tide of Time's rough Sea,
>   And let my Spirit rest amid the Past.[7]

No amount of contemporary teaching could break my addiction to the 18th century—my sense of natural placement therein. At home all the main bookcases in library, parlours, dining-room, & elsewhere were full of standard Victorian junk, most of the brown-leather old-timers (except rare items like the Magnalia or the ancestral bibles & testaments) having been banished to a windowless third-story trunk-room which had sets of shelves. But what did I do? What, pray, but go with candles or kerosene lamp to that obscure & nighted aërial crypt—leaving the snug downstairs 19th century flat, & boring my way back through the decades into the late 17th, 18th & early 19th century by means of innumerable crumbling & long-s'd tomes of every size & nature—Spectator, Tatler, Guardian, Idler, Rambler, Dryden, Pope, Thomson, Young, Tickell, Cooke's Hesiod, Ovid by Various Hands, Francis's Horace & Phaedrus, &c. &c. &c.[8] . . . . golden treasures, & thank gawd I have 'em yet as the *main* items of my own modest collection. Easy enough getting them when family dividing came—for nobody else wanted 'em! Tempora mutantur, sed ego in illis non muto![9] And not alone literature, but dictionaries*, encyclopaedias, & rhetorical text books. Cyclopaedia of Arts & Sciences, compil'd by a Society of Gentlemen (1763), Blair's Rhetorick, Abner Alden's 1797 Reader—old days, old days! It is out of this last-named relique that I carefully

---

*including Johnson's—in an 1800 abridgment

learnt the basic rules of versification at the age of 6—before anybody tried to teach me any modern way. Thus the old Georgian manner is *really* my first, instinctive natural medium of expression. Parker's Aid to Composition (ultra-modern for me—actually as recent as 1844!) was another hereditary thing that I learned backwards & forwards, from cover to cover, before I was 12 years old. It was a great life—& all joined up with my foot & bicycle rambles in quest of ancient houses & archaic streets & centuried villages. The 19th & 20th centuries receded as a dream—& the old Colonial age became the reality. I habitually us'd the long s in writing—& my prose was just as Georgian as my verse. I used forms like *publick, accompt, intitule, shoar, cou'd, ingulph,* &c. &c. as a natural thing, & always elided the *e* of pasts & participles (drown'd, walk'd, &c.) except when I meant them to receive the full original pronunciation with the extra syllable. (drown-ed, walk-ed, &c)

> In Adam's Fall
> We *sinned* all   2 syllables

Thus the old New England Primer, of which we had—& have—3 different editions. Ah, me, but it was hard work climbing down 150 to 200 years to meet the objective external world. Hard work for an old man . . . . . . I think I once told you that I would actually feel more at home in a silver-button'd coat, velvet small-cloaths, three-corner'd hat, buckled shoes, Ramillies bob wig, Steenkirk cravat, & all that goes with such an outfit from sword to snuff-box, than in the plain modern garb that good sense bids me wear in this prosaick aera. Nor did I neglect the satirical spirit of the 18th century. I could shew you couplets written in my amateur journalistick period which attempt to burn up my enemies in the manner of MacFlecknoe, the Dunciad, & English Bards & Scotch Reviewers.[10] This phase lasted down into the Woodrow Wilson aera—that unctuous idealist's "too proud to fight" speech eliciting the following:

> *Horatius* at the Bridge intrepid stands,
> A Branch of Olive in his gentle Hands:
> Th' Etruscan Host draws nearer, as with PRIDE
> The manly Hero bows and steps aside![11]

Ah me! The past, the past! The informal & miscellaneous nature of my early reading made me familiar with many Georgian or Queen Anne works not commonly read today, even in collegiate literary courses—Darwin's "Botanick Garden", Garth's "Dispensary", Oldham's, Parnell's, Tickell's, Dyer's, Warton's, &c. poems, odd periodical essays like The World & The Bee, & such early American Things as Dwight's "Conquest of Canaan", Barlow's "Columbiad", & Trumbull's satires—"MacFingall", & "The Progress of Dulness."[12] God, Sir, but if any mortal has ever really *liv'd* in the 18th century, that bird is myself! And of course the tales of Gothick horror came with the rest—though they didn't give me the wallop Poe did. In general, I felt a sort of kinship with the 19th century down to 1849 or 1850—but then my interest & sense of affiliation went dead. The mid-Victorian world has always been as utterly alien to me as the world of Sumerian Babylon, Achaemenian Persia, or Klarkash-Tonic Commoriom. My nearest *objective* approach to the 18th century consists of an actual conversation with a person born therein. In 1896, when I was six years old, I was taken to visit in the Western Rhode Island region whence my maternal stock came; & there met an ancient gentlewoman—a Mrs. Wood, daughter to a rebel officer in the late unfortunate uprising against His Maj^{ty's} lawful authority—who was celebrating with proper pride her hundredth birthday. Mrs. Wood was born in the year 1796, & could walk & talk when Genl Washington breath'd his last. And now, in 1896, I was conversing with her—with one who had talked to people in periwigs & three-cornered hats, & had studied from schoolbooks with the long s! Young as I was, the idea gave me a tremendous feeling of cosmic victory over time—a sense that I was actually working my way back into that 18th century which had produced the Georgian doorways on the hill & the brown-leather books in the trunk room. This ancient matron— who, even then an old lady, had told stories of the past to my mother & aunts when they were small—was alive when my Abner Alden reader of 1797 was published! It is pleasing to relate that Mrs. Wood survived till about 1903 or 1904, thus actually living in *three* centuries. I did not, however, have a chance to speak with her except in 1896. Another link—at one remove—was supplied by my acquaintance with an old gentleman who, in his early boyhood, (he was born in 1831) had talked much with his own centenarian great-aunt, who remembered the terrors of the Ft. William Henry massacre of 1757, when Montcalm's Indian allies got out of control & worked such lethal slaughter. Old days .... old days .... so near & yet so far!![13]

Well, well, well, Child—how the Old Man rambles! But that's what this ancient river bank always does to me.

About A. Gordon Pym—for Lud's sake read it if you haven't! It is at once realistick & haunting ..... Tekeli-li! Tekeli-li! The thing which you probably mistook for it is the earlier prize story, "MS. Found in a Bottle", which also deals with the antarctic.[14] Poe thought often of the great white south—perhaps even at the moment of his death. Among his last delirious words was the repeated cry "Reynolds! Reynolds!"—& Reynolds is the name of the man who furnished him the antarctic lore from which Pym was evolved.

As to anthologies—Howard tells me that E. Hoffmann Price & W. K. Mashburn are planning an anthology which will include my "Pickman's Model"—though they haven't said anything to me about it.[15]

Weather is variable here as well as in Wisconsin. Yesterday was so cold that I had to seek refuge in the vacant flat of my younger aunt, (now in Maine. #10 still upheaved by steamfitters!) but today is a blazing bit of summer right after my own heart. Squirrels & chipmunks—especially the former—are numerous all over Providence; & it is interesting to see how the *grey* squirrel—almost driven out 30 years ago by his red cousin—has made a gradual comeback & regained his ancient dominance. Exotic birds are infrequent—but the other day I saw a curious woodpecker unlike any other in my recollection. I like dawn, too; but it hasn't quite the spell of sunset for me—& anyway, I seldom stay outdoors late enough to see it from an advantageous point.

Hope we get that warm weather—but by the way, the name "Indian Summer" applies only to a warm spell around St. Martin's day in early Novr. It is the American name for "St. Martin's Summer."

Best wishes—

Grandpa H P

Notes

1. *College Humor* had been founded in 1922 by J. C. Henneberger, the first owner of *WT*.

2. HPL refers to the popular novelists Harold MacGrath (1871–1932) [American], Anthony Hope (pseud. of Anthony Hope Hawkins, 1863–1933) [British], Winston Churchill (1871–1947) [American], Charles Major (1856–1913) [American], Meredith Nicholson (1866–1947) [American], Stanley J. Weyman (1855–1928) [British], and Charles Felton Pidgin (1844–1923) [American].

3. Lewis Mumford (1895–1990) and Joseph Wood Krutch (1893–1970) were leading social and cultural critics of the period. HPL was significantly influenced by Krutch's *The Modern Temper* (1929), an incisive account of human values in an age of science.

4. REH, "College Socks," *Sports Story Magazine* (25 September 1931).

5. Austin Dobson (1840–1921), British poet who harked back to eighteenth-century models in his poetry. He also wrote biographies of Hogarth, Steele, Goldsmith, and other eighteenth-century figures.

6. "Quinsnicket Park" (1913), ll. 19–28 (but somewhat altered here).

7. "Ode to Selena or Diana," *Poemata Minora, Volume II* (1902), ll. 13–16.

8. See LL 7, 9–10 (*Spectator*), 8 (*Tatler* and *Guardian*), 240 (*Idler*), 484 (*Rambler*), 267 (Dryden), 705 (Pope), 883 (Thomson), 421 (Cooke's Hesiod), 664 (Garth's Ovid), and 439–40 (Philip Francis's translation of Horace and Phaedrus).

9. "Times change; but I will not change with them." A deliberate alteration of the anonymous Latin axiom *Tempora mutantur, nos et mutamur in illis* ("Times change, and we change with them also").

10. HPL refers to three of the great poetic satires in English: John Dryden's *MacFlecknoe* (1682), Alexander Pope's *Dunciad* (1728/1742), and Lord Byron's *English Bards and Scotch Reviewers* (1809).

11. "Gems from *In a Minor Key*" (1915), ll. 9–12.

12. See LL 222 (Erasmus Darwin's *The Botanick Garden*), 343 (Garth's *The Dispensary*), and 192 (poetical works of John Trumbull). HPL did not own the other works cited here: the works of John Oldham (1653–1683; cf. HPL's poem "John Oldham: A Defence"), Thomas Parnell (1679–1718), Thomas Tickell (1685–1740), John Dyer

(1699–1757), Joseph Warton (1722–1800), the periodicals *The World* (1753–56) and Oliver Goldsmith's *The Bee* (1759), *The Conquest of Canaan* (1785) by Timothy Dwight (1752–1817), and *The Columbiad* (1807) by Joel Barlow (1754–1812; cf. *SL* 5.168).

13. HPL refers to Jonathan E. Hoag (1831–1927). Reminiscences of this sort find their way into the person of Zadok Allen in HPL's "The Shadow over Innsmouth."

14. "MS. Found in a Bottle" was a short story contest sponsored by the *Baltimore Sunday Visiter* (announced 12 October 1833).

15. The anthology never appeared.

[222]   [ALS]

Septr 18, 1931

Dear A W:—

Here is another dose (vide enc.) of our young friend Shea—a mature appraisal of my "Mountains of Madness", which lately reached him on its rounds. Draw your own conclusions. I won't let the child drive me exactly to desperation, since grey hairs breed perspective as regards youth. Ah, me—could I but capture some fraction of the sublime arrogance & self-confidence of 19! I hate to jolt a youth off of that all-too-transient pinnacle of subjective eminence—for how soon will it melt beneath his feet in the course of nature leaving him to face the greyness of the terrestrial scene as it is! While it lasts it often gives the aspirant a momentum toward achievement which long survives the pleasing mirage itself—so that I prefer to temper it gently with suggestions of broader perspectives, rather than annihilate it by means of contrasts as fatal as the splendours of Jove when display'd to the hapless Semele. Young Shea is a little cruder in taste than most equally educated boys of his years, tho' scarcely more so than I was at 19. He has led a very secluded life—almost as coddled as little Belknap—& has not had many chances to assimilate or correlate his ample but uneven reading. A few years—unless his abundant energies get switched in another direction—will work wonders with him. He enters the Univ. of Pittsburgh this month, & will probably derive a great deal from the intellectual discipline that lies ahead. Meanwhile he is as friendly & well-meaning a kid as one could wish to see—& with a highly inspiring degree of exuberance. I was quite amused & edified by his epistle to you—in which he has your future as an important minor writer all mapped out! Fortunately my grandpaternal years save me from a corresponding prophecy on his part—my future, as the ancient bull runs, being wholly behind me!

Yesterday I sent you under separate cover the tales you mentioned—though I am sure you must have seen most of them. Some are in the pseudo-Dunsanian vein to which I was once so violently addicted, while at least one—"From Beyond"—is so commonplace that I wonder how I ever came to write it . . . . . . or how Wright ever came to reject it! "In the Vault" is the one which Bre'r Farnie rather absurdly on the ground that it is too horrible for his wholesome family journal. As for "The Shunned House"—didn't I mention that all hope of that book is virtually gone? Cook's financial wreckage is complete, & the unbound edition has doubtless been lost in the shuffle. Cook, by the way, has secured a typographical job near Boston, & is now to be addressed at 17 Chambers St. (in the lee of old Beacon Hill) in that venerable town. He will probably get on his own feet again, but will hardly be in a position to undertake any extra ventures for a long time to come. The sheets I am sending form the completed book except for Belknap's introduction. You will note that the proofreading (five times performed by me) is absolutely perfect—at least, a professional proofreader once failed to find a single slip. When I regret all the work gone to waste, I think of Cook's own wasted labour in setting the thing up & printing it, & feel ruefully consoled on the principle that misery loves company! I couldn't very well send on "The Dream-Quest of Unknown Kadath" & "The Case of Charles Dexter Ward" because they are not typed—& you couldn't possibly decipher the scrawled & interlined MSS. Wandrei tried it with indifferent success during his fortnight here in 1927, & failed to become enthusiastic about either. Kadath is 110 pp. long, & Ward 150—which makes typing too vast a job for me to face. I don't think any editor would even look at Kadath—my last fling at Dunsanianism—while Ward is too full of antiquarian material (the big scene is in the Providence of 1771) to be acceptable in its present form. I do like the plot of Ward, though; & may tinker with the tale some day. Both were written in the winter of 1926–27.

Thanks exceedingly for the vivid portraiture of Rasputin, the Black Monk! Your vestments are surely coming in their exotic fashion, though a few sashes, medals, tiaras, mitres, or kindred decorations would help to land a certain brilliancy to the ensemble. I must some day get snapped in a three-cornered hat, periwig, & small-clothes—which reminds me that when young a friend & I did snap each other in false beards & other theatrical accessories.

Addresses requested:

Robert E. Howard, Lock Box 313, Cross Plains, Texas.
Wilfred B. Talman, 2215 Newkirk Ave., Brooklyn, N.Y.

Howard's story, "College Socks", is in *Sports Stories* for Septr. 25. I'll enclose it herewith, since despite my admiration for the author's vivid letters on Texas history & tradition I have no burning urge to retain this especial narrative. No further news of the Price-Mashburn anthology—but Belknap tells me he has seen a review of the Hammett affair in the N.Y. Tribune. Neither he nor I has received any cheque or notification, so we are wondering whether we were both left out at the last moment. You lose at least 10 bucks if we are thus ditched!

Bad news about *Amazing*—for once Macfadden gets hold of a thing, farewell to anything like an even semicivilised standard![1] Well—it was a fairly good magazine while it lasted! I wonder how the new editors will manage to debase "scientifiction" to the levels of the anencephalous sub-homonidae forming the Macfadden public?

As for M R James—I don't think his lightness has the real essence of the sardonic (as in Bierce), no matter what his intention may be. There is just enough suggestion of the blandly & jauntily whimsical to make me put him below Blackwood & Machen. But heaven knows some of his tales are so good in substance that they triumph over every handicap of style, & I would be the last to demote "Count Magnus" or "The Treasure of Abbot Thomas" from the list of supreme weird tales. So far as ghosts—specifically—are concerned, I doubt if anyone will care to challenge his supremacy.

About old Aitchell[2]—of course he has his weak & redundant spots, but I still find it hard to deny him substantial stature. I don't agree with the conventional platitude about not pulling anything down when you haven't anything to replace it—that is, in the world of ideas as distinguished from that of politics. It is often important to call attention to the hollowness of some absurd doctrine, standard, or practice, even when no immediate substitute is at hand—since if such attention is not called, the false idol will continue to be blindly worshipped, & search for a saner perspective never begun. Some gratitude is due the man who tells us that we need a better perspective—whether or not he has any to offer—for we'll never start an honest search until we realise the necessity. What is more, Mencken's iconoclasms are not always of such a sort as to call for any replacement. There are many silly superstitions which are simply better out of the way—our course of action in their absence being a self-evident one dictated by common reason. Perhaps some of the problems attacked by H L are not quite so simple—but enough of them are to make an impressive showing. All of which reminds me that I haven't followed the old boy very closely these last few years. His Mercury does get rather repetitious—but I still think it's a useful influence. At his worst, he can't be as absurd as the half-baked intellectual underworld he lampoons!

Yes—it'll take more than young Shea to shake Grandpa loose from the past! It wouldn't do that same kid any harm to get at least a moderate sense of chronological orientation himself—for surely no age or set of folkways is really significant or intelligible except in terms of the endless time-stream of which it forms a single momentary point. One does not need to be a confirmed antiquarian, or to delve backward for any specific number of years or centuries; but it is important to get one's own scene somehow correlated in the endless flux, & to understand that what is is merely the offspring of what was, & the parent of what will be. About the pastoral—I fear that most of our standard examples are sprung from Theocritus & Virgil rather than from the soil itself; though many contain, either consciously or otherwise, certain added elements of greater directness & originality. The first nature-poem founded on direct observation is Thomson's "Seasons"—a very authentic growth of the soil despite the undeniably pompous blank verse & air of Virgilian urbanity. I never tire of reading & re-reading this, especially in a rural setting. Pocket editions—two of which I have—used to be printed all over New England & adjacent territory; one of mine, with engravings by Richard Westall, being a New York imprint of 1819.

Speaking of the rural scene—I am highly grateful for the splendid coloured views of pastoral Wisconsin. It is surely a landscape to admire & revel in, & the Milwaukee Journal seems especially felicitous in catching its choicest aspects. I return the one you wish back—with the nice view of our fellow-litterateur Edgar A. Guest on the other side. It gave me an almost fatal shock to learn last month that Edgar & I share the same birthday—Aug. 20—though the Bard of the People preceded me into the world by several years.[3] Alas—now the day is quite ruined for me! I used to note with pride that it was the same as that of the statesman who cut his birthday cake in the White House even as I emitted my first melancholy wail—Benjamin Harrison, born Aug. 20, 1833, & in the curule chair on Aug. 20, 1890.

Thanks very much for the glimpse of the MSS. The satire[4] is very sprightly, & I trust it will land advantageously. All of the "fillers" are adequate so far as I can see—"The Man from the Islands" striking me most forcibly. I have not annotated these pieces—though I did change a "stomped" to "*stamped*" in "A Message for His Majesty."

Warm weather continued till 2 or 3 days ago, & it still is far from chilly. Open air writing periods continue—though the treat of autumn looms nigh. Sun crosses the equinox next Wednesday at 7:24 p.m. according to the Old Farmer's Almanack—which we have had in our family, I fancy, ever since its founding in 1793. (the surviving file dates brokenly from 1805 & continuously from 1836 to date) Foliage not yet touched by autumnal change—but it won't be long now. I only hope October has a hot spell—as in 1920 & 1928—so that I can enjoy the prismatic splendour of the dying woods under favourable conditions.

Best wishes—

Yr most ob^t h^{ble} Servt

H P

Notes

1. Teck Publishing Corp. took over *Amazing Stories* in October 1931. It does not appear that Bernarr Macfadden had anything to do with Teck, and *Amazing's* editor, T. O'Connor Sloane, was retained in his position.

2. I.e., H. L. Mencken.

3. Edgar A. Guest (1881–1959), British-born American poet whose work—widely syndicated in newspapers—became a byword for triteness and conventionality.
4. "These Childless Marriages."

[223]   [ALS]

The Old River Bank—
Sept[r] 24, 1931

Dear A W:—

Another reprieve from freezing! Mercury stood at 89° Tuesday, 75° yesterday, & can't be very low today. Hence my hibernation is somewhat delayed.

A thousand & one thanks for your generosity in typing "In the Vault"—a job I wouldn't have undertaken myself for any amount! Putnam's treated my MSS. barbarously, so that a good many items will be dropping out of circulation soon. Your alterations are all right, except that in certain places I like to use a semicolon, for the sake of neatness & balance, where others are apt to use a comma. "Old Father Death" was distinctly affected—shewing the difference between what I wrote in 1925 & what I would write now.[1] "Soul", however, is commonly used in rural New England in the sense of "person" .... 'good soul', 'a lazy soul', &c. &c. &c. No one here could possibly find any lack of fitness in the expression as used. The mythological connotation would not even be thought of. Wright rejected this in 1925 on the ground that it was "too horrible to print", & a year later the former W.T. owner J. C. Henneberger expressed a similar opinion. Bates rejected it several months ago, simply on the ground that it wasn't good enough for his uniformly submediocre periodical. I doubt if it would do much good to sent it again to Wright—I hate the cheapening involved in persistent peddling. But I'll think the matter over—& am meanwhile more grateful than I can say for your kindness in saving the tale from probable total annihilation. Now that its lease of life is extended, it may yet find a home some day. As for the others, "Iranon" is mawkish tripe, & I'm afraid Wandrei didn't serve the cause of art very well by preserving it a few years ago as you have just preserved "In the Vault". It is a typical product of my 1921 phase of Dunsanity, & I doubt if I would even wish to see it printed under my own signature. "Celephaïs" isn't quite so bad—but belongs to the same mood & period. Ditto "The Other Gods." I don't know about having The Other Gods seen—somehow that seems to me like coming too closely to grips with an ultimate horror. I don't believe it has many professional possibilities anyway. Regarding "From Beyond"—all your suggestions are good; but I don't know that there's enough in the damn thing to warrant salvaging. The same amount of effort would be spent more advantageously in a wholly new tale. The idea at the bottom of the thing was that of having strange, non-terrestrial sounds filter into a lonely attic—& it could surely find any number of better embodiments than the existing specimen. W.T. rejected "The Shunned House" most emphatically in 1925, & I doubt very much if its attitude would be changed today. I am not overly stuck on this thing myself, though for some reason or other it especially pleased one or two of the gang—notably W. Paul Cook & Samuel Loveman. Cook will be here next Saturday, & if I can tactfully manage it I shall ask him about the possibility of salvaging a dozen or two copies of the doomed edition for private binding & presentation to various friends.

Your "Silken Mask" sounds admirably promising, & I hope to see it soon. Klarkash-Ton has aroused my interest in Yoh-Vombis, & I hope to receive it soon from Wandrei.[2] Bates rejected Belknap's "Brain-Eaters" on the ground that it is 'too horrible & depressing'. Oh, violets & roses, but aren't we dainty & wholesome these day! Nothing gruesome or weird must intrude to spoil the sunny optimism of a clean & inspiring family paper!! It's a safe bet that nothing of mine will ever land with that damned ass. I've not read the first *Strange Tales* through, & can sense immediately that its atmosphere is antipodally alien to me. Conventionality, juvenile psychology, tameness, & crudeness form the keynote of virtually all the contents—& a palpable air of insincerity & artificiality hangs over the whole venture. As I get old & crabbed, this kind of thing wears more & more on my patience. If I tried to dicker with the editor of a thing like that, I'd develop homicidal tendencies inside of a month! The rejection of "The Brain Eaters" is one of the most incredible bits of stupidity I've ever seen.

What Belknap saw in the Tribune about "Creeps by Night" seems to have been both an advertisement & a paragraph of comment with extracts from Hammett's preface. Whether it could have been in advance of publication is more than I can say. Shea saw the thing also. Still no cheque or word from the John Day Co.—hence Belknap & I are beginning to think that we may indeed have been left out at the last moment. It interests me, by the way, to learn that the Harré flop has been reissued as a dollar book. Better luck this time!

Sorry the "Left Wing" came back, & hope "Wind Walker' will escape a like fate. Klarkash-Ton shares my extreme liking for this tale.

Little Shea will get a good deal of benefit from your advice & remarks if he takes them in the right spirit—as I rather think he will in the end. Young kids are often much better able to imbibe ideas from persons only slightly older than themselves—persons closer to their own stage in point of time, & moulded by the same set of chronological influences—than from members of the preceding generation. I imagine that "The Earth Taint" must be rather a sorry & immature concoction of popular fictional formulae, though with vivid passages here & there. Shea wants me to read it after you have thoroughly dissected it.

As for the "Rats"—my own opinion of it is midway betwixt yours & JV's. I'm not very fond of it; yet upon reading the reprint after a lapse of years, my opinion goes up instead of down as in the case of the "Outsider".

Much that you say in regard to Mencken is undoubtedly true—indeed, it scarcely occurred to me to judge him by the reiterated journalistic polemics of the *Mercury*. Those performances, I imagine, are simply commercial phenomena; his cloth-bound utterances being what represent his actual ideas. Still—it undeniably argues a certain lack of fineness of personality to be willing to indulge in such antics before the public.

I shall send you a copy of Thomson's "Seasons" with my compliments the moment I can find one among the local book marts. I honestly don't understand how it could be left out of any well-balanced college curriculum, for its place in the development of English literature is really a highly significant one. Artificial though its outward form undoubtedly is, its substance marks almost the earliest foreshadowing of the return to nature found in later 18th century literature—for it was written (in separate sections, "Autumn" being first) in the decade of the 1720's. Its popularity in the 18th & early 19th centuries was unbounded—& I can hardly comprehend its omission even today from a representative university course. Thomson was the chap who, as part of an oratorio, wrote the immortal lines now sung separately as "Rule, Britannia".[3] Apart from this & the "Seasons", his only celebrated work was "The Castle of Indolence", written in the Spenserian stanza. This also shewed a sort of *foreshadowing* tendency—an archaism to be more consistently followed by the Gothick romantics of the late 18th century, & finally by Scott & the pseudo-mediaevals of the 19th century. Another effusion of Thomson's was the tragedy of "Sophonisba"—a mawkish mess which all the critics, including Pope, ridiculed. One of the lines—"O Sophonisba, Sophonisba, O!" was popularly parodied as "O Jemmy Thomson, Jemmy Thomson, O!" Pope, by the way, revised "The Seasons", & is responsible for 12 lines of the now current version of "Autumn".

Six books for a morning's recreation! Bless my old bones! After which light prologue, I presume you settled down to do some really continuous reading! Ah, me—how unevenly are the world's energies distributed!

Well—best wishes, & thanks again for the embalming of "In the Vault".

Yr obt grandsire—

H P

P.S. Arthur Leeds has just lent me "The Shadowy Thing", by H B. Drake, which I am about to peruse.

Notes

1. See "In the Vault": "I believe his eye-for-an-eye fury could beat old Father Death himself" (*DH* 11).
2. CAS, "The Vaults of Yoh-Vombis," *WT* (May 1932).
3. The song appears in Thomas Augustine Arne's opera *Alfred* (1740).

[224]   [ALS]

9/30/31

Dear A W:—

Well, well! So Sonny Belknap & Grandpa H P *are* in "Creeps" after all! No word or cheque, however, from the John Day Co. I am sorry that none of your stories was included, but glad that Wandrei's "Red Brain" got in. I have heard of William Faulkner as an important new arrival in literature, & have thought of looking up some of his material.[1] With *five* of your choices adopted, I think Hammett ought to have set you down as a full-fledged co-editor—& most certainly you ought to get the fifty bucks due you according to schedule. I think the contributors ought to get at least one complimentary copy each, (the Harré-Macaulay outfit gave me *three*) though I believe this is not always the rule. I shall see about buying one if none comes gratuitously.

The bird at Putnam's with whom I corresponded was the book editor—by name Winfield Shiras. Hope you have better luck than Whitehead or I did—& don't submit anything unless you are willing to have your MSS. woefully manhandled. I feel like suing the damn company for the way they messed up the already badly worn pages I sent them!

I hope to see "The Satin Mask" & "The Telephone in the Library" in due season, & have high expectations regarding them. Glad the latest "Not at Night" will have a tale of yours—but did not know another was due so soon. How about the one which was to have my "Rats in the Walls" & something of Belknap's? They promised to send a copy, but none ever came—although I was paid for the story. Did you receive a copy? I think you were represented. Glad Wandrei's "Tree Man" was accepted by W.T., & hope your "Panelled Room" likewise lands. Wish you could get that temporary editorial job—you might help Brother Farnsworth develop some taste! Glad "Old Ladies" is accepted in an important quarter, & hope the magazine will survive long enough to print it.[2]

As for *Strange Tales*—I surely hope the later issues won't be like #1! Bates's preference for "The Awful Injustice"[3]—tame & trite in essence—does not argue well for really original work; though I dare say one or two things of merit (yours among them I hope) will manage to creep in by accident now & then. The worst sign so far is the rejection of Belknap's "Brain Eaters"—indicating as it does a state of mind unfavourable to everything genuine in the field of the macabre. I have a strong presentiment that nothing of mine will ever adorn any magazine in which either Bates or Clayton is connected.

About "In the Vault"—well, since you went to all the bother of typing, it would be churlish in me not to accede to your wish for its re-submission to Wright; so here it goes! It will probably come back—although as you say, Wright was rather more afraid of really weird stiff in 1925 than he probably is now. You shall certainly be among the first to receive a permanent copy of

"The Shunned House" if I manage to salvage any copies. W. Paul Cook was here last Saturday & Sunday—looking so miraculously recovered from his 1930 breakdown that I hadn't the heart to remind him of anything connected with his fallen fortunes. I expect to see him again in Boston next Saturday.

I thought Little Shea's "Earth Taint" would be pretty bad—& shall not complain if he decides not to send it to me! Your advice will certainly do him good, even though it may jolt his ego a bit at first—for in many ways he seems eminently reasonable & teachable. He needs to have his whole perspective rectified—to realise better just where he stands. Has he sent you his "Brother & Sister" yet? Its style is after your own in "People" . . . . a long way after. Its chief merit is a rudimentary breaking away from his ordinarily flamboyant & redundant diction.

Tried unsuccessfully to get Thomson's "Seasons" down town—but hope for better luck in Boston next Saturday. If I can't pick up a copy, I'll lend you my duplicate—for this is something you really ought to read. James Thomson was born in 1700 & died in 1748. He was the subject of a biography in Dr. Johnson's "Lives of the Poets", & certainly deserves his always prominent place in English literature. Another rustic poem you ought to read is Robert Bloomfield's "Farmer's Boy" (1800)—of which I have an edition printed in New York in 1803.

Hope your walk proved pleasant. You have a greater variety of birds, evidently, than we commonly have in southern R.I. Probably the widespread urbanisation of the region has driven many away. In Florida I noticed great numbers of birds—especially of the wading variety—that I never saw before in my life. I am not a good ornithologist, & cannot identify many species— but your mysterious specimen sounds very interesting. I took a ramble with Cook last Sunday, but it is now too cold for me to do much outdoor reading & writing. The leaves, however, have not yet turned. New steam heat is now working at #10—& seems quite adequate so far. From now till May I shall be more or less a prisoner indoors!

With best wishes—

Yr most ob^t h^ble Servt

H P

Notes

1. Faulkner's "A Rose for Emily" was included in *Creeps by Night*. See further letters 234f.

2. "Old Ladies" also was rewritten and incorporated into *Evening in Spring* in the section "Take Arms!"

3. S. B. H. Hurst, "The Awful Injustice," *Strange Tales of Mystery and Terror* (September 1931).

[225]   [ANS][1]

[Postmarked Boston, Mass.,
5 October 1931]

Here is a typical example of New England scenery in the region W. Paul Cook & I have been traversing today. ¶ Having a great time. Went to Boston Saturday, met Cook, & was taken by him on a motor ride south of Boston, where the scenery is exquisitely unspoiled & all the villages are still quaint & idyllic. We stopped at Hingham & saw the Old Ship Church (1681)—the oldest continuously used house of worship in the U.S. ¶ Today—Sunday—we went up to Haverhill to see the sterling old-time amateur C. W. Smith, (pub. of *Tryout*) & afterward went to Amesbury & Newburyport. A glorious day— in fact, both days have been warm & magnificent. Foliage is more turned in the Boston region than in Rhode Island. Newburyport is probably the quaintest city I have ever seen. Even the main business section remains as it was around 1820. ¶ Hope you've received the copy of Thomson's "Seasons" mailed from Boston yesterday. It was harder to get than I had expected & I must apologise for the tattered nature of the copy. Trust you'll enjoy it. Regards—H P

Am following your work with interest. W. P. Cook

Notes

1. Front: The Newburyport Turnpike, Newbury, Mass.

[226]   [ALS]

Octr 9, 1931

Dear A W:—

Well, Son, Grandpa will hand it to you for once! Wright *has* accepted "In the Vault" for 55 bucks—& it is wholly to you that I owe this unexpected prospective influx. Thanks several dozen times! You are a public benefactor of the first magnitude! As for writing commercial tales—I simply haven't the knack. We can't all be high-pressure producers like you & Klarkash-Ton. What I write in the fictional line has to conform to certain realistic & proportioning impulses of my own, else it loses all its motive power. The employment of unctuous & insincere popular devices wrecks the whole creative mood & makes composition impossible—or at least, as difficult as pushing a freight car single-handed. Besides which, the products of such a process would have a laboured woodenness precluding sale. Of all businesses, I think the writing of commercial fiction would be most repulsive to me—involving as it does a parody or debasement of the genuine processes of expression whereby one obtains imaginative gratification. But of course, I am always glad when an honestly-conceived tale of mine happens to find a market.

Glad to hear news of "Creeps"—though nothing has so far come my way. I shall purchase a copy if no free one comes within a reasonable time. You surely ought to get more than a single ten spot, even though others may have anticipated you on one or two suggestions. It is virtually certain that "Erich Zann", "Visitor from Egypt', & "Red Brain" are primarily your suggestions, & only a very reprehensible kind of sharp practice could deprive you of the promised rewards.

Good luck with Putnam's—though I place no more high hopes with that firm. Your selections for a possible anthology sound good to me—though I'd hesitate in preferring Klarkash-Ton's "Halman Carnby" to "Satampra Zeiros" or "City of the Singing Flame." Also—Whitehead's best are unquestionably "Passing of a God" & "Black Beast." Of Suter, I prefer "Beyond the Door" to "The Guard of Honour"—& I wouldn't leave Humphreys' "Floor Above" out.[1] Well—in any case I wish you luck.

I'll wait a while before buying the Rat-containing Not at night—for it seems to me they did send me a belated copy once. Moreover, they very definitely promised me a copy of the present anthology this spring. Same with Belknap—who has received none so far.

I've purchased the new W.T., but have had no chance to read it as yet. Senf's improvement is notable—though I always realised he *could* draw if he only *would*. However—he hasn't the imagination Rankin had. Rankin could cross the borderline into pure phantasy to an extent his competitors seem unable to duplicate.

Your suggestions for little Shea's "Brother & Sister" strike me as splendid—indeed, I can almost picture the subtilised tale as part of "People"! Of course the theme is unpleasant according to usual standards—but as you point out, such standards are now greatly relaxed in the interest of realistic life-portrayal. You will be a great help in the kid's literary development—for I feel sure his superabundant energy can lead to something if intelligently harnessed. He quoted some of your "Earth Taint" remarks, with most of which I can unqualifiedly agree.

By this time you doubtless have the copy of Thomson's "Seasons" which I found in Boston. Sorry about the tattered copy, but I am told that the book is harder to get than it used to be—probably owing to a general buying-up of editions around 1926, when the 200th anniversary of the poem's publication was quite generally observed. You may not, of course, care for the thing—but no harm will be done if you don't. As I said before, it is undeniably pompous & formal in its exterior—but upon analysis it displays an observation & comprehension of nature quite new to literature in its day.

You also, no doubt, have my card telling of the scenic jaunts of Cook & myself north & south of Boston. No sooner had I returned from the Boston zone than I found a telegram summoning me to Hartford for a personal conference connected with the book-revising job (for Vrest Orton's Stephen Daye Press of Brattleboro, Vt.) which I have mentioned to you as looming ahead. This took me through another delectable countryside—which, despite its relative proximity to my own doorstep, I had never before visited in all my long years of existence. On my return trip I chose an indirect route for variety's sake—passing through Norwich & Plainfield. Here I found the autumnal scenery still more magnificent—with bold hills & valleys, & some fairly breath-taking panoramas. Hartford is not especially distinctive, but Norwich (where I paused to explore antiquities) is exceedingly quaint—built on the steep terrains that rise from a bend in the river Thames. The turning of the leaves is more manifest each day, & parts of my 'bus ride were gorgeous beyond description. As for the job—it will keep me dead to the world for a week or more, & may possibly necessitate a brief trip to Brattleboro. I am to edit & proofread the text of a long history of Dartmouth College by a professor therein. Pay is only 50 bucks & expenses, but it may prove the opening wedge for a good deal of work from the Stephen Daye—especially if they continue to handle the printing for the Dartmouth University Press.

You will be sorry to hear that Whitehead is somewhat worse. The scar tissues from the ulcers have obstructed the outlet of his stomach, & he will have to undergo an operation in about 3 weeks. He also has an ear tumour. He has just changed his address to Box 414, Dunedin Isles, Dunedin, Fla.—a bit north of old 1859. ¶ Best wishes—& thanks again about "In the Vault".

Yr obt Grandsire—

H P

Notes

1. J. Paul Suter, "The Guard of Honor," *WT* (July–August 1923).

[227]   [TLS, JHL]

Sauk City, Wisconsin   12 October, 1931

Dear H. P.,

Well, I *am* glad that In the Vault landed, and feel amply repaid for my retyping. You see, it's just as if I took a copy for myself, since W. T. will have it.

But—poor deluded grandpa! Lordhelpus, I wasn't suggesting that you conform to commercial standards. I should have made myself clearer. What I meant was that with your style, you could bring commercial magazines around without any damage to your weird ideals. And you could. Do a story of a lurking horror from the coral reef or island, do it in the manner of The Rats in the Walls, and you will land with Bates at 2¢ a word. Ah, how I wish I could be there. You could make four times as much with your writing than by revision work.

Re Creeps: I finally got $20.00, which is something. As routine, I shall protest, mildly, for a letter this morning informs that a second volume will definitely be published in the fall of 1932, to which I also hope to contribute. Keep this under your hat, please.

Thanks for the comments on the projected anthology, which will probably not materialize; still I might as well try. I have already put The Floor Above into the list. Beyond the Door having already seen publication in book form was left out in favour of The Guard of Honour, which may also be eliminated in time. The Whitehead selections are tentative; I liked The Shadows very much personally. I may oust Hill Drums and put in The Black Beast. The whole thing is very tentative. I shall probably use only one of my tales, unless I decided at the last moment to shoot in The Telephone in the Library, for which I have a high regard.

I enclose herewith my two latest, The Satin Mask, and the Telephone in the Library. Please give these your close attention; I like the latter very much, but am chary of the former. [Send 'em on to Shea!] Seems to me that I haven't done the Satin Mask very well. Can you make any suggestions for the betterment of either? They will be appreciated. I am not preparing to do the rewrite of The Lost Path, am outlining a new tale, The Wind from the River. These, and those above, plus The Panelled Room, The Sheraton Mirror, The Return of Miss Sarah, The Shuttered House, In the Pool and The Rector Sits Alone would make a nice book of my best shorts.

Many thanks for The Seasons, and no apologies for a worn copy, please. The book is a fine old copy, and it is an easy matter to have it rebound. I've had no time to read it, as yet, but will be getting around to it fairly soon. I'm on a detective and mystery story spree, and Lord, how I'm going it. Reading virtually night and day.

[Conclusion non-extant.]

[228]   [ALS]

Friday the 23d [23 October 1931]

Dear A W:—

Hard work keeping within the 14-day limit amidst the turmoil of that book job, but here goes! I owe 18 other letters—including a small verse-revision job—but anyhow, I have disposed of the main item. Don't know yet whether I'll have to go to Brattleboro. With autumn advancing, I'd hardly make the trip for pleasure!

Thanks for the glimpse of the new tales, which I forwarding to young Shea as per request. The "Telephone" is certainly a fine piece of work, & I can't think of any especial way to improve it.* All I did to the MS. was to change a *him* to a *he* on p. 16 where the grammar called for it. ("Yes—it must have been *he*") "The Satin Mask", as you remark, does seem to have a need of a little tightening up; though it is an excellent tale & has a magnificent central idea. I don't know just what is needed most—but do you suppose the style is a little too matter-of-fact & conversational? Ought the subject matter to have a tenser & more menacing atmosphere, & ought the characters to react more complexly & affrightedly to the hints of incredible events? As for details—could you describe the mask more concretely—whether it was just yellow silk or whether it had some sort of depicted face? Also—is it not rather melodramatic to have the thing hanging up in a sealed chamber? Why not let it be packed away in a storeroom, & why not have Monica take more time in finding it? Also—why not let *one* wearing alone occur? The motivation of the return & second wearing seems a trifle strained. There is room for some acute terror in this story—especially when the mask is found. It can assume hideous expressions—on the order of James's "face of crumpled linen."[1] The air of ineffable menace can be intensified throughout the story, & can rise to a hideous extreme at the last. It is doubtful, I think, whether a weird tale gains much from the careful restraint & blandly smooth style which can help out a more realistic narrative. If you wanted to make an entirely different story—a real horror-story in every sense—you could have Aunt Monica become a sort of intangible semi-vampire & haunt the house. Then it would be all right to keep your sealed room. The letters could be discovered *by accident*—Aunt Monica's name being an unmentioned one in the family. But of course this is only a suggestion. The tale is really very good as it is, & if it lands in this form you won't have to worry any more about it.

"Creeps" & the 25 duly came at last—though I have as yet had no time to read the former. Shea got $10.00 for suggesting "Beyond the Door". Your 20, I imagine, are for "Erich" & "Egypt"—& I hope your protest will bring more. They wrote about that new volume & asked for suggestions—which latter I may or may not try to make.[2] Anyhow, I'll wait till you're through suggesting, so that I shan't cut into your territory. I shall urge "The House of Sounds" even though it has been in book form; since it is virtually unobtainable, & has never been seen by the present generation. What tales of yours would you like boosted? I'll recommend the ones you yourself name, so as to back you up & create a larger favourable vote.

As for commercial fiction on my part—I'm no good at accomodating myself to external demands. That is an attribute of cleverer souls than I.

---

*One may overlook the coincidence of having the telephone service broken at exactly the season to forward the climax of the tale.

I have to write what's in me at the time, or not at all. Every time I've written even slightly to order, the result has been a lamentable mess. Besides—the moment I try to write with external demands in mind, the process loses all its savour & becomes as ineffably repulsive as revision. I'd like to get hold of some other source of revenue—such as the light revision & proofreading job I've just finished—& never feel obliged to send a story to an editor again. The only thing that will ever start me writing again with the vigour of 1920 will be a complete emancipation from even the shadow of surveillance—an absolute freedom to set down anything I like, irrespective of any prevailing standard or any opinion save my own. I think it would be better if I never tried to exhibit stories till I have a fair number of them fully written. But at any rate, commercial fiction as a source of steady revenue is definitely ruled out for me. It is one of those things for which, like salesmanship, I have a conspicuous lack of natural qualifications.

Haven't had time to read much of the Nov. W.T., but agree with you in weeping over "Subterranea." And yet—what a splendid *synopsis for a story* that is . . . . if only someone would write the story! Wright surely is a provoking cuss—& I don't feel any kindlier toward him since learning that he pays Seabury Quinn for *reprints* (which he isn't legally compelled to do) without extending a similar mark of regard to Grandpa! He obviously exercises favouritism toward those (like Quinn & Kline) from whom he has reason to expect much catchily popular material. Well—it'll be a long while before he gets anything more from #10 Barnes!

Too bad young Grayson has been delaying "The Early Years"—but he freely confesses to a lack of orderliness. I haven't heard from the young scamp since I was in New York last July—but fortunately he has none of my property in his custody.

Sorry I missed the article with your data in *Time*.[3] I used to see T. regularly when one of my aunts took it; but since the lapse of subscription due to economy I have had only occasional glimpses.

Today, to add to my troubles, the steamfitting mess has been reopened on a small scale. The system as installed heats so unevenly that a new boiler & cellar piping are to be tried out. Well—thank gawd, it at least doesn't mean any more furniture moving in this room! Weather of late has been visually fine, but not warm enough for my taste. Haven't been out of the house for a week, but may try a short expedition today—just a last look at the woodlands before the trees lose their fevered autumnal glory.

Best wishes—

H P

Notes

1. This is the climactic scene in M. R. James's "'Oh, Whistle, and I'll Come to You,

My Lad,'" in *Ghost-Stories of an Antiquary.*

2. The John Day Co. was planning a second anthology of weird tales, for publication in 1932, but it never materialized.

3. HPL probably refers to the unsigned article "Modest Attempt," *Time* 18, No. 15 (12 October 1931): 49–50, about the *Midland.*

[229]   [TLS, JHL]

26 October [1931]

Dear H. P.,

Glad you liked the stories, especially the Telephone. I agree with you anent The Satin Mask; it doesn't seem meaty enough. Yes, I too think the coincidence of the telephone service being broken is easily overlooked. The prejudice against coincidence is hardly valid anymore, saving of course such as are outrageously implausible. Coincidence is so great a part of a busy person's life, that I never even thought of the broken telephone service as a coincidence.

Re Creeps by Night. The $10.00 that went to Shea should have gone to me, as should $20.00 more. I know definitely that Shea suggested Beyond the Door after I did, could prove it to John Day by a letter from him, and furthermore they set up the story out of my magazine sent them at their request. No, my $20.00 they said renumerates [*sic*] for Erich and Red Brain. But, of course, I don't mind. They might easily have made an error or two at the office. As to the second volume, I shall add my voice to yours in urging The House of Sounds. As to my own tales—Hammett himself liked He Shall Come, and from the copy I sent them and which they returned this morning, I see that the story was originally scheduled for about page 43 of the book, was cut out only at the last moment. So you might suggest that tale to them. But I wish I could tear down their prejudice against unprinted tales, for I think The Panelled Room or The Telephone in the Library might go well in a collection like that.

I send herewith some things from Shea, which he suggested I send on to you. I have just received Smith's latest tale, will shoot it out to Don tomorrow or day after.

Bates finally accepted The Thing That Walked on the Wind; the $100.00 check was most welcome, I can assure you. At the same time Wright rejected The Lair of the Star Spawn, They Shall Rise, and In the Junction Station, accepted Laughter in the Night, a short. He seems determined to keep me doing short things for him. ... Re paying for reprints: on the contrary, if author sells only "First North American Serial Rights", editor is legally compelled to pay for reprint rights unless author specifically releases him from such payment. If author sells all rights, editor can reprint as often as he wants to, can even sell the story and make ten times what the author did. ... Wright liked The Lair of the Star-Spawn but it "didn't click" for some reason. I'll shoot it back to him, retyped or something. He'll take it in the end. Put in a word for it, please, if you should happen to write him, but don't write just for that.

The weather up here has been simply grand—only one very light & uneven frost; nothing more. The country is simply brilliant, and as you may imagine, I am doing very little writing. I have learned a good deal of mushrooms etc in the last week or so, am returning to tutoring this week as a slight income. I am starting The Rector Sits Alone, revising The Tree Near the Window.

as always,
August

[230]   [ALS]

Friday [30 October 1931]

Dear A W:—

    Yes—coincidences do often occur in real life, but they seldom form the pivotal point of major occurrences. Telephone breakdowns are by no means common, & to have one occur just as a highly unusual phenomenon is taking place is at least enough to attract attention. But as I said, this case is by no means obtrusive. If you did want to iron it out you could have the ghost exert a sort of paralysing influence on the service, so that it would later be reported that all calls failed inexplicably for a period around the time of the phenomena. However, such a change would doubtless necessitate much reconstruction, & might subtract considerably from the verisimilitude of the tale—so I fancy it's all right to leave it as it is. Is is assuredly an extremely vivid & "convincing" piece of work.

    Too bad the "Creeps" awards were so carelessly made. I'd have said, on a guess, that others would have been much more likely to select "The Red Brain" (which was notably popular in W.T.) than the "Visitor". In writing the John Day I shall name "He Shall Come", "Panelled Room", & "Telephone in Library." I shall also name Whitehead's "Passing of a God", "Black Beast", & "Cassius" (if the latter's complete form warrants it), Belknap's "Black Druid", & possibly others. I am omitting those you want for your contemplated anthology.

    I have now read the current "Creeps", & am forced to admit myself a trifle disappointed. There is too much mechanical cleverness & too little of the really weird in the sense that Blackwood & Machen achieve it. The majority of the tales are simply more or less gruesome *contes cruels*, with artificial jack-in-the-box endings which I could predict far in advance in a great number of cases. I think you liked the Faulkner story best, but to me it seems artificial.

All but the last touch (the *grey* hair on the pillow) is predictable *in essence* from the very moment the *smell* is mentioned, & even this last touch is merely dark realism rather than imaginative liberation. Of all the contents, Ewers' "Spider" gave me the greatest sense of the weird despite an early predictability. Benet's "King of the Cats" is absurdly trivial, & has no place in a book of this sort. It is as silly as the allegedly comic efforts of Poe. Seabrook & Frisbie likewise present poor stuff—& "Green Thoughts" is inane & ridiculous. Second to "The Spider" I'd put our old friend "Beyond the Door"—& "The Kill" is splendid despite early predictability. "Ten o'Clock" is a good *conte cruel*, though I had a very early idea of what was in that basket. "Mr. Arcularis" has real power—especially the *destination* of the hero's shipboard wanderings—though here again I knew very soon what the whole thing was going to amount to. On the whole, I don't care nearly so much for this collection as Harré's—though perhaps it will command a wider market. Unfortunately Hammett has been guided too much by his own precept that "atmosphere may be used to set the stage, but is seldom a great help thereafter & in fact more often an encumbrance than not."[1]

I duly note the material from little Jehvish-Êi. He was quite excited by that Pittsburgh exhibition—especially since he chanced to be among those interviewed & photographed. For my part, I think the winning picture has a good deal of subjective power despite a technique more modern than I relish. Shall be glad to see Klarkash-Ton's new tale when young Melmoth shoots it along.

Glad Wind-Walker has landed definitely at last—but damn Wright for his rejections! About my reprints—no, they have so far been only of early tales submitted without any reservation of rights. The noble Farnsworth once told me how magnanimous he was to allow me to get Selwyn & Blount returns on "Red Hook" when as a matter of fact I had not retained any legal hold on it. But possibly astute Sequin[2] did reserve his rights from the first—being an attorney, he naturally would have his eyes open for such points. I shall certainly urge the acceptance of "Star-Spawn" the next time I have occasion to drop a line to Farny. The current issue, as you have remarked, is very mediocre. "Satampra" is good, & Talman's little sketch has a certain effectiveness. Howard's "Black Stone" gave me a kick despite the awkward management of the pseudo-erudition, & "Subterranea" is an excellent *synopsis* for a story—if only somebody would write the story! I am told the new *Strange Tales* is out, & must look up a copy soon to see what the completed "Cassius" is like.[3] No news from Dunedin, though H S must be having his operation by this time.

Glad you've had good weather—though frost as early as this sound rather shivery to a Rhodinsularian. I've been tied indoors by that damned book job* till lately, & even now I've had too much imperative writing to let me get far from my desk. I did, though, take advantage of a warm day Wednesday, & went out to my old river-bank with my work. The autumn colours are still bright, though a heavy rain yesterday didn't do them any good. I am scheduled to visit W. Paul Cook in Boston tomorrow, Sunday, & Monday, & hope the weather will be clement. November . . . . ugh! We may possibly visit a wild & picturesque region north of the city—the Middlesex Falls Reservation, which (like R.I.'s Quinsnicket region) has been preserved in its natural woodland state—& we may take in the antiquities of "Kingsport" & "Arkham" (Marblehead & Salem) or we might conceivably dart up to Portsmouth, N.H., which I haven't seen since 1927.

 Good luck with your new tales—
Yr obt grandsire
H P

Notes

1. HPL refers to Hanns Heinz Ewers, "The Spider"; Stephen Vincent Benét, "The King of the Cats"; W. B. Seabrook, "The Witch's Vengeance"; Robert Dean Frisbie, "The Ghost of Alexander Perks, A.B."; John Collier, "Green Thoughts"; Paul Suter, "Beyond the Door"; Peter Fleming, "The Kill"; Philip MacDonald, "Ten o'Clock"; and Conrad Aiken, "Mr. Arcularis." HPL quotes from Hammett's introduction (p. [10]).

2. I.e., Seabury Quinn.

3. Henry S. Whitehead, "Cassius," *Strange Tales of Mystery and Terror* (November 1931); in *SNM*. Based on entry 133 from HPL's *CB*: "Man has miniature shapeless Siamese twin—exhib. in circus—twin surgically detached—disappears—does hideous things with malign life of his own." See also letter 190.

[231] [ANS][1]

[Postmarked Boston, Mass.,
1 November 1931]

Wandering about ancient & picturesque New England towns—Portsmouth & Newburyport. You ought to do this region!
Regards—HP

W. Paul Cook

Notes

1. Front: Abram Wendell Doorway, Portsmouth, N.H.

*which pleased the Stephen Daye Press so well that they promise to give me the revision of all their books. Let's see how well they live up to that promise.

[232]   [ANS][1]

[Postmarked Salem, Mass.,
2 November 1931]

History with about 200 years' start on Sauk City!
Now for Marblehead.
Yr obt grandfather
    H P

Notes

1. Front: Dwellings of Settlers of 1630 Reproduced / Wigwams and Dwellings at
Pioneers' Village, Forest River Park, Salem, Mass.

[233]   [TLS, JHL]

2 November [1931]

Dear H. P.,

I enclose herewith Don's latest tale,[1] of which, to be frank, I don't think much.
As Smith pointed out, the idea of atomic shrinking is a good one, but the rest
of the story is the usual pseudoscience claptrap. I am drawing farther and farther away from the scientific tale, and all those I do regard highly are primarily weird tales, rather than scientific tales. This is undoubtedly due to my
tremendous reading and its wide variety, which is putting the weird tale and
its bastard growth, the scientific tale, in a place more in perspective.

My preference for A Rose for Emily (which I now have also in Faulkner's
These 13, his new book), is easily understandable when I say that it is because
of 1) his striking style; 2) his environment and general atmosphere used in the
tale. This hinges, I believe, on the fundamental difference in our respective
preferences. The weird tale can, I believe, be divided into two rough classes—
those hinting of cosmic evil and horror—and those only vaguely suggesting
something beyond, something beyond the surface, the appearance, and range all the
way from vague fright to utmost horror. You prefer the former group, to which
we would according to this grouping, parcel such tales as The Yellow Sign, your
Cthulhu et al[.] tales, the White People, etc; I prefer the latter group, in which
fall Mary E. Wilkins-Freeman's tales, your own Rats in the Walls, Strange High
House, my Panelled Room, etc., The Monkey's Paw, The Yellow Wall Paper.
And so on. The vast majority of the first-raters belong in this latter class.

By the way, before I forget it, Lady Cynthia Asquith has just brought out
WHEN CHURCHYARDS YAWN, a new anthology of new ghost and weird
stories, by Walpole, Maugham, Onions, Chesterton, and the usual group, ex-
cepting only, I think, M. R. James. I have it on order, will let you know how it

is as soon as I get it. It is not yet printed in the U. S.

Returning to Creeps By Night—while I agree in the main with what you say, I do not agree with all of it. Ewers' Spider will not bear a second reading, I think. I had read it somewhere before this, did not react so favourably to it this time. I don't agree that Green Thoughts (save for the title) is inane and ridiculous. The ending is bad, but the telling is whimsical enough to entertain.

As to The Telephone in the Library—I'm not going to touch it. Shea liked The Satin Mask better; while you and I thought it too vague, lacking substance, he thought it excellent because of that.

By the way—in suggesting tales to John Day, don't omit anything I have specified I might use; after all, my primary interest is in seeking a good anthology, no matter who does it.

[Conclusion non-extant.]

Notes

1. "Raiders of the Universes."

[234] [ALS]

Novr 6, 1931

Dear A W:—

Wandrei story duly received & passed on to its creator. I am forced to agree that it does not escape very far from the conventional Edmond Hamilton mould, either in setting or in action & motivation; but can at least commend it as original in some respects—such as the metallic nature of the invaders, the atomic shrinkage mentioned by Klarkash-Ton, &c. The science is rather poor—especially the illogical assumption that a mind-reading entity (necessarily dealing with abstract images, & knowing *no* terrestrial language) could be baffled by thinking in Greek. Also, the different gravity on the synthetic planet, as affecting the hero, is not allowed for. I don't think the conventional "scientifiction" tale has any artistic possibilities, although I *do* think that tremendously effective yarns could be woven around intrusions from *outside* if handled with the proper development & emotional stresses—dispensing with the glib, machine-made conventional style, & the cheap stereotyped perspective. These tales would, of course, be *weird* in basic nature—with nothing of the brisk, matter-of-fact atmosphere which treats incredible mechanisms with the utmost casualness.

As for "Creeps"—I'm far from denying the Faulkner yarn a high place as a realistic story. It is a fine piece of work—but it is *not weird.* This sort of gruesomeness does *not* suggest anything beyond ordinary physical life & commonplace nature. Necrophily is horrible enough—but only *physically* so, like other repellent abnormalities. It excites loathing—but does not call up anything beyond Nature. We are horrified at Emily as at a cannibal—or as at some practitioner of nameless Sabbat-rites—but we do not feel the stark terror that is suggested by some blasphemous glimpse or monstrous doubt hinting at subversions of basic natural law. There is no chill-breeding sapping at the very foundations of things. Your classification doesn't quite work—for "The Monkey's Paw", "The Panelled Room", & most of the Freeman tales *do* suggest subversions of natural law. Choice in such matters is largely a matter of personal taste—except that such Grand-Guignol shudders as Faulkner's or Level's ought to seek their deservedly ample laurels in their own class—the *conte cruel*—rather than in the domain of the truly weird. About "The Spider"—I had read something like it before, & could foresee the ending from a very early period; (say p. 158 or 159) but it gave me the biggest kick of the book, just the same. Next—in order—I'd put "Beyond the Door", "The Kill", & "Mr. Arcularis". I take back nothing about "Green Thoughts". It is utterly punk—in fact, anything that is *whimsical* is basically tawdry, insincere, & the very opposite of the authentically weird. Incidentally, how can such a self-consciously wide reader as yourself find the *title* any more inane than the rest of the thing? It has the same cheap cleverness as the rest—coming, as you doubtless know, from Andrew Marvell's famous lines in his "Thoughts in a Garden"—

> "Annihilating all that's made
>   To a green thought in a green shade."[1]

"Perchance to Dream" was a very good story—not really weird, but first rate as a *conte cruel*.[2] The best touch was not the machine-made shiver, but the suggestion of *what* the boy might have become if the mad father's dosing had continued. In general, "Creeps" is all right of its kind, but I vastly prefer the Harré anthology.

I'll be glad to hear your report on "When Churchyard's Yawn". These anthologies come thick & fast, & some of them are excellent. I intend to get "The Omnibus of Crime" (whose second half you described to me) now that it is issued for a dollar.[3] All right—I won't exempt your anthology choices in writing John Day. About "Cassius"—it is hard for me to give an unbiassed judgment, since the development is so antithetical to that which I had in mind when offering the central idea. To me it seems that a vast number of atmospheric & other horror-possibilities have been left unrealised, & that the typically bland, urbane, & almost unctuous style (the stereotyped Kipling tradition) wrecks the sort of hideous tensity really needed. Yet on the other hand I can see where Whitehead has used a fertile cleverness in incident-devising that I could never have approached. The chief scientific objection is, of course, the part played by "hereditary memory"—a thing wholly repudiated by responsible biologists, though still favoured by weird writers. I'd call "Cassius" a typical anthology item—for "sophisticated" professionals love that unctuous urbanity which to me is so markedly unsatisfying. I shall certainly suggest "Cassius" to John Day, though placing it below "Passing of a God" & "Black Beast." I haven't read "Guatemozin"[4]—for I gave my S.T. to W. Paul Cook before I had a chance to read it through. He can't seem to find it on sale in Boston, though it's readily obtainable enough in Providence.

Good luck with your recent fiction—& don't let Bates wholly ruin your "Magnolias." Such cold-blooded mutilation is enough to drive anybody out of the hack fictional field.

About "Arkham" & "Kingsport"—bless my soul! but I thought I'd told you all about them years ago![5] They are typical but imaginary places—like the river "Miskatonic", whose name is simply a jumble of Algonquin roots. Vaguely, "Arkham" corresponds to Salem (though Salem has no college), while "Kingsport" corresponds to Marblehead. Similarly, there is no "Dunwich"—the place being a vague echo of the decadent Massachusetts countryside around Springfield—say Wilbraham, Monson, & Hampden. It would be impossible to make any real place the scene of such bizarre happenings as those which beset my hypothetical towns. At the same time, I take pains to make these places wholly & realistically characteristic of genuine New England seaports—always being authentic concerning architecture, atmosphere, dialect, manners & customs, &c. As for that rocky promontory—the coast north of Boston *is* composed of high rocky cliffs, which in several places rise to considerable altitudes as bold headlands. Of course, though, there is nothing as dizzy as the fabled seat of the Strange High House. If I had any promontory specifically in mind when writing that tale, it was the headland near Gloucester called "Mother Ann"—though that has no such relation to the city as my mysterious cliff has to "Kingsport". Marblehead has rocky cliffs—though of no great height—along the neck to the south of the ancient town.

As you may see from recent cards, (I enclose another of "Kingsport") I have just made my farewell 1931 round of my favourite coastal antiquities—Portsmouth, Newburyport, Salem, & Marblehead. Cook accompanied me to the first two places, but the last two I took in alone. They are very little changed from year to year—though in Salem a whole slum district near the railway station (with ancient gambrel-roofed houses, one of which was a lodging-place of the painter Copley)[6] has just been torn down. Also—the quaint back streets & byways of Marblehead have just been *macadamised*. O tempora! O mores! The weather is getting pretty bitter & overcoatish now, & I fancy my time of close hibernation is just beginning. May heaven speed the spring! Best wishes—

Yr obt Servt

H P

Notes

1. Andrew Marvell (1621–1678), "The Garden" (1681), ll. 47–48.

2. Michael Joyce, "Perchance to Dream."

3. Dorothy L. Sayers, ed., *The Omnibus of Crime*.

4. Arthur J. Burks, "Guatemozin the Visitant," *Strange Tales of Mystery and Terror* (November 1931).

5. HPL first pointed this out in September 1927 (see letter 57).

6. John Singleton Copley (1738–1815), the greatest early American portraitist.

[235]   [TLS, JHL]

9 November [1931]

Dear H. P., Yes, but the point is, that a "weird Tale" does not necessarily need to suggest something from OUTSIDE, or even supernatural. It needs to suggest only something unknown, a mystery so designed that a natural explanation fails to fit it. Re the Faulkner story, for instance—I must confess, that though I am steeped in abnormal sex, having studied all kinds of perverts at first hand, the suspicion of necrophilia in A Rose for Emily never once entered my mind. The human mind is so complex that three or four other solutions immediately suggested themselves. Here is a woman starved for something—what is it, love perhaps? Let us assume it is. But she knows nothing about it. Love to her means a possession, a having. What she had come to regard as hers seems to be too independent. She kills. Thus, she keeps, she possesses, she loves. Necrophilia may or may not enter into this relation; it's a minor point to me, since my own experience with people in this existence has led me to look on such things as part and parcel of life, though I am still conservative enough to be horrified by them, deeply. Yet I would be the first to jump to the defense of a necrophiliac, a homosexual, etc., largely because I know that so often these poor creatures are incapable of helping themselves, have had their nerve systems tortured and twisted permanently from birth. But I am digressing inexcusably. It is not necessary to, as you say, "feel the stark terror that is suggested by some blasphemous glimpse .. hinting at subversions of natural law." What I am trying to make clear here is that you are biased in favour of the outre, the outsideness of evil, etc. May I try to clarify my stand somewhat, by quoting you the same figure or example I recently quoted to Shea: Let us take two stories, The Whisperer in Darkness and A Telephone in the Library. (At the outset you and I agree that The Whisperer is vastly to be preferred to The Telephone.) Given two readers. A is an average intellectual man, has read widely, in many fields, and much; B is also an average intellectual man, has read widely, but prefers the weird, has read almost everything he can get hold of in the field. These two readers take up the two stories; what will their verdicts be as to the better of the two. A will say The Telephone is better—is closer to reality as he understands it, The Whisperer is for him too far-fetched; B will say The Whisperer is better, the other he will say is too common-place. Both will be right. Now in this discussion I am taking the position of A, while you are distinctly in that of B. B has had so much weird in his diet, that only a very shuddery chilling thing will rouse his jaded appetite—if I may use such a poor hackneyed figure. (Don't take me to mean that your appetite is jaded!) The difference I wanted to suggest was not subversions of natural law; I did not intend to classify weird tales as those which did suggest subversions and those which did not; at the outset, I would say in this regard, that all the best weird tales suggested such subversions. My line was drawn between stories of cosmic horror which were farther from reality than those close to reality where the terror was not so obviously cosmic, where merely a ghost might enter instead of stupendous beings. It is the difference between The Whisperer and The Telephone. I maintain that it is essentially easier to convince the reader of a horror in the Vermont hills where few of them have ever been, than to convince him that a ghost has walked into your commonplace little library and strangled somebody, or to make someone believe that a god of evil lives on Rigel than to make the same person believe that this fellow has taken up residence in your back yard.

The reason I thought the title Green Thoughts as a title inane, was because I did not realize its source. As for the story, your objections to it are primarily Okeh, and I must perforce agree with them; yet I stick to what I originally said of the story. It is to me a distinct relief after reading so many trashy tales in W. T. about monstrous plants which ate people and which just miss the heroine for supper. For the same reason I like tremendously Oscar Wilde's hilariously funny Canterville Ghost.

The point about When Churchyards Yawn is that all the tales are new, haven't even seen magazine printing before, and all by masters of writing. I order such a book posthaste without any further notice. The 2nd Omnibus of Crime hasn't been published here yet; but in England it is out. Colin de la Mare's anthology The Walk Again has just been printed here; it sells at $2.50. I am finding out what it contains. No fear that Bates will succeed in mutilating Magnolias; I'll keep up the general tone nevertheless, though some of the atmosphere in the beginning will unfortunately have to go. Yesterday I did a new short after 14 days of depression; not weird, but unusual, The Hunt.

Many thanks for the various postcards of old Massachusetts, and for the information about Arkham etc. Really, I had completely deceived myself. That is very amusing, and you can readily feel flattered, for your descriptions are so real that even Mark who has been in many of the real towns recognized the thorough Massachusetts atmosphere. Yes, I think Mark had the Mother Ann headland in mind also when he wrote with me In the Left Wing, or the hook there, isn't that the same thing?

The weather here is positively splendid. Yesterday and today I spent outside in shirtsleeves, rolled up, too. A damp springish wind is blowing, much to my delight, and I have Henry Williamson's early books—Lone Swallows and The Peregrine's Saga—to read.[1] His nature books are exquisite; Mark has just done a paper on him. He was home for the first time this weekend, and we went quickly through Magnolias for a final (I hope) revision.

The new W. T. is execrable. The Haunted Chair pleased me most; so you can see how bad I thought it. The January, however, looks good, with Smith and Long in it, and Smith's story in part burlesquing the scientific tale. Wright writes of my own as a tale of elementals but for the life of me I can't remember the elementals.

as always,

August

Notes

1. Henry Williamson (1895–1977), prolific British author of novels about the natural world and social history.

[236]   [ALS]

Novr. 14, 1931

Dear A W:—

There is, of course, a vast similarity between the merely gruesome or terrestrially mysterious tale & the true weird article; but I think the line, hazy though it is, can be drawn a trifle more definitely than you are disposed to draw it. You admit to the weird category any story suggesting something which no existing natural explanation fits. I would narrow the class to tales of something which no natural explanation fits, & *which it is very probable that no natural explanation can fit*. It is this predominant *unlikelihood* of a natural explanation which makes a really weird tale; for certainly, the essence of weirdness is its implication of the violation of natural law. By this text, Faulkner's story *is not weird*, although it is an exceedingly fine & adroit specimen of its realistically gruesome kind. As for its exact interpretation—I fancy a letter to the author would reveal more than any amount of conjecture. In using the term "necrophilia" I had no precise idea of any literal process in mind, for I am no abnormal psychologist, amateur or professional. Probably Emily was fonder of her betrayer alive than dead—but the point is that (being, as you suggest, starved for affection & of keen possessive tendencies) she violated ordinary repugnances in prolonging the symbolism of affection under ghoulish & hideous conditions. And that is all the story suggests—a disordered mind, & a violation of ordinary repugnances. There is no indication of any suspension or doubt of any natural law. Not by any stretch of the definition could this be called a *weird tale*.

There is some confusion in your exposition of the two kinds of weird tale, because it is evident that you actually do admit the need of having natural law violated or called in question in order to produce a genuine specimen of either sort. The distinction between the two kinds is merely one of method, setting, & degree; the basic element being identical for both. Without the hint of sub-verted natural law, there is no weirdness. Choice between the two types is largely a matter of personal preference—the partisans of each being able to conceive in rather supercilious terms the mind which relishes & creates the other. Probably each form has as many aesthetic potentialities as the other, & there are times when the same person may vary his preference according to mood. Both are necessarily minor manifestations of literature, though genuine in a limited way because they furnish an authentic emotional catharsis for many distinct types of people. It is hardly relevant to say that some persons can become sophisticated beyond the emotional reach of the weird. We know that—& likewise that in this generation many can become sophisticated beyond the emotional reach of human tragedy. As for the two kinds of weird story—it is certainly a substantial artistic feat to bring the unreal into the midst of the every-day; & only an illiberal critic, whatever his personal predilections, could judge any atmospherically effective performance of this feat tame or common-place. For example—I have never heard any dissenting word as to the greatness of Henry James's "Turn of the Screw". But it is equally illiberal—or, what is worse, irrelevant & futile—for any critic to attack the intensely or exotically weird tale as a type. This tale furnishes as valuable a catharsis & escape as the other, & in a direction sufficiently different to cause no conflict or overlapping. The function & raison d'etre are often totally different, being in many cases at-tempts at crystallising certain natural sentiments connected with distant or rarely observed scenes or phenomena. That is, they are not so much attempts to drag weird emotions by the heels into every-day situations which do not or-dinarily suggest them, as they are to dramatise, substantialise, or symbolise cer-tain definitely existing perspectives which naturally evoke vague emotions of a mystical sort. The important factor *is* the remoteness & uncommonness rather than the weird emotion—so that the author of such things, if compelled to vary his theme, would prefer to write something non-weird about the remote object or perspective rather than find another setting & theme for his weirdness. To use a personal example—my object in writing "The Whisperer" was not just to be weird, but primarily to crystallise a powerful imaginative impression given me by a certain landscape. Likewise, "At the Mountains of Madness" is simply an endeavour to get on paper the emotions evoked by the conception of the dead, remote, antarctic waste. And a *really good* interplanetary story would be no more than an effort to crystallise the burning & provocative curiosity which the unplumbed existence of the outer void inevitably inflames in any really sensitive imagination. As yet, though, no first-rate tale of outer space has been written. To deny that these powerful & characteristic emotions regarding remote vistas exist, is quite absurd. Naturally—as with tragedy, or the weird as a whole—certain individuals may become jaded & sophisticated beyond such sensitiveness; but this does not necessarily invalidate the emotions where they do exist. The one trouble with the 'remote & intense' weird tale is the difficulty of making it really fulfil its function. A 'local & mild' weird tale, when it is inadequate, seems merely flat & tame; but a 'remote & intense' weird tale under such conditions becomes extravagant & ridiculous. However—the value of an art form is not to be gauged by so arbitrary a measure as that of difficulty or facility of achievement. Incidentally, you rather miss the point of many complaints against the common ghost tale. One does not object because it has an every-day setting, or because the abnormal element is not a titanic & overpowering monster of Tsathogguan horror. One objects merely because the indicated abnormality *is not sufficiently original to produce the delicate effect of slightly subverted natural law intended.* When conventional images & methods are too closely followed, they convey no emotion whatsoever; since the reader is so familiar with all the little twists & turns as part of hackneyed folklore & previous reading, *that they do not represent subjectively visualisable happenings,* but are merely cold repetitions of well-known stock wooden images, clearly & boresomely recognisable as such. This, of course, is equally true of the purely conventional 'remote & intense' tale—like Edmond Hamilton's—& is the subject of just as much complaint here as in the 'local & mild' class. A *ghost story* cannot at this date depend simply upon the appearance of a ghost—per se—for its emotional effect. Ghosts, as such, are so wholly stock symbols that they cannot escape utter flatness & unconvincingness unless buttressed by implications, conditions, & atmospheric preparation of the most strikingly *original* & expert sort. M. R. James fulfils the conditions very well, & succeeds quite often. So does Algernon Blackwood. So do you, in a great number of your tales. But more don't than do—as any issue of the current weird magazines & almost any anthology will prove—hence a certain amount of reiterated complaint is inevitable. Actually, almost all legitimate objections against either kind of weird tale must be levelled *at its unskilful examples rather than at the type itself.* To use a personal example again—I am so dissatisfied with any product of mine that I have almost decided to write nothing further. In no case have I come near conveying the mood or image I wish to convey; & when one has not done this at 41 there is not much use in wasting time on further attempts. I am now making certain "laboratory experiments" in handling various images & conceptions—writing up the same plot idea in a wide diversity of ways—& upon the result of this test, as judged by myself alone, will depend my ultimate course in the matter.[1] Of course—in any event I might later concoct crude verbal recreations for my own mild amusement. By "further writing" I mean serious attempts to attain a certain aesthetic standard, or the preparation of material for publication.

Concerning the de la Mare anthology—here are a couple of Sideshows referring to it, (only copies—please return) in which I am incidentally mentioned.[2] I hardly fancied that B K H would print a postcard which merely disclaimed knowledge in the desired field—but anything makes copy. I hope to see the book eventually, as well as the other anthologies under discussion. B K H agrees with you in liking comic "weird" tales, but I must say that I can't see anything in them. A really subtle & mordant satire on clumsy weird writing—such as a sly burlesque of Cthulhu—would be intensely clever & interesting; but most of the existing comic "weird" stuff is merely Victorian-spirited slop. Junk like Brander Matthews' "Rival Ghosts" or Frank R. Stockton's "Transferred Ghost" put me to sleep—& I can't say much different for Middleton's "Ghost Ship." "The Canterville Ghost" had traces of a real wit which gave it considerable value as comedy—indeed, one does not regard such a thing as belonging to the province of the weird at all.

Since you are striking some successful bargains with Bates, you might be interested in the enclosed snapshot of him, which Whitehead has just sent me. You might return it, since I believe other correspondents of mine would like to get a look at their new potential market. Good old H S, by the way, has had an up-grade physical turn; so that his physician once more thinks he can escape an operation. I surely hope he can get on his feet again without surgery.

I have not had time to read the new W.T. yet, but many correspondents concur with you in calling it the dullest in a long while. Not that it is ever a very notable galaxy of achievement, taken as a whole!

Glad your collaborator found my Massachusetts atmosphere convincing. The plot I am now experimenting on concerns another fictitious Mass. town—"Innsmouth"—which is vaguely suggested by the ancient & almost dead city of Newburyport. Of course, there is no sinister, un-human shadow over poor old Newburyport—but then, there never was a festival of worms at Marblehead (Kingsport)![3]

We have had some Indian summer here, too, thank heaven. Yesterday & Tuesday were so warm that I took my work out to my favourite river-bank—revelling in a mystical autumn landscape with brown earth & almost denuded boughs. All the north seems to have been favoured this fall—in contrast to which, subnormal temperatures are prevailing in the south. I must look up some things of Henry Williamson's. Are they anything like the good old "Natural History of Selborne"?[4] That has always delighted my rustic 18th century soul.

I enjoyed the de Sitter lecture on The Size of The Universe[5]—which contained one or two points I had not absorbed elsewhere. It seemed odd to be watching one of the greatest living minds on the planet—for de Sitter is all of that.

With best wishes—

Yr obt h^ble Servt

H P

Notes

1. HPL refers to the writing of "The Shadow over Innsmouth." See *The Shadow over*

Innsmouth (West Warwick, RI: Necronomicon Press, 1994) about the origins and composition of the story.

2. B. K. Hart, "The Sideshow," *Providence Journal* 103, No. 269 (10 November 1931): 14; 103, No. 272 (13 November 1931): 14. A postcard by HPL is quoted in the second article.

3. As in "The Festival."

4. By Gilbert White.

5. The physicist Willem de Sitter (1872–1934) lectured in Providence on 9 November. HPL mentioned him by name in "The Whisperer in Darkness."

[237]   [TLS, JHL]

17 November [1931]   Sauk City, Wisconsin

Dear H. P.,

Many thanks for the view of Bates, which I return to you herewith. He is rather a handsome brute, and younger than I suspected he was. I placed him at about 35, since I could tell from his letters that he was young. Speaking of snapshots reminds me that Shea was quite pleased with the view of me in Yvonne which I think you sent him some time ago, writing that he had no idea I was so good looking, which amused me very much because if there's one thing I've an inferiority on, its [*sic*] my personal appearance, which reminds me always of a football player. How inadequately some of us are clothed, eh?

The Sideshow columns were valuable to me insofar as they decided me against buying de la Mare's anthology. I did not know what was in the book, whether new or old tales; all the tales here mentioned I already have in some form or other, mostly in anthologies and in original volumes such as Blackwood and James and de la Mare Sr. I sent today for When Churchyards Yawn, the anthology of brand new tales by Asquith, which has just reached Chicago from England. I will let you have a report on this as soon as it reaches me and I have read it through. I agree with you re le Fanu. It is very surprising to know that Colin has included Dunsany's Electric King which is inferior even to many of my own tales. Looking over some of the titles Hart mentions one begins to see the aptitude of de la Mare's title THEY WALK *AGAIN!*

The past week bought me two welcome items—Wright replied finally, sending me advance sheets of Those Who Seek, the illustration for which I must admit could have been worse, and accepting In the Left Wing at $65.00, another of the summer's collaborations though he cut off 500 of my listed wordage. Of this tale he wrote that he liked it as well as anything of mine he had seen, despite the inclusion of 2 hackneyed incidents, the cab-driver's refusal to take the narrator to the Thraves estate, and the fire at the end. I at once offered to change the two incidents providing he could show me how, for as you perhaps know I pondered them, especially the latter at your own direction some time before I finally revised the tale; I had to leave them in or do an entirely different story. I heard also from The Midland, which is using Old Ladies in the January–February issue. The editor was most grateful, attributing the fact that the magazine could continue largely to my efforts, due to the TIME article for which I was responsible. I am continuing my struggle for the magazine which I regard as the best literary mag in the U. S. I've promised him 10 subscriptions, 5 of which are already in, three more of which are promised. I have just sent an article on Midland to the Nation, offering it to them gratis; will do another gratis for The New Republic, should Nation accept this article. Then I am planning long historical articles for American Mercury and The Bookman, with both of the editors of which I am now in correspondence over said articles. The magazine is worth keeping alive; with so few really good magazines in being, I shall do all I can to keep The Midland here with us. It can continue now, says Editor Frederick, through 1932.

I am glad to hear that H. S. is on the upgrade, and shall drop him a note of encouragement tomorrow, at the same time mentioning how much I liked Cassius.

I am also very glad to know that you are working on another plot, and hope that the story will materialize shortly. I look forward to it, as I am sure all of us do.

Yes, the weather is certainly marvellous—today I went down into the marshes in shirtsleeves, and for the first time in my life, gathered pussy willows, bittersweet, and winter berries (holly family) all at once. I hope that those catkins now prematurely out will bear again in spring, for the marshes would surely be dull without them.

Re Williamson—you will like especially The Lone Swallows, The Old Stag, The Peregrine's Saga, The Village Book, and Tarka the Otter. His Flax of Dream volumes—Dandelion Days, The Beautiful Years, Dream of Fair Women, and The Pathway are beautiful also, but his nature sketches appeal very strongly to me, as I am sure they would to you. By all means try them. Look them up at the public library there, where I am sure most of them will be—you have a public library, I hope. Of course.

As to *liking* comic weird tales—I must take exception to your phrasing this. I like The Canterville Ghost, would like any tale like this, but I cannot be said to like comic weird tales. I do not feel any particular antipathy towards either them or their authors, nor any particular liking. They amuse me, that's all. But I fully agree with you when you say that they are not to be taken into serious consideration.

I think we are at cross purposes in our letters—we are both on the same side of the fence, but we aren't convincing each other of it. I agree with all you say insofar as the argument is between us. But what I am trying to do is to show you how the average intelligent man is going to react, trying to show you that what *we* as genuine *weird talers* understand as embraced by the WEIRD is NOT what the average intelligent man understands as embraced by the weird, but that the latter classification is wide enough to take in at one and the same time The Whisperer, An Adventure in the 4th Dimension,[1] and A Rose for Emily, while we, were we to limit the strictly weird, would include only The Whisperer. Now, at the same time that I, strictly weirdly speaking, agree with you, I still classify these other two weird tales as weird tales because they are so classed by the average reader.

Now, when you say "which it is very probable that no natural explanation can fit", you are saying something which is okeh to one part of me yet fundamentally wrong. I am getting very abstruse, I fear. Let me put it this way: everything on this earth or off it has a natural explanation, but we have not yet found this natural explanation. Thus you can easily see why I say your statement is wrong. Now you can say that you do not believe that everything etc has a natural explanation; then you will be admitting a belief in the supernatural purely supernatural. But it is so much easier saying that we do not know the natural explanation; therefore the weird.

My postulate re the relative values of weird tales set in familiar and exotic settings did not include critics—only readers, the reader familiar to weird tales, and one not so familiar. No attack on either tale was intended. As the outset we eliminate any such tales as set out to be just weird and no more. Re the objections you list that I miss: I wasn't even intending to class as a weird tale a mere narrative of the appearance of a ghost, nor have I written anything recently which did not have some very good reason for the appearance of the ghost, mostly the revenge motif, true. I realize and agree with such objections as you list, but what I do not agree with is the stretching of such objections by persons none too careful to include really good weird tales—such as Wright for instance.

But now I have a real bone to pick with you. You write: "In no case have I come near conveying the mood or image I wish to convey; and when one has not done this at 41 years there is not much use in wasting time on further attempts." So grandpa is getting pessimistic; fie on thee. Needless to say, I flatly disagree with your statement in all points. I want to wager that you can get absolutely no one to agree with you. It may sound ridiculous for me to disagree so violently with something which must of necessity be a purely personally knowledge, but there is something about creative work which all artists have in common. Had such tales as Dunwich Horror, Colour out of Space, Rats in the Walls, Music of Erich Zann etc. embodied further intense mood or images, they would have suffered; it is because these tales are just rightly turned, just correctly done that they are so strongly appreciated by yrs. truly and others. Furthermore, even should we admit your first statement, the second part does not follow. Because you haven't done a thing say in 25 yrs. is no proof that you can't do it thereafter; not at all, though it may indicate a pessimistic philosophy etc. Of course, fundamentally, you know best what to do with your work; but I should advise you to go on with the lab experiments, then discard them, and continue with "further writing" regardless. I often have depressed periods when I feel I will never touch a typewriter again to create, but I always go back. When I wrote The Early Years I was far from satisfied; now I feel that it is almost perfect. Thus it goes. When I wrote The Panelled Room, I felt I had failed; now I regard it not only as my best, but ranking among the best ever done by anyone. On the other hand, things that satisfied me immediately almost invariably disappointed me later on.

Ah, well, words words words.   as always,
                                                                        August

Notes

1. FW, "An Adventure in the Fourth Dimension," *WT* (October 1923).

[238]   [ALS]

Novr. 20, 1931

Dear A W:—

    Well—why *don't* you like to look like a football player? Don't the very finest & most virile of all youths play football? And is that game incompatible with the very best of looks? Bless my soul, but I wish I *did* look like the sort of person who might have played football in his long-departed heyday! As a matter of fact, you have no complaint at all to make according to the pictures I've seen—& I don't believe so many cameras could be uniformly mendacious in the same direction. Odd that little Jehvish-Êi preferred the Robed Abbot of the Black Mass to the other view I loaned him. I think I like the outdoor one best—the latest one you sent.

    I want to get a look at that de la Mare anthology, if only to see Le Fanu's "Green Tea", which B K H praises so highly. It is possible that I did the fellow an injustice—though I can scarcely imagine a really weird tale by the author of "The House by the Churchyard" & other Victorian products which I have seen. In general, the contents of the book does seem rather hackneyed. I shall welcome your report on "When Churchyards Yawn". The first Asquith anthology had some good stuff in it.

Glad that professional matters progress well—& that the Left Wing has landed. Congratulations on the *Midland* acceptance—& good luck with your campaign for the preservation of the magazine.[1] I am not sure that I have ever seen the publication, though its name is familiar to me from quoted extracts & allusions. It would be unfortunate indeed if such a publication were forced to succumb.

Glad your warm weather is continuing. Ours likewise continues, though in conjunction with a continuous mistiness & occasional rain preclusive of outdoor enjoyment. I rather like mist visually, though, because of the ethereal glamour it imparts to distant prospects such as the outspread lower town as seen from the precipice whereon I dwell. Since armistice day our marble state house dome has been illuminated by the most intensive & vivid flood-lighting system I have ever seen, & the effect of this glimpsed through a haze from the hilltop is indescribably exquisite & imagination-stirring. I must look up Williamson—yes, Providence has one of the finest & amplest public libraries in the country, in addition to notable subscription & university libraries.

As for our recent argument on the province of the weird—assuredly the field is complex, & full of opportunities for varied interpretation. Just what set of criteria ought to be employed is likewise debatable. There is no more reason for choosing the complete layman than for choosing the complete specialist, since most persons who enjoy weird tales at all are usually part way betwixt the two. But certainly, no contention is valid or clear unless terms & standards be well defined. Concerning "A Rose for Emily"—I still insist that it is *not weird* even according to the 'layingest' layman. Any casual reader would pronounce it *gruesome*, but he could not possibly associate it with tales of ghosts or other impossible unrealities. It simply belongs to a different species, as is obvious from the first. Manifestly, this is a dark & horrible thing which *could happen*, whereas the crux of a *weird* tale is something which *could not possibly happen*. If any unexpected advance of physics, chemistry, or biology were to indicate the *possibility* of any phenomena related by the weird tale, that particular set of phenomena would cease to be *weird* in the ultimate sense because it would become surrounded by a different set of emotions. It would no longer represent imaginative liberation, because it would no longer indicate a suspension or violation of the natural laws against whose universal dominance our fancies rebel. It would not even represent the shudder formerly felt when people believed in non-material phenomena; since that shudder was based upon mystery & unplumbed possibilities, whereas today we know that anything which can exist at all exists in strict mathematical relationship to all other cosmic energy-manifestations. However—one may add that in the event of such a discovery a certain aura of vague quasi-weirdness would continue to linger around the affected field through the force of tradition until it became very thoroughly understood & explored. The foregoing will shew you why I insist on the definition "which it is very probable that no natural explanation can possibly fit". Everything *which really exists* most certainly has a natural explanation. But it is my contention that real *weirdness* or imaginative liberation depends on the depiction of something *which does not exist,* or which probably does not exist. If ghosts, Tsathogguan monsters, or any sort of a "spiritual" world *existed,* weird fiction would sink to commonplaceness. It was, indeed, a much less potent & poignant field in the days when the supernatural was believed in, & is probably still so to the vestigial types who still believe in the supernatural.

As for my fiction—the Putnam incident has convinced me that it falls between two stools. It has been tainted enough with the cheap W.T. ideal to be unacceptable as literature, yet does not conform enough to the cheap herd standard to be marketable. Whether it can ever pull out of the slough remains to be seen. As I have said, I am gradually experimenting with various manners—but it may be that silence is the more dignified policy. Thus I decided in 1908, when I swore off & kept sworn off for nine years. But we shall see. I have just destroyed the third version of my "laboratory" plot & am planning to try a fourth when opportunity offers.

Best wishes—

Yr most obt Grandsire

H P

Notes

1. See "Plight of the Midland," a letter by AWD to *Commonweal* explaining the need to support the foundering *Midland* magazine, which published the work of Midwestern authors.

[239]   [ALS]

10 Barnes—
Woden's-Dag
[25 November 1931]

Dear A W:—

Well—I can't get personally interested in athletic games (or any other kind, from marbles to bridge or chess to crap-shooting) but I do think they form a salutary influence for the person of good physique & average psychology, & rather regret that absence of the competitive instinct which leaves me cold to them. They teach endurance, fearlessness, coördination, & determination—all qualities which any unbiassed critic must judge superior, & without which no civilisation could last long. Sport can be overdone, & probably is— but I still think it's a good thing if one can be moderately interested.

I must get hold of "Green Tea" in some form or other. Sorry the new Asquith anthology doesn't equal the first—but would give a good deal to see that new Machen tale! The Blackwood tale in "They Walk Again" is one I don't recall seeing—according to B K H's description.[1]

Congratulations on the high-grade sales! Sooner or later, I have not the least doubt, you'll be regularly making the standard magazines—which is more than any other of the gang is ever likely to do. Hope you win your *Midland* campaign—the *Bookman* ought to be a good medium for publicity on that theme.

"Bishop Kroll" sounds good. Dwyer would dote on it, & I hardly think even little Jevish-Êi could object very violently to its amiable clerical hero. Hope it lands in highly exclusive circles! Good luck, too, with the revised tales of more popular cast.

The astonishing second summer continues here, & I am constantly out around my river-bank—learning for the first time the charm of the brown & bare-boughed winter woods so often dwelt upon by Machen. Temperatures hover around 70° or 71°. But sudden disaster is in the offing, I fear, for last night's paper threatened a cold wave before the lapse of many hours. Hope your crocus-blooming won't mean their absence next spring—I'm really not enough of a botanist to know what the probabilities are in such a matter. I've noticed quite a few birds, too—although we have a good many perennial species here. I hope the mildness will last over tomorrow, so that I can persuade my semi-invalid aunt to go out for a good Thanksgiving dinner.

I've never read "A Son of the Middle Border".[2] Main roads in Massachusetts aren't much as they were in '85; since concrete, hot dog stands, billboards, & filling stations are all too evident. But quiet back roads do carry a great deal of the aspect of the past if one knows where to look for them. The region south of Boston—Hingham, Scituate, &c., which I visited for the first time last month—is less spoiled in proportion than any other section of Massachusetts I have seen. Hope you'll like the new O'Neill play, at which I must myself get a look sooner or later.[3]

Good luck with your John Day persuasions—though I can't promise any new material. My present experimenting has gone back to zero—since I've torn up the last of the consciously modelled versions & am slowly writing the thing out just as I would have written it in the first place. Readers will consider it too long, detailed, atmospheric, & slow-moving—though I don't intend to bother very many readers with it. You can see it if you like—that is, if it gets as far as a legible copy. The coral key idea doesn't seem to pan out— largely, perhaps, because I cannot readily associate the macabre with the South. Somehow, my idea of the sinister seems basically bound up with northern cold.

As for the discussion—I still doubt if it would occur to any average reader to call "A Rose for Emily" more than realistically gruesome. Wish I had the facilities for assembling a symposium of readers' views! About possibility versus weirdness—I think an actual proof of the objective existence of Cthulhu or of a ghost at #10 would be the first step toward removing these themes from the weird. They would continue to be *strange* themes, but as soon as they became recognised as fact their imaginative status would change. The act of assuming them to be possible would no longer form an emotional liberation of the fullest sort, since that liberation comes only when we temporarily persuade ourselves of the possibility of something which our deepest instincts & sharpest comprehension recognise to be basically & unalterably impossible. Unless we feel sure that a thing absolutely *can't* happen, we do not derive the fullest kick from the sport of deluding ourselves into the momentary pseudo-belief that it can happen or has happened. We know that ghosts don't exist, & that sincere accounts of them are due to mistakes, exaggerations, hallucinations, & the like. That is *why* we enjoy reading about them—because the story half-persuades us to distrust the basic realities of the universe. If acceptance of the fiction did not involve such a contradiction of known fact, the appeal would be distinctly diluted. There would be no real liberation.

Well, as you say, this leads nowhere!

Best wishes—

Grandpa H P

Notes

1. Arthur Machen, "Opening the Door"; Algernon Blackwood, "Keeping His Promise" (reprinted from *The Empty House*).

2. By Hamlin Garland.

3. Eugene O'Neill (1888–1953), *Mourning Becomes Electra* (1931).

[240]   [ALS]

Decr. 10, 1931

Dear A W:—

I don't think the experimenting came to very much. The result, 68 pages long, has all the defects I deplore—especially in point of style, where hackneyed phrases & rhythms have crept in despite all precautions. Use of any other style was like working in a foreign language—hence I was left high & dry. Possibly I shall try experimenting with another plot—of as widely different nature as I can think of—but I think an hiatus like that of 1908 is the best thing. I have been paying too much attention to the demands of markets & the opinions of others—hence if I am ever to write again I must begin afresh; writing only for myself & getting into the old habit of non-self-conscious storytelling without any technical thoughts. No—I don't intend to offer "The Shadow over Innsmouth" for publication, for it would stand no chance of acceptance. I shall probably use it as a quarry to furnish material for later tales if I write them. If I ever try to type it, you shall at once see it; but I fancy nobody but myself could read it now.

Glad to hear that you fare well with the high-grade markets, & hope you keep it up. As for Schorer's new opinion of the weird tale—I think he goes too far if he considers it essentially inartistic, yet the fact remains that weird fiction is indeed a very minor & specialised field.

As for our controversy—all one can say is that we 'know' of the non-existence of ghosts *as well as we know anything which rests on competitive probabilities & evidence of a negative sort.* They 'exist' as psychological phenomena just as dreams & other illusions 'exist'—that is, as images caused by fancy & credulity, though without objective counterparts. I don't think I'm too easily satisfied with the probable explanations of such illusions—for you must remember that hardly any scientific man of standing takes such things seriously. On the other hand, I think you flagrantly underestimate the *overwhelming improbabilities* involved in the conception of a ghost-breeding world of spirit. There are far fewer difficulties in accounting for reported 'occult' phenomena than in accepting the absurdities involved in belief in human personality apart from the living cellular organism.

Thus the question resolves itself into two phases:

I.   The utter & abysmal improbability of a non-corporeal human existence.

II. The causes of the perplexing illusions which lead certain persons to believe in the extravagant & untenable doctrine of non-corporeal human existence.

The first phase is not hard to outline—in fact, Haeckel did it so well a generation or two ago that further elaboration is mere repetition. Briefly—there is no such conceivable thing as a stable or permanent human personality. The existence of every living mammal is something new & (apart from ultimate determinism) fortuitous, depending wholly on the accident of what parental elements happened to combine. Every fresh organism is something wholly new—the result of a fresh cell-combination—& to fancy that its essence has any coherence or reality apart from the growth of these creative cells is so *wild & unmotivated* a vagary as to have no standing whatever in the light of reason. As the cells develop & follow natural ancestral patterns, the natural irritability of the protoplasm flowers into the phenomena of consciousness & personality; but there is never any *one* stage of this development which we may take as a permanent growth & call "the person." On the other hand, the developing organism creates a whole series of personalities—the child, the youth, the adult, the senescent, & the senile—only vaguely resembling one another, & each equally basic for the time being. As the cells change, so does the personality change—& accident can bring as many changes as nature. Let something cripple certain cerebral cells, or let something cause a disproportionate functioning of the endocrine glands, & the whole personality of the moment vanishes & gives place to another. Personality, then, is an obvious attribute of cellular organism—having no existence before the parent elements united to form the organism, & being subject to change as the organism ages or suffers other modifications. To fancy that this attribute (a mode of motion in matter of certain complex natural form) has any existence apart from its causative material, or that it can survive the death & dispersal of that material, (when as a matter of fact it often fails to survive, in full, even a decade within the lifetime of that material!) is a delusion so childish that few biologists of the present even begin to consider it seriously. To cling to primitive myths of this sort is like believing the earth to be flat, or accepting the Ptolemaic theory of the solar system. Three-quarters of all the religious piffle & ghostly legendry extant would vanish in a flash if the majority of people had the patience & common sense to look at this matter as it really is. The mistake of the herd is to harbour a totally false idea about the nature of life. Life is not a *thing* but a *process;* & a process ceases when its component parts are dispersed. Life is like a flame—which cannot survive the candle which produces it. It is a lack of comprehension of the *utter improbability* of non-corporeal human existence which lays certain minds open to suggestions of 'occult' phenomena.

So much for Phase I. Phase II is much more complex, & of course begins at the opposite end. It takes a miscellaneous body of alleged phenomena of all degrees of crudity or puzzling subtlety, cited as evidence *against* the normal conclusion reached in Phase I, & endeavours to see how such phenomena can be reported when all the bulk of evidence is overwhelmingly against non-corporeal existence. Modern observation does not find the alleged phenomena of occultism as impressive as past generations did, because recent anthropological & psychological researches have emphasised the feeble hold which our consciousnesses have on reality. Everything we seem to perceive & know depends on a curious filtration & colouration imposed by our mental & emotional backgrounds, so that we can be sure of nothing unless it will bear testing & objective demonstration. What we think we remember of yesterday may at times bear only an approximate relationship to what really happened; & many an acute & self-analytical man can spot in himself dozens of wholly erroneous *pseudo-memories* & *mnemonic transpositions* by means of objective checking up—things which he would have sworn were true if he had not been honest & intelligent enough to analyse them & track them down to their illusory birth. We also come to recognise the tremendous force of myth-building, & the well-nigh incredible persistence of unreal myth-patterns—as well as the accretive nature of repetition as applied to stories, anecdotes, &

reports. We find that all those reported phenomena which do not savour plainly of hallucination, error, mendacity, or transposed memory, are those to which we can never get closer than third or fourth hand. Taking Phase II as a whole, we may say inclusively that the one great cause of 'occult' belief is the defenceless state of mind bequeathed by our justly credulous (because necessarily uninformed) ancestral past. It was absolutely inevitable that our forbears should believe in supernatural & spiritual phenomena, because they had no other way of accounting for the phenomena of nature & the delusive paradoxes created by dreams, shadows, memories, & the like. Animism & dualism were essential stages which we had to pass through; & their crystallisation in dogmatic & compulsory religions served to drive them so far into the subconsciousness of the race that they have long survived their rational term. Our minds are crippled—biassed & predisposed toward the acceptance of supernaturalism as a matter of course—by the religious instruction we receive at the most impressionable period of early childhood. Psychologists know that almost any sort of emotional & imaginative bias, be it ever so absurd, can be drilled into one if he be taken at a suitably early age. That is why our subjective feelings—crippled as they are—form no evidence whatever one way or the other in the stern quest for reality. If we were not so injured in childhood, we would today laugh the notion of the spiritual out of court at the very outset. It is, then, no wonder that the minds of the non-analytical form fertile soil for delusions. Now—how can we classify the various types of occult delusion with respect to origin & implantation? There seem to be two types of false evidences here involved:

(1.) Phenomena which have a basis in reality, but which suffer misinterpretation.

(2.) Reports of phenomena which have never occurred at all.

First let us look back into class (1.) It would be impossible to analyse & classify, in the compass of a single letter, all the delusions so confidently, sincerely, & ingeniously brought forward by men like Flammarion & Chevreuil; one may take a few salient types as illustrations of the sources of apparent 'evidence for spirituality.'

(a.) Direct error. Vapour interpreted as ghost. Wind in hollow walls mistaken for spectral music.* Given the phenomena, it weaves its own legend & creates its own mythical antecedents in the course of a few repetitions.

(b) Transposition of memory. A. says that he saw a certain indication of a given happening *before* it occurred or before he learned of its occurrence. Investigation always shews that the alleged indication

---

*actual case in Halsey Mansion (built 1801) just around the corner from 10 Barnes St. In the 1850's this fine old brick house was actually feared by the ignorant.[1]

was in fact *subsequent,* even though the narrator sincerely believes that it was antecedent.

(c) Mnemonic selection. B. insists that he had an advance dream or vague premonition of something which actually occurs. The fact is, that the situation was one which (although it may not *seem* so) called for speculation in advance, with the eventual alternative among others. After the outcome is known, B. remembers thinking or dreaming of the correct alternative, & forgets that he thought or dreamed about others just as strongly. This type of myth is of course fostered by the measurable number of pure accidental coincidences in which the subject really happens to guess a correct alternative in advance. But for every such case of accidentally correct guessing, there are naturally a hundred cases of incorrect guessing. People remember the one striking accident & forget the humdrum hundred bad guesses.

(d) Auto-hypnosis due to volition. Most people, irritated by man's real insignificance & helplessness in the cosmos, ardently wish that a spiritual world existed to give them the unreal importance formerly assured them by religion. Natural limitations of time, space, & natural law are galling to them—especially in the light of the delusive & grandiloquent tradition on which they were suckled—hence some consciously take to weird fiction, whilst others prefer to kid themselves along & cling to a vestigial love of the obsolescent spiritual mythology. The subconscious strength of this wish is often so great as to become translated into downright hallucination, causing the subject to experience illusory evidences of the supernatural, or even to construct elaborate day-dreams of occultism revolving around himself. In some cases, it drives otherwise truthful persons to grotesque extremes of uncontrollable (even when not wholly unconscious) mendacity in the direction of establishing or corroborating illusions which bolster up their cherished conception of the spiritual. This is especially marked in abnormally egotistical types, whose sense of importance & centrality is enhanced by the weaving of supernatural illusions around their personality.* The two greatest occult liars I know are New England poets of considerable conceit & artificiality. Egotism also enhances the sincere occult belief which

---

*a psychiatric study of the Rev. Montague Summers—who claims, among other marvels, to have "seen" a priest bodily levitated several feet into the air during the performance of some sacerdotal rite—would be a highly important contribution to science. Here we have an extraordinarily profound scholar & author subject to wish-hallucinations of the most extreme type. He is probably not technically insane in a general sense as yet, but the baldness & crudeness of his delusions will make his future worth watching.

does not involve mendacity, as is revealed by a census of all the civilised occult believers I personally know. It may seem an odd connexion to the casual observer, but the tabulation is impressive. At the base of the condition is the egotist's love of deeming himself 'finer' or 'more spiritually sensitive' than the common man. At least three females for every male are occult believers, which further corroborates the influence of self-centred non-impersonalism as a factor. Of course, the lower classes or even the frivolous & non-thoughtful upper classes do not count at all. They have no well-divined thought processes, hence are just as naturally subject to primitive beliefs as were the uninformed dawn-races among whom such beliefs originally rose. All peasants are religious & superstitious, & 0.9 of all thoughtless fashionables believe in deity, astrology, luck charms, & kindred rubbish.

(e) Sincere errors in reporting—similar to case (a) but less crude & direct. This is the case of those who read & accept elaborate presentations of alleged occult phenomena such as those in Chevreuil & Flammarion. Because the data in such books is so detailed & sincere, & so coherently & forcefully presented, the susceptible reader allows his larger conception of cosmic probability to be lulled to sleep by something which merely *looks* irrefutable. He forgets that it is much more likely for these rare alleged events (events which very suspiciously follow certain hackneyed myth-patterns in a majority of instances) to involve a hidden error or falsehood somewhere along the chain of transmission & verification, than for the basic facts of human existence & perishability to be other than what the overwhelming bulk of tested evidence & common sense indicates. This forgetfulness & predisposition would undoubtedly be less marked if people would realise how natural it is for seemingly convincing ghostly legends to take their rise. The stage was all set for such hallucinations in primitive times, so that anthropologists know they would have occurred in any case—whether or not any similar reality existed. With the general lines of the myth-pattern all marked out, it is inevitable that it should have been transmitted, with suitable accretions & adaptations to varying sets of manners & customs, down the long line of ages. It is amusing to analyse certain ghost tales current in certain nations, & to discover in them half-submerged elements unmistakably bespeaking their earlier formulation in lands widely separated from the place of alleged occurrence. We read of an 'occult' phenomenon occurring yesterday in a house in Boston—but can trace in the account features which could not have developed except in France, or Italy, or Hungary, as the case may be, or in centuries more recent than the 17th, 16th, 15th, & so on. Such analysis breaks up a vast number of the most apparently circumstantial cases, whilst *actual investigation almost invariably rips away one of them to tatters.* It is inconceivable to a believer how many discrepancies there are betwixt the actual conditions in such a case as finally tracked down, & the plausible case-history as written up in the pages of a Flammarion. One false link alters the whole thing. The character of witnesses, psychological & otherwise—the actual thing first reported—the conditions of visibility &c—the motivations uncovered—the number of accretive repetitions—&c. &c. &c. It is the same old story whenever one these plausible yarns is really tracked down—& sometimes, of course, one finds that the alleged anecdote is wholly fictitious. Let any occultist choose any case at random, & a thoroughly searching investigation will either shew flaws, or shew an endless chain of repetitions hinting at ultimate nullity, or prove the whole thing a fake. Obviously, nobody can bother to track down every single case that the occultists put forward; but it is enough to shew that any casually picked case always ends in an exposé when it can be pinned down as having happened at all. Irish mediums, New England haunted houses, Nova Scotia poltergeists—all come to the same thing. And all the while we must keep in mind that strong natural reasons for the outburst of these alleged phenomena exist. They always follow patterns established by known primitive folklore, even when such patterns belie the geographical & chronological milieu; & in a vast number of cases they involve the presence of low-grade ego-centred persons (especially of an adolescent, exhibitionistic type) whose psychology strongly motivates them toward the fostering or creation of supernatural delusions. As for the element of reporting & transmission—we have only to see how common rumour grows by repetition, and how the honest testimony of two eye-witnesses to the same event differs, in order to appreciate the development of myths as they circulate. A. hears the blinds slamming on a house & tells B. B. tells C. that the blinds slammed without any wind. C. tells D. that a ghostly hand slammed the blinds. D. tells E. that a transparent man in white slammed the blinds. E. tells F. that in a house where a murder took place 150 years ago, a periwigged ghost opened the blinds of a long-sealed room—& so on, & so on. All in all, *if we keep our sense of proportion intact,* we can see that it is impossible & silly to accept these specious embodiments of myth-patterns as real evidence against the natural conditions which all our direct & sober observations attest; just as it is foolish to accept subjective impressions & hallucinations when we know so well the capriciousness & wish-swayed unreliability of our perceptive faculties. With things as they are, it is not to be wondered at that virtually no modern thinkers of any standing—not even those who vaguely harbour the old cosmic-purpose delusion—have any credence in the claims of mediums & ghost-seers. Against the fantastic minority represented by Flammarion (who was not a physicist or biologist) & two or three other Frenchmen, by Sir William Crookes, Sir Oliver Lodge, & one or two Americans, *we have as complete occult sceptics the entire body of responsible investigative intellect throughout the world,* including Einstein, Jeans, Eddington, Millikan, Compton, de Sitter, Julian Huxley, Santayana, Bertrand Russell, Freud, Jung, Adler, Watson, Pavlov, ... but there's no need of reproducing an international Who's Who. Be it enough to say that your cocksure belief that certain phenomena 'will not fit' into normally conceived nature is rejected by about 95 out of 100 of the world's recognised first-rate investigators. If you can prove them "too blissfully conservative" & "too easily satisfied", go ahead & do it! The world would enjoy the privilege of lindberghing a new super-mind to replace Einstein!

There now remains for consideration Class (2.) or reported occult phenomena—things which never occurred in *any* form, but which have been created by imagination, tradition, or mendacity, & developed by plausible repetition. We have touched upon these in connexion with group (e) of Class (1.), but it will be well to cite certain classic instances. That of the Hindoo fakir is the best case. For a century we have heard of yogis & mahatmas who throw a rope into the air so that it stands up straight & extends aloft out of sight— whereupon a boy climbs up & likewise vanishes in the distance. This became a popular traveller's tale—as having been told one by Colonel C—— who heard it from Major M—— as early as the 1850's; & for fully thirty years was accepted by the general western public as a marvellous & unexplained bit of actual sleight-of-hand. Nobody but occult dupes (& there was a wave of that delusion in the middle 19th century, somewhat resembling the present popular wave) believed it to be supernatural, but everyone joined in a wondering admiration of the clever turbaned performers. Then an *explanation* was reported. *Mass hypnotism* was the answer, & there began to be frequent reports of a photographer who snapped the spectacle at the crucial moment when he thought he saw the boy climbing the rope, but who found on developing his negative that the rope was on the ground & the boy simply scuttling away around the nearest corner. This was the general public belief after about 1880, & probably still is with many. But what are the facts? The matter was actually taken up seriously early in the 20th century through a systematic tracking down of reports. Colonel C—— was asked just what Major M—— told him, & Major M—— was asked where he got his account. Who, as a matter of fact, had ever *seen* this rope & boy trick as opposed to merely *hearing about it?* Who was the photographer who had revealed it as mass-hypnotism? Well—the result was that the whole thing was relegated to the domain of *pure folklore*. Nobody had ever seen the trick—*& nobody had ever performed it!* It was a typical case of pure myth-pattern—utterly fictitious to start with, but eventually believed all over the world. The same was proved concerning other Hindoo tricks, although long-term living burials (in some cases of which the subject died) were shewn to exist occasionally as a result of a special physiological aptitude or of some hidden breathing connexion with the surface. What is significant—as shewing how myth-patterns can originate in recent times as well as in antiquity—is the fact that the tale of the photographer was found to be as baseless as all the rest. Yet in the fin de siecle period this plausible anecdote was widely credited by the most thoughtful men alive. One of the best-informed persons in this field was the late showman Houdini[2]—a tremendously intelligent & hard-headed soul despite his many crudities—for whom I did a great deal of revision in the last years of his life. He had delved very thoroughly into the Hindoo fakir question himself, & was convinced that all the more spectuacular tricks attributed to them were sheer legend, although their residue of genuine legerdemain was surely clever enough. Such is a typical case of the myth which grows by report. Reaching back to mediaeval history, we find entire episodes—once widely believed—to be mere growths of folk legend or applications of the solar & other myth-patterns. There never was a Wilhelm Tell, nor was Richard III a hunchback. Coming down again—the old haunted well of Middleboro, Mass. was created by a Boston American reporter, & the haunted house at Henniker N.H. received its traditional ghosts when the present tearoom exploiters bought & opened it. In these last two cases myth-patterns are in the making—at least one 'historical' ballad apiece having been innocently & independently launched from sources wholly unconnected with the original fakes. And of course Arthur Machen's bowmen of Mons form the one perfect modern classic instance. You ought to see the "authentic" reports of people who "saw" people who "had seen" the shining phantoms on the battlefield before Machen invented them! And pretty soon people began to "remember" the peculiar arrow wounds found on the German dead . . . . . "doctors" (who could somehow never be located) gave testimony about those wounds . . . . . . & poor credulous Harold Begbie (the late "Gentleman with a Duster") wrote the whole thing piously up & accused Machen of not writing his own story[3] . . . . & so on . . . . & so on . . . It's a great life if you can believe all you hear!

But I can't believe all I hear, & I am too familiar with pseudo-memories, selective 'premonitions', & so on—many of which I have traced in myself & those around—to have any illusions about the experience of these things. Much as I would like to live in a cosmos full of my favourite Cthulhus, Yog-Sothoths, Tsathogguas, & the like, I find myself forced into agreement with men like Russell, Santayana, Einstein, Eddington, Haeckel, & so on. Prose is less attractive than poetry, but when it comes to a choice between probability

& extravagance, I have to let common sense be my guide. If you want to find a kindred soul in the pro-occult realm, Whitehead is the boy to tackle. He actually half-swallows some of the nigger magic of the Indies, though he isn't so credulous about Caucasian ghosts in the States. A jumbee, I infer, is rather more plausible than a white misty form in a Scottish castle or Virginia manorhouse! Incidentally—I find that there is still a whole region in the U.S. where witchcraft is believed as uniformly & implicitly as in the Salem of 1692. It is the Lehigh Valley region of Pennsylvania, where the "hex" murders attracted attention a few years ago. I thought those a rather isolated vestigial case, but I now have two bright young correponsents in Allentown[4] who (themselves as sceptical as I) indicate a widespread surviving belief. "Hex" doctors have a strong hold on the imaginations of the people; & only last week one of them kept at a distance, by some quasi-hypnotic psychological menace, a sheriff who wanted to search his garage. The country folk paint on their barn gables great circles filled with labyrinthine lines—to entrap any "hexes" who may have designs on their livestock & grain. I must visit around there some time—picturesque country!

I'd like to see your region, too. The calling custom you describe seems refreshingly unique for the modern world, though it recalls the New-Year customs of early New York. Winter has hit us now, though there are warm & rainy interludes. I succeeded in getting my aunt out to a good Thanksgiving dinner, & fancy it will take less persuasion to incite a corresponding trip Christmas. ¶ Best wishes—& apologies for the length & argumentativeness of this document! ¶ Yr obt Servt

H P

P.S. I surely intend to get hold of "Mourning Becomes Electra." ¶ Belknap & others didn't care much for "How the Old Woman Got Home".[5] ¶ I've just got the new W.T.—glad to see "Those Who Seek". ¶ Heard an interesting lecture on Whitehead's (not our H S!) philosophy last night,[6] but can't say it gave me any greater fondness for the would-be unifier than I had before. W. gets *more* rather than *less* chimerical as he "progresses", & he never made his case against scientific supremacy very plausible in the first place.

Notes

1. The Thomas Lloyd Halsey House (c. 1800, c. 1825), 140 Prospect Street; the home of Charles Dexter Ward in HPL's *The Case of Charles Dexter Ward*.

2. Harry Houdini (born Ehrich Weiss, 1874–1926), escape artist and debunker of spiritualism, for whom HPL ghost-wrote "Under the Pyramids." HPL owned his exposé *A Magician among the Spirits* (1924; *LL* 443).

3. Harold Begbie, *On the Side of the Angels*.

4. Carl Ferdinand Strauch and Harry Kern Brobst.

5. By M. P. Shiel.

6. The lecture by Alfred E. Murphey (1901–1962) was on the British philosopher Alfred North Whitehead.

[241]   [ALS]

Decr. 23, 1931

Dear A W:—

I'll give the "Shadow over Innsmouth" another glance, & see if it looks worth salvaging. But I doubt if you could decipher the existing copy. Probably I can't myself, in parts. Most of it is in pencil, & the blurring is extreme. After a rest, I may try some more experimenting, but not in any media alien enough to make the process self-conscious. That is what dries me up altogether. What I must do—if I try to write more—is to forget about everybody, (especially Farnsworth Wright, Harry Bates, &c.) & attempt some mood-fixing for my own private consumption. The idea of any audience or critics is death to production.

As for the controversy, your point that 'negative evidence in the absence of positive evidence is nil' is not a very good one except in theory. It is true that in a matter where no probabilities exist on either side, negative evidence can scarcely figure. Here, however, the case is different. The alleged thing whose existence is under discussion is an *improbability* of the most overwhelming sort; all our knowledge of the universe & its workings pointing against its possibility. Nothing, then, could justify the serious consideration of such a thing as a possibility except the very strongest sort of positive evidence. If this positive evidence is lacking, the absence becomes *in effect* a strong— almost irrefutably strong—piece of "negative evidence"; because it leaves the field clear for these *other* general evidences regarding the structure of the cosmos, whereby the existence of the alleged thing is shewn as an improbability just short of absolute impossibility. There is no use trying to evade the force of this truth. To embody the principle concretely—suppose I asserted, without a raison d'etre, & in the face of all opposing evidence, that there is a city of brick houses inhabited by lizard-headed entities on a planet revolving around the star ζ Ursae Majoris. Who the hell can *disprove* what I say? The only thing which makes it virtually certain that such a race & city do *not* exist, is the fact that my statement is not founded on any basis of evidence; so that there is nothing to invalidate the general probabilities which declare against the existence of the hypothetical things. In other words, the principle of negative evidence is that whereby we recognise, in practical thinking, *that there is no reason to believe in the existence of anything whose claim to reality can be shewn to depend on nothing but error, caprice, or irrelevantly motivated guesswork.* When we come to realise that certain types of cosmic assumption are inevitable products of natural error as handled by the known psychology of mankind—& that we know that these assumptions would positively exist in any case, irrespective of the truth or falsity of that which they assume—we have a right to say that their reality is very wildly improbably at best, & almost impossible in cases where general evidence is adverse. It would, common intelligence tells us, be altogether too absurd to fancy that there is any likelihood of a still-unplumbed mystery's real solution being exactly the same as some wild guess formulated by somebody who had no means of knowing anything about the mystery's real conditions & explanation. Chance coincidence simply does not extend that far. So when anthropologically evolved folklore makes a claim of "explaining" some natural secret through an arbitrary myth determined by circumstances apart from true knowledge, we may bank on it that the identity of the myth & the unknown reality is an *improbability* of the strongest sort. We *know* that the imaginative experiences of primitive mankind *must inevitably* create a delusion of spirit life, whether or not any such thing actually exists. Apart from these known delusions, there is no evidence for spirit life; but on the other hand, all nature hints in the strongest possible way that no such thing exists. Draw your own conclusions. I refuse to descend to the quibbling which would balk at the *working assertion* that we virtually "know" spirit life does not exist.

Your attitude toward the "legendary infallibility" of science shews a disposition to misvalue your adversaries. All that science claims is to shew a set of *extreme probabilities,* & it has certainly done this by an extension of the same method which causes us to discriminate betwixt heat & cold, & light & darkness.

As for Charles Fort & his analogues—there is no absurdity whatever in asserting that all their data, *in its details as interpreted by them,* are false. They are hunting feverishly for a certain type of report, commonly evolved in folklore & through error, which has always existed & always must exist according to the natural structure of the human mind & human society. That an infinity of diverse specimens can exist is not at all remarkable, for all myth-patterns tend toward infinite repetition with variations. Some of the illusions can be readily seen through, whilst others are more complex; but both the resolved & the unresolved possess evolutionary marks of a common origin. The different items, of course, may fall within any of the several sub-classes of such illusion. There will be some false reports, some imperfectly perceived & misinterpreted realities, some material which may be incomprehensible now but which will later be explained according to normal cosmic laws, &c. &c. &c. It would be incredible if the day's grist of news did not contain much of this hazy material in addition to the more accurately defined material—& any curio-collector may anthologise at will if he have the time & perseverance.

Your personal case as reported does not, of course, involve the *spiritual* in any strict sense; since purely mental communication *between living persons* (i.e., between those who are *really* persons instead of imaginary abstractions without a place in the biochemical scheme) is certainly an *hypothetical possibility* according to the known laws of material & electrical organisation. However, it must be insisted that even this material "telepathy" is far from probable. Almost all alleged cases break down under investigation, & I gather from reviews that the latest book of Alfred Edward Wiggam[1] contains a section disposing (so far as present evidence is concerned) of telepathic belief. Looking at your case—the first thing to break down is your claim of previous scepticism* on the part of both parties. If Schorer was a sceptic, why did he send you a special delivery after his dream? Do you suppose I'd write to anybody—even my most cherished relatives—on the mere strength of a dream? My aunts would think I was getting soft-headed if, during a visit away, I should send one of them an alarmed message describing a "vision" of her illness & asking if she were indeed indisposed! Of course, if she happened to be really ill at the time, a credulous believer might try to connect the phenomena & subtly colour the circumstances of the illness to conform to the picture of the dream—thus heightening the original coincidence. That is irrelevant. The main point is that *no real sceptic would even think of writing at all.* It is absurd to try to distinguish an alleged "waking" vision from any other sort of dreaming. We have no real means of discriminating betwixt the dreaming & waking states. Sometimes we know we are dreaming, but more often we do not. Doubtless you yourself have had *dreams of awaking,* where a known dream passes into a state of dream with your familiar bedroom setting—recognisable as a dream only in case of a *direct* real awaking which reveals differences betwixt the familiar room as just dreamed of & as now seen. This process of apparent & real waking, indeed, can occur in *more* than two stages, a whole Chinese-box set of dream states being gone through before actual consciousness is gained. And if instead of a direct awaking there comes some turn of dream which carries the mind into other visions, there will never be any way of proving whether the interval of prosaic bedroom-perception (if remembered, as it sometimes is) was a phase of dream or a momentary actual awakening. I have noted such phenomena carefully in myself, & have made inquiries of others which corroborate my own experience. It is impossible for us to be *really sure,* at any moment, whether we are asleep or awake. There are merely *different grades of probability* on both sides.

But to continue with your phenomenon. Schorer probably knows what your room looks like, in furniture & architecture, as well as how you yourself look in various postures. If he was at all worried about your health, it is very probable that he would visualise you as sitting up in bed just about as you would characteristically sit up. The ghostly effect—transparent chair, &c.—would be natural because of his familiarity with the folklore of such matters,

---

*unless, of course, you are using the word in its historic rather than common meaning—applying it to an "open" attitude ready to receive myth as well as probability.

& because of the lack of scepticism revealed by his act in writing your. At this point a really thorough investigator would thoroughly work out the question of your antecedent health as known to Schorer—his reasons or lack of reasons for a state of apprehension.

Now as for yourself. Being alarmed & in pain, you go through—or think then or later you go through—certain risings & sinkings fairly characteristic of you. On the following day, when presumably better, you receive & read the letter, & have the suggestion of telepathy planted in your mind through the fact that the general description chances to resemble what actually occurred—even though that occurrence was of a really generalised type which any sick man might duplicate. Granting a certain amount of real coincidence, (conditioned by the amount of reason Schorer had for worrying about your health) your own hazy recollections of the pain-racked night at once snapped into a *precise* conformity with that written account to which your real nocturnal acts had only *vaguely & casually* conformed. From that moment onward, you "recalled" what the letter had suggested to you—the acceptance of this suggestion being facilitated by your own basic credulity regarding occult phenomena. It may seem to you that your recollection is real enough—but other false recollections which we all have seem equally real until their illusory nature is proved. I have had scores of "memories" which subsequent researches have resolved into post facto suggestions. They seemed real while they lasted, but their origin later became very clear.

But of course, this especial interpretation of your phenomenon is merely a crude illustrative specimen, made at a distance without any of the detailed data which one needs to study such things intelligently. I may have missed many vital elements—& in any case, the proportioning of sheer coincidence & suggestion may be different from what I have assumed. Theoretically, too, it would not do to exclude the bare possibility of some still-unrecognised force of "telepathic" nature—though I really think the degree of probablility against such a condition is very great. All sorts of seemingly inexplicable things take place under the recognised laws of nature—sometimes to be ultimately explained, & sometimes not. However, let me make it plain that the one *great* objection to occultism is its chimerical assumption that consciousness can exist apart from the localised organisms whose internal motions constitute consciousness—that is, that life & personality can exist after the death & dispersal of the organism.

I have just obtained & partly read the new *Strange Tales*—without having read the preceding issue, which I gave away to Cook in the vain expectation of getting another on the stands. It is certainly a vast improvement on #1, & I am glad to see you represented. Whitehead's story unfortunately reflects a facile romanticism carried to annoying extremes. It grates on me to hear men of the Restoration period using the language of stage Elizabethans! I'm glad to see that "The Trap"—which I revised & totally recast last summer—has landed with Bates. When you read it, see if you can recognise Grandpa's style in the central part. I tried, of course, to be as Canevinical as possible; but fear I did not attain perfection in this respect. Edmond Hamilton almost bewilders one by developing a new plot.[2] Hope he'll devise a third some day.

About "Mive"[3]—of course I'd have been glad to say a good word whether I liked it or not, but fortunately I am really quite enthusiastic about the tale! It has the pervasive, insidious atmosphere so discouragingly lacking in almost all cheap weird fiction; & I gave it a puff on a postal sent in ostensible acknowledgment of the Yuletide likeness of small Bobby Wright. Glad that Nellie & the Spawn have landed, & hope P.R. & Shall Rise may ultimately share their happy fate. Good luck with Magnolias.

What you say of "The Lady Who Came to Stay"[4] greatly interests me. I must try to get hold of it. Klarkash-Ton's MS. was Dunsanianly appealing, despite certain romantic artificialities. You & he certainly have mastered the secret of quantity production! Hope to see your own new work in the course of time.

I'm enclosing a cutting bearing on our controversy, & also illustrating the marvellous survivial of primitive superstition in the Lehigh Valley of Pennsylvania. My data comes from two very bright young fellows in Allentown who got hold of me through W.T., & who are full of anecdotes of local "hex" beliefs & apparent marvels. If you ever want a new field of scenic setting for your work, you ought to get in touch with these boys, for their regional information is ample & accurate. One of them—Carl Strauch, 616 N. Penn St., Allentown, Pa—is in college, & about to publish a volume of poetry. He is exceedingly tasteful & intelligent. The other—Harry Brobst, 1321 Gordon St., Allentown, Pa—is less scholarly, but very bright & genial. Their joint description of the "hex" country is so alluring that I shall try to see it some day—especially since Allentown is only a brief bus ride from my favourite Philadelphia.

Well—merry christmas, & don't let the spooks catch you!

Yr obt Servt

H P

Notes

1. I.e., *The Marks of a Clear Mind* (1931).

2. AWD, "The Shadow on the Sky"; Henry S. Whitehead, "Cassius"; "Edmond Hamilton, "Dead Legs," *Strange Tales of Mystery and Terror* (January 1932).

3. Carl Jacobi, "Mive," *WT* (January 1932).

4. R. E. Spencer, *The Lady Who Came to Stay* (1931). HPL included the novel in his list of "Books to mention in new edition of weird article," but the book was not in fact mentioned in any revised edition of SHL.

CPSIA information can be obtained
at www.ICGtesting.com
Printed in the USA
BVHW04s0739130318
510160BV00003B/235/P

9 781614 980605